500 SOUP RECIPES

500 SOUP RECIPES

An unbeatable collection including chunky winter warmers, oriental broths, spicy fish chowders and hundreds of classic, chilled, clear, creamy, meat, bean and vegetable soups

Expert step-by-step guidance on blending sensational soups from fresh ingredients with ideas for all occasions and appetites shown in more than 500 glorious photographs

Contributing Editor: Bridget Jones

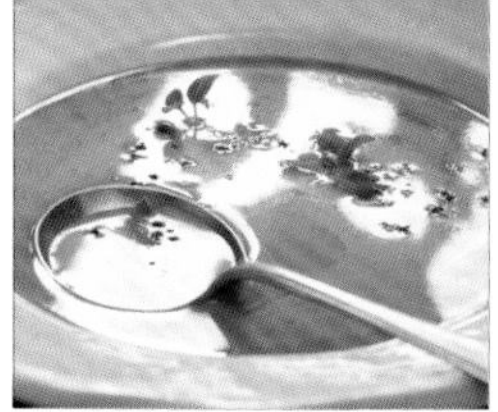

This edition is published by Hermes House,
an imprint of Anness Publishing Ltd, Hermes House,
88–89 Blackfriars Road, London SE1 8HA
tel. 020 7401 2077; fax 020 7633 9499

www.hermeshouse.com; www.annesspublishing.com

If you like the images in this book and would like to investigate using them for publishing, promotions or advertising, please visit our website www.practicalpictures.com for more information.

Publisher: Joanna Lorenz
Editorial Director: Helen Sudell
Project Editor: Catherine Stuart
Copy-editor: Bridget Jones
Design: SMI and Diane Pullen
Jacket Design: Adelle Morris
Production: Pirong Wang

ETHICAL TRADING POLICY

At Anness Publishing we believe that business should be conducted in an ethical and ecologically sustainable way, with respect for the environment and a proper regard to the replacement of the natural resources we employ.

As a publisher, we use a lot of wood pulp to make high-quality paper for printing, and that wood commonly comes from spruce trees. We are therefore currently growing more than 750,000 trees in three Scottish forest plantations: Berrymoss (130 hectares/320 acres), West Touxhill (125 hectares/305 acres) and Deveron Forest (75 hectares/185 acres). The forests we manage contain more than 3.5 times the number of trees employed each year in making paper for the books we manufacture.

Because of this ongoing ecological investment programme, you, as our customer, can have the pleasure and reassurance of knowing that a tree is being cultivated on your behalf to naturally replace the materials used to make the book you are holding.

Our forestry programme is run in accordance with the UK Woodland Assurance Scheme (UKWAS) and will be certified by the internationally recognized Forest Stewardship Council (FSC). The FSC is a non-government organization dedicated to promoting responsible management of the world's forests. Certification ensures forests are managed in an environmentally sustainable and socially responsible way. For further information about this scheme, go to www.annesspublishing.com/trees

A CIP catalogue record for this book is available from the British Library.

Main image on front cover:
Spiced Red Lentil Soup with Smoky Bacon, see page 61

Notes

Bracketed terms are intended for American readers.

For all recipes, quantities are given in both metric and imperial measures and, where appropriate, in standard cups and spoons. Follow one set, but not a mixture, because they are not interchangeable. Standard spoon and cup measures are level. 1 tsp = 5ml, 1 tbsp = 15ml, 1 cup = 250ml/8fl oz. Australian standard tablespoons are 20ml. Australian readers should use 3 tsp in place of 1 tbsp for measuring small quantities of gelatine, flour, salt etc.

The nutritional analysis given for each recipe is calculated per portion (i.e. serving or item), unless otherwise stated. If the recipe gives a range, such as Serves 4–6, then the nutritional analysis will be for the smaller portion size, i.e. 6 servings.

Medium (US large) eggs are used unless otherwise stated.

Important: pregnant women, the elderly, the ill and very young children should avoid recipes using raw or lightly cooked eggs.

PUBLISHER'S NOTE

Although the advice and information in this book are believed to be accurate and true at the time of going to press, neither the authors nor the publisher can accept any legal responsibility or liability for any errors or omissions that may be made nor for any inaccuracies nor for any harm or injury that comes about from following instructions or advice in this book.

Contents

Introduction

Soup is a ubiquitous dish: it has origins in cheap and nourishing rustic fare, but is still an integral part of fine dining. Soups feature in every cuisine around the world – as gumbos, potages, chowders, broths and consommées – and can be as delicious when composed of a handful of ingredients as when packed full of vegetables, meat and pasta or noodles.

Perhaps the greatest culinary advantage of soup is its sheer adaptability. At its simplest, a successful soup requires little more than chopping up your favourite vegetables, adding some well-flavoured stock to the pan and letting the mixture bubble away for a short while. If, however, you want to experiment, there are literally hundreds of possibilities for creating flavoursome blends. This collection contains 500 fresh ideas for every conceivable kind of soup, including chilled and iced soups, classic cream soups with twists on the familiar, superb seafood soups – a glorious way to cook firm-bodied fish and succulent shellfish; stew-like soups made from fried, roasted or simmered meats, vegetarian varieties; and hearty bowls of noodles, pasta and rice in delicious, steaming stock. From a light, lunchtime vichyssoise to a chunky stew-like main course dish, there is a recipe to suit every possible occasion and preference.

Soups are an important part of international cooking, particularly Asian cuisine, and now that once-unfamiliar ingredients are readily available in specialist food shops and many supermarkets, you can bring all kinds of exciting cross-cultural fusions into your own soup-making. When it might prove tricky to get hold of certain specialist items, substitutes are given. Spicy, aromatic or floral flavourings can be created with more readily-to-hand ingredients, and the result will be just as good. In addition, depending on taste and diet, meat soups can easily be made vegetarian or vice versa; light dishes can be made heartier; indulgent soups can be slimmed down; and heat and spice can be taken up a level or toned down. The recipes in these pages contain so many suggestions for variations that in fact you have far more than 500 ideas at your fingertips.

Very little specialist equipment is needed to make soups. You will find that a food processor or hand-held blender is invaluable and will save time and effort when you want to purée soup mixtures before serving. However, pressing the soup through a sieve (strainer) is a reasonably good alternative. You will probably already have in your kitchen a good-quality, heavy-based pan, a sharp knife and chopping board, and a vegetable peeler.

A well-flavoured stock, preferably home-made, is essential. Stock (bouillon) cubes and stock powder save time, but it is hard to beat the flavour and quality of home-made stocks. Better quick-fix alternatives are the chilled fresh stock products available from some supermarkets and delicatessens. The pages immediately following from these contain foolproof recipes for chicken, fish, meat and vegetable stocks. Fresh stocks will keep well for a time if refrigerated or frozen.

Finally, the addition of an attractive garnish, perhaps a sprinkling of chopped fresh herbs, some vegetables cut into julienne strips, crispy spring onions, a swirl of cream or a dash of paprika will enhance even the simplest of recipes. More substantial serving suggestions and accompaniments range from sesame naan croûtons to spicy dumplings, omelette-style "egg knots", smoked fish pieces, sauces and salsas. Or you can simply serve with a wedge of crusty bread to soak up the juices – what better partner could there be?

Soup-making Strategies

MAKING STOCKS

Stock-making is simple, quick and inexpensive. It is a good idea to freeze stock in useful 600ml/1 pint/2½ cup quantities. Line a deep plastic container with a freezer bag, pour in the stock and cover the container. Freeze until solid, then remove the bag of frozen stock from the container, and seal and label the bag.

The following are basic recipes, but you can add more or less what you like to stock. Remember that very strong or distinct flavours will be prominent in the finished stock (for example, parsnips) and root vegetables make the liquid cloudy. Clean vegetable peelings and stalks from fresh herbs will all add flavour to stocks.

Chicken stock

900g/2lb chicken bones and/or chicken wings
2 leeks, roughly chopped
1 large carrot, roughly chopped
1 celery stick, roughly chopped
1 bay leaf
6 black peppercorns
2 sprigs fresh thyme
1.75 litres/3 pints/7½ cups cold water

Makes 1.5 litres/2½ pints/6¼ cups

1 Put all the ingredients into a large saucepan. Bring slowly to the boil, then use a spoon to skim off the scum.

2 Reduce the heat and simmer the stock very gently for 2–3 hours, skimming the surface occasionally to remove any scum. It is important to simmer the stock gently, as rapid boiling will make the stock cloudy.

3 Leave to cool slightly, then strain through a fine sieve (strainer) (line with muslin [cheesecloth] if the sieve is not fine). Cool the stock, then chill it for up to 3 days or freeze.

Fish stock

1.5kg/3–3½ lb fish bones, washed
2 large onions, roughly chopped
1 large leek, roughly chopped
1 celery stick, roughly chopped
6 button mushrooms, sliced
6 black peppercorns
a few fresh parsley stalks
1.2 litres/2 pints/5 cups cold water

Makes 1.2 litres/2 pints/5 cups

1 Cut large bones into two or three pieces and place in a large pan. Add the vegetables, peppercorns and parsley stalks. Pour in the water, bring to the boil, then skim. Reduce the heat and simmer for 20 minutes.

2 Strain the stock through a muslin (cheese-cloth) lined sieve (strainer) and leave until just cool. Chill for up to 3 days or freeze.

Vegetable stock

1 large onion, roughly chopped
1 large leek, roughly chopped
2 carrots, sliced
1 celery stick, roughly chopped
2 garlic cloves
8 white peppercorns
a few fresh parsley stalks
1 bay leaf
2 sprigs fresh thyme
1.2 litres/2 pints/5 cups cold water

Makes 1.2 litres/2 pints/5 cups

1 Put all the ingredients in a large saucepan. Bring to the boil and skim off the scum that rises to the surface, then reduce the heat and simmer for 1 hour, skimming occasionally.

2 Sieve (strain) the stock through a fine strainer (line with muslin [cheesecloth] if not very fine) and leave to cool. Chill for up to 3 days or freeze.

Meat stock

1.5kg/3–3½2lb beef, veal or lamb bones
1 large onion, unpeeled and quartered
1 large leek, roughly chopped
2 carrots, sliced
1 celery stick, roughly chopped
30ml/2 tbsp tomato purée (paste)
1 fresh bouquet garni
6 black peppercorns
3 litres/5¼ pints/13 cups cold water

Makes 2.75 litres/4½ pints/11 cups

1 Preheat the oven to 230°C/450°F/Gas 8. Put the bones in a roasting tin and roast them for 20 minutes. Add the vegetables, stir and roast for a further 20 minutes. Transfer the ingredients to a large pan, pour a little hot water into the roasting tin and stir well.

2 Place the roasting tin on the stove and heat, stirring continuously, until boiling. Scrape the sticky residue off the roasting tin and boil for 2–3 minutes until all the residue is dissolved in the water. Add this to the pan.

3 Add the remaining ingredients. Bring to the boil and skim off the scum. Reduce the heat and simmer for 3 hours, skimming occasionally.

4 Sieve (strain) the stock through a fine strainer and leave to cool. Chill for up to 3 days or freeze.

COOKING SOUPS

Use a wooden spoon to stir soups at all stages of cooking. This will not damage the base of the saucepan (important if the pan is non-stick). However, wood absorbs flavours, so wash and dry the spoon well after use. And don't leave the spoon in the soup while it is cooking.

WHISKING SOUPS

A whisk is ideal for incorporating ingredients such as eggs and cream that could curdle, or flour mixtures that can form lumps.

SIEVING SOUPS

A wooden mushroom (or champignon), which looks like a large, flat toadstool, is useful for pressing ingredients through a fine sieve (strainer) to give a smooth purée. The back of a large spoon or ladle also works, but it is a little slower.

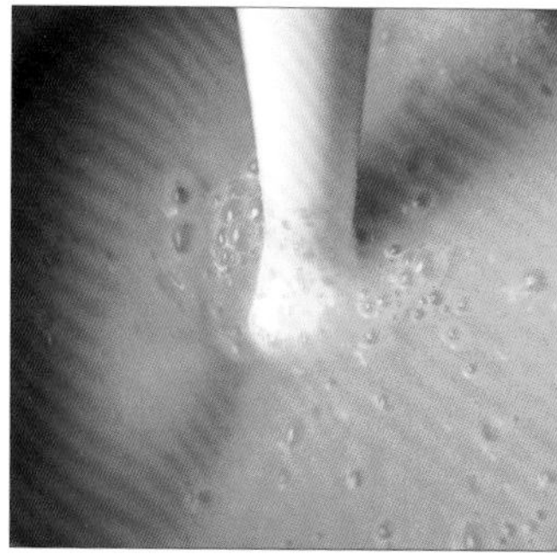

PURÉEING SOUPS

A hand-held blender is brilliant for simple, mess-free soup-making as it allows you to blend the mixture directly in the pan. Controlling the speed is easy to give the required consistency.

A more traditional method is to use a Mouli-legume, a type of mechanical sieve (strainer). This sits over a bowl and has a

blade to press the food through two fine sieves. The blade is turned by hand.

Food processors and free-standing blenders. are quick and efficient, but the food processor does not produce as smooth a result as a blender and some soups also need to be sieved.

THICKENING SOUPS

Beurre manié

This smooth flour and butter paste is used to thicken soups at the end of the cooking time. Equal quantities of plain flour and butter are kneaded together, then a small knob of the paste is added to the soup and whisked until it is fully incorporated before adding the next. The soup is brought to the boil and simmered for

approximately 1 minute, until thickened and to avoid an unpleasant raw flour flavour. A similarly useful paste can be made using flour and cream.

Breadcrumbs

Use fresh white breadcrumbs to thicken smooth soups. Whisk them into the soup and simmer for approximately 5 minutes, stirring occasionally until the bread has completely disappeared into the liquid. Season after thickening with bread, as the bread will contribute some salt to the soup. Bread is also used for thickening cold soups.

Cream

Double (heavy) cream can be used to thicken and enrich fine soup. Add towards the end of cooking, and then heat the soup without boiling. If the soup boils, the cream will curdle.

Cornflour (corn starch) or arrowroot

Mix these flours with a little cold water to make a smooth, thick, but runny, paste. (This method is known as slaking.) Stir the paste into the hot soup and simmer, stirring constantly, until boiling. Simmer cornflour for about 3 minutes to thicken completely. Arrowroot achieves maximum thickness on boiling and becomes slightly thinner if simmered. Cornflour gives an opaque result, but arrowroot becomes clear when it boils.

Eggs

Beaten eggs, egg yolks, or a mixture of eggs and a little cream can be used to enrich and slightly thicken a smooth soup. Whisk a little of the hot liquid into the eggs or egg yolks and cream before adding them to the saucepan of hot soup.

Heat gently and do not allow the soup to boil once they are added or it will curdle. In some recipes, egg is cooked in the soup.

FLAVOURING SOUPS

Oils, vinegars and alcohol

Vinegars and oils pack a punch into finished soups. Try chilli oil for a hot flavour, or basil oil in fish soup. Vinegar adds piquancy –

balsamic or fruit vinegars are milder. Boil off strong alcohol, leaving the flavour of wines, Pernod or sherry.

Colourful creams

Crème fraîche or double (heavy) cream can be flavoured with herbs, chopped grilled peppers or sun-dried tomatoes, or infused with saffron.

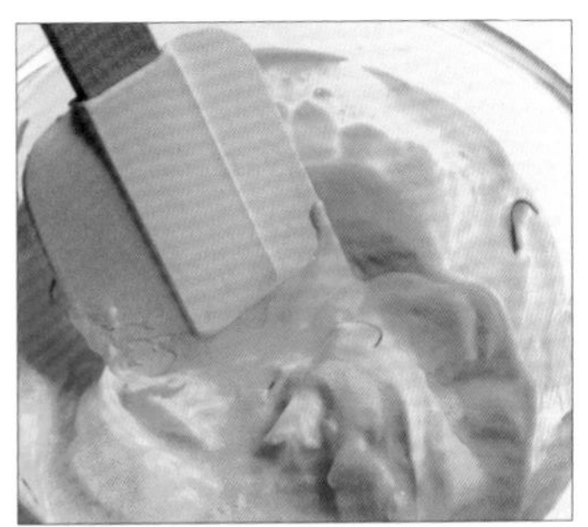

Sauces

Table sauces include Thai fish sauce (*nam pla*) and soy sauce for seasoning Asian broths. Pound garlic, basil, pine nuts and Parmesan into pesto and stir it into vegetable soups.

Chilled Almond Soup

This chilled Moorish soup is a perfect balance of three key ingredients: crushed almonds, garlic and vinegar, in a smooth purée made luscious with oil.

Serves 6

115g/4oz day-old white bread
115g/4oz/1 cup blanched almonds
2 garlic cloves, sliced
75ml/5 tbsp olive oil
25ml/1½ tbsp sherry vinegar
salt and ground black pepper

For the garnish

toasted flaked almonds
green and black grapes, halved and seeded
chopped fresh chives

1 Break the bread into a bowl. Pour in 150ml/¼ pint/⅔ cup cold water, leave to soak for about 5 minutes, then squeeze dry.

2 Put the almonds and garlic in a food processor or blender and process until very finely ground. Add the soaked white bread and process again until thoroughly combined.

3 Continue to process, gradually adding the oil until the mixture forms a smooth paste. Add the sherry vinegar, followed by 600ml/1 pint/2½ cups cold water and process until the mixture is smooth.

4 Transfer the soup to a bowl and season with plenty of salt and pepper, adding a little more water if the soup is very thick. Cover with clear film (plastic wrap) and chill for at least 2 hours.

5 Ladle the soup into bowls. Scatter the almonds, halved grapes and chopped chives over to garnish.

Cook's Tip

To accentuate the flavour of the almonds, dry roast them in a frying pan until they are lightly browned before grinding them. This will produce a slightly darker soup.

Walnut and Cucumber Yogurt Soup

This is a particularly refreshing cold soup, using a classic combination of cucumber and yogurt. The walnuts contribute the delightfully crunchy texture.

Serves 5–6

1 cucumber
4 garlic cloves
2.5ml/½ tsp salt
75g/3oz/¾ cup walnut pieces
40g/1½oz day-old bread, torn into pieces
30ml/2 tbsp walnut or sunflower oil
400ml/14 fl oz/1⅔ cups natural (plain) yogurt
120ml/4 fl oz/½ cup cold water or chilled still mineral water
5–10ml/1–2 tsp lemon juice

For the garnish

40g/1½oz/scant ½ cup walnuts, coarsely chopped
25ml/1½ tbsp olive oil
sprigs of fresh dill

1 Cut the cucumber in half and peel one half of it. Dice the cucumber flesh and set aside.

2 Using a large mortar and pestle, crush together the garlic and salt well, then add the walnuts and bread.

3 When the mixture is smooth, slowly add the walnut or sunflower oil and combine well.

4 Transfer the mixture into a large bowl and beat in the yogurt and diced cucumber. Add the cold water or mineral water and lemon juice to taste.

5 Pour the soup into chilled soup bowls to serve. Garnish with the chopped walnuts and drizzle with the olive oil. Finally, arrange the sprigs of dill on top and serve immediately.

Cook's Tip

Peeling half the cucumber retains the flavour and colour of the peel without having too much, which would make the soup slightly bitter. A food processor can be used instead of the mortar and pestle for speedy preparation.

Chilled Almond: Energy 245kcal/1017kJ; Protein 5.7g; Carbohydrate 10.8g, of which sugars 1.3g; Fat 20.2g, of which saturates 2.2g; Cholesterol 0mg; Calcium 67mg; Fibre 1.7g; Sodium 102mg.
Walnut and Cucumber: Energy 175kcal/728kJ; Protein 6g; Carbohydrate 9.2g, of which sugars 6g; Fat 13.1g, of which saturates 1.5g; Cholesterol 1mg; Calcium 152mg; Fibre 0.7g; Sodium 92mg.

Chilled Coconut Soup

Refreshing, cooling and not too filling, this soup is the perfect antidote to hot weather. For a formal meal, it would be excellent after a starter, to refresh the palate before the main course. Use light coconut milk as a reduced-fat alternative to subdue the creaminess.

Serves 6

1.2 litres/2 pints/5 cups milk
225g/8oz/2⅔ cups unsweetened desiccated coconut
400ml/14fl oz/1⅔ cups coconut milk
400ml/14fl oz/1⅔ cups chicken stock
200ml/7fl oz/scant 1 cup double (heavy) cream
2.5ml/½ tsp salt
2.5ml/½ tsp ground white pepper
5ml/1 tsp caster sugar
small bunch of fresh coriander (cilantro)

1 Pour the milk into a large pan. Bring it to the boil, stir in the coconut, lower the heat and allow to simmer for 30 minutes. Spoon the mixture into a food processor and process until smooth. This may take a while – up to 5 minutes – so pause frequently and scrape down the sides of the bowl.

2 Rinse the pan to remove any coconut that remains, pour in the processed mixture and add the coconut milk. Stir in the chicken stock (home-made, if possible, which gives a better flavour than a stock cube), cream, salt, pepper and sugar. Bring the mixture to the boil, stirring occasionally, then lower the heat and cook for 10 minutes.

3 Reserve a few coriander leaves to garnish, then chop the rest finely and stir into the soup. Pour the soup into a large bowl, let it cool, then cover and put into the refrigerator until chilled. Just before serving, taste the soup and adjust the seasoning, as chilling will alter the flavour. Serve in chilled bowls, garnished with the coriander leaves.

Cook's Tip
Avoid using sweetened desiccated coconut, which would spoil the flavour of this soup.

Yogurt and Cucumber Soup

Yogurt is frequently used in Greek and Middle Eastern cooking, and the best yogurt is usually home-prepared. Sometimes yogurt is added during the very last stage of cooking a soup, as a healthier alternative to cream. Like cream, it will also curdle if simmered or boiled. In this chilled soup, however, the yogurt is one of the key ingredients, and there is no heating involved. It blends beautifully with the cucumber and mint.

Serves 4

1 large cucumber, peeled
300ml/½ pint/1¼ cups single (light) cream
150ml/¼ pint/⅔ cup natural (plain) yogurt
2 garlic cloves, crushed
30ml/2 tbsp white wine vinegar
15ml/1 tbsp chopped fresh mint
salt and ground black pepper
sprigs of fresh mint, to garnish

1 Grate the cucumber coarsely. Use a coarse hand grater or do this in a food processor or blender. Alternatively, it can be coarsely chopped in a blender. Pour the cucumber into a bowl or large jug (pitcher).

2 Stir in the cream, yogurt, garlic, vinegar and mint. Season to taste. Cover the container tightly and then chill the soup for at least 2 hours before serving.

3 Stir well before serving. Ladle the soup into small bowls and garnish with mint.

Cook's Tips
- *Although it takes a little longer, peeling the cucumber gives the soup a light flavour and colour, and provides a delicate background for the garlic and mint in the yogurt.*
- *This soup can be made with all yogurt, if you would prefer to omit the cream completely. Simply use three times the amount of yogurt indicated above. Strained, whole-milk yogurt is deliciously creamy, and still relatively low in fat.*

Chilled Coconut: Energy 597kcal/2474kJ; Protein 10.8g; Carbohydrate 16.9g, of which sugars 16.9g; Fat 54.7g, of which saturates 40.8g; Cholesterol 69mg; Calcium 317mg; Fibre 6.7g; Sodium 188mg.
Yogurt and Cucumber: Energy 170Kcal/704kJ; Protein 4.7g; Carbohydrate 5g, of which sugars 4.8g; Fat 14.8g, of which saturates 9.3g; Cholesterol 42mg; Calcium 151mg; Fibre 0.2g; Sodium 54mg.

Spiced Mango Soup

Mangoes may seem an unusual choice for a savoury soup, but this is actually a delicious invention by Chutney Mary's, the Anglo-Indian restaurant in London. It is best when served lightly chilled. Gram flour, or chickpea flour also known as besan, is available from Asian stores.

Serves 4

2 ripe mangoes
15ml/1 tbsp gram flour
120ml/4fl oz/½ cup natural (plain) yogurt
900ml/1½ pints/3¾ cups cold or chilled water
2.5ml/½ tsp grated fresh root ginger
2 fresh red chillies, seeded and finely chopped
30ml/2 tbsp olive oil
2.5ml/½ tsp mustard seeds
2.5ml/½ tsp cumin seeds
8 curry leaves
salt and ground black pepper
fresh mint leaves, shredded, to garnish
natural (plain) yogurt, to serve

1 Peel the mangoes, remove the stones and cut the flesh into chunks. Purée in a food processor or blender until smooth. Pour into a saucepan and stir in the gram flour, yogurt, water, ginger and chillies.

2 Bring the ingredients slowly to the boil, stirring occasionally. Simmer for 4–5 minutes until thickened slightly, then set aside off the heat.

3 Heat the oil in a frying pan over medium to low heat. Add the mustard seeds and cook for a few seconds until they begin to pop, then add the cumin seeds.

4 Add the curry leaves and then cook for 5 minutes. Stir the spice mixture into the soup, return it to the heat and cook for 10 minutes.

5 Press through a sieve (strainer), if you like, then season to taste. Leave the soup to cool completely, then chill for at least 1 hour.

6 Ladle the soup into bowls, and top each with a dollop of yogurt. Garnish with shredded mint leaves and serve.

Iced Melon Soup

Use different varieties of melon for this cool soup and ice sorbet to create subtle contrast. Try a mix of Charentais and Ogen or cantaloupe and Galia.

Serves 6–8

2.25kg/5–5¼lb very ripe melon
45ml/3 tbsp orange juice
30ml/2 tbsp lemon juice
mint leaves, to garnish

For the melon and mint sorbet

25g/1oz/2 tbsp sugar
120ml/4fl oz/½ cup water
2.25kg/5–5¼lb very ripe melon
juice of 2 limes
30ml/2 tbsp chopped fresh mint

1 To make the melon and mint sorbet, put the sugar and water into a saucepan and heat gently until the sugar dissolves. Bring to the boil and simmer for 4–5 minutes, then remove from the heat and leave to cool.

2 Halve the melon. Scrape out the seeds, then cut it into large wedges and cut the flesh out of the skin. Weigh about 1.5kg/3–3½lb melon.

3 Purée the melon in a food processor or blender with the cooled syrup and lime juice.

4 Stir in the mint and pour the melon mixture into an ice-cream maker. Churn, following the manufacturer's instructions, or until the sorbet is smooth and firm. Alternatively, pour the mixture into a suitable container and freeze until icy around the edges. Transfer to a food processor or blender and process until smooth. Repeat the freezing and processing two or three times or until smooth and holding its shape, then freeze until firm.

5 To make the chilled melon soup, prepare the melon as in step 2 and purée it in a food processor or blender. Pour the purée into a bowl and stir in the orange and lemon juice. Place the soup in the fridge for 30–40 minutes, but do not chill it for too long as this will dull its flavour.

6 Ladle the soup into bowls and add a large scoop of the sorbet to each. Garnish with mint leaves and serve at once.

Spiced Mango Soup: Energy 83kcal/354kJ; Protein 3g; Carbohydrate 14.4g, of which sugars 12.7g; Fat 2g, of which saturates 0.5g; Cholesterol 0mg; Calcium 72mg; Fibre 2g; Sodium 28mg.
Iced Melon Soup: Energy 150kcal/636kJ; Protein 2.9g; Carbohydrate 35.3g, of which sugars 35.3g; Fat 0.6g, of which saturates 0g; Cholesterol 0mg; Calcium 75mg; Fibre 2.3g; Sodium 175mg.

Tomato and Chilli Soup

Pure clean flavours and a chilli kick make great soup.

Serves 2

1 fresh red or green chilli, chopped
250g/9oz carrots, chopped
3 tomatoes, quartered
juice of 1 orange
crushed ice

1 If you prefer a milder flavour, remove the seeds and white pith from the chilli before chopping it. Push the carrots through a juicer, then follow with the tomatoes and chilli. Alternatively, purée the ingredients in a blender and press through a sieve (strainer).

2 Add the orange juice and stir well to mix. Fill two tumblers or glass bowls with crushed ice, pour the soup over and serve.

Ultra-light Gazpacho

This is a light version of the classic Spanish soup, made without the usual bread.

Serves 4–5

½ fresh red chilli
800g/1¾lb tomatoes, skinned
½ cucumber, roughly sliced
1 red (bell) pepper, seeded and cut into chunks
1 celery stick, chopped
1 spring onion (scallion), roughly chopped
a small handful of fresh coriander (cilantro), stalks included, plus extra to decorate
juice of 1 lime
salt
ice cubes

1 Using a sharp knife, seed the chilli. Add to a blender or food processor with the tomatoes, cucumber, red pepper, celery, spring onion and coriander.

2 Blend well until smooth, scraping the vegetable mixture down from the side of the bowl, if necessary. Add the lime juice and a little salt and blend. Pour into glasses or small bowls. Add ice cubes and a few coriander leaves to serve.

Tomato and Peach Soup

American-style soups, made from the clear juices extracted from vegetables or fruits and referred to as "water" soups by chefs, provide the inspiration for this recipe.

Serves 6

1.5kg/3–3½lb ripe peaches, peeled, stoned and cut into chunks
1.2kg/2½lb beef tomatoes, peeled and cut into chunks
30ml/2 tbsp white wine vinegar
1 lemon grass stalk, crushed and chopped
2.5cm/1in fresh root ginger, grated
1 bay leaf
150ml/¼ pint/⅔ cup water
18 tiger prawns (jumbo shrimp), shelled with tails on and deveined
olive oil, for brushing
salt and ground black pepper
handful of fresh coriander (cilantro) leaves and 2 vine-ripened tomatoes, peeled, seeded and diced, to garnish

1 Purée the peaches and tomatoes in a food processor or blender. Stir in the vinegar and seasoning. Line a large bowl with muslin (cheesecloth). Pour the purée into the bowl, gather up the ends of the muslin and tie tightly. Suspend over the bowl and leave at room temperature for 3 hours or until about 1.2 litres/2 pints/5 cups juice have drained through.

2 Meanwhile, put the lemon grass, ginger and bay leaf into a pan with the water, and simmer for 5–6 minutes. Set aside to cool. Strain the mixture into the tomato and peach juice and chill for at least 4 hours.

3 Using a sharp knife, slit the prawns down their curved sides, cutting about three-quarters of the way through and keeping their tails intact. Open them out flat.

4 Heat a griddle or frying pan and brush with a little oil. Sear the prawns for 1–2 minutes on each side, until tender and slightly charred. Pat dry on kitchen paper to remove any remaining oil. Cool, but do not chill.

5 Ladle the soup into bowls and place three prawns in each. Add torn coriander leaves and diced tomato to each bowl.

Tomato and Chilli: Energy 84kcal/351kJ; Protein 2.7g; Carbohydrate 16.9g, of which sugars 16.3g; Fat 1g, of which saturates 0.3g; Cholesterol 0mg; Calcium 52mg; Fibre 4.6g; Sodium 49mg.
Ultra-light Gazpacho: Energy 43kcal/183kJ; Protein 1.8g; Carbohydrate 7.9g, of which sugars 7.8g; Fat 0.7g, of which saturates 0.2g; Cholesterol 0mg; Calcium 24mg; Fibre 2.5g; Sodium 21mg.
Tomato and Peach: Energy 188kcal/797kJ; Protein 12.7g; Carbohydrate 25.2g, of which sugars 25.2g; Fat 4.8g, of which saturates 0.8g; Cholesterol 98mg; Calcium 71mg; Fibre 5.8g; Sodium 116mg.

Chilled Cherry Soup

Soups made from seasonal fruits are a favourite Central European treat. Cherry soup, one of the glories of the Hungarian table, is also a Jewish speciality, often served during the festival of Shavuot when dairy foods are traditionally feasted upon. It is served with sour cream – and the test is whether you can resist that extra spoonful!

Serves 6

1kg/2¼lb fresh, frozen or canned sour cherries, such as Morello or Montmorency, pitted
175–250g/6–9oz/about 1 cup sugar, to taste
1–2 cinnamon sticks, each about 5cm/2in long
750ml/1¼ pints/3 cups dry red wine
5ml/1 tsp almond extract, or to taste
250ml/8fl oz/1 cup single (light) cream
250ml/8fl oz/1 cup sour cream or crème fraîche

1 Add the pitted cherries, 250ml/8 fl oz/1 cup water, sugar, cinnamon and wine in a large pan. Bring to the boil, reduce the heat and simmer for 20–30 minutes, until the cherries are tender. Remove from the heat and pour into a bowl.

2 Stir the almond extract into the soup and leave until cool. Then cover and chill.

3 In a bowl, stir a few tablespoons of single cream into the sour cream or crème fraîche to thin it down, then stir in the rest until the mixture is smooth. Stir half the cream into the soup and chill until ready to serve. Chill the remaining cream.

4 To serve, ladle the soup into small bowls and swirl in the remaining cream.

Variation
When plums are in season, use them instead of cherries.

Yogurt Soup with Quick Chilli Salsa

The refreshing flavours of cucumber and yogurt in this soup fuse with the cool salsa and the smoky flavour of the charred salmon topping to bring a taste of summer to the table.

Serves 4

3 medium cucumbers
300ml/½ pint/1¼ cups Greek (strained plain) yogurt
250ml/8fl oz/1 cup vegetable stock, chilled
120ml/4fl oz/½ cup crème fraîche
15ml/1 tbsp chopped fresh chervil
15ml/1 tbsp snipped fresh chives
15ml/1 tbsp chopped fresh flat leaf parsley
1 small red chilli, seeded and very finely chopped
a little oil, for brushing
225g/8oz salmon fillet, skinned and cut into eight thin slices
salt and ground black pepper
fresh chervil or chives, to garnish

1 Peel two of the cucumbers and halve them lengthways. Scoop out and discard the seeds, then roughly chop the flesh. Purée in a food processor or blender, then add the yogurt, stock, crème fraîche, chervil, chives and seasoning, and process until smooth. Chill.

2 Peel, halve and seed the remaining cucumber. Cut the flesh into small neat dice. Mix with the chopped parsley and chilli. Chill until required.

3 Brush a griddle or frying pan with oil and heat until very hot. Sear the salmon slices for 1–2 minutes on each side, until tender and charred.

4 Ladle the chilled soup into soup bowls. Top with two slices of the salmon, then pile a portion of salsa into the centre of each. Garnish with the chervil or chives and serve.

Cook's Tip
Fresh tuna can be used instead of salmon. For a vegetarian alternative, make this soup with brown halved cherry tomatoes and diced halloumi cheese.

Chilled Cherry: Energy 484Kcal/2037kJ; Protein 3.7g; Carbohydrate 64.1g, of which sugars 64.1g; Fat 16.3g, of which saturates 10.3g; Cholesterol 48mg; Calcium 125mg; Fibre 1g; Sodium 53mg.
Yogurt Soup: Energy 226kcal/942kJ; Protein 15.8g; Carbohydrate 9.1g, of which sugars 5.9g; Fat 14.4g, of which saturates 2.3g; Cholesterol 29mg; Calcium 177mg; Fibre 0.6g; Sodium 91mg.

Beetroot and Cranberry Soup

Although it sounds complex, this soup is ridiculously easy to make. The sweet, earthy flavour of fresh, cooked beetroot is combined with zesty orange and tart cranberry.

Serves 4

350g/12oz cooked beetroot, roughly chopped
grated rind and juice of 1 orange
600ml/1 pint/2½ cups unsweetened cranberry juice
450ml/¾ pint/scant 2 cups Greek (strained plain) yogurt
a little Tabasco
4 slices brioche
60ml/4 tbsp mascarpone
salt and ground black pepper

For the garnish

sprigs of mint
cooked cranberries

1 Purée the beetroot with the orange rind and juice, half the cranberry juice and the yogurt in a blender until smooth.

2 Press the purée through a sieve (strainer) into a clean bowl. Stir in the remaining cranberry juice, Tabasco and salt and pepper to taste. Chill for at least 2 hours.

3 Preheat the grill (broiler). Using a large pastry cutter, stamp a round out of each slice of brioche and toast until golden. Ladle the soup into bowls and top each with brioche and mascarpone. Garnish with mint and fresh cranberries.

Variation

Raspberries are superb with beetroot. Use raspberry juice instead of the cranberry juice and add a few fresh raspberries for the garnish.

Cook's Tip

If the oranges you use are a little tart, add a pinch or two of caster sugar to the soup.

Tomato Soup with Rocket Pesto

Baby tomatoes make sweet, flavour-packed soup.

Serves 4

225g/8oz baby cherry tomatoes
225g/8oz baby plum tomatoes
225g/8oz vine-ripened tomatoes
2 shallots, roughly chopped
25ml/1½ tbsp sun-dried tomato paste
600ml/1 pint/2½ cups vegetable stock
salt and ground black pepper
ice cubes, to serve

For the rocket pesto

15g/½oz rocket (arugula) leaves
75ml/5 tbsp olive oil
15g/½oz/2 tbsp pine nuts
1 garlic clove
25g/1oz/⅓ cup freshly grated Parmesan cheese

1 Purée all the tomatoes, shallots and the sun-dried tomato paste in a blender. Press through a sieve (strainer) into a pan. Add the stock and heat gently for 5 minutes. Season, cool and chill well.

2 For the pesto, blend the rocket, oil, pine nuts and garlic in a food processor. Transfer the paste to a bowl and stir in the Parmesan. Serve the soup topped with ice cubes and pesto.

Broccoli and Beansprout Soup

Green grapes naturally sweeten this thin and juicy vegetable soup, which is ideal for detox.

Serves 3–4

150g/5oz broccoli, broken up
2 large pears, cored and cubed
150g/5oz/1 cup beansprouts
300g/11oz green grapes

For the garnish

ice cubes
sliced green grapes

1 Push all the ingredients through a juicer. Alternatively, blend them until smooth and then press through a fine sieve (strainer).

2 Pour the soup into glasses or small glass dishes and serve garnished with ice cubes and sliced green grapes.

Beetroot Soup: Energy 365kcal/1544kJ; Protein 13.9g; Carbohydrate 63.7g, of which sugars 40.5g; Fat 8g, of which saturates 1.9g; Cholesterol 18mg; Calcium 316mg; Fibre 1.7g; Sodium 331mg.
Tomato Soup: Energy 217kcal/900kJ; Protein 4.8g; Carbohydrate 7.4g, of which sugars 7.1g; Fat 18.9g, of which saturates 3.6g; Cholesterol 6mg; Calcium 99mg; Fibre 2.2g; Sodium 104mg.
Broccoli and Beansprout: Energy 119kcal/505kJ; Protein 3.9g; Carbohydrate 25.5g, of which sugars 24.6g; Fat 0.8g, of which saturates 0.1g; Cholesterol 0mg; Calcium 56mg; Fibre 4.2g; Sodium 10mg.

Tomato and Basil-flower Soup

This fresh tomato soup is deliciously flavoured with garlic and bursting with aromatic basil. This herb flowers in early spring and flower heads are often removed to promote leaf growth, but here they work well as an attractive garnish.

Serves 4

15ml/1 tbsp olive oil
1 onion, finely chopped
1 garlic clove, crushed
600ml/1 pint/2½ cups vegetable stock
900g/2lb tomatoes, roughly chopped
20 fresh basil leaves
a few drops of balsamic vinegar
juice of ½ lemon
150ml/¼ pint/⅔ cup natural (plain) yogurt
sugar and salt, to taste

For the garnish

30ml/2 tbsp natural (plain) yogurt
8 small basil leaves
10ml/2 tsp basil flowers, all green parts removed

1 Heat the oil in a pan and add the finely chopped onion and garlic. Fry the onion and garlic in the oil for 2–3 minutes, until soft and transparent, stirring occasionally.

2 Add 300ml/½ pint/1¼ cups of the vegetable stock and the chopped tomatoes to the pan. Bring to the boil, then lower the heat and simmer the mixture for 15 minutes. Stir it occasionally to prevent it from sticking to the base of the pan.

3 Allow the mixture to cool slightly, then transfer it to a food processor and process until smooth. Press through a sieve placed over a bowl to remove the tomato skins and seeds.

4 Return the mixture to the food processor and add the remainder of the stock, half the basil leaves, the vinegar, lemon juice and yogurt. Season with sugar and salt to taste. Process until smooth. Pour into a bowl and chill.

5 Just before serving, finely shred the remaining basil leaves and add them to the soup. Pour the chilled soup into individual bowls. Garnish with yogurt topped with a few small basil leaves and a sprinkling of basil flowers.

Chilled Tomato and Cucumber Soup

Basil is perfect with light, refreshing cucumber and summery ripe tomatoes.

Serves 1–2

½ cucumber, peeled and quartered
a handful of fresh basil, plus extra sprigs to garnish
350g/12oz tomatoes
ice cubes

1 Juice the cucumber with the basil, then do the same with the tomatoes. Alternatively, process the ingredients in a blender until smooth and press through a sieve (strainer). Serve on ice, garnished with basil.

Vegetable and Herb Soup

Make this soup when the tomato season is at its peak.

Serves 4

15ml/1 tbsp olive oil
1 large onion, chopped
1 carrot, chopped
1kg/2¼lb ripe tomatoes, quartered
2 garlic cloves, chopped
5 sprigs of fresh thyme, or 1.5ml/¼ tsp dried thyme
4 or 5 sprigs fresh marjoram, or 1.5ml/¼ tsp dried marjoram
1 bay leaf
45ml/3 tbsp crème fraîche, soured cream or natural (plain) yogurt, plus a little extra to garnish
salt and freshly ground black pepper

1 Heat the olive oil in a pan. Add the onion and carrot and cook for 3–4 minutes, until the vegetables are just softened, stirring occasionally.

2 Add the quartered tomatoes, chopped garlic and herbs. Reduce the heat and simmer, covered, for 30 minutes.

3 Discard the bay leaf and press the soup through a sieve (strainer). Stir in the cream or yogurt and season to taste. Leave to cool, then chill in the refrigerator.

Tomato and Basil: Energy 117kcal/491kJ; Protein 4.4g; Carbohydrate 16.3g, of which sugars 14.8g; Fat 4.4g, of which saturates 0.9g; Cholesterol 1mg; Calcium 100mg; Fibre 2.3g; Sodium 55mg.
Tomato and Cucumber: Energy 40kcal/168kJ; Protein 1.9g; Carbohydrate 7g, of which sugars 6.8g; Fat 0.7g, of which saturates 0.2g; Cholesterol 0mg; Calcium 31mg; Fibre 2.4g; Sodium 19mg.
Vegetable and Herb: Energy 172kcal/723kJ; Protein 4.9g; Carbohydrate 24.9g, of which sugars 8g; Fat 6.6g, of which saturates 3.8g; Cholesterol 15mg; Calcium 80mg; Fibre 3.7g; Sodium 68mg.

Chilled Pepper Soup

The secret is to serve this soup very cold, but not over-chilled.

Serves 4

1 onion, quartered
4 garlic cloves, unpeeled
2 red (bell) peppers, seeded and quartered
2 yellow (bell) peppers, seeded and quartered
30–45ml/2–3 tbsp olive oil
grated rind and juice of 1 orange
200g/7oz can chopped tomatoes
600ml/1 pint/2½ cups cold water
salt and ground black pepper
30ml/2 tbsp snipped fresh chives, to garnish (optional)

For the hot Parmesan toast
1 medium baguette
50g/2oz/¼ cup butter
175g/6oz Parmesan cheese

1 Preheat the oven to 200°C/400°F/Gas 6. Put the onion, garlic and peppers in a roasting tin. Drizzle the oil over the vegetables and mix well, then turn the pieces of pepper skin sides up. Roast for 25–30 minutes, until slightly charred. Cool slightly.

2 Squeeze the garlic flesh into a food processor or blender. Add the roasted vegetables, orange rind and juice, tomatoes and water. Process until smooth, then press through a sieve (strainer) into a bowl. Season well and chill for 30 minutes.

3 Make the Parmesan toasts when you are ready to serve the soup. Preheat the grill (broiler) to high. Tear the baguette in half lengthways, then tear or cut it across to give four large pieces. Spread the pieces of bread with butter.

4 Pare most of the Parmesan into thin slices or shavings using a swivel-bladed vegetable knife or a small paring knife, then finely grate the remainder. Arrange the sliced Parmesan on the toasts, then dredge with the grated cheese. Transfer to a large baking sheet or grill rack and toast under the grill for a few minutes, until the topping is well browned.

5 Ladle the chilled soup into large, shallow bowls and sprinkle with snipped fresh chives, if using, and plenty of freshly ground black pepper. Serve the hot Parmesan toast with the chilled soup.

Classic Gazpacho

This classic chilled soup is deeply rooted in the region of Andalusia, southern Spain. The soothing blend of tomatoes, sweet peppers and garlic is sharpened with sherry vinegar, and enriched with olive oil. Serving it with saucerfuls of garnishes has virtually become a tradition.

Serves 4

1.3–1.6kg/3–3½lb ripe tomatoes
1 green (bell) pepper, seeded and roughly chopped
2 garlic cloves, finely chopped
2 slices day-old bread, crusts removed
60ml/4 tbsp extra virgin olive oil
60ml/4 tbsp sherry vinegar
150ml/¼ pint/⅔ cup tomato juice
300ml/½ pint/1¼ cups iced water
salt and ground black pepper
ice cubes, to serve (optional)

For the garnishes
30ml/2 tbsp olive oil
2–3 slices day-old bread, diced
1 small cucumber, peeled and finely diced
1 small onion, finely chopped
1 red (bell) and 1 green (bell) pepper, seeded and finely diced
2 hard-boiled eggs, chopped

1 Skin the tomatoes, then quarter them and remove the cores and seeds, saving the juices. Put the pepper in a food processor or blender and process for a few seconds. Add the tomatoes, reserved juices, garlic, bread, oil and vinegar and process. Add the tomato juice and blend to combine.

2 Season the soup, then pour into a large bowl, cover with clear film (plastic wrap) and chill for at least 12 hours.

3 Prepare the garnishes. Heat the olive oil in a frying pan and fry the bread cubes for 4–5 minutes until golden brown and crisp. Drain well on kitchen paper, then arrange in a small dish. Place each of the remaining garnishes in separate small dishes.

4 Just before serving, dilute the soup with the ice-cold water. The consistency should be thick but not too stodgy. If you like, stir a few ice cubes into the soup, then spoon into bowls and serve with the garnishes.

Pepper: Energy 678kcal/2842kJ; Protein 28.7g; Carbohydrate 71.2g, of which sugars 17.1g; Fat 32.9g, of which saturates 16.8g; Cholesterol 70mg; Calcium 671mg; Fibre 5.9g; Sodium 1182mg.
Classic Gazpacho: Energy 356kcal/1494kJ; Protein 7.6g; Carbohydrate 41.9g, of which sugars 21.5g; Fat 18.8g, of which saturates 2.9g; Cholesterol 0mg; Calcium 90mg; Fibre 6.7g; Sodium 346mg.

Green Pea and Mint Soup

Peas and mint really capture the flavours of summer.

Serves 4

4 spring onions (scallions), sliced
50g/2oz/4 tbsp butter
450g/1lb fresh or frozen peas
600ml/1 pint/2½ cups stock
2 large sprigs of fresh mint
600ml/1 pint/2½ cups milk
a pinch of sugar (optional)
salt and freshly ground black pepper
fresh mint and single (light) cream

1 Soften the spring onions in the butter. Stir in the peas, stock and mint. Bring to the boil, cover and simmer for 30 minutes (15 minutes for frozen peas).

2 Remove 45ml/3 tbsp peas. Purée the soup until smooth, adding the milk, sugar, and seasoning. Cool and chill. Serve with cream and peas.

Chilled Melon Soup with Basil

This is a refreshing, chilled fruit soup. The soft melon flesh is easy to blend.

Serves 4–6

2 Charentais or rock melons, halved and seeds removed
75g/3oz/scant ½ cup caster (superfine) sugar
finely grated rind and juice of 1 lime
45ml/3 tbsp shredded fresh basil, plus whole leaves, to garnish

1 Using a melon baller, scoop out 20–24 melon balls and set aside. Scoop out the remaining flesh into a blender.

2 Dissolve the sugar in 175ml/6fl oz/¾ cup water with the lime rind in a small pan over a low heat. Bring to the boil, reduce the heat and simmer for 2–3 minutes. Leave to cool slightly. Blend half the mixture with the melon flesh until smooth, adding the remaining syrup and lime juice to taste.

3 Pour the soup into a bowl, stir in the basil and chill. Serve garnished with whole basil leaves and melon balls.

Watercress and Orange Soup

This is a healthy soup, which is just as good served either hot or chilled.

Serves 4

1 large onion, chopped
15ml/1 tbsp olive oil
2 bunches or bags of watercress
grated rind and juice of 1 large orange
600ml/1 pint/2½ cups vegetable stock
150ml/¼ pint/⅔ cup single (light) cream
10ml/2 tsp cornflour (corn starch)
salt and freshly ground black pepper
a little double (heavy) cream or natural (plain) yogurt, to garnish
4 orange wedges, to serve

1 Soften the onion in the oil in a large pan. Add the watercress, unchopped, to the onion. Cover and cook for about 5 minutes until the watercress is softened.

2 Add the orange rind and juice and the stock to the watercress mixture. Bring to the boil, cover and simmer for 10–15 minutes.

3 Purée the soup in a blender or food processor until thoroughly smooth. For a satin-smooth result, press the soup through a fine sieve (strainer) to remove any trace of watercress fibres. Return the soup to the rinsed-out pan.

4 Blend the cream with the cornflour until no lumps remain, then add to the soup. Season to taste.

5 Bring the soup gently back to the boil, stirring, until just slightly thickened. Check the seasoning.

6 Serve the soup ladled into bowls, topped with a swirl of cream or yogurt, and a wedge of orange to squeeze in at the last moment.

7 If serving the soup chilled, thicken and leave to cool, before chilling in the fridge. Garnish with cream or yogurt and orange, as above.

Pea and Mint: Energy 242kcal/1012kJ; Protein 12.1g; Carbohydrate 18.3g, of which sugars 10.5g; Fat 13.9g, of which saturates 8.4g; Cholesterol 36mg; Calcium 226mg; Fibre 5.9g; Sodium 247mg.
Melon Soup with Basil: Energy 129kcal/550kJ; Protein 1.7g; Carbohydrate 31.7g, of which sugars 31.7g; Fat 0.3g, of which saturates 0g; Cholesterol 0mg; Calcium 50mg; Fibre 1.3g; Sodium 104mg.
Watercress and Orange: Energy 144kcal/599kJ; Protein 3.6g; Carbohydrate 9.4g, of which sugars 5.6g; Fat 10.6g, of which saturates 5.1g; Cholesterol 21mg; Calcium 136mg; Fibre 1.7g; Sodium 40mg.

Chilled Asparagus Soup

This delicate, pale green soup, garnished with a swirl of cream or yogurt, is as pretty as it is delicious.

Serves 6

900g/2lb fresh asparagus
60ml/4 tbsp butter or olive oil
175g/6oz/1½ cups sliced leeks or spring onions (scallions)
45ml/3 tbsp plain (all-purpose) flour
1.5 litres/2½ pints/6¼ cups chicken stock or water
120ml/4 fl oz/½ cup single (light) cream or natural (plain) yogurt
15ml/1 tbsp chopped fresh tarragon or chervil
salt and freshly ground black pepper

1 Remove the top 6cm/2½in of the asparagus spears and blanch in boiling water for 5–6 minutes until just tender. Drain thoroughly. Cut each tip into two or three pieces and set aside.

2 Trim the ends of the stalks, removing any brown or woody parts. Chop the stalks into 1cm/½in pieces.

3 Heat the butter or oil in a heavy-based saucepan. Add the sliced leeks or spring onions and cook over a low heat for about 5 minutes until softened but not browned. Stir in the chopped asparagus stalks, cover and then cook for a further 6–8 minutes until the stalks are tender.

4 Add the flour and stir well to blend. Cook for 3–4 minutes, uncovered, stirring occasionally.

5 Add the stock or water. Bring to the boil, stirring frequently, then reduce the heat and simmer for 30 minutes. Season with salt and pepper.

6 Purée the soup. If necessary, sieve (strain) it to remove any coarse fibres. Stir in the asparagus tips, most of the cream or yogurt, and the herbs. Chill well.

7 Stir before serving and check the seasoning. Garnish each bowl with a swirl of cream or yogurt.

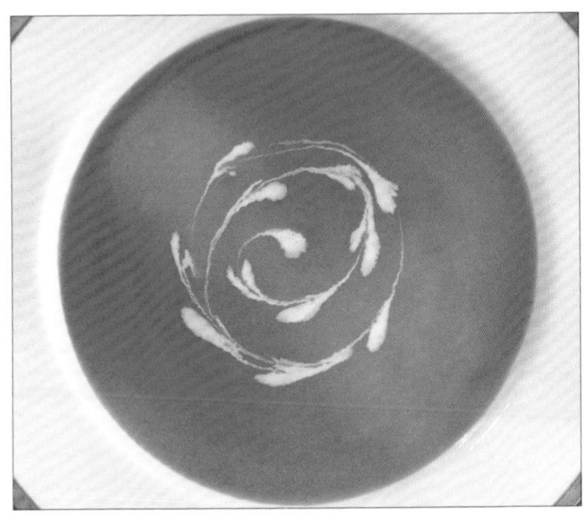

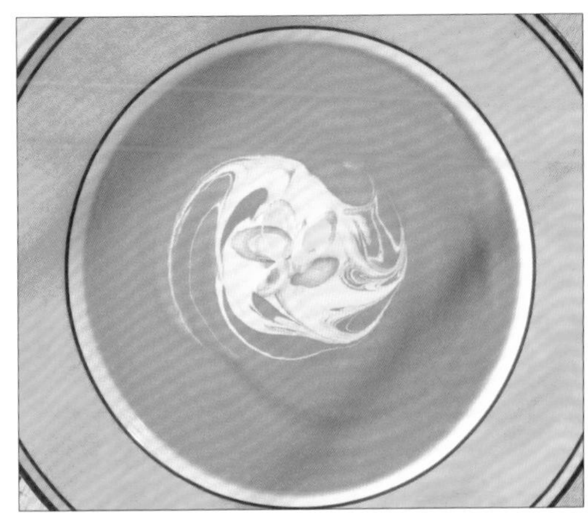

Avocado and Cucumber Soup

Avocados are combined with lemon juice, dry sherry and an optional dash of hot pepper sauce, to make this subtle chilled soup an absolute winner. The pepper sauce will not be to everyone's taste – so check with guests before you add.

Serves 4

2 large or 3 medium ripe avocados
15ml/1 tbsp fresh lemon juice
75g/3oz/¾ cup coarsely chopped peeled cucumber
30ml/2 tbsp dry sherry
25g/1oz/¼ cup coarsely chopped spring onions (scallions), with some of the green stems
475ml/16fl oz/2 cups mild-flavoured chicken stock
5ml/1 tsp salt
hot pepper sauce (optional)
natural yogurt or single (light) cream, to garnish

1 Cut the avocados in half, remove the stones and peel. Roughly chop the flesh and place in a food processor or blender. Add the lemon juice and process until very smooth.

2 Add the cucumber, sherry and most of the spring onions, reserving a few for the garnish. Process again until smooth.

3 In a large bowl, combine the avocado mixture with the chicken stock. Whisk until well blended. Season with the salt and a few drops of hot pepper sauce, if liked. Cover the bowl and place in the refrigerator to chill thoroughly.

4 To serve, fill individual bowls with the soup. Place a spoonful of yogurt or cream in the centre of each bowl and swirl with a spoon. Sprinkle with the reserved chopped spring onions.

Variation

For a refreshing, zesty avocado and lemon soup, use 3 avocados and add the grated rind and juice of 1 lemon (instead of the 15ml/1 tbsp juice). Omit the cucumber and add 25ml/8fl oz/1 cup unsweetened apple juice.

Asparagus Soup: Energy 157kcal/649kJ; Protein 5.7g; Carbohydrate 4.4g, of which sugars 4.2g; Fat 13.1g, of which saturates 7.8g; Cholesterol 32mg; Calcium 72mg; Fibre 3g; Sodium 70mg.
Avocado and Cucumber: Energy 155kcal/638kJ; Protein 1.7g; Carbohydrate 2g, of which sugars 0.9g; Fat 14.5g, of which saturates 3.1g; Cholesterol 0mg; Calcium 15mg; Fibre 2.8g; Sodium 498mg.

Chilled Avocado Soup with Cumin

Andalusia in southern Spain is home to both avocados and gazpacho, so it is not surprising that this chilled avocado soup, which is also known as green gazpacho, was invented there. Here, this mild, creamy soup is known simply as *sopa de aguacate* – avocado soup.

Serves 4

3 ripe avocados
1 bunch spring onions (scallions), white parts only, trimmed and roughly chopped
2 garlic cloves, chopped
juice of 1 lemon
1.5ml/¼ tsp ground cumin
1.5ml/¼ tsp paprika
450ml/¾ pint/scant 2 cups fresh chicken stock, cooled, and all fat skimmed off
300ml/½ pint/1¼ cups iced water
salt and ground black pepper
roughly chopped fresh flat leaf parsley, to serve

1 Starting half a day, or several hours ahead to allow time for chilling, put the flesh of one avocado in a food processor or blender. Add the spring onions, garlic and lemon juice and purée until smooth. Add the second avocado and purée, then the third, with the spices and seasoning. Purée until smooth.

2 Gradually add the chicken stock. Pour the soup into a metal bowl or other suitable container and chill.

3 To serve, stir in the iced water, then season to taste with plenty of salt and black pepper. Garnish with chopped parsley and serve immediately.

Cook's Tip
When avocados are plentiful and inexpensive, peel them, remove their stones (pits) and mash the flesh with lemon juice, then place in small containers in the freezer. Thaw in the refrigerator and they are ideal for soups or dips.

Parsnip and Fennel Soup

Instead of the usual hearty, winter versions of parsnip soup, this recipe is made with raw ingredients, using a juicer. With refreshing fennel, apple and pear as the perfect foils for the intense sweetness of parsnip, the result is excitingly different. More chilled soup than juice, thanks to the typically thick texture of the puréed parsnips, this is the perfect choice for a hand-around informal first course. It also makes a worthy partner to a lunchtime sandwich.

Serves 2

115g/4oz fennel
200g/7oz parsnips
1 apple
1 pear
a small handful of flat leaf parsley
crushed ice

1 Using a sharp knife, cut the fennel and parsnips into large similar-sized chunks. Quarter the apple and pear, carefully removing the core, then cut the quartered pieces in half.

2 Push half the prepared fruit and vegetables through a juicer, then follow with the parsley and, finally, process the remaining fruit and vegetables.

3 Fill short glasses with ice and pour the soup over the top. Serve immediately.

Cook's Tips
- *Parsnips are at their sweetest a few weeks after the first frost, so try serving shots of this wonderful soup when you are most in need of a little winter boost.*
- *For a slightly thicker soup, to eat with a spoon, remove the tough core of the parsnips and purée them with the other ingredients in a blender, adding unsweetened apple juice. Pour through a sieve (strainer).*

Avocado with Cumin: Energy 148kcal/613kJ; Protein 1.9g; Carbohydrate 2.2g, of which sugars 1.1g; Fat 14.6g, of which saturates 3.1g; Cholesterol 0mg; Calcium 18mg; Fibre 2.9g; Sodium 6mg.
Parsnip and Fennel: Energy 113kcal/477kJ; Protein 2.7g; Carbohydrate 24g, of which sugars 17.2g; Fat 1.3g, of which saturates 0.2g; Cholesterol 0mg; Calcium 65mg; Fibre 8.2g; Sodium 19mg.

Avocado and Lime Soup with Zesty Tomato Salsa

Inspired by guacamole, the popular avocado dip, this creamy soup relies on good-quality ripe avocados for its flavour and colour.

Serves 4

3 ripe avocados
juice of 1½ limes
1 garlic clove, crushed
handful of ice cubes
400ml/14fl oz/1⅔ cups vegetable stock, chilled
400ml/14fl oz/1⅔ cups milk, chilled
150ml/¼ pint/⅔ cup soured cream, chilled
few drops of Tabasco
salt and ground black pepper
fresh coriander (cilantro), to garnish
extra virgin olive oil, to serve

For the salsa

4 tomatoes, peeled, seeded and finely diced
2 spring onions (scallions), finely chopped
1 green chilli, seeded and finely chopped
15ml/1 tbsp chopped fresh coriander (cilantro)
juice of ½ lime

1 Prepare the salsa first. Mix all the ingredients and season well. Chill until required.

2 Halve and stone the avocados. Scoop the flesh out of the avocado skins and place in a food processor or blender. Add the lime juice, garlic, ice cubes and 150ml/¼ pint/⅔ cup of the vegetable stock.

3 Process the soup until smooth. Pour into a large bowl and stir in the remaining stock, milk, soured cream, Tabasco and seasoning. Cover and chill until required, but for no longer than about 2 hours or the avocado will discolour.

4 Ladle the soup into bowls or glasses and spoon a little salsa on top. If you like, serve small portions to start and take the main bowl, along with the salsa and olive oil, to the table. Add a splash of olive oil to each portion and garnish with fresh coriander leaves. Serve at once.

Sorrel and Spinach Soup with Smoked Fish

The warm taste of horseradish and the aniseed flavour of dill meld with sorrel and spinach to make this unusual Russian soup. It is an excellent summer soup, served chilled.

Serves 6

25g/1oz/2 tbsp butter
225g/8oz sorrel, stalks removed
225g/8oz young spinach, stalks removed
25g/1oz fresh horseradish, grated
750ml/1¼ pints/3 cups cider
1 pickled cucumber, finely chopped
30ml/2 tbsp chopped fresh dill
225g/8oz cooked fish, such as pike, perch or salmon, skinned and boned
salt and ground black pepper
sprig of dill, to garnish

1 Melt the butter in a large pan. Add the prepared sorrel and spinach leaves together with the grated fresh horseradish. Cover the pan and allow to cook gently for 3–4 minutes, or until the sorrel and spinach leaves have wilted.

2 Tip the vegetables into a food processor or blender and process to a fine purée (paste). Ladle into a tureen or bowl and stir in the cider, cucumber and dill.

3 Cut or break the fish into bitesize pieces. Add to the soup, then season well. Chill for at least 3 hours before serving, garnished with a sprig of dill.

Cook's Tips

Sorrel is a herb with a sharp, tangy flavour that is best compared with lemon juice. The soft leaves are best freshly picked as they are easily damaged and bruised. If sorrel is not available, increase the quantity of spinach and add some freshly squeezed lemon juice.

Avocado and Lime: Energy 335kcal/1390kJ; Protein 7.3g; Carbohydrate 12g, of which sugars 10.6g; Fat 28.9g, of which saturates 10g; Cholesterol 28mg; Calcium 176mg; Fibre 4.7g; Sodium 76mg.
Sorrel and Spinach: Energy 162kcal/676kJ; Protein 9.7g; Carbohydrate 4.5g, of which sugars 4.4g; Fat 8.2g, of which saturates 3g; Cholesterol 28mg; Calcium 146mg; Fibre 1.6g; Sodium 156mg.

Summer Pea and Ham Soup

This quick and simple soup is light and refreshing. Using frozen petits pois cuts out the labour involved in shelling fresh peas – you simply add them straight to the pan with the hot stock and herbs. Petits pois are much loved for their sweetness, and using frozen produce will produce a better flavour than canned.

Serves 6

25g/1oz/2 tbsp butter
1 leek, sliced
1 garlic clove, crushed
450g/1lb/4 cups frozen petits pois (baby peas)
1.2 litres/2 pints/5 cups vegetable stock
small bunch of fresh chives, coarsely snipped
300ml/½ pint/1¼ cups double (heavy) cream
90ml/6 tbsp Greek (strained plain) yogurt
4 slices prosciutto, roughly chopped
salt and ground black pepper
fresh chives, to garnish

1 Melt the butter in a pan. Add the leek and garlic, cover and cook gently for 4–5 minutes, until softened. Stir in the petits pois, stock and chives. Bring slowly to the boil, then simmer for 5 minutes. Cool slightly.

2 Process the soup in a food processor or blender until smooth. Pour into a bowl, stir in the cream and season. Chill for at least 2 hours.

3 Ladle the soup into bowls and add a spoon of Greek yogurt to the centre of each. Scatter the chopped prosciutto over the top and garnish with chives before serving.

Cook's Tips

- *Use kitchen scissors to trim and cut prosciutto – for best results do this straight into the soup, so that the pieces fall neatly rather than sticking together.*
- *For a clever garnish, cut five lengths of chives to about 6cm/2½in, then use another chive to tie them together. Lay this on top of the soup.*

Chilled Leek and Potato Soup

This creamy-smooth cold version of the classic vichyssoise is served with the refreshing tang of yogurt as a topping.

Serves 4

25g/1oz/2 tbsp butter
15ml/1 tbsp vegetable oil
1 small onion, chopped
3 leeks, sliced
2 floury potatoes, diced
600ml/1 pint/2½ cups vegetable stock
300ml/½ pint/1¼ cups milk
45ml/3 tbsp single (light) cream
a little extra milk (optional)
salt and ground black pepper
60ml/4 tbsp natural (plain) yogurt and fried leeks, to serve

1 Heat the butter and oil in a large pan and add the onion, leeks and potatoes. Cover and cook for 15 minutes, stirring occasionally, until the leeks have wilted and given up their juices. Bring to the boil, reduce the heat and simmer for 10 minutes.

2 Stir in the stock and milk and heat until simmering. Cover again and cook for a further 15 minutes, until the vegetables are completely tender.

3 Ladle the vegetables and liquid into a blender or a food processor in batches and purée until smooth. Pour into a bowl or jug (pitcher) for chilling. Stir in the cream and season.

4 Leave the soup to cool, and then chill for 3–4 hours, or longer until ready to serve. You may need to add a little extra milk to thin down the soup, as it will thicken slightly as it cools.

5 Ladle the soup into soup bowls and serve topped with a spoonful of natural yogurt and a sprinkling of leeks.

Variation

The classic soup is also delicious when spiced up slightly. Scrape out the seeds from eight green cardamoms, grind them to a powder in a mortar, and add them with the leeks in the first step. Add the grated rind of one small lemon with the cream.

Pea and Ham: Energy 386kcal/1610kJ; Protein 20.6g; Carbohydrate 32.8g, of which sugars 4.5g; Fat 20.1g, of which saturates 6.9g; Cholesterol 53mg; Calcium 47mg; Fibre 5.3g; Sodium 682mg.
Leek and Potato: Energy 410kcal/1695kJ; Protein 3.5g; Carbohydrate 13.2g, of which sugars 5.1g; Fat 38.5g, of which saturates 23.8g; Cholesterol 97mg; Calcium 59mg; Fibre 2.7g; Sodium 77mg.

Vichyssoise with Watercress Cream

This cold French version of leek and potato soup is one of the classic old-timers.

Serves 6

50g/2oz/¼ cup butter
1 onion, sliced
450g/1lb leeks, sliced
225g/8oz potatoes, sliced
750ml/1¼ pints/3 cups chicken stock
300ml/½ pint/1¼ cups milk
45ml/3 tbsp single (light) cream
salt and ground black pepper
fresh chervil, to garnish

For the watercress cream
1 bunch watercress, about 75g/3oz, stalks removed
small bunch of fresh chervil, finely chopped
150ml/¼ pint/⅔ cup double (heavy) cream
pinch of freshly grated nutmeg

1 Melt the butter in a large pan. Add the onion and leeks, cover and cook gently for 10 minutes, stirring occasionally, until softened. Stir in the potatoes and stock, and bring to the boil. Reduce the heat and simmer for 20 minutes or until the potatoes are tender. Cool slightly.

2 Process the soup in a food processor or blender until smooth, then press through a sieve (strainer) into a clean bowl.

3 Stir in the milk and single cream. Season the soup well and chill for at least 2 hours.

4 To make the watercress cream, process the watercress in a food processor or blender until finely chopped, then stir in the chervil and cream. Pour into a bowl and stir in the nutmeg with seasoning to taste. Ladle the vichyssoise into bowls and spoon the watercress cream on top. Garnish with chervil and serve.

Cook's Tip
Parsley and mint can be used instead of watercress to make a deliciously fresh cream garnish.

Chilled Sorrel Soup

This refreshingly sharp, chilled sorrel soup is a culinary souvenir of the Ashkenazim of Russia. The sorrel, also known as sour spinach or sour grass, gives a wonderful pale green colour and tangy flavour.

Serves 4–6

500g/1¼lb sorrel leaves, stems removed
1 medium–large onion, thinly sliced
1.5 litres/2½ pints/6¼ cups vegetable stock
15–30ml/1–2 tbsp sugar
60ml/4 tbsp lemon juice
2 eggs
150ml/¼ pint/⅔ cup sour cream
salt
3–4 spring onions (scallions), thinly sliced, to serve

1 Finely shred the sorrel, then put in a large pan with the onion and stock. Bring to the boil, then reduce the heat and simmer for 10–15 minutes.

2 Add the sugar and half the lemon juice to the pan, stir and simmer for a further 5–10 minutes.

3 In a bowl, beat the eggs and mix in the sour cream, then stir in about 250ml/8fl oz/1 cup of the hot soup. Add another 250ml/8fl oz/1 cup of soup, stirring to ensure a smooth texture.

4 Slowly pour the egg mixture into the hot soup, stirring constantly to prevent the eggs from curdling and ensuring a smooth texture. Cook for just a few moments over a low heat until the soup thickens slightly. Season with a little salt to taste and stir in the remaining lemon juice.

5 Leave the soup to cool, then chill for at least 2 hours. Taste again for seasoning (it may need more salt or lemon juice) and serve sprinkled with the spring onions.

Cook's Tip
Shred the sorrel across the grain. This will help to prevent it from becoming stringy when it is cooked.

Vichyssoise: Energy 407kcal/1682kJ; Protein 5.5g; Carbohydrate 16.8g, of which sugars 8.6g; Fat 35.7g, of which saturates 21.7g; Cholesterol 88mg; Calcium 118mg; Fibre 5.3g; Sodium 255mg.
Chilled Sorrel Soup: Energy 116Kcal/479kJ; Protein 5.5g; Carbohydrate 6.9g, of which sugars 6.2g; Fat 7.6g, of which saturates 3.7g; Cholesterol 78mg; Calcium 182mg; Fibre 2.1g; Sodium 151mg.

Coriander Cream Soup

This light, creamy soup is usually served warm, but it is just as delicious cold. It is the perfect choice as a chilled appetizer for an *al fresco* meal.

Serves 4

90ml/6 tbsp olive oil
3 onions, halved and sliced
1 garlic clove, chopped
2 bunches fresh coriander (cilantro), about 300g/11oz, chopped
300g/11oz potatoes, diced
8 cherry tomatoes, peeled
150g/5oz cheese, cut into cubes
salt and ground black pepper

1 Heat half the oil in a large pan. Add the onions, garlic and coriander and cook over a low heat, stirring occasionally, for 5 minutes, until softened.

2 Add the potatoes and 1 litre/1¾ pints/4 cups water. Bring to the boil, lower the heat and cook for 20–30 minutes, until the potatoes are tender. Preheat the oven to 160°C/350°F/Gas 3.

3 Transfer the soup to a food processor or blender and process to a purée. Season to taste with salt. If you are serving the soup hot, re-heat gently. Otherwise, leave to cool, then chill in the refrigerator.

4 Place the tomatoes in a small casserole, drizzle them with the remaining olive oil and season with salt and pepper. Bake them for 10 minutes. If serving the soup cold, the tomatoes can be baked ahead and cooled, or served hot, as preferred.

5 Serve the soup hot or cold in bowls with two tomatoes each, the cubed cheese and sprinkled with some of the olive oil used to cook the tomatoes.

Cook's Tip

Firm, mild fresh goat's cheese is delicious in the soup or try feta. For a milder flavour add white cheese (Cheshire or Lancashire) or for a kick, add blue cheese (Stilton or Danish).

Juniper and Apple Soup

This is an example of the savoury fruit soups that are popular throughout northern Europe. The apple and juniper flavours are particularly Norwegian. Here it's the berries that are being used, not the fresh young shoots.

Serves 4

15ml/1 tbsp juniper berries
4 green cardamom pods
3 whole allspice
1 small cinnamon stick
bunch of fresh parsley
30ml/2 tbsp olive oil
3 cooking apples, peeled, cored and diced
2 celery sticks, finely chopped
2 shallots, chopped
2.5cm/1in piece fresh root ginger, finely chopped
1 litre/1¾ pints/4 cups light chicken stock
250ml/8fl oz/1 cup cider
250ml/8fl oz/1 cup double (heavy) cream
75ml/5 tbsp Armagnac (optional)
salt and ground black pepper
chopped fresh parsley, to garnish

1 Put the juniper berries, cardamom pods, allspice and cinnamon stick in a piece of muslin (cheesecloth) and tie together with string. Tie the parsley together.

2 Heat the oil in a pan, add the apples, celery, shallots and ginger, and season with salt and pepper. Place a piece of dampened baking parchment on top, cover the pan and cook gently for 10 minutes. Discard the parchment.

3 Add the stock and cider and stir well. Add the spices and parsley. Bring the soup slowly to the boil, then lower the heat and cover the pan. Simmer for 40 minutes, until the apples are reduced to a pulp and the vegetables are soft. Remove the spices and parsley.

4 Pour the soup into a food processor or blender and blend until smooth. Then pass it through a sieve (strainer) into a clean pan. Reheat, stirring occasionally, until boiling. Reduce the heat or turn it off, so that the soup barely simmers, then stir in the cream and Armagnac, if using. Taste the soup and add salt and pepper if necessary. Ladle the soup into bowls and serve hot, garnished with parsley.

Coriander Soup: Energy 439kcal/1820kJ; Protein 15g; Carbohydrate 26.4g, of which sugars 11.5g; Fat 30.3g, of which saturates 10.6g; Cholesterol 36mg; Calcium 470mg; Fibre 6.7g; Sodium 310mg.
Juniper and Apple: Energy 406kcal/1677kJ; Protein 1.4g; Carbohydrate 8.5g, of which sugars 8.1g; Fat 39.2g, of which saturates 21.7g; Cholesterol 86mg; Calcium 48mg; Fibre 1.2g; Sodium 29mg.

Apple Soup with Mixed Vegetables

This delicious and unusual soup makes the most of freshly picked apples.

Serves 6

45ml/3 tbsp oil
1 kohlrabi, diced
3 carrots, diced
2 celery sticks, diced
1 green (bell) pepper, seeded and diced
2 tomatoes, diced
2 litres/3½ pints/9 cups chicken stock
6 large green apples
45ml/3 tbsp plain (all-purpose) flour
150ml/¼ pint/⅔ cup double (heavy) cream
15ml/1 tbsp sugar
30–45ml/2–3 tbsp lemon juice
salt and freshly ground black pepper
lemon wedges and crusty bread, to serve

1 Heat the oil in a large pan. Add the kohlrabi, carrots, celery, green pepper and tomatoes and fry for 5–6 minutes to soften.

2 Pour in the chicken stock, bring to the boil, then reduce the heat and simmer for about 45 minutes.

3 Meanwhile, peel and core the apples, then chop into small cubes. Add to the pan and simmer for a further 15 minutes.

4 In a bowl, mix together the flour and cream, then pour slowly into the soup, stirring well, and bring to the boil. Add the sugar and lemon juice before seasoning. Serve immediately with lemon wedges and crusty bread.

Cook's Tip
Firm, sweet-sour eating apples are ideal for this soup as they hold their shape and complement the vegetable mixture. For a vegetarian version, use vegetable stock. For a meaty variation, dice and fry some firm meaty sausage, such as ham sausage, kabanos or salami, and use to garnish the soup before serving.

Simple Cream of Celeriac and Spinach Soup

Celeriac has a wonderful flavour that is reminiscent of celery, but also adds a slightly nutty taste. Despite its tough, warty exterior, it is relatively quick to cook, and is often used mashed or puréed in soups and stews.

Serves 6

1 litre/1¾ pints/4 cups water or stock
250ml/8fl oz/1 cup dry white wine
1 leek, thickly sliced
500g/1¼lb celeriac, diced
200g/7oz spinach leaves
freshly grated nutmeg
salt and freshly ground black pepper
25g/1oz/¼ cup pine nuts, to garnish

1 Mix the water or stock and wine in a jug (pitcher). Place the leek, celeriac and spinach in a deep pan and pour the liquid over them. Bring to the boil, lower the heat and simmer for 10–15 minutes until the vegetables are soft.

2 Pour the celeriac mixture into a blender or food processor and purée until smooth, in batches if necessary. Return to the clean pan and season to taste with salt, ground black pepper and nutmeg. Reheat gently.

3 Heat a non-stick frying pan (do not add any oil) and add the pine nuts. Roast until golden brown, stirring frequently so that they do not stick. Sprinkle them over the soup and serve.

Cook's Tip
If the soup is too thick, thin it with a little water, stock or semi-skimmed milk when puréeing. Vegetable stock can be used for a meat-free soup, or ham stock is delicious with celeriac and spinach. Cider can be used instead of the wine, or increase the quantity of stock or water and omit the alcohol completely.

Apple with Vegetables: Energy 278kcal/1159kJ; Protein 2.4g; Carbohydrate 24.8g, of which sugars 18.8g; Fat 19.5g, of which saturates 9.2g; Cholesterol 34mg; Calcium 63mg; Fibre 4.6g; Sodium 54mg.
Celeriac and Spinach Soup: Energy 77kcal/319kJ; Protein 2.5g; Carbohydrate 2.6g, of which sugars 2.3g; Fat 3.4g, of which saturates 0.3g; Cholesterol 0mg; Calcium 102mg; Fibre 2.3g; Sodium 99mg.

Salmon and Rocket Soup

In Scotland, where this soup originates, the kiln-smoked salmon used to garnish is actually "cooked" during the smoking process, producing a delicious flaky texture. Kiln-smoked salmon is available at some specialist shops and delicatessens – it is a delightful partner for this soup if you can find it.

Serves 4

15ml/1 tbsp olive oil
1 small onion, sliced
1 garlic clove, crushed
150ml/¼ pint/⅔cup double (heavy) cream
350ml/12fl oz/1½ cups vegetable stock
350g/12oz rocket (arugula)
4 fresh basil leaves
salt and ground black pepper
flaked kiln-smoked salmon, to garnish

1 Heat the olive oil in a pan over a medium heat. Add the onion and sweat for a few minutes, stirring continuously. Add the garlic and continue to sweat gently until soft and transparent, but not browned.

2 Add the cream and stock, stir in gently and bring slowly to the boil. Allow to simmer gently for about 5 minutes. Add the rocket, reserving a few leaves to garnish, and the basil. Return briefly to the boil and turn off the heat. Add a little cold water and allow to cool for a few minutes.

3 Purée the soup in a blender until smooth, adding a little salt and pepper to taste. Reheat gently but do not allow to boil. Serve topped with a few flakes of salmon, a leaf or two of rocket and a drizzle of virgin olive oil over the top.

Variation
Cold-smoked salmon is also very good with this soup. Simply cut a few slices into medium-thick strips and add to the hot soup. Warming the smoked salmon for a few minutes increases its flavour. Take care when seasoning as cold smoked salmon is very salty.

Cream of Asparagus Soup

This Dutch soup is made without meat or meat stock (rare for their traditional soups). White asparagus is less common than its more familiar green relative as it can be difficult and time-consuming to cultivate.

Serves 4

500g/1¼lb white or green asparagus, peeled and trimmed
1.2 litres/2 pints/5 cups asparagus stock or water
65g/2½oz/5 tbsp butter
75g/3oz/2⁄3 cup plain (all-purpose) flour
120ml/4fl oz/½ cup whipping cream
salt and ground white pepper
finely chopped fresh parsley, to garnish

1 Cut the asparagus spears into 5cm/2in pieces and set the tips aside in some water.

2 Bring the stock or water to the boil in a pan, add the pieces of asparagus stalk, cover and simmer for 20 minutes, until the asparagus is tender. Remove the asparagus with a slotted spoon and pass it through a sieve (strainer) into a bowl or process it in a blender or food processor and then sieve it to remove fibres. Reserve the stock.

3 Melt the butter in a large pan over a low heat, but do not let it brown. Stir in the flour and cook, stirring constantly, for about 2 minutes. Gradually stir in the stock and bring to the boil, stirring. Then add the asparagus purée and the cream.

4 Strain the soup into a clean pan, then return it to the heat and bring to the boil, stirring constantly.

5 Drain the asparagus tips, add them to the soup and simmer, stirring occasionally, for 10 minutes, until they are tender.

6 Taste the soup and add salt and pepper. Ladle the soup into bowls and serve immediately, garnished with chopped parsley.

Salmon and Rocket: Energy 258kcal/1063kJ; Protein 6.8g; Carbohydrate 3.2g, of which sugars 2.8g; Fat 24.3g, of which saturates 13.1g; Cholesterol 56mg; Calcium 174mg; Fibre 2.1g; Sodium 395mg.
Asparagus Soup: Energy 331kcal/1368kJ; Protein 6.1g; Carbohydrate 18g, of which sugars 3.6g; Fat 26.5g, of which saturates 16.2g; Cholesterol 66mg; Calcium 80mg; Fibre 2.7g; Sodium 108mg.

Asparagus and Pea Soup

This bright and tasty soup is good for using a glut of asparagus.

Serves 6

350g/12oz asparagus
2 leeks
1 bay leaf
1 carrot, roughly chopped
1 celery stick, chopped
few stalks of fresh parsley
1.75 litres/3 pints/7½ cups cold water
25g/1oz/2 tbsp butter
150g/5oz fresh garden peas
15ml/1 tbsp chopped fresh parsley
120ml/4 fl oz/½ cup double (heavy) cream
grated rind of ½ lemon
salt and ground black pepper
shavings of Parmesan cheese, to serve

1 Cut the woody ends from the asparagus, then set the spears aside. Roughly chop the woody ends and place them in a large pan. Cut off and chop the green parts of the leeks and add to the asparagus stalks with the bay leaf, carrot, celery, parsley stalks and the cold water. Bring to the boil and simmer for about 30 minutes. Strain the stock and discard the vegetables.

2 Cut the tips off the asparagus and set aside, then cut the stems into short pieces. Chop the remainder of the leeks.

3 Melt the butter in a large pan and add the leeks. Cook for 3–4 minutes until softened. Add the asparagus stems, peas and parsley. Pour in 1.2 litres/2 pints/5 cups of the asparagus stock. Boil, reduce the heat and cook for 6–8 minutes. Season well.

4 Purée the soup in a food processor or blender. Press through a fine sieve (strainer) into the rinsed-out pan. Stir in the cream and lemon rind.

5 Bring a small pan of water to the boil and cook the asparagus tips for 2–3 minutes or until tender. Drain and refresh under cold water. Reheat the soup, but do not boil.

6 Ladle the soup into six warmed bowls and garnish with the asparagus tips. Serve immediately, with shavings of Parmesan cheese and plenty of ground black pepper.

Mushroom Soup Thickened with Bread

This rich mushroom soup is warming and satisfying, and the perfect antidote to cold winter days. It makes a particularly hearty lunch. Adding pieces of bread to soup during cooking is a very easy, traditional way of thickening up the texture.

Serves 8

75g/3oz/6 tbsp unsalted (sweet) butter
900g/2lb field (portabello) mushrooms, sliced
2 onions, roughly chopped
600ml/1 pint/2½ cups milk
8 slices white bread
60ml/4 tbsp chopped fresh parsley
300ml/½ pint/1¼ cups double (heavy) cream
salt and freshly ground black pepper

1 Melt the butter and sauté the sliced mushrooms and chopped onions for about 10 minutes until soft but not browned. Add the milk and heat until just simmering, then remove from the heat.

2 Cut the crusts off the bread and tear the slices into pieces. Drop the pieces of bread into the soup, cover and leave to soak for 15 minutes.

3 Purée the soup in a food processor or blender and return it to the pan. Reheat gently, stirring all the time to prevent the soup from burning on the bottom of the pan.

4 Add 45ml/3 tbsp of the parsley, the cream and seasoning to the soup, then reheat, without boiling. Serve garnished with the remaining parsley.

Variation
Use close-textured walnut bread for a rich, nutty soup. Cook the mushrooms in olive oil instead of butter and drizzle a little walnut oil into the soup before serving.

Asparagus and Pea: Energy 184kcal/759kJ; Protein 4.9g; Carbohydrate 7.2g, of which sugars 4.4g; Fat 15.3g, of which saturates 9.1g; Cholesterol 36mg; Calcium 56mg; Fibre 3.9g; Sodium 39mg.
Mushroom with Bread: Energy 296kcal/1243kJ; Protein 9.9g; Carbohydrate 34.4g, of which sugars 7.7g; Fat 14.3g, of which saturates 6.8g; Cholesterol 28mg; Calcium 205mg; Fibre 1.8g; Sodium 373mg.

Mushroom Soup with Croûtes

This classic soup is still a favourite, especially with crisp and garlicky croûtes.

Serves 6

1 onion, chopped
1 garlic clove, chopped
25g/1oz/2 tbsp butter
450g/1lb/6 cups chestnut or brown cap mushrooms, roughly chopped
15ml/1 tbsp plain (all-purpose) flour
45ml/3 tbsp dry sherry
900ml/1½ pints/3¾ cups vegetable stock
150ml/¼ pint/⅔ cup double (heavy) cream
salt and ground black pepper
sprigs of fresh chervil, to garnish

For the crostini

15ml/1 tbsp olive oil, plus extra for brushing
1 shallot, chopped
115g/4oz/1½ cups button mushrooms, finely chopped
15ml/1 tbsp chopped fresh parsley
6 brown cap mushrooms
6 slices baguette
1 small garlic clove
115g/4oz/1 cup soft goat's cheese

1 Cook the onion and garlic in the butter for 5 minutes. Add the mushrooms, cover and cook for 10 minutes, stirring often. Stir in the flour and cook for 1 minute. Stir in the sherry and stock and bring to the boil, then simmer for 15 minutes. Cool slightly, then purée it in a food processor or blender.

2 For the croûtes, heat the oil in a small pan. Add the shallot and button mushrooms, and cook for 8–10 minutes, until softened. Drain well and transfer to a food processor. Add the parsley and process until finely chopped.

3 Preheat the grill (broiler). Brush the brown cap mushrooms with oil and grill for 5–6 minutes. Toast the baguette, rub with the garlic and top with goat's cheese. Add the grilled mushrooms and fill these with the mushroom mixture.

4 Return the soup to the pan and stir in the cream. Season, then reheat gently. Ladle the soup into six bowls. Float a croûte in the centre of each and garnish with chervil.

Cream of Wild Mushroom Soup

Wild mushrooms are at their best in late summer and early Autumn.

Serves 4

10g/¼oz/1 tbsp dried mushrooms, such as ceps, if wild are unavailable
400g/14oz mushrooms, preferably wild, sliced
1.25 litres/2¼ pints/5½ cups vegetable or chicken stock
50g/2oz/4 tbsp butter
30–45ml/2–3 tbsp plain (all-purpose) flour
60ml/4 tbsp double (heavy) cream, plus extra to garnish
a squeeze of fresh lemon juice
15–30ml/1–2 tbsp medium sherry (optional)
salt and ground black pepper
chopped fresh parsley, to garnish

1 If using dried mushrooms, put in a small bowl and pour over plenty of boiling water. Leave to soak for at least 20 minutes, until soft. Using a slotted spoon, remove the mushrooms, then strain the liquid and reserve. Chop the soaked mushrooms.

2 Put the sliced mushrooms in a pan, cover with the stock and simmer for 10 minutes. Strain the stock and reserve.

3 Melt the butter in a large pan, add the sliced mushrooms and the soaked mushrooms and fry gently for 2–3 minutes. Stir in seasoning and the flour and cook gently for 1–2 minutes, without colouring. Remove from the heat and gradually stir in the reserved stock and soaking liquid to form a smooth sauce. Return to the heat and bring to the boil, stirring. Lower the heat and simmer gently for 5–10 minutes.

4 Add the cream, lemon juice to taste and sherry, if using. Pour into bowls and top with a little cream and chopped parsley.

Cook's Tips

- *Wild mushrooms have an intense flavour that makes this soup rich and satisfying.*
- *Choose a single type of wild mushroom or combine varieties, adding some cultivated mushrooms, if liked, according to whatever is available and personal preference.*

Mushroom with Croûtes: Energy 368kcal/1533kJ; Protein 10.3g; Carbohydrate 25.1g, of which sugars 3.1g; Fat 25g, of which saturates 14.5g; Cholesterol 61mg; Calcium 99mg; Fibre 2.4g; Sodium 399mg.
Wild Mushroom: Energy 154kcal/638kJ; Protein 3.2g; Carbohydrate 9.3g, of which sugars 0.5g; Fat 11.8g, of which saturates 7.2g; Cholesterol 29mg; Calcium 26mg; Fibre 1.6g; Sodium 82mg.

Mushroom, Leek and Shallot Soup

The Italian dried wild porcini mushrooms are quite expensive, but they have an intense flavour, so only a small amount is needed for this recipe. Beef stock may seem unusual for a vegetable soup, but it helps strengthen the earthy flavour of the mushrooms.

Serves 4

25g/1oz/½ cup dried porcini mushrooms
30ml/2 tbsp olive oil
15g/½oz/1 tbsp butter
2 leeks, thinly sliced
2 shallots, roughly chopped
1 garlic clove, roughly chopped
225g/8oz/3 cups fresh wild mushrooms, such as ceps or chanterelles
about 1.2 litres/2 pints/5 cups beef stock
2.5ml/½ tsp dried thyme
150ml/¼ pint/⅔ cup double (heavy) cream
salt and ground black pepper
fresh thyme sprigs, to garnish

1 Put the dried porcini in a bowl, add 250ml/8fl oz/1 cup warm water and leave to soak for 20–30 minutes. Lift out of the liquid and squeeze over the bowl to remove the soaking liquid. Strain the liquid and reserve. Finely chop the porcini.

2 Heat the oil and butter in a large pan until foaming. Add the leeks, shallots and garlic and cook gently for about 5 minutes, stirring frequently, until softened but not coloured.

3 Chop or slice the fresh mushrooms and add to the pan. Stir over medium heat for a few minutes until the mushrooms begin to soften. Add the stock and bring to the boil. Add the porcini, soaking liquid, thyme and salt and pepper. Lower the heat, half cover the pan and simmer gently for 30 minutes, stirring occasionally.

4 Pour about three-quarters of the soup into a blender or food processor and process until smooth. Return to the soup remaining in the pan, stir in the cream and heat through. Check the consistency and add more stock if the soup is too thick. Taste for seasoning. Serve hot, garnished with thyme sprigs.

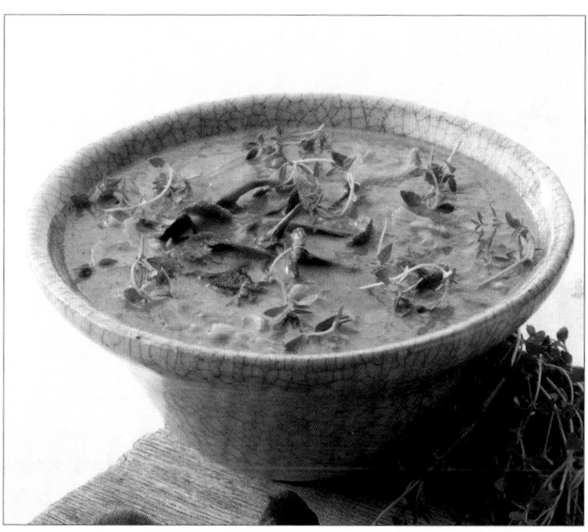

Courgette Soup with Cheese

The beauty of this soup is its delicate colour, rich and creamy texture and subtle flavour. If you prefer a more pronounced cheese flavour, use Gorgonzola instead of Dolcelatte.

Serves 4–6

30ml/2 tbsp olive oil
15g/½oz/1 tbsp butter
1 onion, roughly chopped
900g/2lb courgettes (zucchini), trimmed and sliced
5ml/1 tsp dried oregano
about 600ml/1 pint/2½ cups vegetable or chicken stock
115g/4oz Dolcelatte cheese, rind removed, diced
300ml/½ pint/1¼ cups single (light) cream
salt and ground black pepper
fresh oregano and extra Dolcelatte, to garnish

1 Heat the oil and butter in a large pan until foaming. Add the onion and cook gently for about 5 minutes, stirring frequently, until softened but not brown.

2 Add the courgettes and oregano to the pan, with salt and pepper to taste. Cook over medium heat for 10 minutes, stirring frequently.

3 Pour in the stock and bring to the boil, stirring. Lower the heat, half cover the pan and simmer gently, stirring occasionally, for about 30 minutes. Stir in the diced Dolcelatte and heat gently, still stirring, until it has melted.

4 Process the soup in a food processor or blender until smooth, then press through a sieve (strainer) back into the rinsed-out pan.

5 Add two-thirds of the cream and stir over low heat until hot, but not boiling. Check the consistency and add more stock if the soup is too thick. Taste and adjust the seasoning.

6 Pour the soup into heated bowls. Swirl in the remaining cream and sprinkle with a little extra cheese. Garnish each portion with a few sprigs of oregano and serve.

Courgette with Cheese: Energy 248kcal/1024kJ; Protein 8.5g; Carbohydrate 5.4g, of which sugars 4.8g; Fat 21.5g, of which saturates 11.7g; Cholesterol 47mg; Calcium 181mg; Fibre 1.6g; Sodium 266mg.
Mushroom and Leek: Energy 287kcal/1184kJ; Protein 2.8g; Carbohydrate 3.1g, of which sugars 2.4g; Fat 29.4g, of which saturates 15.4g; Cholesterol 59mg; Calcium 41mg; Fibre 2.3g; Sodium 35mg.

Celery Soup with Stilton

Stilton – known as the "king of English cheeses" – and celery are traditional partners, whether on the cheeseboard or in this deliciously warming winter soup. The two flavours complement each other beautifully, with the fresh, clean taste of the celery setting off the rich, creamy texture and tang of the famous blue-veined cheese.

Serves 6

40g/1½oz/3 tbsp butter
1 large onion, finely chopped
1 potato, cut into small cubes
1 head of celery, thinly sliced
900ml/1½ pints/3¾ cups vegetable or chicken stock
100g/3¾oz Stilton cheese, crumbled
150ml/¼ pint/⅔ cup single (light) cream
salt and ground black pepper

1 Melt the butter in a large pan and add the onion. Cook over a medium heat for 5 minutes, stirring occasionally, until soft but not browned.

2 Stir in the potato and celery and cook for a further 5 minutes until the vegetables soften and begin to brown.

3 Add the stock, bring to the boil, then cover the pan and simmer gently for about 30 minutes, until all the vegetables are very soft.

4 Process or blend about three-quarters of the soup until smooth, then return it to the pan with the rest of the soup. For a smoother soup, process a larger batch.

5 Bring the soup just to the boil, stirring, and season to taste with salt and ground black pepper.

6 Remove the pan from the heat and stir in the cheese, reserving a little for the garnish. Stir in three-quarters of the cream, reserving just a little for garnish, and reheat the soup gently, if necessary, without boiling.

7 Serve topped with the reserved crumbled cheese and drizzled with the remaining cream.

Onion Soup with Chives

This wonderfully soothing soup has a deep, buttery flavour that is complemented by crisp croûtons and snipped chives, sprinkled over just before serving.

Serves 4

115g/4oz/½ cup unsalted (sweet) butter
1kg/2¼lb onions, sliced
1 fresh bay leaf
105ml/7 tbsp dry white vermouth
1 litre/1¾ pints/4 cups good chicken or vegetable stock
150ml/¼ pint/⅔ cup double (heavy) cream
a little lemon juice (optional)
salt and ground black pepper
snipped fresh chives, to garnish
croûtons, to serve

1 Melt 75g/3oz/6 tbsp of the butter in a large heavy-based pan. Set about 200g/7oz of the onions aside and add the rest to the pan with the bay leaf. Stir to coat in the butter, then cover and cook very gently for about 30 minutes. The onions should be very soft and tender, but not browned.

2 Add the vermouth, increase the heat and boil rapidly until the liquid has evaporated. Add the stock, about 5ml/1 tsp salt and pepper to taste. Bring to the boil, lower the heat and simmer for 5 minutes, then remove from the heat.

3 Leave the soup to cool, then discard the bay leaf and process the soup in a food processor or blender until smooth. Return the soup to the rinsed pan.

4 Meanwhile, melt the remaining butter in another pan and cook the remaining onions slowly, covered, until soft but not browned. Uncover and continue to cook gently until the onions are golden yellow.

5 Add the cream to the soup and reheat it gently until hot, but do not allow it to boil. Taste and adjust the seasoning, adding a little lemon juice if liked. Add the buttery onions and stir for 1–2 minutes, then ladle the soup into bowls. Sprinkle with snipped chives and serve with croûtons.

Celery with Stilton: Energy 199kcal/826kJ; Protein 5.9g; Carbohydrate 7.5g, of which sugars 2.4g; Fat 16.2g, of which saturates 10.4g; Cholesterol 44mg; Calcium 117mg; Fibre 1.4g; Sodium 233mg.
Onion with Chives: Energy 233Kcal/965kJ; Protein 7.2g; Carbohydrate 16.2g, of which sugars 12.3g; Fat 16g, of which saturates 5.2g; Cholesterol 27mg; Calcium 51mg; Fibre 3.3g; Sodium 398mg.

Cream of Corn Soup

Quick and easy to prepare, this colourful soup has a sweet and creamy flavour. Children love it.

Serves 6

2 red (bell) peppers
30ml/2 tbsp vegetable oil
1 onion, finely chopped
500g/1¼lb/3–4 cups corn, thawed if frozen
750ml/1¼ pints/3 cups chicken stock
150ml/¼ pint/⅔ cup single (light) cream
salt and ground black pepper

1 Dry fry the peppers in a frying pan griddle pan over a moderate heat, turning them frequently until the skins are blistered all over. Place them in a strong plastic bag and tie the top to keep the steam in. Set aside for 20 minutes, then remove the peppers from the bag and peel off the skin.

2 Cut the peppers in half and scoop out the seeds and cores. Set one aside. Cut the other into 1cm/½in dice.

3 Heat the oil in a large pan. Add the onion and fry over a low heat for about 10 minutes, until it is translucent and soft. Stir in the diced pepper and corn and fry for 5 minutes over a moderate heat.

4 Spoon the contents of the pan into a food processor or blender, pour in the chicken stock and process until almost smooth. This processing can be done in batches if necessary.

5 Return the soup to the pan and reheat it until almost boiling. Stir in the cream with salt and pepper to taste. Core, seed and cut the reserved pepper into thin strips and add half of these to the pan. Serve the soup in heated bowls, garnished with the remaining pepper strips.

Cook's Tip
Look out for roasted red (bell) peppers in jars. These come ready-skinned and are useful in all sorts of recipes. Used here, they would make a quick soup even speedier.

Aubergine and Mozzarella Soup

Gremolata is a classic Italian garnish combining garlic, lemon and parsley. It is easy to make, and adds a flourish of fresh flavour to this rich cream soup.

Serves 6

30ml/2 tbsp olive oil
2 shallots, chopped
2 garlic cloves, chopped
1kg/2¼lb aubergines (eggplants), trimmed and roughly chopped
1 litre/1¾ pints/4 cups chicken stock
150ml/¼ pint/⅔ cup double (heavy) cream
30ml/2 tbsp chopped fresh parsley
175g/6oz mozzarella cheese, thinly sliced
salt and ground black pepper

For the gremolata
2 garlic cloves, finely chopped
grated rind of 2 lemons
60ml/4 tbsp chopped fresh parsley

1 Heat the oil in a large pan and add the shallots and garlic. Cook for 4–5 minutes, until softened. Add the aubergines and cook for about 25 minutes, stirring occasionally, until they are very soft and browned.

2 Pour in the chicken stock and bring to the boil. Reduce the heat, cover the pan and simmer the soup for about 5 minutes, until the aubergines are very soft. Leave the soup to cool slightly before processing.

3 Purée the soup in a food processor or blender until smooth. Pour it back into the rinsed-out pan. Add the cream and seasoning to taste. Stir in the parsley, and heat through.

4 Mix the ingredients for the gremolata. Ladle the soup into bowls and lay the mozzarella on top. Scatter with gremolata and serve.

Cook's Tip
Buffalo mozzarella is the creamiest type. The large blocks of Danish mozzarella tend to be dense and rubbery.

Cream of Corn: Energy 218kcal/914kJ; Protein 4.2g; Carbohydrate 27.4g, of which sugars 12.8g; Fat 11g, of which saturates 4.5g; Cholesterol 17mg; Calcium 39mg; Fibre 2.2g; Sodium 237mg.
Aubergine/Mozzarella: Energy 261kcal/1079kJ; Protein 7.5g; Carbohydrate 4.9g, of which sugars 4.3g; Fat 23.7g, of which saturates 13.1g; Cholesterol 51mg; Calcium 137mg; Fibre 3.5g; Sodium 124mg.

Potato and Fennel Soup

Savoury scones are delicious with this lightly spiced soup.

Serves 4

75g/3oz/6 tbsp butter
2 onions, chopped
5ml/1 tsp fennel seeds, crushed
3 bulbs fennel, coarsely chopped
900g/2lb potatoes, thinly sliced
1.2 litres/2 pints/5 cups chicken stock
150ml/¼ pint/⅔ cup double (heavy) cream
salt and ground black pepper
handful of fresh herb flowers and 15ml/1 tbsp snipped fresh chives, to garnish

For the rosemary scones

225g/8oz/2 cups self-raising (self-rising) flour
2.5ml/½ tsp salt
5ml/1 tsp baking powder
10ml/2 tsp chopped fresh rosemary
50g/2oz/¼ cup butter
150ml/¼ pint/⅔ cup milk
1 egg, beaten, to glaze

1 Melt the butter in a pan. Add the onions and cook gently for 10 minutes, stirring occasionally, until very soft. Add the fennel seeds and cook for 2–3 minutes. Stir in the fennel and potatoes. Cover with wet greaseproof paper. Cover and simmer gently for 10 minutes, until very soft. Remove the paper. Pour in the stock, bring to the boil, cover and simmer for 35 minutes.

2 Meanwhile, make the scones. Preheat the oven to 230°C/450°F/Gas 8 and grease a baking tray. Sift the flour, salt and baking powder into a bowl. Stir in the rosemary, then rub in the butter. Add the milk and mix to form a soft dough.

3 Knead very lightly on a floured surface. Roll out to 2cm/¾in thick. Stamp out 12 rounds with a cutter and place on the baking tray. Brush with egg and bake for 8–10 minutes, until risen and golden. Cool on a wire rack until warm.

4 Purée the soup in a food processor or blender until smooth. Press through a sieve into the rinsed-out pan. Stir in the cream with seasoning to taste. Reheat gently but do not boil.

5 Ladle the soup in bowls, and scatter with a few herb flowers and snipped chives. Serve with the warm rosemary scones.

Leek and Potato Soup with Rocket

Rocket adds its distinctive, peppery flavour to this wonderfully satisfying soup. Serve it hot, garnished with a generous sprinkling of tasty ciabatta croûtons.

Serves 4–6

50g/2oz/4 tbsp butter
1 onion, chopped
3 leeks, chopped
2 floury potatoes, diced
900ml/1½ pints/3¾ cups light chicken stock or water
2 large handfuls rocket (arugula), roughly chopped
150ml/¼ pint/⅔ cup double (heavy) cream
salt and ground black pepper
garlic-flavoured ciabatta croûtons, to serve

1 Melt the butter in a large heavy-based pan then add the onion, leeks and potatoes and stir until the vegetables are coated in butter. Heat the ingredients until they are sizzling and then reduce the heat to low.

2 Cover the pan and sweat the vegetables for 15 minutes. Pour in the stock or water and bring to the boil, then reduce the heat. Cover again and simmer for 20 minutes or until the vegetables are tender.

3 Press the soup through a sieve (strainer) or pass through a food mill and return to the rinsed-out pan. Add the chopped rocket to the pan and cook the soup gently, uncovered, for 5 minutes.

4 Stir in the cream, then season to taste and reheat gently. Ladle the soup into warmed soup bowls and serve with a scattering of garlic-flavoured ciabatta croûtons in each.

Variation

When puréeing the soup, a mill or sieve (strainer) gives a good, smooth texture. A food processor or blender can – very quickly – make the soup glue-like in texture.

Potato/Fennel: Energy 797kcal/3331kJ; Protein 12.2g; Carbohydrate 84g, of which sugars 8.8g; Fat 48.1g, of which saturates 29.5g; Cholesterol 120.3mg; Calcium 315mg; Fibre 7.6g; Sodium 703mg.
Leek and Potato: Energy 235kcal/972kJ; Protein 2.8g; Carbohydrate 9.4g, of which sugars 3.2g; Fat 20.9g, of which saturates 12.8g; Cholesterol 52mg; Calcium 75mg; Fibre 2.3g; Sodium 97mg.

Leek and Potato with Heart of Palm Soup

This delicate soup has a luxurious, creamy, almost velvety texture. The subtle yet distinctive flavour of the palm hearts is like no other, although it is mildly reminiscent of artichokes and asparagus. Serve with fresh bread for a really satisfying lunch.

Serves 4

25g/1oz/2 tbsp butter
10ml/2 tsp olive oil
1 onion, finely chopped
1 large leek, finely sliced
15ml/1 tbsp plain (all-purpose) flour
1 litre/1¾ pints/4 cups well-flavoured chicken stock
350g/12oz potatoes, peeled and cubed
2 x 400g/14oz cans hearts of palm, drained and sliced
250ml/8fl oz/1 cup double (heavy) cream
salt and ground black pepper
cayenne pepper and chopped fresh chives, to garnish

1 Heat the butter and oil in a large pan over a low heat. Add the onion and leek and stir well until coated in butter. Cover and cook for 5 minutes until softened and translucent.

2 Sprinkle the flour into the pan over the vegetables. Stir and cook, still stirring, for 1 minute.

3 Pour in the stock and add the potatoes. Bring to the boil, stirring, then lower the heat and simmer for 10 minutes. Stir in the hearts of palm and the cream, and simmer gently for a further 10 minutes.

4 Process the soup in a food processor or blender until smooth. Pour it back into the rinsed-out pan and heat gently, adding a little water if necessary. The consistency should be thick but not too heavy. Do not allow to boil. Season with salt and ground black pepper.

5 Ladle the soup into warm bowls and garnish each portion with a pinch of cayenne pepper and a scattering of fresh chives. Serve immediately.

Cream of Parsnip Soup

This lightly spiced soup has become popular in recent years, and variations abound, including a traditional combination of parsnip and apple in equal proportions.

Serves 6

900g/2lb parsnips
50g/2oz/¼ cup butter
1 onion, chopped
2 garlic cloves, crushed
10ml/2 tsp ground cumin
5ml/1 tsp ground coriander
about 1.2 litres/2 pints/5 cups hot chicken stock
150ml/¼ pint/⅔ cup single (light) cream
salt and ground black pepper
chopped fresh chives or parsley and/or croûtons, to garnish

1 Peel and thinly slice the parsnips. Heat the butter in a large heavy pan and add the peeled parsnips and chopped onion with the crushed garlic. Cook until softened but not coloured, stirring occasionally.

2 Add the cumin and coriander to the vegetable mixture and cook, stirring, for 1–2 minutes. Then gradually stir in the hot chicken stock and bring to the boil, stirring.

3 Cover the pan and simmer the soup for about 20 minutes, or until the parsnips are soft. Purée the soup; adjust the texture with extra stock or water if it seems too thick.

4 Add the cream and check the seasoning, then reheat the soup gently without boiling.

5 Serve immediately, sprinkled with chopped chives or parsley and/or croûtons, to garnish.

Variation
For fabulous root vegetable soup, perfect as colourful winter fare, use a mixture of parsnips, carrots and swede (rutabaga) instead of all parsnips.

Leek and Potato: Energy 486kcal/2013kJ; Protein 5.2g; Carbohydrate 25.1g, of which sugars 7.9g; Fat 41.2g, of which saturates 24.5g; Cholesterol 99mg; Calcium 147mg; Fibre 4.9g; Sodium 184mg.
Cream of Parsnip: Energy 325Kcal/1355kJ; Protein 5.9g; Carbohydrate 32.1g, of which sugars 15.9g; Fat 20.1g, of which saturates 11.5g; Cholesterol 47mg; Calcium 138mg; Fibre 10.9g; Sodium 233mg.

Spiced Parsnip Soup with Sherry

Parsnips are a naturally sweet vegetable and curry powder complements them perfectly, while a dash of sherry lifts the soup into the dinner-party realm. Swirling some natural yogurt into this deeply flavoured dish when serving will prettify presentation and enrich the result.

Serves 4

115g/4oz/½ cup butter
2 onions, sliced
1kg /2¼lb parsnips, peeled
10ml/2 tsp curry powder
30ml/2 tbsp medium sherry
1.2 litres/2 pints/5 cups chicken or vegetable stock
salt and ground black pepper
natural (plain) yogurt, to serve (optional)

1 Melt the butter in a pan, add the onions and sweat gently without allowing them to colour.

2 Cut the parsnips into even-sized pieces, add to the pan and coat with butter. Stir in the curry powder.

3 Pour in the sherry and cover with a cartouche (see Cook's Tip) and a lid. Cook over a low heat for 10 minutes or until the parsnips are softened, making sure they do not colour.

4 Add the stock and season to taste. Bring to the boil then simmer for about 15 minutes or until the parsnips are soft. Remove from the heat. Allow to cool for a while then purée in a food processor or blender.

5 When ready to serve, reheat the soup, stirring to prevent it from sticking to the bottom of the pan, and check the seasoning. Add a swirl of natural (plain) yogurt, if you like.

Cook's Tip
A cartouche is a circle of greaseproof (waxed) paper that helps to keep in the moisture, so the vegetables cook in their own juices along with the sherry.

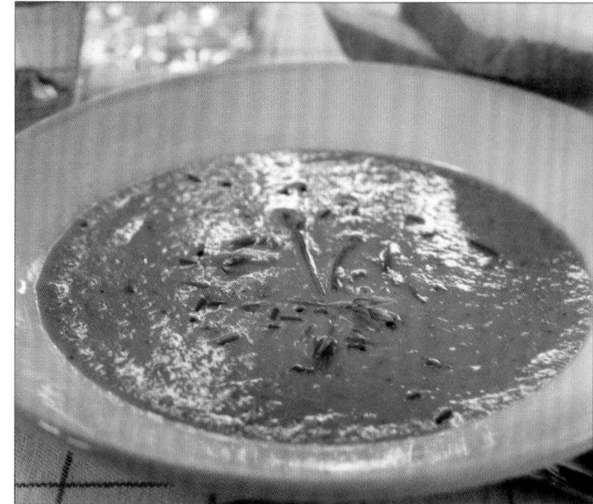

Cream of Pea and Spinach Soup with Mint and Chives

Peas, spinach and mint picked fresh from the garden are still truly seasonal treats. Together they make a velvety, fresh-tasting soup. When fresh peas and spinach are out of season, use frozen peas.

Serves 6

25g/1oz/2 tbsp butter
1 onion, finely chopped
675g/1½lb shelled fresh peas
1.5ml/¼ tsp sugar
1.2 litres/2 pints/5 cups chicken or vegetable stock
handful of fresh mint leaves
450g/1lb young spinach leaves
150ml/¼ pint/⅔ cup double (heavy) cream
salt and ground black pepper
snipped fresh chives, to serve

1 Melt the butter in a large pan and add the onion. Cook over a low heat for about 10 minutes, stirring occasionally, until soft and just brown.

2 Add the peas, sugar, stock and half the mint. Cover and simmer gently for 10 minutes, until the peas are tender. Stir in the spinach and simmer for a further 5 minutes, until the leaves have wilted and the peas are tender.

3 Leave to cool slightly. Add the remaining mint and process or blend until smooth. Return the soup to the rinsed-out pan and season to taste.

4 Stir in the cream and reheat gently without boiling. Serve garnished with snipped chives.

Variation
Tender broccoli is also delicious with peas and spinach in soup. Add the chopped stems for 10 minutes and the tops of the chopped florets for 5 minutes (with the spinach).

Spiced Parsnip: Energy 437kcal/1820kJ; Protein 5.9g; Carbohydrate 39.5g, of which sugars 20.2g; Fat 28.7g, of which saturates 16.8g; Cholesterol 67mg; Calcium 134mg; Fibre 12.9g; Sodium 218mg.
Pea and Spinach Soup: Energy 121kcal/506kJ; Protein 6.1g; Carbohydrate 9.2g, of which sugars 5.2g; Fat 7g, of which saturates 4.2g; Cholesterol 18mg; Calcium 113mg; Fibre 3g; Sodium 123mg.

Artichoke and Fennel Soup with Bruschetta

Jerusalem artichokes are nutty and delicious in soup.

Serves 6

squeeze of lemon juice
450g/1lb Jerusalem artichokes, peeled and diced
65g/2½oz/5 tbsp butter
175g/6oz potatoes, roughly diced
1 small onion, chopped
1 garlic clove, chopped
1 celery stick, chopped
1 small fennel bulb, chopped
1.2 litres/2 pints/5 cups vegetable stock
300ml/½ pint/1¼ cups double (heavy) cream
pinch of freshly grated nutmeg
salt and ground black pepper
basil leaves, to garnish

For the bruschetta

6 thick slices French bread
1 garlic clove
50g/2oz/¼ cup unsalted (sweet) butter
400g/14oz can artichoke hearts, drained and halved
45ml/3 tbsp tapenade
9 salted anchovy fillets, halved lengthways

1 Prepare a bowl of water with lemon juice. Add artichokes to the water to prevent discoloration.

2 Melt the butter in a large pan. Drain the artichokes and add to the pan with the potatoes, onion, garlic, celery and fennel. Cook for 10 minutes, stirring occasionally, until softening.

3 Add the stock, bring to the boil, and simmer for 10–15 minutes, until all the vegetables are soft. Cool slightly, then purée until smooth. Add the cream and nutmeg, and season well.

4 For the bruschetta, lightly toast the French bread on both sides. Rub with the garlic. Melt the butter in a small pan. Add the artichoke hearts and cook for 3–4 minutes, turning once.

5 Spread the tapenade on the toast and arrange the artichoke hearts on top. Top with anchovy fillets and garnish with basil.

6 Reheat the soup without boiling, then ladle it into shallow bowls. Serve the bruschetta with the soup.

Old-English Cream of Jerusalem Artichoke Soup

Related to the sunflower and also known as root artichoke or sunchoke, Jerusalem artichoke was introduced to England in the 17th century. At first it was prized but then became so common an ingredient that people began to lose their taste for it. The tubers can be knobbly, so choose those with a fairly smooth surface for easier cleaning or peeling. Roast in advance to bring out their nuttiness.

Serves 4–6

500g/1¼lb Jerusalem artichokes
1 onion, roughly chopped
4 celery sticks, roughly chopped
2 carrots, roughly chopped
4 garlic cloves
45ml/3 tbsp olive oil
1.2 litre/2 pints/5 cups vegetable or chicken stock
60ml/4 tbsp double (heavy) cream
salt and ground black pepper

1 Preheat the oven to 200°C/400°F/Gas 6. Scrub the artichokes well and halve them lengthways.

2 Toss the artichokes, onion, celery, carrots and garlic together in a roasting tin. Add the olive oil, mix well and spread the vegetables out on the pan.

3 Roast the vegetables in the hot oven for 30–40 minutes, until they are soft and golden brown. Stir them once during cooking so that the edges brown evenly.

4 Tip the roasted vegetables into a large pan, scraping any bits from the roasting pan.

5 Add the stock and bring to the boil. Reduce the heat, cover and simmer the soup for 15 minutes. Process or blend until smooth, then return the soup to the rinsed-out pan.

6 Add the cream and reheat the soup gently, stirring to prevent it from sticking. Do not boil. Season to taste and serve seasoned with freshly ground black pepper.

Artichoke and Fennel: Energy 533kcal/2212kJ; Protein 7.2g; Carbohydrate 25.9g, of which sugars 4.3g; Fat 45.3g, of which saturates 27.1g; Cholesterol 114mg; Calcium 167mg; Fibre 3.4g; Sodium 787mg.
Jerusalem Artichoke: Energy 310kcal/1277kJ; Protein 2.7g; Carbohydrate 4.7g, of which sugars 4.3g; Fat 31.3g, of which saturates 19.4g; Cholesterol 80mg; Calcium 116mg; Fibre 1.5g; Sodium 168mg.

Tomato and Blue Cheese Soup

This is a great variation on tomato soup. The concentrated flavour of roasted tomatoes strikes a great balance with strong blue cheese.

Serves 4

1.5kg/3lb ripe tomatoes, peeled, quartered and seeded
2 garlic cloves, minced
30ml/2 tbsp vegetable oil or butter
1 leek, chopped
1 carrot, chopped
1.2 litres/2 pints/5 cups chicken stock
115g/4oz blue cheese, crumbled
45ml/3 tbsp whipping cream
several large fresh basil leaves, or 1–2 sprigs fresh parsley, plus extra to garnish
175g/6oz rindless bacon, cooked and crumbled, to garnish
salt and freshly ground black pepper

1 Preheat the oven to 200°C/400°F/Gas 6. Spread the tomatoes in a shallow ovenproof dish. Sprinkle with the garlic and some salt and pepper. Place in the oven and bake for 35 minutes.

2 Heat the oil or butter in a large pan. Add the leek and carrot and season lightly with salt and pepper. Cook over low heat, stirring often, for about 10 minutes until softened.

3 Stir in the stock and baked tomatoes. Bring to the boil, then lower the heat, cover and simmer for about 20 minutes.

4 Add the blue cheese, cream and basil or parsley. Transfer to a food processor or blender and process until smooth (work in batches if necessary). Taste and adjust the seasoning.

5 Reheat the soup, but do not boil. Serve garnished with bacon and a sprig of fresh herbs.

Variation
For a meat-free soup use vegetable stock and chopped walnuts instead of the bacon.

Classic Tomato Soup

Until the late 19th century, the English viewed the tomato with great suspicion in case it caused sickness. When it was used, it was usually cooked in soups and stews, and was rarely eaten raw. This creamy soup owes its good flavour to a mix of fresh and canned tomatoes – in summer you could, of course, use all fresh, but do make sure they are really ripe and full of flavour.

Serves 4–6

25g/1oz/2 tbsp butter
1 onion, finely chopped
1 small carrot, finely chopped
1 celery stick, finely chopped
1 garlic clove, crushed
450g/1lb ripe tomatoes, roughly chopped
400g/14oz can chopped tomatoes
30ml/2 tbsp tomato purée (paste)
30ml/2 tbsp sugar
1 tbsp chopped fresh thyme or oregano leaves
600ml/1 pint/2½ cups chicken or vegetable stock
600ml/1 pint/2½ cups milk
salt and ground black pepper

1 Melt the butter in a large pan. Add the onion, carrot, celery and garlic. Cook over a medium heat for about 5 minutes, stirring occasionally, until soft and just beginning to brown.

2 Add the tomatoes, purée, sugar, stock and herbs, retaining some to garnish.

3 Bring to the boil, then cover and simmer gently for about 20 minutes until all the vegetables are very soft.

4 Process or blend the mixture until smooth, then press it through a sieve (strainer) to remove the skins and seeds.

5 Return the sieved soup to the cleaned pan and stir in the milk. Reheat gently.

6 Stir, without allowing it to boil. Season to taste with salt and ground black pepper. To serve, ladle the soup into bowls and garnish with the remaining herbs.

Tomato and Cheese: Energy 365kcal/1519kJ; Protein 16.8g; Carbohydrate 14.7g, of which sugars 14.3g; Fat 27g, of which saturates 12.1g; Cholesterol 57mg; Calcium 191mg; Fibre 5.2g; Sodium 1067mg.
Classic Tomato Soup: Energy 107kcal/447kJ; Protein 2.3g; Carbohydrate 11.4g, of which sugars 10.9g; Fat 6.1g, of which saturates 3.5g; Cholesterol 13mg; Calcium 50mg; Fibre 3.9g; Sodium 71mg.

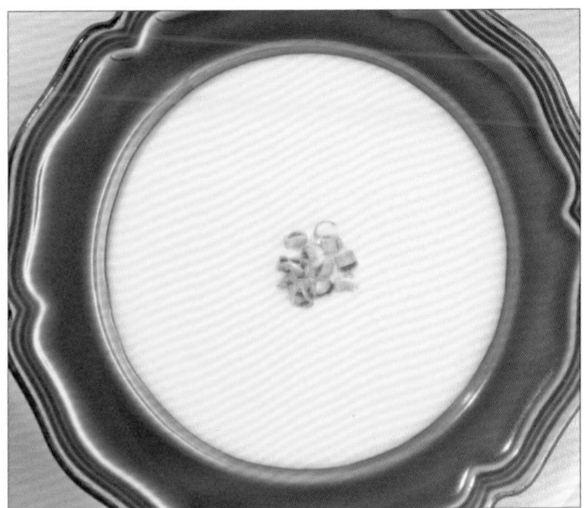

Cream of Spring Onion Soup

The sumptuous onion flavour of this soup is surprisingly delicate, thanks to the quantity of stock and addition of lemon juice.

Serves 4–6

25g/1oz/2 tbsp butter
1 small onion, chopped
150g/5oz/1¾ cups spring onions (scallions), chopped
225g/8oz potatoes, peeled and chopped
600ml/1 pint/2½ cups vegetable stock
350ml/12fl oz/1½ cups single (light) cream
30ml/2 tbsp lemon juice
salt and freshly ground white pepper
chopped spring onions (scallions) or fresh chives, to garnish

1 Melt the butter in a pan and add all the onions. Cover and cook over a very low heat for about 10 minutes or until soft.

2 Add the potatoes and the stock. Bring to the boil, then cover the pan again and simmer over a moderately low heat for about 30 minutes. Cool slightly.

3 Purée the soup until smooth in a food processor or blender.

4 If serving the soup hot, pour it back into the pan. Add the cream and season with salt and pepper. Reheat gently, stirring occasionally. Add the lemon juice.

5 If serving the soup cold, pour it into a bowl. Stir in the cream and lemon juice and season with salt and pepper. Cover the bowl and cool, then chill for at least 1 hour.

6 Serve sprinkled with the chopped spring onions or chives.

Variation
For a lighter version that is still satisfyingly creamy, use olive oil instead of butter and plain (natural) yogurt instead of cream and omit the lemon juice.

Bean and Parmesan Soup

Green beans and Parmesan are delicious together.

Serves 4

25g/1oz/2 tbsp butter
225g/8oz green beans, trimmed
1 garlic clove, crushed
450ml/¾ pint/scant 2 cups vegetable stock
40g/1½oz/½ cup grated Parmesan cheese
50ml/2fl oz/¼ cup single (light) cream
salt and freshly ground black pepper
30ml/2 tbsp chopped fresh parsley, to garnish

1 Melt the butter in a pan. Add the beans and garlic and cook for 2–3 minutes, stirring. Add the stock and seasoning, and bring to the boil. Simmer for 15 minutes until the beans are tender.

2 Purée the soup in a food processor or blender and reheat gently. Stir in the Parmesan and cream, then serve sprinkled with parsley.

Speedy Pea Soup

This soup is quick, simple and delicious. Use decent bought stock.

Serves 2–3

3 shallots, chopped
1 garlic clove, crushed
a small knob of butter
400g/14oz/3 cups frozen peas
2.5ml/½ tsp sugar
grated rind of ½ lemon
500ml/17fl oz/2¼ cups stock
60ml/4 tbsp whipping cream
salt and freshly ground black pepper
croûtons, to garnish

1 Cook the shallots and garlic gently in the butter for 5 minutes. Add the peas, sugar, lemon rind, stock and seasoning. Boil, lower the heat and cover. Simmer 5 minutes.

2 Strain the peas and purée them with some of the stock in a food processor or blender until smooth. Return the purée and remaining stock to pan. Stir in the cream, gently reheat, without boiling, and taste for seasoning. Serve in warmed bowls, garnished with a few croûtons.

Spring Onion Soup: Energy 179kcal/744kJ; Protein 3.2g; Carbohydrate 8.9g, of which sugars 3.1g; Fat 14.8g, of which saturates 9.3g; Cholesterol 41mg; Calcium 67mg; Fibre 0.9g; Sodium 48mg.
Bean and Parmesan: Energy 462kcal/1952kJ; Protein 43.2g; Carbohydrate 48.4g, of which sugars 11.7g; Fat 12g, of which saturates 4.3g; Cholesterol 58mg; Calcium 240mg; Fibre 18.6g; Sodium 204mg.
Speedy Pea Soup: Energy 143kcal/591kJ; Protein 9.5g; Carbohydrate 16.7g, of which sugars 4.2g; Fat 4.8g, of which saturates 2.1g; Cholesterol 7mg; Calcium 34mg; Fibre 6.5g; Sodium 22mg.

Cauliflower and Dumpling Soup

This pureéd soup is Czechozlovakian, with all the luxuriously smooth texture typical of Czech soups and the bouncy, plump dumplings so beloved of all Czech people.

Serves 6–8

1 large cauliflower, cut into florets
1.5 litres/2½ pints/6¼ cups vegetable stock
40g/1½oz/3 tbsp butter
40g/1½oz/⅓ cup plain (all-purpose) flour
pinch of nutmeg or mace
2 egg yolks
300ml/½ pint/1¼ cups whipping cream
flat leaf parsley, to garnish
crusty bread, to serve

For the dumplings

75g/3oz/1½ cups white breadcrumbs
10g/¼oz/½ tbsp butter, softened
1 egg, beaten
10ml/2 tsp chopped fresh flat leaf parsley
a little milk, to bind
salt and ground black pepper

1 Cook the cauliflower in the vegetable stock for 12 minutes or until just tender. Remove and reserve the cooking liquid and a few florets of the cauliflower.

2 Make a sauce by melting the butter in a small pan. Add the flour and cook for 1–2 minutes, before adding about 150ml/¼ pint/⅔ cup of the reserved cauliflower cooking liquid and stirring well. Remove from the heat.

3 Purée the cooked cauliflower in a food processor or blender until smooth. Beat a good pinch of nutmeg or mace and the egg yolks into the cauliflower, then add to the pan of sauce.

4 Add enough cauliflower liquid to make the quantity of soup up to 1.2 litres/2 pints/5 cups. Reheat the soup.

5 Make up the dumplings by mixing all the ingredients together. Roll into balls.

6 Poach the dumplings gently in the soup for 3–5 minutes before adding the whipping cream. Serve garnished with the sprigs of parsley and reserved cauliflower.

Cream of Vegetable Soup

This soup is light in flavour yet satisfying enough for a lunchtime snack.

Serves 6

30ml/2 tbsp olive oil
2 large onions, finely diced
1 garlic clove, crushed
3 large floury potatoes, finely diced
3 celery sticks, finely diced
1.75 litres/3 pints/7½ cups vegetable stock
2 carrots, finely diced
1 cauliflower, chopped
15ml/1 tbsp chopped fresh dill
15ml/1 tbsp lemon juice
5ml/1 tsp mustard powder
1.5ml/¼ tsp caraway seeds
300ml/½ pint/1¼ cups single (light) cream
salt and ground black pepper
shredded spring onions (scallions), to garnish

1 Heat the oil in a large pan, add the onions and garlic and fry them for a few minutes until they soften. Add the potatoes, celery and stock and simmer for 10 minutes. Stir in the carrots and simmer for a further 10 minutes.

2 Add the cauliflower, dill, lemon juice, mustard powder and caraway seeds and stir well, then simmer for 20 minutes. The cauliflower should be soft.

3 Process the soup in a food processor or blender until smooth, return it to the pan and stir in the cream. Season to taste and serve garnished with shredded spring onions.

Cook's Tip

All sorts of vegetables can be married in a mixed soup, so the variations on this "cream of vegetable" recipe are endless. However, the trick for continual success is to combine complementary flavours in balanced quantities. Parsnips and swede (rutabaga) can be added in relatively small proportions (too much will dominate). Courgettes (zucchini) and squash are good and they lighten the heavier vegetables. Add tender broccoli tops, spinach, lettuce and/or watercress about 5 minutes before the end of cooking for a fresh flavour.

Cauliflower: Energy 293Kcal/1216kJ; Protein 6.9g; Carbohydrate 14.8g, of which sugars 3.5g; Fat 23.3g, of which saturates 13.5g; Cholesterol 127mg; Calcium 72mg; Fibre 1.9g; Sodium 138mg.
Vegetable Soup: Energy 202kcal/840kJ; Protein 5.1g; Carbohydrate 16.5g, of which sugars 9.4g; Fat 13.2g, of which saturates 6.7g; Cholesterol 28mg; Calcium 100mg; Fibre 3.9g; Sodium 38mg.

Butternut Squash Soup

This is a fragrant, creamy and delicately flavoured soup – excellent as a first course or for a light lunch. The lovely bright colour is also part of the appeal.

Serves 4

25g/1oz/2 tbsp butter
2 small onions, finely chopped
450g/1lb butternut squash, peeled, seeded and cubed
1.2 litres/2 pints/5 cups chicken stock
225g/8oz potatoes, cubed
5ml/1 tsp paprika
120ml/4fl oz/½ cup whipping cream (optional)
25ml/1½ tbsp snipped fresh chives, plus a few whole chives to garnish
salt and freshly ground black pepper

1 Melt the butter in a large pan. Add the onions and cook for about 5 minutes until soft but not browned.

2 Add the squash, stock, potatoes and paprika. Bring to the boil. Reduce the heat to low, cover the pan and simmer for about 35 minutes or until all the vegetables are soft.

3 Pour the soup into a food processor or blender and process until smooth. Return the soup to the pan and stir in the cream, if using. Season to taste with salt and pepper. Reheat gently without boiling.

4 Stir in the snipped chives just before serving. Garnish each serving with a few whole chives.

Variations
- *For a vegetarian soup use vegetable stock instead of the chicken stock.*
- *The recipe can be used for pumpkin soup – simply use pumpkin instead of butternut squash.*
- *Try a carrot and butternut squash soup, with a hint of orange: add 250g/9oz diced carrots with the potatoes and the grated rind and juice of 1 orange with the stock. Omit the paprika.*

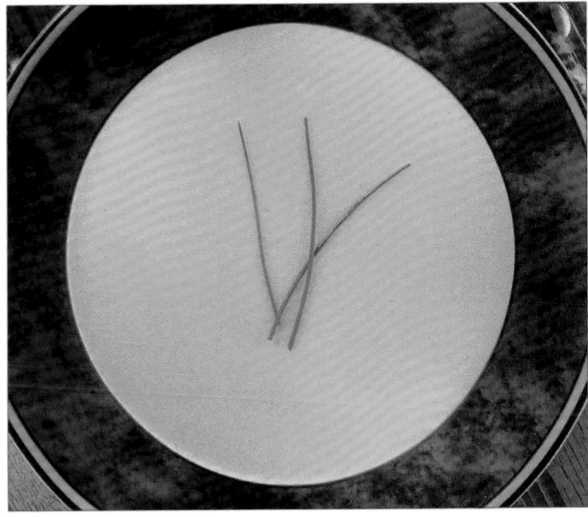

Mussel and Wine Soup

Mussels are either loved or loathed: this is a real treat for those who love them.

Serves 4

1 bottle (750ml/1½ pints/3 cups) dry white wine
1.2 litres/2 pints/5 cups water
1 chicken leg
1 large carrot, thinly sliced
pinch of powdered saffron
4kg/8¾lb live mussels
4 onions, sliced into rings
2 bay leaves
2 celery sticks
6 black peppercorns, lightly crushed
2 leeks, thinly sliced
75g/3oz/2/3 cup cornflour (cornstarch)
200ml/7fl oz/scant 1 cup whipping cream
salt and ground black pepper
celery leaves, to garnish
buttered soft rolls filled with cress, to serve (optional)

1 Pour the wine and 1 litre/1¾ pints/4 cups of the water into a large pan. Add the chicken leg, carrot and saffron and season. Bring to the boil, lower the heat, cover and simmer for 1 hour.

2 Scrub the mussels under cold water and pull off the "beards". Discard any with broken shells or those that do not shut immediately when tapped. Put them, with the onions, bay leaves, celery, peppercorns and remaining water into a pan, cover and cook over a high heat, shaking the pan three times, for 5 minutes, until the shells have opened.

3 Strain the mussels, reserving the liquid. Discard any mussels that remain closed and remove the rest from their shells.

4 Strain 500ml/17fl oz/generous 2 cups of the cooking liquid through a sieve (strainer) lined with muslin (cheesecloth) twice; add to the soup. Remove the chicken, cut off the meat and chop.

5 Add the leeks to the pan and cook for 2 minutes. Mix the cornflour with just enough cold water to form a pouring paste and stir into the soup. Bring to the boil, stirring continuously.

6 Remove the pan from the heat and stir in the cream, mussels and chicken meat. Sprinkle with celery leaves and serve immediately with buttered soft rolls filled with cress, if liked.

Butternut Squash: Energy 68kcal/287kJ; Protein 1.2g; Carbohydrate 4.7g, of which sugars 3.4g; Fat 0.7g, of which saturates 0.2g; Cholesterol 110mg; Calcium 82mg; Fibre 1.7g; Sodium 108mg.
Mussel and Wine: Energy 692kcal/2910kJ; Protein 62g; Carbohydrate 32.9g, of which sugars 12.1g; Fat 22.6g, of which saturates 14.5g; Cholesterol 150mg; Calcium 712mg; Fibre 4.2g; Sodium 713mg.

Mussel and Fennel Cream Soup

Every country that gathers mussels has its version of mussel soup and this one is from Scotland, where the small local mussels would be used for exceptionally good flavour. You will need two pans for this dish, one to cook the mussels and one for the liquor. The leaves and bulb of the fennel are also cooked separately.

Serves 4

1kg/2¼lb fresh mussels
1 fennel bulb, leaves retained
120ml/4fl oz/½ cup dry white wine
1 leek, finely sliced
olive oil
25g/1oz/2 tbsp butter
splash of Pernod or Ricard
150ml/¼ pint/⅔ cup double (heavy) cream
25g/1oz fresh parsley, chopped

1 Clean the mussels thoroughly, removing any beards and scraping off any barnacles. Discard any that are broken or open.

2 Strip off the outer leaves of the fennel and roughly chop them. Set to one side. Then take the central core of the fennel and chop it very finely. Set it aside in a separate dish or bowl.

3 Place the roughly chopped fennel leaves, the mussels and the wine in a large pan, cover and cook gently until all the mussels open, about 5 minutes. Discard any that remain closed.

4 In a second pan sweat the leek and finely chopped core of the fennel gently in the oil and butter until soft.

5 Meanwhile remove the mussels from the first pan and either leave in the shell or remove. Set aside.

6 Strain the liquor on to the leek mixture and bring to the boil. Add a little water and the Pernod or Ricard and simmer for a few minutes. Stir in the cream and parsley and heat gently without allowing the soup to boil.

7 Place the mussels in a serving tureen and pour over the soup. Serve with crusty bread for mopping up the juices.

Scallops in Artichoke Cream Broth

The best scallops are hand-collected, when divers literally dive down and collect them from the seabed, which is why they can be expensive. This way, though, the divers can be selective and choose only the right size, and they do not disturb the seabed. Scallops have a remarkable affinity with Jerusalem artichokes, and this simple soup is evidence that they are a superb combination.

Serves 4

450g/1lb Jerusalem artichokes
75g/3oz/6 tbsp butter
1 large onion, chopped
5ml/1 tsp sea salt
120ml/4fl oz/½ cup double (heavy) cream
8 fresh king scallops
chopped fresh parsley, to garnish

1 Roughly peel the artichokes, but don't be too fussy as the knobbly bits can be hard to get into and it is very time-consuming. It is most important to remove all the earth otherwise the soup can be gritty. Chop roughly.

2 Heat a pan, melt the butter and gently sweat the onion until softened but not coloured. Add the artichokes and stir to coat in the butter.

3 Cover the pan with a well-fitting lid and leave to stew gently for about 10 minutes, giving the pan a shake occasionally to prevent the artichokes from sticking to the base of the pan.

4 Pour in enough water just to cover the artichokes, and add the salt. Bring to the boil then reduce the heat and simmer gently for 30 minutes. Purée in a blender until smooth, then strain into a clean pan. Add the cream and check the seasoning.

5 Slice the scallops in two horizontally. When the soup is ready, remove the pan from the heat and immediately add the scallops. Leave to stand briefly – the scallops will cook in the soup off the heat in a couple of minutes.

6 Serve the soup garnished with chopped fresh parsley, allowing four slices of scallop per person.

Mussel and Fennel: Energy 392kcal/1624kJ; Protein 13.4g; Carbohydrate 5.7g, of which sugars 3g; Fat 33g, of which saturates 16.9g; Cholesterol 105mg; Calcium 95mg; Fibre 2.8g; Sodium 297mg.
Scallops Broth: Energy 383kcal/1586kJ; Protein 13.5g; Carbohydrate 8.1g, of which sugars 5g; Fat 33.3g, of which saturates 20.4g; Cholesterol 106mg; Calcium 94mg; Fibre 2.1g; Sodium 280mg.

Seared Scallops in Vermouth Soup

Seared scallops form an elegant tower in this crème de la crème of fine soups. The caviar garnish is superb.

Serves 4

25g/1oz/2 tbsp butter
5 shallots, sliced
300ml/½ pint/1¼ cups dry white wine
300ml/½ pint/1¼ cups good-quality vermouth,
900ml/1½ pints/3¾ cups fish stock
300ml/½ pint/1¼ cups double (heavy) cream
300ml/½ pint/1¼ cups single (light) cream
15ml/1 tbsp olive oil
12 large scallops
salt and ground black pepper
15ml/1 tbsp red lumpfish roe or caviar and snipped chives, to garnish

For the rocket (arugula) oil
115g/4oz rocket (arugula) leaves
120ml/4 fl oz/½ cup olive oil

1 Prepare the rocket oil. Process the rocket and olive oil in a food processor or blender to give a green paste. Line a small bowl with muslin (cheesecloth) and scrape the paste into it. Gather up the muslin and squeeze it well to extract the oil.

2 Melt the butter in a large pan. Add the shallots and cook over a gentle heat for 8–10 minutes, until soft but not browned. Add the wine and vermouth and boil for 8–10 minutes, until reduced by about three-quarters of the volume.

3 Add the stock and bring back to the boil. Boil until reduced by half. Pour in the double and single creams, and return to the boil. Reduce the heat and simmer for 12–15 minutes, until just thick enough to coat the back of a spoon. Strain the soup through a fine sieve (strainer) into the rinsed-out pan, and set aside.

4 Heat a griddle or frying pan. Brush the scallops with oil and sear them for 1–2 minutes on each side, until just cooked.

5 Reheat the soup gently, then taste and season. Arrange three scallops, one on top of the other, in the centre of each of four warm soup plates. Ladle the hot soup around the scallops and top them with a little of the lumpfish roe or caviar. Drizzle some rocket oil over the surface of the soup, then sprinkle with chives.

Cream of Crab Soup with Sherry

Although crab is available all the year round, it is at its best and is least expensive during the summer months – the perfect time to make this lovely creamy soup. Many people profess to favour the white body meat, which is more plentiful, to the darker meat from the claws, but this recipe wisely notes that both have much to contribute in terms of their flavour.

Serves 4–6

25g/1oz/2 tbsp butter
1 onion, finely chopped
1 celery stick, finely chopped
1 garlic clove, crushed
25ml/1½ tbsp plain (all-purpose) flour
225g/8oz cooked crab meat, half dark and half white
1.2 litres/2 pints/5 cups fish stock
150ml/¼ pint/⅔ cup double (heavy) cream
30ml/2 tbsp dry sherry
salt and ground black pepper

1 Melt the butter in a pan and add the onion, celery and garlic. Cook over a medium heat for about 5 minutes, stirring frequently, until the vegetables are soft but not browned.

2 Remove from the heat and quickly stir in the flour, then the brown crab meat. Gradually stir in the stock.

3 Bring the mixture just to the boil, then reduce the heat and simmer for about 30 minutes. Process or blend the soup and return it to the rinsed pan. Season to taste.

4 Chop the white crab meat and stir it into the soup with the cream and sherry. Reheat the soup without allowing it to boil and serve immediately.

Cook's Tip

When fresh crab is not available, make a mixed white fish and crab soup, using 225g/8oz skinless, boneless white fish fillet (plaice or lemon sole are good but any white fish will do) in the soup and processing until smooth. Finish the soup and stir in flaked canned or frozen crab meat at the end with the cream and sherry.

Scallops in Vermouth: Energy 557kcal/2303kJ; Protein 13.1g; Carbohydrate 4.7g, of which sugars 2.6g; Fat 48.9g, of which saturates 28.9g; Cholesterol 140mg; Calcium 63mg; Fibre 0.2g; Sodium 148mg.
Crab with Sherry: Energy 209kcal/867kJ; Protein 7.8g; Carbohydrate 4.6g, of which sugars 1.2g; Fat 17.3g, of which saturates 10.6g; Cholesterol 70mg; Calcium 69mg; Fibre 0.3g; Sodium 241mg.

Creamy Clam Chowder

A traditional chowder from New England in the United States, the mixture of clams and pork, with potatoes and cream, is rich and utterly delicious.

Serves 8

48 clams, scrubbed
1.5 litres/2½ pints/6¼ cups water
40g/1½oz/¼ cup finely diced salt pork or bacon
3 onions, finely chopped
1 bay leaf
3 potatoes, diced
475ml/16fl oz/2 cups milk, warmed
250ml/8fl oz/1 cup single (light) cream
salt and freshly ground black pepper
chopped fresh parsley, to garnish

1 Rinse the clams well in cold water and drain. Place them in a deep pan with the water and bring to the boil. Cover and steam for about 10 minutes or until the shells open. Remove from the heat.

2 When the clams have cooled slightly, remove them from their shells. Discard any clams that have not opened. Chop the clams coarsely. Pour the cooking liquid through a sieve (strainer) lined with muslin (cheesecloth) and reserve.

3 In a large, heavy pan, fry the salt pork or bacon until it renders its fat and begins to brown. Add the onions and cook over a low heat for 8–10 minutes until softened.

4 Stir in the bay leaf, potatoes, and clam cooking liquid. Bring to the boil and cook for 5–10 minutes.

5 Stir in the chopped clams. Continue to cook until the potatoes are tender, stirring from time to time. Season lightly.

6 Stir the warmed milk into the soup, followed by the cream and heat very gently for a further 5 minutes. Do not allow the soup to boil as it will curdle. Discard the bay leaf once heated through, adjust the seasoning and serve sprinkled with chopped fresh parsley.

Corn and Scallop Chowder

Fresh, canned or frozen corn can be used for this chowder, which is almost a meal in itself and makes a perfect lunch.

Serves 4–6

2 corn cobs or 200g/7oz/generous 1 cup frozen or canned corn
600ml/1 pint/2½ cups milk
15g/½oz butter
1 small leek or onion, chopped
40g/1½oz/¼ cup smoked streaky (fatty) bacon, finely chopped
1 small garlic clove, crushed
1 small green (bell) pepper, seeded and diced
1 celery stick, chopped
1 potato, diced
15ml/1 tbsp plain (all-purpose) flour
300ml/½ pint/1¼ cups chicken or vegetable stock
4 scallops
115g/4oz cooked fresh mussels
pinch of paprika
150ml/¼ pint/⅔ cup single (light) cream (optional)
salt and freshly ground black pepper

1 Using a sharp knife, slice down the corn cobs to remove the kernels. Place half the kernels in a food processor or blender and process with a little of the milk. Set the other half aside.

2 Melt the butter in a large pan and gently fry the leek or onion, bacon and garlic for 4–5 minutes, until the leek is soft but not browned. Add the green pepper, celery and potato. Cover the pan and sweat the ingredients over a gentle heat for a further 3–4 minutes, stirring occasionally.

3 Stir in the flour and cook for about 1–2 minutes. Stir in a little milk and the corn mixture, the stock, remaining milk and corn kernels and seasoning.

4 Bring to the boil. Then lower the heat and part cover the pan. Simmer for 15–20 minutes until the vegetables are tender.

5 Remove any corals from the scallops and cut the white flesh into 5mm/¼in slices. Stir the scallops into the soup and cook for about 4 minutes. Then stir in the corals, mussels and paprika. Heat briefly, then stir in the cream, if using. Taste to check the seasoning before serving.

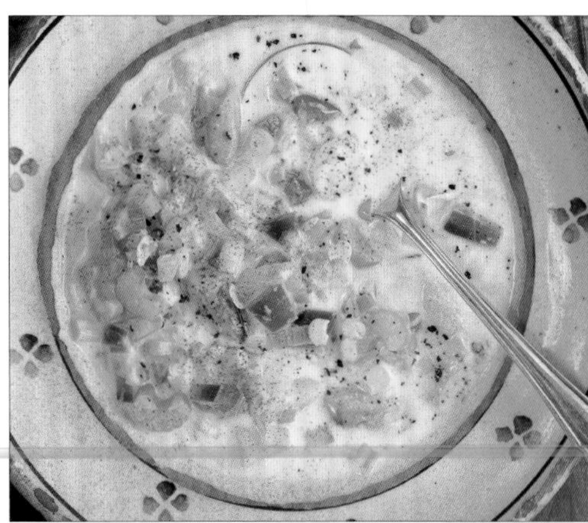

Clam Chowder: Energy 374kcal/1556kJ; Protein 23.9g; Carbohydrate 11.3g, of which sugars 5.3g; Fat 26.2g, of which saturates 15.1g; Cholesterol 136mg; Calcium 189mg; Fibre 0.5g; Sodium 1629mg.
Corn and Scallop: Energy 200kcal/845kJ; Protein 13g; Carbohydrate 23.6g, of which sugars 10.5g; Fat 6.7g, of which saturates 3.2g; Cholesterol 31mg; Calcium 150mg; Fibre 1.9g; Sodium 326mg.

Shrimp and Corn Bisque

Hot pepper sauce brings a touch of spice to this mild, creamy soup, which is a classic combination of shrimp, corn and fresh herbs.

Serves 4

30ml/2 tbsp olive oil
1 onion, finely minced
50g/2oz/4 tbsp butter
25g/1oz/¼ cup plain (all-purpose) flour
750ml/1¼ pints/3 cups fish stock
250ml/8fl oz/1 cup milk
115g/4oz/1 cup peeled cooked small shrimps, deveined if necessary
225g/8oz/1½ cups corn
2.5ml/½ tsp chopped fresh dill or thyme
hot pepper sauce
120ml/4fl oz/½ cup single (light) cream
salt
sprigs of fresh dill, to garnish

1 Heat the olive oil in a large heavy pan. Add the onion and cook over a low heat for 8–10 minutes until softened.

2 Meanwhile, melt the butter in a second pan. Add the flour and cook for 1–2 minutes, stirring. Stir in the stock and milk, bring to the boil and cook for 5–8 minutes, stirring frequently.

3 Cut each shrimp into two or three pieces and add to the onion with the corn and dill or thyme. Cook for 2–3 minutes, then remove from the heat.

4 Add the soup to the shrimp and corn mixture, and mix well. Remove 750ml/1¼ pints/3 cups of the soup and purée in a food processor or blender. Stir it into the rest of the soup in the pan. Season with salt and hot pepper sauce to taste.

5 Add the cream and stir to blend. Heat the soup, stirring, but do not allow it to boil. Pour it into bowls and serve hot, garnished with sprigs of dill.

Cook's Tip
When tiny shrimp are not available, use prawns (shrimp). For a simple everyday snack-soup, use drained canned tuna.

Cream of Prawn Bisque

The classic French method for making a bisque requires pushing the shellfish through a tamis, or drum sieve. This recipe is simpler.

Serves 6–8

675g/1½lb small or medium whole cooked prawns (shrimp)
25ml/1½ tbsp vegetable oil
2 onions, halved and sliced
1 large carrot, sliced
2 celery sticks, sliced
2 litres/3½ pints/9 cups water
a few drops of lemon juice
30ml/2 tbsp tomato purée (paste)
bouquet garni
50g/2oz/4 tbsp butter
50g/2oz/⅓ cup plain (all-purpose) flour
45–60ml/3–4 tbsp brandy
150ml/¼ pint/⅔ cup whipping cream

1 Remove the heads from the prawns and peel away the shells. Reserve the heads and shells for the stock. Place the prawns in a covered bowl in the refrigerator.

2 Heat the oil in a large pan, add the heads and shells and cook over a high heat, stirring, until they start to brown. Reduce the heat to medium, add the vegetables and fry, stirring occasionally, for 5 minutes until the onions soften.

3 Add the water, lemon juice, tomato purée and bouquet garni. Bring to the boil, then reduce the heat, cover and simmer gently for 25 minutes. Strain the stock through a sieve.

4 Melt the butter in a heavy pan over a medium heat. Stir in the flour and cook until just golden, stirring occasionally.

5 Add the brandy. Gradually pour in half the prawn stock, whisking vigorously until smooth, then whisk in the remaining liquid. Season if necessary. Reduce the heat, cover and simmer for 5 minutes, stirring frequently.

6 Strain the soup into a clean pan. Add the cream and a little extra lemon juice to taste, then stir in most of the reserved prawns and cook over a medium heat, stirring frequently, until hot. Do not allow the soup to boil. Serve at once, garnished with the remaining reserved prawns.

Shrimp and Corn: Energy 195kcal/821kJ; Protein 15.4g; Carbohydrate 17.9g, of which sugars 10g; Fat 7.4g, of which saturates 4.2g; Cholesterol 162mg; Calcium 92mg; Fibre 1.1g; Sodium 407mg.
Cream of Prawn Bisque: Energy 220kcal/915kJ; Protein 9g; Carbohydrate 9.7g, of which sugars 4g; Fat 15g, of which saturates 8.3g; Cholesterol 122mg; Calcium 73mg; Fibre 1.1g; Sodium 566mg.

Lobster Soup with Brandy

The blue and black clawed lobster is known as the king of the shellfish. When cooked, it turns brilliant red. This is an extravagant soup, ideal for a celebration meal.

Serves 4

1 cooked lobster (about 675g/1½lb)
30ml/2 tbsp vegetable oil
115g/4oz/½ cup butter
2 shallots, finely chopped
juice of ½ lemon
45ml/3 tbsp brandy
1 bay leaf
sprig of fresh parsley, plus extra to garnish
1 blade of mace
1.2 litres/2 pints/5 cups fish stock
40g/1½oz/3 tbsp plain (all-purpose) flour
45ml/3 tbsp double (heavy) cream
salt and ground black pepper
a pinch of cayenne pepper, to garnish

1 Preheat the oven to 180°C/350°F/Gas 4. Lay the lobster out flat and split it in half lengthways. Remove and discard the little stomach sac from the head, the thread-like intestine and the coral (if any).

2 In a large, heavy-based roasting tin (pan), heat the oil with 25g/1oz/2 tbsp of the butter. Sauté the lobster, flesh-side down, for 5 minutes. Add the shallots, lemon juice and brandy, then cook in the oven for 15 minutes.

3 Remove the lobster meat from the shell. Place the shell and the juices in a large pan and simmer with the bay leaf, parsley, mace and stock for 30 minutes. Strain the stock.

4 Finely chop 15ml/1 tbsp of the lobster meat. Process the rest with 40g/1½oz/3 tbsp of the butter and set aside. Melt the remaining butter in the rinsed pan, add the flour and cook gently for 30 seconds. Gradually add the stock and bring to the boil, stirring constantly. Stir in the processed lobster and butter, the cream and seasoning.

5 Ladle the soup into individual serving dishes and serve immediately. Garnish with the chopped lobster, parsley sprigs and a sprinkling of cayenne.

Haddock Chowder

This traditional soup never fails to please, whether it is made with milk or, more luxuriously, with a generous quantity of cream.

Serves 4

3 thick-cut bacon rashers
1 large onion
675g/1½ potatoes
1 litre/1¾ pints/4 cups fish stock
450g/1lb skinless haddock, cut into 2.5 cm/1 in cubes
30ml/2 tbsp chopped fresh parsley
15ml/1 tbsp snipped fresh chives
300ml/½ pint/1¼ cups whipping cream or whole milk
salt and ground black pepper

1 Remove the rind from the bacon and discard it; cut the bacon into small pieces. Chop the onion and cut the potatoes into 2cm/¾in cubes.

2 Fry the bacon in a deep pan until the fat is rendered. Add the onion and potatoes and cook over low heat, without browning, for about 10 minutes. Season to taste.

3 Pour off excess bacon fat from the pan. Add the fish stock to the pan and bring to the boil. Simmer until the vegetables are tender, about 15–20 minutes.

4 Stir in the cubes of fish, the parsley and chives. Simmer for about 3–4 minutes, until the fish is just cooked.

5 Stir the cream or milk into the chowder and reheat gently, but do not bring to the boil. Season to taste and serve.

Variations

- *Smoked haddock makes delicious, golden chowder, or use half and half smoked and white fish.*
- *Any white fish may be used instead of haddock – cod or hoki are both good alternatives.*
- *Add salmon fillet instead of haddock to make a rich soup. Sprinkle in the grated rind of 1 lemon with the salmon.*
- *Canned tuna is a great emergency fish for chowder.*

Lobster with Brandy: Energy 443kcal/1837kJ; Protein 15g; Carbohydrate 8.6g, of which sugars 0.9g; Fat 36.3g, of which saturates 19.6g; Cholesterol 144mg; Calcium 65mg; Fibre 0.5g; Sodium 381mg.
Haddock Chowder: Energy 205kcal/863kJ; Protein 16.1g; Carbohydrate 19g, of which sugars 6.4g; Fat 7.8g, of which saturates 4.7g; Cholesterol 41mg; Calcium 142mg; Fibre 1g; Sodium 536mg.

Cream of Oyster Soup

Oysters make a delicious and distinctive soup that is really special. It may take a little while to shuck the oysters but it is part of the fun! Just be sure to use a sharp knife. Don't discard the liquor from the shucked shells as it makes a fantastic base for the soup. As oysters are expensive, you can adjust the quantity or type used – see Variations.

Serves 6

475ml/16fl oz/2 cups milk
475ml/16fl oz/2 cups single (light) cream
1.2 litres/2 pints/5 cups shucked oysters, drained, with their liquor reserved
a pinch of paprika
25g/1oz/2 tbsp butter
salt and freshly ground black pepper
15ml/1 tbsp chopped fresh parsley, to garnish

1 Combine the milk, single cream, and oyster liquor in a heavy pan. Heat the mixture over a medium heat until small bubbles appear around it at the edge of the pan, being careful not to allow it to boil. Reduce the heat to low and add the oysters.

2 Cook, stirring occasionally, until the oysters plump up and their edges begin to curl. Add the paprika and season to taste.

3 Meanwhile, warm six soup plates or bowls. Cut the butter into six pieces and put one piece in each bowl.

4 Ladle the oyster soup into the bowls and sprinkle with chopped parsley. Serve immediately.

Variations

- *Serve a poached egg in each portion of soup.*
- *For an economical version, combine the oysters with peeled cooked prawns (shrimp). Use half the quantity of oysters and an equal quantity of prawns.*
- *For a punchy soup, use peeled cooked prawns and canned smoked oysters instead of fresh oysters. Add the prawns instead of the fresh oysters. Then serve the soup garnished with the drained canned smoked oysters.*

Salmon Chowder

Dill is the perfect partner for salmon in this classic, full-flavoured dish. Use the best possible boneless fish.

Serves 4

20g/¾oz/1½ tbsp butter
1 onion, finely chopped
1 leek, finely chopped
1 small fennel bulb, finely chopped
25g/1oz/¼ cup plain (all-purpose) flour
1.75 litres/3 pints/7½ cups fish stock
2 potatoes, cut into 1cm/½in cubes
450g/1lb boneless, skinless salmon, cut in 2cm/¾in cubes
175ml/6fl oz/¾ cup milk
120ml/4fl oz/½ cup whipping cream
30ml/2 tbsp chopped fresh dill
salt and ground black pepper

1 Melt the butter in a large pan. Add the onion, leek and chopped fennel and cook over a medium heat for 5–8 minutes until softened, stirring from time to time.

2 Stir in the flour. Reduce the heat to low and cook for 3 minutes, stirring occasionally.

3 Add the fish stock and potatoes. Season with salt and ground black pepper. Bring to the boil, then reduce the heat, cover and simmer for about 20 minutes or until the potatoes are tender.

4 Add the salmon and simmer gently for 3–5 minutes until it is just cooked.

5 Stir in the milk, cream, and dill. Cook until just warmed through, but do not boil. Adjust the seasoning and then serve.

Variation

Fresh young mackerel fillets are delicious in soup. They are particularly good in this recipe, which has lots of vegetables. Add a crushed garlic clove, if liked, and use tarragon instead of dill. For a zesty flavour to cut the fish, add the grated rind of 1 lemon and season with a hint of cayenne pepper.

Cream of Oyster: Energy 385kcal/1609kJ; Protein 26.5g; Carbohydrate 17.6g, of which sugars 12.2g; Fat 22.6g, of which saturates 13.8g; Cholesterol 174mg; Calcium 430mg; Fibre 0g; Sodium 1112mg.
Salmon Chowder: Energy 301kcal/1254kJ; Protein 18.3g; Carbohydrate 13g, of which sugars 3.8g; Fat 19.9g, of which saturates 8.6g; Cholesterol 67mg; Calcium 83mg; Fibre 1.5g; Sodium 78mg.

Creamy Salmon Soup with Dill

Dill is the natural partner for fresh and smoked salmon. This classic soup is enriched with cream.

Serves 4

20g/¾oz/1½ tbsp butter
1 onion, finely chopped
25g/1oz/¼ cup plain (all-purpose) flour
1.75 litres/3 pints/7 cups fish stock
2 potatoes, cut in 1cm/½in cubes
50–75g/2–3oz smoked salmon scraps, cut into small pieces
250g/½lb salmon fillet, skinned and cut into 2cm/¾in cubes
175ml/6fl oz/¾ cup milk
120ml/4fl oz/½ cup whipping cream
30ml/2 tbsp chopped fresh dill
salt and ground black pepper

1 Melt the butter in a large pan. Add the onion and cook for 6 minutes until softened.

2 Stir in the flour. Reduce the heat to low and cook for 3 minutes, stirring occasionally with a wooden spoon.

3 Add the fish stock and potatoes to the mixture in the pan. Season with a little ground black pepper. Bring to the boil, then reduce the heat. Cover the pan and simmer the soup gently for about 20 minutes or until the potatoes are tender.

4 Add the smoked salmon scraps and the cubed salmon, then simmer gently for 3–5 minutes until it is just cooked.

5 Stir the milk, cream and chopped dill into the soup. Heat until just warmed through, stirring occasionally, but do not allow to boil. Adjust the seasoning to taste, then ladle the soup into warmed soup bowls to serve.

Cook's Tip

When cooking smoked salmon or adding it to a cooked dish, do not add salt until just before serving. Taste to check the seasoning as smoked salmon becomes very salty on cooking and extra salt is rarely needed.

Salmon Soup with Salsa and Rouille

Tangy sorrel goes well with salmon but dill or fennel are delicious alternatives.

Serves 4

90ml/6 tbsp olive oil
1 onion, chopped
1 leek, chopped
1 celery stick, chopped
1 fennel bulb, roughly chopped
1 red (bell) pepper, seeded and sliced
3 garlic cloves, chopped
grated rind and juice of 2 oranges
1 bay leaf
400g/14oz can chopped tomatoes
1.2 litres/2 pints/5 cups fish stock
pinch of cayenne pepper
800g/1¾lb salmon fillet, skinned
300ml/½ pint/1¼ cups double (heavy) cream
salt and ground black pepper
4 thin slices baguette, to serve

For the ruby salsa

2 tomatoes, peeled, seeded and diced
½ small red onion, very finely chopped
15ml/1 tbsp cod's roe
15ml/1 tbsp chopped fresh sorrel

For the rouille

120ml/4fl oz/½ cup mayonnaise
1 garlic clove, crushed
5ml/1 tsp sun-dried tomato paste

1 Heat the oil in a large pan. Add the onion, leek, celery, fennel, pepper and garlic. Cover and cook gently for 20 minutes.

2 Add the orange rind and juice, bay leaf and tomatoes. Cover and cook for 4–5 minutes, stirring occasionally. Add the stock and cayenne, cover the pan and simmer for 30 minutes.

3 Add the salmon and poach it for 8–10 minutes, until just cooked. Lift out the fish and flake it coarsely, discarding bones.

4 Mix all the salsa ingredients and set aside. For the rouille, mix the mayonnaise with the garlic and the sun-dried tomato paste. Toast the baguette slices on both sides and set aside.

5 Purée the soup and sieve it back into the rinsed pan. Stir in the cream, seasoning and salmon. Heat gently but do not boil.

6 To serve, ladle the soup into bowls. Top the baguette slices with rouille, float on the soup and spoon over the salsa.

Creamy Salmon: Energy 373Kcal/1556kJ; Protein 18.8g; Carbohydrate 20.8g, of which sugars 5.9g; Fat 24.5g, of which saturates 12g; Cholesterol 79mg; Calcium 107mg; Fibre 1.4g; Sodium 234mg.
Salmon with Salsa: Energy 1153kcal/4772kJ; Protein 44.9g; Carbohydrate 13.7g, of which sugars 12.5g; Fat 102.5g, of which saturates 34.9g; Cholesterol 225mg; Calcium 127mg; Fibre 4.7g; Sodium 268mg.

Creamy Haddock Soup with Saffron

Filling yet not too rich, this golden soup makes a delicious meal served with lots of hot, fresh bread.

Serves 4
1 parsnip, quartered
2 carrots, quartered
1 onion, quartered
2 celery sticks, quartered
2 smoked bacon rashers (strips), rinds removed
juice of 1 lemon
pinch of saffron strands
450g/1lb fish heads
900ml/1½ pints/3¾cups water
450g/1lb live mussels, scrubbed
1 leek, shredded
2 shallots, finely chopped
30ml/2 tbsp chopped dill, plus extra sprigs to garnish
450g/1lb haddock, skinned and boned
3 egg yolks
30ml/2 tbsp double (heavy) cream
salt and ground black pepper

1 Put the parsnip, carrots, onion, celery, bacon, lemon juice, saffron strands and fish heads in a large pan with the water. Bring to the boil. Cook for 20 minutes or until reduced by half.

2 Discard any mussels that are open and do not close when tapped sharply. Add the rest to the pan of stock. Cook for about 4 minutes, until they have opened. Strain the soup and return the liquid to the pan. Discard any unopened mussels, then remove the remaining ones from their shells and set aside.

3 Add the leek and shallots to the soup, bring to the boil and cook for 5 minutes. Add the dill and haddock, and simmer for a further 5 minutes, until the fish is tender. Remove the haddock, with a slotted spoon, then flake it into a bowl, using a fork.

4 In another bowl, whisk together the eggs and double cream. Whisk in a little of the hot soup, then stir the mixture back into the hot, but not boiling, liquid. Continue to stir for several minutes as the soup heats through and thickens slightly, but do not let it boil.

5 Add the flaked haddock and mussels to the soup and check the seasoning. Ladle the soup into bowls and serve garnished with tiny sprigs of dill.

Cullen Skink

This familiar soup comes from the small fishing port of Cullen on the east coast of Scotland. The word "skink" means an essence or soup. Traditionally, the local fishermen smoked the smaller fish from their catch and, by adding locally grown potatoes, they formed their staple diet and created a world-renowned soup.

Serves 6
1 Finnan haddock, about 350g/12oz
1 onion, chopped
bouquet garni
900ml/1½ pints/3¾ cups water
500g/1¼lb potatoes, quartered
600ml/1 pint/2½ cups milk
40g/1½oz/3 tbsp butter
salt and pepper
snipped chives, to garnish

1 Put the haddock, onion, bouquet garni and water into a large pan and bring to the boil. Skim the surface with a slotted spoon, discarding any fish skin, then cover. Reduce the heat and gently poach for 10–15 minutes, until the fish flakes easily.

2 Lift the fish from the pan, using a fish slice, and remove the skin and any bones. Return the skin and bones to the pan and simmer, uncovered, for a further 30 minutes. Flake the cooked fish flesh and leave to cool.

3 Strain the fish stock and return it to the pan, then add the potatoes and simmer for about 25 minutes, or until tender. Carefully remove the potatoes from the pan using a slotted spoon, and place in a bowl. Mash the potatoes with the butter.

4 Add the milk to the soup and bring to the boil. A little at a time, whisk the potatoes into the soup, until it is thick and creamy. Stir in the flaked fish and adjust the seasoning.

5 Serve sprinkled with chives, with fresh crusty bread.

Cook's Tip
When small whole finnan haddock are not available, use natural smoked haddock fillet, without dye or flavouring.

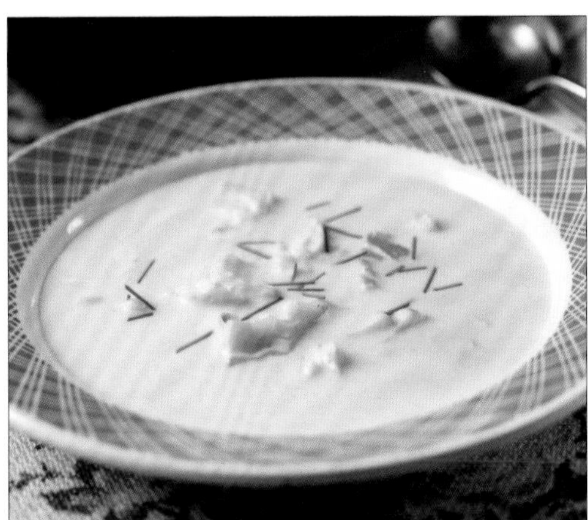

Creamy Haddock: Energy 283kcal/1188kJ; Protein 33.7g; Carbohydrate 9.7g, of which sugars 6.3g; Fat 12.5g, of which saturates 4.8g; Cholesterol 222mg; Calcium 168mg; Fibre 4.2g; Sodium 367mg.
Cullen Skink: Energy 205kcal/864kJ; Protein 16.1g; Carbohydrate 19g, of which sugars 6.4g; Fat 7.8g, of which saturates 4.7g; Cholesterol 41mg; Calcium 137mg; Fibre 1g; Sodium 132mg.

Fish and Sweet Potato Cream Soup

The subtle sweetness of the potato combines with the stronger flavours of fish and oregano to make this an appetizing soup, popular throughout the Caribbean.

Serves 4

175g/6oz white fish fillet, skinned
½ onion, chopped
1 sweet potato, about 175g/6oz, peeled and diced
1 small carrot, about 50g/2oz, chopped
5ml/1 tsp chopped fresh oregano or 2.5ml/½ tsp dried oregano
2.5ml/½ tsp ground cinnamon
1.35 litres/2¼ pints/5½ cups fish stock
75ml/5 tbsp single (light) cream
chopped fresh parsley, to garnish

1 Remove any bones from the fish and put it in a pan. Add the onion, sweet potato, carrot, oregano, cinnamon and half the stock. Bring to the boil, then simmer for 20 minutes or until the potatoes are cooked.

2 Leave to cool, then pour into a food processor or blender and blend until smooth. Return the soup to the pan, stir in the remaining fish stock and gently bring to the boil. Reduce the heat.

3 Stir the cream into the soup, then gently heat it through without boiling. If the soup boils the cream will curdle. Serve hot, garnished with the chopped parsley.

Variations

- *Omit the fish and use ham or chicken stock. Serve the soup topped with crisp fried bacon or pancetta.*
- *Use ordinary potato instead of sweet potato and omit the cinnamon. Add a pinch of ground mace.*
- *For a chicken and sweet potato soup, use 2 diced, skinless boneless chicken breast fillets instead of the fish and chicken stock instead of the fish stock.*
- *For a ham and sweet potato soup, use 1 trimmed, diced gammon steak (cured or smoked ham) instead of the fish, and ham or chicken stock.*

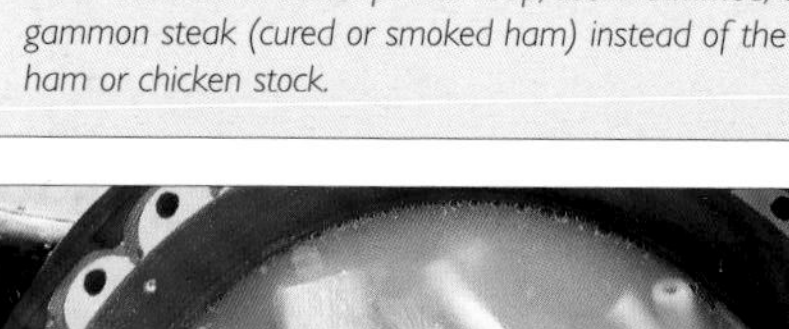

Spicy Chicken Soup with Almonds

This recipe brings slightly different seasoning to a classic soup, making it deliciously different for lunch or supper. Serve with naan bread.

Serves 4

75g/3oz/6 tbsp unsalted (sweet) butter
1 leek, chopped
2.5ml/½ tsp shredded fresh root ginger
75g/3oz/¾ cup ground almonds
5ml/1 tsp salt
2.5ml/½ tsp crushed black peppercorns
1 fresh green chilli, seeded and chopped
1 carrot, sliced
50g/2oz/½ cup frozen peas
115g/4oz/1 cup chicken, skinned, boned and cubed
30ml/2 tbsp chopped fresh coriander (cilantro)
450ml/¾ pint/scant 2 cups stock or water
250ml/8fl oz/1 cup single (light) cream
4 sprigs fresh coriander (cilantro)

1 Melt the unsalted (sweet) butter in a deep, round-bottomed frying pan, and sauté the leek and the ginger until soft and only just turning brown.

2 Lower the heat and add the ground almonds, salt, peppercorns, chilli, carrot, peas and chicken. Fry for about 10 minutes or until the chicken is completely cooked, stirring constantly. Add the chopped fresh coriander.

3 Remove the pan from the heat and allow to cool slightly. Transfer the mixture to a food processor or blender and process until smooth. Pour in the stock or water and blend briefly, until smooth and combined.

4 Pour the soup back into the pan and bring to the boil, stirring occasionally. Lower the heat and gradually stir in the cream. Cook gently for a further 2 minutes, stirring from time to time.

5 Ladle the soup into bowls and serve garnished with the sprigs of fresh coriander.

Fish and Sweet Potato: Energy 119kcal/501kJ; Protein 9.4g; Carbohydrate 11.9g, of which sugars 4.7g; Fat 4.1g, of which saturates 2.4g; Cholesterol 30mg; Calcium 38mg; Fibre 1.6g; Sodium 53mg.
Chicken with Almonds: Energy 425kcal/1760kJ; Protein 14.6g; Carbohydrate 5.5g, of which sugars 3.5g; Fat 38.5g, of which saturates 18.4g; Cholesterol 94mg; Calcium 119mg; Fibre 3g; Sodium 153mg.

Chicken Soup with Mushrooms and Coriander

This creamy spiced chicken soup makes a hearty meal. Serve it piping hot with fresh garlic bread.

Serves 4

75g/3oz/6 tbsp unsalted (sweet) butter
2.5ml/½ tsp crushed garlic
5ml/1 tsp garam masala
5ml/1 tsp crushed black peppercorns
5ml/1 tsp salt
1.5ml/¼ tsp freshly grated nutmeg
225g/8oz skinless, boneless chicken breast
1 leek, sliced
75g/3oz/generous 1 cup mushrooms, sliced
50g/2oz/⅓ cup corn
300ml/½ pint/1¼ cups chicken stock or water
250ml/8fl oz/1 cup single (light) cream
30ml/2 tbsp chopped fresh coriander (cilantro)
5ml/1 tsp crushed dried red chillies or chilli powder, to garnish (optional)

1 Melt the butter in a medium pan. Lower the heat slightly and add the garlic and garam masala. Lower the heat even further and add the black peppercorns, salt and nutmeg.

2 Cut the chicken pieces into very fine strips and add to the pan with the leek, mushrooms and corn. Cook stirring constantly, for 5–7 minutes, until the chicken is cooked through and the mixture is aromatic.

3 Remove from the heat and allow to cool slightly. Transfer three-quarters of the mixture to a food processor or blender. Add the stock or water and process until smooth.

4 Pour the resulting purée back into the pan with the rest of the soup and bring to the boil over a medium heat. Stir occasionally to prevent the soup from sticking to the bottom of the pan. Lower the heat and stir in the cream.

5 Add the fresh coriander. Taste and adjust the seasoning. Ladle the soup into bowls. Sprinkle with crushed red chillies or a little chilli powder, if liked, and serve immediately.

Classic Cream of Chicken Soup

A rich and flavoursome creamy chicken soup makes a fabulous lunch served with crispy bread. It is essential to use a really strong, home-made chicken stock for this recipe to give the soup a delicious, full flavour.

Serves 6

50g/2oz/¼ cup butter
2 onions, chopped
2 potatoes, chopped
1 large carrot, diced
1 celery stick, diced
750ml/1¼ pints/3 cups chicken stock
25g/1oz/¼ cup plain (all-purpose) flour
150ml/¼ pint/⅔ cup milk
175g/6oz cooked chicken
300ml/½ pint/1¼ cups single (light) cream
salt and ground black pepper
parsley leaves, to garnish

1 Melt the butter in a large pan and cook the onions, potatoes, carrot and celery gently for 5 minutes. Do not allow the vegetables to brown.

2 Add the stock and simmer gently for 30 minutes. Season with salt and pepper to taste. Purée the soup in a food processor or blender until smooth and then return it to the pan. Blend the flour with the milk and stir this into the soup. Cook over a low heat, stirring, until the soup boils and thickens.

3 Meanwhile, chop the chicken finely. Add to the soup and heat through for 5 minutes. Add 75ml/2½fl oz/⅓ cup of the cream and simmer for 5 minutes more.

4 Serve in individual bowls topped with a swirl of the remaining cream and garnished with ground black pepper and parsley leaves.

Variations
- *Add 30ml/2 tbsp chopped fresh tarragon with the cream.*
- *Add the grated rind of 1 small orange and serve the soup garnished with chopped walnuts.*

Chicken with Mushrooms: Energy 335kcal/1388kJ; Protein 17.1g; Carbohydrate 3.1g, of which sugars 2.7g; Fat 28.3g, of which saturates 17.6g; Cholesterol 114mg; Calcium 75mg; Fibre 1.4g; Sodium 310mg.
Cream of Chicken: Energy 233kcal/974kJ; Protein 13.1g; Carbohydrate 14.6g, of which sugars 5.4g; Fat 14.1g, of which saturates 8.4g; Cholesterol 60mg; Calcium 102mg; Fibre 1.3g; Sodium 154mg.

Tomato and Steak Soup

This unusual meatball soup hails from southern Holland.

Serves 4

2kg/4½lb ripe tomatoes, halved
25g/1oz/2 tbsp butter
1 onion, finely chopped
1 leek, finely chopped
25g/1oz/¼ cup plain (all-purpose) flour
500ml/17fl oz/generous 2 cups hot beef stock
1 bay leaf
150ml/¼ pint/⅔ cup milk
200g/7oz minced (ground) steak
15ml/1 tbsp soft brown sugar
50ml/2fl oz/¼ cup whipping cream
salt and ground black pepper
chopped fresh basil, chives, parsley and celery leaves, to garnish

1 Cook the tomatoes gently in a heavy pan, stirring often, for 10 minutes, until pulpy. Purée and sieve (strain) them. Heat gently, stirring occasionally, until reduced to 1 litre/1¾ pints/4 cups. Remove from the heat and set aside.

2 Melt the butter in a large pan. Add the onion and leek and cook over a low heat, stirring occasionally, for 5 minutes, until softened. Stir in the flour. Gradually stir in the stock and milk, followed by the tomato purée. Add the bay leaf. Bring to the boil, stirring, lower the heat and simmer gently.

3 Season the steak and shape it into small balls. Bring a small pan of salted water to the boil. Reduce the heat so that the water simmers. Add the meatballs and simmer for 10 minutes, until cooked. Drain well.

4 Stir the sugar and cream into the soup. Then stir in the meatballs. Season to taste and ladle into bowls, then serve sprinkled with chopped herbs.

Variation
For a healthier alternative, use all stock to replace the milk and cream. Add finely chopped leek and some chopped fresh lovage at the end, to garnish.

Cream of Duck Soup

This rich soup is ideal for smart autumn meals.

Serves 4

2 duck breasts
4 rindless streaky bacon rashers (strips), chopped
1 onion, chopped
1 garlic clove, chopped
2 carrots, diced
2 celery sticks, chopped
4 large mushrooms, chopped
15ml/1 tbsp tomato purée (paste)
2 duck legs, chopped into pieces
15ml/1 tbsp plain (all-purpose) flour
45ml/3 tbsp brandy
150ml/¼ pint/⅔ cup port
300ml/½ pint/1¼ cups red wine
900ml/1½ pints/3¾ cups chicken stock
1 bay leaf
2 sprigs fresh thyme
15ml/1 tbsp redcurrant jelly
150ml/¼ pint/⅔ cup double (heavy) cream
salt and ground black pepper

For the blueberry relish
150g/5oz/1¼ cups blueberries
15ml/1 tbsp caster sugar
grated rind and juice of 2 limes
15ml/1 tbsp chopped fresh parsley
15ml/1 tbsp balsamic vinegar

1 Score the skin and fat on the duck breasts. Brown in a hot heavy pan, skin down, for 8–10 minutes. Turn and cook for 5–6 minutes, until tender. Remove the duck. Drain off some of the duck fat, leaving about 45ml/3 tbsp in the pan.

2 Add the bacon, onion, garlic, carrots, celery and mushrooms and cook for 10 minutes, stirring. Stir in the tomato purée and cook for 2 minutes. Remove the skin and bones from the duck legs and chop the flesh. Add to the pan and cook for 5 minutes.

3 Stir in the flour, then the brandy, port, wine and stock. Boil, stirring. Stir in the bay, thyme and jelly. Reduce the heat and simmer for 1 hour. Sieve the soup and simmer for 10 minutes.

4 Mix all the ingredients for the relish, crushing some berries.

5 Discard the skin and fat from the duck breasts. Cut the meat into thin strips and add to the soup with the cream. Season and reheat, then ladle into bowls and serve topped with relish.

Tomato and Steak: Energy 369kcal/1547kJ; Protein 48.8g; Carbohydrate 14g, of which sugars 0.9g; Fat 13g, of which saturates 5.4g; Cholesterol 328mg; Calcium 45mg; Fibre 0.6g; Sodium 160mg.
Cream of Duck: Energy 642kcal/2673kJ; Protein 39.2g; Carbohydrate 14.2g, of which sugars 13.6g; Fat 35g, of which saturates 17.2g; Cholesterol 252mg; Calcium 83mg; Fibre 2.8g; Sodium 384mg.

Split Pea and Bacon Soup

This popular soup is great on really cold days.

Serves 4–6

350g/12oz/1½ cups dried split yellow or green peas
25g/1oz/2 tbsp butter
6 rashers (strips) rindless streaky (fatty) bacon, finely chopped
1 onion, finely chopped
1 carrot, thinly sliced
1 celery stick, thinly sliced
1.75 litres/3 pints/7½ cups ham or chicken stock
60ml/4 tbsp double (heavy) cream
salt and ground black pepper
croûtons and fried bacon, to serve

1 Soak the split peas in boiling water to cover. Melt the butter in a large pan. Add the bacon, onion, carrot and celery and cook for 10–15 minutes, stirring until soft and browning.

2 Drain and add the peas and stock. Bring to the boil, cover and simmer gently for 1 hour or until the peas are very soft. Process or blend until smooth. Season, add the cream and reheat. Serve with croûtons and pieces of crisp bacon on top.

Chicken and Leek Soup

This is a simple variation of an old French recipe.

Serves 4

1 boiling fowl (stewing chicken)
7.5ml/1½ tsp salt
1 small leek
1 bouquet garni
1 mace blade
1.5 litres/2½ pint/6¼ cups water
65g/2½oz/⅓ cup rice
1 egg yolk
50ml/2fl oz/¼ cup whipping cream

1 Put the fowl, salt, leek, bouquet garni, mace and water in a large pan. Boil, cover and simmer for 2 hours. Remove the fowl and cool. Strain the stock into a clean pan. Add the rice, bring to the boil and cook for 30 minutes. Purée the soup.

2 Dice the meat from the fowl. Add it to the soup and boil again. Remove from the heat. Beat the egg yolk with a ladleful of the soup, then stir it into the pan with the cream. Warm through, but do not boil. Season to taste and serve.

Cauliflower Soup with Broccoli and Bacon

Creamy cauliflower soup is given real bite by adding chunky cauliflower and broccoli florets and crusty bread piled high with melting Cheddar cheese.

Serves 4

1 onion, chopped
1 garlic clove, chopped
50g/2oz/¼ cup butter
2 cauliflowers, broken into florets
1 large potato, cut into chunks
900ml/1½ pints/3¾ cups chicken stock
225g/8oz broccoli, broken into florets
150ml/¼ pint/⅔ cup single (light) cream
6 rindless streaky bacon rashers
1 small baguette, cut in 4 pieces
225g/8oz/2 cups medium-mature Cheddar cheese, grated
salt and ground black pepper
roughly chopped fresh parsley, to garnish

1 Cook the onion and garlic in the butter for 4–5 minutes. Add half the cauliflower, all the potato and the stock. Bring to the boil, reduce the heat and simmer for 20 minutes.

2 Boil the remaining cauliflower for about 6 minutes, or until just tender. Use a draining spoon to remove the the florets and refresh under cold running water, then drain well. Cook the broccoli in the water for 3–4 minutes, until just tender. Drain, refresh under cold water, then drain. Add to the cauliflower.

3 Cool the soup slightly, then purée it until smooth and return it to the rinsed pan. Add the cream and seasoning, then heat gently. Add the cauliflower and broccoli and heat through.

4 Preheat the grill (broiler) to high. Grill the bacon until crisp, then cool slightly. Ladle the soup into flameproof bowls.

5 Place a piece of baguette in each bowl. Scatter grated cheese over the top and grill for 2–3 minutes, until the cheese is melted and bubbling. Take care when serving the hot bowls.

6 Crumble the bacon and sprinkle it over the melted cheese, then scatter the parsley over the top and serve immediately.

Split Pea and Bacon: Energy 378kcal/1584kJ; Protein 20.2g; Carbohydrate 34.9g, of which sugars 3.1g; Fat 18.5g, of which saturates 8.7g; Cholesterol 47mg; Calcium 45mg; Fibre 3.4g; Sodium 527mg.
Chicken and Leek: Energy 194kcal/811kJ; Protein 13g; Carbohydrate 20.1g, of which sugars 1.8g; Fat 6.8g, of which saturates 3.6g; Cholesterol 66mg; Calcium 45mg; Fibre 0.8g; Sodium 320mg.
Cauliflower/Broccoli: Energy 737kcal/3071kJ; Protein 34.8g; Carbohydrate 45.5g, of which sugars 9.2g; Fat 46.2g, of which saturates 26.4g; Cholesterol 121mg; Calcium 589mg; Fibre 6.6g; Sodium 1206mg.

Green Pea Soup with Garlic

The best thing about this soup is if you keep peas in the freezer, you can rustle it up in minutes. Despite using just a few simple ingredients, it has a wonderfully sweet taste and smooth texture and is great served with crusty bread and garnished with mint.

Serves 4

25g/1oz/2 tbsp butter
1 garlic clove, crushed
900g/2lb/8 cups frozen peas
1.2 litres/2 pints/5 cups chicken stock
salt and ground black pepper
sprigs of mint, to garnish

1 Heat the butter in a large pan and add the garlic. Fry gently for 2–3 minutes, until softened, then add the peas. Cook for 1–2 minutes more, then pour in the stock.

2 Bring the soup to the boil, then reduce the heat so that the soup cooks at a simmer. Cover the pan and simmer gently for 5–6 minutes, until the peas are tender. Leave to cool slightly, then transfer the mixture to a food processor or blender and process until smooth (you may have to do this in two batches).

3 Return the soup to the pan and heat through gently. Season with salt and pepper. Serve garnished with mint.

Variations

- *Ham stock makes a delicious base for pea soup. To complement the flavour garnish the soup with diced cooked ham and a little finely shredded fresh sage.*
- *For a vegetarian version use a good vegetable stock instead of chicken stock.*
- *Iced pea soup is good on hot summer days. Use frozen petit pois (baby peas) for a sweet flavour and add the grated rind and juice of 1 lime to the cold soup. Chill before serving.*
- *Crisp cubes of pan-fried halloumi cheese are delicious in this plain pea soup. Have the pan hot, the soup ready in warm bowls and then cook cubes of cheese quickly until brown outside and tender inside. Float in the soup and serve.*

Green Lentil Soup

High in fibre, lentils make a particularly tasty soup. Red or puy lentils make an equally good substitute for the green lentils used in this version.

Serves 4–6

225g/8oz/1 cup green lentils
75ml/5 tbsp olive oil
3 onions, finely chopped
2 garlic cloves, finely sliced
10ml/2 tsp cumin seeds, ground, or 5ml/1 tsp ground cumin
1.5ml/¼ tsp ground turmeric
600ml/1 pint/2½ cups vegetable stock
salt and ground black pepper
30ml/2 tbsp roughly chopped fresh coriander (cilantro), to garnish
warm crusty bread, to serve

1 Put the lentils in a saucepan and cover with cold water. Bring to the boil and boil rapidly for 10 minutes. Drain.

2 Heat 30ml/2 tbsp of the oil in a pan and fry two of the onions with the garlic, cumin and turmeric for approximately 3 minutes, or until golden brown, stirring. Add the lentils, stock and 600ml/1 pint/2½ cups water. Bring to the boil, reduce the heat, cover and simmer gently for 30 minutes until the lentils are soft.

3 Heat the remaining oil and fry the third onion until golden brown, stirring frequently.

4 Use a potato masher to lightly mash the lentils and make the soup pulpy in texture. Reheat gently and season with salt and freshly ground pepper to taste.

5 Pour the soup into bowls. Stir the fresh coriander in with the fried onion and scatter over the soup as a garnish. Serve with warm crusty bread.

Cook's Tip

Unlike other dried beans and legumes, the lentils do not need to be soaked before cooking.

Green Pea with Garlic: Energy 236kcal/977kJ; Protein 15.7g; Carbohydrate 25.4g, of which sugars 5.2g; Fat 9g, of which saturates 1.5g; Cholesterol 0mg; Calcium 48mg; Fibre 10.6g; Sodium 112mg.
Green Lentil Soup: Energy 220kcal/921kJ; Protein 9.5g; Carbohydrate 25.1g, of which sugars 3.7g; Fat 9.8g, of which saturates 1.4g; Cholesterol 0mg; Calcium 32mg; Fibre 2.5g; Sodium 15mg.

Spicy Lentil Dhal

This chunky lentil soup makes a sustaining meal in a bowl.

Serves 4–6

40g/1½oz/3 tbsp butter or ghee
1 onion, chopped
2 green chillies, seeded and chopped
15ml/1 tbsp chopped fresh root ginger
225g/8oz/1 cup yellow or red lentils
45ml/3 tbsp roasted garlic purée
5ml/1 tsp ground cumin
5ml/1 tsp ground coriander
200g/7oz tomatoes, peeled and diced
a little lemon juice
salt and ground black pepper
30–45ml/3–4 tbsp coriander (cilantro) sprigs, and fried onion and garlic slices, to garnish

For the whole spice mix

30ml/2 tbsp groundnut (peanut) oil
4–5 shallots, sliced
2 garlic cloves, thinly sliced
15g/½oz/1 tbsp butter or ghee
5ml/1 tsp cumin seeds
5ml/1 tsp mustard seeds
3–4 small dried red chillies
8–10 fresh curry leaves

1 Melt the butter or ghee in a large pan and cook the onion, chillies and ginger for 10 minutes, until golden. Stir in the lentils and 900ml/1½ pints/3¾ cups water. Bring to the boil, reduce the heat and part-cover. Simmer, stirring occasionally, for 50–60 minutes, until the lentils are broken down completely.

2 Stir in the roasted garlic purée, cumin, ground coriander and salt and pepper to taste. Cook for 10–15 minutes, stirring. Stir in the tomatoes. Adjust the seasoning, adding lemon juice to taste.

3 For the whole spice mix, heat the oil in a small pan. Add the shallots and fry, stirring occasionally, until crisp and browned. Add the garlic and cook, stirring, until it colours slightly. Use a draining spoon to remove the mixture from the pan; set aside.

4 Melt the butter or ghee in the same pan. Add the cumin and mustard seeds and fry until the mustard seeds pop. Stir in the chillies, curry leaves and shallot mixture, then swirl the mixture into the cooked dhal. Garnish with coriander sprigs, onions and garlic, and serve immediately.

Split Pea and Bottle Gourd Soup

Chana dhal, also known as Bengal gram, is a very small type of chickpea grown in India. It has a nutty taste and gives a fabulous earthy flavour to the food. Chana dhal is available from good Indian stores, and is at its best in spicy stew-type dishes like this one. Yellow split peas make a good substitute and require the same cooking time, but the flavour is not quite the same.

Serves 4–6

175g/6oz/⅔ cup chana dhal or yellow split peas, washed
1 litre/1¾ pints/4 cups stock or water
60ml/4 tbsp vegetable oil
2 fresh green chillies, chopped
1 onion, chopped
2 cloves garlic, crushed
5cm/2in piece fresh root ginger, grated
6–8 fresh curry leaves
5ml/1 tsp chilli powder
5ml/1 tsp ground turmeric
450g/1lb bottle gourd or marrow (large zucchini), courgettes (zucchini), squash or pumpkin, peeled, pithed and sliced
60ml/4 tbsp tamarind juice
6 tomatoes, chopped
salt
a handful fresh coriander (cilantro) leaves, chopped

1 In a large pan, cook the chana dhal in the stock or water for about 30 minutes until the chana dhal grains are tender but not mushy. Set aside without draining.

2 Heat the oil in a large pan and fry the chillies, onion, garlic, ginger, curry leaves, chilli powder and turmeric with salt to taste until the onions have softened. Add the gourd (or other vegetable) pieces and mix.

3 Pour in the chana dhal and liquid and bring to the boil. Add the tamarind juice, tomatoes and coriander. Cover and simmer for about 20 minutes, until the gourd is cooked. Serve hot.

Cook's Tip
If using courgettes (zucchini), add them along with the tamarind juice, tomatoes and coriander (cilantro) in step 3.

Spicy Lentil Dhal: Energy 262kcal/1095kJ; Protein 10.3g; Carbohydrate 26.9g, of which sugars 4.6g; Fat 13.3g, of which saturates 6.2g; Cholesterol 23mg; Calcium 36mg; Fibre 3.1g; Sodium 84mg.
Split Pea Soup: Energy 186kcal/783kJ; Protein 9g; Carbohydrate 20.9g, of which sugars 4.9g; Fat 8g, of which saturates 1g; Cholesterol 0mg; Calcium 44mg; Fibre 2.7g; Sodium 203mg.

Spiced Red Lentil Soup with Onion and Parsley

In this Turkish recipe the garnishes are vital and the onion, parsley and lemon may be placed in a separate bowl for adding as required.

Serves 4

30–45ml/2–3 tbsp olive or vegetable oil
1 large onion, finely chopped
2 garlic cloves, finely chopped
1 fresh red chilli, seeded and chopped
5–10ml/1–2 tsp cumin seeds
5–10ml/1–2 tsp coriander seeds
1 carrot, finely chopped
scant 5ml/1 tsp ground fenugreek
5ml/1 tsp sugar
15ml/1 tbsp tomato purée (paste)
250g/9oz/generous 1 cup split red lentils
1.75 litres/3 pints/7½ cups chicken stock
salt and ground black pepper

For serving

1 small red onion, finely chopped
1 large bunch of fresh flat leaf parsley, finely chopped
4–6 lemon wedges

1 Heat the oil in a heavy pan and stir in the onion, garlic, chilli, cumin and coriander seeds. When the onion begins to colour slightly, toss in the carrot and cook for 2–3 minutes.

2 Add the fenugreek, sugar and tomato purée and stir in the lentils. Pour in the stock, stir well and bring to the boil. Lower the heat, part-cover the pan and simmer for 30–40 minutes, until the lentils have broken up.

3 If the soup is too thick for your preference, thin it down to the desired consistency with a little water. Season with salt and pepper to taste.

4 Serve the soup as it is or, if you prefer a smooth texture, leave it to cool slightly, then whizz it in a blender and reheat it gently if necessary.

5 Ladle the soup into bowls and sprinkle liberally with the chopped onion and parsley. Serve with a wedge of lemon to squeeze over the soup.

Red Lentil and Coconut Soup

Hot, spicy and richly flavoured, this substantial soup is almost a meal in itself. If you are really hungry, serve with chunks of warmed naan bread or thick slices of toast.

Serves 4

30ml/2 tbsp sunflower oil
2 red onions, finely chopped
1 birds' eye chilli, seeded and finely sliced
2 garlic cloves, chopped
2.5cm/1in piece fresh lemon grass, outer layers removed and inside finely sliced
200g/7oz/scant 1 cup red lentils, rinsed
5ml/1 tsp ground coriander
5ml/1 tsp paprika
400ml/14fl oz/1⅔ cups coconut milk
900ml/1½ pints/3¾ cups vegetable stock or water
juice of 1 lime
3 spring onions (scallions), chopped
20g/¾oz/scant 1 cup fresh coriander (cilantro), finely chopped
salt and ground black pepper

1 Heat the oil in a large pan and add the onions, chilli, garlic and lemon grass. Cook for 5 minutes or until the onions have softened but not browned, stirring occasionally.

2 Add the lentils and spices. Pour in the coconut milk and stock or water, and stir until well mixed. Bring to the boil, stir, then reduce the heat and simmer for 40–45 minutes or until the lentils are soft and mushy.

3 Pour in the lime juice and add the spring onions and fresh coriander, reserving a little of each for the garnish. Season, then ladle into bowls. Garnish the soup with the reserved spring onions and coriander.

Cook's Tip

For a lower-fat version (coconut milk is rich in saturated fat), omit the coconut milk and add unsweetened apple juice instead. Stir in a little Greek (strained plain) yogurt at the end of cooking.

Spiced Red Lentil: Energy 203kcal/856kJ; Protein 11.1g; Carbohydrate 31.8g, of which sugars 7.3g; Fat 4.4g, of which saturates 0.6g; Cholesterol 0mg; Calcium 45mg; Fibre 3.5g; Sodium 26mg.
Lentil and Coconut: Energy 263kcal/1109kJ; Protein 13.6g; Carbohydrate 39.5g, of which sugars 10.8g; Fat 6.8g, of which saturates 1g; Cholesterol 0mg; Calcium 96mg; Fibre 4.1g; Sodium 134mg.

Red Lentil and Garlic Soup

Lentil soup is an eastern Mediterranean classic, and varies in its spiciness according to each region. Lentils are a popular choice as, unlike many pulses, they do not require soaking before being cooked. Red lentils contribute a real splash of colour to soups such as this.

Serves 6

225g/8oz/1 cup red lentils, rinsed and drained
2 onions, finely chopped
2 large garlic cloves, finely chopped
1 carrot, finely chopped
30ml/2 tbsp olive oil
2 bay leaves
a generous pinch of dried marjoram or oregano
1.5 litres/2½ pints/6¼ cups vegetable stock
30ml/2 tbsp red wine vinegar
salt and ground black pepper
celery leaves, to garnish
crusty bread rolls, to serve

1 Put all the ingredients except for the vinegar, seasoning and garnish in a large, heavy-based pan. Bring to the boil over a medium heat, then lower the heat and simmer for 1½ hours, stirring the soup occasionally to prevent the lentils from sticking to the bottom of the pan.

2 Remove the bay leaves and add the red wine vinegar, with salt and pepper to taste. If the soup is too thick, thin it with a little extra vegetable stock or water.

3 Serve the soup in heated bowls, garnished with celery leaves and accompanied by warm crusty rolls.

Cook's Tips

- *If you buy lentils loose, remember to put them into a sieve (strainer) or colander and pick them over, removing any pieces of grit, before rinsing them.*
- *The soup freezes well, especially puréed until smooth. Thin it down when thawed with a little stock or milk.*

Chunky Split Pea, Mushroom and Barley Soup

This hearty soup from Eastern Europe is perfect on a freezing cold day. Serve it in warmed bowls, with plenty of rye (pumpernickel) bread. This is a vegetarian version. For a meat version, use meat stock instead of vegetable and add chunks of tender, long-simmered beef to the soup.

Serves 6–8

30–45ml/2–3 tbsp small haricot (navy) beans, soaked overnight
45–60ml/3–4 tbsp green split peas
45–60ml/3–4 tbsp yellow split peas
90–105ml/6–7 tbsp pearl barley
1 onion, chopped
2 carrots, sliced
3 celery sticks, diced or sliced
½ baking potato, peeled and cut into chunks
10g/¼oz or 45ml/3 tbsp mixed dried mushrooms
5 garlic cloves, sliced
2 litres/3½ pints/8 cups vegetable stock or water with 2 vegetable stock (bouillon) cubes
salt and ground black pepper
30–45ml/2–3 tbsp chopped fresh parsley, to garnish

1 Put the beans, green and yellow split peas, pearl barley, onion, carrots, celery, potato, mushrooms, garlic and stock or water and stock cubes into a large pan.

2 Bring the mixture to the boil, then reduce the heat, cover and simmer gently for about 1½ hours, or until the beans are completely tender.

3 Crumble the stock cubes into the soup and taste for seasoning. Ladle into warmed bowls, garnish with parsley and serve with rye or pumpernickel bread.

Cook's Tip

Do not add the stock cubes until the end of cooking, as the salt they contain will prevent the beans from becoming tender.

Lentil and Garlic: Energy 130Kcal/553kJ; Protein 6.7g; Carbohydrate 26.1g, of which sugars 2.2g; Fat 0.6g, of which saturates 0.1g; Cholesterol 0mg; Calcium 24mg; Fibre 1.8g; Sodium 20mg.
Chunky Split Pea: Energy 162kcal/689kJ; Protein 6.8g; Carbohydrate 34.1g, of which sugars 4.3g; Fat 0.8g, of which saturates 0.1g; Cholesterol 0mg; Calcium 34mg; Fibre 2.9g; Sodium 30mg.

Split Pea and Pumpkin Soup

This is a tasty vegetarian version of a traditional dried pea soup.

Serves 4

225g/8oz/1 cup split peas
25g/1oz/2 tbsp butter
1 onion, finely chopped
225g/8 oz pumpkin, chopped
3 tomatoes, peeled and chopped
5ml/1 tsp dried tarragon, crushed
15ml/1 tbsp chopped fresh coriander (cilantro)
2.5ml/½ tsp ground cumin
1 vegetable stock cube, crumbled
chilli powder, to taste
sprigs of fresh coriander (cilantro), to garnish

1 Soak the split peas overnight in enough water to cover them completely, then drain. Place the split peas in a large saucepan, add 1.2 litres/2 pints/5 cups water and bring to the boil, then cook for about 30 minutes until tender.

2 In a separate pan, melt the butter and sauté the onion until soft but not browned.

3 Add the pumpkin, tomatoes, tarragon, coriander, cumin, vegetable stock cube and chilli powder and bring to the boil over high heat.

4 Stir the vegetable mixture into the cooked split peas and their liquid. Simmer the soup gently for about 20 minutes or until the vegetables are tender. If the soup is too thick, add another 150ml/¼ pint/⅔ cup water and reheat gently.

5 Ladle the soup into bowls and serve hot, garnished with sprigs of coriander.

Variations

- *Use butternut squash instead of the pumpkin.*
- *For a fresh, zesty soup, use 15ml/1 tbsp ground ginger instead of the cumin and add the grated rind of 1 large lemon.*
- *Chopped watercress is good instead of coriander (cilantro).*

Tarka-Dhal Red Lentil Soup

This thick soup-like dish is based on classic Indian tarka dhal. Also spelt tadka, tarka is the term for the hot oil seasoning that is drizzled over and folded into a dish before serving. Dhal varies in thickness according to the particular recipe, cook's preference and type of meal. Served slightly thin, it makes a fabulous meal-in-a-bowl.

Serves 4–6

115g/4oz/½ cup red lentils, washed
50g/2oz/¼ cup chana dhal or yellow split peas, washed
900ml/1½ pints/3¾ cups unsalted vegetable or chicken stock, or water
5ml/1 tsp grated fresh root ginger
3 garlic cloves, crushed
2.5ml/¼ tsp ground turmeric
2 fresh green chillies, chopped
7.5ml/1½ tsp salt

For the tarka

30ml/2 tbsp vegetable oil
1 onion, sliced
2.5ml/¼ tsp mixed mustard and onion seeds
4 dried red chillies
1 tomato, sliced

For the garnish

15ml/1 tbsp chopped fresh coriander (cilantro)
1–2 fresh green chillies, seeded and sliced
15ml/1 tbsp chopped fresh mint

1 Pick over the washed chana dhal or lentils for any stones, then place in a large pan. Add the stock or water with the ginger, garlic, turmeric and chopped green chillies. Bring to the boil, then reduce the heat and simmer for 15–20 minutes or until the lentils are soft.

2 Mash the lentils with the back of a spoon until they are of the same consistency as chicken soup. If the mixture looks too dry, add a little more water.

3 To prepare the tarka, heat the oil in another pan and fry the onion with the mustard and onion seeds, dried red chillies and sliced tomato for 2 minutes.

4 Pour the tarka over the dhal in the pan and garnish with the chopped fresh coriander, fresh green chillies and chopped mint. Serve piping hot.

Pea and Pumpkin: Energy 207kcal/881kJ; Protein 14.8g; Carbohydrate 36.7g, of which sugars 5.7g; Fat 1.2g, of which saturates 0.3g; Cholesterol 0mg; Calcium 71mg; Fibre 4.7g; Sodium 30mg.
Tarka-Dhal Red Lentil: Energy 235kcal/991kJ; Protein 13g; Carbohydrate 28.4g, of which sugars 3.7g; Fat 8.8g, of which saturates 2.2g; Cholesterol 0mg; Calcium 66mg; Fibre 2.9g; Sodium 40mg.

Spiced Bean Soup with Tofu

Long-life packs of tofu are widely available from supermarkets and Asian stores. It is silky in texture and delicious with crisp beans and little mushrooms in this spicy soup.

Serves 4–6

600ml/1 pint/2½ cups coconut milk
4 kaffir lime leaves, torn
15ml/1 tbsp red curry paste
45ml/3 tbsp Thai fish sauce
10ml/2 tsp palm sugar or soft light brown sugar
225g/8oz button (white) mushrooms
115g/4oz French (green) beans, trimmed
175g/6oz tofu, rinsed and cut into 2cm/¾in cubes
2 fresh red chillies, sliced
fresh coriander (cilantro) sprigs, to garnish

1 Put about one-third of the coconut milk in a wok or large pan. Add the lime leaves and bring to the boil, then reduce the heat and simmer until an oily sheen appears on the surface.

2 Add the red curry paste, fish sauce and sugar to the coconut milk. Mix together thoroughly.

3 Add the button mushrooms. Stir well and cook over a medium heat for about 1 minute. Stir in the rest of the coconut milk and bring back to the boil.

4 Add the French beans and cubes of tofu and allow to simmer gently for another 4–5 minutes, until the beans are tender. Do not cook too fast or the tofu will break up.

5 Ladle the soup into bowls and sprinkle with the chillies and coriander, then serve piping hot.

Cook's Tip
For an intense heat, add the chillies to the first batch of coconut milk, with the lime leaves. For a less fiery flavour, remove the seeds from the red chillies, adding them at the end.

Thick Curried Bean Soup

This spiced and chunky bean feast of a soup is delicious scooped up in torn-off pieces of warmed naan.

Serves 4

225g/8oz/1¼ cups dried red kidney beans
30ml/2 tbsp vegetable oil
2.5ml/½ tsp cumin seeds
1 onion, thinly sliced
1 fresh green chilli, finely chopped
2 garlic cloves, crushed
2.5cm/1in piece fresh root ginger, grated
30ml/2 tbsp curry paste
5ml/1 tsp ground cumin
5ml/1 tsp ground coriander
2.5ml/½ tsp chilli powder
2.5ml/½ tsp salt
400g/14oz can chopped tomatoes
30ml/2 tbsp chopped fresh coriander (cilantro)

1 Place the kidney beans in a large bowl of cold water and then leave them to soak overnight.

2 Drain the beans and place in a large pan with plenty of water. Boil vigorously for 10 minutes. Drain, rinse and return the beans to the pan. This process is essential in order to remove the toxins that are present in dried kidney beans. Add plenty of fresh water and bring to the boil. Reduce the heat, then cover and cook for 1–1½ hours, or until the beans are soft.

3 Meanwhile, heat the oil in a large pan and fry the cumin seeds for 2 minutes, until they begin to splutter. Add the onion, chilli, garlic and ginger and fry for 5 minutes. Stir in the curry paste, ground cumin, coriander, chilli powder and salt, and cook for 5 minutes.

4 Add the tomatoes and simmer for 5 minutes. Add the beans and fresh coriander, reserving a little for the garnish. Cover and cook for 15 minutes, adding a little water if necessary. Serve garnished with the reserved coriander.

Cook's Tip
Drained and well-rinsed canned beans work very well as an alternative to the dried beans.

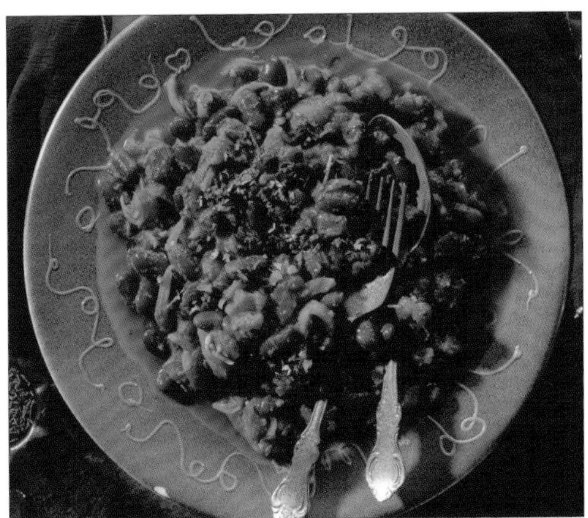

Spiced Bean Soup: Energy 65kcal/276kJ; Protein 4g; Carbohydrate 8.3g, of which sugars 7.3g; Fat 2.1g, of which saturates 0.4g; Cholesterol 0mg; Calcium 204mg; Fibre 1.4g; Sodium 124mg.
Curried Bean Soup: Energy 161kcal/682kJ; Protein 9.9g; Carbohydrate 23g, of which sugars 3g; Fat 3.5g, of which saturates 0.6g; Cholesterol 0mg; Calcium 47mg; Fibre 5.6g; Sodium 507mg.

Lentil and Vegetable Potage

Red lentils and vegetables are cooked and puréed, then sharpened with lots of lemon juice in this garlic-laden pot full of goodness. Made with vegetable stock, it is an excellent choice for a vegetarian light meal. Try serving with dark rye bread and cream cheese.

Serves 4

45ml/3 tbsp olive oil
1 onion, chopped
2 celery sticks, chopped
1–2 carrots, sliced
8 garlic cloves, chopped
1 potato, diced
250g/9oz/generous 1 cup red lentils
1 litre/1¾ pints/4 cups vegetable stock
2 bay leaves
1–2 lemons, halved
2.5ml/½ tsp ground cumin, or to taste
cayenne pepper or Tabasco sauce, to taste
salt and ground black pepper
lemon slices and chopped fresh flat leaf parsley or coriander (cilantro) leaves, to serve

1 Heat the oil in a large pan. Add the onion and cook for about 5 minutes, or until softened. Stir in the celery, carrots, half the garlic and all the potato. Cook for a few minutes until beginning to soften.

2 Add the lentils and stock to the pan and bring to the boil. Reduce the heat, cover and simmer for about 30 minutes, until the potato and lentils are tender.

3 Add the bay leaves, remaining garlic and half the lemons to the pan and cook the soup for a further 10 minutes. Remove the bay leaves. Squeeze the juice from the remaining lemons, then stir into the soup, to taste.

4 Pour the soup into a food processor or blender and process until smooth. (You may need to do this in batches.) Transfer the soup back into the pan, stir in the cumin, cayenne pepper or Tabasco sauce, and season with salt and pepper.

5 To serve, ladle the soup into bowls and top each portion with lemon slices and a sprinkling of parsley or coriander.

Braised Bean and Wheat Soup

This dish is wonderfully easy to make, but it is vital that you start soaking the pulses and wheat a day in advance. Offer tasty extra virgin olive oil at the table, ready for drizzling over the soup.

Serves 4

200g/7oz/1¼ cups mixed beans and lentils
25g/1oz/2 tbsp whole wheat grains
150ml/¼ pint/⅔ cup extra virgin olive oil
1 large onion, finely chopped
2 garlic cloves, crushed
5–6 fresh sage leaves, chopped
juice of 1 lemon
3 spring onions (scallions), thinly sliced
60–75ml/4–5 tbsp chopped fresh dill
salt and ground black pepper

1 Put the pulses and wheat in a large bowl and cover with cold water. Leave to soak overnight.

2 Next day, drain the pulse mixture, rinse it under cold water and drain again. Put the mixture in a large pan. Cover with plenty of cold water and cook for about 1½ hours, by which time all the ingredients will be quite soft.

3 Strain the bean mixture, reserving 475ml/16fl oz/2 cups of the cooking liquid. Return the bean mixture to the clean pan.

4 Heat the oil in a frying pan and fry the onion until light golden. Add the garlic and sage. As soon as the garlic becomes aromatic, add the mixture to the beans.

5 Stir in the reserved liquid, add plenty of seasoning and simmer for about 15 minutes, or until the pulses are piping hot. Stir in the lemon juice, then spoon into serving bowls, top with a sprinkling of spring onions and dill and serve.

Cook's Tip
Be sure to buy uncooked whole-wheat grains, not cracked wheat or bulgur, which is cracked and part-cooked.

Lentil and Vegetable: Energy 327Kcal/1379kJ; Protein 16.4g; Carbohydrate 47.4g, of which sugars 4.5g; Fat 9.3g, of which saturates 1.4g; Cholesterol 0mg; Calcium 51mg; Fibre 4.3g; Sodium 39mg.
Braised Bean Soup: Energy 442kcal/1844kJ; Protein 14.1g; Carbohydrate 39.2g, of which sugars 5.9g; Fat 26.5g, of which saturates 3.7g; Cholesterol 0mg; Calcium 76mg; Fibre 4.7g; Sodium 27mg.

Lentil and Tomato Soup

This soup of lentils and tiny pasta, sharpened by a shake of vinegar, is based on an old Greek recipe.

Serves 4

275g/10oz/1¼ cups brown-green lentils, preferably the small variety
150ml/¼ pint/⅔ cup extra virgin olive oil
1 onion, thinly sliced
5 garlic cloves, sliced into thin batons
1 carrot, sliced into thin discs
400g/14oz can chopped tomatoes
15ml/1 tbsp tomato purée (paste)
2.5ml/½ tsp dried oregano
1 litre/1¾ pints/4 cups hot vegetable stock or water
60g/2oz/½ cup tiny pasta, such as orzo
salt and ground black pepper
30ml/2 tbsp roughly chopped parsley leaves, to garnish
a few shakes of vinegar

1 Rinse the lentils, drain them and put them in a large pan with cold water to cover. Bring to the boil and boil for 3–4 minutes. Strain, discarding the liquid, and set the lentils aside.

2 Wipe the pan clean, heat the olive oil in it, then add the onion and sauté until translucent. Stir in the garlic, then, as soon as it becomes aromatic, return the lentils to the pan.

3 Add the carrot, tomatoes, tomato purée and oregano. Stir in the hot stock or water and a little pepper to taste.

4 Bring to the boil, then lower the heat, cover the pan and cook gently for 20–30 minutes until the lentils feel soft but have not begun to disintegrate. Halfway through, add the tiny pasta.

5 Add salt, the chopped parsley and a few shakes of vinegar just before serving the soup.

Variation
Try black Puy lentils in this recipe. For a simple non-vegetarian variation, add some sliced cooked good-quality sausages just before serving.

Frothy Lentil and Lobster Soup

Adding ice-cold butter a little at a time is the secret of whipping up the good froth that gives the clever cappuccino effect.

Serves 6

450–675g/1–1½lb live lobster
150g/5oz/⅔ cup Puy lentils
1 carrot, halved
1 celery stick, halved
1 small onion, halved
1 garlic clove
1 bay leaf
large bunch of tarragon, well tied
1 litre/1¾ pints/4 cups fish stock
120ml/4fl oz/½ cup double (heavy) cream
25g/1oz/2 tbsp butter, finely diced and chilled until ice cold
salt and ground black pepper
fresh tarragon sprigs, to garnish

1 Bring a large pan of water to the boil. Lower the live lobster into the water and cover the pan. Cook for 15–20 minutes, then drain the lobster and leave to cool.

2 Put the lentils in a pan and cover with cold water. Add the vegetables, garlic and herbs. Bring to the boil and simmer for 20 minutes. Drain the lentils and discard the vegetables and herbs. Purée the lentils in a food processor or blender until smooth. Set aside.

3 Break the claws off the lobster, crack them open and remove the meat from inside. Break off the tail, split it open and remove the meat. Cut all the meat into bitesize pieces.

4 Pour the fish stock into a large clean pan and bring to the boil. Lightly stir in the lentil purée and cream, but do not mix too much at this point otherwise you will not be able to create the cappuccino effect. The mixture should still be quite watery in places. Season well.

5 Using either a hand-held blender or electric beater, whisk up the soup mixture, adding the butter one piece at a time, until it is very frothy.

6 Divide the lobster meat among the bowls and carefully pour in the soup. Garnish with sprigs of tarragon and serve at once.

Lentil and Tomato: Energy 601Kcal/2523kJ; Protein 21.9g; Carbohydrate 72.3g, of which sugars 8.2g; Fat 26.9g, of which saturates 3.9g; Cholesterol 0mg; Calcium 60mg; Fibre 6.1g; Sodium 40mg.
Lentil and Lobster: Energy 232kcal/969kJ; Protein 12.4g; Carbohydrate 12.6g, of which sugars 0.7g; Fat 15.1g, of which saturates 9g; Cholesterol 66mg; Calcium 45mg; Fibre 2.2g; Sodium 123mg.

Chicken and Lentil Broth

An old-fashioned soup, this version is given more body by adding Puy lentils.

Serves 4

2 leeks, cut into 5cm/2in fine julienne
115g/4oz/½ cup Puy lentils
1 bay leaf
few sprigs of fresh thyme
2 skinless, boneless chicken breasts
900ml/1½ pints/3¾ cups good chicken stock
8 ready-to-eat prunes, cut into strips
salt and ground black pepper
fresh thyme sprigs, to garnish

1 Bring a small pan of salted water to the boil and cook the julienne of leeks for 1–2 minutes. Drain and refresh under cold running water. Drain again and set aside.

2 Pick over the lentils to check for any small stones or grit. Put into a saucepan with the bay leaf and thyme and cover with cold water. Bring to the boil and cook for 25–30 minutes until tender. Drain and refresh under cold water.

3 Put the chicken breasts in a saucepan and pour over enough stock to cover them. Bring to the boil and poach gently for 15–20 minutes until tender. Using a draining spoon, remove the chicken from the stock and leave to cool.

4 When the chicken is cool enough to handle, cut it into strips. Return it to the stock in the pan and add the lentils and the remaining stock. Bring just to the boil and add seasoning.

5 Divide the leeks and prunes among four warmed bowls. Ladle over the hot chicken and lentil broth. Garnish each portion with a few fresh thyme sprigs and serve immediately.

Cook's Tip
Julienne is a name for foods cut into long, thin strips – usually vegetables, but also meat and fish. For perfect julienne leeks, cut them into 5cm/2in lengths. Cut each piece in half lengthways, then with the cut side down, slice the leek into thin strips.

Lentil and Bacon Soup

Ready-prepared, puréed versions of this winter warmer are sometimes so thick you could stand your spoon in them. This chunkier version is delightful served with chunks of warm, crusty Granary (whole-wheat) bread. The addition of bacon and herbs boosts the otherwise mild flavour of this popular classic.

Serves 4

450g/1lb thick-sliced bacon, cubed
1 onion, roughly chopped
1 small turnip, roughly chopped
1 celery stick, chopped
1 potato, roughly chopped
1 carrot, sliced
75g/3oz/scant ½ cup lentils
1 bouquet garni
ground black pepper
fresh flatleaf parsley, to garnish

1 Heat a large pan and add the bacon. Cook for a few minutes, allowing the fat to run out.

2 Add the onion, turnip, celery, potato and carrot. Cook for about 4 minutes, stirring from time to time.

3 Add the lentils, bouquet garni, seasoning and pour in enough water to cover the ingredients. Bring to the boil, then reduce the heat and cover the pan. Simmer for 1 hour or until the lentils are tender.

4 Taste the soup and adjust the seasoning. Then ladle the soup into warmed bowls and serve garnished with flat-leaf parsley.

Variation
If you have a little more time to invest in cooking, and want to create a heartier, main course dish, you can substitute the sliced bacon with a whole piece of bacon. Simmer the joint in enough water to cover, adding a sliced onion, carrot and bay leaf. The usual cooking time is 20 minutes per 450g/1lb, plus 20 minutes extra. Use the stock for the soup and cube some of the cooked bacon. Cook the vegetables in a little oil in step 2, then add the cooked meat at the end of the cooking time. This is also a good way of producing well-flavoured cooking stock from a piece of gammon (smoked or cured ham).

Chicken and Lentil: Energy 210kcal/891kJ; Protein 26.3g; Carbohydrate 23.8g, of which sugars 9.8g; Fat 1.7g, of which saturates 0.3g; Cholesterol 53mg; Calcium 43mg; Fibre 5g; Sodium 52mg.
Lentil and Bacon: Energy 260kcal/1091kJ; Protein 14.8g; Carbohydrate 24.6g, of which sugars 3.9g; Fat 12.1g, of which saturates 3.8g; Cholesterol 29mg; Calcium 42mg; Fibre 3.2g; Sodium 370mg.

Spiced Red Lentil Soup with Smoky Bacon

Crispy shallots and a parsley cream top this rich soup.

Serves 6

5ml/1 tsp cumin seeds
2.5ml/½ tsp coriander seeds
5ml/1 tsp ground turmeric
30ml/2 tbsp olive oil
1 onion, chopped
2 garlic cloves, chopped
1 smoked bacon (ham) hock
1.2 litres/2 pints/5 cups vegetable stock
275g/10oz/1¼ cups red lentils
400g/14oz can chopped tomatoes
15ml/1 tbsp vegetable oil
3 shallots, thinly sliced

For the parsley cream
45ml/3 tbsp chopped fresh parsley
150ml/¼ pint/⅔ cup Greek (US strained plain) yogurt
salt and ground black pepper

1 Roast the cumin and coriander seeds in a hot, dry pan over a high heat for a few seconds, shaking the pan, until they are aromatic. Crush in a mortar and pestle. Add the turmeric.

2 Heat the oil in a large pan. Add the onion and garlic and cook for 4–5 minutes, until softened. Add the spices and cook for 2 minutes, stirring. Add the bacon and stock. Bring to the boil, reduce the heat, cover and simmer gently for 30 minutes.

3 Add the red lentils and cook for 20 minutes or until the lentils and bacon hock are tender. Stir in the tomatoes and cook for a further 5 minutes.

4 Remove the bacon. Leave the soup to cool slightly, then purée until almost smooth. Return the soup to the rinsed-out pan. Cut the meat from the hock, discarding skin and fat, then stir it into the soup and reheat.

5 Heat the vegetable oil in a frying pan and fry the shallots for 10 minutes until crisp and golden. Drain on kitchen paper.

6 For the parsley cream, stir the parsley into the yogurt and season. Serve the soup topped with parsley cream and shallots.

Yellow Pea Soup with Pork or Bacon

This soup is an old favourite that always tastes so good.

Serves 6–8

500g/1¼lb yellow split peas
30ml/2 tbsp vegetable oil
1 Spanish onion, sliced
500g/1¼lb/2¾ cups salted pork belly or bacon
2 litres/3½ pints/8 cups water or ham stock
1 bay leaf
1 bunch thyme sprigs
5ml/1 tsp chopped fresh thyme and/or marjoram
crispbread and Swedish mustard, to serve

1 Soak the yellow split peas in cold water overnight. The next day, drain them and put to one side.

2 Heat the oil in a large, heavy pan, add the onion and pork belly and, when browned, add the water or ham stock. Heat until simmering then skim off any foam and cook for 1 hour.

3 Add the peas, bay leaf and thyme sprigs and leave to cook for about a further hour until the peas are soft and the pork is cooked and falling apart.

4 Remove the pork from the pan and cut it into cubes, then return it to the pan with the fresh thyme and/or marjoram.

5 Season the soup with salt to taste before serving, Remember that the meat is salty, so the soup may not need extra seasoning. Serve the soup with Swedish mustard and good crispbread, such as knäckebröd.

Cook's Tip

Often served as a main course, this is a Swedish version of the internationally popular soup. Swedes dip their spoons into the mustard before taking a spoonful of soup. Any mild mustard can be used as a substitute.

Spiced Red Lentil Soup: Energy 235kcal/991kJ; Protein 13g; Carbohydrate 28.4g, of which sugars 3.7g; Fat 8.8g, of which saturates 2.2g; Cholesterol 21mg; Calcium 66mg; Fibre 2.9g; Sodium 40mg.
Pea Soup with Bacon: Energy 374kcal/1569kJ; Protein 25.8g; Carbohydrate 38.3g, of which sugars 3.7g; Fat 14g, of which saturates 4.3g; Cholesterol 33mg; Calcium 57mg; Fibre 3.9g; Sodium 988mg.

Lentil, Bacon and Frankfurter Soup

This is a wonderfully hearty German soup, but a lighter version can be made by omitting the frankfurters, if preferred.

Serves 6

225g/8oz/1 cup brown lentils
15ml/1 tbsp sunflower oil
1 onion, finely chopped
1 leek, finely chopped
1 carrot, finely diced
2 celery sticks, chopped
115g/4oz lean bacon, in one piece
2 bay leaves
30ml/2 tbsp chopped fresh parsley, plus extra to garnish
225g/8oz frankfurters, sliced
salt and ground black pepper

1 Rinse the lentils thoroughly under cold running water, then drain well and set aside.

2 Heat the oil in a large pan and gently fry the onion for about 5 minutes or until soft. Add the leek, carrot, celery, bacon and bay leaves.

3 Add the lentils. Pour in 1.5 litres/2½ pints/6¼ cups water, then slowly bring to the boil. Skim the surface, then reduce the heat and simmer, half-covered, for about 45–50 minutes, or until the lentils are soft.

4 Remove the piece of bacon from the soup and cut into small cubes. Trim off any fat. Return the bacon to the soup with the parsley and sliced frankfurters, and season well with freshly ground black pepper. The soup may need a little salt. Simmer for 2–3 minutes, then remove the bay leaves.

5 Transfer to individual soup bowls and serve garnished with chopped parsley.

Cook's Tip
Unlike most beans and pulses, lentils do not need to be soaked before cooking.

Chunky Lentil Soup with Rosemary and Bacon

This is a classic rustic Italian soup flavoured with rosemary, delicious served with chunks of garlic bread.

Serves 4

225g/8oz/1 cup dried green or brown lentils
45ml/3 tbsp extra virgin olive oil
3 rindless streaky (fatty) bacon slices, cut into small dice
1 onion, finely chopped
2 celery sticks, finely chopped
2 carrots, finely diced
2 fresh rosemary sprigs, finely chopped
2 bay leaves
400g/14oz can chopped plum tomatoes
1.75 litres/3 pints/7½ cups vegetable stock
salt and ground black pepper
bay leaves and rosemary sprigs, to garnish

1 Place the lentils in a bowl and cover with cold water. Leave to soak for 2 hours. Rinse and drain well.

2 Heat the oil in a large pan. Add the bacon and cook for about 3 minutes, then stir in the onion and cook for 5 minutes, until softened.

3 Stir in the celery, carrots, rosemary, bay leaves and lentils. Toss over the heat for 1 minute, until thoroughly coated in the oil.

4 Add the tomatoes and stock and bring to the boil. Lower the heat, half cover the pan, and simmer for about 1 hour, or until the lentils are perfectly tender.

5 Remove the bay leaves from the soup and add seasoning to taste. Serve garnished with bay leaves and rosemary sprigs.

Cook's Tip
Look out for the small brown Italian lentils that are grown in the area around Umbria – they do not break up during cooking and, in Italian cuisine, they are often mixed with small pasta shapes or rice for a contrast of flavours and textures.

Lentil and Frankfurter: Energy 275kcal/1154kJ; Protein 18.1g; Carbohydrate 21.4g, of which sugars 3.1g; Fat 13.6g, of which saturates 4.8g; Cholesterol 39mg; Calcium 49mg; Fibre 4.6g; Sodium 655mg.
Lentil with Rosemary: Energy 334kcal/1403kJ; Protein 18.2g; Carbohydrate 38.1g, of which sugars 7.3g; Fat 13.1g, of which saturates 2.8g; Cholesterol 12mg; Calcium 53mg; Fibre 4.7g; Sodium 392mg.

Split Pea and Ham Soup

Another fabulous variation on the popular pea and ham favourite, the main ingredient for this dish is bacon hock, which is the narrow piece of bone cut from a leg of ham. You could use a piece of pork belly instead, if you prefer, and remove it with the herbs before serving.

Serves 4

450g/1lb/2½ cups green split peas
4 rindless bacon rashers (strips)
1 onion, roughly chopped
2 carrots, sliced
1 celery stick, sliced
1 sprig of fresh thyme
2 bay leaves
1 large potato, roughly diced
1 bacon hock
ground black pepper

1 Put the split peas into a bowl, cover with plenty of cold water and leave to soak overnight.

2 Cut the bacon into small pieces. In a large pan, dry fry the bacon for 4–5 minutes or until crisp. Remove from the pan with a slotted spoon.

3 Add the chopped onion, carrots and celery to the fat in the pan and cook for 3–4 minutes or until the onion is softened but not browned. Return the bacon to the pan and stir, then pour in 2.4 litres/4¼ pints/10½ cups water.

4 Drain the split peas and add to the pan with the thyme, bay leaves, potato and bacon hock. Bring to the boil, reduce the heat, cover and cook gently for 1 hour.

5 Remove the thyme, bay leaves and hock. Process the soup in a blender or food processor until smooth. Then pour it back into a clean pan.

6 Cut the meat from the hock, discarding the fat and skin. Dice the meat and add it to the soup. Heat gently, stirring to prevent the soup from sticking to the pan. Season with plenty of pepper. Ladle into warm soup bowls and serve.

Bean and Lentil Soup with Lamb

This hearty Moroccan meat, bean and lentil soup is known as harira. The ingredients are simmered with warming spices.

Serves 4

450g/1lb well-flavoured tomatoes
225g/8oz lamb, cut into 1cm/½in pieces
2.5ml/½ tsp ground turmeric
2.5ml/½ tsp ground cinnamon
25g/1oz/2 tbsp butter
60ml/4 tbsp chopped fresh coriander (cilantro)
30ml/2 tbsp chopped fresh parsley
1 onion, chopped
50g/2oz/¼ cup red lentils
75g/3oz/½ cup dried chickpeas, soaked overnight and drained
4 baby onions or small shallots, peeled
25g/1oz/¼ cup soup noodles
salt and ground black pepper
chopped fresh coriander (cilantro), lemon slices and ground cinnamon, to garnish

1 Plunge the tomatoes into boiling water for 30 seconds, then rinse in cold water. Peel, seed and roughly chop.

2 Put the lamb, turmeric, cinnamon, butter, coriander, parsley and onion into a large pan, and cook over a moderate heat, stirring, for 5 minutes. Add the chopped tomatoes and continue to cook for 10 minutes.

3 Rinse the lentils and add to the pan with the chickpeas and 600ml/1 pint/2½ cups water. Bring to the boil, cover, and simmer gently for 1 hour or until the lentils are soft. Add the baby onions and continue to cook for a further 30 minutes.

4 Add the soup noodles about 5 minutes before the end of the cooking time. Season to taste. Garnish with the coriander, lemon slices and cinnamon.

Cook's Tip

Soup noodles are fine, quick-cook noodles; tiny pasta shapes can be used instead, if preferred. They will take the same amount of time to cook.

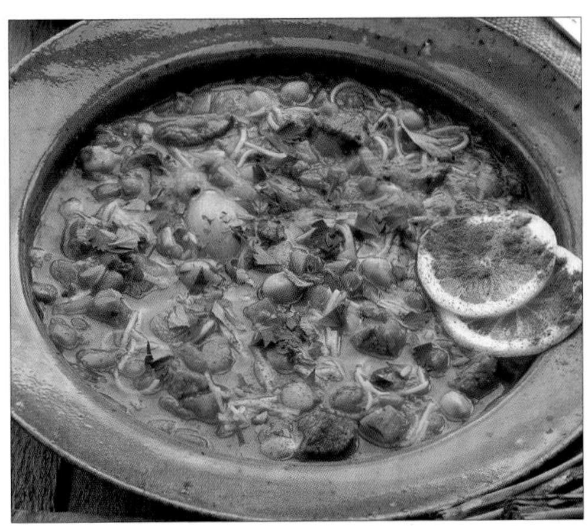

Split Pea and Ham: Energy 466kcal/1974kJ; Protein 32.2g; Carbohydrate 75.6g, of which sugars 6.2g; Fat 5.9g, of which saturates 1.9g; Cholesterol 13mg; Calcium 75mg; Fibre 7g; Sodium 443mg.
Bean and Lentil: Energy 297kcal/1248kJ; Protein 19.6g; Carbohydrate 26.4g, of which sugars 5.4g; Fat 13.1g, of which saturates 6.4g; Cholesterol 56mg; Calcium 75mg; Fibre 4.5g; Sodium 113mg.

Creamy Black Lentil Soup

Black lentils are available whole, split and skinned and split. All three types make a very thick and delicious dhal, especially when enriched by cream. If you are feeling decadent, you can even serve this dish with extra cream at the table.

Serves 4–6

175g/6oz/¾ cup black lentils, soaked
50g/2oz/¼ cup red split lentils
1.5 litres/2 pints/5 cups vegetable or chicken stock
120ml/4fl oz/½ cup double (heavy) cream
120ml/4fl oz/½ cup natural (plain) yogurt
5ml/1 tsp cornflour (cornstarch)
45ml/3 tbsp ghee or vegetable oil
1 onion, finely chopped
5cm/2in piece fresh root ginger, crushed
4 fresh green chillies, chopped
1 tomato, chopped
2.5ml/½ tsp chilli powder
2.5ml/½ tsp ground turmeric
2.5ml/½ tsp ground cumin
2 garlic cloves, sliced
salt
coriander (cilantro) sprigs and sliced red chilli, to garnish

1 Drain the black lentils and place in a large pan with the red lentils. Pour in the stock and bring to the boil. Reduce the heat, cover the pan and simmer for about 30 minutes, or until tender. Mash with a spoon or vegetable masher.

2 In a bowl, mix together the cream, yogurt and cornflour until smooth and then stir the paste into the soup and bring to the boil, stirring. Remove from the heat.

3 Heat 15ml/1 tbsp of the ghee or oil in a frying pan, and fry the onion, ginger, two green chillies and the tomato until the onion is soft. Add the chilli powder, turmeric and cumin, and fry for a further 2 minutes. Stir into the lentil soup and mix well.

4 Heat the remaining ghee or oil in a frying pan over a low heat and fry the garlic slices and remaining chillies until the garlic slices are golden brown.

5 Ladle the lentils into bowls and top each portion with a little of the garlic and chillies. Add coriander leaves and red chilli to garnish, and serve at once.

Green Bean and Almond Soup

Any seasonal vegetables can be added or substituted for the beans in this recipe. If preferred, the lemon wedges can be served on the side.

Serves 8

225g/8oz green beans
1 garlic clove, roughly chopped
2 macadamia nuts or 4 almonds, finely chopped
1cm/½in cube shrimp paste
10–15ml/2–3 tsp coriander seeds, dry fried
15ml/1 tbsp sunflower oil
1 onion, finely sliced
400ml/14fl oz can reduced-fat coconut milk
2 bay leaves
225g/8oz/4 cups beansprouts
8 thin lemon wedges
30ml/2 tbsp lemon juice
salt and ground black pepper

1 Cut them into small pieces. Bring 1.2 litres/2 pints/5 cups water to the boil with a little salt. Add the beans and cook for 3–4 minutes. Drain, reserving the cooking water. Set the water and beans aside.

2 Finely grind the chopped garlic, macadamia nuts or almonds, shrimp paste and the coriander seeds to a paste using a pestle and mortar or in a food processor.

3 Heat the oil in a wok or pan, and fry the onion until transparent. Remove with a slotted spoon. Add the nut paste to the wok and fry it for 2 minutes without allowing it to brown.

4 Add the reserved vegetable water to the wok or pan and stir well. Add the reduced-fat coconut milk, bring to the boil and add the bay leaves. Reduce the heat and simmer the soup, uncovered, for 15–20 minutes.

5 Just before serving, reserve a few green beans, fried onions and beansprouts for garnish and stir the rest into the soup and heat through without boiling.

6 Add the lemon wedges, lemon juice and seasoning to the soup and stir well. Pour or ladle the soup into soup bowls and garnish with the reserved green beans, onion and beansprouts. Serve piping hot.

Creamy Black Lentil: Energy 291kcal/1216kJ; Protein 11.3g; Carbohydrate 23.3g, of which sugars 3g; Fat 17.8g, of which saturates 7.6g; Cholesterol 28mg; Calcium 84mg; Fibre 3.2g; Sodium 30mg.
Green Bean: Energy 51kcal/212kJ; Protein 2.2g; Carbohydrate 5.2g, of which sugars 4.2g; Fat 2.5g, of which saturates 0.4g, of which polyunsaturates 1.2g; Cholesterol 3mg; Calcium 43mg; Fibre 1.2g; Sodium 84mg.

Runner Bean Soup

This is an ideal recipe for making the most of tender young runner beans or other green beans. You can buy canned white beans to save time, but the flavour will not be as good. This soup is traditionally served with buttered white bread – select a good country loaf, with a firm close texture, and be generous with the butter.

Serves 4

250g/9oz/1⅓ cups dried white beans, soaked over night
800g/1¾lb rib of beef
800g/1¾lb celeriac, cubed
800g/1¾lb runner (green) beans, cut into short lengths
250g/9oz potatoes, coarsely diced
2 leeks, thickly sliced
salt
chopped fresh parsley or celery leaves, to garnish
buttered white bread, to serve

1 Drain the white beans and rinse under cold running water.

2 Put the beef in a pan and add 2 litres/3½ pints/8¾ cups water. Bring to the boil. Skim off any scum that rises to the surface, lower the heat, cover and simmer for 1 hour.

3 Add the white beans to the pan, re-cover and simmer for a further 1 hour, until the beans are just tender.

4 Add the celeriac, runner beans, potatoes and leeks to the soup and simmer for 20 minutes, until all the vegetables are tender. Remove the meat and carve it into slices.

5 Taste the soup and adjust the seasoning. Ladle the soup into bowls and sprinkle with parsley or celery leaves.

6 Serve the soup with the meat and buttered bread.

Cook's Tip
The soup is seasoned at the end of cooking when the white beans are tender. If the water is salted at first, the beans will not become tender as the salt toughens them.

Green Bean and Cabbage Soup

Summer savory is essential to the success of this simple vegetable soup. An aromatic, pungent herb, it does have a natural affinity with all kinds of beans. Winter savory can also be used, although its flavour is slightly stronger.

Serves 4

500g/1¼lb floury potatoes, cut into pieces
2 onions, chopped
300g/11oz green beans, cut into 1cm/½in lengths
500g/1¼ lb green cabbage, roughly chopped
1 small bunch of fresh summer savory, chopped
50ml/2fl oz/¼ cup olive oil
salt

1 Put the potatoes and onions in a large pan, add 1 litre/1¾ pints/4 cups water and bring to the boil. Cover and simmer for about 20 minutes, until tender.

2 Transfer the vegetables and cooking liquid to a food processor or blender and process to a purée. Return to the rinsed-out pan.

3 Cut the cabbage in quarters, cut out the core and slice in 2.5cm/1in pieces. Add the cabbage, beans and summer savory to pan and cook over a medium heat for a few minutes until the cabbage is cooked, and the beans are tender but still slightly crisp.

4 Season the soup with salt to taste, stir in the olive oil and serve immediately.

Variation
The soup is delicious made with tender young broad (fava) beans instead of green beans. Blanch the broad beans in boiling water for 3–5 minutes, until they are just cooked. For a very special version, skin the little beans, removing the pale green pods and leaving the bright green beans. Heat them for a few seconds in the soup before serving.

Runner Bean: Energy 462kcal/1952kJ; Protein 43.2g; Carbohydrate 48.4g, of which sugars 11.7g; Fat 12g, of which saturates 4.3g; Cholesterol 58mg; Calcium 240mg; Fibre 18.6g; Sodium 204mg.
Bean and Cabbage: Energy 239kcal/998kJ; Protein 6.2g; Carbohydrate 34.2g, of which sugars 11.7g; Fat 9.6g, of which saturates 1.4g; Cholesterol 0mg; Calcium 96mg; Fibre 6.1g; Sodium 20mg.

Snake Bean and Pumpkin Soup with Coconut

This tasty soup is from Java, where it is served on its own with rice or as an accompaniment to a poached or grilled fish dish.

Serves 4

30ml/2 tbsp palm, groundnut (peanut) or corn oil
150g/5oz pumpkin or squash flesh
115g/4oz snake beans (yardlong beans)
220g/7½oz can bamboo shoots, drained and rinsed
900ml/1½ pints/3¾ cups coconut milk
10–15ml/2–3 tsp palm sugar (jaggery)
130g/4½oz fresh coconut, shredded
salt

For the spice paste
4 shallots, chopped
25g/1oz fresh root ginger, chopped
4 red chillies, seeded and chopped
2 garlic cloves, chopped
5ml/1 tsp coriander seeds
4 candlenuts, toasted and chopped

For serving
cooked rice
chilli sambal

1 For the spice paste, using a mortar and pestle, grind all the ingredients together or whiz them in an electric spice mill.

2 Heat the oil in a large pan, stir in the spice paste and fry until fragrant. Stir in the pumpkin, snake beans and bamboo shoots, then the coconut milk. Add the sugar and bring to the boil. Cook gently for 5–10 minutes, until the vegetables are tender.

3 Stir in salt to taste and half the coconut. Ladle into bowls, sprinkle with the remaining coconut and serve with cooked rice and a chilli sambal for adding to taste.

Cook's Tip
Chilli sambal is a thick, spicy paste that can be easily made at home by pounding chillies with shrimp paste and lime juice, or with ginger and garlic.

American Red Bean Soup

This soup is in Tex-Mex style, and it is served with a cooling avocado and lime salsa. If you relish chillies, add a little more cayenne for a truly fiery experience.

Serves 6

30ml/2 tbsp olive oil
2 onions, chopped
2 garlic cloves, chopped
10ml/2 tsp ground cumin
1.5ml/¼ tsp cayenne pepper
15ml/1 tbsp paprika
15ml/1 tbsp tomato purée (paste)
2.5ml/½ tsp dried oregano
400-g/14-oz can chopped tomatoes
2 x 400g/14oz cans red kidney beans, drained and rinsed
salt and ground black pepper
Tabasco, to serve

For the guacamole salsa
2 avocados
1 small red onion, finely chopped
1 green chilli, seeded and finely chopped
15ml/1 tbsp chopped fresh coriander (cilantro)
juice of 1 lime

1 Heat the oil in a large pan and add the onions and garlic. Cook for about 4–5 minutes, until softened. Add the cumin, cayenne and paprika, and cook for 1 minute, stirring.

2 Stir in the tomato purée and cook for a few seconds, then stir in the oregano. Add the chopped tomatoes, kidney beans and 900ml/1½ pints/3¾ cups water.

3 Bring the tomato and bean mixture to the boil. Reduce the heat and cover the pan, then simmer for 15–20 minutes. Cool the soup slightly, then purée it in a food processor or blender until smooth. Return to the rinsed-out pan and add seasoning to taste.

4 To make the guacamole salsa, halve, stone (pit) and peel the avocados, then dice them finely. Place in a small bowl and gently, but thoroughly, mix with the finely chopped red onion and chilli, and the coriander and lime juice.

5 Reheat the soup and ladle it into bowls. Spoon a little guacamole salsa into the middle of each and serve, offering Tabasco for those who want to spice up their soup.

Snake Bean Soup: Energy 333kcal/1388kJ; Protein 6g; Carbohydrate 26g, of which sugars 23.8g; Fat 23.6g, of which saturates 11.7g; Cholesterol 0mg; Calcium 115mg; Fibre 4.9g; Sodium 258mg.
Red Bean Soup: Energy 302kcal/1265kJ; Protein 11.7g; Carbohydrate 33.2g, of which sugars 11.8g; Fat 14.5g, of which saturates 2.8g; Cholesterol 0mg; Calcium 125mg; Fibre 11.8g; Sodium 537mg.

Spiced Black-eyed Bean Broth

These black-eyed beans are delicious in their turmeric-tinted tomato broth, which is flavoured with tangy lemon and speckled with chopped fresh coriander.

Serves 4

175g/6oz/1 cup dried black-eyed beans (peas)
15ml/1 tbsp olive oil
2 onions, chopped
4 garlic cloves, chopped
1 medium-hot or 2–3 mild fresh chillies, chopped
5ml/1 tsp ground cumin
5ml/1 tsp ground turmeric
250g/9oz fresh or canned tomatoes, diced
600ml/1 pint/2½ cups chicken, beef or vegetable stock
25g/1oz fresh coriander (cilantro) leaves, roughly chopped
juice of ½ lemon
pitta bread, to serve

1 Put the beans in a pan, cover with cold water, bring to the boil, then cook for 5 minutes. Remove from the heat, cover and leave to stand for 2 hours.

2 Drain the beans, return them to the rinsed-out pan, cover with fresh cold water, then bring to the boil. Reduce the heat, cover and simmer for 35–40 minutes, or until the beans are tender. Drain and set aside.

3 Heat the oil in a pan, add the onions, garlic and chilli and cook for 5 minutes, or until the onions are soft. Stir in the cumin, turmeric, tomatoes, stock, half the coriander and the beans and bring to the boil. Reduce the heat, cover the pan and simmer for 20–30 minutes.

4 Stir the lemon juice and remaining coriander into the soup and serve immediately with pitta bread.

Cook's Tip
When cooking dried beans and pulses, boil them in unsalted water. Salt prevents the beans from becoming tender or toughens them if it is added when they are only part cooked.

Chestnut and White Bean Soup

This substantial Portuguese soup is a traditional peasant dish. Chestnuts have a long history of cultivation in southern and alpine Europe, and were eaten long before potatoes, which were imported from the Americas. You can freeze chestnuts if you buy too many – so long as you remember to peel them first (see Cook's Tip).

Serves 4

100g/3¾oz/½ cup dried white beans, soaked overnight in cold water and drained
90g/3½oz peeled chestnuts, thawed if frozen
1 bay leaf
50ml/2fl oz/¼ cup olive oil
1 onion, chopped
salt

1 Put the beans, chestnuts and bay leaf in a large pan. Pour in 1 litre/3¾ pints/4 cups water and bring to the boil. Lower the heat, cover the pan and simmer the beans for about 1½ hours, until they are tender.

2 Meanwhile, heat the oil in a frying pan. Add the onion and cook over a low heat, stirring occasionally, for 5 minutes, until softened. Do not allow the oil to overheat.

3 Add the onion and its cooking oil to the soup. Stir well, seasoning to taste with salt. Remove and discard the bay leaf. Mash the beans and chestnuts with a fork or vegetable masher, so they are crushed into the soup but not smooth.

4 Ladle the soup into bowls and serve immediately, while piping hot and freshly laced with the olive oil and onion.

Cook's Tip
If using fresh chestnuts, do not store them for more than a week. The easiest way to shell them and remove their inner skins is to make a small cut in each one and par-boil or roast in the oven at 180°C/350°F/Gas 4 for about 5 minutes. Remove the shells and rub off the skins with a dish towel. Peeled frozen chestnuts are a simpler option.

Black-eyed Bean Broth: Energy 172Kcal/727kJ; Protein 10.9g; Carbohydrate 25.4g, of which sugars 6g; Fat 3.7g, of which saturates 0.6g; Cholesterol 0mg; Calcium 73mg; Fibre 8.5g; Sodium 17mg.
Chestnut and Bean: Energy 184kcal/773kJ; Protein 6.2g; Carbohydrate 20.5g, of which sugars 3.1g; Fat 9.2g, of which saturates 1.4g; Cholesterol 0mg; Calcium 39mg; Fibre 5.1g; Sodium 8mg.

Broad Bean Soup with Gammon

The combination of bean soup with a cake of herb-flavoured pan-fried potatoes is delicious.

Serves 4

2 onions, thinly sliced
800g/1¾lb gammon (smoked or cured ham), rind removed
1.2–1.6kg/2½–3½lb shelled broad (fava) beans
15g/½oz/1 tbsp butter
1 bunch spring onions (scallions), diced
30ml/2 tbsp cornflour (cornstarch)
1 bunch parsley, chopped
single (light) cream, to serve
salt and ground black pepper

Summer savory cake

500g/1¼lb potatoes, grated
2 eggs, lightly beaten
pinch of freshly grated nutmeg
30ml/2 tbsp finely chopped fresh summer savory
25g/1oz/2 tbsp butter

1 Place half the sliced onions and the meat in a pan. Pour in 1.5 litres/2½ pints/6¼ cups water in a pan. Bring to the boil, then lower the heat, cover and simmer for 1 hour.

2 For the cake, mix the potatoes, eggs, nutmeg, savory and seasoning. Melt half the butter in a non-stick frying pan. Add the potato mixture, pressing it out evenly. Cook over low heat until set. Loosen the edges and turn out on to a plate.

3 Melt the remaining butter in the pan, slide the cake back in, cooked side up, and fry until browned underneath. Keep warm.

4 Remove the meat from the pan. Add the beans and cook for 15–20 minutes, until tender. Melt the butter in a frying pan. Lightly brown the piece of meat with the remaining onion and for about 10 minutes over low heat.

5 Remove and purée about half the beans from the soup, then stir the purée into the soup with the spring onions. Mix the cornflour to a paste with 60ml/4 tbsp water, stir into the soup and bring to the boil, stirring. Season and sprinkle with parsley.

6 Serve the soup with the cake, sliced meat and onion mixture. A jug (pitcher) of cream may be offered at the table.

Broad Bean and Potato Soup

Coriander provides a refreshing twist to this creamy soup of fresh beans and hearty potatoes.

Serves 4

30ml/2 tbsp olive oil
2 onions, chopped
3 large floury potatoes, diced
450g/1lb fresh shelled broad (fava) beans
1.75 litres/3 pints/7½ cups vegetable stock
1 bunch fresh coriander (cilantro), roughly chopped
150ml/¼ pint/⅔ cup single (light) cream, plus a little extra, to garnish
salt and ground black pepper

1 Heat the oil in a large pan and fry the onions, stirring, for about 5 minutes, until they are soft.

2 Add the potatoes. Reserve a few of the beans for garnish, then add the rest to the pan. Pour in the stock, and bring it to the boil. Simmer the soup for 5 minutes, then add the coriander and simmer for a further 10 minutes.

3 Blend the soup in batches in a food processor or blender until smooth, then return it to the rinsed-out pan.

4 Reheat the soup until almost boiling, stirring to prevent it from sticking to the pan. Stir in the cream and heat for a few seconds, but do not allow the soup to simmer or boil.

5 Blanch the reserved beans in boiling water for 1 minute, then drain them and remove their skins.

6 Taste and season the soup, then ladle it into bowls and garnish with beans, cream and coriander.

Variation

Instead of the broad (fava) beans, try a combination of peas – shelled fresh or frozen – and a bunch of watercress in this recipe. The peas and watercress are delicious with the coriander (cilantro).

Bean with Bacon: Energy 428kcal/1793kJ; Protein 46g; Carbohydrate 26.2g, of which sugars 5.1g; Fat 16g, of which saturates 5.2g; Cholesterol 46mg; Calcium 108mg; Fibre 9.2g; Sodium 1777mg.
Bean and Potato: Energy 236kcal/990kJ; Protein 9.3g; Carbohydrate 30.3g, of which sugars 4.6g; Fat 9.4g, of which saturates 3.8g; Cholesterol 14mg; Calcium 94mg; Fibre 6.8g; Sodium 30mg.

Pasta-free Minestrone

Minestrone is the famous Italian soup that can be made with almost any combination of seasonal vegetables. Here pesto is added for intense flavour.

Serves 6

1.75 litres/3 pints/7½ cups vegetable stock
1 large onion, chopped
3 celery sticks, chopped
2 carrots, finely diced
2 large floury potatoes, finely diced
½ head of cabbage, very finely diced
225g/8oz runner (green) beans, sliced diagonally
2 x 400g/14oz cans cannellini beans, drained
60ml/4 tbsp ready-made pesto sauce
salt and ground black pepper
crusty bread, to serve
freshly grated Parmesan cheese, to serve

1 Pour the stock into a large pan. Add the onion, celery and carrots. Bring to the boil, reduce the heat and cover the pan. Then simmer for 10 minutes.

2 Add the potatoes, cabbage and beans to the soup and simmer for 10–12 minutes or until the potatoes are tender.

3 Stir in the cannellini beans and pesto, and bring the soup to the boil, stirring frequently.

4 Season the soup to taste and serve hot, with crusty bread and plenty of freshly grated Parmesan cheese for adding to individual portions as required.

Variation
Rice or barley can be added to minestrone instead of pasta. Try adding a handful of either grain with the vegetables in step 1 above. Instead of floury potatoes, dice small, waxy salad potatoes that will hold their shape and stay firm but tender during cooking to complement the rice or barley.

Chunky Bean, Leek and Cabbage Soup

There are lots of versions of this wonderful Italian soup from Tuscany. This one uses cannellini beans, leeks, cabbage and good olive oil – and tastes even better reheated.

Serves 4

45ml/3 tbsp extra virgin olive oil
1 onion, roughly chopped
2 leeks, roughly chopped
1 large potato, diced
2 garlic cloves, finely chopped
1.2 litres/2 pints/5 cups vegetable stock
400g/14oz can cannellini beans, drained, liquid reserved
175g/6oz Savoy cabbage, shredded
45ml/3 tbsp chopped fresh flat leaf parsley
30ml/2 tbsp chopped fresh oregano
75g/3oz/1 cup shaved Parmesan cheese
salt and ground black pepper

For the garlic toasts
30–45ml/2–3 tbsp extra virgin olive oil
6 thick slices country bread
1 garlic clove, peeled and bruised

1 Heat the oil in a large pan, add the onion, leeks, potato and garlic and cook gently for 4–5 minutes. Pour on the stock and the liquid from the beans (reserving the beans). Cover and simmer for 15 minutes.

2 Stir in the cabbage and beans, with half the herbs. Season and cook for 10 minutes more. Spoon about one-third of the soup into a food processor or blender and process until fairly smooth. Return the purée to the soup in the pan, taste for seasoning and heat through for 5 minutes.

3 Meanwhile make the garlic toasts. Drizzle a little oil over the slices of bread, then rub both sides of each slice with the garlic. Toast until browned on both sides.

4 Ladle the soup into bowls. Sprinkle with the remaining herbs and the Parmesan shavings. Add a drizzle of olive oil and serve immediately with the garlic toasts.

Pasta-free Minestrone: Energy 241kcal/1007kJ; Protein 9.7g; Carbohydrate 21.7g, of which sugars 9.3g; Fat 13.4g, of which saturates 4g; Cholesterol 13mg; Calcium 204mg; Fibre 3.6g; Sodium 165mg.
Bean and Cabbage: Energy 200kcal/838kJ; Protein 7.3g; Carbohydrate 21.7g, of which sugars 10.3g; Fat 9.9g, of which saturates 1.5g; Cholesterol 0mg; Calcium 92mg; Fibre 7.6g; Sodium 330mg.

Cannellini Bean Soup

Bursting with authentic Italian flavour, this chunky soup from Tuscany is very quick and easy to make. Offer it as a substantial starter or, for a nourishing lunch dish, serve it with warmed ciabatta bread.

Serves 4

2 x 400g/14oz cans chopped tomatoes with herbs
250g/9oz cavolo nero leaves
400g/14oz can cannellini beans
60ml/4 tbsp extra virgin olive oil
salt and ground black pepper

1 Pour the tomatoes into a large pan and add a canful of cold water. Season with salt and pepper and bring to the boil, then reduce the heat so that the tomatoes simmer.

2 Roughly shred the cavolo nero leaves and add them to the tomatoes. Partially cover the pan and continue to simmer the tomatoes gently for about 15 minutes, or until the cabbage is just tender.

3 Drain the cannellini beans through a strainer, then rinse them under cold running water. Add the beans to the tomato mixture and warm them through for a few minutes without boiling fiercely.

4 Check and adjust the seasoning, then ladle the soup into bowls, drizzle with a little olive oil and serve immediately.

Cook's Tips

- *Cavolo nero is a very dark green cabbage from Tuscany and southern Italy. It has a delicious nutty flavour and adds an authentic taste to this traditional recipe. Cavolo nero is available in most large supermarkets but, if you can't find it, Savoy cabbage is a perfectly good substitute.*
- *Olive oil is traditionally drizzled into the soup to add flavour, but instead you could spoon a little green pesto into each bowl and add a sprinkling of Parmesan shavings.*
- *Toasted Italian bread, rubbed with garlic and drizzled with olive oil, makes a classic accompaniment.*

Minestrone with Pesto

The variations on this vegetarian minestrone are endless. This version is packed with heaps of vegetables to make a hearty lunch when served with warm crusty bread.

Serves 6

1.5 litres/2½ pints/6¼ cups stock or water, or a combination of both
45ml/3 tbsp olive oil
1 large onion, finely chopped
1 leek, sliced
2 carrots, finely chopped
1 celery stick, finely chopped
2 garlic cloves, finely chopped
2 potatoes, diced
1 bay leaf
1 sprig fresh thyme, or 1.5ml/¼ tsp dried thyme
115g/4oz/¾ cup shelled fresh or frozen peas
2–3 courgettes (zucchini), finely chopped
3 tomatoes, peeled and finely chopped
425g/15oz/3 cups cooked or canned beans, such as cannellini
45ml/3 tbsp pesto
salt and ground black pepper
freshly grated Parmesan cheese, to serve

1 In a medium pan, heat the stock or water until simmering.

2 Heat the olive oil in a large pan. Stir in the onion and leek, and cook for 5–6 minutes, or until the onion softens. Add the carrots, celery and garlic, and cook over moderate heat, stirring frequently, for another 5 minutes. Add the potatoes and cook for 2–3 minutes more.

3 Pour in the hot stock or water and stir well. Add the herbs and season with salt and pepper. Bring to the boil, reduce the heat slightly and cook for 10–12 minutes.

4 Stir in the peas, if fresh, and the courgettes. Simmer for a further 5 minutes. Add the frozen peas, if using, and the tomatoes. Cover the pan, and simmer for 5–8 minutes.

5 About 10 minutes before serving the soup, uncover and stir in the beans. Simmer for 10 minutes. Stir in the pesto sauce and adjust the seasoning. Simmer for a further 5 minutes, then remove from the heat. Allow the soup to stand for a few minutes before serving with the grated Parmesan.

Cannellini Bean: Energy 416kcal/1756kJ; Protein 24.4g; Carbohydrate 53.4g, of which sugars 11.8g; Fat 13.1g, of which saturates 2g; Cholesterol 0mg; Calcium 145mg; Fibre 19g; Sodium 41mg.
Minestrone with Pesto: Energy 570kcal/2396kJ; Protein 26.9g; Carbohydrate 72.8g, of which sugars 12.5g; Fat 21g, of which saturates 6g; Cholesterol 35mg; Calcium 247mg; Fibre 9g; Sodium 1636mg.

Beetroot and Butter Bean Soup with Orange and Sour Cream

This soup is a simplified version of borscht and is prepared in a fraction of the time. Served with a spoonful of soured cream and a scattering of chopped fresh parsley, it is delicious.

Serves 4

30ml/2 tbsp vegetable oil
1 onion, sliced
5ml/1 tsp caraway seeds
finely grated rind of ½ orange
250g/9 oz cooked beetroot, grated
1.2 litres/2 pints/5 cups beef stock or rassol (see Cook's Tip)
400g/14oz can butter (lima) beans, drained and rinsed
15ml/1 tbsp wine vinegar
60ml/4 tbsp sour cream
60ml/4 tbsp chopped fresh parsley, to garnish

1 Heat the oil in a large pan and cook the onion, caraway seeds and orange rind until soft but not coloured.

2 Add the beetroot, stock or rassol, butter beans and vinegar and bring to the boil. Reduce the heat and cover the pan, then simmer over low heat for a further 10 minutes.

3 Taste the soup for seasoning before serving. Then ladle it into bowls and add a spoonful of soured cream to each. Scatter with chopped parsley to garnish.

Variation

Add the rind of a whole orange and the squeezed juice. Cook 1 crushed garlic clove with the onion and add 5ml/1 tsp sugar with the stock. Omit the beans. Chill well before serving.

Cook's Tip

Rassol is a beetroot broth, which is used to impart a strong beetroot colour and flavour. You are most likely to find it in Kosher speciality sections of large supermarkets.

Chunky Plum Tomato and Cannellini Bean Soup

This is a rich and satisfying soup. Serve olive ciabatta or a good substantial loaf to make a delicious meal.

Serves 4

900g/2lb ripe plum tomatoes
30ml/2 tbsp olive oil
275g/10oz onions, roughly chopped
2 garlic cloves, crushed
900ml/1½ pints/3¾ cups vegetable stock
30ml/2 tbsp sun-dried tomato purée (paste)
10ml/2 tsp paprika
15ml/1 tbsp cornflour (cornstarch)
425g/15oz can cannellini beans, rinsed and drained
30ml/2 tbsp chopped fresh coriander (cilantro)
salt and ground black pepper
olive ciabatta, to serve

1 First, peel the tomatoes. Using a sharp knife, make a small cross in each one and place in a bowl. Pour over boiling water to cover and leave to stand for 30–60 seconds.

2 Drain the tomatoes and quickly peel off the skins. Quarter them and then cut each piece in half again. If the tomatoes are firm, process them in two batches, otherwise the skins are difficult to peel when the tomatoes have cooled.

3 Heat the oil in a large pan and cook the onions and garlic for 3 minutes or until just beginning to soften.

4 Add the tomatoes and stir in the stock, sun-dried tomato purée and paprika. Season with a little salt and pepper. Bring to the boil, reduce the heat and cover the pan. Then simmer the soup for 10 minutes.

5 Mix the cornflour to a smooth paste with 30ml/2 tbsp water. Stir the beans into the soup, then stir in the cornflour paste. Cook, stirring, for a further 5 minutes, until thickened.

6 Adjust the seasoning and stir in the chopped coriander just before serving with olive ciabatta.

Beetroot and Bean: Energy 189kcal/790kJ; Protein 7.9g; Carbohydrate 19.8g, of which sugars 7.1g; Fat 9.2g, of which saturates 2.6g; Cholesterol 9mg; Calcium 65mg; Fibre 6.5g; Sodium 471mg.
Tomato and Cannellini: Energy 216kcal/911kJ; Protein 9.3g; Carbohydrate 31g, of which sugars 13.3g; Fat 7g, of which saturates 1.1g; Cholesterol 0mg; Calcium 70mg; Fibre 8.8g; Sodium 492mg.

Spicy Black and Red Bean Soup

This filling soup is made with two kinds of beans flavoured with cumin.

Serves 6–8

175g/6oz/1 cup dried black beans, soaked overnight and drained
175g/6oz/1 cup dried kidney beans, soaked overnight and drained
2 bay leaves
30ml/2 tbsp olive or vegetable oil
3 carrots, chopped
1 onion, chopped
1 celery stick
1 garlic clove, crushed
5ml/1 tsp ground cumin
1.5–2.5ml/¼–½ tsp cayenne pepper
2.5ml/½ tsp dried oregano
50ml/2 fl oz/¼ cup red wine
1.2 litres/2 pints/5 cups beef stock
salt and ground black pepper

For the garnish
soured cream
chopped fresh coriander (cilantro)

1 Put the black beans and kidney beans in two separate pans with cold water to cover and a bay leaf in each. Boil rapidly for 10 minutes, then cover and simmer for 50 minutes, until the beans are tender. Drain.

2 Heat the oil in a large pan. Add the carrots, onion, celery and garlic and cook over a low heat for 8–10 minutes, stirring, until softened. Stir in the cumin, cayenne, oregano and salt to taste.

3 Add the wine, stock and 250ml/8 fl oz/1 cup water and stir to thoroughly mix all the ingredients. Remove the bay leaves from the cooked beans and add the beans to the pan.

4 Bring to the boil, reduce the heat, then cover the pan and simmer the soup for about 20 minutes, stirring occasionally.

5 Transfer half the soup, with the beans and vegetables, to a food processor or blender. Process until smooth. Return the purée to the pan and stir thoroughly.

6 Reheat the soup, stirring to prevent it from sticking to the pan, and adjust the seasoning to taste. Serve hot, garnished with soured cream and chopped coriander.

Black and White Bean Soup

This soup, as its appearance suggests, is prepared as two separate components, which are then combined when serving. Although the dish takes a while to prepare, the results are stunning – and the swirl of dark and light is not difficult to achieve.

Serves 8

350g/12oz/2 cups dried black beans, soaked overnight and drained
2.4 litres/4¼ pints/10½ cups unsalted chicken or vegetable stock or water
6 garlic cloves, crushed
350g/12 oz/2 cups dried white beans, soaked overnight and drained
90ml/6 tbsp balsamic vinegar
4 jalapeño peppers, seeded and chopped
6 spring onions (scallions), finely chopped
juice of 1 lime
50ml/2 fl oz/¼ cup olive oil
15g/½ oz/¼ cup chopped fresh coriander (cilantro), plus extra to garnish
salt and ground black pepper

1 Place the black beans in a large pan with half the stock or water and half the garlic. Bring to the boil. Reduce the heat to low, cover the pan and simmer for about 1½ hours or until the beans are soft.

2 Meanwhile, put the white beans in another pan with the remaining water and garlic. Bring to the boil, cover the pan and simmer for about 1 hour until soft.

3 Purée the cooked white beans in a food processor or blender. Stir in the vinegar, jalapeños, and half the spring onions. Return to the pan and reheat gently.

4 Purée the cooked black beans in the food processor or blender. Return to the pan and stir in the lime juice, olive oil, coriander and remaining spring onions. Reheat gently.

5 Season both soups with salt and freshly ground black pepper. To serve, place a ladleful of each puréed soup in each soup bowl, side by side. Swirl the two soups together with a cocktail stick or skewer. Garnish with fresh coriander and serve.

Spicy Bean Soup: Energy 160kcal/675kJ; Protein 10g; Carbohydrate 22.6g, of which sugars 4.1g; Fat 3.5g, of which saturates 0.5g; Cholesterol 0mg; Calcium 55mg; Fibre 7.8g; Sodium 18mg.
Black and White Bean: Energy 281kcal/1189kJ; Protein 19.7g; Carbohydrate 40.2g, of which sugars 3.7g; Fat 5.7g, of which saturates 0.8g; Cholesterol 0mg; Calcium 92mg; Fibre 14.2g; Sodium 17mg.

White Bean Soup

A thick purée of cooked dried beans makes a satisfying base for this warming winter lunch or supper soup.

Serves 6

350g/12oz/scant 2 cups dried cannellini or other white beans
1 bay leaf
75ml/5 tbsp olive oil
1 onion, finely chopped
1 carrot, finely chopped
1 celery stick, finely chopped
3 tomatoes, peeled and finely chopped
2 garlic cloves, finely chopped
5ml/1 tsp fresh thyme leaves, or 2.5ml/½ tsp dried thyme
750ml/1¼ pints/3½ cups boiling water
salt and ground black pepper
extra virgin olive oil, to serve

1 Pick over the beans carefully, discarding any stones or other particles. Soak the beans in a large bowl of cold water for about 12 hours or overnight.

2 Drain the beans and place them in a large pan of water. Bring to the boil and cook for 20 minutes. Drain. Return the beans to the pan, cover with cold water and bring to the boil again. Add the bay leaf and cook for 1–2 hours, until the beans are tender. Drain again. Remove the bay leaf.

3 Process about three-quarters of the beans in a blender or food processor, or pass them through a food mill, adding a little water if necessary.

4 Heat the oil in a large pan. Add the onion and cook, stirring, until it softens. Add the carrot and celery and cook for a further 5 minutes.

5 Stir in the tomatoes, garlic and thyme. Continue to cook for 6–8 minutes, stirring frequently. Pour in the boiling water. Stir in the beans and the bean purée. Season with salt and pepper and simmer for 10–15 minutes.

6 Ladle the soup into bowls and drizzle with a little extra virgin olive oil, then serve piping hot.

Flageolet Bean and Cauliflower Soup

The sweet, anise-liquorice flavour of the fennel seeds gives a delicious edge to this hearty soup.

Serves 4–6

15ml/1 tbsp olive oil
1 garlic clove, crushed
1 onion, chopped
10ml/2 tsp fennel seeds
1 cauliflower, cut into small florets
2 x 400g/14oz cans flageolet (small cannellini) beans, drained and rinsed
1.2 litres/2 pints/5 cups vegetable stock or water
salt and ground black pepper
chopped fresh parsley, to garnish
toasted slices of French bread, to serve

1 Heat the olive oil in a large pan. Add the garlic, onion and fennel seeds and cook gently for 5 minutes or until the onion is softened but not browned.

2 Add the cauliflower florets, half the beans and the vegetable stock or water. Bring to the boil. Reduce the heat and cover the pan, then simmer the soup for about 10 minutes or until the cauliflower is tender.

3 Purée the soup in a food processor or blender until smooth, then return it to the rinsed-out pan.

4 Stir in the remaining beans and add seasoning to taste. Reheat the soup, stirring to prevent it from sticking to the pan.

5 Pour the soup into bowls. Sprinkle with chopped parsley and serve with toasted slices of French bread.

Cook's Tip

Beans and pulses, such as flageolet (small cannellini), are relatively expensive canned compared to dried. The dried beans can be soaked and cooked in large batches, then cooled and frozen in small portions. Soak the beans overnight, drain and boil for 10 minutes, then drain and simmer steadily for 40–60 minutes, until tender. Drain, cool and pack in bags or pots, then freeze. Use the beans from frozen or thaw them in the microwave.

White Bean Soup: Energy 220kcal/926kJ; Protein 11.5g; Carbohydrate 30.6g, of which sugars 8.4g; Fat 6.7g, of which saturates 0.9g; Cholesterol 0mg; Calcium 91mg; Fibre 9.8g; Sodium 31mg.
Flageolet and Cauliflower: Energy 145kcal/611kJ; Protein 9.6g; Carbohydrate 20.8g, of which sugars 6g; Fat 3.1g, of which saturates 0.5g; Cholesterol 0mg; Calcium 101mg; Fibre 7.9g; Sodium 399mg.

Cannellini Bean Soup with Salami

This popular Greek soup is always served with bread and olives, and perhaps raw onion quarters (or even some raw garlic for those with robust palates). The salami, added at the end, is a nice touch, but of course easily omitted for a vegetarian version.

Serves 4

275g/10oz/1½ cups dried cannellini beans, soaked overnight in cold water
1 large onion, thinly sliced
1 celery stick, sliced
2 or 3 carrots, sliced
400g/14oz can tomatoes
15ml/1 tbsp tomato purée (paste)
150ml/¼ pint/⅔ cup extra virgin olive oil
5ml/1 tsp dried oregano
50g/2oz salami, sliced (optional)
30ml/2 tbsp finely chopped fresh flat leaf parsley
salt and ground black pepper

1 Drain the beans, rinse them and drain again. Tip them into a large pan, pour in enough water to cover and bring to the boil over a medium heat. Boil for about 10 minutes, then drain.

2 Return the beans to the pan, pour in fresh water to cover them by about 3cm/1¼in, then add the onion, celery, carrots, and tomatoes.

3 Stir in the tomato purée, olive oil and dried oregano. Season to taste with a little freshly ground black pepper, but do not add salt at this stage, as it would toughen the beans.

4 Bring to the boil, lower the heat and cook for about 1 hour, or until the beans are just tender. Season with salt, stir in the salami, if adding, and parsley and serve.

Cook's Tip
For a more substantial meal serve this soup with feta cheese (or any other hard cheese) and olives, adding fried squid, marinated anchovies or keftedes, if liked. Plenty of crusty bread is the essential accompaniment.

Spiced Chickpea, Broad Bean and Lentil Soup

Ginger and cinnamon are fabulous in this lentil, chickpea and vegetable soup. Warm, aromatic fennel seed rolls really complement the savoury-sweetness of this soup, or you can serve it with savoury brioche.

Serves 8

30–45ml/2–3 tbsp olive oil
2 onions, halved and sliced
2.5ml/½ tsp ground ginger
2.5ml/½ tsp ground turmeric
5ml/1 tsp ground cinnamon
pinch of saffron threads
2 x 400g/14oz cans chopped tomatoes
5–10ml/1–2 tsp caster (superfine) sugar
175g/6oz/¾ cup brown or green lentils, picked over and rinsed
about 1.75 litres/3 pints/7½ cups meat or vegetable stock, or water
200g/7oz/1 generous cup dried chickpeas, soaked overnight, drained and boiled until tender
200g/7oz/1 generous cup dried broad (fava) beans, soaked overnight, drained and boiled until tender
small bunch of fresh coriander (cilantro), chopped
small bunch of flat leaf parsley, chopped
bread rolls or savoury brioche, to serve
salt and ground black pepper

1 Heat the olive oil in a large pan. Add the onions and stir over a low heat for about 15 minutes, or until they are soft.

2 Add the ginger, turmeric, cinnamon and saffron, then the tomatoes and a little sugar. Stir in the lentils and pour in the stock or water. Bring to the boil, then reduce the heat and cover the pan. Simmer the soup for about 25 minutes, or until the lentils are tender.

3 Stir in the cooked chickpeas and beans. Bring the soup back to the boil, then reduce the heat again and cover the pan. Simmer the soup for a further 10–15 minutes.

4 Add the coriander and parsley. Taste and season the soup, then serve piping hot with herb or lightly spiced bread.

Cannellini Bean: Energy 490Kcal/2,051kJ; Protein 17.9g; Carbohydrate 47.8g, of which sugars 11.3g; Fat 26.6g, of which saturates 4.1g; Cholesterol 0mg; Calcium 89mg; Fibre 8.4g; Sodium 45mg.
Chickpea and Lentil: Energy 376Kcal/1594kJ; Protein 18.7g; Carbohydrate 66.4g, of which sugars 12g; Fat 5.9g, of which saturates 1g; Cholesterol 2mg; Calcium 181mg; Fibre 8.6g; Sodium 70mg.

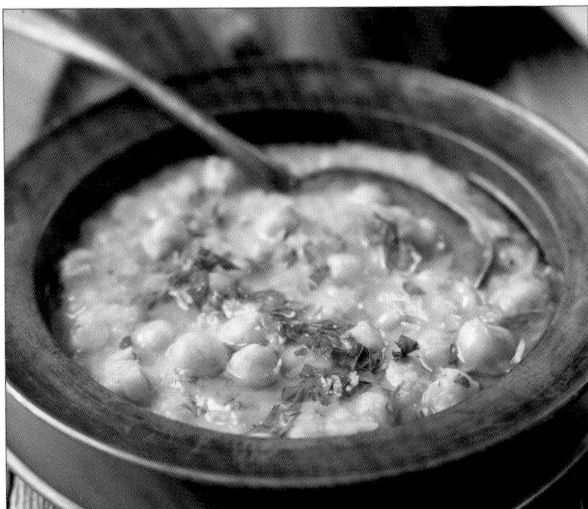

Garlic-laced Chickpea Soup

This is a relatively light soup for one made with pulses but it is big on flavour with rosemary and sautéed garlic. Crusty bread goes well.

Serves 4

150ml/¼ pint/⅔ cup extra virgin olive oil, plus extra for drizzling and serving
6 garlic cloves, sliced
1 large onion, chopped
350g/12oz/1¾ cups dried chickpeas, soaked in cold water overnight
2 large fresh rosemary sprigs
15ml/1 tbsp plain (all-purpose) flour
juice of 1 lemon, or to taste
45ml/3 tbsp chopped fresh flat leaf parsley
salt and ground black pepper

1 Heat the extra virgin olive oil in a heavy pan, add the garlic and cook very gently for 5 minutes. Stir in the onion and cook for a further 5 minutes, until it softens and starts to colour.

2 Meanwhile, drain the chickpeas, rinse them and drain thoroughly. Add them to the onion and garlic and stir to coat them well in the oil. Add the rosemary. Pour in enough hot water to cover the chickpeas by about 4cm/1½in.

3 Slowly bring to the boil. Lower the heat so that the soup simmers and add some freshly ground black pepper. Cover and cook for 1–1¼ hours, or until the chickpeas are soft. Remove the rosemary.

4 Put the flour in a cup and stir in the lemon juice to make a smooth paste. When the chickpeas are perfectly soft, stir in the flour paste and bring to the boil, stirring. Stir in salt to taste. Cover the pan and cook the soup gently for 5–10 minutes more, stirring occasionally.

5 To thicken the soup slightly, take out about two cupfuls of the chickpeas and put them in a food processor or blender. Process briefly so that the chickpeas are broken up, but remain slightly rough. Stir back into the soup in the pan.

6 Add the parsley and add more lemon juice to taste. Serve with extra olive oil for drizzling.

Chickpea and Parsley Soup

Chickpeas are a popular ingredient in Italian country cooking and this thick and tasty soup is a classic example of good, comforting rustic food. If short of time, use canned chickpeas.

Serves 6

225g/8oz/1¾ cups chickpeas, soaked overnight
1 onion, halved
1 bunch fresh parsley, about 40g/1½oz
30ml/2 tbsp olive oil and sunflower oil, mixed
1.2 litres/2 pints/5 cups chicken stock
grated rind of 2 lemons and juice of ½ lemon
salt and ground black pepper
lemon wedges and finely pared strips of rind, to garnish
crusty bread, to serve

1 Drain the chickpeas and rinse them under cold running water. Cook in rapidly boiling water for 10 minutes, then reduce the heat, cover and simmer for 1–1½ hours until tender. Drain.

2 Place the onion and parsley in a food processor or blender and process until finely chopped.

3 Heat the olive and sunflower oils in a large pan. Add the onion mixture and cook for 5 minutes over low heat, stirring occasionally, until the onion is slightly softened.

4 Add the chickpeas, cook gently for 1–2 minutes and pour in the chicken stock. Add the lemon rind and season well with salt and pepper. Bring the soup to the boil, then cover and simmer for about 20 minutes.

5 Allow the soup to cool a little, then coarsely purée it in a food processor or blender. Alternatively, coarsely mash the chickpeas with a vegetable masher or fork. The soup should be thick, with a rough texture, not smooth.

6 If necessary, return the soup to a clean pan. Add the lemon juice and taste for seasoning, adding more salt and pepper, if required. Heat gently and serve, garnished with lemon wedges and finely pared lemon rind, and accompanied by crusty bread.

Garlic Chickpea: Energy 544Kcal/2,274kJ; Protein 20.1g; Carbohydrate 51.6g, of which sugars 6.1g; Fat 30g, of which saturates 4g; Cholesterol 0mg; Calcium 184mg; Fibre 10.9g; Sodium 40mg.
Chickpea and Parsley: Energy 140kcal/591kJ; Protein 8.1g; Carbohydrate 19.4g, of which sugars 1.5g; Fat 3.9g, of which saturates 0.5g; Cholesterol 0mg; Calcium 63mg; Fibre 4.2g; Sodium 15mg.

Clear Chickpea and Potato Broth with Sausage

Chickpeas form part of the staple diet in the Balkans and Mediterranean, used either whole or ground. They are versatile and go well with all sorts of ingredients. They are terrific in soups and the flavour can be varied according to the herbs and spices used.

Serves 4–6

500g/1¼lb/3½ cups chickpeas, rinsed and drained
2 litres/3½ pints/8 cups vegetable stock
3 garlic cloves, sliced
3 large waxy potatoes, peeled and cut into bitesize chunks
50ml/2fl oz/¼ cup olive oil
50g/2oz salami, sliced
225g/8oz spinach leaves, washed and drained well
a little freshly grated nutmeg
salt and ground black pepper

1 Place the chickpeas in a large bowl of cold water and leave to soak overnight. The next day, drain them well and place in a large pan with the stock.

2 Bring to the boil, then reduce the heat and cook gently for about 1 hour. Add the garlic, potatoes, olive oil, salami and seasoning and cook for a further 15 minutes, until the potatoes are tender but not broken.

3 Add the spinach leaves to the soup and bring it back to simmering point, then cook for a further 5 minutes, until the spinach has wilted.

4 Season the soup with a little freshly grated nutmeg and taste, adding salt and pepper, if necessary. Ladle into bowls to serve.

Variation
Instead of salami, slice Polish sausage, ham sausage or garlic sausage to add to the soup with the potatoes. Grilled (broiled) fresh sausages can be sliced and added if liked.

Baked Bean and Vegetable Soup

This classic vegetarian soup, better known as pistou, has a mixed bean base and is flavoured with a home-made garlic, fresh basil and Parmesan pistou sauce.

Serves 4–6

150g/5oz/scant 1 cup dried haricot (navy) beans, soaked overnight in cold water
150g/5oz/scant 1 cup dried flageolet or cannellini beans, soaked overnight in cold water
1 onion, chopped
1.2 litres/2 pints/5 cups hot vegetable stock
2 carrots, roughly chopped
225g/8oz Savoy cabbage, shredded
1 large potato, roughly chopped
225g/8oz French (green) beans, chopped
salt and ground black pepper
basil leaves, to garnish

For the pistou

4 garlic cloves
8 large basil sprigs
90ml/6 tbsp olive oil
60ml/4 tbsp freshly grated Parmesan cheese

1 Drain the haricot and flageolet or cannellini beans. Place in a large casserole. Add the onion and cold water to cover the beans by 5cm/2in. Cover and place in the oven. Set the oven at 200°C/400°F/Gas 6 and cook for 1½ hours, until the beans are tender. Reduce the oven temperature to 180°C/350°F/Gas 4.

2 Drain the beans and onions, and purée half the mixture in a food processor or blender and process. Return the whole beans and purée to the casserole.

3 Add the hot vegetable stock, carrots, cabbage, potato and French beans. Season, cover and replace in the oven. Cook for 1 hour or until all the vegetables are tender.

4 Make the pistou: place the garlic and basil in a mortar and pound with a pestle, then gradually beat in the oil. Stir in the grated Parmesan.

5 Stir half the pistou into the soup and then ladle it into warmed soup bowls. Top each bowl of soup with a spoonful of the remaining pistou and serve garnished with basil.

Chickpea Broth: Energy 399Kcal/1681kJ; Protein 20.5g; Carbohydrate 58g, of which sugars 4g; Fat 10.9g, of which saturates 1.4g; Cholesterol 0mg; Calcium 203mg; Fibre 10.7g; Sodium 96mg.
Bean and Vegetable: Energy 338kcal/1416kJ; Protein 17.2g; Carbohydrate 34.6g, of which sugars 7.5g; Fat 15.5g, of which saturates 3.8g; Cholesterol 10mg; Calcium 215mg; Fibre 10.8g; Sodium 133mg.

Cinnamon-spiced Chickpea and Vegetable Soup

Cinnamon, ginger and turmeric are a warming mix of spices to perfectly complement nutty chickpeas.

Serves 6

1 large onion, chopped
1.2 litres/2 pints/5 cups vegetable stock
5ml/1 tsp ground cinnamon
5ml/1 tsp turmeric
15ml/1 tbsp grated fresh root ginger
pinch of cayenne pepper
2 carrots, diced
2 celery sticks, diced
400g/14oz can chopped tomatoes
450g/1lb floury potatoes, diced
pinch of saffron strands
400g/14oz can chickpeas, drained
30ml/2 tbsp chopped fresh coriander (cilantro)
15ml/1 tbsp lemon juice
salt and ground black pepper
fried wedges of lemon, to serve

1 Place the onion in a large pot with 300ml/½ pint/1¼ cups of the vegetable stock. Bring to the boil, reduce the heat and simmer gently for about 10 minutes.

2 Meanwhile, mix the cinnamon, turmeric, ginger, cayenne pepper and 30ml/2 tbsp of stock to form a paste. Stir into the onion mixture with the carrots, celery and remaining stock.

3 Bring to the boil, stirring continuously, and reduce the heat. Cover and simmer gently for 5 minutes.

4 Add the tomatoes and potatoes and heat until simmering gently again, then cover and cook for 20 minutes.

5 Add the saffron, chickpeas, coriander and lemon juice. Season to taste and heat briefly, then serve with fried wedges of lemon.

Cook's Tip
Frying lemon wedges – or halves, if the fruit are small – caramelizes them, giving the juice a particularly rich flavour.

Bean Soup with Pesto

Italian ribollita is similar to minestrone, but with beans and not pasta. Traditionally, it is ladled over bread and green vegetables.

Serves 6–8

45ml/3 tbsp olive oil
2 onions, chopped
2 carrots, sliced
4 garlic cloves, crushed
2 celery sticks, thinly sliced
1 fennel bulb, trimmed and chopped
2 large courgettes (zucchini), thinly sliced
400g/14oz can chopped tomatoes
30ml/2 tbsp home-made or ready-made pesto
900ml/1½ pints/3¾ cups vegetable stock
400g/14oz can haricot (navy) or borlotti beans, drained
salt and ground black pepper

To finish
450g/1lb young spinach
15ml/1 tbsp extra virgin olive oil, plus extra for drizzling
6–8 slices white bread
Parmesan cheese shavings

1 Heat the oil in a large pan. Add the onions, carrots, garlic, celery and fennel and fry gently for 10 minutes. Add the courgettes and fry for a further 2 minutes.

2 Stir in the tomatoes, pesto, stock and beans and bring to the boil. Reduce the heat, cover the pan and simmer gently for 25–30 minutes, until the vegetables are completely tender. Season with salt and pepper to taste.

3 To serve, fry the spinach in the oil for 2 minutes, or until wilted. Place the bread in large soup bowls and spoon the wilted spinach on top.

4 Ladle the soup into the bowls. Serve with extra virgin olive oil for drizzling on to the soup and Parmesan cheese to sprinkle on top.

Variation
Use other dark greens, such as chard or cabbage, instead of the spinach. Shred and cook them until tender.

Chickpea and Vegetable: Energy 399kcal/1685kJ; Protein 20.6g; Carbohydrate 58.1g, of which sugars 4.1g; Fat 11g, of which saturates 1.4g; Cholesterol 0mg; Calcium 209mg; Fibre 10.8g; Sodium 101mg.
Bean Soup with Pesto: Energy 104kcal/436kJ; Protein 5.6g; Carbohydrate 14.5g, of which sugars 6.9g; Fat 3g, of which saturates 0.5g; Cholesterol 0mg; Calcium 78mg; Fibre 5.9g; Sodium 218mg.

Pear and Roquefort Soup

Like most fruit-based soups, this is served in small portions. It makes an unusual and seasonal starter for an autumn dinner party.

Serves 4

30ml/2 tbsp sunflower oil
1 onion, chopped
3 pears, peeled, cored and chopped
400ml/14fl oz/1⅔ cups vegetable stock
2.5ml/½ tsp paprika
juice of ½ lemon
175g/6oz Roquefort cheese
salt and ground black pepper
watercress sprigs, to garnish

For the caramelized pears
50g/2oz/¼ cup butter
2 pears, halved, cored and cut into wedges

1 Heat the oil in a pan. Add the onion and cook for 4–5 minutes until soft. Add the pears and stock, then bring to the boil. Cook for 8–10 minutes, until the pears are very soft. Stir in the paprika, lemon juice, cheese and seasoning.

2 Cool the soup slightly before puréeing it in a food processor or blender until smooth. Pass the soup through a fine sieve (strainer) and return it to the pan.

3 To make the caramelized pears, melt the butter in a frying pan and add the pears. Cook for 8–10 minutes, turning occasionally, until golden and beginning to caramelize.

4 Reheat the soup gently, then ladle into small, shallow bowls. Add a few caramelized pear wedges to each portion. Garnish with tiny sprigs of watercress and serve at once.

Cook's Tip
Pears discolour quickly when peeled, so prepare them at the last minute. Adding the peeled fruit to a bowl of cold water with a little lemon juice added helps to prevent them from turning brown. This is not so important for the soup but the caramelized pears should not be discoloured before cooking.

Pomegranate Broth

Clear and refreshing, this Persian soup is usually served as a sophisticated palate cleanser between courses, or as a light appetizer at the start of a meal. Sour pomegranates are often available in Middle Eastern stores.

Serves 4

5–6 sour or sweet pomegrantes
1.2 litres/2 pints/5 cups clear chicken stock
juice of 1 lemon, if using sweet pomegranates
seeds of 1 sweet pomegranate
salt and ground black pepper
fresh mint leaves, to garnish

1 For 150ml/¼ pint/⅔ cup juice, you will need 5–6 sour pomegranates. Cut the pomegranates in half and extract the juice by turning the fruit on a stainless-steel, glass or wooden lemon squeezer.

2 Pour the stock into a pan and bring to the boil. Lower the heat, and stir in the pomegranate juice and lemon juice if using sweet pomegranates. Bring the stock back to the boil.

3 Reduce the heat again and stir in half the pomegranate seeds, then season the broth to taste and turn off the heat.

4 Ladle the broth into warmed bowls. Sprinkle the remaining pomegranate seeds into the bowls. Garnish with mint leaves and serve.

Variation
Try unsweetened white grape juice and water, mixed half and half, instead of the stock. Cool and chill before adding the seeds. This can also be served for dessert: open freeze small scoops of whipped cream until firm and add to each portion.

Cook's Tip
Do not use any metal other than stainless-steel for squeezing or it will cause the juice to discolour and taste unpleasant.

Pear and Roquefort: Energy 381kcal/1579kJ; Protein 10.1g; Carbohydrate 21.8g, of which sugars 20.9g; Fat 28.7g, of which saturates 15.6g; Cholesterol 59mg; Calcium 246mg; Fibre 4.7g; Sodium 616mg.
Pomegranate: Per portion Energy 62kcal/260kJ; Protein 2g; Carbohydrate 3.9g, of which sugars 2.3g; Fat 4.4g, of which saturates 0.4g; Cholesterol 0mg; Calcium 14mg; Fibre 0.6g; Sodium 205mg.

Curried Apple Soup

South-east Asian food has become popular in Norway, the home of this soup, and the coconut milk in this recipe replaces the traditional cream.

Serves 4

50g/2oz/4 tbsp butter
2 shallots, finely chopped
1 cooking apple, peeled, cored and chopped
10ml/2 tsp curry paste
30ml/2 tbsp plain (all-purpose) flour
1.25 litres/2¼ pints/5½ cups chicken or beef stock
400ml/14fl oz can unsweetened coconut milk
salt and ground black pepper

For the garnish

60ml/4 tbsp double (heavy) cream or coconut milk
chopped fresh parsley

1 Melt the butter in a pan, add the shallots and cook gently for about 5 minutes until softened but not coloured. Add the apple, season with salt and pepper and cook for another 2 minutes, until the apple is slightly softened.

2 Stir in the curry paste and flour, and cook over low heat, stirring, for 1–2 minutes, without colouring. Remove from the heat and gradually stir in the stock to form a smooth sauce.

3 Return the pan to the heat and bring to the boil, stirring all the time; cook until the soup thickens. Reduce the heat and simmer gently for 10 minutes.

4 Stir in the coconut milk. Check the seasoning, adding salt and pepper if necessary. Pour the soup into bowls and serve with a swirl of cream or coconut milk in each portion. Add chopped parsley to garnish.

Cook's Tips

• *For a smooth soup, blend the soup in a blender or food processor before reheating and serving.*
• *For a lower-fat version, use reduced-fat coconut milk and swirl a little natural (plain) yogurt into the soup instead of cream.*

Cheese and Celeriac Soup

Cheese and celeriac are brilliant together, especially in this Dutch Gouda soup.

Serves 4

40g/1½oz/3 tbsp butter
1 onion, chopped
50g/2oz/½ cup plain (all-purpose) flour
1.2 litres/2 pints/5 cups milk
150g/5oz/1¼ cups grated mature (sharp) Gouda cheese
1 small celeriac
salt
snipped fresh chives, to garnish
toast, to serve

1 Melt the butter in a pan. Add the onion and cook over low heat, stirring occasionally, for 5 minutes, until softened.

2 Stir in the flour and cook, stirring constantly, for 2 minutes, then gradually stir in the milk.

3 Continue to cook, stirring, until slightly thickened. Add 50g/2oz/½ cup of the grated Gouda and cook, stirring occasionally, for about 15 minutes.

4 Meanwhile, peel and finely dice the celeriac, then cook it in boiling water for about 10 minutes, or until tender.

5 Drain the celeriac and add to the soup with the remaining cheese. Stir until the cheese has melted.

6 Season to taste with salt, then ladle the soup into warm bowls and garnish with chives. Serve immediately with hot crisp toast and butter.

Variations

• *For a smooth soup, purée the cooked celeriac and soup, then return it to the pan and stir in the remaining cheese.*
• *Use half and half celeriac and swede (rutabaga), and add a carrot to the soup.*
• *Try other cheeses: mature Cheddar or Spanish manchego are suitable, or add Stilton or Danish blue for a punchy flavour.*

Curried Apple Soup: Energy 195kcal/812kJ; Protein 1.7g; Carbohydrate 14.3g, of which sugars 7.6g; Fat 15g, of which saturates 9.2g; Cholesterol 37mg; Calcium 66mg; Fibre 1.3g; Sodium 200mg.
Cheese and Celeriac: Energy 407kcal/1703kJ; Protein 21.5g; Carbohydrate 25.7g, of which sugars 15.9g; Fat 25.2g, of which saturates 16.1g; Cholesterol 71mg; Calcium 704mg; Fibre 1.4g; Sodium 582mg.

Avgolemono

This is a vegetarian version of the classic, light and refreshing soup from Greece, which traditionally uses chicken stock. It is quick and simple to make.

Serves 4

1.2 litres/2 pints/5 cups light vegetable stock
4 large eggs
juice of 2 large lemons
salt and ground black pepper
fresh chives, to garnish

1 Pour the stock into a large pan and bring it slowly to the boil. Meanwhile, break the eggs into a large bowl and thoroughly whisk in the lemon juice.

2 Cool the stock very slightly, then whisk a little into the egg and lemon mixture until thoroughly combined. Pour the lemon and egg mixture back into the main batch of stock and cook over a very low heat, stirring continuously, until the soup is slightly thickened. Do not let the soup boil.

3 Taste the soup and season it lightly, if required, then ladle it into warmed bowls. Cut the chives into short lengths and scatter a few pieces on top of each portion. Serve immediately.

Cook's Tips

- *It is important to cook this delicate soup very gently over a low heat, stirring constantly with a wooden spoon. Do not allow it to boil, or the eggs will curdle. The soup is best eaten as soon as it is made – this is not one to make ahead.*
- *A good, light vegetable stock is essential, and this is the part that should be prepared ahead. Select delicate and light-coloured ingredients and a good mixture of them for the stock. For example, try celery, fennel, onion, a little carrot and a few cauliflower florets, with bay leaves, parsley, thyme and a sprig of tarragon. Add a strip of lemon peel for a more pronounced lemon flavour.*
- *You can create a delicious sauce from this soup simply by adding 5ml/1 tsp cornflour (cornstarch), mixed to a smooth cream with a little water, to the egg-lemon mixture at the start.*

Nettle Soup with Egg Butterballs

Nettle soup is extremely nutritious, but, as nettles cannot be found all year around, as an alternative you can use spinach, which goes equally well with the butterballs.

Serves 6–8

a knob (pat) of butter
1 onion, roughly chopped
225g/8oz nettles (top 4 leaves from each plant only) or young spinach leaves
600ml/1 pint/2½ cups vegetable stock
30ml/2 tbsp sherry
150ml/¼ pint/⅔ cup double (heavy) cream
5ml/½ tsp freshly grated nutmeg
salt and ground black pepper

For the butterballs

115g/4oz/½ cup butter
2 hard-boiled egg yolks
salt and ground black pepper

1 First make the butterballs. Put the butter and hard-boiled egg yolks in a bowl and mash together. Season the mixture with salt and pepper to taste. Roll into balls approximately 2cm/1in in diameter and chill in the refrigerator until ready to serve.

2 To make the soup, melt the butter in a pan, add the onion and fry until softened. Add the nettles or spinach, stir in the stock and season with salt and pepper. Bring to the boil then cook over a medium heat for 1 minute.

3 Pour the soup into a food processor or blender and whiz until roughly chopped. Return to the pan, add the sherry, stir in the cream and sprinkle with nutmeg. Heat gently until warm but do not allow the soup to boil. Serve in warmed bowls with the butterballs bobbing on the surface and just beginning to melt.

Cook's Tip

Wild nettles are best picked in early spring, before they flower. Avoid the really towering ones as the stalks may be too tough. Use rubber gloves when handling nettles to avoid stinging your hands. If you have only a few nettles, mix them with spinach and lettuce for delicious soup.

Avgolemono: Energy 104kcal/438kJ; Protein 5.5g; Carbohydrate 14.3g, of which sugars 0.7g; Fat 3.2g, of which saturates 0.8g; Cholesterol 95mg; Calcium 20mg; Fibre 0.6g; Sodium 117mg.
Nettle Soup with Egg: Energy 239kcal/982kJ; Protein 2g; Carbohydrate 1.5g, of which sugars 1.3g; Fat 24.5g, of which saturates 14.8g; Cholesterol 109mg; Calcium 68mg; Fibre 0.7g; Sodium 141mg.

Forest Curry Soup

This is a thin, soupy curry with lots of fresh green vegetables and robust flavours. It originated in the forested regions of Thailand, where it would be made using wild leaves and roots.

Serves 2

600ml/1 pint/2½ cups water
5ml/1 tsp Thai vegetarian red curry paste
5cm/2in piece fresh galangal or fresh root ginger
90g/3½oz/scant 1 cup green beans
2 kaffir lime leaves, torn
8 baby corn cobs, halved widthways
2 heads Chinese broccoli, chopped
90g/3½oz/generous 3 cups beansprouts
15ml/1 tbsp drained bottled green peppercorns, crushed
10ml/2 tsp granulated sugar
5ml/1 tsp salt

1 Heat the water in a large pan. Add the red curry paste and stir until it has dissolved completely. Bring to the boil.

2 Meanwhile, using a sharp knife, peel and finely chop the fresh galangal or root ginger.

3 Add the galangal or ginger, green beans, lime leaves, baby corn cobs, broccoli and beansprouts to the pan. Stir in the crushed peppercorns, sugar and salt. Bring back to the boil, then reduce the heat to low and simmer for 2 minutes. Serve immediately.

Cook's Tip
Serve this soup with rice or noodles for a simple lunch or quick-fix supper.

Variation
Garnish the soup with some thinly sliced hard-boiled egg just before serving, or, if you prefer, provide a couple of whole hard-boiled eggs to serve on the side.

Egg and Spinach Soup

Fresh dill invigorates this terrific vegetable soup.

Serves 4–6

1 small turnip, cut into chunks
2 carrots, sliced or diced
1 small parsnip, cut into large dice
1 potato, peeled and diced
1 onion, chopped
1 garlic clove, finely chopped
¼ celeriac bulb, diced
1 litre/1¾ pints/4 cups vegetable stock
200g/7oz spinach chopped
1 small bunch fresh dill, chopped
2 hard-boiled eggs, sliced
1 lemon, cut into slices
salt and ground black pepper
30ml/2 tbsp chopped fresh parsley and dill, to garnish

1 Bring the turnip, carrots, parsnip, potato, onion, garlic, celeriac and stock to the boil in large pan. Simmer for 25–30 minutes.

2 Add the spinach and cook for 5 minutes. Season, stir in the dill and ladle the soup into bowls. Top with egg and lemon. Serve garnished with parsley and dill.

Omelette Soup with Cabbage

This very satisfying soup is quick and easy to prepare.

Serves 4

15ml/1 tbsp vegetable oil
1 egg, lightly whisked
900ml/1½ pints/3¾ cups well-flavoured vegetable stock
2 large carrots, finely diced
4 outer leaves Savoy cabbage or pak choi (bok choy), shredded
30ml/2 tbsp soy sauce
2.5ml/½ tsp sugar
2.5ml/½ tsp ground black pepper
fresh coriander (cilantro) leaves, to garnish

1 Heat the oil in a small frying pan. Pour in the egg, swirling the pan to coat the base. Cook until the egg is golden underneath. Roll up, slide out of the pan and slice thinly. Set aside.

2 Bring the stock, carrots and cabbage to the boil in a large pan. Simmer for 5 minutes. Add the soy sauce, sugar and pepper. Serve topped with the omelette and coriander leaves.

Forest Curry: Energy 154kcal/643kJ; Protein 14.9g; Carbohydrate 14.1g, of which sugars 11.8g; Fat 4.5g, of which saturates 0.8g; Cholesterol 0mg; Calcium 173mg; Fibre 9.1g; Sodium 678mg.
Egg and Spinach: Energy 109kcal/457kJ; Protein 5g; Carbohydrate 17.3g, of which sugars 10.2g; Fat 2.7g, of which saturates 0.7g; Cholesterol 63mg; Calcium 119mg; Fibre 4.2g; Sodium 99mg.
Omelette Soup: Energy 64kcal/264kJ; Protein 2.3g; Carbohydrate 4.3g, of which sugars 4.1g; Fat 4.3g, of which saturates 0.7g; Cholesterol 48mg; Calcium 27mg; Fibre 1.1g; Sodium 560mg.

Roasted Garlic Soup with Poached Egg

Spanish soup and Italian polenta marry wonderfully well in this recipe.

Serves 4

15ml/1 tbsp olive oil
1 bulb garlic, unpeeled, in cloves
4 slices day-old ciabatta bread, broken into pieces
1.2 litres/2 pints/5 cups vegetable stock
pinch of saffron
15ml/1 tbsp white wine vinegar
4 eggs
salt and ground black pepper
chopped fresh parsley, to garnish

For the polenta

750ml/1 ¼ pints/3 cups milk
175g/6oz/1 cup quick-cook polenta
50g/2oz/¼ cup butter

1 Preheat the oven to 200°C/400°F/Gas 6. Brush the oil over a baking tin (pan), and add the garlic and bread. Roast for 20 minutes. Cool.

2 Make the polenta: boil the milk in a large, heavy pan. Pour in the polenta, stirring. Cook for 5 minutes, or according to packet instructions, stirring until the polenta comes away from the pan. Spread out to 1cm/½in thick on a board. Allow to cool and set.

3 Squeeze the softened garlic cloves from their skins into a food processor or blender. Add the dried bread and 300ml/½ pint/1 ¼ cups of the stock, then process until smooth. Pour into a pan. Pound the saffron in a mortar and stir in a little of the remaining stock, then add to the soup with enough of the remaining stock to thin the soup to the required consistency.

4 Cut the polenta into 1cm/½in dice. Melt the butter in a frying pan and cook the polenta over a high heat for 1–2 minutes, tossing until beginning to brown. Drain on kitchen paper.

5 Season and reheat the soup. Bring a frying pan of water to the boil. Add the vinegar and reduce the heat to a simmer. Crack an egg on to a saucer. Swirl the water and drop the egg into the swirl. Repeat with the remaining eggs and poach for 2–3 minutes. Remove the eggs on a draining spoon, then place in bowls. Ladle in the soup, add polenta and parsley, and serve.

Tomato and Pepper Soup with Egg

This popular Turkish street food is known as *menemen*. Depending on the cook, the eggs are either stirred in to scramble them or cracked on top and cooked until set.

Serves 4

15ml/1 tbsp olive oil
15ml/1 tbsp butter
2 red onions, halved and sliced
1 red or green (bell) pepper, halved lengthways, seeded and sliced
2 garlic cloves, roughly chopped
1 fresh red chilli, seeded and sliced
400g/14oz can chopped tomatoes
5–10ml/1–2 tsp sugar
4 eggs
salt and ground black pepper

For serving

90ml/6 tbsp thick and creamy natural (plain) yogurt
1–2 garlic cloves, crushed
handful of fresh flat leaf parsley, roughly chopped

1 Heat the oil and butter in a heavy frying pan. Stir in the onions, pepper, garlic and chilli and cook until the vegetables begin to soften but not brown.

2 Mix in the tomatoes and sugar. Cook for about 10 minutes, or until the liquid has reduced and the mixture is quite thick, then season with salt and pepper to taste.

3 Crack the eggs over the top of the tomato mixture, cover the pan and cook until the eggs are just set.

4 Beat the yogurt with the garlic, salt and pepper. Serve bowls of soup topped with parsley and garlic-flavoured yogurt.

Cook's Tips

- *Instead of cracking the eggs into the soup, scramble or poach them separately and serve them on top of the soup, ladled into bowls, before adding the parsley and yogurt mixture.*
- *The tomato mixture can be divided among four small pans, then an egg can be cracked into each one. The egg-topped soup is garnished and served from the pans.*

Roasted Garlic: Energy 415kcal/1731kJ; Protein 13.4g; Carbohydrate 43.9g, of which sugars 0.9g; Fat 20.8g, of which saturates 8.6g; Cholesterol 217mg; Calcium 57mg; Fibre 1.9g; Sodium 247mg.
Tomato Soup: Energy 190kcal/790kJ; Protein 8.6g; Carbohydrate 14.9g, of which sugars 12.4g; Fat 11.2g, of which saturates 3.5g; Cholesterol 196mg; Calcium 65mg; Fibre 3.1g; Sodium 101mg.

Summer Herb Soup with Radicchio

The sweetness of shallots and leeks in this soup is balanced beautifully by the slightly acidic sorrel, with its hint of lemon, and a bouquet of summer herbs.

Serves 4–6
30ml/2 tbsp dry white wine
2 shallots, finely chopped
1 garlic clove, crushed
2 leeks, sliced
1 potato, about 225g/8oz, roughly chopped
2 courgettes (zucchini), chopped
600ml/1 pint/2½ cups boiling water
115g/4oz sorrel, torn
large handful of fresh chervil
large handful of fresh flat leaf parsley
large handful of fresh mint
1 round or butterhead lettuce, separated into leaves
600ml/1 pint/2½ cups vegetable stock
1 small head radicchio
5ml/1 tsp groundnut oil
salt and ground black pepper

1 Put the wine, shallots and garlic into a heavy-based pan and bring to the boil. Cook for 2–3 minutes, until softened. Add the leeks, potato and courgette with enough of the water to come about halfway up the vegetables. Lay a wetted piece of greaseproof (waxed) paper over the vegetables and put a lid on the pan, then cook gently for 10–15 minutes, until softened. Remove the paper and add the fresh herbs and lettuce. Cook for 1–2 minutes, or until wilted.

2 Pour in the remaining water and vegetable stock and simmer for 10–12 minutes. Cool the soup slightly, then process it in a food processor or blender until smooth. Return the soup to the rinsed-out pan and season well.

3 Cut the radicchio into thin wedges that hold together, then brush the cut sides with the oil. Heat a ridged griddle or frying pan until very hot and add the radicchio wedges. Cook the radicchio wedges for about 1 minute on each side until very well browned and slightly charred in places.

4 Reheat the soup over a low heat, stirring occasionally, then ladle it into warmed shallow bowls. Serve a wedge of charred radicchio on top of each portion.

Avocado, Spinach and Sorrel Soup

Sorrel has a sharp lemony flavour. It is easy to cultivate and delicious in salads and soups, especially with rich buttery avocado and fresh green-tasting spinach.

Serves 4
30ml/2 tbsp olive oil
2 onions, chopped
1kg/2¼lb spinach
900ml/1½ pints/3¾ cups vegetable stock
4 garlic cloves, crushed with salt
1 bunch sorrel leaves
2 avocados, peeled and stoned (pitted)

1 Pour the olive oil into a large heavy pan and sweat the onions over a gentle heat until soft but not coloured. Meanwhile, wash the spinach thoroughly and remove the stalks.

2 Add the spinach to the onions and cook for about 2 minutes, stirring, to wilt the leaves. Cover and increase the heat slightly, then cook for a further 3 minutes. Pour in the stock, cover again and simmer for about 10 minutes.

3 Add the garlic, sorrel and avocados to the soup and heat through, then remove from the heat.

4 Allow the soup to cool then purée it in a blender. Reheat the soup before serving with warmed crusty bread.

Cook's Tips

- *Crushing garlic in salt helps to bring out the oils of the garlic and also stops any being wasted in a garlic press. Use a coarse salt and try to keep a chopping board or at least a corner of one for this sole purpose, as it is hard to get rid of the scent of garlic and it can taint other foods.*
- *When using avocados in soup do not let them boil as this makes them taste bitter. They are best added at the end and just heated through.*
- *This soup freezes for up to a month. Freeze it the day you make it.*

Avocado and Sorrel: Energy 282kcal/1161kJ; Protein 9.3g; Carbohydrate 11.4g, of which sugars 8.3g; Fat 22.1g, of which saturates 4.1g; Cholesterol 0mg; Calcium 452mg; Fibre 8.9g; Sodium 357mg.
Summer Herb: Energy 199kcal/837kJ; Protein 10.2g; Carbohydrate 29.2g, of which sugars 12.6g; Fat 4.4g, of which saturates 0.9g; Cholesterol 0mg; Calcium 227mg; Fibre 8.6g; Sodium 94mg.

Hot and Spicy Broth

This is a colourful and soothing broth for cold evenings. Asafoetida is a pungent Indian spice which tastes better than it smells!

Serves 2–4

30ml/2 tbsp vegetable oil
2.5ml/½ tsp ground black pepper
5ml/1 tsp cumin seeds
2.5ml/½ tsp mustard seeds
1.5ml/¼ tsp asafoetida powder
2 whole dried red chillies
4–6 curry leaves
2.5ml/½ tsp ground turmeric
2 garlic cloves, crushed
300ml/½ pint/1¼ cups tomato juice
juice of 2 lemons
salt
fresh coriander (cilantro) leaves, chopped, to garnish

1 Heat the oil in a large pan. Fry the spices and garlic until the chillies are nearly black and the garlic golden. Lower the heat.

2 Add the tomato and lemon juices, 120ml/4fl oz/½ cup water and salt to taste. Bring to the boil, then simmer for 10 minutes. Garnish with coriander and serve piping hot.

Curried Carrot and Apple Soup

This curried carrot and fruit soup is delicious.

Serves 4

10ml/2 tsp sunflower oil
15ml/1 tbsp mild korma curry powder
500g/1¼lb carrots, chopped
1 large onion, chopped
1 tart cooking apple, chopped
750ml/1¼ pints/3 cups vegetable stock
salt and ground black pepper
yogurt and carrot curls, to garnish

1 Heat the oil in a large pan. Add the curry powder and fry for 2–3 minutes. Stir in the carrots, onion and apple until coated with the curry powder. Cover and cook gently for 15 minutes, then purée with half the stock in a blender.

2 Return to the pan and pour in the remaining stock. Bring to the boil. Season and serve garnished with yogurt and carrot, and serve with extra yogurt, sprinkled with paprika, if you like.

Yogurt and Chilli Soup

Hot chillies, cool yogurt – this is an unusual and tasty soup with a real punch.

Serves 2–3

450ml/¾ pint/scant 2 cups natural (plain) low-fat yogurt, beaten
60ml/4 tbsp gram flour
2.5ml/½ tsp chilli powder
2.5ml/½ tsp ground turmeric
2 fresh green chillies, finely chopped
30ml/2 tbsp vegetable oil
4 whole dried red chillies
5ml/1 tsp cumin seeds
3 or 4 curry leaves
3 garlic cloves, crushed
5cm/2in piece fresh root ginger, grated
salt
fresh coriander (cilantro) leaves, chopped, to garnish

1 Mix the yogurt, gram flour, chilli powder, turmeric and salt to taste in a bowl. Press the mixture through a strainer into a pan. Add the green chillies and simmer for 10 minutes, stirring occasionally.

2 Heat the vegetable oil in a heavy pan and fry the remaining spices, crushed garlic and fresh ginger until the dried chillies turn black.

3 Pour the oil and the spices over the yogurt soup, cover the pan and leave to rest for 5 minutes off the heat.

4 Mix the soup well and reheat it gently for 5 minutes, stirring often. Take care not to let the soup boil or it may curdle.

5 Ladle the soup into warmed soup bowls and serve hot, garnished with the coriander leaves.

Cook's Tips

- *For a lower fat version drain off some of the oil before adding it to the yogurt. Low-fat yogurt makes this a healthy soup.*
- *Adjust the amount of chilli according to how hot you want the soup to be.*

Hot and Spicy Broth: Energy 79kcal/328kJ; Protein 1.7g; Carbohydrate 4.3g, of which sugars 2.6g; Fat 6.3g, of which saturates 0.7g; Cholesterol 0mg; Calcium 42mg; Fibre 1.1g; Sodium 178mg.
Curried Carrot and Apple: Energy 90kcal/376kJ; Protein 1.7g; Carbohydrate 17.3g, of which sugars 15g; Fat 2.1g, of which saturates 0.3g; Cholesterol 0mg; Calcium 51mg; Fibre 4.3g; Sodium 34mg.
Yogurt and Chilli: Energy 226kcal/942kJ; Protein 15.8g; Carbohydrate 9.1g, of which sugars 5.9g; Fat 14.4g, of which saturates 2.3g; Cholesterol 29mg; Calcium 177mg; Fibre 0.5g; Sodium 90mg.

Nettle Soup with Vegetables

A country-style soup which is a tasty variation of the classic Irish potato soup. Use wild nettles if you can find them – they tend to grow well in sunny and protected areas, usually at the edge of a woodland. Alternatively, a washed head of round lettuce will do just as well if you prefer.

Serves 4

115g/4oz/½ cup butter
450g/1lb onions, sliced
450g/1lb potatoes, cut into chunks
750ml/1¼ pints/3 cups vegetable stock
25g/1oz nettle leaves
small bunch of chives, snipped
salt and ground black pepper
double (heavy) cream, to serve

1 Melt the butter in a large pan and add the sliced onions. Cover and cook gently for about 5 minutes, until just softened. Add the potatoes to the pan with the stock. Bring to the boil, reduce the heat and cover the pan. Continue to cook gently for 25 minutes.

2 Wearing rubber gloves to avoid stinging your hands, remove the nettle leaves from their stalks. Wash the leaves under cold running water, then dry them on kitchen paper. Add to the pan and simmer for a further 5 minutes.

3 Ladle the soup into a blender or food processor and process until smooth. Return the soup to the rinsed-out pan and season well. Stir in the chives and serve with a swirl of cream and a sprinkling of pepper.

Variation
Try a mixture of lettuce and parsley instead of nettles, adding a handful of watercress and a few sprigs of rocket (arugula).

Cook's Tip
If you prefer, cut the vegetables finely and leave the cooked soup chunky rather than puréeing it.

Mushroom, Celery and Garlic Soup

This is a robust dish in which the dominant flavour of mushrooms is enhanced with garlic, while celery introduces a slightly fresh, contrasting note. It is a lovely thick soup and can also be served as a sauce, so do freeze any leftovers.

Serves 4

350g/12oz mushrooms, chopped
4 celery sticks, chopped
3 garlic cloves, crushed
45ml/3 tbsp dry sherry or white wine
750ml/1¼ pints/3 cups vegetable stock
freshly grated nutmeg
salt and ground black pepper
celery leaves, to garnish

1 Place the mushrooms, celery and garlic in a pan and stir in the sherry or wine. Bring to the boil, reduce the heat and cover the pan. Then cook over a low heat for 30–40 minutes, until the mushrooms are greatly reduced and the celery and garlic are quite tender.

2 Stir in half the stock and then purée the vegetables in a food processor or blender until smooth. Return the purée to the pan and stir in the remaining stock with nutmeg to taste.

3 Bring the soup to the boil and season to taste with salt and pepper. Serve hot, garnished with celery leaves.

Variations
- *Add 1 finely chopped onion with the mushrooms and celery.*
- *For a thicker texture, and more mellow flavour, add 1 large peeled and diced potato to the mushrooms halfway through cooking in step 1.*
- *The robust soup is delicious flavoured with port instead of sherry or wine, and swirled with single (light) cream when serving. Sprinkle generously with snipped chives.*
- *For a more substantial meal, cook some potato gnocchi or cheese-filled pasta in a separate pan of boiling water. Cook 1 finely sliced leek in a little olive oil. Divide the pasta and leeks among the bowls before ladling in the soup.*

Nettle with Vegetables: Energy 335kcal/1390kJ; Protein 3.6g; Carbohydrate 27.3g, of which sugars 8g; Fat 24.3g, of which saturates 15.1g; Cholesterol 61mg; Calcium 51mg; Fibre 2.8g; Sodium 199mg.
Mushroom, Celery and Garlic: Energy 26kcal/109kJ; Protein 1.9g; Carbohydrate 1.9g, of which sugars 1.6g; Fat 0.5g, of which saturates 0.1g; Cholesterol 0mg; Calcium 33mg; Fibre 1.3g; Sodium 113mg.

Plantain and Corn Soup

Cameroon is the home of this colourful and unusual soup. It is important to use ripe plantains, which cook down and become beautifully tender. Nutmeg adds the final touch.

Serves 4

25g/1oz/2 tbsp butter
1 onion, finely chopped
1 garlic clove, crushed
275g/10oz yellow plantains or green bananas (see Cook's Tip), peeled and thickly sliced
1 large tomato, peeled and chopped
175g/6oz/1½ cups corn
5ml/1 tsp dried tarragon, crushed
900ml/1½ pints/3¾ cups vegetable stock
1 green chilli, seeded and chopped
pinch of freshly grated nutmeg
salt and ground black pepper

1 Melt the butter in a pan over a medium heat, add the onion and garlic and sauté for a few minutes until the onion is soft.

2 Add the plantains or green bananas, tomato and corn and cook for a further 5 minutes, stirring frequently.

3 Stir in the tarragon, pour in the vegetable stock and add the chilli. Season with a little nutmeg and salt and pepper and bring to the boil. Reduce the heat, cover the pan and simmer the soup for 10 minutes or until the plantain is tender.

4 Taste for seasoning, adding a little extra nutmeg, if liked, and then ladle the soup into bowls and serve while piping hot.

Cook's Tip

Green bananas are simply fruit that has been picked while still under-ripe. They should never be eaten raw as they contain indigestible fatty acids. If plantain or green bananas are not available, do not use familiar ripened sweet bananas. Try sliced new potatoes, marrow or butternut squash instead. The result is not the same, but it is equally delicious.

Tamarind Soup with Peanuts and Vegetables

Chayote is a member of the gourd family.

Serves 4

5 shallots or 1 red onion, sliced
3 garlic cloves, crushed
2.5cm/1in piece galangal root, peeled and sliced
1–2 fresh red chillies, seeded and sliced
25g/1oz/¼ cup unroasted peanuts
1.2 litres/2 pints/5 cups vegetable stock
50–75g/2–3oz/½–¾ cup salted peanuts, lightly crushed
15–30ml/1–2 tbsp soft dark brown sugar
5ml/1 tsp tamarind pulp, soaked in 75ml/5 tbsp warm water for 15 minutes
salt

For the vegetables

1 chayote (christophene) or ½ marrow, thinly peeled, seeds removed, flesh finely sliced
115g/4oz French (green) beans, trimmed and finely sliced
50g/2oz/½ cup corn
a handful of green leaves, such as watercress, rocket or Chinese leaves, finely shredded
1 green chilli, sliced, to garnish

1 Grind the shallots or onion, garlic, galangal, chillies and unroasted peanuts to a paste in a food processor or blender, or using a pestle and mortar.

2 Pour in some of the stock to moisten the paste, then pour the mixture into a pan, adding the rest of the stock. Bring to the boil, then reduce the heat and add the crushed salted peanuts and sugar. Simmer for 15 minutes.

3 Strain the tamarind pulp, discarding the seeds, and reserve the juice.

4 About 5 minutes before serving, add the chayote slices, beans and sweetcorn to the soup and cook fairly rapidly. At the last minute, add the green leaves and salt to taste.

5 Add the tamarind juice and adjust the seasoning. Serve at once, garnished with slices of green chilli.

Plantain and Corn: Energy 185Kcal/775kJ; Protein 5.8g; Carbohydrate 22.6g, of which sugars 5.2g; Fat 8.3g, of which saturates 1.9g; Cholesterol 0mg; Calcium 66mg; Fibre 3.3g; Sodium 75mg.
Tamarind with Peanuts: Energy 80kcal/334kJ; Protein 3.8g; Carbohydrate 6.2g, of which sugars 4.9g; Fat 4.7g, of which saturates 0.9g; Cholesterol 0mg; Calcium 46mg; Fibre 1.8g; Sodium 19mg.

Yam and Vegetable Soup

This hearty vegetable soup is filling enough to be served on its own for lunch.

Serves 4

25g/1oz/2 tbsp butter
1 onion, chopped
1 garlic clove, crushed
2 carrots, sliced
1.5 litres/2½ pints/6¼ cups vegetable stock
2 bay leaves
2 fresh thyme sprigs
1 celery stick, finely chopped
2 green bananas, peeled and quartered
175g/6oz white yam or eddoe, peeled and cubed
25g/1oz/2 tbsp red lentils
1 chayote (christophene) or ½ marrow, peeled and chopped
25g/1oz/2 tbsp macaroni (optional)
salt and ground black pepper
chopped spring onion (scallion), to garnish

1 Melt the butter in a pan and fry the onion, garlic and carrots for a few minutes, stirring occasionally. Pour in the stock, then add the bay leaves and thyme, and bring to the boil.

2 Stir in the celery, green bananas, white yam or eddoe, lentils, chayote and macaroni, if using. Season with salt and ground black pepper. Reduce the heat and cover the pan.

3 Simmer the soup for 25 minutes or until the vegetables are cooked through and soft. Stir occasionally to make sure that the soup does not stick to the pan. Taste for seasoning before serving, garnished with chopped spring onion.

Cook's Tip

The soup can be prepared in advance and reheated. Do not add the macaroni until reheating, when it is best to cook it in boiling water before adding to the hot soup when serving.

Variation

Use other root vegetables, such as potatoes or sweet potatoes, if yam or eddoes are not available.

Groundnut Soup

Groundnut paste is available from many health food shops and is worth seeking out as it makes a rich and creamy soup.

Serves 4

45ml/3 tbsp pure groundnut paste or peanut butter
1.5 litres/2½ pints/6¼ cups vegetable stock
30ml/2 tbsp tomato purée (paste)
1 onion, chopped
2 slices fresh root ginger, peeled and finely chopped
1.5ml/¼ tsp dried thyme
1 bay leaf
salt
chilli powder
225g/8oz white yam or sweet potato, diced
10 small okras, trimmed (optional)

1 Place the groundnut paste or peanut butter in a bowl. Gradually stir in 300ml/½ pint/1½ cups of the stock and the tomato purée and blend together to make a smooth paste.

2 Transfer the nut mixture to a pan and add the onion, chopped ginger, thyme, bay leaf, salt and chilli powder to taste, and the remaining stock. Heat the soup gently until it is simmering, stirring to prevent it from sticking to the bottom of the pan.

3 Cover the pan and cook the soup gently for 1 hour, stirring from time to time to prevent the nut mixture from sticking to the pan.

4 Bring a pan of water to the boil. Add the white yam and simmer for 5 minutes, until almost tender. Drain and add to the soup with the okra, if using. Simmer for a further 5 minutes, until the vegetables are tender. Taste for seasoning and serve piping hot.

Cook's Tip

Use peanut butter in place of groundnut paste, but only use the smooth variety for this recipe.

Yam and Vegetable: Energy 209kcal/880kJ; Protein 4.2g; Carbohydrate 37.4g, of which sugars 18.5g; Fat 5.8g, of which saturates 3.4g; Cholesterol 13mg; Calcium 48mg; Fibre 3.5g; Sodium 55mg.
Groundnut Soup: Energy 198Kcal/837kJ; Protein 2.7g; Carbohydrate 35.6g, of which sugars 11g; Fat 6g, of which saturates 3.4g; Cholesterol 13mg; Calcium 20mg; Fibre 2.3g; Sodium 162mg.

Peanut and Potato Soup with Coriander

In this Latin-American soup, the peanuts are used as a thickening agent, with unexpectedly delicious results.

Serves 6

60ml/4 tbsp groundnut (peanut) oil
1 onion, finely chopped
2 garlic cloves, crushed
1 red (bell) pepper, seeded and chopped
250g/9oz potatoes, peeled and diced
2 fresh red chillies, seeded and chopped
200g/7oz canned chopped tomatoes
150g/5oz/1 ¼ cups unsalted peanuts
1.5 litres/2 ½ pints/6 ¼ cups vegetable stock
salt and ground black pepper
30ml/2 tbsp chopped fresh coriander (cilantro), to garnish

1 Heat the oil in a large heavy pan over low heat. Stir in the onion and cook for 5 minutes. Add the garlic, pepper, potatoes, chillies and tomatoes. Stir well, cover and cook for 5 minutes.

2 Meanwhile, toast the peanuts by gently cooking them in a large dry frying pan. Turn and stir the peanuts until they are evenly golden. Take care not to burn them.

3 Set 30ml/2 tbsp of the peanuts aside for garnish. Grind the remaining nuts in a food processor or blender. Add the vegetables and process until smooth. Return the mixture to the pan and stir in the stock. Boil, lower the heat and simmer for 10 minutes.

4 Pour the soup into heated bowls. Garnish with a generous scattering of coriander and the remaining peanuts.

Cook's Tip
Replace the unsalted peanuts with peanut butter if you like. Use equal quantities of chunky and smooth peanut butter for the ideal texture.

Tortilla and Tomato Soup

There are several tortilla soups. This one is an aguada – or liquid – version, and is intended for serving as a starter or light meal. The crisp tortilla pieces add an unusual texture.

Serves 4

4 corn tortillas, freshly made or a few days old
15ml/1 tbsp vegetable oil, plus extra, for frying
1 small onion, finely chopped
2 garlic cloves, crushed
400g/14oz can plum tomatoes, drained
1 litre/1 ¾ pints/4 cups vegetable stock
small bunch of fresh coriander (cilantro), chopped
salt and ground black pepper

1 Cut each tortilla into four or five strips, each about 2cm/¾in wide. Pour oil to a depth of 2cm/¾in into a frying pan. Heat until a small piece of tortilla floats and bubbles at the edges. Fry the tortilla strips in batches, until golden, turning occasionally. Remove with a slotted spoon and drain on kitchen paper.

2 Heat the 15ml/1 tbsp vegetable oil in a large heavy-based pan. Add the onion and garlic and cook over for 2–3 minutes, stirring, until the onion is soft and translucent. Do not let the garlic turn brown or it will give the soup a bitter taste.

3 Chop the tomatoes and add them to the onion mixture. Stir in the stock. Bring to the boil, then lower the heat and simmer for about 10 minutes, until the liquid has reduced slightly.

4 Add the coriander, reserving a little for garnish, and season to taste. Place a few of the crisp tortilla pieces in the bottom of four warmed soup bowls. Ladle the soup on top. Sprinkle each portion with the reserved chopped coriander and serve.

Cook's Tip
An easy way to chop the coriander (cilantro) is to put the leaves in a mug and snip with a pair of scissors. Hold the scissors vertically in both hands and work the blades back and forth until the coriander is finely chopped.

Peanut and Potato: Energy 260kcal/1079kJ; Protein 8g; Carbohydrate 14.7g, of which sugars 6.2g; Fat 19.2g, of which saturates 3.6g; Cholesterol 0mg; Calcium 30mg; Fibre 3g; Sodium 20mg.
Tortilla and Tomato: Energy 270kcal/1135kJ; Protein 8.3g; Carbohydrate 36.9g, of which sugars 7.2g; Fat 10.7g, of which saturates 3.6g; Cholesterol 12mg; Calcium 164mg; Fibre 3.3g; Sodium 248mg.

Cabbage and Dill Pickle Soup

Cabbage and pickles are a classic combination in Eastern European and Jewish cooking. Here, kosher pickle brine and fresh dill add a sparky savour to awaken the tastebuds.

Serves 4–6

1 small turnip
2 carrots
40g/1½oz/3 tbsp butter
1 large onion, sliced
2 celery sticks, sliced
1 white cabbage, about 675g/1½lb
1.2 litres/2 pints/5 cups vegetable stock
1 sharp eating apple, cored, peeled and chopped
2 bay leaves
15ml/1 tbsp chopped fresh dill
15–30ml/1–2 tbsp pickled cucumber juice (preferably dill or kosher dill) or lemon juice
salt and ground black pepper
fresh herbs, to garnish
sour cream and black bread or dark rye bread, to serve

1 Cut the turnip and carrots into matchstick strips. Melt the butter in a large pan and fry the turnip, carrot, onion and celery for 10 minutes.

2 Shred the cabbage and add it to the pan with the stock, apple, bay leaves and dill and bring to the boil. Reduce the heat and cover the pan. Simmer the soup for 40 minutes or until the vegetables are really tender.

3 Remove the bay leaves, then stir in the pickled cucumber juice or lemon juice to taste and season the soup with plenty of salt and pepper.

4 Serve the soup piping hot, garnished with fresh herbs and accompanied by sour cream and black bread.

Variation
For a non-vegetarian soup, use beef stock in place of vegetable stock, and omit the butter and sour cream (use oil instead of butter). Add one or two potatoes in place of the apple.

Cabbage and Potato Soup with Caraway

Earthy floury potatoes are essential to the texture of this soup, so it is best not to use waxy salad potatoes. Caraway seeds come from a plant in the parsley family. They are aromatic and nutty, with a delicate anise flavour, adding a subtle accent to this smooth and satisfying dish.

Serves 4

30ml/2 tbsp olive oil
2 small onions, sliced
6 garlic cloves, halved
350g/12oz green cabbage, shredded
4 potatoes, unpeeled
5ml/1 tsp caraway seeds
5ml/1 tsp sea salt
1.2 litres/2 pints/5 cups boiling water

1 Pour the olive oil into a large pan and add the onions. Cook, stirring occasionally, for 10 minutes, until the onions are softened, but not browned.

2 Add the garlic and the cabbage and continue to cook over a low heat for 10 minutes, stirring occasionally to prevent the cabbage from sticking.

3 Add the potatoes, caraway seeds, sea salt and water. Bring to the boil. Reduce the heat and cover the pan, then simmer until all the vegetables are cooked through, about 20–30 minutes.

4 Remove the pan from the heat and allow the soup to cool slightly before mashing it into a purée or processing in a food processor. Pass the soup through a sieve (strainer), if liked.

5 Return the soup to the rinsed-out pan and reheat gently, stirring until almost boiling before serving.

Cook's Tip
Use floury potatoes to achieve the correct texture for this soup. King Edward or Maris Piper (US russet or Idaho) are excellent choices. Peel the potatoes if preferred or if they are old.

Cabbage and Pickle: Energy 106kcal/442kJ; Protein 2.4g; Carbohydrate 11.5g, of which sugars 10.5g; Fat 5.9g, of which saturates 3.5g; Cholesterol 14mg; Calcium 81mg; Fibre 3.9g; Sodium 62mg.
Cabbage and Potato: Energy 144kcal/601kJ; Protein 3.1g; Carbohydrate 20.4g, of which sugars 8.1g; Fat 6g, of which saturates 0.9g; Cholesterol 0mg; Calcium 60mg; Fibre 3.3g; Sodium 507mg.

Watercress Soup

In Roman times, eating watercress was thought to prevent baldness. Later on it became the food of the working classes and was often eaten for breakfast in a sandwich. Both stalks and leaves are used in this soup for a lovely peppery flavour.

Serves 6
2 bunches of watercress, about 175g/6oz in total
25g/1oz/2 tbsp butter
1 onion, finely chopped
1 potato
900ml/1½ pints/3¾ cups vegetable stock
300ml/½ pint/1¼ cups milk
salt and ground black pepper
single (light) cream, to serve

1 Roughly chop the watercress, reserving a few small sprigs for the garnish.

2 Melt the butter in a large pan and add the onion. Cook over a medium heat for about 5 minutes, stirring occasionally, until the onion is soft and just beginning to brown.

3 Stir in the potato and the chopped watercress, then add the stock. Bring to the boil, reduce the heat and cover the pan. Simmer gently for 15–20 minutes, until the potato is very soft.

4 Remove from the heat, leave to cool slightly and then stir in the milk. Process or blend the soup until it is completely smooth. Return the soup to the rinsed-out pan and adjust the seasoning to taste.

5 Reheat gently and ladle the soup into bowls. Top each serving with a spoonful of cream and a few watercress leaves. Serve immediately.

Cook's Tips
• *Try adding a little finely grated orange rind and the juice of an orange in step 4.*
• *You can gather wild watercress from the banks of streams – though do check that the water course is not polluted.*

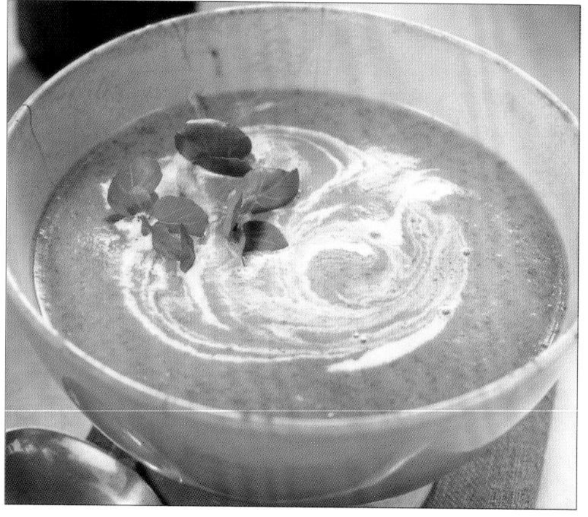

Rocket and Potato Soup

This filling and hearty soup is based on a traditional Italian peasant recipe. If rocket is unavailable, watercress or baby spinach leaves make an equally delicious alternative.

Serves 4
900g/2lb new potatoes
900ml/1½ pints/3¾ cups well-flavoured vegetable stock
1 carrot
115g/4oz rocket (arugula)
2.5ml/½ tsp cayenne pepper, or less to taste
½ loaf stale ciabatta bread, torn into chunks
4 garlic cloves, thinly sliced
60ml/4 tbsp olive oil
salt and ground black pepper

1 Dice the potatoes, then place them in a pan. Pour in the stock and add a little salt. Bring to the boil, reduce the heat and cover then pan. Simmer the potatoes for 10 minutes, until they are tender.

2 Finely dice the carrot and add to the potatoes and stock, then tear the rocket leaves and drop them into the pan. Simmer the soup for a further 15 minutes, until the vegetables are tender.

3 Gradually add the cayenne pepper – try a little at first and taste after each addition, until the soup is sufficiently hot for your taste. Adding all the cayenne at once may make the soup too fiery. Then add salt and black pepper to taste.

4 Add the chunks of bread to the soup. Remove the pan from the heat, cover the pan tightly and leave the soup to stand for about 10 minutes, so that the bread softens and the flavours mingle and mellow.

5 Meanwhile, heat the olive oil in a frying pan and add the garlic. Fry the garlic, stirring often, until golden brown.

6 Warm the serving bowls and then pour or ladle the soup into them (it should not need reheating). Add a little of the sautéed garlic to each bowl and serve immediately.

Watercress Soup: Energy 68kcal/280kJ; Protein 1.5g; Carbohydrate 1.4g, of which sugars 1g; Fat 6.3g, of which saturates 2.4g; Cholesterol 8mg; Calcium 79mg; Fibre 0.9g; Sodium 45mg.
Rocket and Potato: Energy 336kcal/1413kJ; Protein 7.3g; Carbohydrate 50.7g, of which sugars 5.1g; Fat 12.9g, of which saturates 2g; Cholesterol 0mg; Calcium 96mg; Fibre 3.7g; Sodium 203mg.

Spicy Peanut Soup

This distinctive soup is made with an unusual combination of ingredients. It has a rich peanut and chilli flavour and a thick texture – a good, filling autumnal dish.

Serves 6

30ml/2 tbsp oil
1 large onion, finely chopped
2 garlic cloves, crushed
5ml/1 tsp mild chilli powder
2 red (bell) peppers, seeded and finely chopped
225g/8oz carrots, finely chopped
225g/8oz potatoes, peeled and cubed
3 celery sticks, sliced
900ml/1½ pints/3¾ cups vegetable stock
90ml/6 tbsp crunchy peanut butter
115g/4oz/1 cup corn
salt and ground black pepper
roughly chopped unsalted roasted peanuts, to garnish

1 Heat the oil in a large pan and cook the onion and garlic for about 3 minutes. Add the chilli powder and cook for a further 1 minute.

2 Add the peppers, carrots, potatoes and celery to the pan. Stir well, then cook for a further 4 minutes, stirring occasionally.

3 Stir in the stock, peanut butter and corn until combined.

4 Season well. Bring to the boil, cover and simmer for 20 minutes, or until all the vegetables are tender. Adjust the seasoning before serving, and sprinkle with the chopped roasted peanuts, to garnish.

Variation
Try using other nut butters instead of peanut butter. Mixed nut butter or hazelnut butter is very good in soup. These are becoming more widely available, and there are simple recipes for making your own. Omit the peppers and add leeks instead for a sweeter, more mellow flavour to complement the slightly milder flavour of the hazelnuts.. Baby broad (fava) beans are good instead of corn.

Artichoke and Vegetable Soup

Fresh coriander, parsley and mint complement the summery flavours of the vegetables in this tagine-style dish, while turmeric contributes its earthy warmth. Prepare the artichokes yourself by removing the outer leaves, cutting off the stems, and scooping out the choke and hairy bits with a teaspoon, or buy frozen ready prepared hearts.

Serves 4–6

6 fresh artichoke hearts
juice of 1 lemon
30–45ml/2–3 tbsp olive oil
1 onion, chopped
675g/1½lb potatoes, peeled and quartered
small bunch of flat leaf parsley, chopped
small bunch of coriander (cilantro), chopped
small bunch of mint, chopped
pinch of saffron threads
5ml/1 tsp ground turmeric
900ml/1½ pints/3¾ cups vegetable stock
finely chopped rind of ½ preserved lemon
250g/9oz/2¼ cups shelled peas
salt and ground black pepper
flat bread, such as pitta, to serve

1 Poach the artichoke hearts very gently in plenty of simmering water with half the lemon juice, for 10–15 minutes until tender. Drain and refresh under cold water, then drain.

2 Heat the olive oil in a heavy pan. Add the chopped onion and cook over a low heat for about 15 minutes, or until softened but not browned.

3 Add the potatoes, most of the parsley, the coriander, mint, the remaining lemon juice, and the saffron and turmeric to the pan. Pour in the vegetable stock, bring the soup to the boil, then reduce the heat. Cover the pan and simmer the soup for about 15 minutes, or until the potatoes are almost tender.

4 Stir in the lemon rind, artichoke hearts and peas. Cover the pan and cook gently for a further 10 minutes. Season the soup to taste, sprinkle with the remaining parsley, and ladle it into warmed bowls. If preferred, serve the vegetables first, moistened with some broth, and finish with a second bowl or tasty broth. Serve with plenty of flat bread.

Spicy Peanut Soup: Energy 222kcal/925kJ; Protein 6g; Carbohydrate 23.4g, of which sugars 12.1g; Fat 12.2g, of which saturates 2.6g; Cholesterol 0mg; Calcium 41mg; Fibre 4g; Sodium 130mg.
Artichoke and Vegetable: Energy 141kcal/591kJ; Protein 3g; Carbohydrate 19.5g, of which sugars 2.4g; Fat 6.2g, of which saturates 0.9g; Cholesterol 0mg; Calcium 62mg; Fibre 2.7g; Sodium 48mg.

Avocado Soup

This delicious and very pretty soup is perfect for dinner parties and has a fresh, delicate flavour. You might want to add a dash more lime juice just before serving for added zest.

Serves 4

2 large ripe avocados
300ml/½ pint/1¼ cups crème fraîche
1 litre/1¾ pints/4 cups well-flavoured vegetable stock
5ml/1 tsp salt, or to taste
juice of ½ lime
small bunch of fresh coriander (cilantro)
ground black pepper

1 Cut the avocados in half, remove the peel and lift out the stones (pits). Chop the flesh coarsely and place it in a food processor or blender with 45–60ml/3–4 tbsp of the crème fraîche. Process until smooth.

2 Heat the vegetable stock in a pan. When it is hot, but still below simmering point, stir in the rest of the crème fraîche, with the salt.

3 Add the lime juice to the avocado mixture, process briefly to mix, then gradually stir the mixture into the hot stock. Heat gently but do not let the mixture approach boiling point.

4 Chop the coriander. Pour the soup into warmed bowls and sprinkle each portion with coriander and black pepper to taste. Serve immediately.

Cook's Tip

Because this soup contains avocados, it may discolour if left to stand, so make it just before serving. For a chilled version, heat and mix the stock and half the crème fraîche, then cool and chill. Shortly before you are ready to serve the soup, prepare and purée the avocados with the remaining crème fraîche. Stir into the chilled stock, season and serve sprinkled with coriander.

Chunky Courgette and Tomato Soup

This brightly coloured, fresh-tasting tomato soup makes the most of summer vegetables in season. Add lots of sweet, ripe red and yellow (bell) peppers to make a sweeter version.

Serves 4

450g/1lb ripe plum tomatoes
225g/8oz ripe yellow tomatoes
45ml/3 tbsp olive oil
1 large onion, finely chopped
15ml/1 tbsp sun-dried tomato purée (paste)
225g/8oz courgettes (zucchini), trimmed and roughly chopped
225g/8oz yellow courgettes (zucchini), trimmed and roughly chopped
3 waxy new potatoes, diced
2 garlic cloves, crushed
about 1.2 litres/2 pints/5 cups vegetable stock or water
60ml/4 tbsp shredded fresh basil
50g/2oz/⅔ cup freshly grated Parmesan cheese
salt and ground black pepper

1 Plunge all the tomatoes in boiling water for 30 seconds. Then drain, peel and chop finely them.

2 Heat the oil in a large pan, add the onion and cook gently for about 5 minutes, stirring constantly, until softened. Stir in the sun-dried tomato purée, chopped tomatoes, courgettes, diced potatoes and garlic. Mix well and cook gently for 10 minutes, shaking the pan often.

3 Pour in the stock or water. Bring to the boil, lower the heat, half cover the pan and simmer for 15 minutes or until the vegetables are tender. Add more stock or water if necessary.

4 Remove from the heat. Stir in the basil, half the cheese and seasoning. Serve sprinkled with the remaining cheese.

Cook's Tip

Any summer squash or pumpkin can be used in this soup instead of, or with, the courgettes (zucchini).

Avocado Soup: Energy 282kcal/1169kJ; Protein 6.6g; Carbohydrate 10.4g, of which sugars 9.4g; Fat 23.9g, of which saturates 8.9g; Cholesterol 28mg; Calcium 171mg; Fibre 3.5g; Sodium 71mg.
Courgette Soup: Energy 277kcal/1157kJ; Protein 10.7g; Carbohydrate 29.3g, of which sugars 12.7g; Fat 13.7g, of which saturates 4.1g; Cholesterol 13mg; Calcium 215mg; Fibre 4.8g; Sodium 166mg.

Roasted Aubergine and Courgette Soup

A fusion of Greek flavours, this fabulous soup is served with tzatziki, the popular combination of cucumber and creamy yogurt.

Serves 4

2 large aubergines (eggplant), roughly diced
4 large courgettes (zucchini), roughly diced
1 onion, roughly chopped
4 garlic cloves, roughly chopped
45ml/3 tbsp olive oil
1.2 litres/2 pints/5 cups vegetable stock
15ml/1 tbsp chopped fresh oregano
salt and ground black pepper
mint sprigs, to garnish

For the tzatziki

1 cucumber, peeled, seeded and diced
10ml/2 tsp salt
225g/8oz/1 cup Greek (US strained plain) yogurt
2 garlic cloves, crushed
5ml/1 tsp white wine vinegar
a little fresh mint, chopped

1 Preheat the oven to 200°C/400°F/Gas 6. Place the aubergines and courgettes in a roasting tin. Add the onion and garlic, drizzle the oil over and spread out the vegetables. Roast for 35 minutes, turning once, until tender and slightly charred.

2 For the tzatziki, place the cucumber in a colander. Sprinkle with the salt. Place on a bowl and leave for 30 minutes.

3 Dry the cucumber on kitchen paper and add to the yogurt with the garlic, vinegar, seasoning and mint. Chill until required.

4 Place half the roasted vegetables in a food processor or blender. Add the stock and process until almost smooth. Then pour into a large pan and add the remaining vegetables.

5 Bring the soup slowly to the boil and season well. Stir in the chopped oregano. Ladle the soup into four bowls. Garnish with mint sprigs and serve immediately. Hand round the bowl of tzatziki so that your guests can add a dollop or two to their soup as required.

Chunky Roasted Tomato Soup

Slow roasting tomatoes gives a rich, full flavour. The costeno amarillo chilli is fresh and light, making it perfect with rich tomatoes.

Serves 6

500g/1 ¼lb tomatoes
4 small onions, peeled but left whole
5 garlic cloves
sea salt
1 fresh rosemary sprig chopped
2 costeno amarillo chillies
grated rind and juice of ½ small lemon
30ml/2 tbsp extra virgin olive oil
300ml/½ pint/1 ¼ cups tomato juice
1.5ml/¼ tsp soft dark brown sugar

1 Preheat the oven to 160°C/325°F/Gas 3. Cut the tomatoes in half and place them in a roasting pan. Peel the onions and garlic and add them to the tin. Sprinkle with sea salt. Roast for 1 ¼ hours or until the tomatoes are beginning to dry. Do not let them burn or blacken or they will have a bitter taste.

2 Peel the tomatoes and place them in a food processor with the onions and garlic. Process until coarsely chopped and transfer to a pan. Add 350ml/12fl oz/1 cup water to the roasting pan and bring it to the boil, stirring to scrape all the residue off the pan. Boil for a minute, then pour the liquid into the pan.

3 Soak the chillies in hot water for about 10 minutes until soft. Drain, remove the stalks, slit them and scrape out the seeds. Chop the flesh finely and add it to the tomato mixture.

4 Stir in the lemon rind and juice, the olive oil, tomato juice and sugar. Bring to the boil, stirring, then reduce the heat, cover and simmer gently for 5 minutes. Taste for seasoning before serving sprinkled with the remaining rosemary.

Cook's Tip
Use plum tomatoes or vine tomatoes, which tend to have more flavour than tomatoes grown for their keeping properties.

Aubergine and Courgette: Energy 222kcal/920kJ; Protein 9.7g; Carbohydrate 12.7g, of which sugars 11g; Fat 15.7g, of which saturates 4.5g; Cholesterol 0mg; Calcium 192mg; Fibre 6.3g; Sodium 1034mg.
Roasted Tomato Soup: Energy 74kcal/310kJ; Protein 1.8g; Carbohydrate 8.6g, of which sugars 6.1g; Fat 3.9g, of which saturates 0.6g; Cholesterol 0mg; Calcium 24mg; Fibre 1.7g; Sodium 119mg.

Fiery Tomato Soup

This dazzling soup can be made as fiery as you like by increasing the chillies.

Serves 4

1.5kg/3–3½lb plum tomatoes, halved
5 fresh red chillies, seeded
1 red (bell) pepper, halved and seeded
2 red onions, roughly chopped
6 garlic cloves, crushed
30ml/2 tbsp sun-dried tomato paste
45ml/3 tbsp olive oil
400ml/14fl oz/1⅔ cups vegetable stock
salt and ground black pepper
wild rocket (arugula) leaves, to garnish

For the pepper cream

1 red (bell) pepper, halved and seeded
10ml/2 tsp olive oil
120ml/4fl oz/½ cup crème fraîche
few drops of Tabasco

1 Preheat the oven to 200°C/400°F/Gas 6. Toss the tomatoes, chillies, red pepper, onions, garlic and tomato paste with the oil in a roasting tin. Roast for 40 minutes, until slightly charred.

2 For the pepper cream. Lay the red pepper halves skin side up on a baking tray and brush with the olive oil. Roast with the mixed vegetables for about 30–40 minutes, until blistered.

3 Transfer the pepper for the cream to a bowl. Cover with clear film (plastic wrap) and cool. Peel and purée the flesh with half the crème fraîche. Pour into a bowl and stir in the remaining crème fraîche. Season and add a dash of Tabasco. Chill until required.

4 Process the roasted vegetables in batches, adding a ladleful of stock to each batch to make a smooth, thick purée. Depending on how juicy the tomatoes are, you may not need all the stock.

5 Press the purée through a sieve (strainer) into a pan and stir in more stock if you want to thin the soup. Heat the soup gently and season it well.

6 Ladle the soup into bowls and spoon red pepper cream into the centre of each portion. Pile wild rocket leaves on top to garnish and serve immediately.

Garlic and Tomato Soup with Basil

A soup for late summer when fresh tomatoes are at their most plentiful and flavoursome. You can use canned tomatoes out of season.

Serves 4–6

15ml/1 tbsp olive oil
25g/1oz/2 tbsp butter
1 onion, finely chopped
6 garlic cloves, roughly chopped
900g/2lb ripe plum tomatoes, roughly chopped
about 750ml/1¼ pints/3 cups vegetable stock
120ml/4fl oz/½ cup dry white wine
30ml/2 tbsp sun-dried tomato paste
30ml/2 tbsp shredded fresh basil,
150ml/¼ pint/⅔ cup double (heavy) cream
salt and ground black pepper
a few whole basil leaves, to garnish

1 Heat the oil and butter in a large pan until foaming. Add the onion and garlic, and cook gently for about 5 minutes, stirring frequently, until softened but not brown.

2 Stir in the chopped tomatoes and garlic, then add the stock, white wine and sun-dried tomato paste, with salt and pepper to taste. Bring to the boil, then lower the heat, half cover the pan and simmer gently for 20 minutes, stirring occasionally to stop the tomatoes sticking to the base of the pan.

3 Process the soup with the shredded basil in a food processor or blender, then press through a sieve (strainer) into a clean pan.

4 Add the double cream and heat through, stirring. Do not allow the soup to approach boiling point. Add more stock if necessary and then taste for seasoning. Pour into heated bowls and garnish with basil. Serve at once.

Variation

The soup can also be served chilled. Transfer to a bowl at the end of step 3 and chill for at least 4 hours.

Fiery Tomato Soup: Energy 319kcal/1330kJ; Protein 5.3g; Carbohydrate 23.5g, of which sugars 22g; Fat 23.4g, of which saturates 10g; Cholesterol 34mg; Calcium 67mg; Fibre 6.2g; Sodium 72mg.
Garlic and Tomato with Basil: Energy 97kcal/409kJ; Protein 2.4g; Carbohydrate 9.6g, of which sugars 9.2g; Fat 3.7g, of which saturates 1.4g; Cholesterol 4mg; Calcium 32mg; Fibre 2.7g; Sodium 42mg.

Tomato and Ciabatta Soup with Basil Oil

Throughout Europe, bread is a popular ingredient for thickening soup and this recipe shows how wonderfully quick and easy this method can be.

Serves 4

45ml/3 tbsp olive oil
1 red onion, chopped
4 garlic cloves, chopped
300ml/½ pint/1¼ cups white wine
12 plum tomatoes, quartered
2 x 400g/14oz cans plum tomatoes
2.5ml/½ tsp sugar
½ ciabatta loaf, broken into bitesize pieces
salt and ground black pepper
basil leaves, to garnish

For the basil oil

115g/4oz basil leaves
120ml/4fl oz/½ cup olive oil

1 To make the basil oil, process the basil leaves and oil in a food processor or blender for 1–2 minutes to make a paste. Line a small bowl with muslin (cheesecloth) and scrape the paste into it. Gather up the muslin and squeeze it firmly around the paste to extract all the basil-flavoured oil. Set aside.

2 Heat the oil in a large pan and cook the onion and garlic for 4–5 minutes until softened.

3 Add the wine, 150ml/¼ pint/⅔ cup water, fresh and canned tomatoes. Boil, reduce the heat, cover and simmer for 3–4 minutes. Add the sugar and seasoning. Stir in the bread.

4 Ladle the soup into bowls. Garnish with basil and drizzle the basil oil over each portion.

Variation

Try different breads for adding a variety of flavours as well as thickening the soup. Walnut bread is particularly good in this soup. Bread with green olives also works well. Light rye bread with caraway seeds contributes a pleasing tang.

Spicy Tomato Soup with Poached Eggs

Served on its own with chunks of crusty bread, or accompanied by jasmine or ginger rice, this is a tasty dish for a light supper.

Serves 4

30ml/2 tbsp vegetable oil
3 shallots, finely sliced
2 garlic cloves, finely chopped
2 fresh red chillies, seeded and finely sliced
25g/1oz galangal, shredded
8 large, ripe tomatoes, skinned, seeded and finely chopped
15ml/1 tbsp sugar
30ml/2 tbsp fish sauce
4 lime leaves
900ml/1½ pints/3¾ cups chicken stock
15ml/1 tbsp wine vinegar
4 eggs
salt and ground black pepper

For the garnish

chilli oil, for drizzling
1 small bunch fresh coriander (cilantro), finely chopped
1 small bunch fresh mint leaves, finely chopped

1 Heat the oil in a wok or heavy pan. Stir in the shallots, garlic, chillies and galangal and cook until golden and fragrant. Add the tomatoes with the sugar, fish sauce and lime leaves. Stir until the mixture resembles a sauce. Pour in the stock and bring to the boil. Reduce the heat and simmer for 30 minutes. Season.

2 Just before serving, bring a wide pan of water to the boil. Add the vinegar and half a teaspoon of salt. Break the eggs into individual cups or small bowls.

3 Stir the water rapidly to create a swirl and drop an egg into the centre of the swirl. Follow immediately with the others, or poach two at a time, and keep the water boiling to throw the whites up over the yolks. Turn off the heat, cover the pan and leave to poach until firm enough to lift. Poached eggs are traditional, but you could use lightly fried egg instead.

4 Using a slotted spoon, lift the eggs out of the water and slip them into the hot soup. Drizzle a little chilli oil over the eggs, sprinkle with the coriander and mint, and serve.

Tomato and Ciabatta: Energy 273kcal/1150kJ; Protein 6g; Carbohydrate 28.6g, of which sugars 16g; Fat 10.6g, of which saturates 1.8g; Cholesterol 0mg; Calcium 72mg; Fibre 5.3g; Sodium 179mg.
Tomato with Egg: Energy 181kcal/756kJ; Protein 8g; Carbohydrate 12.3g, of which sugars 11.5g; Fat 11.7g, of which saturates 2.4g; Cholesterol 190mg; Calcium 52mg; Fibre 2.3g; Sodium 284mg.

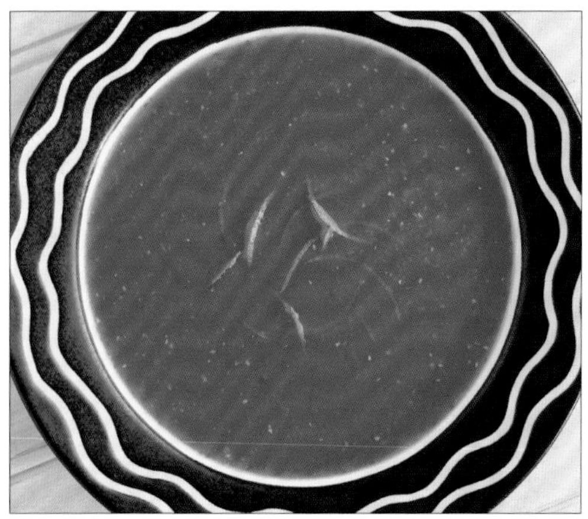

Red Pepper Soup with Lime

The dash of citrus flavouring makes this a wonderfully refreshing and fragrant soup. The beautiful, rich red colour is a large part of the appeal, and, as a finishing touch, simply toast some tiny croûtons to serve sprinkled over the top.

Serves 4–6

1 large onion, chopped
4 red (bell) peppers, seeded and chopped
5ml/1 tsp olive oil
1 garlic clove, crushed
1 small fresh red chilli, sliced
45ml/3 tbsp tomato purée (paste)
900ml/1½ pints/3¾ cups vegetable stock
finely grated rind and juice of 1 lime
salt and ground black pepper
shreds of lime rind, to garnish

1 Cook the onion and peppers gently in the oil in a covered pan for about 5 minutes, shaking the pan occasionally, until the peppers are just softened.

2 Stir in the garlic, chilli and tomato purée. Add half the stock, then bring to the boil. Cover and simmer for 10 minutes.

3 Cool slightly, then purée in a food processor or blender. Return to the pan and add the remaining stock, the lime rind and juice and salt and pepper.

4 Bring the soup back to the boil, then serve at once, with a few strips of lime rind scattered into each bowl.

Cook's Tips

• *This soup can be made with canned red peppers, or a jar of red peppers. Drain the peppers and roughly chop them. Cook the onion for 5 minutes, then add the peppers. Continue as in the main recipe.*

• *When peppers are plentiful and inexpensive, make a large batch of this soup and freeze some for winter. Do not add the lime rind and juice until thawing and reheating.*

Roasted Aubergine Soup

Traditionally, the aubergine is roasted over charcoal, but a hot electric or gas oven will produce similar results, although the smoky flavour will be missing.

Serves 4

2 large aubergines (eggplants)
45ml/3 tbsp vegetable oil
2.5ml/½ tsp black mustard seeds
1 bunch spring onions (scallions), finely chopped
115g/4oz button (white) mushrooms, halved
2 garlic cloves, crushed
1 fresh red chilli, finely chopped
2.5ml/½ tsp chilli powder
5ml/1 tsp ground cumin
5ml/1 tsp ground coriander
1.5ml/¼ tsp ground turmeric
5ml/1 tsp salt
400g/14oz can chopped tomatoes
475ml/16fl oz/2 cups vegetable stock
15ml/1 tbsp chopped fresh coriander (cilantro), plus a few extra sprigs to garnish

1 Preheat the oven to 200°C/400°F/Gas 6. Brush the aubergines with 15ml/1 tbsp of oil, prick them all over and bake for 30–35 minutes until soft.

2 Meanwhile, heat the remaining oil and fry the black mustard seeds for about 2 minutes until they splutter. Add the onions, mushrooms, garlic and chilli, and fry for 5 minutes more. Stir in the chilli powder, cumin, coriander, turmeric and salt and fry for 3–4 minutes. Add the tomatoes and simmer for 5 minutes.

3 Cut the aubergines in half lengthwise and scoop out the soft flesh into a large mixing bowl. Mash the flesh to a course texture, using a fork.

4 Add the aubergines to the pan with the coriander. Stir in the stock and bring to the boil. Reduce the heat, cover the pan and simmer for 5 minutes. Serve garnished with coriander.

Cook's Tip

Roast the aubergines (eggplants) over a barbecue for an authentic smoky flavour.

Red Pepper with Lime: Energy 66kcal/274kJ; Protein 2.1g; Carbohydrate 12.5g, of which sugars 11g; Fat 1.1g, of which saturates 0.2g; Cholesterol 0mg; Calcium 25mg; Fibre 2.8g; Sodium 24mg.
Roasted Aubergine: Energy 141kcal/589kJ; Protein 4g; Carbohydrate 9.3g, of which sugars 6.4g; Fat 10.3g, of which saturates 1.4g; Cholesterol 0mg; Calcium 45mg; Fibre 4.2g; Sodium 509mg.

Fresh Tomato Soup with Cheddar Cheese Croûtes

Choose the ripest-looking tomatoes and add sugar and balsamic vinegar to taste. The quantity will depend on the natural sweetness of the fresh tomatoes. On a hot day, this soup is also delicious chilled.

Serves 6

1.3–1.6kg/3–3½lb ripe tomatoes
400ml/14fl oz/1⅔ cups vegetable stock
45ml/3 tbsp sun-dried tomato purée (paste)
30–45ml/2–3 tbsp balsamic vinegar
10–15ml/2–3 tsp sugar
a small handful of fresh basil leaves, plus extra to garnish
salt and ground black pepper

For serving

toasted cheese croûtes
crème fraîche

1 Plunge the tomatoes into boiling water for 30 seconds, then drain. Peel off the skins and quarter the tomatoes.

2 Put the tomatoes in a large pan and pour over the vegetable stock. Bring just to the boil, reduce the heat, cover and simmer gently for 10 minutes until the tomatoes are pulpy.

3 Stir in the tomato purée, vinegar, sugar and basil. Season with salt and pepper, then cook gently, stirring, for 2 minutes.

4 Process the soup in a food processor or blender, then return it to a clean pan and reheat gently.

5 Serve in bowls, topping each portion with one or two toasted cheese croûtes and a spoonful of crème fraîche. Garnish with basil leaves.

Cook's Tip

Use a sharp knife to cut a cross in the base of each tomato before plunging it into the boiling water. The skin will then peel back easily from the crosses.

Simple Tomato and Coriander Soup

The simplest variations on the tomato soup theme are often the best. True to the culture of thrift in traditional soup-making, this classic thin soup makes great use of a few familiar ingredients, but it is the addition of coriander that brings a burst of flavour. Sprinkle generously with black pepper and serve with crusty bread for a satisfying lunch.

Serves 4

15ml/1 tbsp vegetable oil
1 onion, finely chopped
900g/2lb tomatoes, peeled, seeded and chopped
475ml/16fl oz/2 cups vegetable stock
2 large fresh coriander (cilantro) sprigs
salt and ground black pepper

1 Heat the oil in a pan and gently fry the finely chopped onion, stirring frequently, for about 5 minutes, or until it is soft and translucent but not brown.

2 Add the chopped tomatoes, stock and coriander sprigs to the pan. Bring to the boil, then lower the heat, cover the pan and simmer gently for about 15 minutes.

3 Remove and discard the coriander. Press the soup through a sieve (strainer) and return it to the clean pan. Season and heat through. Serve sprinkled with ground black pepper.

Variations

- *Instead of the coriander, add fresh tarragon to the soup. For a pronounced flavour, do not remove it but chop it very finely instead.*
- *Mixed herbs are good with the tomato soup. Instead of the classic, pungent Mediterranean mix, try lots of chopped fresh parsley, a hint of chopped fresh thyme, just one or two leaves of fresh sage and a small bunch of chives. Ensure all the herbs are finely cut or chopped and add them to the soup after reheating instead of the pepper.*

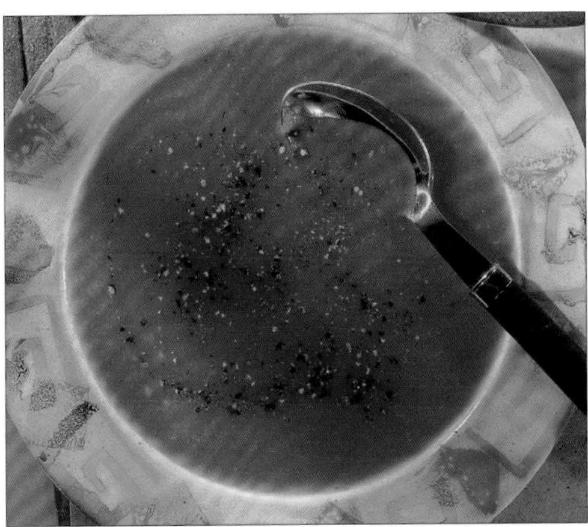

Tomato with Croûtes: Energy 49kcal/210kJ; Protein 1.9g; Carbohydrate 9.5g, of which sugars 9.5g; Fat 0.7g, of which saturates 0.2g; Cholesterol 0mg; Calcium 19mg; Fibre 2.4g; Sodium 38mg.
Tomato and Coriander: Energy 63kcal/267kJ; Protein 2g; Carbohydrate 9.5g, of which sugars 6g; Fat 2.2g, of which saturates 1.1g; Cholesterol 4mg; Calcium 48mg; Fibre 2.5g; Sodium 24mg.

Tomato and Spring Onion Soup with Coriander

Although basil is traditionally used to partner tomatoes, fresh coriander also complements its flavour. This warming soup is excellent on a winter's day.

Serves 4

675g/1½lb tomatoes
30ml/2 tbsp vegetable oil
1 bay leaf
4 spring onions (scallions), chopped
5ml/1 tsp salt
1 garlic clove, crushed
5ml/1 tsp black peppercorns, crushed
30ml/2 tbsp chopped fresh coriander (cilantro)
750ml/1¼ pints/3 cups vegetable stock or water
15ml/1 tbsp cornflour (cornstarch)
30ml/2 tbsp single (light) cream, to garnish

1 Plunge the tomatoes into boiling water for 30 seconds, then drain. Peel away the skins and chop the tomatoes.

2 Heat the oil in a pan and fry the chopped tomatoes, bay leaf and spring onions for a few minutes until the spring onions are soft and the tomatoes have cooked down a little.

3 Add the salt, garlic, peppercorns and fresh coriander to the tomato mixture. Add the stock or water and bring to the boil, lower the heat and simmer for 15–20 minutes.

4 Mix the cornflour to a paste with a little cold water. Remove the soup from the heat and press it through a sieve. Return the soup to a clean pan, add the cornflour paste and bring to the boil, stirring, then cook gently for about 3 minutes until thickened. Serve the soup garnish with the cream.

Cook's Tip
In winter when fresh tomatoes can be rather pale and under-ripe, add 15ml/1 tbsp tomato purée (paste).

Tomato and Bread Soup

This colourful recipe was created to use up stale, leftover bread. It can be made with very ripe fresh or canned plum tomatoes.

Serves 4

90ml/6 tbsp olive oil
small piece of dried chilli, crumbled (optional)
175g/6oz/1½ cups stale coarse white bread, cut into 2.5cm/1in cubes
1 onion, finely chopped
2 garlic cloves, finely chopped
675g/1½lb ripe tomatoes, peeled and chopped, or 2 x 400g/14oz cans peeled plum tomatoes, chopped
45ml/3 tbsp chopped fresh basil
1.5 litres/2½ pints/6¼ cups home-made or ready-prepared stock or water, or a combination of both
salt and ground black pepper
extra virgin olive oil, to serve (optional)

1 Heat 4 tbsp of the oil in a large pan. Add the chilli, if using, and stir for 1–2 minutes. Add the bread cubes and cook until golden. Transfer to a plate and drain on paper towels.

2 Add the remaining oil to the pan with the onion and garlic, and cook until the onion softens. Stir in the tomatoes, bread and basil. Season with salt. Cook over medium heat, stirring occasionally, for about 15 minutes.

3 Meanwhile, heat the stock or water to simmering. Add to the pan of tomato mixture and mix well. Bring to the boil. Lower the heat slightly and simmer for 20 minutes.

4 Remove the soup from the heat. Use a fork to mash the tomatoes and the bread together. Season with pepper, and more salt if necessary. Allow to stand for 10 minutes.

5 Just before serving the soup, swirl in a little extra virgin olive oil, if wished.

Variation
Mix in grated Pecorino or other hard Italian cheese at step 4.

Tomato and Spring Onion: Energy 112kcal/467kJ; Protein 2g; Carbohydrate 9.4g, of which sugars 5.9g; Fat 7.7g, of which saturates 1.7g; Cholesterol 4mg; Calcium 43mg; Fibre 2.4g; Sodium 23mg.
Tomato and Bread: Energy 285kcal/1194kJ; Protein 5g; Carbohydrate 28g, of which sugars 7.2g; Fat 17.9g, of which saturates 2.5g; Cholesterol 0mg; Calcium 64mg; Fibre 2.6g; Sodium 243mg.

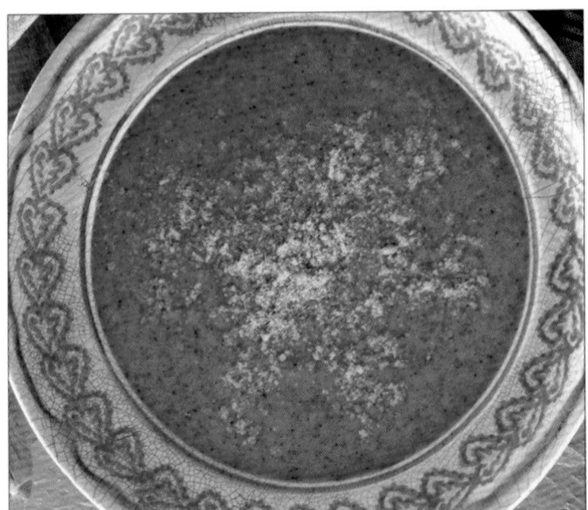

Broccoli and Almond Soup

The creaminess of the toasted almonds combines perfectly with the full flavour of the broccoli.

Serves 4–6

50g/2oz/½ cup ground almonds
675g/1½lb broccoli
900ml/1½ pints/3¾ cups vegetable stock or water
300ml/½ pint/1¼ cups skimmed milk
salt and ground black pepper

1 Preheat the oven to 180°C/350°F/Gas 4. Spread the ground almonds evenly on a baking sheet and toast in the oven for about 10 minutes, until golden. Reserve one-quarter of the almonds and set aside to garnish the finished dish.

2 Cut the broccoli into small florets and steam for about 6–7 minutes until tender.

3 Place the remaining toasted almonds, broccoli, stock or water and milk in a food processor or blender and blend until smooth. Season with salt and pepper to taste.

4 Reheat the soup and serve sprinkled with the reserved toasted almonds.

Cook's Tip

Instead of steaming the broccoli, it can be cooked in boiling water. Cut off the stalks and dice them finely, then cook in the water for 3–5 minutes, until tender, before adding the tender tops of the florets. Simmer for 2–3 minutes to cook completely.

Variation

Use cauliflower instead of broccoli. Dice the cauliflower and cook in boiling water or stock for about 5 minutes, until tender. Use the cooking liquor for the soup. For a super-creamy flavour use whole milk and stir in a little single (light) cream just before sprinkling with the almonds.

Broccoli and Bread Soup

Tender young purple-sprouting broccoli has the most fabulous flavour, so try it in this soup. While it may give a slightly murky green colouring to the soup, it will taste good.

Serves 6

675g/1½lb broccoli spears
1.75 litres/3 pints/7½ cups vegetable stock
15ml/1 tbsp lemon juice
salt and ground black pepper

For serving

6 slices white bread
1 large garlic clove, cut in half
freshly grated Parmesan cheese (optional)

1 Using a small sharp knife, peel the broccoli stems, starting from the base of the stalks and pulling gently up towards the florets. (The peel comes off very easily.) Chop the broccoli into small chunks.

2 Bring the stock to a boil in a large pan. Add the broccoli and simmer for 30 minutes, or until soft.

3 Transfer about half of the broccoli soup to a food processor or blender and process until smooth. Return the purée to the soup in the pan and stir well together. Season with salt, pepper and lemon juice, to taste.

4 Just before serving, reheat the soup to just below boiling point. Toast the bread, rub with garlic and cut into quarters. Place three or four pieces of toast on the bottom of each soup plate. Ladle on the soup. Serve at once, with Parmesan if you wish.

Cook's Tip

The Italian idea of placing garlic-flavoured toast in the bowl before adding the soup is quite delicious. The toast soaks up the liquid and adds not only a wonderful texture to the soup, but also a subtle touch of garlic.

Broccoli and Almond: Energy 104kcal/435kJ; Protein 8.4g; Carbohydrate 4.8g, of which sugars 4.2g; Fat 5.8g, of which saturates 0.7g; Cholesterol 2mg; Calcium 144mg; Fibre 3.5g; Sodium 32mg.
Broccoli and Bread: Energy 101kcal/429kJ; Protein 7.3g; Carbohydrate 15.5g, of which sugars 2.4g; Fat 1.5g, of which saturates 0.2g; Cholesterol 0mg; Calcium 93mg; Fibre 3.4g; Sodium 150mg.

Red Onion and Beetroot Soup

This beautiful, ruby-red soup, with the contrasting yogurt, will look stunning at any dinner party and is very quick and simple to prepare as an appetizer.

Serves 4–6
15ml/1 tbsp olive oil
350g/12oz red onions, sliced
2 garlic cloves, crushed
275g/10oz cooked beetroot, cut into sticks
1.2 litres/2 pints/5 cups vegetable stock or water
50g/2oz/1 cup cooked soup pasta
30ml/2 tbsp raspberry vinegar
salt and ground black pepper

For the garnish
natural (plain) yogurt or fromage blanc
snipped fresh chives

1 Heat the olive oil in a large pan or flameproof casserole and add the onions and garlic.

2 Cook gently for about 20 minutes or until soft and tender, stirring occasionally.

3 Add the beetroot, stock or water, cooked pasta and vinegar and heat through. Season and garnish with a spoonful of yogurt or fromage blanc and chives.

Variations
- *Use mushroom-stuffed pasta, such as tortellini, instead of soup pasta.*
- *Add a little very finely shredded red cabbage with the onion.*
- *Stir a little grated or creamed horseradish into the yogurt for fromage blanc.*
- *Omit the garlic and add finely diced red apple and a little finely chopped fresh root ginger with the onions.*

Cook's Tip
Try substituting cooked barley for the pasta to give extra nuttiness to the flavour.

Leek, Parsnip and Ginger Soup

This soup makes a substantial and flavoursome winter warmer, with the added spiciness of fresh root ginger.

Serves 4–6
30ml/2 tbsp olive oil
225g/8oz leeks, sliced
25g/1oz fresh root ginger, peeled and finely chopped
675g/1½lb parsnips, roughly chopped
300ml/½ pint/1¼ cups dry white wine
1.2 litres/2 pints/5 cups vegetable stock or water
salt and ground black pepper

For the garnish
fromage blanc
paprika

1 Heat the oil in a large pan and add the leeks and ginger. Cook gently for 2–3 minutes until the leeks start to soften.

2 Add the parsnips and cook for a further 7–8 minutes until they are beginning to soften.

3 Pour in the wine and stock or water and bring to the boil. Reduce the heat, cover the pan and simmer for 20–30 minutes or until the parsnips are tender.

4 Purée the soup in a food processor or blender until smooth. Return the soup to the rinsed-out pan.

5 Season to taste. Reheat and garnish with a swirl of fromage blanc and a light dusting of paprika.

Variations
- *To add a dash more colour, use half and half carrot and parsnip instead of all parsnips.*
- *Omit the ginger and add 15ml/1 tbsp grated horseradish when processing the soup.*
- *Use celeriac instead of the parsnips and omit the paprika. Add a sprinkling of freshly grated nutmeg instead.*

Red Onion and Beetroot: Energy 87kcal/366kJ; Protein 2.8g; Carbohydrate 15.1g, of which sugars 7.6g; Fat 2.2g, of which saturates 0.3g; Cholesterol 0mg; Calcium 30mg; Fibre 1.9g; Sodium 52mg.
Leek, Parsnip and Ginger: Energy 146kcal/613kJ; Protein 2.7g; Carbohydrate 15.5g, of which sugars 7.5g; Fat 5.1g, of which saturates 0.8g; Cholesterol 0mg; Calcium 60mg; Fibre 6g; Sodium 14mg.

Leek and Thyme Soup

This is a filling, heart-warming soup, which can be processed to a smooth purée or served as it is here, in its original peasant style.

Serves 4

900g/2lb leeks
450g/1lb potatoes
115g/4oz/½ cup butter
1 large sprig of fresh thyme, plus extra to garnish (optional)
300ml/½ pint/1¼ cups milk
salt and ground black pepper
60ml/4 tbsp double (heavy) cream, to serve

1 Top and tail the leeks. If you are using big winter leeks, strip away all the coarse outer leaves, then cut the leeks into thick slices. Wash thoroughly under cold running water.

2 Cut the potatoes into rough dice, about 2.5cm/1in, and dry them on kitchen paper.

3 Melt the butter in a large pan and add the leeks and 1 sprig of thyme. Cover and cook for 4–5 minutes until softened. Add the potato pieces and just enough cold water to cover the vegetables. Re-cover and cook over a low heat for about 30 minutes.

4 Pour in the milk and season with salt and pepper. Cover and simmer for a further 30 minutes. You will find that some of the potato breaks up, leaving you with a semi-puréed and rather lumpy soup.

5 Remove the sprig of thyme (the leaves will have fallen into the soup) and serve, adding 15ml/1 tbsp cream and a garnish of thyme to each portion, if using.

Cook's Tip

If you want to use all the leeks, especially if they are large and mature, then wash and chop them, then purée the soup. This reduces the tougher parts and makes a delicious soup.

Spiced Cauliflower Soup

Light and tasty, this creamy, mildly spicy vegetable soup is multi-purpose. It makes a wonderful warming first course or an appetizing quick meal and is delicious chilled.

Serves 4–6

1 large potato, diced
1 small cauliflower, chopped
1 onion, chopped
15ml/1 tbsp oil
1 garlic clove, crushed
15ml/1 tbsp grated fresh root ginger
10ml/2 tsp ground turmeric
5ml/1 tsp cumin seeds
5ml/1 tsp black mustard seeds
10ml/2 tsp ground coriander
1 litre/1¾ pints/4 cups vegetable stock
300ml/½ pint/1¼ cups natural (plain) low-fat yogurt
salt and ground black pepper
fresh coriander (cilantro) or parsley, to garnish

1 Put the potato, cauliflower and onion into a large, heavy pan with the oil and 45ml/3 tbsp water. Heat until hot and bubbling, then stir well, cover the pan and turn the heat down. Continue cooking the mixture for about 10 minutes.

2 Add the garlic, ginger and spices. Stir well, and cook for another 2 minutes, stirring occasionally. Pour in the stock and season well. Bring to the boil, then cover and simmer for about 20 minutes. Purée in a food processor or blender and return to the pan. Stir in the yogurt, adjust the seasoning, and serve garnished with coriander or parsley.

Cook's Tip

A freshly made stock always tastes best. To make home-made vegetable stock, add to 3.5 litres/6 pints/15 cups of water: 2 sliced leeks, 3 chopped celery sticks, 1 chopped onion, 1 chopped parsnip, 1 seeded and chopped yellow (bell) pepper, 3 crushed garlic cloves, fresh herbs and 45ml/3 tbsp light soy sauce. Season, then slowly bring to the boil. Lower the heat and simmer for 30 minutes, stirring from time to time. Leave to cool. Sieve (strain), discard the vegetables, and use the stock as indicated in the recipe.

Leek and Thyme: Energy 377kcal/1570kJ; Protein 8.2g; Carbohydrate 28.3g, of which sugars 10.1g; Fat 26.4g, of which saturates 16.1g; Cholesterol 66mg; Calcium 156mg; Fibre 6.1g; Sodium 223mg.
Spiced Cauliflower: Energy 120kcal/501kJ; Protein 7.9g; Carbohydrate 14.1g, of which sugars 7.1g; Fat 4g, of which saturates 0.9g; Cholesterol 1mg; Calcium 129mg; Fibre 2.4g; Sodium 57mg.

Curried Cauliflower Soup

This spicy, creamy soup is perfect for lunch on a cold winter's day served with crusty bread and garnished with fresh coriander.

Serves 4
750ml/1¼ pints/3 cups milk
1 large cauliflower
15ml/1 tbsp garam masala
salt and ground black pepper

1 Pour the milk into a large pan and place over a medium heat. Cut the cauliflower into florets and add to the milk with the garam masala and season with salt and pepper.

2 Bring the milk to the boil, then reduce the heat, partially cover the pan with a lid and simmer for about 20 minutes, or until the cauliflower is tender.

3 Let the mixture cool for a few minutes, then transfer to a food processor or blender and process until smooth (you may have to do this in two batches).

4 Return the purée to the rinsed-out pan and heat through gently, checking and adjusting the seasoning. Ladle into warm bowls and serve immediately.

Variation
Cauliflower lends itself beautifully to mildly curried recipes, but you can also make broccoli soup in the same way, using the same weight of broccoli in place of the cauliflower.

Cook's Tip
There is no need to discard all the outer leaves from a cauliflower when making soup. Trim off any wilted or badly damaged green parts and stalks, and any very tough stalk. Then cut off the florets and dice the larger parts of the stalk. Thinly slice the leafy parts from around the sides. Add all these to the pan and they will bring excellent flavour to the soup. When they are cut smaller they cook as quickly as florets.

Spicy Carrot Soup

Garlic croûtons are very easy to make, and, once you know how, they can of course be used to top all kinds of soups.

Serves 6
15ml/1 tbsp olive oil
1 large onion, chopped
675g/1½lb carrots, sliced
5ml/1 tsp each ground coriander, ground cumin and hot chilli powder
900ml/1½ pints/3¾ cups vegetable stock
salt and ground black pepper
sprigs of fresh coriander (cilantro), to garnish

For the garlic croûtons
a little olive oil
2 garlic cloves, crushed
4 slices bread, crusts removed, cut into 1cm/½in cubes

1 Heat the oil in a large pan, add the onion and carrots and cook gently for 5 minutes, stirring occasionally. Add the ground spices and cook gently for 1 minute, continuing to stir.

2 Stir in the stock, bring to the boil, then cover and cook gently for about 45 minutes until the carrots are tender.

3 Meanwhile, make the garlic croûtons. Heat the oil in a frying pan, add the garlic and cook gently for 30 seconds, stirring. Add the bread cubes, turn them over in the oil and fry over a medium heat for a few minutes until crisp and golden brown all over, turning frequently. Drain on kitchen paper and keep warm.

4 Purée the soup in a food processor or blender until smooth, then season to taste with salt and pepper. Return the soup to the rinsed-out pan and reheat gently. Serve hot, sprinkled with garlic croûtons and garnished with coriander sprigs.

Cook's Tip
There is a confusing array of curry powders and pastes available. Many of the pastes are too complicated in flavour for a simple soup, but a basic, good-quality curry powder can be used instead of the three separate spices.

Curried Caulflower: Energy 136kcal/575kJ; Protein 11.5g; Carbohydrate 13.3g, of which sugars 12g; Fat 4.6g, of which saturates 2.2g; Cholesterol 11mg; Calcium 259mg; Fibre 3.1g; Sodium 100mg.
Spicy Carrot Soup: Energy 124kcal/517kJ; Protein 2.5g; Carbohydrate 19.7g, of which sugars 10.6g; Fat 4.4g, of which saturates 0.6g; Cholesterol 0mg; Calcium 55mg; Fibre 3.4g; Sodium 116mg.

Squash Soup with Hot Horseradish Cream

The partnering of squash and apple in this curried soup is superb. For fans of horseradish, the cream topping is an absolute must.

Serves 6

1 butternut squash
1 cooking apple
25g/1oz/2 tbsp butter
1 onion, finely chopped
5–10ml/1–2 tsp curry powder, plus extra to garnish
900ml/1½ pints/3¾ cups vegetable stock
5ml/1 tsp chopped fresh sage
150ml/¼ pint/⅔ cup apple juice
salt and ground black pepper
lime shreds, to garnish (optional)

For the horseradish cream (optional)
60ml/4 tbsp double (heavy) cream
10ml/2 tsp horseradish sauce
2.5ml/½ tsp curry powder

1 Peel the squash, remove the seeds and chop the flesh. Peel, core and chop the apple.

2 Heat the butter in a large pan. Add the onion and cook, stirring occasionally, for 5 minutes until soft. Stir in the curry powder. Cook to bring out the flavour, stirring constantly, for about 2 minutes.

3 Add the stock, squash, apple and sage. Bring to the boil, lower the heat, cover and simmer for 20 minutes until the squash and apple are soft.

4 If making the horseradish cream, whip the cream in a bowl until stiff, then stir in the horseradish sauce and curry powder. Cover and chill until required.

5 Purée the soup in a food processor or blender. Return to the clean pan and add the apple juice, with salt and pepper to taste. Reheat gently, without boiling.

6 Serve the soup in bowls, topped with a spoonful of horseradish cream, if liked, and a dusting of curry powder. Garnish with a few lime shreds.

Sweet Potato and Parsnip Soup

The sweetness of two of the most popular root vegetables – which are used in both the main part of the dish and the garnish – comes through beautifully in this delicious soup.

Serves 6

15ml/1 tbsp sunflower oil
1 large leek, sliced
2 celery sticks, chopped
450g/1lb sweet potatoes, diced
225g/8oz parsnips, diced
900ml/1½ pints/3¾ cups vegetable stock
salt and ground black pepper

For the garnish
15ml/1 tbsp chopped fresh parsley
roasted strips of sweet potatoes and parsnips

1 Heat the oil in a large pan and add the leek, celery, sweet potatoes and parsnips. Cook gently for about 5 minutes, stirring to prevent them browning or sticking to the pan.

2 Stir in the vegetable stock and bring to the boil, then cover and simmer gently for about 25 minutes, or until the vegetables are tender, stirring occasionally. Season to taste. Remove the pan from the heat and allow the soup to cool slightly.

3 Purée the soup in a food processor or blender until smooth, then return the soup to the pan and reheat gently.

4 Ladle the soup into warmed soup bowls to serve and sprinkle over the chopped parsley and roasted strips of sweet potatoes and parsnips.

Cook's Tip

Making and freezing soup is a practical way of preserving a glut of root vegetables that are unlikely to keep well. Not only can excess raw vegetables be used this way, but leftover boiled, mashed or roasted root vegetables can all be added to soup, puréed, cooled or frozen.

Squash with Cream: Energy 118kcal/489kJ; Protein 1.3g; Carbohydrate 7.7g, of which sugars 6.7g; Fat 9.3g, of which saturates 5.7g; Cholesterol 23mg; Calcium 50mg; Fibre 1.7g; Sodium 44mg.
Sweet Potato and Parsnip: Energy 113kcal/479kJ; Protein 2.1g; Carbohydrate 21.6g, of which sugars 7.2g; Fat 2.6g, of which saturates 0.4g; Cholesterol 0mg; Calcium 45mg; Fibre 4.3g; Sodium 40mg.

Chunky Spiced Vegetable Soup

Coconut crops up in many popular Cameroon dishes, including their famous beef and pineapple curry. Here it is teamed with sweet potato and spices to make a tasty soup.

Serves 4

30ml/2 tbsp butter
½ red onion, finely chopped
175g/6oz each turnip, sweet potato and pumpkin, peeled and roughly chopped
5ml/1 tsp dried marjoram
2.5ml/½ tsp ground ginger
1.5ml/¼ tsp ground cinnamon
15ml/1 tbsp chopped spring onion (scallion)
1 litre/1¾ pints/4 cups vegetable stock
30ml/2 tbsp flaked (sliced) almonds
1 fresh red or green chilli, seeded and chopped
5ml/1 tsp sugar
25g/1oz creamed coconut or 60ml/4 tbsp coconut cream
salt and ground black pepper
chopped fresh coriander (cilantro), to garnish

1 Melt the butter in a large non-stick pan. Fry the onion for 4–5 minutes. Add the chopped vegetables and fry for a further 3–4 minutes.

2 Add the marjoram, ginger, cinnamon, spring onion, salt and pepper. Sauté over a low heat for about 10 minutes, stirring frequently.

3 Add the vegetable stock, flaked almonds, chilli and sugar and stir well to mix, then cover and simmer gently for 10–15 minutes, until the vegetables are just tender.

4 Grate the creamed coconut into the soup, or add the coconut cream, and stir to mix. Spoon the soup into warmed bowls and serve, sprinkled with chopped coriander.

Cook's Tip
Take care when preparing fresh chillies. Avoid touching your eyes and wash your hands thoroughly afterwards (or wear disposable gloves).

Spiced Pumpkin Soup

The sweet flavour of pumpkin is excellent in soups, teaming well with other savoury ingredients, such as onions and potatoes, to make a warm and comforting dish. For super flavour, try roasting the pumpkin chunks for 30–40 minutes, until tender, before adding them to the soup with the stock.

Serves 4–6

15ml/1 tbsp sunflower oil
25g/1oz/2 tbsp butter
1 large onion, sliced
675g/1½lb pumpkin, cut into large chunks
450g/1lb potatoes, sliced
600ml/1 pint/2½ cups vegetable stock
a good pinch of freshly grated nutmeg
5ml/1 tsp chopped fresh tarragon
600ml/1 pint/2½ cups milk
about 5–10ml/1–2 tsp lemon juice
salt and ground black pepper

1 Heat the oil and butter in a heavy-based pan and fry the onion for 4–5 minutes over a gentle heat until soft but not browned, stirring frequently.

2 Add the pumpkin and sliced potatoes, stir well, then cover and sweat over a low heat for about 10 minutes until the vegetables are almost tender, stirring occasionally.

3 Stir in the stock, nutmeg, tarragon and seasoning. Bring to the boil and then simmer for about 10 minutes or until the vegetables are completely tender.

4 Allow to cool slightly, then pour into a food processor or blender and process until smooth. Pour back into a clean pan and add the milk. Heat gently and then taste, adding the lemon juice and extra seasoning, if necessary. Serve piping hot.

Cook's Tip
This soup works well with a mixture of marrow (large zucchini) and pumpkin or butternut squash.

Spiced Vegetable: Energy 168Kcal/701kJ; Protein 2.3g; Carbohydrate 13.2g, of which sugars 5.5g; Fat 12.2g, of which saturates 7.9g; Cholesterol 16mg; Calcium 50mg; Fibre 2.4g; Sodium 66mg.
Spiced Pumpkin Soup: Energy 136kcal/565kJ; Protein 4.6g; Carbohydrate 7.2g, of which sugars 6.2g; Fat 10g, of which saturates 2.4g; Cholesterol 11mg; Calcium 58mg; Fibre 2.6g; Sodium 235mg.

Winter Vegetable Soup

Eight varieties of vegetable are packed into this soup.

Serves 8

30ml/2 tbsp corn oil
1 Savoy cabbage, shredded
4 carrots, finely sliced
2 celery stalks, finely sliced
2 parsnips, diced
1.5 litres/2½ pints/6¼ cups vegetable stock
3 potatoes, diced
2 courgettes (zucchini), sliced
1 small red (bell) pepper, seeded and diced
115g/4oz cauliflower florets
2 tomatoes, seeded and diced
2.5ml/½ tsp fresh thyme leaves
30ml/2 tbsp chopped fresh parsley
salt and ground black pepper

1 Heat the oil in a large pan. Add the cabbage, carrots, celery and parsnips and cook for 10–15 minutes, stirring. Add all the remaining ingredients. Bring to the boil. Reduce the heat, cover and simmer for 20 minutes. Serve piping hot.

Gingered Vegetable Soup with Dill

If time is tight, a mixed pack of fresh vegetables is ideal for this soup.

Serves 6

3 carrots, chopped
1 each of potato, parsnip, turnip and onion, chopped
1 piece fresh root ginger, peeled and grated
30ml/2 tbsp sunflower oil
300ml/½ pint/1¼ cups milk
45ml/3 tbsp crème fraîche
30ml/2 tbsp chopped fresh dill
salt and ground black pepper

1 Cook all the vegetables and ginger in the oil in a large covered, pan, for 15 minutes, shaking the pan occasionally.

2 Pour in 1.5 litres/2½ pints/6¼ cups water. Bring to the boil, season and cover. Simmer for 20 minutes. Purée the soup. Return it to the pan. Add the milk and reheat gently, stirring.

3 Remove from the heat and stir in the crème fraîche and dill. Season and serve immediately.

Vegetable and Herb Chowder

A medley of fresh vegetables and herbs combine to make a delicious lunchtime soup.

Serves 4

25g/1oz/2 tbsp butter
1 onion, finely chopped
1 leek, finely sliced
1 celery stalk, diced
1 yellow or green (bell) pepper, seeded and diced
30ml/2 tbsp chopped fresh parsley
15ml/1 tbsp plain (all-purpose) flour
1.2 litres/2 pints/5 cups vegetable stock
350g/12oz potatoes, diced
a few sprigs of fresh thyme or 2.5ml/½ tsp dried thyme
1 bay leaf
115g/4oz/1 cup young runner (green) beans, thinly sliced on the diagonal
120ml/4fl oz/½ cup milk
salt and ground black pepper

1 Melt the butter in a heavy pan and add the onion, leek, celery, yellow or yellow or green pepper and parsley. Cover and cook gently over low heat until the vegetables are soft.

2 Stir in the flour until well blended. Slowly add the stock, stirring to combine. Bring to the boil, stirring frequently.

3 Add the potatoes, thyme and bay leaf. Bring back to the boil, reduce the heat and simmer, uncovered, for about 10 minutes.

4 Add the beans and simmer for a further 10–15 minutes until all the vegetables are tender.

5 Stir in the milk. Season with salt and pepper and heat through without boiling. Before serving, discard the thyme stalks and bay leaf. Serve hot.

Cook's Tip
For a super-hearty winter's meal, serve bought falafel (chickpea balls or fritters) or onion bhaji in the soup. Heat the balls according to the packet instructions, then add two or three to each bowl of soup and serve immediately.

Winter Vegetable: Energy 105kcal/441kJ; Protein 3.4g; Carbohydrate 15.4g, of which sugars 8.2g; Fat 3.7g, of which saturates 0.6g; Cholesterol 0mg; Calcium 56mg; Fibre 3.9g; Sodium 23mg.
Gingered Vegetable: Energy 167kcal/700kJ; Protein 4g; Carbohydrate 20.6g, of which sugars 11.4g; Fat 8.3g, of which saturates 3.2g; Cholesterol 11mg; Calcium 105mg; Fibre 3.8g; Sodium 45mg.
Vegetable and Herb: Energy 172kcal/723kJ; Protein 4.9g; Carbohydrate 24.9g, of which sugars 8g; Fat 6.6g, of which saturates 3.8g; Cholesterol 15mg; Calcium 80mg; Fibre 3.7g; Sodium 68mg.

Pumpkin and Parsnip Soup

The textures of carrot, parsnip and pumpkin go so very well together, making a soup that is wonderfully rich in texture and flavour.

Serves 4

15ml/1 tbsp olive or sunflower oil
15g/½oz/1 tbsp butter
1 onion, chopped
225g/8oz carrots, chopped
225g/8oz parsnips, chopped
225g/8oz pumpkin
about 900ml/1½ pints/3¾ cups vegetable stock
lemon juice, to taste
salt and ground black pepper

For the garnish

7.5ml/1½ tsp olive oil
½ garlic clove, finely chopped
45ml/3 tbsp chopped fresh parsley and coriander (cilantro), mixed
a good pinch of paprika

1 Heat the oil and butter in a large pan and fry the onion for about 3 minutes until softened, stirring occasionally. Add the carrots and parsnips, stir well, cover and cook over a gentle heat for a further 5 minutes.

2 Cut the pumpkin into chunks, discarding the skin and pith, and stir into the pan. Cover and cook for a further 5 minutes, then add the stock and seasoning, and slowly bring to the boil. Reduce the heat if necessary. Cover the pan and simmer the soup for 35–40 minutes until the vegetables are tender.

3 Allow the soup to cool slightly, then pour it into a food processor or blender and purée until smooth. Add a little extra stock or water if the soup seems too thick. Pour the soup back into the rinsed-out pan and reheat gently.

4 To make the garnish, heat the oil in a small pan and fry the garlic and herbs for 1–2 minutes. Add the paprika and stir well.

5 Taste the soup and adjust the seasoning, then stir in lemon juice to taste. Pour the soup into bowls and spoon a little of the prepared garnish on each portion. Carefully swirl the garnish through the soup using a skewer or cocktail stick (toothpick), or the point of a knife. Serve immediately.

Roasted Pumpkin Soup

The pumpkin is roasted whole, then split open and scooped out to make this real treat of a soup.

Serves 6–8

1.5kg/3–3½lb pumpkin
90ml/6 tbsp olive oil
2 onions, chopped
3 garlic cloves, chopped
7.5cm/3in piece fresh root ginger, grated
5ml/1 tsp ground coriander
2.5ml/½ tsp ground turmeric
pinch of cayenne pepper
1 litre/1¾ pints/4 cups vegetable stock
salt and ground black pepper
15ml/1 tbsp sesame seeds and fresh coriander leaves (cilantro) to garnish

For the pumpkin crisps

wedge of fresh pumpkin, seeded
120ml/4fl oz/½ cup olive oil

1 Preheat the oven to 200°C/400°F/Gas 6. Prick the pumpkin on top several times. Brush with plenty of the oil and bake for 45 minutes or until tender. Leave until cool enough to handle.

2 Taking care as there may be hot steam inside, split and scoop out the pumpkin, discarding the seeds. Chop the flesh.

3 Heat 60ml/4 tbsp of the remaining oil in a large pan. Add the onions, garlic and ginger. Cook for 4–5 minutes, then stir in the coriander, turmeric and cayenne, and cook for 2 minutes. Stir in the pumpkin and stock. Bring to the boil, reduce the heat and simmer for 20 minutes.

4 Cool the soup slightly, then purée it in a food processor or blender until smooth. Return the soup to the rinsed-out pan and season well.

5 Meanwhile, prepare the pumpkin crisps. Using a swivel-blade potato peeler, pare long thin strips off the wedge of pumpkin. Heat the oil in a small pan and fry the pumpkin strips in batches for 2–3 minutes, until crisp. Drain on kitchen paper.

6 Reheat the soup and ladle it into bowls. Top with the pumpkin crisps and garnish each portion with sesame seeds and coriander leaves. Serve immediately.

Pumpkin and Parsnip: Energy 137kcal/568kJ; Protein 2.3g; Carbohydrate 14.3g, of which sugars 9.5g; Fat 8.2g, of which saturates 2.7g; Cholesterol 8mg; Calcium 83mg; Fibre 5.3g; Sodium 47mg.
Roasted Pumpkin Soup: Energy 203kcal/839kJ; Protein 2.3g; Carbohydrate 8.3g, of which sugars 6.2g; Fat 18.1g, of which saturates 2.7g; Cholesterol 0mg; Calcium 82mg; Fibre 2.8g; Sodium 2mg.

Curried Pumpkin and Leek Soup

Ginger and cumin give this Middle-Eastern pumpkin soup a terrifically warm and spicy flavour. It makes a hearty, full-flavoured meal.

Serves 4

900g/2lb pumpkin, peeled and seeds removed
30ml/2 tbsp extra virgin olive oil
2 leeks, sliced
1 garlic clove, crushed
5ml/1 tsp ground ginger
5ml/1 tsp ground cumin
900ml/1½ pints/3¾ cups vegetable stock
salt and ground black pepper
coriander (cilantro) leaves, to garnish
60ml/4 tbsp Greek (strained plain) yogurt, to serve

1 Cut the pumpkin flesh into evenly sized chunks. Heat the oil in a large pan and add the leeks and garlic. Cover and cook gently, stirring occasionally, for about 15 minutes, until the vegetables are softened.

2 Add the ground ginger and cumin and cook, stirring, for a further 1 minute. Add the pumpkin chunks and the chicken stock and season with salt and pepper. Bring the mixture to the boil, reduce the heat and cover the pan. Then simmer for 30 minutes, or until the pumpkin is tender.

3 Process the soup, in batches if necessary, in a food processor or blender until smooth. Then return it to the rinsed-out pan.

4 Reheat the soup gently, and ladle out into four warmed individual bowls. Add a spoonful of Greek yogurt on the top of each and swirl it through the top layer of soup. Garnish with chopped fresh coriander leaves.

Variations

- *Use marrow (large zucchini) instead of pumpkin and replace half the stock with coconut milk.*
- *For a slighty spicy twist, add 1 seeded and chopped fresh green chilli to the yogurt before swirling it into the soup.*
- *Use double the ginger and omit the cumin.*

Pumpkin and Coconut Soup with Fluffy White Rice

This simple, yet punchy, winter soup is rich with coconut balanced by an intriguing hint of sugar and spice. Just firm, but still fluffy, white rice provides an unusual garnish, but it is the perfect contrast for the silken texture of this soup. Following the amount given here, you should have just enough left over to serve as an accompaniment.

Serves 4

about 1.1kg/2lb 7oz pumpkin
750ml/1¼ pints/3 cups vegetable stock
750ml/1¼ pints/3 cups coconut milk
10–15ml/2–3 tsp sugar
115g/4oz/1 cup white rice
salt and ground black pepper
5ml/1 tsp ground cinnamon, to garnish

1 Remove any seeds or strands of fibre from the pumpkin, cut off the peel and chop the flesh. Put the prepared pumpkin in a pan and add the stock, coconut milk, sugar and seasoning.

2 Bring to the boil, reduce the heat and cover. Simmer for about 20 minutes, until the pumpkin is tender. Purée the soup in a food processor or blender. Return it to the rinsed-out pan.

3 Place the rice in a pan and rinse it in several changes of cold water. Then drain in a sieve (strainer) and return it to the pan. Add plenty of fresh cold water to cover and bring to the boil. Stir once, reduce the heat and simmer for 15 minutes, until the grains are tender. Drain in a sieve.

4 Reheat the soup and taste it for seasoning, then ladle into bowls. Spoon a little rice into each portion and dust with cinnamon. Serve immediately, offering more rice at the table.

Variations

Use butternut squash in place of pumpkin, and brown rice in place of white rice, if preferred.

Pumpkin and Leek Soup: Energy 98kcal/409kJ; Protein 3g; Carbohydrate 7.5g, of which sugars 5.8g; Fat 6.4g, of which saturates 1.1g; Cholesterol 0mg; Calcium 86mg; Fibre 4.2g; Sodium 2mg.
Pumpkin and Coconut: Energy 148kcal/627kJ; Protein 8.8g; Carbohydrate 20.7g, of which sugars 13.5g; Fat 4g, of which saturates 2.3g; Cholesterol 11mg; Calcium 308mg; Fibre 2.8g; Sodium 81mg.

Corn and Potato Chowder

This creamy, yet chunky, soup is filled with the sweet taste of corn. Punchy Cheddar cheese rounds off the fabulous flavour.

Serves 4

1 onion, chopped
1 garlic clove, crushed
1 baking potato, chopped
2 celery sticks, sliced
1 small green (bell) pepper, seeded, halved and sliced
30ml/2 tbsp sunflower oil
25g/1oz/2 tbsp butter
600ml/1 pint/2½ cups vegetable stock or water
300ml/½ pint/1¼ cups milk
200g/7oz can flageolet (small cannellini) beans
300g/11oz can corn
good pinch of dried sage or a few small fresh sage leaves
salt and ground black pepper
Cheddar cheese or Monterey Jack, grated, to serve

1 Put the onion, garlic, potato, celery and green pepper into a large heavy-based pan with the oil and butter.

2 Heat until the ingredients are sizzling, then reduce the heat to low. Cover and cook gently for about 10 minutes, shaking the pan occasionally.

3 Pour in the stock or water, season with salt and pepper and bring to the boil. Reduce the heat, cover again and simmer gently for about 15 minutes or until the vegetables are tender.

4 Add the milk, beans and corn, including the liquor from the cans. Stir in the dried or fresh sage. Heat until simmering, then cook gently, uncovered, for 5 minutes. Check the seasoning before ladling the chowder into bowls. Sprinkle with cheese and serve immediately.

Variations

- *Chickpeas are delicious with corn – add a can as well as the flageolet (small cannellini), or use them instead of the flageolet.*
- *For refreshingly spicy, zesty flavour, peel and chop a large chunk of fresh root ginger and cook it with the vegetables. Then add the grated rind of one lemon with the sage.*

Corn and Red Chilli Chowder

Sweetcorn and chillies are traditional buddies, and here the cool combination of creamed corn and milk is the perfect foil for the raging heat of the chillies.

Serves 6

2 tomatoes, skinned
1 onion, roughly chopped
375g/13oz can creamed corn
2 red (bell) peppers, halved and seeded
15ml/1 tbsp olive oil, plus extra for brushing
3 fresh red chillies, seeded and chopped
2 garlic cloves, chopped
5ml/1 tsp ground cumin
5ml/1 tsp ground coriander
600ml/1 pint/2½ cups milk
350ml/12fl oz/1½ cups vegetable stock
3 cobs of corn, kernels removed
450g/1lb potatoes, finely diced
60ml/4 tbsp double (heavy) cream
60ml/4 tbsp chopped fresh parsley
salt and ground black pepper

1 Process the tomatoes and onion in a food processor or blender to a smooth purée. Add the creamed corn and process again, then set aside. Preheat the grill to high.

2 Put the peppers, skin sides up, on a grill rack (broiler) and brush with oil. Grill for 8–10 minutes, until the skins blacken and blister. Transfer to a bowl and cover with clear film (plastic wrap), then leave to cool. Peel and dice the peppers, then set them aside.

3 Heat the oil in a large pan and add the chopped chillies and garlic. Cook, stirring, for 2–3 minutes, until softened.

4 Add the ground cumin and coriander, and cook for a further 1 minute. Stir in the sweetcorn purée and cook for about 8 minutes, stirring occasionally.

5 Pour in the milk and stock, then stir in the corn kernels, potatoes, red pepper and seasoning to taste. Cook for 15–20 minutes, until the corn and potatoes are tender.

6 Pour the soup into deep bowls and add the cream, pouring it slowly into the middles of the bowls. Scatter with the chopped parsley and serve at once.

Corn and Potato: Energy 320kcal/1347kJ; Protein 9.4g; Carbohydrate 43.2g, of which sugars 15.7g; Fat 13.5g, of which saturates 5g; Cholesterol 18mg; Calcium 119mg; Fibre 5g; Sodium 500mg.
Corn and Chilli: Energy 294kcal/1241kJ; Protein 8.9g; Carbohydrate 47.8g, of which sugars 20.8g; Fat 8.9g, of which saturates 4.8g; Cholesterol 20mg; Calcium 168mg; Fibre 4.2g; Sodium 299mg.

Mixed Mushroom Soup

This intense mushroom soup is delicious with little boiled potatoes on the side, to cut up and add as desired. The tart flavours of pickled cucumber, capers and lemon add extra bite to this rich mushroom medley.

Serves 4

2 onions, chopped
1.2 litres/2 pints/5 cups vegetable stock
450g/1lb mixed mushrooms, sliced
25ml/1½ tbsp tomato purée (paste)
1 pickled cucumber, or dill pickle, chopped
1 bay leaf
15ml/1 tbsp capers in brine, drained
pinch of salt
6 peppercorns, crushed
675g/1½lb baby new potatoes
a little butter

For the garnish

lemon rind curls
green olives
spring onions (scallions)
sprigs of flat leaf parsley

1 Put the onions in a large pan with 50ml/2fl oz/¼ cup of the stock. Cook, stirring occasionally, until the liquid has evaporated. Add the remaining vegetable stock with the sliced mushrooms. Bring to the boil, reduce the heat and cover the pan. Then simmer gently for 30 minutes.

2 In a small bowl, blend the tomato purée to a smooth, thin paste with about 30ml/2 tbsp of stock from the soup. Then stir the tomato mixture into the soup.

3 Add the pickled cucumber, bay leaf, capers, salt and peppercorns. Simmer the soup gently for another 10 minutes.

4 Meanwhile, place the potatoes in a pan and add water to cover. Bring to the boil, reduce the heat slightly and cook for about 10 minutes or until tender. Drain, place in a serving bowl and top with a little butter.

5 Ladle the soup into bowls. Sprinkle lemon rind curls, a few olives, sliced spring onions and a sprig of flat leaf parsley over each portion. Serve with the potatoes on the side.

Potato and Mushroom Soup

Using a mixture of mushrooms gives this soup character. This makes a flavoursome light meal when served with fresh crusty bread, or a superb appetizer served solo.

Serves 4–6 as a light meal or 6–8 as a soup course

20g/¾oz/1½ tbsp butter
15ml/1 tbsp oil
1 onion, roughly chopped
4 potatoes, about 250–350g/9–12oz, roughly chopped
350g/12oz mixed mushrooms, such as Paris Browns, field (portabello) and button (white), roughly chopped
1 or 2 garlic cloves, crushed
150ml/¼ pint/⅔ cup white wine or dry (hard) cider
1.2 litres/2 pints/5 cups vegetable stock
bunch of fresh parsley, chopped
salt and ground black pepper
whipped or sour cream, to garnish

1 Heat the butter and oil in a large pan, over medium heat. Add the onion and potatoes. Cover and sweat over a low heat for 5–10 minutes until softened but not browned.

2 Add the mushrooms, garlic and white wine or cider and stock. Season, bring to the boil and cook for 15 minutes, until all the ingredients are tender.

3 Put the mixture through a mouli-légumes (food mill), using the coarse blade, or purée in a food processor or blender.

4 Return the soup to the rinsed-out pan, and add three-quarters of the parsley. Reheat and taste for seasoning. Serve garnished with cream and the remaining parsley.

Variation

Mustard and tarragon together go very well with mushrooms. Add 15ml/1 tbsp wholegrain mustard to the onions and potatoes before stirring in the stock. For a hint of sweetness, use a medium sherry instead of the wine or cider, and add the leaves from a large sprig of fresh tarragon.

Mixed Mushroom Soup: Energy 54kcal/224kJ; Protein 3.4g; Carbohydrate 8.9g, of which sugars 6.4g; Fat 0.8g, of which saturates 0.1g; Cholesterol 0mg; Calcium 33mg; Fibre 2.8g; Sodium 18mg.
Potato and Mushroom: Energy 155kcal/648kJ; Protein 3.3g; Carbohydrate 13.6g, of which sugars 3.4g; Fat 7.6g, of which saturates 3.1g; Cholesterol 11mg; Calcium 23mg; Fibre 2.1g; Sodium 117mg.

Garlic Soup

This interesting and surprisingly subtly flavoured soup makes good use of an ingredient that is not only delicious but also has great health-giving properties. It certainly brings a great sense of well-being and is a real treat for garlic-lovers.

Serves 8

12 large garlic cloves, crushed
15ml/1 tbsp olive oil
15ml/1 tbsp melted butter
1 small onion, finely chopped
15g/½oz/2 tbsp plain (all-purpose) flour
15ml/1 tbsp white wine vinegar
1 litre/1¾ pints/4 cups vegetable stock
2 egg yolks
croûtons, to serve

1 Heat the oil and butter into a pan, add the garlic and onion, and cook them gently for 20 minutes, stirring occasionally.

2 Stir in the flour and make a smooth paste. Cook for a few minutes, stirring, without letting the mixture brown. Then stir in the wine vinegar, stock and 1 litre/1¾ pints/4 cups water. Bring to the boil, reduce the heat and cover the pan. Simmer gently for 30 minutes.

3 Just before serving, lightly whisk the egg yolks in a bowl. Remove the pan from the heat and add a ladleful of soup to the yolks. Stir with the whisk until the yolks are well mixed with the soup, then pour the mixture into the pan.

4 Heat the soup over low heat, stirring, for a few seconds but do not allow it to simmer or boil or the yolks will curdle. Put the croûtons into soup bowls and pour the hot soup over them, then serve immediately.

Cook's Tip

Once the yolks are added the soup is difficult to reheat from cold. If the whole batch is not going to be served, pour half into a pan and add just 1 egg yolk. Finish the rest when required.

Chestnut Mushroom Soup with Tarragon

This is a light mushroom soup, subtly flavoured with tarragon.

Serves 6

15g/½oz/1 tbsp butter
4 shallots, finely chopped
450g/1 lb chestnut mushrooms, finely chopped
300ml/½ pint/1¼ cups vegetable stock
300ml/½ pint/ 1¼ cups milk
15–30ml/1–2 tbsp chopped fresh tarragon
30ml/2 tbsp dry sherry (optional)
salt and ground black pepper
sprigs of fresh tarragon, to garnish

1 Melt the butter in a large pan, add the shallots and cook gently for 5 minutes, stirring occasionally. Add the mushrooms and continue to cook gently for 3 minutes, stirring.

2 Pour in the stock and milk, stirring. Bring to the boil, then reduce the heat and cover the pan. Simmer the soup gently for about 20 minutes or until the vegetables are soft.

3 Stir in the tarragon and season to taste with salt and pepper. Allow the soup to cool slightly, then purée it in a food processor or blender, in batches if necessary, until smooth. Return the soup to the rinsed-out pan and reheat gently.

4 Stir in the sherry, if using, then ladle the soup into warmed bowls and serve garnished with sprigs of tarragon.

Variations

- *Use a mild onion instead of the shallots. Add a bay leaf, a pinch of ground mace and a tiny pinch of ground cloves. Omit the milk but add single (light) cream when reheating.*
- *For a stronger flavour, use a mixture of wild and chestnut mushrooms, or add a few dried cultivated mushrooms.*
- *For a delicate soup, use pale button (white) mushrooms instead of the stronger chestnut variety. Use a little chopped fresh parsley and chopped fresh dill instead of the tarragon.*

Garlic Soup: Energy 55kcal/229kJ; Protein 1.3g; Carbohydrate 3g, of which sugars 0.5g; Fat 4.4g, of which saturates 1.6g; Cholesterol 54mg; Calcium 12mg; Fibre 0.3g; Sodium 50mg.
Mushroom with Tarragon: Energy 55kcal/230kJ; Protein 3.2g; Carbohydrate 3.5g, of which sugars 3.1g; Fat 3.3g, of which saturates 1.9g; Cholesterol 8mg; Calcium 68mg; Fibre 1g; Sodium 41mg.

French Onion Soup

This is perhaps the most famous of all onion soups.

Serves 6

50g/2oz/¼ cup butter
15ml/1 tbsp olive or groundnut (peanut) oil
2kg/4½lb onions, sliced
5ml/1 tsp chopped fresh thyme
5ml/1 tsp caster (superfine) sugar
15ml/1 tbsp sherry vinegar
1.5 litres/2½ pints/6¼ cups good vegetable stock
25ml/1½ tbsp plain (all-purpose) flour
150ml/¼ pint/⅔ cup dry white wine
45ml/3 tbsp brandy
salt and ground black pepper

For the croûtes

6–12 thick slices day-old French bread, about 2.5cm/1in thick
1 garlic clove, halved
15ml/1 tbsp French mustard
115g/4oz Gruyère cheese, grated

1 Heat the butter and oil in a large pan. Add the onions and stir. Cook over a medium heat for 5–8 minutes, stirring once or twice, until the onions begin to soften. Stir in the thyme. Reduce the heat to very low, cover and cook the onions for 20–30 minutes, stirring frequently, until very soft and golden.

2 Uncover the pan and increase the heat slightly. Stir in the sugar and cook for 5–10 minutes, until the onions start to brown. Add the sherry vinegar and increase the heat again, then continue cooking, stirring frequently, until the onions turn a deep, golden brown – this could take up to 20 minutes.

3 Bring the stock to the boil in another pan. Stir the flour into the onions and cook for 2 minutes, then gradually stir in the stock, wine, brandy and seasoning to taste. Bring to the boil, stirring, reduce the heat and simmer for 10–15 minutes.

4 For the croûtes, preheat the oven to 150°C/300°F/Gas 2. Place the bread on a greased baking tray and bake for 15–20 minutes, until lightly browned. Rub with the garlic and spread with mustard, then sprinkle with the cheese.

5 Preheat the grill on the hottest setting. Ladle the soup into six flameproof bowls. Add the croûtes and grill until the cheese melts, bubbles and browns. Serve immediately.

Garlic and Coriander Soup

A simple soup of Portuguese origin, this should be made with the best ingredients – plump garlic, fresh coriander, high-quality country bread and extra virgin olive oil.

Serves 6

25g/1oz fresh coriander (cilantro), leaves and stalks chopped separately
1.5 litres/2½ pints/6¼ cups vegetable stock, or water
5–6 plump garlic cloves, peeled
5ml/1 tsp vinegar
6 eggs
275g/10oz day-old bread, most of the crust removed, torn into bitesize pieces
salt and ground black pepper
90ml/6 tbsp extra virgin olive oil, plus extra to serve

1 Place the coriander stalks in a pan. Add the stock or water and bring to the boil. Lower the heat, cover and simmer for 10 minutes. Process the soup in a food processor or blender and then press it through a sieve (strainer) back into the rinsed-out pan.

2 Crush the garlic with 5ml/1 tsp salt in a mortar or small bowl. Stir in 120ml/4fl oz/½ cup of the hot soup and then pour the mixture back into the pan.

3 Meanwhile, poach the eggs: heat a large frying pan of water, adding the vinegar, until boiling. Crack an egg into a cup or saucer. Reduce the heat so that the water simmers, swirl the water and drop the egg into the middle of the swirl. Poach for 3–4 minutes, until just set. Add the remaining eggs in the same way. (Cook them in two batches if the pan is too small to hold all six at once.) Use a draining spoon to remove the eggs from the pan and transfer them to a warmed plate. Trim off any untidy bits of white with a sharp knife or scissors.

4 Bring the soup back to the boil and add seasoning. Stir in the chopped coriander leaves and remove from the heat.

5 Place the bread in six soup plates or bowls and drizzle the oil over it. Ladle in the soup and stir. Add a poached egg to each portion and serve immediately, offering olive oil at the table so that it can be drizzled over the soup to taste.

French Onion: Energy 415kcal/1745kJ; Protein 13g; Carbohydrate 61.6g, of which sugars 12.6g; Fat 14.1g, of which saturates 6.7g; Cholesterol 25mg; Calcium 240mg; Fibre 4.1g; Sodium 1022mg.
Garlic and Coriander: Energy 290kcal/1212kJ; Protein 10.9g; Carbohydrate 24.1g, of which sugars 1.4g; Fat 17.5g, of which saturates 3.1g; Cholesterol 190mg; Calcium 89mg; Fibre 1.2g; Sodium 310mg.

Sherried Onion Soup with Saffron

The Spanish combination of onions, sherry and saffron is delicious in this golden soup thickened with almonds. It is also good chilled, perhaps with a little extra salt and pepper, as chilling tends to suppress seasoning slightly.

Serves 4

40g/1½oz/3 tbsp butter
2 large onions, thinly sliced
1 small garlic clove, finely chopped
pinch of saffron threads
50g/2oz blanched almonds, toasted and finely ground
750ml/1¼ pints/3 cups vegetable stock
45ml/3 tbsp fino sherry
2.5ml/½ tsp paprika
salt and ground black pepper

For the garnish

30ml/2 tbsp flaked or slivered almonds, toasted
chopped fresh parsley

1 Melt the butter in a heavy pan over a low heat. Add the onions and garlic, and stir for about a minute to ensure that they are thoroughly coated in the melted butter.

2 Cover the pan and cook the onions very gently, stirring frequently, for about 20 minutes, until they are soft and golden.

3 Add the saffron threads to the pan and cook, uncovered, for 3–4 minutes. Add the almonds and cook, stirring constantly, for a further 2–3 minutes.

4 Pour in the stock and sherry with 5ml/1 tsp salt and the paprika. Season with plenty of black pepper. Bring to the boil, stirring, then lower the heat, cover the pan and simmer gently for about 10 minutes.

5 Pour the soup into a food processor or blender and process until smooth, then return it to the rinsed-out pan. Reheat gently, without allowing the soup to boil, stirring occasionally. Taste for seasoning, adding more salt and pepper if required.

6 Ladle the soup into bowls. Garnish with the toasted flaked or slivered almonds and add a little chopped fresh parsley, then serve immediately.

Leek Soup with Feta

Flavoured with dill and topped with crumbled white feta cheese, this Turkish-style leek soup is deliciously different. Serve with chunks of fresh, crusty bread as an appetizer, or as a light meal on its own. The butter is optional, but enriches the soup beautifully.

Serves 3–4

30ml/2 tbsp olive or sunflower oil
3 leeks, roughly chopped
1 onion, chopped
5ml/1 tsp sugar
bunch of fresh dill, chopped
300ml/½ pint/1¼ cups milk
15ml/1 tbsp butter (optional)
115g/4oz feta cheese, crumbled
salt and ground black pepper
paprika and dill, to garnish

1 Heat the oil in a heavy pan and stir in the leeks and onion. Cook for about 10 minutes, or until the vegetables are soft.

2 Add the sugar and dill, and pour in 600ml/1 pint/2½ cups water. Bring to the boil, lower the heat and cover the pan. Simmer for about 15 minutes. Leave the soup to cool a little, then purée in a blender until smooth.

3 Return the soup to the rinsed-out pan, pour in the milk and reheat gently without allowing the soup to boil. Season with a little salt and plenty of ground black pepper, bearing in mind that the feta is salty. If using the butter, drop it on to the surface of the soup and let it melt.

4 Ladle the soup into bowls and top with the crumbled feta. Serve immediately, garnished with a little paprika and dill fronds.

Cook's Tips

- *The saltiness and punchy flavour of feta is excellent in this soup. Roquefort, Danish blue, Pecorino or Parmesan cheese can be used for a different, but equally full, flavour.*
- *Cheese freezes well (feta and other types), and is particularly useful diced or crumbled. This way, it thaws quickly and can be used for topping a wide variety of vegetarian soups, bringing food value and flavour.*

Sherried Onion: Energy 255kcal/1054kJ; Protein 5.8g; Carbohydrate 11.5g, of which sugars 8.1g; Fat 19.6g, of which saturates 6.1g; Cholesterol 21mg; Calcium 82mg; Fibre 3.2g; Sodium 68mg.
Leek with Feta: Energy 205kcal/853kJ; Protein 8.2g; Carbohydrate 7.9g, of which sugars 2.2g; Fat 15.7g, of which saturates 9.9g; Cholesterol 40mg; Calcium 188mg; Fibre 2.2g; Sodium 347mg.

Leek and Cheese Soup

The cheese is an integral part of this substantial Irish soup, which makes full use of ingredients that have always been important in the country's cooking. It can be a good way to use up cheese left over from the cheeseboard. Serve with freshly baked brown bread.

Serves 6
3 large leeks
50g/2oz/¼ cup butter
30ml/2 tbsp oil
115g/4oz farmhouse cheese, such as Cashel Blue
15g/½oz/2 tbsp plain (all-purpose) flour
15ml/1 tbsp wholegrain mustard, or to taste
1.5 litres/2½ pints/6¼ cups vegetable stock
ground black pepper

For the garnish
50g/2oz cheese, grated
snipped chives or chopped spring onion (scallion) greens

1 Slice the leeks thinly. Heat the butter and oil together in a large heavy pan and add the leeks. Cover and cook gently for 10–15 minutes, until the leeks are just softened but not brown.

2 Grate the cheese coarsely and add it to the pan, stirring over a low heat, until it is melted. Add the flour and cook for 2 minutes, stirring constantly with a wooden spoon, then add ground black pepper and wholegrain mustard to taste.

3 Gradually add the stock, stirring constantly to blend it in well, and bring the soup to the boil.

4 Reduce the heat, cover and simmer very gently for about 15 minutes. Check the seasoning and serve the soup garnished with the extra grated cheese and chives or spring onion greens. Offer plenty of fresh bread with the soup.

Variation
Any melting cheese can be used – to retain the Irish flavour, try Cooleeney, a soft white cheese from County Tipperary, or St Killian or Milleens, from West Cork.

Leek and Potato Soup

This is a hearty Scottish staple and a widely travelled soup, served as everything from a warming lunch to a hot drink from a flask on a cold winter's walk. The chopped vegetables produce a chunky soup. If you prefer a smooth texture, press the mixture through a sieve.

Serves 4
50g/2oz/¼ cup butter
2 leeks, chopped
1 small onion, finely chopped
350g/12oz potatoes, peeled and chopped
900ml/1½ pints/3¾ cups vegetable stock
salt and ground black pepper
chopped fresh parsley, to garnish
warmed bread, to serve

1 Heat 25g/1oz/2 tbsp of the butter in a large pan over a medium heat. Add the leeks and onion and cook gently, stirring occasionally, for about 7 minutes, until the vegetables are softened but not browned.

2 Add the potatoes to the pan and cook for about 2–3 minutes, then add the stock and bring to the boil. Reduce the heat, cover and simmer for 30–35 minutes.

3 Season the soup to taste and remove the pan from the heat. Dice the remaining butter and stir it into the soup until it has just melted. Ladle the soup into bowls. Serve immediately, garnished with the chopped parsley, with generous chunks of warm, fresh bread.

Cook's Tips
- *Don't use a food processor or blender to purée this soup as it can give the potatoes a gluey consistency. The potatoes should be left to crumble and disintegrate naturally as they boil, making the consistency of the soup thicker the longer you leave them.*
- *Make a full-flavoured vegetable stock by simmering peelings and trimmings, as well as onions, celery, carrots and other vegetables in water for 2 hours and straining the liquid.*

Leek and Potato Soup: Energy 179kcal/747kJ; Protein 3.2g; Carbohydrate 17.9g, of which sugars 4g; Fat 11g, of which saturates 6.7g; Cholesterol 27mg; Calcium 32mg; Fibre 3g; Sodium 88mg.
Leek and Cheese: Energy 187kcal/773kJ; Protein 5.6g; Carbohydrate 4.3g, of which sugars 1.9g; Fat 16.6g, of which saturates 8.6g; Cholesterol 32mg; Calcium 118mg; Fibre 1.8g; Sodium 407mg.

Parsnip and Apple Soup

Choose a sharp apple juice to complement the sweetness of the parsnips and the warmth of the spices in this tempting soup.

Serves 4–6

25g/1oz/2 tbsp butter
1 onion, finely chopped
1 garlic clove, finely chopped
500g/1¼lb parsnips, thinly sliced
5ml/1 tsp curry paste or powder
300ml/½ pint/1¼ cups apple juice
600ml/1 pint/2½ cups vegetable stock
300ml/½ pint/1¼ cups milk
salt and ground black pepper
thick natural yogurt, to serve
chopped fresh herbs such as mint or parsley, to serve

1 Melt the butter in a large pan and add the onion, garlic and parsnips. Cook gently, without browning, for about 10 minutes, stirring often.

2 Add the curry paste or powder and cook, stirring, for 1 minute. Pour in the apple juice and stock and bring to the boil. Reduce the heat, cover the pan and simmer gently for about 20 minutes or until the parsnips are soft.

3 Process or blend the soup until smooth and return it to the rinsed-out pan. Stir in the milk and season to taste with salt and pepper. Reheat the soup gently, without boiling, and serve topped with a spoonful of yogurt and a sprinkling of herbs.

Variations

- *Omit the curry paste or powder and season the soup with a little cinnamon and freshly grated nutmeg, adding it at the beginning of cooking to give an integrated, mellow flavour.*
- *Instead of apple juice, peel, core and finely chop 4 eating apples and cook them with the onion. Replace the juice with extra stock.*
- *Add a fruity garnish to the soup – core and thinly slice a red-skinned eating apple and sprinkle over the soup before adding the chives.*
- *Garnish with toasted cashew nuts and chives.*

Irish Potato Soup

This most Irish of all soups is not only excellent as it is, but versatile too, as it can be used as a base for numerous other soups. For the best results, use a floury potato, such as Golden Wonder.

Serves 6–8

50g/2oz/¼ cup butter
2 large onions, finely chopped
675g/1½lb potatoes, diced
about 1.75 litres/3 pints/7½ cups vegetable stock
sea salt and ground black pepper
a little milk, if necessary
snipped fresh chives, to garnish

1 Melt the butter in a large heavy pan and add the onions, turning them in the butter until well coated. Cover and leave to sweat over a very low heat.

2 Add the potatoes to the pan, and mix well with the butter and onions. Season with salt and pepper, cover and cook over a gentle heat for about 10 minutes, without browning. Add the stock, bring to the boil and simmer for 20–30 minutes, or until the vegetables are tender.

3 Remove from the heat and allow to cool slightly. Purée the soup in batches in a food processor or blender.

4 Reheat over a low heat and adjust the seasoning. If the soup seems too thick, add a little extra stock or milk to achieve the required consistency. Serve very hot, sprinkled with chives.

Variations

- *Add 2 leeks to make a leek and potato soup.*
- *Add a bunch of watercress 10 minutes before the end of the simmering time.*
- *Finely chop a large bunch of fresh parsley and add to the soup when it is reheated.*
- *Add 1 small cauliflower, broken up, with the potatoes and season with a little freshly grated nutmeg before serving.*

Irish Potato Soup: Energy 178kcal/746kJ; Protein 3.5g; Carbohydrate 26.1g, of which sugars 5.4g; Fat 7.4g, of which saturates 4.3g; Cholesterol 18mg; Calcium 29mg; Fibre 2.6g; Sodium 328mg.
Parsnip and Apple: Energy 130kcal/548kJ; Protein 3.4g; Carbohydrate 18.5g, of which sugars 12.6g; Fat 5.3g, of which saturates 2.9g; Cholesterol 12mg; Calcium 101mg; Fibre 4g; Sodium 56mg.

Curried Parsnip Soup

The mild sweetness of parsnips and mango chutney is given an exciting lift with a blend of spices in this simple soup.

Serves 4

30ml/2 tbsp olive oil
1 onion, chopped
1 garlic clove, crushed
1 small green chilli, seeded and finely chopped
15ml/1 tbsp grated fresh root ginger
5 large parsnips, diced
5ml/1 tsp cumin seeds
5ml/1 tsp ground coriander
2.5ml/½ tsp ground turmeric
30ml/2 tbsp mango chutney
1.2 litres/2 pints/5 cups water
juice of 1 lime
salt and ground black pepper
60ml/4 tbsp natural (plain) yogurt and mango chutney, to serve
chopped fresh coriander (cilantro), to garnish (optional)

For the sesame naan croûtons

45ml/3 tbsp olive oil
1 large naan, cut into small dice
15ml/1 tbsp sesame seeds

1 Heat the oil in a large pan and add the onion, garlic, chilli and ginger. Cook for 4–5 minutes, until the onion has softened. Add the parsnips and cook for 2–3 minutes. Sprinkle in the cumin seeds, coriander and turmeric, and cook for 1 minute, stirring.

2 Add the chutney and the water. Season well and bring to the boil. Reduce the heat, cover and simmer for 15 minutes, until the parsnips are soft.

3 Cool the soup slightly, then purée it in a food processor or blender and return it to the pan. Stir in the lime juice.

4 To make the naan croûtons, heat the oil in a large frying pan and cook the diced naan for 3–4 minutes, stirring, until golden all over. Remove from the heat and drain off any excess oil. Add the sesame seeds and return the pan to the heat for no more than 30 seconds, until the seeds are pale golden.

5 Ladle the soup into bowls. Spoon a little yogurt into each portion, then top with a little mango chutney and some of the sesame naan croûton mixture. Garnish with chopped fresh coriander, if you like.

Potato Soup with Garlic Samosas

Soup and samosas are the ideal partners. Bought samosas are given an easy, but clever, flavour lift in this simple recipe.

Serves 4

60ml/4 tbsp sunflower oil
10ml/2 tsp black mustard seeds
1 large onion, chopped
1 fresh red chilli, seeded and chopped
2.5ml/½ tsp ground turmeric
1.5ml/¼ tsp cayenne pepper
900g/2lb potatoes, cut into cubes
4 fresh curry leaves
750ml/1¼ pint/3 cups vegetable stock
225g/8oz spinach leaves, torn if large
400ml/14fl oz/1⅔ cups coconut milk
handful of fresh coriander leaves (cilantro)
salt and black pepper

For the garlic samosas

1 large garlic clove, crushed
25g/1oz/2 tbsp butter
6 vegetable samosas

1 Heat the oil in a large pan. Add the mustard seeds, cover and cook until they begin to pop. Add the onion and chilli and cook for 5–6 minutes, until softened.

2 Stir in the turmeric, cayenne, potatoes, curry leaves and stock. Bring to the boil, reduce the heat and cover the pan. Simmer for 15 minutes, stirring occasionally, until the potatoes are tender.

3 Meanwhile, prepare the samosas. Preheat the oven to 180°C/350°F/Gas 4. Melt the butter with the garlic in a small pan, stirring and crushing the garlic into the butter.

4 Place the samosas on an ovenproof dish – a gratin dish or quiche dish is ideal. Brush them lightly with the butter, turn them over and brush with the remaining butter. Heat through in the oven for about 5 minutes, until piping hot.

5 Add the spinach to the soup and cook for 5 minutes. Stir in the coconut milk and cook for a further 5 minutes.

6 Season and add the coriander leaves before ladling the soup into bowls. Serve with the garlic samosas.

Curried Parsnip: Energy 150kcal/623kJ; Protein 4.7g; Carbohydrate 7.8g, of which sugars 6.8g; Fat 11.4g, of which saturates 7g; Cholesterol 32mg; Calcium 170mg; Fibre 0.8g; Sodium 112mg.
Potato with Samosas: Energy 658kcal/2744kJ; Protein 8.8g; Carbohydrate 63.4g, of which sugars 15.5g; Fat 42.8g, of which saturates 5.1g; Cholesterol 13mg; Calcium 184mg; Fibre 5.9g; Sodium 375mg.

Roasted Garlic and Butternut Soup with Tomato Salsa

Hot and spicy tomato salsa gives bite to this sweet squash and garlic soup.

Serves 4–5

2 garlic bulbs, outer skin removed
a few fresh thyme sprigs
75ml/5 tbsp olive oil
1 large butternut squash, halved and seeded
2 onions, chopped
5ml/1 tsp ground coriander
1.2 litres/2 pints/5 cups vegetable stock
30–45ml/2–3 tbsp chopped fresh oregano or marjoram
salt and ground black pepper

For the salsa

4 large ripe tomatoes, halved and seeded
1 red (bell) pepper, seeded
1 large fresh red chilli, halved and seeded
30ml/2 tbsp extra virgin olive oil
15ml/1 tbsp balsamic vinegar
pinch of caster (superfine) sugar

1 Preheat the oven to 220°C/425°F/Gas 7. Wrap the garlic and thyme, drizzled with half the oil, in foil. Place on a baking sheet. Add the squash, brushing with 15ml/1 tbsp of the remaining oil. Add the tomatoes, pepper and chilli for the salsa. Roast the vegetables for 25 minutes. Remove the tomatoes, pepper and chilli. Reduce the setting to 190°C/ 375°F/Gas 5 and cook the squash and garlic for 20–25 minutes more.

2 Heat the remaining oil gently in a pan. Cook the onions and coriander for 10 minutes, until soft and beginning to brown. Squeeze the roasted garlic out into the onions and scoop the squash out of its skin into the pan. Add the stock, salt and pepper. Bring to the boil, then simmer for 10 minutes.

3 Skin the pepper and chilli, then process them in a food processor or blender with the tomatoes and the oil for the salsa. Stir in the vinegar, seasoning and sugar.

4 Stir half the fresh oregano or marjoram into the soup and purée until smooth. Reheat without boiling, then season and ladle into bowls. Top with salsa, sprinkle with the remaining oregano or marjoram, and serve.

Roast Vegetable Medley

Winter meets summer in this soup recipe for chunky roasted roots. Serve it with bread baked with a hint of added summer flavour in the form of sun-dried tomatoes.

Serves 4

4 parsnips, quartered lengthways
2 red onions, cut into thin wedges
4 carrots, thickly sliced
2 leeks, thickly sliced
1 small swede (rutabaga), cut into chunks
4 potatoes, cut into chunks
60ml/4 tbsp olive oil
few sprigs of fresh thyme
1 bulb garlic, broken into cloves, unpeeled
1 litre/1¾ pints/4 cups vegetable stock
salt and ground black pepper
fresh thyme sprigs, to garnish

For the sun-dried tomato bread

1 ciabatta loaf
75g/3oz/6 tbsp butter, softened
1 garlic clove, crushed
4 sun-dried tomatoes, finely chopped
30ml/2 tbsp chopped fresh parsley

1 Preheat the oven to 200°C/400°F/Gas 6. Cut the thick ends of the parsnip quarters into four, then place them in a large roasting pan. Add the onions, carrots, leeks, swede and potatoes, and spread them in an even layer.

2 Drizzle the olive oil over the vegetables. Add the thyme and unpeeled garlic cloves. Toss well and roast for 45 minutes, until all the vegetables are tender and slightly charred.

3 To make the sun-dried tomato bread, slice the loaf, without cutting right through. Mix the butter, garlic, sun-dried tomatoes and parsley. Spread the butter between the slices. Wrap in foil. Bake for 15 minutes, opening the foil for the last 4–5 minutes.

4 Discard the thyme from the vegetables. Squeeze the garlic from its skins over the vegetables and purée half the mixture with the stock. Pour into a pan. Add the remaining vegetables. Bring to the boil and season well.

5 Ladle the soup into bowls and garnish with fresh thyme leaves. Serve the hot bread with the soup.

Garlic and Butternut: Energy 238kcal/986kJ; Protein 2.9g; Carbohydrate 11.9g, of which sugars 10.3g; Fat 20.2g, of which saturates 3.1g; Cholesterol 0mg; Calcium 79mg; Fibre 4.1g; Sodium 11mg.
Vegetable Medley: Energy 511kcal/2146kJ; Protein 13.9g; Carbohydrate 72.6g, of which sugars 18.9g; Fat 20.4g, of which saturates 10.6g; Cholesterol 40mg; Calcium 218mg; Fibre 12.1g; Sodium 521mg.

Borscht

Beetroot is the main ingredient of borscht. Its flavour and colour dominate this well-known soup.

Serves 4–6

900g/2lb uncooked beetroot, peeled
2 carrots, peeled
2 celery sticks
40g/1½oz/3 tbsp butter
2 onions, sliced
2 garlic cloves, crushed
4 tomatoes, peeled, seeded and chopped
1 bay leaf
1 large parsley sprig
2 cloves
4 whole peppercorns
1.2 litres/2 pints/5 cups vegetable stock
150ml/¼ pint/⅔ cup beetroot juice or the liquid from pickled beetroot
vinegar, to taste
sugar, to taste
salt and ground black pepper

For serving
sour cream
snipped fresh chives or dill

1 Cut the beetroot, carrots and celery into fairly thick strips. Melt the butter in a large pan and cook the onions over a low heat for 5 minutes, stirring occasionally.

2 Add the beetroot, carrots and celery and cook for a further 5 minutes, stirring occasionally.

3 Add the garlic and chopped tomatoes to the pan and cook, stirring, for 2 more minutes.

4 Place the bay leaf, parsley, cloves and peppercorns in a piece of muslin (cheesecloth) and tie with string. Add the muslin bag to the pan with the stock. Bring to the boil, reduce the heat, cover and simmer for 1¼ hours, or until the vegetables are very tender.

5 Discard the bag. Stir in the beetroot juice and season. Add sugar and vineger to taste, creating a sweet-sour balance. Bring to the boil.

6 Ladle the soup into bowls and serve with sour cream sprinkled with chives or dill.

Sweet-and-Sour Vegetable Borscht

There are many variations of this classic and colourful Eastern European soup: this one includes plentiful amounts of cabbage, tomatoes and potatoes, and it is served piping hot.

Serves 6

1 onion, chopped
1 carrot, chopped
4–6 raw or plain cooked beetroot, 3–4 diced and 1–2 coarsely grated
400g/14oz can tomatoes
4–6 new potatoes, cut into bitesize pieces
1 small white cabbage, thinly sliced
1 litre/1¾ pints/4 cups vegetable stock
45ml/3 tbsp sugar
30–45ml/2–3 tbsp white wine or cider (apple) vinegar
45ml/3 tbsp chopped fresh dill, plus extra to garnish
salt and ground black pepper
sour cream, to garnish
buttered rye bread, to serve

1 Put the onion, carrot, diced beetroot, tomatoes, potatoes and cabbage in a large pan. Pour in the stock and bring to the boil. Reduce the heat and cover the pan. Simmer the soup for about 30 minutes, or until the potatoes are tender.

2 Add the grated beetroot, sugar, wine or vinegar to the soup and continue to cook for 10 minutes.

3 Taste for a good sweet–sour balance and add more sugar and/or vinegar if necessary. Season to taste.

4 To serve, stir in the chopped dill and ladle the soup into bowls. Garnish each portion with sour cream and more dill. Serve with rye bread.

Variation
To make meat borscht, place 1kg/2¼lb chopped beef in a large pan. Pour over water to cover and crumble in 1 beef stock (bouillon) cube. Bring to the boil, then reduce the heat and simmer until tender. Skim any fat from the surface, then add the vegetables and proceed as above.

Borscht: Energy 137kcal/574kJ; Protein 3.7g; Carbohydrate 18.2g, of which sugars 16.3g; Fat 6g, of which saturates 3.6g; Cholesterol 14mg; Calcium 55mg; Fibre 4.6g; Sodium 157mg.
Sweet-and-Sour Borscht: Energy 46kcal/196kJ; Protein 1.6g; Carbohydrate 9.8g, of which sugars 6.4g; Fat 0.4g, of which saturates 0.1g; Cholesterol 0mg; Calcium 22mg; Fibre 1.9g; Sodium 29mg.

Country Vegetable Soup

Soup-making is a good way to make the most of seasonal vegetables. It is also a great way of making healthy meals from the best selection of frozen foods – plain frozen vegetables that cook fast and taste terrific. Serve this classic mixed vegetable soup with crusty bread and perhaps a wedge of cheese as a light meal.

Serves 6

15ml/1 tbsp oil
25g/1oz/2 tbsp butter
2 onions, finely chopped
4 carrots, sliced
2 celery sticks, sliced
2 leeks, sliced
1 potato, cut into small cubes
1 small parsnip, cut into small cubes
1 garlic clove, crushed
900ml/1½ pints/3¾ cups vegetable stock
300ml/½ pint/1¼ cups milk
25g/1oz/4 tbsp cornflour (cornstarch)
handful of frozen peas
30ml/2 tbsp chopped fresh parsley
salt and ground black pepper

1 Heat the oil and butter in a large pan and add the onions, carrots and celery. Cook over a medium heat for 5–10 minutes, stirring occasionally, until soft and just beginning to turn golden brown. Stir in the leeks, potato, parsnip and garlic.

2 Add the stock to the pan and stir into the vegetables. Bring the mixture slowly to the boil, reduce the heat if necessary and cover the pan. Simmer gently for 20–30 minutes until all the vegetables are soft.

3 Stir the milk into the cornflour to make a smooth paste. Stir into the vegetables. Add the frozen peas. Bring to the boil and simmer for 5 minutes Add seasoning and the parsley, and serve.

Variation
For a freezer soup, use onion as the base, with whatever other fresh vegetables you have. From a typical freezer stock, add any or all of the following: mixed vegetables, broccoli, broad (fava) and runner beans, corn, peas, baby Brussels sprouts and cauliflower.

Creamed Spinach and Potato Soup

This is a delicious low-fat creamy soup. This recipe uses spinach but other vegetables would work just as well, such as cabbage or Swiss chard.

Serves 4

1 large onion, finely chopped
1 garlic clove, crushed
900g/2lb floury potatoes, diced
2 celery sticks, chopped
1.2 litres/2 pints/5 cups vegetable stock
250g/9oz fresh spinach leaves
200g/7oz/scant 1 cup low-fat soft cheese
300ml/½ pint/1¼ cups milk
dash of dry sherry
salt and ground black pepper

For the garnish
croûtons
a few baby spinach leaves or chopped fresh parsley

1 Place the onion, garlic, potatoes, celery and stock in a large pan. Bring to the boil, reduce the heat and cover the pan. Simmer the soup for 20 minutes.

2 Season the soup and add the spinach, then bring back to the boil. Reduce the heat and simmer for a further 10 minutes. Remove from the heat and cool slightly.

3 Process the soup in a food processor or blender until smooth and return it to the rinsed-out pan.

4 Stir in the cream cheese and milk. Reheat gently without boiling and taste for seasoning. Add a dash of sherry.

5 Ladle the soup into bowls and serve topped with croûtons and a few baby spinach leaves or chopped fresh parsley.

Cook's Tip
A hand-held blender is excellent for quickly puréeing soups in the pan. Remove the pan from the heat and let it cool slighlty first. Take care to keep the blender well down in the pan, otherwise the soup will spray everywhere. Start on a low setting to break up some of the ingredients, then increase the speed.

Country Vegetable: Energy 160kcal/665kJ; Protein 3.6g; Carbohydrate 11.5g, of which sugars 10g; Fat 11.4g, of which saturates 6.8g; Cholesterol 27mg; Calcium 72mg; Fibre 5.4g; Sodium 106mg.
Spinach and Potato: Energy 274kcal/1157kJ; Protein 15.3g; Carbohydrate 46.2g, of which sugars 11.6g; Fat 5g, of which saturates 2.7g; Cholesterol 13mg; Calcium 281mg; Fibre 4.4g; Sodium 348mg.

Potato and Garlic Broth

Although there is plenty of garlic in this soup, the end result is not overpowering. Serve it piping hot with wholemeal (whole-wheat) bread, as the perfect winter warmer, or with one of the suggested accompaniments below.

Serves 4

2 small or 1 large head of garlic (about 20 cloves)
4 potatoes, diced
1.75 litres/3 pints/7½ cups vegetable stock
salt and ground black pepper
flat leaf parsley, to garnish

1 Preheat the oven to 190°C/375°F/Gas 5. Place the unpeeled garlic bulbs or bulb in a small roasting pan and bake for about 30 minutes until they are soft in the centre.

2 Meanwhile, place the potatoes in a large pan and pour in water to cover. Add a little salt, if liked. Bring to the boil, reduce the heat and part-cover the pan, then cook for 10 minutes.

3 Meanwhile, simmer the stock for 5 minutes. Drain the potatoes and add them to the stock.

4 Squeeze the garlic pulp from the skins into the soup, reserving a few cloves to garnish. Stir and add seasoning to taste. Simmer the soup for a further 15 minutes before serving, garnished with whole garlic cloves and parsley.

Variations

- *Make the soup more substantial by toasting slices of French bread on one side, then topping the second sides with cheese and toasting until golden. Place a slice or two of toasted cheese in each bowl before ladling in the soup.*
- *Hot herb bread, with lots of chopped fresh parsley and plenty of grated lemon rind, is delicious with the broth. Mix the parsley and lemon rind with butter, and spread it between slices of French bread. Reshape the slices into a loaf and wrap in foil, then heat in the oven.*
- *You could roast shallots with the garlic, or sauté some celery to add to the simmering soup about 10 minutes before serving.*

Sautéed Potato Soup with Garlic

Served in earthenware dishes, this classic Spanish soup should be savoured.

Serves 6

30ml/2 tbsp olive oil
1 large onion, finely sliced
4 garlic cloves, crushed
1 large potato, halved and cut into thin slices
5ml/1 tsp paprika
400g/14oz can chopped tomatoes, drained
5ml/1 tsp thyme leaves
900ml/1½ pints/3¾ cups vegetable stock
5ml/1 tsp cornflour (cornstarch)
salt and ground black pepper
chopped thyme leaves, to garnish

1 Heat the oil in a large pan. Add the onion, garlic, potato and paprika, and cook, stirring often, for 5 minutes, until the onions have softened, but not browned.

2 Add the tomatoes, thyme and stock and simmer for 15–20 minutes until the potatoes have cooked through.

3 Mix the cornflour to a smooth paste with a little water. Stir the paste into the soup, and bring back to the boil, stirring all the time. Then simmer gently for 5 minutes until thickened.

4 Using a wooden spoon, break the potatoes up slightly. Season the soup to taste, ladle it into bowls and serve garnished with chopped thyme leaves.

Cook's Tip

Bring a bit of fresh green flavour to the soup by stirring in some shredded salad leaves just before serving. Any of the lettuces or salad leaves will work very well, as long as they are very finely shredded. For a punchy flavour, include rocket (arugula) and a little watercress. For a hint of crisp texture, use some iceberg lettuce or add Chinese cabbage. The secret to cutting them fine enough is to roll the leaves tightly, or bundle them tightly if they are too small to roll, and use a really sharp knife. Cut them at the last minute and stir them through the soup immediately before ladling it into bowls.

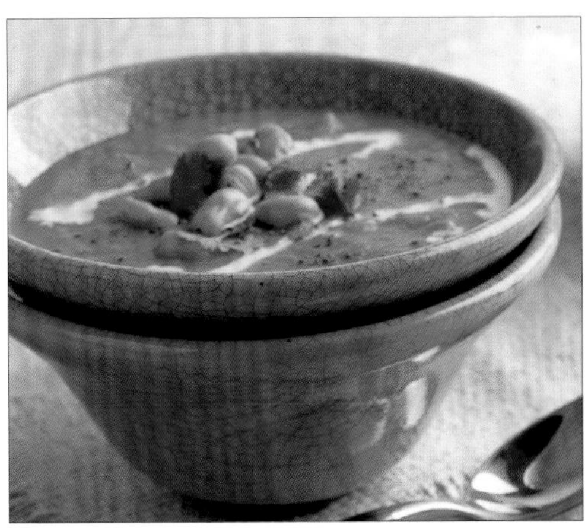

Potato and Garlic: Energy 115kcal/488kJ; Protein 4.3g; Carbohydrate 24.3g, of which sugars 2.1g; Fat 0.7g, of which saturates 0.2g; Cholesterol 0mg; Calcium 14mg; Fibre 2.3g; Sodium 219mg.
Sautéed Potato: Energy 100kcal/419kJ; Protein 1.9g; Carbohydrate 14.7g, of which sugars 5.4g; Fat 4.2g, of which saturates 0.7g; Cholesterol 0mg; Calcium 21mg; Fibre 1.8g; Sodium 13mg.

Tofu and Cos Lettuce Soup

This Chinese-inspired soup is incredibly quick to cook, as all of the ingredients are diced, sliced or shredded during preparation. Use groundnut oil for wok-frying the ingredients if possible as it will contribute well to the flavour.

Serves 4

30ml/2 tbsp groundnut (peanut) or sunflower oil
200g/7oz smoked or marinated tofu, cubed
3 spring onions, sliced diagonally
2 garlic cloves, cut into thin strips
1 carrot, finely sliced
1 litre/1¾ pints/4 cups vegetable stock
30ml/2 tbsp soy sauce
15ml/1 tbsp dry sherry or vermouth
5ml/1 tsp sugar
115g/4oz cos lettuce, shredded
salt and freshly ground black pepper

1 Heat the oil in a preheated wok, then stir-fry the tofu cubes until browned. Drain on kitchen paper and set aside.

2 Add the spring onions, garlic and carrot to the wok and stir-fry for 2 minutes. Add the stock, soy sauce, sherry or vermouth, sugar, lettuce and fried tofu. Heat through gently for 1 minute, season to taste and serve.

Cook's Tips

• Cos, or romaine, lettuce is a hardy leaf from the Greek Island of the same name. Despite its tall, rather stalky-looking green leaves, it is quite a crisp vegetable, and ideal for shredding in soups and stir-fries.

• You can easily marinate tofu overnight, using barbecue sauce and a dash of olive oil. Simply drain and stir-fry as in step 1.

Variation

Chinese rice wine is often recommended as a non-alcoholic substitute for fortified wines.

Tofu Soup with Mushrooms and Tomato

This light, clear Thai soup relies on an aromatic broth. The tofu and dried mushrooms absorb all the delicious flavours.

Serves 4

115g/4oz/scant 2 cups dried shiitake mushrooms, soaked in water for 20 minutes
5ml/1 tsp sunflower oil
2 shallots, halved and sliced
2 Thai chillies, seeded and sliced
4cm/1½in fresh root ginger, peeled and grated
350g/12oz tofu, rinsed, drained and cut into bitesize cubes
4 tomatoes, skinned, seeded and cut into thin strips
salt and ground black pepper
1 bunch coriander (cilantro), stalks removed, finely chopped, to garnish

For the stock

4 celery sticks, sliced
4 carrots, sliced
1 small bulb of fennel, sliced
2 onions, peeled and quartered
6 tomatoes
2 garlic cloves, crushed
7.5cm/3in fresh root ginger, chopped
6 black peppercorns
2 star anise
4 cloves
1 cinnamon stick

1 To make the stock, put all the ingredients in a pan and pour in 2 litres/3½ pints/8 cups water. Bring to the boil, then reduce the heat and simmer with the lid on for 1½–2 hours.

2 Remove the lid and continue simmering for 30 minutes to reduce. Strain and measure out 1.5 litres/2½ pints/6¼ cups.

3 Squeeze the soaked shiitake mushrooms dry, remove the stems and slice the caps into thin strips.

4 Heat the oil in a large pan or wok and stir in the shallots, chillies and ginger. Add the stock.

5 Add the tofu, mushrooms and tomatoes and bring to the boil. Reduce the heat and simmer gently for 5–10 minutes. Season to taste and sprinkle the finely chopped fresh coriander over the top. Serve piping hot.

Tofu and Cos Lettuce: Energy 106kcal/439kJ; Protein 4.8g; Carbohydrate 3.2g, of which sugars 2.8g; Fat 7.8g, of which saturates 1g; Cholesterol 0mg; Calcium 272mg; Fibre 0.8g; Sodium 543mg.
Tofu/Mushrooms: Energy 100kcal/418kJ; Protein 8.8g; Carbohydrate 5.2g, of which sugars 4.5g; Fat 5g, of which saturates 0.7g; Cholesterol 0mg; Calcium 480mg; Fibre 1.8g; Sodium 32mg.

Miso Soup with Wakame

Essential to any Japanese meal is a bowl of rice. Next is miso soup, served in a lacquered bowl.

Serves 4

5g/⅛oz dried wakame
115g/4oz fresh soft tofu or long-life silken tofu
400ml/14fl oz/1⅔ cups dashi stock
45ml/3 tbsp miso
2 spring onions (scallions), finely chopped
shichimi togarashi or sansho (optional), to serve

1 Soak the wakame in cold water for 15 minutes. Drain and chop into stamp-size pieces if using the long or broad type.

2 Cut the tofu into 1cm/½in strips, then cut horizontally through the strips. Cut the thin strips into squares.

3 Bring the dashi stock to the boil. Put the miso in a small cup and mix with 60ml/4 tbsp hot stock. Reduce the heat to low and pour two-thirds of the miso back into the pan of stock.

4 Taste the soup and add more miso if required. Add the wakame and the tofu and increase the heat. Just before the soup comes to the boil again, add the spring onions and remove the pan from the heat. Do not boil.

5 Serve the soup ladled into bowls and sprinkled with shichimi togarashi or sansho, if liked.

Cook's Tips

- *Buy a pack of dried konbu for making dashi stock. If liked, for additional flavour in a vegetarian stock, add shredded spring onion to the water when soaking the konbu. (Fine shreds of dried fish are used in non-vegetarian dashi.)*
- *Sansho is a spice, known as Japanese pepper. It is part of the seven spice mixture known as shichimi togarashi. Look out for Japanese spices in specialist stores or among the Japanese ingredients on deli counters in larger supermarkets.*

Miso Broth with Mushrooms

Shiitake mushrooms give this soup superb flavour.

Serves 4

1.2 litres/2 pints/5 cups boiling water
45ml/3 tbsp light miso paste
3 fresh shiitake mushrooms, sliced
115g/4oz tofu diced
1 spring onion (scallion), green part only, sliced

1 Mix the boiling water and miso in a pan. Add the mushrooms and simmer for 5 minutes.

2 Divide the tofu among four warmed soup bowls, ladle in the soup, scatter with sliced spring onions and serve.

Variations

A wide variety of simple broths can be made using the basic miso stock. The following are some suggestions – experiment with your favourite stir-fry vegetable mixtures and Western-style ingredient combinations.

- *Stir-fry finely shredded cabbage with thinly sliced garlic and place in bowls. Top with snipped garlic chives or ordinary chives and sprinkle with toasted sesame seeds. Pour over the miso broth and serve.*
- *Brush a block of tofu with a little oil and soy sauce, then grill (broil) until well browned. Slice and divide among bowls. Add spring onions (scallions) and pour in the stock.*
- *For a completely different interpretation, cut carrots into fine strips and cook them in the minimum amount of water, with a little butter and seasoning until the liquid evaporates. Serve with the broth, sprinkled with a little finely shredded raw leek.*

Cook's Tip

Look out for Japanese ingredients in health food stores. Miso, konbu and other seaweeds, dried mushrooms, Japanese soy sauce and many similar ingredients are well established among vegetarian and vegan products.

Miso with Wakame: Energy 40kcal/167kJ; Protein 3.8g; Carbohydrate 3.4g, of which sugars 1.3g; Fat 1.3g, of which saturates 0.2g; Cholesterol 0mg; Calcium 156mg; Fibre 0.9g; Sodium 892mg.
Miso with Mushrooms: Energy 25kcal/103kJ; Protein 2.4g; Carbohydrate 2.6g, of which sugars 2.4g; Fat 0.6g, of which saturates 0.1g; Cholesterol 0mg; Calcium 107mg; Fibre 1.6g; Sodium 882mg.

Peppery Vegetable Soup

This lightly spiced soup sharpens the taste buds without being too filling, and is ideal as a starter in a meal that features spicy meat or fish dishes. The fried shallots add texture and make an attractive garnish.

Serves 4

100g/3¾oz carrots, peeled
100g/3¾oz cucumber, peeled and seeded
100g/3¾oz French or long beans
5ml/1 tsp black peppercorns
2 shallots
2 garlic cloves
25g/1oz fresh root ginger
30ml/2 tbsp vegetable oil
700ml/24fl oz/2¾ cups water or vegetable stock
salt
fried shallots, to garnish

1 Cut the carrots and cucumber into 1cm/½in cubes. Trim the beans and slice them into rounds of a size similar to the other vegetables.

2 Using a pestle and mortar, grind the peppercorns, shallots, garlic and ginger to a paste. Alternatively, blend in a food processor until smooth. Heat the oil and fry the paste for 3 minutes. Add the water or stock and bring to the boil.

3 Add the vegetables and simmer for 15 minutes, until tender. Add salt to taste and serve in individual bowls, garnished with fried shallots.

Variation
This soup is a simpler version of the rich, spiced Indonesian soup known as soto. It can be cooked with water, but using a good vegetable stock will give it much more body and flavour.

Cook's Tip
Most supermarkets and ethnic stores now sell fried shallots in small tubs.

Miso Broth with Leek and Tofu

This nutritious soup is standard Japanese breakfast fare. Westerners who are dedicated to blueberry muffins or breakfast muesli may prefer to reserve this delicious broth for a lunch or suppertime treat.

Serves 4

5 baby leeks
15g/½oz fresh coriander (cilantro), including the stalks
3 thin slices fresh root ginger
2 star anise
1 small dried red chilli
1.2 litres/2 pints/5 cups dashi stock or vegetable stock
225g/8oz pak choi (bok choy), thickly cubed
200g/7oz firm tofu, cubed
60ml/4 tbsp red miso
30–45ml/2–3 tbsp shoyu

1 Cut the tops off the leeks and slice the rest finely. Place the tops in a large pan. Chop the coriander leaves and set aside.

2 Add the coriander stalks, ginger, star anise and chilli to the pan. Pour in the dashi or vegetable stock. Bring to the boil, then reduce the heat and simmer for 10 minutes. Strain, return the broth to the pan and reheat.

3 Add the sliced leeks to the stock, with the pak choi and tofu. Cook gently for 2 minutes. Then mix 45ml/3 tbsp of the miso to a thin paste with a little of the hot soup and stir it back into the pan of soup.

4 Stir in the chopped coriander and cook the soup for a further minute before serving, ladled into bowls.

Cook's Tip
Shoyu is Japanese soy sauce, which is different from the Chinese type. It is available as dark or light, and of different qualities. Dark soy sauce is richer and not as salty as the light type. Always add soy sauce carefully, and in stages, tasting after each addition to avoid making the broth too salty. Extra shoyu can be added to taste at the table.

Peppery Vegetable Soup: Energy 72kcal/297kJ; Protein 1.1g; Carbohydrate 4.3g, of which sugars 3.6g; Fat 5.8g, of which saturates 0.7g; Cholesterol 0mg; Calcium 24mg; Fibre 1.5g; Sodium 117mg.
Miso Broth with Leek: Energy 71kcal/297kJ; Protein 7.2g; Carbohydrate 4.2g, of which sugars 3.5g; Fat 2.9g, of which saturates 0.4g; Cholesterol 0mg; Calcium 372mg; Fibre 2.6g; Sodium 884mg.

Fragrant Tofu Vegetable Soup

One of the most refreshing and healthy soups, this fragrant dish would make an ideal light lunch or supper.

Serves 4

30ml/2 tbsp groundnut (peanut) oil
300g/11oz firm tofu, diced
1.2 litres/2 pints/5 cups good vegetable stock
15ml/1 tbsp chilli jam
grated rind of 1 kaffir lime
1 shallot, finely sliced
1 garlic clove, finely chopped
2 kaffir lime leaves, shredded (see Cook's Tip)
3 fresh red chillies, seeded and shredded
1 lemon grass stalk, finely chopped
6 shiitake mushrooms, thinly sliced
4 spring onions (scallions), shredded
30ml/2 tbsp light soy sauce
45ml/3 tbsp lime juice
5ml/1 tsp sugar
45ml/3 tbsp chopped fresh coriander (cilantro)
salt and ground black pepper

1 Heat the oil in a wok and fry the tofu for 4–5 minutes until golden, turning occasionally. Use a slotted spoon to remove it and set aside. Transfer the oil from the wok into a large, heavy pan.

2 Add the stock, chilli jam, kaffir lime rind, shallot, garlic, lime leaves, two-thirds of the chillies and the lemon grass to the pan. Bring to the boil, reduce the heat and simmer for 20 minutes.

3 Strain the stock into a clean pan. Stir in the remaining chilli, the shiitake mushrooms, spring onions, soy sauce, lime juice and sugar. Simmer for 3 minutes.

4 Add the fried tofu and heat through for 1 minute. Mix in the chopped coriander and season with salt and pepper to taste. Serve at once in warmed bowls.

Cook's Tip

Fresh kaffir limes and leaves are available from South-east Asian stores. If you cannot find them, use freeze dried leaves, which are widely available, or ordinary lime rind.

Hot and Sour Soup

This spicy, warming soup really whets the appetite and is the perfect introduction to a simple Chinese meal.

Serves 4

10g/¼oz dried cloud ear (wood ear) mushrooms
8 fresh shiitake mushrooms
900ml/1½ pints/3¾ cups vegetable stock
75g/3oz firm tofu, cubed
50g/2oz/½ cup canned sliced bamboo shoots
15ml/1 tbsp caster (superfine) sugar
45ml/3 tbsp rice vinegar
15ml/1 tbsp light soy sauce
1.5ml/¼ tsp chilli oil
2.5ml/½ tsp salt
large pinch of ground white pepper
15ml/1 tbsp cornflour (cornstarch)
1 egg white
5ml/1 tsp sesame oil
2 spring onions (scallions), sliced into fine rings
white pepper, to serve

1 Soak the dried cloud ear mushrooms in hot water for 20 minutes or until soft. Drain, trim off and discard the hard base from each cloud ear and then chop the fungus roughly.

2 Remove and discard the stems from the shiitake mushrooms. Cut the caps into thin strips.

3 Place the stock, both types of mushroom, tofu and bamboo shoots in a large pan. Bring the stock to the boil, lower the heat and simmer for about 5 minutes.

4 Stir in the sugar, vinegar, soy sauce, chilli oil, salt and pepper. Mix the cornflour to a paste with a little cold water. Add to the soup, stirring constantly, and bring to the boil, stirring until it thickens slightly.

5 Lightly whisk the egg white with a fork, just enough to break it up, then pour it slowly into the soup in a steady stream, stirring constantly so that it forms threads. Add the sesame oil.

6 Ladle the soup into heated bowls and garnish with spring onion rings. Serve immediately, offering white pepper at the table for anyone who wants a hotter soup.

Fragrant Tofu Soup: Energy 122kcal/506kJ; Protein 7.1g; Carbohydrate 3.6g, of which sugars 2.9g; Fat 8.9g, of which saturates 1.5g; Cholesterol 0mg; Calcium 395mg; Fibre 0.7g; Sodium 273mg.
Hot and Sour Soup: Energy 102kcal/429kJ; Protein 7.3g; Carbohydrate 7.3g, of which sugars 0.3g; Fat 5.1g, of which saturates 1g; Cholesterol 44mg; Calcium 135mg; Fibre 0.7g; Sodium 208mg.

Clear Vegetable Soup

In China and Central Asia, this type of clear soup is usually made in large quantities, then stored as appropriate and reheated for consumption over a number of days. To do the same, double or treble the quantities below. Chill leftover soup rapidly and always reheat it thoroughly before serving.

Serves 4

30ml/2 tbsp groundnut (peanut) oil
15ml/1 tbsp magic paste (see Cook's Tip)
100g/3½oz Savoy cabbage or Chinese leaves (Chinese cabbage), finely shredded
100g/3½oz white radish (daikon), finely diced
1 cauliflower, coarsely chopped
4 celery sticks, coarsely chopped
1.2 litres/2 pints/5 cups vegetable stock
130g/4½oz fried tofu, cut into 2.5cm/1in cubes
5ml/1 tsp palm sugar (jaggery) or light muscovado (brown) sugar
45ml/3 tbsp light soy sauce

1 Heat the groundnut oil in a large, heavy pan or wok. Add the magic paste and cook over a low heat, stirring frequently, until it gives off its aroma. Add the shredded Savoy cabbage or Chinese leaves, white radish, cauliflower and celery.

2 Pour in the vegetable stock, increase the heat to medium and bring to the boil, stirring occasionally. Reduce the heat so that the soup simmers then gently stir in the tofu cubes.

3 Add the sugar and soy sauce. Reduce the heat and simmer for 15 minutes, until the vegetables are cooked and tender.

4 Taste the soup and add a little more soy sauce if needed. Serve hot, taking the pan to the table, so that the soup can be ladled into small individual bowls in several helpings. Alternatively, divide among four deep soup bowls.

Cook's Tip
Magic paste, now widely available, is a mixture of crushed garlic, white pepper and coriander (cilantro).

Hot-and-Sweet Vegetable and Tofu Soup

An interesting combination of hot, sweet and sour flavours makes an inspiring low-fat soup. It takes only minutes to make as the spinach and silken tofu are simply placed in bowls and covered with the flavoured hot stock.

Serves 4

1.2 litres/2 pints/5 cups vegetable stock
5–10ml/1–2 tsp Thai red curry paste
2 kaffir lime leaves, torn
40g/1½oz/3 tbsp palm sugar (jaggery) or light muscovado (brown) sugar
30ml/2 tbsp soy sauce
juice of 1 lime
1 carrot, cut into thin strips
50g/2oz baby spinach leaves, any coarse stalks removed

1 Heat the stock in a large pan, then add the red curry paste. Stir constantly over a medium heat until the paste has dissolved. Add the lime leaves, sugar and soy sauce and bring to the boil.

2 Add the lime juice and carrot to the pan. Reduce the heat and simmer for 5–10 minutes.

3 Divide the spinach and tofu among four bowls and pour the hot stock on top. Serve at once.

Variations
The key is to have excellent stock for this and similar recipes – many good 'instant' stock packs are available from specialist stores. Spices and fresh herbs, with soy sauce and mirin (rice wine) or dry sherry are good flavourings. Try the following combinations in the bowl:
- *Shredded spring onion (scallion), tofu, shreds of red (bell) pepper and shreds of white radish.*
- *Finely sliced French beans, thinly sliced canned water chestnuts and shredded plain omelette.*

Clear Vegetable: Energy 205kcal/851kJ; Protein 13.8g; Carbohydrate 8.6g, of which sugars 7.5g; Fat 13g, of which saturates 1.3g; Cholesterol 0mg; Calcium 579mg; Fibre 3.4g; Sodium 845mg.
Hot-Sweet: Energy 98kcal/412kJ; Protein 5.3g; Carbohy. 12.7g, of which sugars 12.3g; Fat 3.3g, of which saturates 0.4g, of which polyunsaturates 1.7g; Cholest. 0mg; Calcium 318mg; Fibre 0.6g; Sodium 558mg.

Mixed Vegetables in Coconut Broth

There are many ways to make a vegetable curry, but this recipe, in which the vegetables are simmered in coconut milk, is typical of South India. Traditionally, it may be served as an accompaniment, but this cross between a soup and stew is perfect for a vegetarian lunch, with warm naan bread or soft chapatis as an accompaniment.

Serves 4

225g/8oz potatoes, cut into 5cm/2in cubes
125g/4oz/¾ cup French (green) beans
150g/5oz carrots, cut into 5cm/2in cubes
500ml/17fl oz/2¼ cups vegetable stock or water
1 small aubergine (eggplant), about 225g/8oz, quartered lengthwise
75g/3oz coconut milk powder
5ml/1 tsp salt, or to taste
30ml/2 tbsp vegetable oil
6–8 fresh or 8–10 dried curry leaves
1–2 dried red chillies, chopped into small pieces
5ml/1 tsp ground cumin
5ml/1 tsp ground coriander
2.5ml/½ tsp ground turmeric

1 Put the potatoes, beans and carrots in a large pan and add 300ml/½ pint/1¼ cups of the stock or water. Bring to the boil. Reduce the heat a little, cover the pan and cook for 5 minutes.

2 Cut the aubergine quarters into 5cm/2in pieces and add them to the soup.

3 Blend the coconut milk powder with the remaining hot water and add it to the soup with the salt. Bring to a slow simmer, cover and cook for 6–7 minutes.

4 In a small pan, heat the oil over a medium heat and add the curry leaves and the chillies. Immediately follow with the cumin, coriander and turmeric. Stir-fry the spices for 15–20 seconds and pour the entire contents of the pan over the vegetables. Stir to distribute the spices evenly and remove from the heat.

5 Ladle the soup into bowls and serve piping hot, with any naan bread or soft chapatis.

Egg Flower Soup

This simple, healthy soup is flavoured with fresh root ginger and Chinese five-spice powder. It is quick and delicious and can be made at the last minute.

Serves 4

1.2 litres/2 pints/5 cups vegetable stock
10ml/2 tsp grated fresh root ginger
10ml/2 tsp light soy sauce
5ml/1 tsp sesame oil
5ml/1 tsp Chinese five-spice powder
15–30ml/1–2 tbsp cornflour (cornstarch)
2 eggs
salt and ground black pepper

For the garnish
1 spring onion (scallion), very finely sliced
15ml/1 tbsp roughly chopped coriander (cilantro)

1 Pour the vegetable stock into a large pan. Add the ginger, soy sauce, sesame oil and five-spice powder. Bring to the boil, reduce the heat and allow to simmer gently for 10 minutes.

2 In a bowl or jug (pitcher) blend the cornflour to a smooth paste with 60–75ml/4–5 tbsp water. Gradually stir the paste into the stock and bring back to the boil, stirring. Cook, stirring constantly, for a few minutes, until slightly thickened. Season to taste with salt and pepper.

3 In a jug (pitcher), beat the eggs with 30ml/2 tbsp cold water until the mixture becomes frothy.

4 Bring the soup back just to the boil and drizzle in the egg mixture, stirring vigorously with chopsticks. Serve at once, ladled into warmed bowls and sprinkled with the sliced spring onions and chopped coriander or parsley.

Cook's Tip

This soup is a good way of using up leftover egg yolks or whites, which have been stored in the freezer and then thawed. When adding the egg to the soup, use a jug (pitcher) with a fine spout to form a very thin drizzle.

Vegetables in Coconut: Energy 80kcal/335kJ; Protein 1.2g; Carbohydrate 5.6g, of which sugars 5.3g; Fat 6.1g, of which saturates 0.9g; Cholesterol 0mg; Calcium 29mg; Fibre 2.3g; Sodium 71mg.
Egg Flower Soup: Energy 58kcal/244kJ; Protein 3.3g; Carbohydrate 3.8g, of which sugars 0.3g; Fat 3.6g, of which saturates 0.9g; Cholesterol 95mg; Calcium 16mg; Fibre 0g; Sodium 304mg.

Vegetable Noodle Soup

Potatoes and noodles are a good combination in soup for those who live in a cold climate. This soup is also easily digested and therefore thought to be suitable for those who are feeling delicate.

Serves 4

1 large onion, finely sliced
25g/1oz/2 tbsp butter
350g/12oz potatoes, peeled and diced
900ml/1½ pints/3¾ cups vegetable stock
1 bay leaf
salt and ground black pepper

For the drop noodles

75g/3oz/⅔ cup self-raising (self-rising) flour
pinch of salt
15g/½oz/1 tbsp butter
15ml/1 tbsp chopped fresh parsley, plus a little extra to garnish
1 egg, beaten
crusty bread, to serve

1 In a wide, heavy pan, cook the onion in the butter gently for 10 minutes, or until it begins to brown.

2 Add the diced potatoes and cook for 2–3 minutes, then pour in the stock. Add the bay leaf, salt and pepper. Bring to the boil, then reduce the heat, cover and simmer for 10 minutes.

3 Meanwhile, make the noodles. Sift the flour and salt into a bowl and rub in the butter. Stir in the parsley, then add the egg to the flour mixture and mix to a soft dough.

4 Drop half-teaspoonfuls of the dough into the simmering soup. Cover and simmer gently for a further 10 minutes.

5 To serve, ladle the soup into warmed deep bowls, sprinkle over a little parsley, and serve immediately with chunks of warm crusty bread.

Cook's Tip
Use old potatoes, of a floury texture, such as King Edwards or Maris Pipers, so that they break down slightly in the soup.

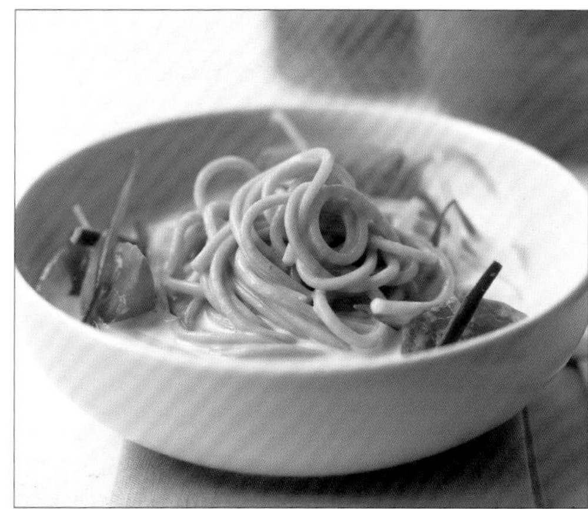

Wheat Noodles in Soybean Soup

Strands of thin wheat noodles taste great in a mild and deliciously nutty chilled soup. This is a perfect choice of satisfying soup for a warm summer's day. The iced broth is topped with succulent strips of cucumber and wedges of tomato, providing refreshing flavours to complement the tender noodles.

Serves 4

185g/6½oz/1 cup soya beans
30ml/2 tbsp sesame seeds
300g/11oz thin wheat noodles
salt

For the garnish

1 cucumber, cut into thin strips
1 tomato, cut into wedges

1 Soak the soya beans overnight. Rinse in cold water and then roll them between your palms to remove the skins.

2 Gently toast the sesame seeds in a dry pan until they are lightly browned. Place the peeled soya beans and the sesame seeds in a food processor or blender. Add 1 litre/1¾ pints/4 cups water and process until the beans and seeds are finely ground.

3 Strain the bean mixture through muslin (cheesecloth), collecting the liquid in a jug (pitcher) – this is soya and sesame milk. Chill the soya and sesame milk in the refrigerator.

4 Bring a pan of water to the boil and cook the noodles, then drain them and rinse in cold water.

5 Place a portion of noodles in each soup bowl, and pour over the chilled milk. Garnish with strips of cucumber and tomato wedges, then season with salt and serve.

Cook's Tip
For a quick and easy version, use 250ml/8fl oz/1 cup unsweetened soya milk rather than soaking and puréeing the soya beans. Simply add the ground sesame seeds to the soya milk and chill to make the soup.

Vegetable Noodle: Energy 241kcal/1010kJ; Protein 5.7g; Carbohydrate 33.6g, of which sugars 4.9g; Fat 10.3g, of which saturates 5.7g; Cholesterol 69mg; Calcium 63mg; Fibre 2.5g; Sodium 91mg.
Wheat Noodles: Energy 268kcal/1121kJ; Protein 20.1g; Carbohydrate 17.9g, of which sugars 3.4g; Fat 13.3g, of which saturates 1.7g; Cholesterol 0mg; Calcium 174mg; Fibre 8.7g; Sodium 6mg.

Spiced Squash Noodle Soup

This full-flavoured soup, or chorba, is the daily dish in many Moroccan households. You can purée the soup, if you prefer, but here it is left chunky and finished with a swirl of yogurt and finely chopped coriander. Garlic lovers may like to add a crushed garlic clove and a little salt to the yogurt.

Serves 4

1 butternut squash
8 large, ripe tomatoes
45–60ml/3–4 tbsp olive oil
3–4 whole cloves
2 onions, chopped
4 celery sticks, chopped
2 carrots, chopped
5–10ml/1–2 tsp sugar
15ml/1 tbsp tomato purée (paste)
5–10ml/1–2 tsp ras el hanout
2.5ml/½ tsp ground turmeric
a big bunch of fresh coriander (cilantro), chopped
1.75 litres/3 pints/7½ cups vegetable stock
handful of dried egg noodles or capellini, broken into pieces
salt and ground black pepper
natural (plain) yogurt, to serve
coriander (cilantro), to garnish

1 Halve the squash, remove the seeds and peel, then cut the flesh into small chunks. Peel and roughly chop the tomatoes.

2 In a deep, heavy pan, heat the oil and add the cloves, onions, squash, celery and carrots. Fry until the vegetables begin to colour, then stir in the chopped tomatoes and sugar. Cook, stirring occasionally, until the liquid reduces and the tomatoes begin to pulp.

3 Stir in the tomato purée, ras el hanout, turmeric and chopped coriander. Pour in the stock and bring to the boil. Reduce the heat and simmer, uncovered, for 30–40 minutes until the vegetables are soft and the liquid is reduced a little.

4 To make a smooth soup, let the soup cool slightly before processing it in a food processor or blender, then pour it back into the pan.

5 Add the pasta to the soup and simmer for 10 minutes, until it is tender. Ladle the soup into bowls and serve topped with yogurt. Garnish with coriander.

Red Onion Laksa

Sliced red onions mimic flour noodles in this soup.

Serves 6

150g/5oz/2½ cups dried shiitake mushrooms
1.2 litres/2 pints/5 cups boiling vegetable stock
30ml/2 tbsp tamarind paste
250ml/8fl oz/1 cup boiling water
6 large dried red chillies, stems removed and seeded
2 lemon grass stalks, finely sliced
5ml/1 tsp ground turmeric
15ml/1 tbsp grated fresh galangal or fresh root ginger
1 onion, chopped
5ml/1 tsp dried shrimp paste
30ml/2 tbsp vegetable oil
10ml/2 tsp palm sugar (jaggery)
175g/6oz rice vermicelli
1 red onion, very finely sliced
1 small cucumber, seeded and cut into strips
handful of fresh mint leaves, to garnish

1 Place the mushrooms in a bowl and pour in enough boiling stock to cover them, then leave to soak for 30 minutes. Put the tamarind paste into a bowl and pour in half the boiling water. Mash, strain and reserve the liquid, discarding the pulp.

2 Soak the chillies in the remaining boiling water for 5 minutes, then drain, reserving the liquid. Place in a food processor or blender and blend with the lemon grass, turmeric, galangal or ginger, onion and shrimp paste, adding a little soaking water to form a paste.

3 Heat the oil in a large, heavy pan and cook the paste over a low heat for 4–5 minutes. Add the tamarind liquid and bring to the boil, then simmer for 5 minutes. Remove from the heat.

4 Drain the mushrooms and reserve the stock. Discard the stems, then halve or quarter the mushrooms, if large. Add the mushrooms to the pan with their soaking liquid, the remaining stock and the sugar. Simmer for 25–30 minutes or until tender.

5 Put the rice vermicelli into a large bowl and cover with boiling water, then leave to soak for 4 minutes until softened. Drain well, then divide among six bowls. Top with onion and cucumber, then ladle in the boiling shiitake soup. Add a small bunch of mint leaves to each bowl and serve.

Squash Noodle: Energy 265Kcal/1108kJ; Protein 6.9g; Carbohydrate 37.8g, of which sugars 20.2g; Fat 10.2g, of which saturates 1.7g; Cholesterol 0mg; Calcium 158mg; Fibre 8.1g; Sodium 64mg.
Red Onion Laksa: Energy 161kcal/671kJ; Protein 4.1g; Carbohydrate 26.6g, of which sugars 2.7g; Fat 4.3g, of which saturates 0.6g; Cholesterol 4mg; Calcium 32mg; Fibre 0.2g; Sodium 41mg.

Noodle Soup with Tofu

This light and refreshing soup is an excellent pick-me-up. The aromatic, spicy broth is simmered first, and then the tofu, beansprouts and noodles are added.

Serves 4

150g/5oz dried thick rice noodles
1 litre/1¾ pints/4 cups vegetable stock
1 fresh red chilli, seeded and thinly sliced
15ml/1 tbsp light soy sauce
juice of ½ lemon
10ml/2 tsp sugar
5ml/1 tsp finely sliced garlic
5ml/1 tsp finely chopped fresh root ginger
200g/7oz firm tofu
90g/3½oz/scant 1 cup beansprouts
50g/2oz/½ cup peanuts
15ml/1 tbsp chopped fresh coriander (cilantro)

For the garnish

spring onion (scallion) slivers
red chilli slivers

1 Spread out the noodles in a shallow dish and pour over boiling water to cover. Soak according to the packet instructions, until they are just tender. Drain, rinse and set aside.

2 Meanwhile, place the stock, red chilli, soy sauce, lemon juice, sugar, garlic and ginger in a wok or pan over high heat. Bring to the boil, cover, reduce to low heat and simmer the mixture gently for 10–12 minutes.

3 Cut the tofu into cubes. Add it to the soup with the drained noodles and the beansprouts. Cook the mixture gently for a further 2–3 minutes.

4 Roast the peanuts in a dry non-stick wok or frying pan, then chop them. Stir the coriander into the soup. Serve the soup ladled into warm bowls with peanuts, spring onions and chilli scattered over the top.

Cook's Tip
It is important to use vegetable stock with plenty of flavour for this simple soup.

Courgette, Carrot and Noodle Soup

If you have the time, it is worth the effort making your own stock – either vegetable, chicken or meat – for this recipe.

Serves 4

1 yellow (bell) pepper
2 large courgettes (zucchini)
2 large carrots
1 kohlrabi
900ml/1½ pints/3¾ cups well-flavoured vegetable stock
50g/2oz rice vermicelli
salt and freshly ground black pepper

1 Cut the pepper into quarters, removing the seeds and core. Cut the courgettes and carrots lengthways into 5 mm/¼in thick slices and slice the kohlrabi into 5 mm/¼in rounds.

2 Using tiny pastry cutters, stamp out shapes from the vegetables or use a very sharp knife to cut the sliced vegetables into stars and other decorative shapes.

3 Place the vegetables and stock in a pan and simmer for 10 minutes, until the vegetables are tender. Season to taste with salt and pepper.

4 Meanwhile, place the vermicelli in a bowl, cover with boiling water and set aside for 4 minutes. Drain, then divide among four warmed soup bowls. Ladle over the soup and serve.

Cook's Tips
- *This is a great soup for children and a good way of getting them to eat vegetables. Try adding potatoes and swede (rutabaga), cut into shapes. Cooked ham can also be cut into shapes and added to the soup. Soup pasta shapes can be used instead of the vermicelli.*
- *Make little crunchy cheese toasts to go with the soup by cutting decorative bread shapes, toasting one side, topping the untoasted side with cheese and toasting until golden.*
- *Sauté the leftover vegetable pieces in a little oil and mix with cooked brown rice to make a tasty risotto.*

Noodle with Tofu: Energy 261kcal/1092kJ; Protein 10g; Carbohydrate 36.4g, of which sugars 4.3g; Fat 8g, of which saturates 1.4g; Cholesterol 0mg; Calcium 275mg; Fibre 1.2g; Sodium 97mg.
Courgette and Carrot: Energy 120kcal/501kJ; Protein 4.1g; Carbohydrate 24.3g, of which sugars 13.6g; Fat 1g, of which saturates 0.3g; Cholesterol 0mg; Calcium 63mg; Fibre 4.6g; Sodium 526mg.

Cellophane Soup with Tofu

The noodles used in this soup go by various names: glass, cellophane, bean thread or transparent.

Serves 4

4 large dried shiitake mushrooms
15g/½oz dried lily buds (optional)
½ cucumber, coarsely chopped
2 garlic cloves, halved
90g/3½oz white cabbage, coarsely chopped
1.2 litres/2 pints/5 cups boiling water
115g/4oz cellophane noodles
30ml/2 tbsp soy sauce
15ml/1 tbsp palm sugar (jaggery) or light muscovado (brown) sugar
90g/3½oz block silken tofu, diced
fresh coriander (cilantro) leaves, to garnish

1 Soak the shiitake mushrooms in warm water for 30 minutes. In a separate bowl, soak the dried lily buds in warm water, also for 30 minutes.

2 Meanwhile, put the cucumber, garlic and cabbage in a food processor or blender and process to a smooth paste. Scrape the mixture into a large pan and add the measured boiling water.

3 Bring to the boil. Reduce the heat and cook for 2 minutes, stirring occasionally. Strain this stock into another pan, return to a low heat and bring to simmering point.

4 Drain the lily buds, rinse under cold running water, then drain again. Cut off any hard ends. Add the lily buds to the stock with the noodles, soy sauce and sugar and cook for 5 minutes more.

5 Strain the mushroom soaking liquid into the soup. Discard the mushroom stems, then slice the caps. Divide them and the tofu among four serving bowls. Pour the hot soup over, garnish with coriander leaves and serve.

Cook's Tip
Dried lily flowers are available at Chinese supermarkets, or can simply be omitted.

Sour Noodle Soup

The sour notes in this classic soup emanate from the tamarind and salted soya beans. It is packed with all kinds of wonderful textures – both soft and chewy.

Serves 4

vegetable oil, for deep-frying
225g/8oz firm tofu, rinsed, drained and cut into cubes
60ml/4 tbsp dried prawns (shrimp), soaked until rehydrated
5ml/1 tsp shrimp paste
4 garlic cloves, chopped
4–6 dried red chillies, soaked to soften, drained, seeded and the pulp scraped out
90g/3½oz/¾ cup roasted peanuts, ground
50g/2oz salted soya beans
2 lemon grass stalks, trimmed, halved and bruised
30ml/2 tbsp sugar
15–30ml/1–2 tbsp tamarind paste
150g/5oz dried rice vermicelli, soaked in hot water until pliable
handful of beansprouts, rinsed and drained
4 quail's eggs, hard-boiled, shelled and halved
2 spring onions (scallions), sliced
salt and ground black pepper
fresh coriander (cilantro) leaves, finely chopped, to garnish

1 In a wok, heat enough vegetable oil for deep-frying. Drop in the tofu and deep-fry until golden. Drain on kitchen paper.

2 Grind the soaked dried prawns with the shrimp paste, garlic and chilli pulp to form a paste.

3 Heat 30ml/2 tbsp vegetable oil in a wok and fry the paste for 1 minute. Add the peanuts, soya beans and lemon grass. Fry for another minute and stir in the sugar and tamarind paste, followed by 900ml/1½ pints/3¾ cups water. Mix well, bring to the boil, then simmer gently for 10 minutes. Season with salt and pepper.

4 Drain the noodles and heat through in the broth. Ladle ths soup into bowls. Sprinkle over the beansprouts and add the tofu, quail's eggs and spring onions. Garnish with the coriander and serve.

Cellophane with Tofu: Energy 148kcal/618kJ; Protein 4.1g; Carbohydrate 29.7g, of which sugars 5.7g; Fat 1.1g, of which saturates 0.1g; Cholesterol 0mg; Calcium 139mg; Fibre 0.7g; Sodium 546mg.
Sour Noodle: Energy 477kcal/1993kJ; Protein 27.5g; Carbohydrate 44.8g, of which sugars 10.7g; Fat 21.2g, of which saturates 3.6g; Cholesterol 71mg; Calcium 376mg; Fibre 2.9g; Sodium 83mg.

Miso Broth with Noodles

This delicate, fragrant soup is flavoured with just a hint of chilli.

Serves 4

45ml/3 tbsp mugi miso
200g/7oz/scant 2 cups udon, soba or Chinese noodles
30ml/2 tbsp sake or dry sherry
15ml/1 tbsp rice or wine vinegar
45ml/3 tbsp soy sauce
115g/4oz asparagus tips or mangetouts (snow peas), sliced
50g/2oz shiitake mushrooms, stalks removed and thinly sliced
1 carrot, sliced into julienne strips
3 spring onions (scallions), thinly sliced diagonally
salt and ground black pepper
5ml/1 tsp dried chilli flakes, to serve

1 Bring 1 litre/1¾ pints/4 cups water to the boil in a pan. Pour 150ml/¼ pint/⅔ cup of the boiling water over the miso in a small bowl or jug (pitcher) and stir until the miso has dissolved, then set aside.

2 Meanwhile, bring another large pan of lightly salted water to the boil for the noodles. Add the noodles and cook according to the packet instructions, until they are just tender. Take care not to overcook the noodles.

3 Drain the noodles in a colander. Rinse under cold running water, then drain again.

4 Add the sake or sherry, rice or wine vinegar and soy sauce to the pan of boiling water. Boil gently for 3 minutes or until the alcohol has evaporated, then reduce the heat and stir in the miso mixture.

5 Add the asparagus or mangetouts, mushrooms, carrot and spring onions, and simmer for about 2 minutes until the vegetables are just tender. Season the soup to taste.

6 Divide the noodles among four warm bowls and pour the soup over the top. Serve, sprinkled with the chilli flakes.

Chinese Fish Ball Soup

Often eaten as a snack or light lunch, this superb Chinese-inspired soup is garnished with spring onions and fresh chillies. In Malaysian adaptations, an extra drizzle of chilli sauce or chilli sambal is often added to the soup. Fish balls are available ready made, chilled or frozen, from Chinese supermarkets.

Serves 4–6

For the fish balls

450g/1lb white fish fillets (such as haddock, cod, whiting or bream), skinned, boned and flaked
15–30ml/1–2 tbsp rice flour
salt and ground black pepper

For the soup

1.5 litres/2½ pints/6 cups fish or chicken stock
15–30ml/1–2 tbsp light soy sauce
4–6 mustard green leaves, chopped
90g/3½oz mung bean thread noodles, soaked in hot water until soft

For the garnish

2 spring onions (scallions), trimmed and finely sliced
1 fresh red or green chilli, seeded and finely sliced
fresh coriander (cilantro) leaves, finely chopped

1 To make the fish balls, remove any stray bones from the fish, then grind the flakes to a paste, using a mortar and pestle, food processor or blender.

2 Season with salt and pepper and stir in 60ml/4 tbsp water. Add enough rice flour to form a paste. Take small portions of fish paste and squeeze them to mould into balls.

3 Meanwhile, bring the stock to the boil in a deep pan and season to taste with soy sauce. Drop in the fish balls and simmer for 5 minutes. Add the shredded mustard greens and cook for 1 minute.

4 Divide the noodles among four to six bowls. Using a slotted spoon, add the fish balls and greens to the noodles, then ladle over the hot stock, being generous with your portions. Garnish with the spring onions and chilli and sprinkle the chopped coriander over the top.

Miso with Noodles: Energy 230kcal/973kJ; Protein 7.7g; Carbohydrate 42.6g, of which sugars 5.1g; Fat 3.5g, of which saturates 0.1g; Cholesterol 0mg; Calcium 34mg; Fibre 2.9g; Sodium 809mg.
Chinese Fish Ball: Energy 127kcal/533kJ; Protein 14.9g; Carbohydrate 14.8g, of which sugars 0.5g; Fat 0.6g, of which saturates 0.1g; Cholesterol 35mg; Calcium 17mg; Fibre 0.2g; Sodium 408mg.

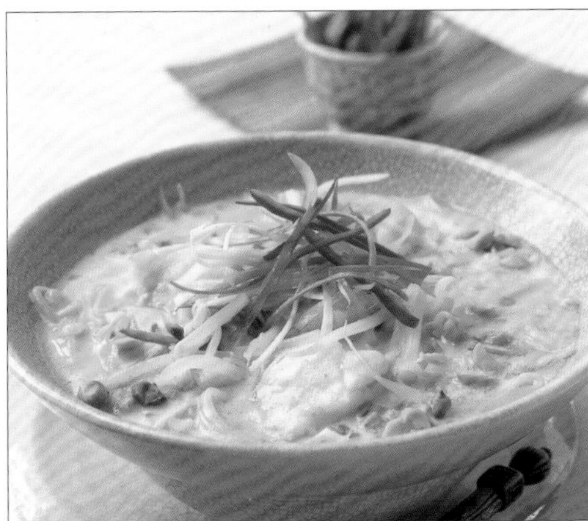

Red Monkfish Soup

This light and creamy coconut soup provides a base for a colourful fusion of red-curried monkfish and rice noodles.

Serves 4

175g/6oz flat rice noodles
30ml/2 tbsp vegetable oil
2 garlic cloves, chopped
15ml/1 tbsp red curry paste
450g/1lb monkfish fillet, cut into bitesize pieces
300ml/½ pint/1¼ cups coconut cream
750ml/1¼ pints/3 cups hot chicken stock
45ml/3 tbsp fish sauce
15ml/1 tbsp palm sugar (jaggery)
60ml/4 tbsp roasted peanuts, roughly chopped
4 spring onions (scallions), shredded lengthways
50g/2oz/½ cup beansprouts
large handful of fresh Thai basil leaves
salt and ground black pepper
1 fresh red chilli, seeded and cut lengthways into slivers, to garnish

1 Soak the noodles in a bowl of boiling water for 10 minutes, or according to the packet instructions. Drain.

2 Heat the oil in a wok or pan over a high heat. Add the garlic and cook for 2 minutes. Stir in the curry paste and cook for 1 minute, until fragrant.

3 Add the monkfish and stir-fry over a high heat for 4–5 minutes, until just tender. Pour in the coconut cream and chicken stock.

4 Stir in the fish sauce and sugar, and bring just to the boil. Add the drained noodles and cook for 1–2 minutes, until tender.

5 Stir in half the peanuts, half the spring onions, half the beansprouts, the basil and seasoning.

6 Ladle the soup into deep individual soup bowls and sprinkle over the remaining peanuts. Garnish with the remaining spring onions, beansprouts and the slivers of red chilli.

Noodle Soup with Crab and Cloud Ear Mushrooms

This is a dish of contrasting textures and flavours. It's quick to cook if you can manage to simmer the noodles in vegetable broth with one hand and gently wok-fry the crab meat with the other!

Serves 4

25g/1oz dried cloud ear (wood ear) mushrooms, soaked in warm water for 20 minutes
115g/4oz dried bean thread (cellophane) noodles, soaked in warm water for 20 minutes
30ml/2 tbsp vegetable or sesame oil
3 shallots, halved and thinly sliced
2 garlic cloves, crushed
2 green or red Thai chillies, seeded and sliced
1 carrot, peeled and cut into thin diagonal rounds
5ml/1 tsp sugar
45ml/3 tbsp oyster sauce
15ml/1 tbsp soy sauce
400ml/14fl oz/1⅔ cups water or chicken stock
225g/8oz fresh, raw crab meat, cut into bitesize chunks
ground black pepper
fresh coriander (cilantro) leaves, to garnish

1 Remove the centres from the soaked wood ear mushrooms and cut the mushrooms in half. Drain the soaked noodles and cut them into 30cm/12in pieces.

2 Heat a wok or heavy pan and add 15ml/1 tbsp of the oil. Stir in the shallots, garlic and chillies, and cook until fragrant. Add the carrot rounds and cook for 1 minute, then add the mushrooms. Stir in the sugar with the oyster and soy sauces, followed by the bean thread noodles. Pour in the water or stock, cover the wok or pan and cook for 3–5 minutes, or until the noodles are softened.

3 Meanwhile, heat the remaining oil in a heavy pan. Add the crab meat and cook until it is nicely pink and tender. Season well with black pepper. Pour the noodle soup into a bowl, arrange the crab meat on top and garnish with coriander.

Red Monkfish: Energy 379kcal/1589kJ; Protein 25.5g; Carbohydrate 41.2g, of which sugars 4.7g; Fat 12g, of which saturates 2g; Cholesterol 18mg; Calcium 49mg; Fibre 0.9g; Sodium 111mg.
Noodle Soup with Crab: Energy 292kcal/1224kJ; Protein 16g; Carbohydrate 30g, of which sugars 5g; Fat 13g, of which saturates 2g; Cholesterol 36mg; Calcium 29mg; Fibre 2.5g; Sodium 1g.

Crab and Chilli Soup

Use prepared fresh crab to create an exotic soup in no time at all. The coriander relish is equally fast to make, and is a worthy accompaniment for its fresh and nutty flavour.

Serves 4

45ml/3 tbsp olive oil
1 red onion, finely chopped
2 fresh red chillies, seeded and finely chopped
1 garlic clove, finely chopped
450g/1lb white crab meat
30ml/2 tbsp chopped fresh parsley
30ml/2 tbsp chopped fresh coriander (cilantro)
juice of 2 lemons
1 lemon grass stalk
1 litre/1¾ pints/4 cups good fish or chicken stock
15ml/1 tbsp fish sauce
150g/5oz vermicelli or angel hair pasta, broken into 5–7.5cm/2–3in lengths
salt and ground black pepper

For the coriander relish

50g/2oz/1 cup fresh coriander (cilantro) leaves
1 green chilli, seeded and chopped
15ml/1 tbsp sunflower oil
25ml/1½ tbsp lemon juice
2.5ml/½ tsp ground roasted cumin seeds

1 Heat the oil in a pan and add the onion, chillies and garlic. Cook until the onion is very soft. Transfer to a bowl. Stir in the crab meat, parsley, coriander and lemon juice. Set aside.

2 Bruise the lemon grass with a pestle. Pour the stock and fish sauce into a pan. Add the lemon grass and bring to the boil, then add the pasta. Simmer, uncovered, for 3–4 minutes or according to the packet instructions, until just tender.

3 Meanwhile, make the relish. Place the fresh coriander, chilli, oil, lemon juice and cumin in a food processor or blender and process to form a coarse paste. Season to taste.

4 Remove and discard the lemon grass from the soup. Stir the chilli and crab mixture into the soup and season it well. Bring to the boil, reduce the heat and simmer for 2 minutes. Ladle the soup into four deep, warmed bowls and put a spoonful of the relish in the centre of each. Serve at once.

Snapper and Tamarind Soup

Tamarind gives this light, fragrant noodle soup a slightly sour taste.

Serves 4

1kg/2¼lb red snapper (or other red fish such as mullet)
1 onion, sliced
50g/2oz tamarind pods
15ml/1 tbsp fish sauce
15ml/1 tbsp sugar
30ml/2 tbsp vegetable oil
2 garlic cloves, finely chopped
2 lemon grass stalks, very finely chopped
4 ripe tomatoes, peeled and coarsely chopped
30ml/2 tbsp yellow bean paste
225g/8oz rice vermicelli, soaked in warm water until soft
115g/4oz/½ cup beansprouts
8–10 fresh basil or mint sprigs
25g/1oz/¼ cup roasted peanuts, ground
salt and ground black pepper

1 Bring 2 litres/3½ pints/8 cups water to the boil in a pan. Lower the heat and add the fish and onion, with 2.5ml/½ tsp salt. Simmer gently until the fish is cooked through.

2 Remove the fish from the pan; set aside. Add the tamarind, fish sauce and sugar to the stock. Cook for 5 minutes, then strain the stock into a large bowl. Carefully remove all of the bones from the fish, keeping the flesh in big pieces.

3 Heat the oil in a large frying pan. Add the garlic and lemon grass and cook for a few seconds. Stir in the tomatoes and bean paste. Cook gently for 5–7 minutes, until the tomatoes are soft. Add the stock, bring back to a simmer and adjust the seasoning. Stir to mix.

4 Drain the vermicelli and divide among individual serving bowls. Add the beansprouts, fish and basil or mint, and sprinkle the ground peanuts on top. Top up each bowl with the hot soup.

Cook's Tip
Use about 15ml/1 tbsp prepared tamarind paste instead of the pods.

Crab and Chilli: Energy 228kcal/951kJ; Protein 23.6g; Carbohydrate 5.4g, of which sugars 5g; Fat 12.6g, of which saturates 3.7g; Cholesterol 90mg; Calcium 199mg; Fibre 1.1g; Sodium 767mg.
Snapper and Tamarind: Energy 495kcal/2079kJ; Protein 43.1g; Carbohydrate 55.5g, of which sugars 9.1g; Fat 11.4g, of which saturates 1.9g; Cholesterol 65mg; Calcium 108mg; Fibre 2.4g; Sodium 165mg.

Noodle and Seared Salmon Soup

Ramen is a Japanese noodle soup. The lightly spiced broth is delicious with slices of fresh salmon and crisp vegetables.

Serves 4

1.5 litres/2½ pints/6¼ cups good vegetable stock
2.5cm/1in piece fresh root ginger, finely sliced
2 garlic cloves, crushed
6 spring onions (scallions), sliced
45ml/3 tbsp soy sauce
45ml/3 tbsp sake
450g/1lb salmon, skinned and boned (fillet or steaks)
5ml/1 tsp groundnut (peanut) oil
350g/12oz ramen or udon noodles
4 small heads pak choi (bok choy)
1 fresh red chilli, seeded and sliced
50g/2oz/¼ cup beansprouts
salt and ground black pepper

1 Pour the stock into a large pan. Add the ginger, garlic, a third of the spring onions, the soy sauce and sake. Bring to the boil, then reduce the heat; simmer for 30 minutes.

2 Remove any bones from the salmon, then cut it on the slant into 12 slices, using a very sharp knife.

3 Brush a ridged griddle or frying pan with the oil and heat until very hot. Sear the salmon slices for 1–2 minutes on each side until just cooked. Set aside.

4 Cook the ramen or udon noodles in boiling water for 4–5 minutes or according to the packet instructions. Drain well and refresh under cold running water. Drain again and set aside.

5 Strain the broth into a clean pan and season to taste, then bring to the boil. Break the pak choi into leaves and add to the pan. Bring back to the boil. Remove from the heat.

6 Use a fork to twist the noodles into four nests and put these into deep bowls. Add three slices of salmon to each bowl, with the remaining spring onions, the chilli and beansprouts.

7 Ladle the steaming hot broth around and over the ingredients and serve immediately.

Prawn and Squid Coconut Laksa

Creamy rice noodles in a spicy coconut-flavoured soup, topped off with seafood, makes a delicious meal. There is a fair amount of work involved in preparing this dish, but you can make the soup base in advance.

Serves 4

4 fresh red chillies, seeded and roughly chopped
1 onion, roughly chopped
1 piece blacan (belacan) or other dried shrimp paste, the size of a stock cube
1 lemon grass stalk, chopped
1 small piece fresh root ginger, peeled and roughly chopped
6 macadamia nuts or almonds
60ml/4 tbsp vegetable oil
5ml/1 tsp paprika
5ml/1 tsp ground turmeric
475ml/16fl oz/2 cups fish stock
600ml/1 pint/2½ cups coconut milk
dash of fish sauce, to taste
12 king prawns (jumbo shrimp), peeled and deveined
8 scallops
225g/8oz prepared squid, cut into rings
350g/12oz rice vermicelli or rice noodles, soaked in warm water until soft
salt and ground black pepper
lime halves, to serve

For the garnish

¼ cucumber, cut into matchsticks
2 fresh red chillies, seeded and finely sliced
30ml/2 tbsp mint leaves
30ml/2 tbsp fried shallots or onions

1 In a food processor or blender, process the chillies, onion, blacan, lemon grass, ginger and nuts until smooth.

2 Heat 45ml/3 tbsp of the oil in a large pan. Add the chilli paste and fry for 6 minutes. Stir in the paprika and turmeric and fry for about 2 minutes more. Pour in the stock and coconut milk. Bring to the boil, then simmer gently for 15–20 minutes. Season with fish sauce.

3 Season the seafood with salt and pepper. Fry quickly in the remaining oil for 2–3 minutes until cooked.

4 Add the noodles to the soup and heat through. Divide among bowls. Top with the seafood. Garnish with the cucumber, chillies, mint and shallots or onions. Serve with the limes.

Noodle and Salmon: Energy 611kcal/2572kJ; Protein 37.8g; Carbohydrate 72.3g, of which sugars 5.5g; Fat 19.6g, of which saturates 2.4g; Cholesterol 56mg; Calcium 227mg; Fibre 5.6g; Sodium 997mg.
Prawn and Squid: Energy 524kcal/2199kJ; Protein 43.1g; Carbohydrate 65.1g, of which sugars 6.3g; Fat 10.1g, of which saturates 2g; Cholesterol 233mg; Calcium 162mg; Fibre 1.9g; Sodium 356mg.

Spicy Seafood and Tofu Laksa

This is the ultimate serve-yourself soup.

Serves 6

675g/1½lb small clams, scrubbed
50g/2oz ikan bilis (dried anchovies)
2–3 aubergines (eggplants)
675g/1½lb raw peeled prawns (shrimp)
10ml/2 tsp sugar
1 head Chinese leaves, thinly sliced
115g/4oz/2 cups beansprouts
2 spring onions (scallions), finely chopped
50g/2oz crispy fried onions
2 x 400ml/14fl oz cans coconut milk
115g/4oz shallots, finely chopped
4 garlic cloves, chopped
6 macadamia nuts, chopped
3 lemon grass stalks
90ml/6 tbsp sunflower oil
1cm/½in cube shrimp paste
25g/1oz/¼ cup curry powder
a few curry leaves
115g/4oz fried tofu
675g/1½lb noodles (laksa, mee or behoon, or mixed), cooked
prawn crackers

1 Put the clams in a large pan with 1cm/½in water. Bring to the boil, cover and steam for 3–4 minutes until opened. Drain.

2 Simmer the ikan bilis in 900ml/1½ pints/3¾ cups water for 20 minutes, then strain into a pan. Cook the aubergines in this for 10 minutes. Lift out, peel and cut into strips. Arrange on a platter. Sprinkle the prawns with sugar. Cook in the stock for 2–4 minutes. Remove. Add to the aubergines with the Chinese leaves, beansprouts, spring onions, fried onions and clams.

3 Make up the coconut milk to 1.2 litres/2 pints/5 cups with water. Purée the shallots, garlic and nuts with the lower 5cm/2in of two lemon grass stalks. Fry the purée in the oil in a pan. Add the remaining lemon grass, shrimp paste, curry powder and a little coconut milk. Stir for 1 minute over low heat. Add the remaining coconut milk and curry leaves and simmer.

4 Stir the remaining stock into the soup and boil. Rinse the tofu in boiling water, cool and squeeze, then cut up and add to the soup. Simmer. Remove the curry leaves and lemon grass. Serve the soup with the noodles, seafood and vegetables, and prawn crackers. Provide big bowls for self-service soup.

Piquant Prawn Laska

Ready-made laksa paste is available from Asian stores.

Serves 3

115g/4oz rice vermicelli or noodles
10ml/2 tsp vegetable oil
750ml/1¼ pints/3 cups fish stock
200ml/7fl oz/scant 1 cup coconut milk
30ml/2 tbsp Thai fish sauce
½ lime
18 peeled cooked prawns (shrimp)
salt and cayenne pepper
60ml/4 tbsp fresh coriander (cilantro) sprigs, chopped, to garnish

For the spicy paste
2 lemon grass stalks, finely chopped
2 fresh red chillies, seeded and chopped
2.5cm/1in piece fresh root ginger, peeled and sliced
2.5ml/½ tsp dried shrimp paste
2 garlic cloves, chopped
2.5ml/½ tsp ground turmeric
30ml/2 tbsp tamarind paste

1 Add the rice vermicelli or noodles to a pan of boiling water. Bring back to the boil, cook for 2 minutes or according to the packet instructions. Drain, then rinse under cold water.

2 To make the spicy paste, place the lemon grass, chillies, ginger, shrimp paste, garlic, turmeric and tamarind paste in a mortar and pound with a pestle. Alternatively, put the ingredients in a food processor or blender and whiz until smooth.

3 Heat the vegetable oil in a large pan, add the spicy paste and fry, stirring constantly, for a few moments to release all the flavours, but be careful not to let it burn.

4 Pour in the fish stock and coconut milk and bring to the boil. Stir in the fish sauce, then simmer for 5 minutes. Season with salt and cayenne to taste, adding a squeeze of lime. Add the prawns and heat through for a few seconds without boiling as this will toughen the prawns.

5 Divide the noodles among three warmed soup bowls. Pour over the very hot soup, making sure that each portion includes an equal number of prawns. Garnish with coriander and serve piping hot.

Seafood and Tofu: Energy 524kcal/2200kJ; Protein 43.1g; Carbohydrate 65.1g, of which sugars 6.3g; Fat 10.1g, of which saturates 2g; Cholesterol 233mg; Calcium 162mg; Fibre 1.9g; Sodium 356mg.
Piquant: Energy 224kcal/939kJ; Protein 15.7g; Carbohy. 33.7g, of which sugars 3.6g; Fat 2.9g, of which saturates 0.5g, of which polyunsaturates 1.4g; Cholest. 130mg; Calcium 108mg; Fibre 0.5g; Sodium 206mg.

Chicken and Crab Noodle Soup

The chicken makes a delicious stock for this light noodle soup.

Serves 6

2 chicken legs, skinned
1.75 litres/3 pints/7½ cups cold water
large bunch of spring onions (scallions)
2.5cm/1in piece fresh root ginger, sliced
5ml/1 tsp black peppercorns
2 garlic cloves, halved
75g/3oz rice noodles
115g/4oz white crab meat
30ml/2 tbsp light soy sauce
salt and ground black pepper
coriander (cilantro) leaves, to garnish

For the omelettes

4 eggs
30ml/2 tbsp chopped fresh coriander (cilantro) leaves
15ml/1 tbsp extra virgin olive oil

1 Put the chicken and water in a pan. Bring to the boil, reduce the heat and cook gently for 20 minutes. Skim the surface occasionally. Slice half the spring onions and add to the pan with the ginger, peppercorns, garlic and salt to taste. Cover and simmer for 1½ hours.

2 Meanwhile, soak the noodles according to the packet instructions. Drain and refresh under cold water. Shred the remaining spring onions and set aside.

3 To make the omelettes, beat the eggs with the coriander and seasoning. Heat a little of the olive oil in a small frying pan and use the mixture to make three omelettes. Roll up the omelettes tightly one at a time and slice thinly.

4 Remove the chicken from the stock and leave to cool. Strain the stock into a clean pan. Remove and finely shred the chicken meat.

5 Bring the stock to the boil. Add the noodles, chicken, spring onions and crab meat, then simmer for 1–2 minutes. Stir in the soy sauce and season. Ladle the soup into bowls and top each with sliced omelette and coriander leaves.

Chicken and Tiger Prawn Laksa

Laksa is a spicy noodle soup enriched with coconut milk.

Serves 6

6 dried red chillies, seeded
225g/8oz vermicelli, broken
15ml/1 tbsp shrimp paste
10 shallots, chopped
3 garlic cloves
1 lemon grass stalk, roughly chopped
25g/1oz/¼ cup macadamia nuts
grated rind and juice of 1 lime
60ml/4 tbsp groundnut (peanut) oil
2.5ml/½ tsp ground turmeric
5ml/1 tsp ground coriander
1.5 litres/2½ pints/6 cups fish or chicken stock
450g/1lb raw tiger prawns (jumbo shrimp), shelled and deveined
450g/1lb skinless, boneless chicken breast portions, cut into long thin strips
2 x 400g/14oz cans coconut milk
115g/4oz/1 cup beansprouts
½ cucumber, cut into strips
small bunch of spring onions (scallions), shredded, plus extra to garnish
salt and ground black pepper
1 lime, cut into wedges, to serve

1 Soak the chillies in hot water for 45 minutes. Cook the vermicelli according to the packet instructions. Drain; set aside. Drain the chillies and put them in a food processor or blender with the shrimp paste, shallots, garlic, lemon grass, nuts, lime rind and juice. Process to form a thick paste.

2 Heat 45ml/3 tbsp of the oil in a large, heavy pan. Add the spice paste and cook for 1–2 minutes, stirring. Add the turmeric and coriander and cook for 2 minutes more. Stir in the stock; simmer for 25 minutes, then strain and set aside.

3 Heat the remaining oil in a clean pan and fry the prawns until pink. Remove and set aside. Add the chicken and fry for 4–5 minutes, until just cooked.

4 Pour in the stock and coconut milk. Reheat gently. Add the vermicelli and prawns, and heat for 2 minutes. Stir in the beansprouts, cucumber and spring onions.

5 Ladle the soup into bowls, garnish with spring onions and serve with lime wedges.

Chicken and Crab: Energy 159kcal/664kJ; Protein 13.5g; Carbohydrate 10.6g, of which sugars 0.4g; Fat 6.9g, of which saturates 1.7g; Cholesterol 157mg; Calcium 46mg; Fibre 0g; Sodium 526mg.
Chicken and Prawn: Energy 414kcal/1734kJ; Protein 36.4g; Carbohydrate 38.9g, of which sugars 8.8g; Fat 12.6g, of which saturates 1.9g; Cholesterol 199mg; Calcium 129mg; Fibre 1.1g; Sodium 352mg.

Red Chicken Curry Soup

This delicious noodle soup has Burmese origins but is now more closely associated with Thailand. It is the Thai equivalent of the Malaysian dish laksa.

Serves 4–6

600ml/1 pint/2½ cups coconut milk
30ml/2 tbsp red curry paste
5ml/1 tsp ground turmeric
450g/1lb chicken thighs, boned and cut into bitesize chunks
600ml/1 pint/2½ cups chicken stock
60ml/4 tbsp fish sauce
15ml/1 tbsp dark soy sauce
juice of ½–1 lime
450g/1lb fresh egg noodles, blanched briefly in boiling water
salt and freshly ground black pepper

For the garnish

3 spring onions (scallions) chopped
4 fresh red chillies, seeded and chopped
4 shallots, chopped
60ml/4 tbsp sliced pickled mustard leaves, rinsed
30ml/2 tbsp fried sliced garlic
fresh coriander (cilantro) leaves
4 fried noodle nests (optional)

1 Pour about one-third of the coconut milk into a large saucepan and bring to the boil, stirring often with a wooden spoon until it separates.

2 Add the curry paste and turmeric, stir and cook for a minute or so. Add the chicken and cook, stirring, for about 2 minutes, ensuring that all the chunks are coated with the paste.

3 Pour in the remaining coconut milk, chicken stock, fish sauce and soy sauce. Season the soup to taste. Bring to the boil, then immediately reduce the heat and simmer gently for 7–10 minutes. Remove from the heat and stir in the lime juice.

4 Reheat the noodles in boiling water, drain and divide among individual bowls. Divide the chicken among the bowls and then ladle in the hot soup.

5 Top each bowl of soup with a little spring onion, chilli, shallot, pickled mustard leaves, garlic and coriander. Serve with fried noodle nests, if liked, for crunching over the soup.

Thai Chicken Soup

This soup makes excellent use of the characteristic Thai flavourings of garlic, coconut, lemon, peanuts, fresh coriander and chilli. The coconut garnish adds a welcome touch of sweetness to this slurpy, savoury soup.

Serves 4

15ml/1 tbsp vegetable oil
1 garlic clove, finely chopped
2 skinless, boneless chicken breasts (175g/6oz each), diced
2.5ml/½ tsp ground turmeric
1.5ml/¼ tsp hot chilli powder
75g/3oz/½ cup creamed coconut
900ml/1½ pints/3¾ cups hot chicken stock
30ml/2 tbsp lemon or lime juice
30ml/2 tbsp crunchy peanut butter
50g/2oz/1 cup thread egg noodles, broken into small pieces
15ml/1 tbsp chopped spring onions (scallions)
15ml/1 tbsp chopped fresh coriander (cilantro)
salt and ground black pepper

For the garnish

desiccated (dry unsweetened) coconut
finely chopped fresh red chilli

1 Heat the oil in a large pan and fry the garlic for 1 minute until lightly golden. Add the chicken and spices. Cook, stirring, for 3–4 minutes.

2 Crumble the creamed coconut into the hot chicken stock and stir until dissolved. Pour on to the chicken and add the lemon or lime juice, and peanut butter. Bring to the boil, stirring, then reduce the heat and add the thread egg noodles.

3 Cover the pan and simmer for 15 minutes. Add the spring onions and fresh coriander, season well with salt and freshly ground black pepper and cook gently for a further 5 minutes.

4 Meanwhile, cook the desiccated coconut and chilli in a small frying pan for 2–3 minutes, stirring frequently, until the coconut is lightly browned.

5 Pour the soup into warmed individual bowls, dividing the chicken and noodles evenly among them. Sprinkle with the dry-fried coconut and chilli, and serve immediately.

Chicken Curry: Energy 420kcal/1777kJ; Protein 26.4g; Carbohydrate 61.6g, of which sugars 7.8g; Fat 9.3g, of which saturates 2.6g; Cholesterol 101mg; Calcium 102mg; Fibre 3.8g; Sodium 871mg.
Thai Chicken: Energy 338kcal/1411kJ; Protein 25.4g; Carbohydrate 11.4g, of which sugars 2.2g; Fat 21.6g, of which saturates 13g; Cholesterol 65mg; Calcium 17mg; Fibre 0.8g; Sodium 107mg.

Chicken and Egg Noodle Soup

In China, noodles in soup (tang mein) are far more popular than fried noodles (chow mein). You can adapt this basic recipe by using different ingredients for the "dressing".

Serves 4

225g/8oz chicken breast fillet
3–4 dried shiitake mushrooms, soaked
115g/4oz canned sliced bamboo shoots, drained
115g/4oz spinach leaves, lettuce hearts, or Chinese leaves
2 spring onions (scallions)
350g/12oz dried egg noodles
600ml/1 pint/2½ cups chicken stock
30ml/2 tbsp vegetable oil
5ml/1 tsp salt
2.5ml/½ tsp soft light brown sugar
15ml/1 tbsp light soy sauce
10ml/2 tsp Chinese rice wine or dry sherry
a few drops of sesame oil
red chilli sauce, to serve

1 Thinly shred the chicken. Drain the shiitake mushrooms and squeeze them dry, then discard any tough stalks. Thinly shred the mushrooms, bamboo shoots, greens and spring onions.

2 Cook the noodles in boiling water according to the instructions on the packet, then drain and rinse under cold water. Place in a serving bowl.

3 Bring the stock to the boil and pour over the noodles. Set aside and keep warm.

4 Heat a wok, then add the oil and heat briefly. Add about half the spring onions. Add the chicken and stir-fry for 1 minute.

5 Add the mushrooms, bamboo shoots and greens, and stir-fry for 1 minute. Add the salt, sugar, soy sauce and rice wine or sherry and blend well.

6 Pour the "dressing" over the noodles, garnish with the remaining spring onions, and sprinkle over a few drops of sesame oil. Ladle into individual bowls and serve hot, with red-chilli sauce.

Pot-cooked Chicken and Udon Soup

Chicken is the main ingredient in this authentic Japanese dish.

Serves 4

200g/7oz chicken breast fillet, skinned
10ml/2 tsp sake
2 deep-fried tofu or abura-age
900ml/1½ pints/3¾ water mixed with 7.5ml/1½ tsp dashi stock granules
6 large shiitake mushrooms, stalks removed, quartered
4 spring onions (scallions), trimmed and chopped into 3mm/⅛in lengths
30ml/2 tbsp mirin
about 90g/3½oz miso
300g/11oz dried udon noodles
4 eggs

1 Cut the chicken into bitesize pieces. Sprinkle with sake and leave to marinate for 15 minutes.

2 Put the tofu in a sieve (strainer) and rinse with hot water from the kettle to wash off the oil. Drain and cut each into four squares.

3 Bring the water and dashi stock granules to the boil in a pan. Add the chicken, shiitake and tofu. Cook for 5 minutes. Remove the pan from the heat and add the spring onions.

4 Put the mirin and miso in a small bowl. Scoop 30ml/2 tbsp soup from the pan and stir this in well.

5 To cook the udon, boil at least 2 litres/3½ pints/9 cups water in a large pan. The water should not be higher than two-thirds the depth of the pan. Cook the udon for 6 minutes and drain.

6 Put the udon in a large, flameproof clay pot or casserole. Mix the miso paste into the soup and taste. Add more miso if required. Ladle enough soup into the pot to cover the udon, and arrange the rest of the soup ingredients on top.

7 Put the soup on a medium heat and break the eggs on top. When the soup bubbles, wait for 1 minute, then cover and remove from the heat. Leave to stand for 2 minutes before serving in individual bowls.

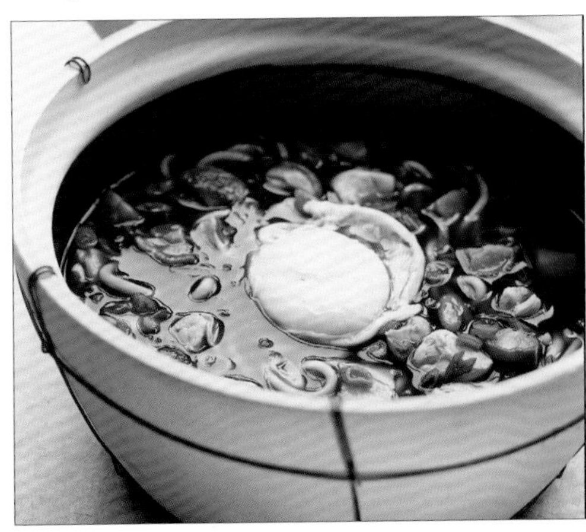

Chicken and Noodle: Energy 372kcal/1576kJ; Protein 12.4g; Carbohydrate 73.3g, of which sugars 6.6g; Fat 5.3g, of which saturates 1.3g; Cholesterol 15mg; Calcium 80mg; Fibre 4.8g; Sodium 129mg.
Chicken and Udon: Energy 439kcal/1855kJ; Protein 28.8g; Carbohydrate 59.5g, of which sugars 3.9g; Fat 11.1g, of which saturates 1.8g; Cholesterol 225mg; Calcium 59mg; Fibre 2.9g; Sodium 1707mg.

Chicken and Vegetable Soup

Hand-made noodles are delicious and easy to make.

Serves 2

½ whole chicken, cut in portions
2 leeks
4 garlic cloves, peeled
40g/1½oz fresh root ginger, sliced
8 dried shiitake mushrooms, soaked until soft and drained
30ml/2 tbsp vegetable oil
100g/4oz carrot, cut in strips
1 courgette (zucchini), in strips
1 onion, finely chopped
10ml/2 tsp sesame oil
light soy sauce, to taste
½ dried chilli, finely chopped

For the seasoning

10ml/2 tsp dark soy sauce
2 spring onions (scallions), finely chopped
2 garlic cloves, crushed
30ml/2 tbsp sesame oil
30ml/2 tbsp sesame seeds
salt and ground white pepper

For the noodles

230g/8oz/2 cups plain (all-purpose) flour
6 eggs, beaten

For the sauce

30ml/2 tbsp light soy sauce
2 spring onions (scallions), finely chopped
2 garlic cloves, crushed
10ml/2 tsp Korean chilli powder
10ml/2 tsp sesame seeds
15ml/1 tbsp sesame oil

1 Simmer the chicken with the leeks, garlic and ginger in water to cover for 20–25 minutes. Remove the chicken and strain the stock. Skin and bone the chicken, cutting the meat in thin strips. Mix the seasoning ingredients with a pinch of salt and white pepper. Add the chicken strips, coat them and set aside.

2 For the noodles, mix the flour, a pinch of salt, eggs and a splash of water to a dough. Knead until smooth. Roll out on a floured surface to 3mm/⅛in thick. Roll or fold and slice thinly.

3 Slice the shiitake. Heat the vegetable oil and stir-fry the shiitake, courgette, carrot and onion. Add the sesame oil and a pinch of salt.

4 Boil the chicken stock and season with the light soy sauce, salt and pepper. Add the noodles and cook for 4 minutes. Serve topped with the chicken, vegetables and a sprinkling of dried chilli. Mix all the sauce ingredients and serve with the soup.

Spicy Chicken Noodle Soup

This fragrant soup is particularly popular in Indonesian and Malay fare. Rempah is one of the main seasoning pastes used in South-east Asia.

Serves 6

1 small chicken, about 900g/2lb
2 lemon grass stalks, bruised
25g/1oz fresh root ginger, peeled and sliced
2 fresh kaffir lime leaves
1 dried red chilli
30ml/2 tbsp vegetable oil
50g/2oz mung bean thread noodles, soaked until pliable
3 hard-boiled eggs, peeled and halved
115g/4oz/½ cup beansprouts
small bunch of fresh coriander (cilantro), roughly chopped, to garnish
2 limes, quartered, chilli oil and soy sauce, to serve

For the rempah

8 shallots, chopped
8 garlic cloves, chopped
6 candlenuts or macadamia nuts
50g/2oz galangal, chopped
2 lemon grass stalks, chopped
4 fresh kaffir lime leaves
15ml/1 tbsp ground coriander
10ml/2 tsp ground turmeric
15ml/1 tbsp vegetable oil

1 Using a mortar and pestle or a food processor or blender, grind all the rempah ingredients to a paste. Set aside.

2 Put the chicken, lemon grass, ginger, lime leaves and chilli into a deep pan and pour in enough water just to cover. Bring to the boil, then cover and simmer for about 1 hour, until the chicken is tender. Remove the chicken, take off and discard the skin and tear the meat into shreds. Strain the stock.

3 Heat the oil in a wok or heavy pan. Stir in the rempah and cook for 1–2 minutes, until fragrant. Pour in the stock and stir well. Season to taste with salt and pepper.

4 Divide the noodles among six bowls. Add the hard-boiled eggs, beansprouts and shredded chicken. Ladle the steaming broth into each bowl and garnish with coriander. Serve immediately with the lime wedges, chilli oil and soy sauce.

Chicken and Veg: Energy 1138kcal/4767kJ; Protein 94.1g; Carbohydrate 70.4g, of which sugars 11.4g; Fat 55.6g, of which saturates 10.5g; Cholesterol 746mg; Calcium 392mg; Fibre 10.1g; Sodium 739mg.
Spicy Chicken Noodle: Energy 411kcal/1708kJ; Protein 30g; Carbohydrate 7.1g, of which sugars 0.8g; Fat 29.3g, of which saturates 7.6g; Cholesterol 215mg; Calcium 39mg; Fibre 0.7g; Sodium 148mg.

Chicken and Chilli Soup

Ginger and lemon grass add an aromatic note to this tasty, refreshing dish, which is more like a mound of tender, pot-simmered vegetables served over delicious noodle soup. It can be served as a light lunch or appetizer. The soft vermicelli rice noodles are the perfect foil to the crunch of the cooked vegetables, and soak up the flavoursome liquid of this soup wonderfully well.

Serves 4

150g/5oz skinless boneless chicken breasts, cut into strips
2.5cm/1in piece fresh root ginger, finely chopped
5cm/2in piece lemon grass stalk, finely chopped
1 fresh red chilli, seeded and thinly sliced
8 baby corn cobs, halved lengthways
1 large carrot, cut into thin sticks
1 litre/1¾ pints/4 cups hot chicken stock
4 spring onions (scallions), thinly sliced
12 small shiitake mushrooms, sliced
115g/4oz/1 cup vermicelli rice noodles
30ml/2 tbsp soy sauce
salt and ground black pepper

1 Place the chicken strips, chopped ginger, chopped lemon grass and sliced chilli in a Chinese sand pot or ovenproof casserole. Add the halved baby corn and the carrot sticks. Pour over the hot chicken stock and cover the pot.

2 Place the Chinese sand pot or casserole in an unheated oven. Set the temperature to 200°C/400°F/Gas 6 and cook the soup for 30–40 minutes, or until the stock is simmering and the chicken and vegetables are tender.

3 Add the spring onions and mushrooms, cover and return the pot to the oven for 10 minutes. Meanwhile place the noodles in a large bowl and cover with boiling water – soak for the required time, following the packet instructions.

4 Drain the noodles and divide among four warmed serving bowls. Stir the soy sauce into the soup and season with salt and pepper. Divide the soup among the bowls and serve.

Chicken Steamboat

This chicken dish is named after the vessel in which it is cooked – like a fondue pot, with a funnel and a moat.

Serves 8

8 dried shiitake mushrooms, soaked for 30 minutes
1.5 litres/2½ pints/6¼ cups chicken stock
10ml/2 tsp rice wine or medium-dry sherry
10ml/2 tsp sesame oil
225g/8oz each lean pork and rump steak, thinly sliced
1 chicken breast, skinned and thickly sliced
2 chicken livers, trimmed and sliced
225g/8oz/2 cups raw prawns (shrimp), peeled
450g/1lb white fish fillets, skinned and cubed
200g/7oz fish balls (from Asian stores)
115g/4oz fried tofu, cut in pieces
leafy green vegetables, such as lettuce, Chinese leaves, spinach leaves and watercress, cut up
225g/8oz Chinese rice vermicelli
8 eggs
½ bunch spring onions (scallions), chopped
salt and ground white pepper
sauces, to serve, such as soy sauce with sesame seeds; soy sauce with crushed ginger; chilli sauce; and plum sauce

1 Drain and slice the mushrooms, reserving the liquid. Pour the stock into a large pan, with the rice wine or sherry, sesame oil and mushroom liquid. Bring to the boil, then season with salt and white pepper. Reduce the heat and simmer gently.

2 Put the meat, fish, tofu, vegetables and mushrooms in bowls on the table. Soak the vermicelli in hot water for 5 minutes, drain and place in eight soup bowls. Crack an egg for each diner into a small bowl. Put the sauces in bowls on the table.

3 Add the spring onions to the stock, and bring to the boil. Pour the liquid into a lighted steamboat at the table. Each guest lowers a few chosen morsels into the boiling stock, using chopsticks or fondue forks. When cooked, after a minute or two, they are removed and eaten with the sauces.

4 When all the ingredients are finished, reduce the rich stock with boiling water if necessary. Ladle it over the soaked noodles and slide an egg into each, stirring until it sets into threads.

Chicken and Chilli: Energy 165kcal/693kJ; Protein 13.3g; Carbohydrate 26g, of which sugars 3.1g; Fat 0.9g, of which saturates 0.2g; Cholesterol 26mg; Calcium 23mg; Fibre 1.4g; Sodium 852mg.
Chicken Steamboat: Energy 547kcal/2295kJ; Protein 78.8g; Carbohydrate 9.1g, of which sugars 1.9g; Fat 21.9g, of which saturates 5.9g; Cholesterol 673mg; Calcium 377mg; Fibre 0.9g; Sodium 684mg.

Duck Broth with Egg

This Chinese-inspired duck and noodle soup makes a delicious meal.

Serves 6

5ml/1 tsp sunflower oil
2 shallots, thinly sliced
4cm/1½in fresh root ginger, peeled and sliced
15ml/1 tbsp soy sauce
5ml/1 tsp five-spice powder
10ml/2 tsp sugar
175g/6oz pak choi (bok choy)
450g/1lb fresh egg noodles
225g/8oz roast duck, thinly sliced
sea salt

For the stock

1 chicken carcass
2 carrots, peeled and quartered
2 onions, peeled and quartered
4cm/1½in fresh root ginger, sliced
2 lemon grass stalks, chopped
30ml/2 tbsp shrimp paste
15ml/1 tbsp soy sauce
6 black peppercorns

For the garnish

4 spring onions (scallions), sliced
1–2 red Serrano chillies, seeded and finely sliced
1 bunch each coriander (cilantro) and basil, leaves chopped

1 For the stock, put the chicken in a pan with all the other stock ingredients and pour in 2.5 litres/4½ pints/10¼ cups water. Boil for a few minutes, skim off any foam, then reduce the heat and simmer gently with the lid on for 2–3 hours. Uncover and simmer for 30 minutes to reduce the stock. Skim off fat, season, then strain. Measure 2 litres/3½ pints/8 cups.

2 Heat the oil in a wok or deep pan and stir in the shallots and ginger. Add the soy sauce, five-spice powder, sugar and stock and bring to the boil. Season with a little salt, reduce the heat and simmer for 10–15 minutes.

3 Meanwhile, cut the pak choi diagonally into wide strips and blanch in boiling water to soften them. Drain and refresh under cold running water to prevent them cooking any further. Bring a large pan of water to the boil, then add the fresh noodles. Cook for 5 minutes, then drain well.

4 Divide the noodles among six soup bowls, lay some of the pak choi and sliced duck over them, and then ladle over generous amounts of the simmering broth. Garnish with the spring onions, chillies and herbs, and serve immediately.

Beef Broth with Egg and Noodles

This chilled broth is refreshing and satisfying.

Serves 2

90g/3½oz beef shank
1 leek, roughly chopped
½ onion, chopped
10g/¼oz fresh root ginger, peeled and roughly chopped
4 garlic cloves, chopped
1 hard-boiled egg
¼ Chinese white radish, peeled
½ cucumber
1 Asian pear
90g/3½oz buckwheat noodles
ice cubes, to serve

For the seasoning

15ml/1 tbsp rice vinegar
15ml/1 tbsp sugar
ready-made English (hot) mustard, sugar, rice vinegar and salt

1 Soak the beef in cold water for 30 minutes, then drain.

2 Bring 1 litre/1¾ pints/4 cups water to the boil in a large pan. Add the beef, reduce the heat and simmer for 1 hour, skimming the fat and foam from the surface throughout. Add the leek, onion, root ginger and garlic, and cook for another 20 minutes. Remove the meat and cut it into thin slices.

3 Strain, cool and chill the soup. Slice the hard-boiled egg in half. Cut the radish into thin julienne strips. Seed the cucumber and cut into thin julienne strips. Peel and core the Asian pear and cut it into thin julienne strips.

4 Place the radish in a bowl and add the rice vinegar, sugar and a pinch of salt for seasoning. Coat the radish and leave to chill.

5 Cook the noodles in a pan of boiling water for 5 minutes. Drain. Rinse two or three times in cold water. Drain and chill.

6 Pour the chilled broth into two serving bowls, adding a ice cubes. Divide the noodles, beef, pear, cucumber and seasoned radish between the dishes. Top each with an egg half.

7 Place the seasonings, mustard, sugar, rice vinegar and salt, in small dishes and serve with the soup. The seasonings are stirred into the broth, to taste, starting with 5ml/1 tsp vinegar and 2.5ml/½ tsp mustard, a pinch of salt and sugar.

Duck Broth: Energy 337kcal/1411kJ; Protein 12.1g; Carboh. 62.5g, of which sugars 1.1g; Fat 3.3g, of which saturates 0.8g, of which polyunsaturates 0.9g; Cholesterol 41mg; Calc. 66mg; Fibre 0.7g; Sodium 269mg.
Beef Broth: Energy 403kcal/1698kJ; Protein 22.2g; Carbohydrate 57.5g, of which sugars 22.9g; Fat 10.9g, of which saturates 2.8g; Cholesterol 131mg; Calcium 100mg; Fibre 6.8g; Sodium 87mg.

Beef Noodle Soup with Oyster Mushrooms

Serve the soup with a bowl of steamed rice.

Serves 2

80g/3oz lean tender beef
30ml/2 tbsp light soy sauce
2 eggs, beaten
50ml/3 tbsp vegetable oil
4 oyster mushrooms
80g/3oz courgette (zucchini)
sesame oil, for drizzling
100g/4oz plain noodles
1 spring onion (scallion), finely chopped
1 dried red chilli, thinly sliced
2 garlic cloves, crushed
salt and ground white pepper
sesame seeds, to garnish

1 Pour 500ml/17fl oz/2¼ cups water into a pan and bring to the boil. Add the beef and cook until tender, about 20 minutes. Remove and slice into thin strips. Strain the stock into a jug (pitcher). Add the light soy sauce and set aside.

2 Season the eggs with salt. Coat a frying pan with 10ml/2 tsp vegetable oil and heat. Add the eggs and cook to a thin omelette, browned each side. Remove and cut into thin strips.

3 Cut the oyster mushrooms and courgette into thin julienne strips. Sprinkle both with a little salt. Pat the courgette dry with kitchen paper after 5 minutes.

4 Coat a frying pan or wok with the remaining vegetable oil and heat. Quickly stir-fry the mushrooms and drizzle with sesame oil before setting them aside. Lightly fry the courgette until it softens, then remove from the wok. Finally, stir-fry the beef until it has lightly browned, and set aside.

5 Bring a pan of water to the boil and cook the noodles, then drain and rinse in cold water. Reheat the reserved beef stock.

6 Place the noodles in a soup dish and cover with the mushrooms, courgette and sliced beef. Top with the spring onion, chilli and garlic, then pour over the beef stock until roughly one-third of the ingredients are covered. Finally, sprinkle with sesame seeds before serving.

Beef Noodles in Oxtail Broth

Nutritious and filling, this much-loved noodle soup makes an intensely satisfying meal at any time of day.

Serves 6

500g/1¼lb dried noodles, soaked in water for 20 minutes
1 onion, halved and finely sliced
6–8 spring onions (scallions), cut into long pieces
2–3 fresh red chillies, seeded and finely sliced
115g/4oz/½ cup beansprouts
1 large bunch each fresh coriander (cilantro) and mint, stalks removed, leaves chopped, to garnish
2 limes, cut in wedges, and hoisin sauce and fish sauce, to serve

For the stock

1.5kg/3lb 5oz oxtail, trimmed of fat and cut into thick pieces
1kg/2¼lb beef shank or brisket
2 large onions
2 carrots
7.5cm/3in fresh root ginger, cut into chunks
6 cloves
2 cinnamon sticks
6 star anise
5ml/1 tsp black peppercorns
30ml/2 tbsp soy sauce
45–60ml/3–4 tbsp fish sauce
salt

1 To make the stock, put the oxtail into a large, deep pan and cover with water. Bring it to the boil and cook for 10 minutes. Drain the oxtail, rinsing off any scum, and return it to the clean pan with the other stock ingredients, apart from the fish sauce. Cover with 3 litres/5¼ pints/12 cups water. Boil, then simmer for 2–3 hours with the lid on, and 1 hour without it. Skim, then strain 2 litres/3½ pints/8 cups stock into another pan.

2 Cut the cooked meat into thin pieces; discard the bones. Bring the stock to the boil, stir in the fish sauce, season to taste, and keep simmering until ready to use.

3 Cook the noodles in boiling water until tender, then drain and divide among six wide soup bowls. Top each serving with beef, onion, spring onions, chillies and beansprouts. Ladle the hot stock over the top, sprinkle with fresh herbs and serve immediately, with the lime wedges to squeeze over and the sauces to pass round.

Beef Noodle: Energy 492kcal/2059kJ; Protein 23.1g; Carbohydrate 40.4g, of which sugars 3.3g; Fat 27.7g, of which saturates 4.9g; Cholesterol 213mg; Calcium 60mg; Fibre 2.3g; Sodium 1167mg.
Beef in Oxtail: Energy 180kcal/748kJ; Protein 10.8g; Carbohydrate 4.8g, of which sugars 4.1g; Fat 4.2g, of which saturates 1.6g; Cholesterol 24mg; Calcium 35mg; Fibre 1g; Sodium 219mg.

Meatball Soup with Noodles

This wonderfully fragrant combination makes for a hearty, warming soup.

Serves 4

10 dried shiitake mushrooms
90g/3½oz bean thread noodles
675g/1½lb minced (ground) beef
10ml/2 tsp finely grated garlic
10ml/2 tsp finely grated fresh root ginger
1 fresh red chilli, seeded and chopped
6 spring onions (scallions), sliced
1 egg white
15ml/1 tbsp cornflour (cornstarch)
15ml/1 tbsp Chinese rice wine
30ml/2 tbsp sunflower oil
1.5 litres/2½ pints/6 cups beef or chicken stock
50ml/2fl oz/¼ cup light soy sauce
5ml/1 tsp sugar
150g/5oz enokitake mushrooms, trimmed
200g/7oz Chinese leaves (Chinese cabbage) very thinly sliced
salt and ground black pepper

1 Place the dried mushrooms in a medium bowl and pour over 250ml/8fl oz/1 cup boiling water. Leave to soak for 30 minutes and then squeeze dry, reserving the liquid. Remove and discard the tough mushroom stems; thickly slice the caps and set aside.

2 Put the noodles in a large bowl and pour over boiling water to cover. Soak for 3–4 minutes, then drain, rinse and set aside.

3 Place the beef, garlic, ginger, chilli, spring onions, egg white, cornflour, rice wine and seasoning in a food processor or blender. Process to combine well. Divide the mixture into 30 portions, then shape each one into a ball. Heat the stock.

4 Heat a wok and add the oil. Fry the meatballs, in batches, for 2–3 minutes on each side. Remove with a slotted spoon and drain on kitchen paper. Add the meatballs to the simmering beef stock with the soy sauce, sugar, shiitake mushrooms and reserved soaking liquid. Cook gently for 20–25 minutes.

5 Add the noodles, enokitake mushrooms and cabbage and cook gently for 4–5 minutes. Serve in wide bowls.

Beef and Tofu Noodle Soup

Use a special cast-iron sukiyaki pan and burner or a similar table top cooker for this dish, as it needs a continuous high heat.

Serves 4

1kg/2¼lb beef topside (pot roast), thinly sliced
lard (or white cooking fat), for cooking
4 leeks, sliced diagonally into 1cm/½in pieces
8 shiitake mushrooms, stems removed
300g/11oz shirataki noodles, boiled for 2 minutes, drained and halved
2 pieces fried tofu, cubed
4 fresh eggs, to serve

For the sukiyaki stock
100ml/3½fl oz/scant ½ cup mirin
45ml/3 tbsp sugar
105ml/7 tbsp soy sauce

For the seasoning mix
200ml/7fl oz/scant 1 cup dashi
100ml/3½fl oz/scant ½ cup sake
15ml/1 tbsp soy sauce

1 Make the sukiyaki stock. Mix the mirin, sugar and soy sauce in a pan, bring to the boil, then set aside. To make the seasoning mix, heat the dashi, sake and soy sauce in a pan. As soon as it boils, set aside.

2 Fan out the beef slices on a large serving plate. Put the lard for cooking on the same plate. Arrange all the remaining ingredients, except the eggs, on one or more large plates.

3 Stand the portable cooker on a suitably heavy mat. Melt the lard or white cooking fat, add three or four slices of beef and some leeks, then pour in the sukiyaki stock. Gradually add the remaining ingredients, except the eggs.

4 Place each egg in a ramekin and beat lightly. When the beef and vegetables are cooked, diners help themselves and dip the food in the raw egg before eating.

5 When the stock has thickened, stir in the seasoning mix and carry on cooking until all the ingredients have been eaten.

Meatball with Noodles: Energy 102kcal/424kJ; Protein 5.4g; Carbohydrate 5.8g, of which sugars 3g; Fat 6.5g, of which saturates 1.9g; Cholesterol 13mg; Calcium 39mg; Fibre 0.9g; Sodium 308mg.
Beef and Tofu: Energy 868kcal/3633kJ; Protein 71.5g; Carbohydrate 51.7g, of which sugars 11.1g; Fat 43.2g, of which saturates 13.1g; Cholesterol 662mg; Calcium 605mg; Fibre 6.5g; Sodium 1695mg.

Spicy Beef and Mushroom Soup

Ginger gives this satisfying soup a delightful tang.

Serves 4

10g/½oz dried porcini mushrooms
6 spring onions (scallions)
115g/4oz carrots
350g/12oz lean rump (round) steak
about 30ml/2 tbsp oil
1 garlic clove, crushed
2.5cm/1in fresh root ginger, grated
1.2 litres/2 pints/5 cups beef stock
45ml/3 tbsp light soy sauce
60ml/4 tbsp sake or dry sherry
75g/3oz dried thin egg noodles
75g/3oz spinach, shredded
salt and ground black pepper

1 Break up the dried porcini, place them in a bowl and pour over 150ml/¼ pint/⅔ cup boiling water. Cover and leave the mushrooms to soak for 15 minutes.

2 Cut the spring onions and carrots into fine 5cm/2in long strips. Trim any fat from the meat and slice into thin strips.

3 Heat the oil in a large pan and cook the beef in batches until browned. Remove and drain on kitchen paper. Add the garlic, ginger, spring onions and carrots to the pan and stir-fry for 3 minutes.

4 Add the beef stock, the mushrooms and their soaking liquid, the soy sauce, sherry and plenty of seasoning. Bring to the boil, reduce the heat and simmer, covered, for 10 minutes.

5 Break up the noodles slightly and add to the pan, with the spinach. Simmer gently for 5 minutes, or until the beef is tender. Adjust the seasoning before serving in warmed bowls.

Cook's Tips

- *Chilling the beef briefly in the freezer will make it much easier to slice into thin strips.*
- *Dried mixed mushrooms are also available to buy and can be used in this recipe.*

Sesame Beef Broth with Wild Mushrooms

In this delicious soup, the mushrooms are simmered in beef broth seasoned with garlic and sesame. Ideal as a winter warmer, it takes a little while to cook, but is well worth it for the earthy flavour spiced with spring onions and chillies.

Serves 2

150g/5oz beef
2 dried shiitake mushrooms, soaked in warm water for about 30 minutes until softened
25g/1oz enoki mushrooms
1 onion, sliced
400ml/14fl oz/1⅔ cups water or beef stock
25g/1oz oyster mushrooms, thinly sliced
6 pine mushrooms, cut into thin strips
10 spring onions (scallions), sliced
2 chrysanthemum leaves (optional), and ½ red and ½ green chilli, seeded and shredded, to garnish
steamed rice, to serve

For the seasoning

30ml/2 tbsp dark soy sauce
3 spring onions (scallions), sliced
2 garlic cloves, crushed
10ml/2 tsp sesame seeds
10ml/2 tsp sesame oilwater

1 Slice the beef into thin strips and place in a bowl. Add the seasoning ingredients and mix well, coating the beef evenly. Leave to absorb the flavours for 20 minutes.

2 Drain the shiitake mushrooms and slice them thinly, discarding the stems. Discard the caps from the enoki mushrooms.

3 Place the seasoned beef and the onion in a heavy pan or flameproof casserole and add the water or beef stock. Add all the mushrooms and the spring onions, and bring to the boil.

4 Once the pan is bubbling reduce the heat and simmer for 20 minutes.

5 Transfer to a serving dish or serve from the casserole. Garnish with the chrysanthemum leaves, if using, and shredded chilli, and then serve with steamed rice to soak up the soup.

Spicy Beef: Energy 315kcal/1316kJ; Protein 23.4g; Carbohydrate 17.4g, of which sugars 4g; Fat 15.5g, of which saturates 4.5g; Cholesterol 56mg; Calcium 57mg; Fibre 1.9g; Sodium 713mg.
Sesame Beef: Energy 227kcal/945kJ; Protein 21.1g; Carbohydrate 5.5g, of which sugars 4.4g; Fat 13.6g, of which saturates 3.9g; Cholesterol 44mg; Calcium 72mg; Fibre 2.4g; Sodium 1125mg.

Lamb and Cabbage Noodle Soup

The hotpot, or Mongolian firepot, was introduced to China by 13th-century invaders. Diners cook the ingredients at the table and then dip them in sauces. A standard pot fondue set can be used instead of a firepot.

Serves 6–8

900g/2lb boned leg of lamb
225g/8oz lamb's liver, trimmed
900ml/1½ pints/3¾ cups hot lamb stock
900ml/1½ pints/3¾ cups hot chicken stock
1cm/½in piece fresh root ginger, peeled and thinly sliced
45ml/3 tbsp rice wine
½ head Chinese leaves (Chinese cabbage) shredded
115g/4oz cellophane noodles
salt and ground black pepper

For the dipping sauce

50ml/2fl oz/¼ cup red wine vinegar
7.5ml/½ tbsp dark soy sauce
1cm/½in piece fresh root ginger, peeled and finely shredded
1 spring onion (scallion), shredded

To serve

tomato sauce, sweet chilli sauce, mustard oil and sesame oil
dry-fried coriander seeds, crushed

1 When buying the lamb, ask your butcher to slice it thinly on a slicing machine. Alternatively, freeze for one hour then slice.

2 Mix both types of stock in a large pan. Add the ginger and rice wine, with salt and pepper to taste. Heat to simmering point; simmer for 15 minutes.

3 Arrange the meats and greens on platters. Soak the noodles, following the instructions on the packet.

4 Mix the dipping sauce ingredients in a small bowl. Place the other accompaniments in separate small dishes.

5 Fill the moat of the hotpot, or the pot of the fondue, with the simmering stock. Each guest cooks a portion of meat in the hot stock, then dips it in sauce and coats it in seeds.

6 Once the meat is eaten, add the vegetables and drained noodles. Cook for a minute or two, then serve as a soup.

Red Lentil Lamb Soup

This attractive meat and vegetable soup, made sweet with cinnamon, is ideal for cold and hungry days, especially after energetic activities and long country walks in fresh frosty air.

Serves 4

25g/1oz/2 tbsp butter
225g/8oz lean boneless lamb, cut into 1cm/½in pieces
1 onion, chopped
450g/1lb well-flavoured tomatoes
60ml/4 tbsp chopped fresh coriander (cilantro)
30ml/2 tbsp chopped fresh parsley
2.5ml/½ tsp ground turmeric
2.5ml/½ tsp ground cinnamon
50g/2oz/¼ cup red lentils
75g/3oz/½ cup dried chickpeas, soaked overnight
600ml/1 pint/2½ cups unsalted chicken or lamb stock, or water
4 baby onions or small shallots, peeled
25g/1oz/¼ cup soup noodles
salt and ground black pepper

For the garnish

chopped fresh coriander (cilantro)
lemon slices
ground cinnamon

1 Heat the butter in a large pan or flameproof casserole and fry the lamb and onion for 5 minutes, stirring frequently.

2 Peel the tomatoes, if you wish, by plunging them into boiling water to loosen the skins. Wait for them to cool a little before peeling off the skins. Then cut them into quarters and add to the lamb with the coriander, parsley, turmeric and cinnamon.

3 Rinse the lentils under cold running water and drain the chickpeas. Add both to the pan with the stock or water. Season with pepper. Do not use salted stock or season with stock as this will prevent the chickpeas from become tender. Bring to the boil, cover and simmer gently for 1½ hours.

4 Add the baby onions or small shallots and cook for a further 25 minutes.

5 Add the noodles, stir well and cook for a further 5 minutes. Serve the soup when the noodles are tender, garnished with the coriander, lemon slices and cinnamon.

Lamb and Cabbage: Energy 144kcal/606kJ; Protein 12.3g; Carbohydrate 12g, of which sugars 1.2g; Fat 5.1g, of which saturates 1.1g; Cholesterol 128mg; Calcium 193mg; Fibre 0.9g; Sodium 49mg.
Red Lentil Lamb: Energy 587kcal/2465kJ; Protein 55.7g; Carbohydrate 34.9g, of which sugars 2.6g; Fat 26g, of which saturates 11.9g; Cholesterol 171mg; Calcium 48mg; Fibre 2.9g; Sodium 216mg.

Chinese Pork Soup with Pickled Mustard Greens

This highly flavoured soup makes an interesting start to a meal.

Serves 4–6

225g/8oz pickled mustard leaves, soaked
50g/2oz cellophane noodles, soaked
15ml/1 tbsp vegetable oil
4 garlic cloves, finely sliced
1 litre/1¾ pints/4 cups chicken stock
450g/1lb pork ribs, cut into large chunks
30ml/2 tbsp fish sauce
a pinch of sugar
freshly ground black pepper
2 fresh red or green chillies, seeded and finely sliced, to garnish

1 Cut the pickled mustard leaves into bitesize pieces. Taste to check the seasoning. If they are too salty, soak them for a little longer and drain well.

2 Drain the cellophane noodles, discarding the soaking water, and cut them into pieces about 5cm/2in long.

3 Heat the oil in a small frying pan, add the garlic and stir-fry until golden. Transfer to a bowl and set aside.

4 Put the stock in a saucepan, bring to the boil, then add the pork ribs and simmer gently for 10–15 minutes.

5 Add the pickled mustard leaves and cellophane noodles. Bring back to the boil. Season to taste with fish sauce, sugar and freshly ground black pepper.

6 Pour the soup into individual serving bowls. Garnish with the fried garlic and the red or green chillies and serve hot.

Cook's Tip
Pickled mustard greens are sold in rustic-looking earthenware or ceramic pots in traditional Chinese supermarkets.

Pork Prawn and Noodle Broth

This delicate, yet satisfying, soup is from Vietnam.

Serves 4–6

350g/12oz pork chops or fillet
225g/8oz raw prawns (shrimp)
150g/5oz thin egg noodles
15ml/1 tbsp vegetable oil
10ml/2 tsp sesame oil
4 shallots or 1 onion, sliced
15ml/1 tbsp finely sliced fresh root ginger
1 garlic clove, crushed
5ml/1 tsp sugar
1.5 litres/2½ pints/6¼ cups chicken stock
2 kaffir lime leaves
45ml/3 tbsp fish sauce
juice of ½ lime

For the garnish

4 sprigs of fresh coriander (cilantro)
2 spring onions (scallions), green parts only, chopped

1 If you are using pork chops rather than fillet, remove any fat and the bones. Place the pork in the freezer for 30 minutes to firm but not freeze it. The cold makes the meat easier to slice thinly. Once sliced, set aside.

2 Peel and devein the prawns.

3 Bring a large pan of salted water to the boil and simmer the egg noodles according to the instructions on the packet. Drain and refresh under cold water. Set the noodles to one side.

4 Heat a wok. Add the vegetable and sesame oils and heat through. When the oil is hot, add the shallots or onion and stir-fry for 3–4 minutes, until evenly browned. Remove from the wok and set aside.

5 Add the ginger, garlic, sugar and chicken stock to the wok and bring to a simmer. Add the lime leaves, fish sauce and lime juice. Add the pork, then simmer for 15 minutes.

6 Add the prawns and noodles and simmer for 4–6 minutes, until the prawns are pink and cooked.

7 Serve garnished with coriander sprigs and the green parts of the spring onion.

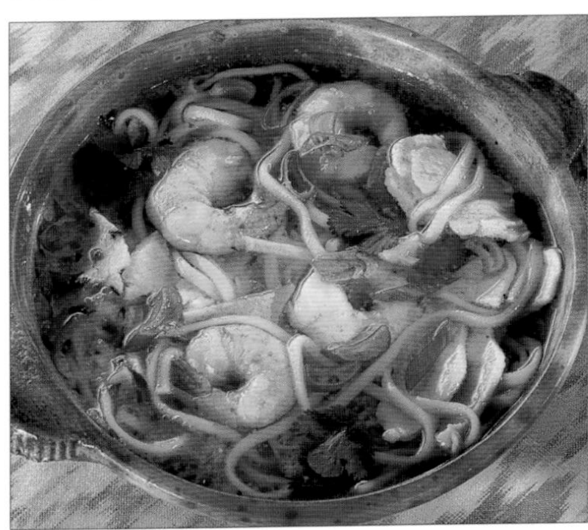

Pork with Greens: Energy 204kcal/851kJ; Protein 16.1g; Carbohydrate 7.3g, of which sugars 0.7g; Fat 12.3g, of which saturates 4.2g; Cholesterol 50mg; Calcium 78mg; Fibre 0.6g; Sodium 627mg.
Pork Prawn: Energy 593kcal/2496kJ; Protein 59.2g; Carbohydrate 48.4g, of which sugars 1.8g; Fat 19.4g, of which saturates 4.7g; Cholesterol 313mg; Calcium 110mg; Fibre 1.9g; Sodium 894mg.

Pork and Spicy Seafood Soup

This is a spicy, garlic-infused soup with squid, prawns and mussels.

Serves 2

90g/3½oz squid, prepared
50g/2oz mussels, scrubbed
15ml/1 tbsp vegetable oil
1 dried chilli, sliced
½ leek, sliced
2 garlic cloves, finely sliced
5ml/1 tsp grated fresh root ginger
50g/2oz pork loin, thinly sliced
30ml/2 tbsp Korean chilli powder
5ml/1 tsp mirin or rice wine
50g/2oz bamboo shoots, sliced
½ onion, roughly chopped
50g/2oz carrot, roughly chopped
50g/2oz prawns (shrimp), peeled
2 Chinese leaves (Chinease cabbage), roughly chopped
750ml/1¼ pints/3 cups beef stock
light soy sauce
300g/11oz udon noodles
salt

1 Score the squid and slice it into 2cm/¾in pieces. Discard any open mussels that do not close when tapped.

2 Heat the oil in a large pan over high heat. Add the chilli, leek, garlic and ginger. Stir-fry until the garlic has lightly browned. Add the pork. Stir-fry quickly, add the chilli powder and mirin or rice wine, and coat the ingredients well.

3 Add the bamboo shoots, onion and carrot, and stir-fry until the vegetables have softened. Stir in the squid, mussels, prawns and cabbage and cook over high heat for 30 seconds.

4 Pour in the beef stock and bring to the boil. Reduce the heat. Season with salt and soy sauce, then reduce the heat. Cover and simmer for 3 minutes. Discard any closed mussels.

5 Cook the udon or wheat noodles in a pan of boiling water until soft, then drain and rinse with cold water. Place a portion of noodles in each soup bowl, ladle over the soup and serve.

Variation
Pak choi (bok choy) can replace the Chinese leaves (Chinese cabbage), and chilli oil can replace the chilli powder.

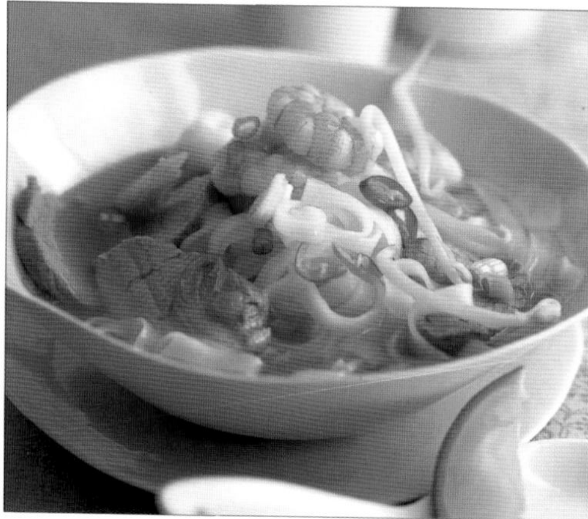

Prawn and Pork Soup with Rice Vermicelli

This low-fat and healthy soup is a popular everyday dish in Cambodia.

Serves 4

225g/8oz rice vermicelli, soaked in lukewarm water for 20 minutes
20 prawns (shrimp), peeled
225g/8oz lean pork tenderloin
115g/4oz/½ cup beansprouts
2 spring onions (scallions), finely sliced
2 fresh green or red Thai chillies, seeded and finely sliced
1 garlic clove, finely sliced
1 bunch each coriander (cilantro) and basil, leaves chopped

For the stock
25g/1oz dried squid
450g/1lb pork ribs
1 onion, peeled and quartered
225g/8oz carrots, cut in chunks
15ml/1 tbsp shrimp paste
15ml/1 tbsp soy sauce
6 black peppercorns
salt

For serving
1 lime, cut into quarters

1 For the stock, soak the squid for 30 minutes, rinse and drain. Put the ribs in a pan. Cover with 2.5 litres/4½ pints/10 cups water. Boil, skim off any fat, and add the squid with all the remaining stock ingredients. Cover. Simmer for 1 hour. Skim and simmer, uncovered, for a further 1½ hours.

2 Strain the stock: there should be 2 litres/3½ pints/8 cups. Boil, reduce the heat, add the tenderlon and simmer for about 25 minutes. Lift out and slice the pork. Keep the stock simmering.

3 Bring a pan of water to the boil. Drain the rice sticks and add to the water. Cook for 5 minutes, or until tender, separating them with chopsticks if they stick together. Drain the rice sticks and divide them among four warm bowls.

4 Drop the prawns into the simmering stock for 1 minute. Lift out with a slotted spoon and lay with the pork on the rice sticks. Ladle the stock over and sprinkle with beansprouts, spring onions, chillies, garlic and herbs. Serve with wedges of lime to squeeze over it.

Pork and Seafood: Energy 778kcal/3288kJ; Protein 39.5g; Carbohydrate 122.8g, of which sugars 9.4g; Fat 17.7g, of which saturates 1.4g; Cholesterol 176mg; Calcium 104mg; Fibre 6.9g; Sodium 734mg.
Prawn: Energy 234kcal/981kJ; Prot. 26.2g; Carbohy. 24.8g, of which sugars 1.6g; Fat 3.3g, of which saturates 1g, of which polyunsaturates 0.6g; Cholesterol 137mg; Calcium 84mg; Fibre 1.1g; Sodium 681mg.

Pork and Pickle Noodle Soup

Despite its European-sounding name, this soup is actually an oriental speciality. This soup is a meal in itself and the hot pickle gives it a delicious tang.

Serves 4

1 litre/1¾ pints/4 cups chicken stock
350g/12oz egg noodles
15ml/1 tbsp dried prawns (shrimp), soaked
30ml/2 tbsp vegetable oil
225g/8oz lean pork, finely shredded
15ml/1 tbsp yellow bean paste
15ml/1 tbsp soy sauce
115g/4oz Szechuan hot pickle, rinsed, drained and shredded
a pinch of sugar
2 spring onions (scallions), finely sliced, to garnish

1 Bring the stock to the boil in a pan. Add the noodles and cook until almost tender. Drain the noodles.

2 Drain the dried prawns, rinse them under cold water, drain again and add to the stock. Lower the heat and simmer for a further 2 minutes. Keep hot.

3 Heat the oil in a frying pan or wok. Add the pork and stir-fry over a high heat for 3 minutes.

4 Add the bean paste and soy sauce to the pork and stir-fry for 1 minute. Add the hot pickle with a pinch of sugar. Stir-fry for 1 minute further.

5 Divide the noodles and soup among individual serving bowls. Spoon the pork mixture on top, then sprinkle with the spring onions and serve at once.

Variation

This is good made with lamb tenderloin instead of pork. Omit the dried prawns (shrimp) and add some finely shredded fresh root ginger and chopped fresh mint with the spring onions (scallions) when serving the soup. Lamb or chicken stock can be used as the base for the lamb soup.

Pork and Egg Ramen-style Soup

This is a famous Japanese soup.

Serves 4

250g/9oz dried ramen noodles

For the stock

4 spring onions (scallions)
7.5cm/3in fresh root ginger, sliced
2 raw chicken carcasses
1 large onion, quartered
4 garlic cloves
1 large carrot, roughly chopped
1 egg shell
120ml/4fl oz/½ cup sake
60ml/4 tbsp shoyu or soy sauce
2.5ml/½ tsp salt

For the pot-roast pork

500g/1¼lb pork shoulder, boned
30ml/2 tbsp vegetable oil
2 spring onions (scallions), chopped
2.5cm/1in fresh root ginger, peeled and sliced
15ml/1 tbsp sake
45ml/3 tbsp shoyu or soy sauce
15ml/1 tbsp sugar

For the toppings

2 hard-boiled eggs
150g/5oz pickled bamboo shoots, soaked for 30 minutes and drained
½ nori sheet, broken into pieces
2 spring onions (scallions), chopped
ground white pepper
sesame oil or chilli oil

1 To make the stock, bruise the spring onions and ginger. Boil 1.5 litres/2½ pints/6¼ cups water in a wok. Add the chicken bones and boil for 5 minutes. Drain and rinse the bones. Bring another 2 litres/3½ pints/9 cups water to the boil. Add the bones and other stock ingredients, except the shoyu and salt. Simmer gently for up to 2 hours, until reduced by half. Strain.

2 For the pork, roll the meat up tightly and tie. Heat the oil, stir in the spring onions and ginger. Add and brown the meat.

3 Sprinkle with sake and add 400ml/14fl oz/1⅔ cups water, the shoyu and sugar. Boil, then cover and cook for 25–30 minutes, turning every 5 minutes. Remove from the heat. Slice the pork.

4 Boil 1 litre/1¾ pints/4 cups soup stock. Add the shoyu and salt. Cook the noodles according to the packet instructions. Drain. Divide among four bowls. Cover with soup. Add the boiled eggs, pork, pickled bamboo shoots, and nori. Sprinkle with spring onions. Serve with pepper and sesame or chilli oil.

Pork and Pickle: Energy 218kcal/911kJ; Protein 24.5g; Carbohydrate 7.8g, of which sugars 0.9g; Fat 9.7g, of which saturates 3g; Cholesterol 74mg; Calcium 90mg; Fibre 0.8g; Sodium 454mg.
Pork and Egg: Energy 521kcal/2193kJ; Protein 38.9g; Carbohydrate 55.6g, of which sugars 8.7g; Fat 17.5g, of which saturates 3.2g; Cholesterol 174mg; Calcium 57mg; Fibre 3g; Sodium 843mg.

Vermicelli Soup

This popular Mexican soup, is delicious as an appetizer.

Serves 4

30ml/2 tbsp olive or corn oil
50g/2oz/⅓ cup vermicelli
1 onion, roughly chopped
1 garlic clove, chopped
450g/1lb tomatoes, chopped
1 litre/1¾ pints/4 cups vegetable or chicken stock
1.5ml/¼ tsp sugar
15ml/1 tbsp finely chopped fresh coriander (cilantro)
salt and ground black pepper
25g/1oz/¼ cup freshly grated Parmesan cheese, to serve

1 Heat the oil in a pan and sauté the vermicelli until golden: do not burn. Remove the vermicelli with a slotted spoon and drain.

2 Purée the onion, garlic and tomatoes. Add to the pan and cook, stirring, for 5 minutes. Add the vermicelli, stock, seasoning and coriander. Boil, lower the heat, cover and simmer until the vermicelli is tender. Serve with Parmesan.

Pumpkin Soup with Spaghetti

Broken spaghetti makes good soup pasta.

Serves 4

50g/2oz/¼ cup butter
1 onion, finely chopped
450g/1lb pumpkin flesh, diced
750ml/1¼ pints/3½ cups chicken stock
475ml/16fl oz/2 cups milk
pinch of freshly grated nutmeg
40g/1½oz spaghetti, broken into small pieces
90ml/6 tbsp freshly grated Parmesan cheese
salt and ground black pepper

1 Heat the butter in a large pan. Add the onion and cook for 6–8 minutes. Stir in the pumpkin and cook for 2–3 minutes. Add the stock and simmer for 15 minutes, until the pumpkin is soft. Cool, purée and return to the pan.

2 Stir in the milk, nutmeg and seasoning. Boil, add the spaghetti and simmer for 10 minutes. Stir in the Parmesan and serve.

Beetroot Soup with Ravioli

Beetroot and pasta are a delicious duo. With bought ravioli and ready cooked beetroot, this substantial soup is ready in minutes. Ideal for a tasty supper or speedy first course.

Serves 4

225g/8oz fresh mushroom ravioli
1 small onion or shallot, finely chopped
2 garlic cloves, crushed
5ml/1 tsp fennel seeds
600ml/1 pint/2½ cups chicken or vegetable stock
225g/8oz cooked beetroot
30ml/2 tbsp fresh orange juice
fresh fennel or dill leaves, to garnish
crusty bread, to serve

1 Bring a large pan of salted water to the boil. Add the ravioli and bring back to the boil, Cook for 3–5 minutes or according to the packet instructions, until the ravioli are tender, but not soft. Drain well and rinse under cold running water, then set aside in a colander.

2 Put the onion, garlic and fennel seeds into a pan. Then pour in 150ml/¼ pint/⅔ cup of the stock. Bring to the boil, cover and simmer for 5 minutes, or until the onion is tender.

3 Peel and finely dice the beetroot, reserving 60ml/4 tbsp for the garnish. Add the rest of the beetroot to the pan and pour in the remaining stock. Bring to the boil.

4 Add the orange juice and cooked ravioli and simmer for 2 minutes. Ladle into shallow soup bowls. Garnish with the reserved diced beetroot and fresh fennel or dill leaves. Serve hot, with crusty bread.

Cook's Tip

Polish-style beetroot soup is often served with pasta filled with dried mushrooms. Cheese-filled pasta is also excellent. Plain pasta shapes can be used and a little diced cooked ham added, then Parmesan cheese sprinkled over when serving.

Vermicelli Soup: Energy 141kcal/589kJ; Protein 4.4g; Carbohydrate 13.3g, of which sugars 3.5g; Fat 7.9g, of which saturates 2.2g; Cholesterol 6mg; Calcium 86mg; Fibre 1.1g; Sodium 79mg.
Pumpkin Soup: Energy 304kcal/1267kJ; Protein 15.2g; Carbohydrate 16.7g, of which sugars 8.8g; Fat 20.1g, of which saturates 12.5g; Cholesterol 56mg; Calcium 454mg; Fibre 1.6g; Sodium 373mg.
Beetroot with Ravioli: Energy 260kcal/1101kJ; Protein 9.9g; Carbohydrate 51g, of which sugars 6.1g; Fat 3.3g, of which saturates 0.7g; Cholesterol 76mg; Calcium 108mg; Fibre 3.1g; Sodium 198mg.

Courgette Soup with Conchigliette

This pretty, fresh-tasting soup combines a popular Italian summer vegetable with attractive little shell-shaped pasta.

Serves 4–6

60ml/4 tbsp olive or sunflower oil
2 onions, finely chopped
1.5 litres/2½ pints/6¼ cups chicken stock
900g/2lb courgettes (zucchini)
115g/4oz/1 cup conchigliette
freshly squeezed lemon juice
30ml/2 tbsp chopped fresh chervil
salt and ground black pepper
soured cream, to serve

1 Heat the oil in a large pan and add the finely chopped onions. Cover and cook gently for about 20 minutes, until very soft but not coloured, stirring occasionally.

2 Add the chicken stock to the pan and bring the soup to the boil.

3 Meanwhile grate the courgettes and stir into the boiling stock with the pasta. Reduce the heat and simmer for about 15 minutes, until the pasta is *al dente*. Season to taste with lemon juice, salt and pepper.

4 Stir in the chopped fresh chervil and add a swirl of soured cream before serving.

Cook's Tip
Courgettes are now available almost all the year round, but they are at their best in spring and summer. Choose smaller ones for the best flavour.

Variation
To ring the changes, try replacing the courgettes with cucumber and use any of the little soup pasta available.

Pasta and Bean Soup

This peasant soup is very thick. In Italy it is made with dried, soaked or fresh beans, never canned, and served hot or at room temperature.

Serves 4–6

300g/11oz/1½ cups dried borlotti or cannellini beans
400g/14oz can plum tomatoes, chopped, with their juice
3 garlic cloves, crushed
2 bay leaves
pinch coarsely ground black pepper
90ml/6 tbsp olive oil
10ml/2 tsp salt
200g/7oz/2¼ cups ditalini or other small soup pasta
45ml/3 tbsp chopped fresh parsley

For serving

extra virgin olive oil (optional)
freshly grated Parmesan cheese

1 Place the beans in a bowl, cover with cold water and leave to soak overnight. Rinse and drain well.

2 Place the beans in a large pan and cover with water. Bring to the boil and cook for 10 minutes. Rinse and drain again.

3 Return the beans to the pan. Add enough water to cover them by 2.5cm/1in. Stir in the coarsely chopped tomatoes with their juice, the garlic, bay leaves, black pepper and the oil.

4 Simmer for 1½–2 hours, or until the beans are tender. If necessary, add more water.

5 Remove the bay leaves. Pass about half of the bean mixture through a food mill or process in a food processor or blender. Stir into the pan with the remaining bean mixture. Add 750ml/1¼ pints/3½ cups water and bring the soup to the boil.

6 Add the salt and the pasta. Stir well, and cook until the pasta is *al dente*. Stir in the parsley.

7 Allow the soup to stand for at least 10 minutes before serving. To serve, drizzle with a little olive oil, if using, and serve with grated Parmesan passed separately.

Courgette Soup: Energy 189kcal/790kJ; Protein 6.1g; Carbohydrate 23.6g, of which sugars 7.9g; Fat 8.5g, of which saturates 1.1g; Cholesterol 0mg; Calcium 68mg; Fibre 3.2g; Sodium 5mg.
Pasta and Bean: Energy 240kcal/1010kJ; Protein 16.7g; Carbohydrate 25.1g, of which sugars 4.8g; Fat 8.8g, of which saturates 2.2g; Cholesterol 32mg; Calcium 60mg; Fibre 5g; Sodium 1009mg.

Egg and Lemon Soup with Pasta

Egg and lemon mixed together, and then cooled to make a creamy soup, has long been a traditional favourite throughout the Mediterranean. This version uses tiny orzo pasta to make a heartier dish than the classic avgolemono. Orzo is tiny pasta, more akin to rice in appearance.

Serves 4–6

1.75 litres/3 pints/7½ cups chicken stock
115g/4oz/½ cup orzo pasta
3 eggs
juice of 1 large lemon
salt and ground black pepper
lemon slices, to garnish

1 Pour the stock into a large pan, and bring to boiling point. Add the pasta and cook for 5 minutes.

2 Beat the eggs until frothy, then add the lemon juice and a tablespoon of cold water. Slowly stir in a ladleful of the hot chicken stock, then add one or two more.

3 Reduce the heat under the pan to the lowest setting. Return the egg mixture to the soup in the pan, stirring all the time. Immediately remove the pan from the heat and stir well. Season with salt and pepper and serve immediately, garnished with lemon slices.

Cook's Tip
Do not let the soup boil once the eggs have been added or it will curdle. Take care when using a heavy bottomed pan that retains heat because the soup may continue to simmer for some time after the heat has been reduced. This can be enough to curdle the eggs in the soup.

Variation
Replace orzo with other small pasta such as stellette (stars) or orecchiette (little ears). The cooking times should be the same.

Roasted Tomato and Pasta Soup

Roasting enhances and concentrates the flavour of tomatoes and, in this recipe, the soup has a wonderful, smoky taste.

Serves 4

450g/1lb ripe plum tomatoes, halved lengthways
1 large red (bell) pepper, quartered lengthways and seeded
1 large red onion, quartered lengthways
2 garlic cloves, unpeeled
15ml/1 tbsp olive oil
1.2 litres/2 pints/5 cups vegetable stock or water
a good pinch of sugar
90g/3½oz/scant 1 cup small pasta shapes, such as tubetti or small macaroni
salt and ground black pepper
fresh basil leaves, to garnish

1 Preheat the oven to 190°C/375°F/Gas 5. Spread out the tomatoes, red pepper, onion and garlic in a roasting pan and drizzle with the olive oil. Roast for 30–40 minutes until the vegetables are soft and charred, stirring and turning them halfway through cooking.

2 Transfer the vegetables into a food processor or blender, add about 250ml/8fl oz/1 cup of the stock or water, and process until puréed. Scrape into a sieve (strainer) placed over a large pan and press the purée through into the pan.

3 Add the remaining stock or water, the sugar and salt and pepper to taste. Bring to the boil.

4 Add the pasta and simmer for 7–8 minutes (or according to the instructions on the packet), stirring frequently, until *al dente*, tender but with a bit of bite. Taste and adjust the seasoning with salt and black pepper. Serve hot in warmed bowls, garnished with the fresh basil leaves.

Cook's Tip
You can roast the vegetables in advance, allow them to cool, then leave them in a covered bowl in the refrigerator overnight before puréeing.

Egg and Lemon: Energy 104kcal/438kJ; Protein 5.5g; Carbohydrate 14.3g, of which sugars 0.7g; Fat 3.2g, of which saturates 0.8g; Cholesterol 95mg; Calcium 20mg; Fibre 0.6g; Sodium 117mg.
Tomato and Pasta: Energy 128kcal/543kJ; Protein 4.5g; Carbohydrate 26.9g, of which sugars 9.7g; Fat 1g, of which saturates 0.2g; Cholesterol 0mg; Calcium 30mg; Fibre 3.2g; Sodium 14mg.

Summer Minestrone

Classic Italian minestrone soup takes on a summer-fresh image in this recipe.

Serves 6

2 onions, finely chopped
2 garlic cloves, finely chopped
30ml/2 tbsp olive oil
2 carrots, very finely chopped
1 celery stick, very finely chopped
1.27 litres/2¼ pints/5⅔ cups boiling water
450g/1lb shelled fresh broad (fava) beans
225g/8oz mangetouts (snow peas), cut into fine strips
3 tomatoes, peeled and chopped
5ml/1 tsp tomato purée (paste)
50g/2oz spaghettini, broken into 4cm/1½in lengths
225g/8oz baby spinach
30ml/2 tbsp chopped fresh parsley
handful of fresh basil leaves
salt and ground black pepper
basil sprigs, to garnish
freshly grated Parmesan cheese, to serve

1 Cook the onions and garlic in the oil for 4–5 minutes. Add the carrots and celery. Cook for 2–3 minutes. Add the water and simmer for 15 minutes, until the vegetables are tender.

2 Cook the beans in boiling water for 4–5 minutes. Remove with a slotted spoon, refresh under cold water and set aside.

3 Bring the pan of water back to the boil, add the mangetouts and cook for 1 minute until tender. Drain, refresh and set aside.

4 Add the tomatoes and the tomato purée to the soup. Cook for 1 minute. Purée two or three large ladlefuls of the soup and a quarter of the broad beans in a food processor or blender until smooth. Set aside.

5 Add the spaghettini to the remaining soup and cook for 6–8 minutes, until tender. Stir in the purée and spinach and cook for 2–3 minutes. Add the rest of the broad beans, the mangetouts and parsley, and season well.

6 When you are ready to serve the soup, stir in the basil leaves and ladle the soup into deep cups or bowls and garnish with sprigs of basil. Serve immediately, with a little grated Parmesan sprinkled over.

Chunky Vegetable Soup with Pasta

This is a delicious chunky vegetable soup from Nice in the south of France, served with tomato pesto, and fresh Parmesan cheese. Serve in small portions as an appetizer, or in larger bowls with crusty bread as a filling lunch.

Serves 4–6

1 courgette (zucchini), diced
1 small potato, diced
1 shallot, chopped
1 carrot, diced
400g/14oz can chopped tomatoes
1.2 litres/2 pints/5 cups vegetable stock
50g/2oz French beans, cut into 1cm/½in lengths
50g/2oz/½ cup frozen petits pois (baby peas)
50g/2oz/½ cup small pasta shapes
60–90ml/4–6 tbsp pesto
15ml/1 tbsp tomato purée (paste)
salt and ground black pepper
freshly grated Parmesan or Pecorino cheese, to serve

1 Place the courgette, potato, shallot, carrot and tomatoes, with the can juices, in a large pan. Add the stock and season well. Bring to the boil over a medium to high heat, then lower the heat, cover the pan and simmer for 20 minutes.

2 Bring the soup back to the boil and add the green beans and petits pois. Cook the mixture briefly, for about a minute. Add the pasta. Cook for a further 10 minutes, until the pasta is tender. Taste and adjust the seasoning.

3 Ladle the soup into bowls. Mix together the pesto and tomato purée, and stir a spoonful into each serving. Sprinkle with freshly grated Parmesan or Pecorino cheese.

Variation
To strengthen the tomato flavour, try using tomato-flavoured spaghetti, broken into small lengths, instead of the small pasta shapes. Sun-dried tomato purée (paste) can be used instead of regular tomato purée.

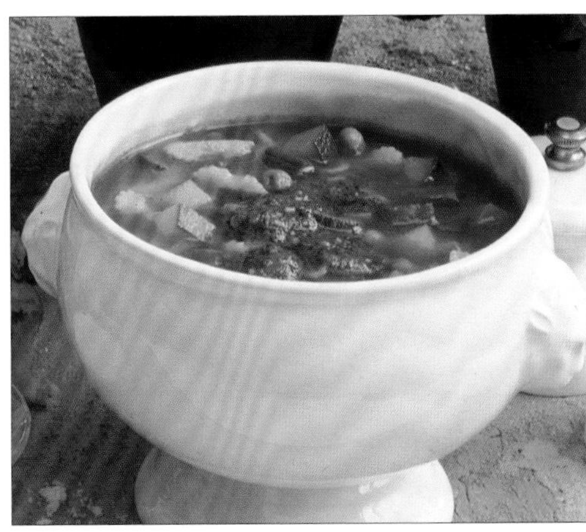

Summer Minestrone: Energy 201kcal/839kJ; Protein 8.1g; Carbohydrate 18.1g, of which sugars 7.8g; Fat 11.2g, of which saturates 3.4g; Cholesterol 10mg; Calcium 170mg; Fibre 3g; Sodium 138mg.
Chunky Vegetable: Energy 204kcal/857kJ; Protein 10.6g; Carbohydrate 23.6g, of which sugars 8.8g; Fat 8.1g, of which saturates 1.9g; Cholesterol 4mg; Calcium 150mg; Fibre 9.3g; Sodium 451mg.

Brown Lentil and Pasta Soup

This rustic vegetarian soup makes a hearty and warming winter meal and goes especially well with Granary or crusty Italian bread.

Serves 4–6

175g/6oz/¾ cup brown lentils
3 garlic cloves, unpeeled
1 litre/1¾ pints/4 cups boiling water
45ml/3 tbsp olive oil
25g/1oz/2 tbsp butter
1 onion, finely chopped
2 celery sticks, finely chopped
30ml/2 tbsp sun-dried tomato purée (paste)
1.75 litres/3 pints/7½ cups vegetable stock
a few fresh marjoram leaves
a few fresh basil leaves
leaves from 1 fresh thyme sprig
50g/2oz/½ cup small pasta shapes, such as macaroni or tubetti
salt and ground black pepper
tiny fresh herb leaves, such as thyme or marjoram, to garnish

1 Put the lentils in a large pan. Smash one of the garlic cloves using the blade of a large knife (there's no need to peel it first), then add it to the lentils. Pour in the water and bring to the boil. Reduce the heat, part-cover and simmer the lentils for about 20 minutes, or until they are tender.

2 Drain the lentils in a sieve, remove the garlic and set it aside. Rinse the lentils under the cold tap and leave to drain.

3 Heat 30ml/2 tbsp of the oil with half the butter in the pan. Add the onion and celery and cook gently for 5 minutes.

4 Crush the remaining garlic, then peel and mash the reserved garlic. Add to the pan with the remaining oil, the tomato purée and the lentils. Stir, then add the stock, marjoram, basil, thyme and salt and pepper. Bring to the boil, stirring. Simmer the soup for 30 minutes, stirring occasionally.

5 Add the pasta and bring the soup back to the boil, stirring. Reduce the heat and simmer until the pasta is just tender. Add the remaining butter and stir until melted. Taste the soup for seasoning, then serve in warmed bowls, sprinkled with herbs.

Borlotti Bean Soup with Pasta

A complete meal in a bowl, this is a version of a classic Italian soup.

Serves 4

1 onion, chopped
1 celery stick, chopped
2 carrots, chopped
75ml/5 tbsp olive oil
1 bay leaf
1 glass white wine (optional)
1 litre/1¾ pints/4 cups vegetable stock
400g/14oz can chopped tomatoes
300ml/½ pint/1¼ cups passata (bottled strained tomatoes)
175g/6oz/1½ cups pasta shapes, such as farfalle or conchiglie
400g/14oz can borlotti beans, drained
salt and ground black pepper
250g/9oz spinach
50g/2oz/⅔ cup freshly grated Parmesan cheese, to serve

1 Place the onion, celery and carrots in a large pan with the olive oil. Cook over a medium heat for 5 minutes.

2 Add the bay leaf, wine, vegetable stock, tomatoes and passata, and bring to the boil. Lower the heat and simmer for 10 minutes until the vegetables are just tender.

3 Add the pasta and beans, and bring the soup back to the boil, then simmer for 8 minutes until the pasta is *al dente*. Stir frequently to prevent the pasta from sticking.

4 Season to taste with salt and pepper. Remove any thick stalks from the spinach and add it to the soup. Cook for a further 2 minutes. Serve in heated bowls, sprinkled with Parmesan.

Variations

- *For a delicious meaty version of this soup, you can add chunks of cooked spicy sausage or pieces of crispy cooked pancetta or bacon. The cooked meat needs to be piping hot before the soup is served, so add at the end of step 3 and stir frequently with the other ingredients.*
- *For vegetarians, you could use fried chunks of smoked or marinated tofu as an alternative to meat.*

Lentil and Pasta: Energy 179kcal/753kJ; Protein 8.4g; Carbohydrate 24.2g, of which sugars 2.3g; Fat 6.1g, of which saturates 0.9g; Cholesterol 0mg; Calcium 25mg; Fibre 2.1g; Sodium 29mg.
Borlotti Bean Soup: Energy 321kcal/1363kJ; Protein 15g; Carbohydrate 57.8g, of which sugars 12.7g; Fat 5g, of which saturates 0.8g; Cholesterol 0mg; Calcium 166mg; Fibre 9.9g; Sodium 762mg.

Cappelletti in Broth

This soup is traditionally served in northern Italy on Santo Stefano (St Stephen's Day), on December 26th, and on New Year's Day as a welcome light change from all the special celebration food. Cappelletti are stuffed pasta shapes, usually filled with meat, which are said to resemble hats.

Serves 4

1.2 litres/2 pints/5 cups home-made chicken stock
90–115g/3½–4oz/1 cup fresh or dried cappelletti
about 45ml/3 tbsp finely chopped fresh flat leaf parsley (optional)
about 30ml/2 tbsp freshly grated Parmesan cheese
salt and ground black pepper

1 Pour the chicken stock into a large pan and bring to the boil. Add a little seasoning to taste, then drop in the pasta.

2 Stir well and bring back to the boil. Lower the heat to a simmer and cook until the pasta is *al dente*, or tender but still with a bit of bite.

3 Swirl in the finely chopped fresh flat leaf parsley, if using, then taste and adjust the seasoning, if necessary.

4 Ladle into four warmed soup plates, then sprinkle with the freshly grated Parmesan cheese and serve immediately.

Cook's Tip
This soup needs a well-flavoured stock as a base. If you don't have home-made stock use two 300g/11oz cans of condensed beef consommé, adding water as instructed. Alternatively, buy chilled commercial chicken stock.

Variation
Use other small filled pasta shapes such as tortellini or, for a very lightweight soup, simply use small, dried soup pasta. Use a meat stock if you prefer.

Red Pepper and Pasta in Broth

This simple soup is ideal for a light supper when served with ciabatta bread and also makes a delicious first course for an *al fresco* supper. Soup pasta is called pastini in Italian and is now widely available. Choose one particular shape or use a mixture of different shapes and colours for a more interesting result.

Serves 4

1.2 litres/2 pints/5 cups well-flavoured vegetable or chicken stock
75g/3oz/¾ cup tiny soup pasta
2 pieces bottled roasted red (bell) pepper, about 50g/2oz
coarsely shaved Parmesan cheese, to serve

1 Bring the stock to the boil in a large pan. Add seasoning to taste, then drop in the dried soup pasta. Stir well and bring the stock back to the boil.

2 Reduce the heat so that the soup simmers and cook for 7–8 minutes, until the pasta shapes are *al dente*, or tender but still firm to the bite.

3 Drain the pieces of roasted pepper and dice them finely. Place them in the base of four warmed soup plates. Taste the soup for seasoning before ladling it into the soup plates. Serve immediately, topped with shavings of Parmesan.

Cook's Tip
There are many different pastini to choose from, including stellette (stars), anellini (tiny thin rounds), risoni (rice-shaped) and farfalline (little butterflies). You could also use the fine "angel hair" pasta, capellini, broken into smaller pieces.

Variation
Use fresh (bell) peppers instead of bottled: first roast them until charred, then remove the skins and seeds and dice.

Cappelletti in Broth: Energy 111kcal/469kJ; Protein 5.8g; Carbohydrate 16.7g, of which sugars 0.8g; Fat 3g, of which saturates 1.6g; Cholesterol 8mg; Calcium 96mg; Fibre 0.7g; Sodium 228mg.
Red Pepper and Pasta: Energy 79kcal/334kJ; Protein 2.9g; Carbohydrate 15.9g, of which sugars 2.4g; Fat 0.8g, of which saturates 0.1g; Cholesterol 0mg; Calcium 10mg; Fibre 1g; Sodium 426mg.

Broccoli, Anchovy and Pasta Soup

This soup is from the region of Apulia in the south of Italy, where anchovies and broccoli are often used together in pasta dishes.

Serves 4

30ml/2 tbsp olive oil
1 small onion, finely chopped
1 garlic clove, finely chopped
¼–⅓ fresh red chilli, seeded and finely chopped
2 canned anchovy fillets, drained
200ml/7fl oz/scant 1 cup passata (bottled strained tomatoes)
45ml/3 tbsp dry white wine
1.2 litres/2 pints/5 cups vegetable stock
300g/11oz broccoli florets
200g/7oz/1¾ cups orecchiette
salt and ground black pepper
grated Pecorino cheese, to serve

1 Heat the oil in a large pan. Add the onion, garlic, chilli and anchovies and cook over a low heat, stirring all the time, for 5–6 minutes, until the onion is softened slightly.

2 Add the passata and wine, with salt and pepper to taste. Bring to the boil, reduce the heat and cover the pan, then cook gently, stirring occasionally, for 12–15 minutes.

3 Pour in the stock. Bring to the boil, then add the broccoli and simmer for about 5 minutes, until half cooked.

4 Add the pasta and bring the soup back to the boil, stirring. Simmer for 7–8 minutes or according to the instructions on the packet, stirring frequently, until the pasta is *al dente* or tender with a bit of bite.

5 Taste and adjust the seasoning. Serve the soup hot, ladled into warmed individual bowls. Hand round the grated Pecorino cheese separately.

Cook's Tip

Look out for jars or cans of anchovy fillets in olive oil. If you are not using the entire contents within 1–2 days, snip the leftovers into pieces and freeze in a small container for up to 2 weeks.

Tomato Soup with Israeli Couscous

Israeli couscous is a toasted, round pasta, much larger than regular couscous. It is delicious in savoury, zesty soups such as this one. It also works really well in spicy fish soups, served with a wedge of lemon. If you like your soup to have a strong garlic flavour, add an extra clove of chopped garlic just before serving.

Serves 4–6

30ml/2 tbsp olive oil
1 onion, chopped
1–2 carrots, diced
400g/14oz can chopped tomatoes
6 garlic cloves, roughly chopped
1.5 litres/2½ pints/6¼ cups vegetable or chicken stock
200–250g/7–9oz/1–1½ cups Israeli couscous
2–3 mint sprigs, chopped, or several pinches of dried mint
1.5ml/¼ tsp ground cumin
¼ bunch fresh coriander (cilantro), or about 5 sprigs, chopped
cayenne pepper, to taste
salt and ground black pepper

1 Heat the oil in a large pan, add the onion and carrots and cook gently for about 10 minutes, or until the vegetables are softened but not browned.

2 Add the tomatoes, half the garlic, the stock, couscous, mint, ground cumin and coriander, with the cayenne pepper, salt and pepper to taste.

3 Bring the soup to the boil, add the remaining chopped garlic, then reduce the heat slightly and simmer the soup gently for 7–10 minutes, stirring occasionally, or until the couscous is just tender.

4 Serve the soup piping hot, ladled into warmed individual serving bowls.

Cook's Tip

Sprinkle mint with a small pinch of sugar when it is on the board and ready to chop. The grainy sugar makes chopping far easier and quicker.

Broccoli and Anchovy: Energy 268kcal/1131kJ; Protein 10.3g; Carbohydrate 41.2g, of which sugars 5.2g; Fat 7.3g, of which saturates 1.1g; Cholesterol 1mg; Calcium 69mg; Fibre 3.9g; Sodium 182mg.
Tomato with Couscous: Energy 138kcal/575kJ; Protein 2.8g; Carbohydrate 23.1g, of which sugars 5.3g; Fat 4.3g, of which saturates 0.6g; Cholesterol 0mg; Calcium 24mg; Fibre 1.6g; Sodium 13mg.

Spicy Couscous in Shellfish Broth

This classic dish includes a soup-like stew, ladled over the couscous.

Serves 4–6

500g/1¼lb/3 cups couscous
5ml/1 tsp salt
600ml/1 pint/2½ cups warm water
45ml/3 tbsp sunflower oil
5–10ml/1–2 tsp harissa
75g/3oz/6 tbsp butter
500g/1¼lb mussels in shells, scrubbed, with beards removed
500g/1¼lb uncooked prawns (shrimp) in their shells
juice of 1 lemon
2 shallots, finely chopped
5ml/1 tsp coriander seeds, roasted and ground
5ml/1 tsp cumin seeds, roasted and ground
2.5ml/½ tsp ground turmeric
2.5ml/½ tsp cayenne pepper
5–10ml/1–2 tsp plain (all-purpose) flour
600ml/1 pint/2½ cups fish stock
120ml/4fl oz/½ cup double (heavy) cream
salt and ground black pepper
small bunch of fresh coriander (cilantro), finely chopped, to serve

1 Preheat the oven to 180°C/350°F/Gas 4. In an ovenproof dish, soak the couscous in the water with the salt for 10 minutes. Stir the oil into the harissa, then rub it into the couscous, breaking up lumps. Dot with 25g/1oz/2 tbsp of the butter. Cover and heat in the oven for 20 minutes.

2 Put the mussels, prawns, lemon juice and 50ml/2fl oz/¼ cup water in a pan. Cover and cook for 3–4 minutes, shaking, until the mussels have opened. Drain, reserving the liquor, and shell about two-thirds of the shellfish. Discard any closed mussels.

3 Heat the remaining butter in a pan, add the shallots and cook for 5 minutes. Add the spices and fry for 1 minute. Stir in the flour, stock and shellfish liquor. Bring to the boil, stirring. Add the cream and simmer, stirring often, for 10 minutes. Season, add the shellfish and most of the coriander. Heat through, then sprinkle with the remaining coriander.

4 Fork up the couscous, mixing in the melted butter. Place some couscous in warmed bowls, then ladle the soup over. Serve the remaining couscous separately, for adding to taste.

Wild Mushroom Soup with Polenta

This rich soup is delicious with Parmesan polenta.

Serves 6

20g/¾oz/scant ½ cup dried porcini mushrooms
175ml/6fl oz/¾ cup hot water
50g/2oz/¼ cup butter
1 large red onion, chopped
3 garlic cloves, chopped
115g/4oz/1¾ cups mixed wild mushrooms, trimmed
120ml/4fl oz/½ cup light red wine
1.2 litres/2 pints/5 cups vegetable stock
2.5ml/½ tsp wholegrain mustard
salt and ground black pepper
chopped fresh parsley, to garnish

For the polenta

750ml/1¼ pints/3 cups milk
175g/6oz/1 cup quick-cook polenta
50g/2oz/¼ cup butter
50g/2oz/⅔ cup freshly grated Parmesan cheese, plus extra to serve

1 Soak the porcini in the hot water for about 30 minutes. Drain, then strain the liquid through a fine sieve (strainer); reserve both the liquid and the mushrooms.

2 Melt the butter in a pan. Add the onion and garlic and cook for 4–5 minutes. Add the wild mushrooms and cook for a further 3–4 minutes. Add the dried mushrooms and strain in the soaking liquid through a muslin-lined sieve. Pour in the wine and stock, and cook for 15 minutes or until reduced by half.

3 Ladle half the soup into a food processor or blender and process until almost smooth. Pour the processed soup back into the soup remaining in the saucepan and set aside.

4 To make the polenta, bring the milk to the boil and pour in the polenta in a steady stream, stirring continuously. Cook for about 5 minutes, or until the polenta begins to come away from the pan. Beat in the butter, then stir in the Parmesan. Cover and keep warm.

5 Reheat the soup until just boiling. Stir in the mustard and season well. Divide the polenta among six bowls and ladle the soup around it. Scatter with grated Parmesan and parsley.

Spicy Couscous: Energy 496kcal/2062kJ; Protein 17.2g; Carbohydrate 45.5g, of which sugars 1.2g; Fat 28.3g, of which saturates 14g; Cholesterol 152mg; Calcium 134mg; Fibre 0.6g; Sodium 636mg.
Mushroom: Energy 2117kcal/8817kJ; Protein 67.3g; Carbohydrate 176.6g, of which sugars 44.8g; Fat 118.3g, of which saturates 70.6g; Cholesterol 307mg; Calcium 1580mg; Fibre 7.9g; Sodium 1495mg.

Speedy Clam and Pasta Soup

This delicious soup is a variation of the pasta dish spaghetti alle vongole. It is ideal for using store-cupboard ingredients. Serve it with hot focaccia or ciabatta for an informal supper with friends.

Serves 4

30ml/2 tbsp olive oil
1 large onion, finely chopped
2 garlic cloves, crushed
400g/14oz can chopped tomatoes
15ml/1 tbsp sun-dried tomato purée (paste)
5ml/1 tsp sugar
5ml/1 tsp dried mixed herbs
about 750ml/1¼ pints/3 cups fish or vegetable stock
150ml/¼ pint/⅔ cup red wine
50g/2oz/½ cup small pasta shapes
150g/5oz jar or can clams in natural juice
30ml/2 tbsp finely chopped fresh flat-leaf parsley, plus a few whole leaves to garnish
salt and freshly ground black pepper

1 Heat the oil in a large pan. Cook the onion gently for 5 minutes, stirring frequently, until softened.

2 Add the garlic, tomatoes, tomato purée, sugar, herbs, stock and wine, with salt and pepper to taste. Bring to the boil. Lower the heat, half-cover the pan and simmer for 10 minutes, stirring occasionally.

3 Add the pasta and continue simmering, uncovered, for about 10 minutes or until *al dente*. Stir occasionally to prevent the pasta shapes sticking together.

4 Add the clams and their juice to the soup and heat through for 3–4 minutes, adding more stock if required. Do not allow it to boil, or the clams will become tough.

5 Remove from the heat, stir in the chopped parsley and adjust the seasoning. Serve hot, sprinkled with coarsely ground black pepper and parsley leaves.

Mediterranean Fish Soup

Packed with fish and shellfish, the fresh flavours of this soup will transport you to the warm, sunny Mediterranean shores of southern Italy.

Serves 4

30ml/2 tbsp olive oil
1 onion, sliced
1 garlic clove, crushed
1 leek, sliced
225g/8oz can chopped tomatoes
pinch of Mediterranean herbs
1.5ml/¼ tsp saffron strands (optional)
115g/4oz/1 cup small pasta shapes
about 8 fresh mussels in the shell
450g/1lb filleted and skinned white fish, such as cod, plaice or monkfish
salt and ground black pepper

To finish

2 garlic cloves, crushed
1 canned pimiento, drained and chopped
15ml/1 tbsp fresh white breadcrumbs
60ml/4 tbsp mayonnaise
toasted bread, to serve

1 Heat the oil in a large pan and add the onion, garlic and leek. Cover and cook gently for 5 minutes, stirring until the vegetables are soft.

2 Pour in 1 litre/1¾ pints/4 cups water, the tomatoes, herbs, saffron, if using, and pasta. Season with salt and ground black pepper and cook for 15–20 minutes.

3 Scrub the mussels and pull off the beards. Discard any that will not close when sharply tapped.

4 Cut the fish into bitesize chunks and add to the soup in the pan, placing the mussels on top. Then simmer with the lid on for 5–10 minutes, until the mussels open and the fish is just cooked. Discard any unopened mussels.

5 To finish, pound the garlic, canned pimiento and breadcrumbs together in a mortar and pestle or process in a food processor or blender. Then stir in the mayonnaise and season well.

6 Spread the pimiento paste on freshly made toast. Ladle the soup into bowls and serve the toasts as an accompaniment.

Clam and Pasta: Energy 196kcal/821kJ; Protein 9.3g; Carbohydrate 20.2g, of which sugars 8.9g; Fat 6.5g, of which saturates 1g; Cholesterol 25mg; Calcium 67mg; Fibre 2.6g; Sodium 466mg.
Mediterranean Fish: Energy 389kcal/1627kJ; Protein 27.4g; Carbohydrate 29g, of which sugars 4.8g; Fat 18.9g, of which saturates 2.8g; Cholesterol 68mg; Calcium 46mg; Fibre 2.7g; Sodium 207mg.

Chicken and Pasta Soup

Simple and great for supper.

Serves 4–6

900ml/1½ pints/3¾ cups chicken stock
4 spring onions (scallions), sliced
225g/8oz button (white) mushrooms, sliced
1 bay leaf
115g/4oz cooked chicken, diced
50g/2oz soup pasta (stellette)
150ml/¼ pint/⅔ cup dry white wine
15ml/1 tbsp chopped parsley
salt and ground black pepper

1 Bring the stock, spring onions, mushrooms and bay leaf, to the boil in a large pan. Add the chicken and season to taste. Heat for 2–3 minutes. Add the pasta, cover and simmer for 7–8 minutes, until tender. Stir in the wine and parsley and heat for 2–3 minutes. Pour in to individual soup bowls and serve.

Seafood Consommé with Pasta

Seafood-filled pasta shapes floating in a clear consommé broth make an elegant and satisfying dish.

Serves 4–6

75g/3oz peeled cooked prawns (shrimp)
75g/3oz canned crab meat, drained
5ml/1 tsp fresh root ginger, peeled and finely grated
15ml/1 tbsp fresh white breadcrumbs
5ml/1 tsp light soy sauce
1 spring onion (scallion), chopped
1 garlic clove, crushed
about 12 pieces fresh lasagne
flour, for dusting
egg white, beaten
400g/14oz can chicken or fish consommé
30ml/2 tbsp sherry or vermouth
salt and ground black pepper

For the garnish

50g/2oz cooked, peeled prawns (shrimp)
fresh coriander (cilantro) leaves, to garnish

1 To make the filling, put the prawns, crab meat, ginger, breadcrumbs, soy sauce, onion, garlic and seasoning into a food processor or blender and process until smooth.

2 Lay out the lasagne on a surface lightly dusted with flour and stamp out 32 rounds with a 5cm/2in fluted pastry cutter from the sheets. Place a small teaspoon of filling in the centre of half the rounds. Brush the edges of each round with egg white and top with a second round. Pinch the edges together firmly to stop the filling seeping out.

3 Cook the pasta, in batches, in a large pan of boiling salted water for 5 minutes. Remove and drop into a bowl of cold water for 5 seconds before placing on a tray.

4 Heat the chicken or fish consommé in a pan with the sherry or vermouth. When piping hot, add the pasta shapes and simmer for 1–2 minutes.

5 Ladle the pasta and soup into shallow soup bowls Garnish with extra peeled prawns and fresh coriander leaves.

Corn Chowder with Smoked Turkey

Sweetcorn, smoked turkey and pasta are delicious.

Serves 6–8

1 small green (bell) pepper, seeded and diced
450g/1lb potatoes, diced
350g/12oz/2 cups canned or frozen corn
1 onion, chopped
1 celery stick, chopped
1 bouquet garni
600ml/1 pint/2½ cups chicken stock
300ml/½ pint/1¼ cups skimmed milk
50g/2oz conchigliette
oil, for frying
150g/5oz smoked turkey breast, skinned and diced
salt and ground black pepper
bread sticks, to serve

1 Soak the pepper in boiling water for 2 minutes. Drain and rinse. Put in a pan with the potatoes, corn, onion, celery, bouquet garni and stock. Bring to the boil, cover and simmer for 20 minutes until tender.

2 Add the milk. Purée half of the soup and return it to the pan with the pasta. Simmer for 10 minutes, until the pasta is tender. Stir in the smoked turkey and serve with bread sticks.

Seafood with Pasta: Energy 43kcal/181kJ; Protein 6.9g; Carbohydrate 2.1g, of which sugars 0.2g; Fat 0.4g, of which saturates 0.1g; Cholesterol 50mg; Calcium 36mg; Fibre 0.1g; Sodium 319mg.
Chicken and Pasta: Energy 75kcal/315kJ; Protein 6.7g; Carbohydrate 6.9g, of which sugars 0.9g; Fat 0.7g, of which saturates 0.1g; Cholesterol 13mg; Calcium 27mg; Fibre 1.2g; Sodium 18mg.
Chowder with Turkey: Energy 156kcal/662kJ; Protein 9.2g; Carbohydrate 29g, of which sugars 8.6g; Fat 1.2g, of which saturates 0.3g; Cholesterol 12mg; Calcium 58mg; Fibre 1.9g; Sodium 154mg.

Chicken Soup with Vermicelli

This is a simplified version of a Moroccan soup that would traditionally be made with a whole chicken.

Serves 4–6

30ml/2 tbsp sunflower oil
15g/½oz/1 tbsp butter
1 onion, chopped
2 chicken legs or breast pieces, halved or quartered
flour, for dusting
2 carrots, cut into chunks
1 parsnip, cut into chunks
1.5 litres/2½ pints/6¼ cups chicken stock
1 cinnamon stick
good pinch of paprika
pinch of saffron
2 egg yolks
juice of ½ lemon
30ml/2 tbsp chopped fresh coriander (cilantro)
30ml/2 tbsp chopped fresh parsley
150g/5oz vermicelli
salt and ground black pepper

1 Heat the oil and butter in a pan. Add and fry the onion for 3–4 minutes until softened. Dust the chicken pieces in seasoned flour, add to the pan and fry gently until evenly browned.

2 Transfer the chicken to a plate and add the carrots and parsnip to the pan. Cook over a gentle heat for 3–4 minutes, stirring frequently, then return the chicken to the pan. Add the stock, cinnamon stick and paprika and season well. Bring to the boil, cover and simmer for 1 hour.

3 Meanwhile, blend the saffron in 30ml/2 tbsp boiling water. Beat the egg yolks with the lemon juice in a separate bowl and add the coriander and parsley. When the saffron water has cooled, stir into the egg and lemon mixture.

4 Transfer the chicken to a plate. Spoon away any excess fat from the soup, then increase the heat a little and stir in the noodles. Cook for 5–6 minutes until the noodles are tender. Meanwhile, remove the skin and bones from the chicken and cut the flesh into bitesize pieces.

5 When the vermicelli is cooked stir in the chicken pieces and the egg, lemon and saffron mixture. Cook over a low heat for 1–2 minutes, stirring. Adjust the seasoning and serve at once.

Pasta Soup with Chicken Livers

This richly flavoured and versatile pasta soup can be served as a first or main course. The fried chicken livers are so delicious, cooked with garlic, herbs and wine, that, even if you do not normally like them, you will probably really enjoy them in this soup.

Serves 4–6

115g/4oz/½ cup chicken livers, thawed if frozen
15ml/1 tbsp olive oil
knob of butter
4 garlic cloves, crushed
3 sprigs each of fresh parsley, marjoram and sage, chopped
1 sprig of fresh thyme, chopped
5–6 fresh basil leaves, chopped
15–30ml/1–2 tbsp dry white wine
2 x 300g/11oz cans condensed chicken consommé
225g/8oz/2 cups frozen peas
50g/2oz/½ cup small pasta shapes, such as farfalle
2–3 spring onions (scallions), sliced diagonally
salt and ground black pepper

1 Cut the chicken livers into small pieces with scissors. Discard any bits of membrane and core from the livers.

2 Heat the oil and butter in a frying pan, add the garlic and herbs, with salt and ground black pepper to taste, and fry gently for a few minutes. Add the livers, increase the heat to high and stir-fry briefly until they change colour and become firm. Add the wine, cook until it evaporates, then remove from the heat.

3 Pour the chicken consommé into a large pan and add water to the condensed soup as directed on the can. Add an extra can of water, then stir in a little salt and pepper to taste and bring to the boil.

4 Add the frozen peas to the soup and simmer for about 5 minutes, then add the pasta and bring the soup back to the boil, stirring. Simmer, stirring frequently, for about 5 minutes or until the pasta is tender but not soft.

5 Add the chicken livers and all their pan juices to the soup. Stir in the spring onions and taste for seasoning before serving.

Pasta with Chicken: Energy 88kcal/367kJ; Protein 6.4g; Carbohydrate 9.2g, of which sugars 1.3g; Fat 2.9g, of which saturates 0.5g; Cholesterol 61mg; Calcium 28mg; Fibre 2.1g; Sodium 355mg.
Chicken Soup: Energy 236kcal/984kJ; Protein 15.8g; Carbohydrate 24.1g, of which sugars 3.3g; Fat 8.5g, of which saturates 2.5g; Cholesterol 108mg; Calcium 40mg; Fibre 1.6g; Sodium 60mg.

Chunky Chicken Minestrone

This is a special minestrone made with fresh chicken. Served with crusty Italian bread, it makes a hearty meal in itself.

Serves 4–6

15ml/1 tbsp olive oil
2 chicken thighs
3 rindless streaky (fatty) bacon rashers (strips), chopped
1 onion, finely chopped
a few fresh basil leaves, shredded
a few fresh rosemary leaves, finely chopped
15ml/1 tbsp chopped fresh flat-leaf parsley
2 potatoes, cut into 1cm/½in cubes
1 large carrot, cut into 1cm/½in cubes
2 small courgettes (zucchini), cut into 1cm/½in cubes
1–2 celery sticks, cut into 1cm/½in cubes
1 litre/1¾ pints/4 cups chicken stock
200g/7oz/1¾ cups frozen peas
90g/3½oz/scant 1 cup stellette or other small soup pasta
salt and ground black pepper
Parmesan cheese shavings, to serve

1 Heat the oil in a large frying pan, add the chicken thighs and fry for about 5 minutes on each side. Remove with a slotted spoon and set aside.

2 Add the bacon, onion and herbs to the pan and cook gently, stirring constantly, for about 5 minutes. Add the potatoes, carrot, courgettes and celery and cook for 5–7 minutes more.

3 Return the chicken thighs to the pan, add the stock and bring to the boil. Reduce the heat. Cover and cook over a low heat for 35–40 minutes, stirring the soup occasionally, until the chicken pieces are cooked. Remove the chicken thighs with a slotted spoon and place them on a board.

4 Stir the peas and pasta into the soup and bring it back to the boil. Reduce the heat and simmer, stirring frequently, for 7–8 minutes until the pasta is cooked.

5 Cut the meat off the chicken, discarding the bones and skin. Dice the meat and add it to the soup. Taste for seasoning and serve sprinkled with Parmesan cheese shavings.

Chicken Tortellini Soup

This traditional Italian soup, was designed to use up leftovers of roast capon served on Christmas day.

Serves 6–8

200g/7oz/1¾ cups plain (all-purpose) flour
2 large eggs, beaten
15ml/1 tbsp oil
2 litres/3½ pints/9 cups beef stock
salt and ground black pepper
freshly grated Parmesan cheese, to serve

For the filling
25g/1oz/2 tbsp butter
250g/9oz minced (ground) chicken or turkey
5ml/1 tsp chopped fresh rosemary
5ml/1 tsp chopped fresh sage
freshly grated nutmeg
250ml/8fl oz/1 cup chicken stock
60ml/4 tbsp freshly grated Parmesan cheese
90g/3½oz mortadella sausage, very finely chopped
1 small egg

1 For the filling, melt the butter in a pan. Add the chicken or turkey, herbs, a little nutmeg and salt and pepper. Cook gently for 5–6 minutes, stirring. Add the stock and simmer, uncovered, for 15–20 minutes, until the meat is cooked and quite dry. Cool. Mix in the Parmesan, mortadella and egg.

2 Sift the flour and a pinch of salt into a bowl. Add the eggs and oil. Gradually mix by hand to a dough. Knead until smooth, then wrap and allow to rest for at least 30 minutes.

3 Roll out one-quarter of the pasta into two 45cm/18in lengths. Cut out 8–10 discs, about 5cm/2in round, from one of the strips. Put a little filling in the centre of each, then brush water on the edge. Fold in half to seal in the filling. Wrap each around a finger and pinch the bottom corners together. Set aside on a floured tray. Repeat to make 64–80 tortellini.

4 Bring the stock to the boil in a large pan. Add the tortellini, bring back to the boil and boil for 4–5 minutes. Taste the stock and season with salt and pepper if necessary.

5 Pour the tortellini and stock into large tureen, sprinkle with Parmesan cheese and serve immediately.

Chicken Minestrone: Energy 198kcal/833kJ; Protein 15.6g; Carbohydrate 23.3g, of which sugars 3.9g; Fat 5.4g, of which saturates 1.4g; Cholesterol 30mg; Calcium 31mg; Fibre 3.2g; Sodium 224mg.
Tortellini Soup: Energy 243kcal/1018kJ; Protein 17.2g; Carbohydrate 20.3g, of which sugars 0.7g; Fat 11.1g, of which saturates 4.7g; Cholesterol 116mg; Calcium 153mg; Fibre 1.2g; Sodium 419mg.

Minestrone with Pasta and Beans

This classic minestrone from the Lombardy region of Italy includes pancetta for a pleasant touch of saltiness. Milanese cooks vary the recipe according to what is on hand, and you can do the same.

Serves 4

45ml/3 tbsp olive oil
115g/4oz pancetta, any rinds removed, roughly chopped
2–3 celery sticks, finely chopped
3 carrots, finely chopped
1 onion, finely chopped
1–2 garlic cloves, crushed
2 x 400g/14oz cans chopped tomatoes
about 1 litre/1¾ pints/4 cups chicken stock
400g/14oz can cannellini beans, drained and rinsed
50g/2oz/½ cup short-cut macaroni
30–60ml/2–4tbsp chopped flat leaf parsley, to taste
salt and ground black pepper
shaved Parmesan cheese, to serve

1 Heat the oil in a large pan. Add the pancetta, celery, carrots and onion and cook over low heat for 5 minutes, stirring constantly, until the vegetables are softened.

2 Add the garlic and tomatoes, breaking them up well with a wooden spoon. Pour in the chicken stock. Add salt and pepper to taste and bring to the boil. Half cover the pan, lower the heat and simmer gently for about 20 minutes, until the vegetables are soft.

3 Drain the beans and add them to the pan with the macaroni. Bring to the boil again. Cover, lower the heat and continue to simmer for about 20 minutes more.

4 Check the consistency and add more stock if necessary. Stir in the parsley and adjust the seasoning. Serve hot, sprinkled with plenty of Parmesan cheese.

Variations
Use long-grain rice instead of the pasta, and chickpeas instead of cannellini beans. Try bacon instead of pancetta.

Meatballs in Pasta Soup

These meatballs are delicious in a hearty soup

Serves 4

400g/14oz can cannellini beans, drained and rinsed
1 litre/1¾ pints/4 cups vegetable stock
45ml/3 tbsp olive oil
1 onion, finely chopped
2 garlic cloves, chopped
1 small fresh red chilli, seeded and finely chopped
2 celery sticks, finely chopped
1 carrot, finely chopped
15ml/1 tbsp tomato purée (paste)
300g/11oz small pasta shapes
large handful of fresh basil, torn
salt and ground black pepper
basil leaves, to garnish
freshly grated Parmesan cheese, to serve

For the meatballs

1 thick slice white bread, crusts removed, made into crumbs
60ml/4 tbsp milk
350g/12oz lean minced (ground) beef or veal
30ml/2 tbsp chopped fresh parsley
grated rind of 1 orange
2 garlic cloves, crushed
1 egg, beaten
30ml/2 tbsp olive oil

1 For the meatballs, mix the bread, milk, meat, parsley, orange rind, garlic, egg and seasoning. Stand for 15 minutes, then shape into balls about the size of a large olive.

2 Heat the oil in a frying pan and fry the meatballs in batches for 6–8 minutes until browned all over. Use a draining spoon to remove them from the pan and set aside.

3 Purée the cannellini beans with a little of the vegetable stock in a food processor or blender until smooth. Set aside.

4 Heat the olive oil in a pan. Add the onion, garlic, chilli, celery and carrot. Cover and cook gently for a 10 minutes, then stir in the tomato purée, bean purée and the remaining stock. Bring the soup to the boil and cook for about 10 minutes.

5 Stir in the pasta and simmer for 8–10 minutes, until the pasta is tender. Add the meatballs and basil and cook for 5 minutes. Season well before ladling it into warmed bowls. Garnish with basil and serve with Parmesan cheese.

Minestrone with Pasta: Energy 371kcal/1558kJ; Protein 17g; Carbohydrate 40.5g, of which sugars 14.5g; Fat 16.8g, of which saturates 3.9g; Cholesterol 19mg; Calcium 113mg; Fibre 12g; Sodium 420mg.
Meatballs in Soup: Energy 277kcal/1158kJ; Protein 19.9g; Carbohydrate 20.5g, of which sugars 1.4g; Fat 14g, of which saturates 6.1g; Cholesterol 89mg; Calcium 133mg; Fibre 1g; Sodium 731mg.

Beef and Veal Soup with Vermicelli

Another meaty soup, and a real weekend favourite.

Serves 4
1 onion
2 cloves
400g/14oz shin (shank) of beef with bone
bunch of parsley
bay leaf
150g/5oz minced (ground) veal
15ml/1 tbsp breadcrumbs
pinch of freshly grated nutmeg
400g/14oz mixed diced vegetables, such as carrots, leeks, green beans, cauliflower, celeriac and Brussels sprouts
40g/1½oz broken vermicelli
salt and ground black pepper
chopped fresh parsley, to garnish

1 Stud the whole onion with the cloves. Put the beef in a pan, add 1.5 litres/2½ pints/ 6¼ cups water and bring to the boil.

2 Skim off any scum that rises to the surface and add the onion, parsley and bay leaf. Season with salt and pepper. Lower the heat, cover and simmer for 3 hours.

3 Remove the beef from the pan, cut the meat off the bone and dice it. Strain the stock through a sieve (strainer) lined with muslin (cheesecloth) into a clean pan.

4 Mix together the veal, breadcrumbs and nutmeg in a bowl and season with salt. Form the mixture into small balls. Bring the stock to the boil, add the meatballs, diced vegetables and vermicelli. Cook for 15 minutes, until the vegetables are tender.

5 Add the beef to the pan and warm it through.

6 Season to taste with salt and pepper, garnish with chopped parsley and serve immediately.

Variations

- *You can use 40g/1½oz/scant ¼ cup pre-boiled rice instead of vermicelli, adding it with the vegetables in step 6.*
- *You can thicken the soup with 15g/½oz potato flour or cornflour (cornstarch).*

Rolled Beef and Pasta Soup

This substantial Dutch soup makes a heartwarming meal.

Serves 4
1kg/2¼lb boned and rolled beef
250g/9oz lean minced (ground) beef
1 rusk, crushed
2.5ml/½ tsp ground mace
2 onions
1 bouquet garni of parsley, sage and bay leaf
500g/1¼lb white asparagus, peeled
100g/3¾oz vermicelli
bunch of celery leaves
salt

To serve
lamb's lettuce (corn salad)
cocktail onions
gherkins
lemon segments
mustard
Dutch brandy
buttered wholemeal (whole-wheat) bread

1 Put the rolled meat in a large pan, pour in 2.5 litres/4½ pints/ 11¼ cups water and bring to the boil. Mix the minced beef, rusk, mace and 5ml/1 tsp salt and shape into small balls.

2 When the water in the pan comes to the boil, add the meatballs, whole onions and bouquet garni and skim off any scum that rises. Lower the heat and simmer for 2 hours.

3 Remove the rolled meat and leave to cool. Strain the stock through a sieve (strainer) lined with muslin (cheesecloth) into a clean pan. Rinse the meatballs and return them to the stock.

4 Cut the asparagus into 5cm/2in pieces. Add to the stock and cook for 10 minutes, then add the vermicelli and cook for a further 10 minutes. Add the celery leaves and salt to taste.

5 Make a bed of lamb's lettuce on a plate. Cut the cold rolled meat into neat slices and arrange them in the middle of the plate. Put the cocktail onions and gherkins around the rim and garnish with lemon segments.

6 Serve buttered bread with the meat, mustard and pickles. Traditionally a drop of lemon juice was squeezed into the soup and spoonfuls of soup were often followed by a sip of brandy.

Beef and Pasta: Energy 331kcal/1368kJ; Protein 6.1g; Carbohydrate 18g, of which sugars 3.6g; Fat 26.5g, of which saturates 16.2g; Cholesterol 66mg; Calcium 80mg; Fibre 2.7g; Sodium 108mg.
Beef and Veal: Energy 318kcal/1330kJ; Protein 32.4g; Carbohydrate 19.8g, of which sugars 8.4g; Fat 12.4g, of which saturates 5g; Cholesterol 81mg; Calcium 44mg; Fibre 2.7g; Sodium 150mg.

Pasta Squares, Peas and Parma Ham in Broth

In Italy, an old-fashioned recipe for this soup would be made with fresh home-made pasta and peas. In this modern version, ready-made pasta is used with frozen peas to save time.

Serves 4–6

25g/1oz/2 tbsp butter
50g/2oz/⅓ cup pancetta or rindless smoked streaky (fatty) bacon, roughly chopped
1 small onion, finely chopped
1 celery stick, finely chopped
400g/14oz/3½ cups frozen peas
5ml/1 tsp tomato purée (paste)
5–10ml/1–2 tsp finely chopped fresh flat-leaf parsley
1 litre/1¾ pints/4 cups chicken stock
300g/11oz fresh lasagne sheets
about 50g/2oz/⅓ cup prosciutto or Parma ham, cut into cubes
salt and ground black pepper
grated Parmesan cheese, to serve

1 Melt the butter in a large pan and add the pancetta or bacon, with the onion and celery. Cook over a low heat, stirring constantly, for 5 minutes.

2 Add the peas and cook, stirring, for 3–4 minutes. Stir in the tomato purée and parsley, then add the stock, with salt and pepper to taste. Bring to the boil. Cover the pan, lower the heat and simmer gently for 10 minutes. Meanwhile, cut the lasagne sheets into 2cm/¾in squares.

3 Taste the soup and adjust the seasoning. Drop in the pasta, stir and bring to the boil. Simmer for 2–3 minutes or until the pasta is *al dente*, then stir in the ham. Serve hot in warmed bowls, with grated Parmesan handed round separately.

Cook's Tip
Take care when adding salt because of the saltiness of the pancetta and the prosciutto.

Cinnamon-spiced Borlotti Bean and Ham Soup

This straightforward soup is made that bit different with warm cinnamon.

Serves 4–6

30ml/2 tbsp olive oil
115g/4oz rindless smoked streaky (fatty) bacon, diced
1 onion, chopped
2 carrots, chopped
2 celery sticks, chopped
1.75 litres/3 pints/7½ cups vegetable stock
1 cinnamon stick or a good pinch of ground cinnamon
90g/3½oz/scant 1 cup small pasta shapes, such as conchiglie or coralini
400g/14oz can borlotti beans, rinsed and drained
1 thick slice cooked ham (about 225g/8oz) diced
salt and ground black pepper
Parmesan cheese shavings, to serve

1 Heat the oil in a large pan, add the bacon and cook, stirring, until lightly browned. Add the vegetables and cook for about 10 minutes, stirring frequently, until lightly coloured. Pour in the stock, add the cinnamon with salt and pepper to taste and bring to the boil. Cover and simmer gently for 15–20 minutes.

2 Add the pasta shapes. Bring back to the boil, stirring. Lower the heat and simmer, stirring often, for 5 minutes. Add the borlotti beans and diced ham and simmer for 2–3 minutes, or according to the instructions on the packet, until the pasta is *al dente*.

3 Remove the cinnamon stick, if used, taste the soup and adjust the seasoning. Serve hot in warmed bowls, sprinkled with Parmesan shavings.

Variation
If you prefer, you can use spaghetti or tagliatelle instead of the small pasta shapes, breaking them into small pieces over the pan. Use cannellini or white haricot (navy) beans instead of the borlotti. Add them to the pan after the stock in step 1. If you like, add 15ml/1 tbsp tomato purée (paste) along with the beans.

Pasta/Peas and Ham: Energy 175kcal/730kJ; Protein 9.5g; Carbohydrate 19.7g, of which sugars 2.6g; Fat 7.1g, of which saturates 3.2g; Cholesterol 19mg; Calcium 24mg; Fibre 4g; Sodium 236mg.
Borlotti and Ham: Energy 260kcal/1091kJ; Protein 16.7g; Carbohydrate 26.9g, of which sugars 6.4g; Fat 10.2g, of which saturates 2.6g; Cholesterol 34mg; Calcium 70mg; Fibre 5.6g; Sodium 967mg.

Pasta and Lentil Soup with Sage and Ham

The small brown lentils which are grown in central Italy are traditionally used in this wholesome soup, but green lentils may be substituted, if preferred.

Serves 4–6

225g/8oz/1 cup green or brown lentils
90ml/6 tbsp olive oil
50g/2oz gammon (cured ham) or salt pork, cut into small dice
1 onion, finely chopped
1 celery stick, finely chopped
1 carrot, finely chopped
2 litres/3½ pints/9 cups chicken stock or water, or a combination of both
1 fresh sage leaf or large pinch of dried
1 sprig fresh thyme or 1.5ml/¼ tsp dried
175g/6oz/2½ cups ditalini or other small soup pasta
salt and ground black pepper

1 Carefully check the lentils for small stones. Place them in a bowl, cover with cold water and soak for 2–3 hours. Rinse and drain well.

2 In a large pan, heat the oil and cook the ham or salt pork for 2–3 minutes. Add the onion, and cook gently until it softens.

3 Stir in the celery and carrot, and cook for a further 5 minutes, stirring frequently. Add the lentils and stir to coat them in the fat.

4 Pour in the stock or water, add the herbs and bring the soup to the boil. Cook over medium heat for about 1 hour, or until the lentils are tender. Add salt and pepper to taste.

5 Stir in the pasta and cook it until *al dente* or tender but still firm to the bite. Allow the soup to stand for a few minutes before serving.

Variation
Add 1 crushed garlic clove with the onion at step 2.

Pea and Ham Soup with Pasta

Peas and ham are a classic combination of ingredients for soup. Here they are presented Italian style, with pasta, to make a deliciously satisfying soup. The recipe works well with frozen peas, which provide fresh flavour and a bright colour.

Serves 4

115g/4oz/1 cup small pasta shapes, such as tubetti
30ml/2 tbsp vegetable oil
1 small bunch spring onions (scallions), chopped
350g/12oz/3 cups frozen peas
1.2 litres/2 pints/5 cups chicken stock
225g/8oz raw unsmoked ham or gammon (cured ham)
60ml/4 tbsp double (heavy) cream
salt and ground black pepper
warm crusty bread, to serve

1 Bring a pan of lightly salted water to the boil, add the small pasta shapes and cook until *al dente* or just tender. Drain thoroughly, then return to the pan again, cover with cold water and set aside until required.

2 Heat the vegetable oil in a large heavy pan and cook the spring onions gently, stirring, until soft but not browned. Add the frozen peas and chicken stock to the pan, then simmer gently over a low heat for about 10 minutes.

3 Process the soup in a food processor or blender, then return it to the pan. Cut the ham or gammon into short fingers and add, with the pasta, to the pan. Simmer for 2–3 minutes and season with salt and pepper to taste.

4 Stir in the double cream and serve the soup immediately with the warm crusty bread.

Cook's Tip
Use petits pois (baby peas) for a more delicate taste. The pea and ham combination also goes well with cheese – try sprinkling the soup with freshly grated Parmesan cheese.

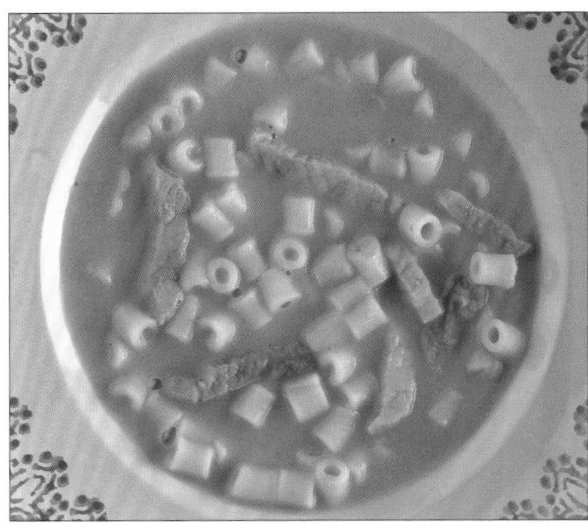

Pasta and Lentil Soup: Energy 206kcal/865kJ; Protein 8.1g; Carbohydrate 23.5g, of which sugars 1.7g; Fat 9.5g, of which saturates 3g; Cholesterol 9mg; Calcium 24mg; Fibre 1.9g; Sodium 42mg.
Pea and Ham: Energy 360kcal/1502kJ; Protein 20.5g; Carbohydrate 32.6g, of which sugars 4.4g; Fat 17.3g, of which saturates 6.6g; Cholesterol 53mg; Calcium 45mg; Fibre 5.3g; Sodium 682mg.

Barley Soup with Ham

This hearty vegetable soup comes from Italy's mountainous north. A thick, nourishing soup, it is the perfect warming food for cold winter days. Serve it with thick chunks of warm crusty bread.

Serves 6–8

225g/8oz/1 cup pearl barley
2 litres/3½ pints/9 cups beef stock or water
45ml/3 tbsp olive oil
2 carrots, finely chopped
1 large onion, finely chopped
2 celery sticks, finely chopped
1 leek, thinly sliced
1 large potato, finely chopped
115g/4oz cooked ham, diced
1 bay leaf
45ml/3 tbsp chopped fresh parsley
1 small sprig fresh rosemary
salt and ground black pepper
freshly grated Parmesan cheese, to serve

1 Pick over the barley and discard any stones or other particles. Rinse in cold water. Leave the barley to soak in cold water for at least 3 hours.

2 Drain the barley and place in a large pan with the stock or water. Bring to the boil, lower the heat and simmer for 1 hour. Skim off any scum.

3 Stir in the oil, all the vegetables and the ham. Add the herbs. If necessary add more water: the ingredients should be covered by at least 2.5cm/1in. Simmer for 1–1½ hours, or until the vegetables and barley are very tender.

4 Season to taste with salt and pepper. Serve hot with grated Parmesan, if wished.

Cook's Tip

The soup is delicious made with the stock left after boiling a large piece of bacon or ham. Ham stock is salty, so the soup may not need extra seasoning. If the meat is a traditionally cured ham or bacon, soak it first. Bring it to the boil, then drain and cook in fresh water, otherwise the stock will be too salty.

Leek and Oatmeal Soup

This is the traditional Irish version of leek and oatmeal soup combining leeks, oatmeal and milk – three ingredients that have been staple foods for centuries. The soup may be referred to as Brotchán foltchep or Brotchán Roy in its mother country. Serve with still-warm freshly baked bread and butter for a simple peasant-style lunch.

Serves 4–6

about 1.2 litres/2 pints/5 cups chicken stock and milk, mixed
30ml/2 tbsp medium pinhead oatmeal
25g/1oz/2 tbsp butter
6 large leeks, sliced into 2cm/¾in pieces
salt and ground black pepper
pinch of ground mace
30ml/2 tbsp chopped fresh parsley

For the garnish

single (light) cream
chopped fresh parsley leaves or chives

1 Bring the stock and milk mixture to the boil over a medium heat and sprinkle in the oatmeal. Stir well to prevent lumps from forming, and then simmer gently, still stirring.

2 Wash the leeks in a bowl. Melt the butter in a separate pan and cook the leeks over a gentle heat until softened slightly, then add them to the stock mixture.

3 Simmer for a further 15–20 minutes, or until the oatmeal is cooked. Extra stock or milk can be added if the soup is too thick – stir well while pouring in extra liquid.

4 Season with salt, pepper and mace, stir in the parsley and serve in warmed bowls. Decorate with a swirl of cream and some chopped fresh parsley or chives, if you like.

Variation

Make nettle soup in the spring, when the nettle tops are young and tender. Strip about 10oz/275g nettle tops from the stems, chop them and add to the leeks.

Barley with Ham: Energy 227kcal/958kJ; Protein 8.6g; Carbohydrate 34.6g, of which sugars 4.5g; Fat 6.9g, of which saturates 1.6g; Cholesterol 15mg; Calcium 61mg; Fibre 2.3g; Sodium 276mg.
Leek and Oatmeal: Energy 199kcal/834kJ; Protein 10g; Carbohydrate 19.5g, of which sugars 12.4g; Fat 9.6g, of which saturates 5.1g; Cholesterol 22mg; Calcium 243mg; Fibre 5.8g; Sodium 219mg.

Vegetable Broth with Oatmeal

This is one of many versions of this famous Irish oatmeal soup, which is best flavoured with strong chicken stock.

Serves 4

25g/1oz/2 tbsp butter
1 onion, finely chopped
1 celery stick, finely chopped
1 carrot, finely chopped
25g/1oz/¼ cup plain (all-purpose) flour
900ml/1½ pints/3¾ cups chicken stock
25g/1oz/¼ cup medium oatmeal
115g/4oz spinach, chopped
30ml/2 tbsp single (light) cream
salt and ground black pepper
chopped fresh parsley, to garnish

1 Place the butter, onion, celery and carrot in a large pan. Cook for 5 minutes until the onion softens. Stir in the flour and cook gently for 1 minute, stirring. Pour in the stock, boil and cover. Reduce the heat and simmer for 30 minutes.

2 Stir in the oatmeal and spinach. Cook for 15 minutes, stirring often. Stir in the cream and seasoning. Serve garnished with chopped fresh parsley.

Egg, Cheese and Semolina Soup

In this classic Roman soup, eggs are slightly scrambled in the stock.

Serves 6

3 eggs
45ml/3 tbsp fine semolina
90ml/6 tbsp freshly grated Parmesan cheese
pinch of nutmeg
1.5 litres/2½ pints/6¼ cups cold meat or chicken stock
salt and ground black pepper
country bread, toasted, to serve

1 Beat the eggs, then beat in the semolina, cheese, nutmeg and 250ml/8fl oz/1 cup of the stock. Heat the remaining stock in a large pan until simmering gently.

2 Whisk the egg mixture into the stock and bring it barely to the boil. Season and cook for 3–4 minutes. Place the toasted bread in soup plates and ladle on the soup. Serve immediately.

Egg and Lemon Soup with Rice

This is a great favourite in Greece and is a fine example of how a few ingredients can make a marvellous dish if carefully chosen and cooked. It is essential to use a well-flavoured stock. Add as little or as much rice as you like.

Serves 4

900ml/1½ pints/3¾ cups chicken stock, preferably home-made
50g/2oz/generous ⅓ cup long grain rice
3 egg yolks
30–60ml/2–4 tbsp lemon juice
30ml/2 tbsp finely chopped fresh parsley
salt and freshly ground black pepper
lemon slices and parsley sprigs, to garnish

1 Pour the stock into a pan, bring to simmering point, then add the drained rice. Half cover and cook for about 12 minutes until the rice is just tender. Season with salt and pepper.

2 Whisk the egg yolks in a bowl, then add about 30ml/2 tbsp of the lemon juice, whisking constantly until the mixture is smooth and bubbly. Add a ladleful of soup and whisk again.

3 Remove the soup from the heat and slowly add the egg mixture, whisking all the time. The soup will turn a pretty lemon colour and will thicken slightly.

4 Taste and add more lemon juice if necessary. Stir in the parsley. Serve at once, without reheating, garnished with lemon slices and parsley sprigs.

Cook's Tip

The key to a successful egg and lemon soup is to add the egg mixture to the hot liquid without it curdling. Avoid whisking the mixture into boiling liquid. It is safest to remove the soup from the heat entirely and then whisk in the mixture in a slow but steady stream. Do not reheat the soup as curdling would be almost inevitable.

Vegetable with Oatmeal: Energy 170kcal/711kJ; Protein 4g; Carbohydrate 22.5g, of which sugars 3.2g; Fat 7.7g, of which saturates 4.3g; Cholesterol 17mg; Calcium 98mg; Fibre 2.4g; Sodium 93mg.
Egg, Cheese, Semolina: Energy 245kcal/1030kJ; Protein 14.1g; Carbohydrate 27.5g, of which sugars 1.3g; Fat 9.4g, of which saturates 4.1g; Cholesterol 110mg; Calcium 246mg; Fibre 1.1g; Sodium 424mg.
Egg and Lemon with Rice: Energy 96kcal/404kJ; Protein 3.3g; Carbohydrate 10.9g, of which sugars 0.2g; Fat 4.7g, of which saturates 1.2g; Cholesterol 151mg; Calcium 39mg; Fibre 0.4g; Sodium 10mg.

Rice and Broad Bean Soup

This a lovely thick risotto-style soup, this makes the most of fresh broad beans while they are in season. It also works well with frozen beans for the rest of the year. It is ideal as a substantial supper.

Serves 4

1kg/2lb broad (fava) beans in their pods, or 400g/14oz shelled frozen beans, thawed
90ml/6 tbsp olive oil
1 onion, finely chopped
2 tomatoes, peeled and finely chopped
200g/7oz/1 cup risotto or other uncooked rice
25g/1oz/2 tbsp butter
1 litre/1¾ pints/4 cups boiling water
salt and ground black pepper
freshly grated Parmesan cheese, to serve (optional)

1 Shell the beans if they are fresh. Bring a large pan of water to the boil and blanch the beans, fresh or frozen, for 3–4 minutes. Rinse under cold water, then peel off the skins.

2 Heat the oil in a large pan. Add the chopped onion and cook over low to medium heat, until it softens. Stir in the broad beans, and cook for about 5 minutes, stirring often to coat them with the oil. Season with salt and pepper. Add the tomatoes, and cook for a further 5 minutes, stirring often.

3 Stir in the rice and cook for 1–2 minutes. Add the butter and stir until it melts. Pour in the water, a little at a time, until the whole amount has been added. Taste for seasoning.

4 Continue cooking the soup until the rice is tender. Serve hot, with grated Parmesan if wished.

Cook's Tip

Risotto rice, such as arborio, is particularly good for this soup. A short grain rice, it has rounder grains than the long grain variety. This type of rice has the ability to absorb water and cook to a creamy smoothness yet still retain its shape.

Spinach and Rice Soup

Use very young spinach leaves to prepare this light and fresh-tasting soup.

Serves 4

675g/1½lb fresh spinach leaves, washed
45ml/3 tbsp extra virgin olive oil
1 small onion, finely chopped
2 garlic cloves, finely chopped
1 small fresh red chilli, seeded and finely chopped
225g/8oz/generous 1 cup risotto rice, such as arborio
1.2 litres/2 pints/5 cups vegetable stock
salt and ground black pepper
Parmesan or Pecorino cheese shavings, to serve

1 Place the spinach in a large pan with just the water that clings to its leaves after washing. Add a large pinch of salt. Heat gently until the spinach has wilted, then remove from the heat and drain, reserving any liquid.

2 Either chop the spinach finely using a large kitchen knife or place in a food processor or blender and process the leaves to a fairly coarse purée.

3 Heat the oil in a large pan and gently cook the onion, garlic and chilli for 4–5 minutes, until softened. Stir in the rice until well coated with the oil, then pour in the stock and reserved spinach liquid. Bring to the boil, lower the heat and simmer for 10 minutes.

4 Add the spinach, with salt and pepper to taste. Cook for 5–7 minutes, until the rice is tender. Check the seasoning. Serve in heated bowls, topped with the shavings of cheese.

Cook's Tip

Buy Parmesan or Pecorino cheese as a small block from a reputable supplier, as it will be full of flavour and easy to grate or shave with a vegetable peeler. The hard cheeses will keep for a long time if well wrapped and refrigerated.

Rice and Bean: Energy 507kcal/2111kJ; Protein 14.4g; Carbohydrate 61.3g, of which sugars 3.1g; Fat 22.7g, of which saturates 5.8g; Cholesterol 13mg; Calcium 87mg; Fibre 8.5g; Sodium 50mg.
Spinach and Rice: Energy 293kcal/1215kJ; Protein 13g; Carbohydrate 26.8g, of which sugars 3.4g; Fat 14.7g, of which saturates 4.4g; Cholesterol 15mg; Calcium 476mg; Fibre 3.8g; Sodium 400mg.

Risotto-style Squash and Blue Cheese Soup

This is, in fact, a very wet risotto, but it bears more than a passing resemblance to soup and makes a very smart first course for a dinner party. The combination of blue cheese and creamy rice is irresistible, and the perfect base for the nutty squash.

Serves 4

25g/1oz/2 tbsp butter
30ml/2 tbsp olive oil
2 onions, finely chopped
½ celery stick, finely sliced
1 small butternut squash, peeled, seeded and cut into small cubes
15ml/1 tbsp chopped sage
300g/11oz/1½ cups risotto or arborio rice
1.2 litres/2 pints/5 cups hot chicken stock
30ml/2 tbsp double (heavy) cream
115g/4oz blue cheese, finely diced
30ml/2 tbsp olive oil
salt and ground black pepper
4 large fresh sage leaves

1 Place the butter in a large pan with the oil and heat gently. Add the onions and celery, and cook for 4–5 minutes, until softened. Stir in the butternut squash and cook for a further 3–4 minutes, then add the sage.

2 Add the rice and cook for 1–2 minutes, stirring, until the grains are slightly translucent. Add the chicken stock a ladleful at a time.

3 Cook until each ladleful of stock has been absorbed before adding the next. Continue adding the stock in this way until you have a very wet rice mixture. Season and stir in the cream.

4 Meanwhile, heat the oil in a frying pan and fry the sage leaves for a few seconds until crisp. Drain. Stir the blue cheese into the risotto soup and ladle it into bowls. Garnish with fried sage leaves.

Bamboo Shoot, Fish and Rice Soup

This is a spicy Thai-style freshwater fish soup.

Serves 4

75g/3oz/scant ½ cup long grain rice, well rinsed
250ml/8fl oz/1 cup reduced-fat coconut milk
2 lemon grass stalks, crushed
25g/1oz galangal, thinly sliced
2–3 fresh Thai chillies, seeded and chopped
4 garlic cloves, crushed
15ml/1 tbsp palm sugar (jaggery)
225g/8oz can sliced bamboo shoots, drained
450g/1lb freshwater fish fillets, such as carp or catfish, skinned and cut into bitesize pieces
1 small bunch fresh basil leaves
rice or noodles, to serve

For the garnish

1 small bunch fresh coriander (cilantro), chopped
1 chilli, finely sliced

For the stock

450g/1lb pork ribs
1 onion, quartered
225g/8oz carrots, cut into chunks
25g/1oz dried squid or dried shrimp, soaked in water for 30 minutes, rinsed and drained
15ml/1 tbsp Thai fish sauce
15ml/1 tbsp soy sauce
6 black peppercorns
salt

1 To prepare the stock, put the ribs in a large pan and cover with 2.5 litres/4¼ pints/10 cups water. Bring to the boil, skim off any fat, and add the remaining stock ingredients. Cover the pan and simmer for 1 hour, then skim off any foam or fat.

2 Simmer the stock, uncovered, for a further 1–1½ hours, until reduced, then strain it into another pan. There should be about 2 litres/3½ pints/7¾ cups of stock.

3 Bring the pan of stock to the boil. Stir in the rice and reduce the heat. Add the coconut milk, lemon grass, galangal, chillies, garlic and sugar. Simmer for about 10 minutes to let the flavours mingle. The rice should be just cooked, with bite to it.

4 Add the bamboo shoots and fish. Simmer for 5 minutes, until the fish is cooked. Check the seasoning and stir in the basil leaves. Ladle the soup into bowls, garnish with the chopped coriander and chilli, and serve with the rice or noodles.

Risotto-style Squash: Energy 505kcal/2100kJ; Protein 9.2g; Carbohydrate 63.7g, of which sugars 5.7g; Fat 23g, of which saturates 8.3g; Cholesterol 26mg; Calcium 110mg; Fibre 2.7g; Sodium 91mg.
Bamboo Shoot: Energy 269kcal/1130kJ; Protein 35.5g; Carbohydrate 23.2g, of which sugars 7.9g; Fat 3.8g, of which saturates 1.1g; Cholesterol 87mg; Calcium 109mg; Fibre 2.6g; Sodium 214mg.

Classic Seafood Broth

Adding rice makes this a substantial main-meal soup.

Serves 4–6

450g/1lb fresh mussels, scrubbed
250ml/8fl oz/1 cup white wine
675–900g/1½–2lb mixed white fish fillets, cut into cubes
6 large scallops
30ml/2 tbsp olive oil
3 leeks, chopped
1 garlic clove, crushed
1 red (bell) pepper, seeded and cut into 2.5cm/1in pieces
1 yellow (bell) pepper, seeded and cut into 2.5cm/1in pieces
175g/6oz fennel bulb, diced
400g/14oz can chopped tomatoes
150ml/1/4 pint/⅔ cup passata (bottled strained tomatoes)
about 1 litre/1¾ pints/4 cups well-flavoured fish stock
pinch of saffron threads, soaked in 15ml/1 tbsp hot water
175g/6oz/scant 1 cup white long grain rice, soaked
8 large raw prawns (shrimp), peeled and deveined
salt and ground black pepper
30–45ml/2–3 tbsp fresh dill, to garnish

1 Discard any mussels that do not close when tapped. Place in a pan. Add 90ml/6 tbsp of the wine, cover, bring to the boil on high heat and cook for 3 minutes or until all the mussels open.

2 Strain, reserving the liquid. Discard any closed mussels, set aside half in their shells; shell the rest and put them in a bowl.

3 Detach the corals from the scallops and slice the white flesh. Add the slices to the fish and the corals to the shelled mussels.

4 Heat the olive oil in a pan. Fry the leeks and garlic for 3–4 minutes, until soft. Add the pepper and fennel, and fry for 2 minutes more. Add the tomatoes, passata, stock, saffron water, mussel liquid and wine. Season and cook for 5 minutes. Drain the rice, stir it in, cover and simmer for 10 minutes.

5 Stir in the white fish. Cook gently for 5 minutes. Add the prawns, cook for 2 minutes, then add the scallop corals and shelled mussels and cook for 2–3 minutes, until all the fish is tender. Add a little extra white wine or stock if needed. Spoon into warmed soup dishes, top with mussels in their shells and sprinkle with the dill. Serve immediately.

Seafood and Rice Chowder

Chowder takes its name from the French word for cauldron – chaudière – the type of pot once traditionally used for soups and stews.

Serves 4–6

200g/7oz/generous 1 cup drained, canned corn
600ml/1 pint/2½ cups milk
15g/½oz/1 tbsp butter
1 small leek, sliced
1 small garlic clove, crushed
2 rindless smoked streaky (fatty) bacon rashers (strips), chopped
1 small green (bell) pepper, seeded and diced
1 celery stalk, chopped
115g/4oz/generous ½ cup white long grain rice
5ml/1 tsp plain (all-purpose) flour
about 450ml/¾ pint/scant 2 cups hot chicken or vegetable stock
4 large scallops, with corals
115g/4oz white fish fillet, such as monkfish or plaice
15ml/1 tbsp finely chopped fresh parsley
good pinch of cayenne pepper
30–45ml/2–3 tbsp single (light) cream (optional)
salt and ground black pepper

1 Process half the corn in a food processor or blender with a little of the milk until thick and creamy.

2 Melt the butter in a large pan. Gently fry the leek, garlic and bacon for 4–5 minutes until soft but not brown. Add the pepper and celery and cook gently for 3–4 minutes, stirring.

3 Stir in the rice. Cook for a few minutes. Sprinkle over the flour. Cook, stirring, for 1 minute, then gradually stir in the remaining milk and the stock. Boil, lower the heat and stir in the corn mixture, with the whole corn. Season well.

4 Cover and simmer gently for 20 minutes until the rice is tender, stirring often. Add a little stock or water if the mixture thickens too quickly or the rice sticks to the pan.

5 Pull the corals off the scallops and slice the white flesh into 5mm/¼in pieces. Cut the fish fillet into bite-size chunks.

6 Stir the scallops and fish into the chowder, cook for 4 minutes, then stir in the corals, parsley and cayenne. Cook for a few minutes, then stir in the cream, if liked. Season and serve.

Classic Seafood: Energy 267kcal/1112kJ; Protein 20.1g; Carbohydrate 25.2g, of which sugars 18.7g; Fat 9g, of which saturates 1.3g; Cholesterol 96mg; Calcium 96mg; Fibre 4.8g; Sodium 262mg.
Seafood and Rice: Energy 488kcal/2050kJ; Protein 46g; Carbohydrate 36.2g, of which sugars 11.3g; Fat 18.7g, of which saturates 9.6g; Cholesterol 127mg; Calcium 163mg; Fibre 3.4g; Sodium 771mg.

Mixed Seafood and Rice Gumbo

Gumbo is a soup served over rice as a main course.

Serves 6

450g/1lb fresh mussels, cooked and shelled, with cooking liquor
450g/1lb raw prawns (shrimp), with shells
1 cooked crab, about 1kg/2¼lb
small bunch of parsley, leaves chopped and stalks reserved
150ml/¼ pint/⅔ cup cooking oil
115g/4oz/1 cup plain (all-purpose) flour
1 green (bell) pepper, seeded and chopped
1 large onion, chopped
2 celery sticks, sliced
3 garlic cloves, finely chopped
75g/3oz smoked spiced sausage, skinned and sliced
275g/10oz/1½ cups white long grain rice
6 spring onions (scallions), shredded
cayenne pepper, to taste
Tabasco sauce, to taste
salt

1 Make the mussel liquor up to 2 litres/3½ pints/8 cups with water and place in a pan. Peel the prawns, reserving a few for the garnish. Put the shells and heads in the pan. Remove all the meat from the crab, separating the brown and white meat. Add the shell to the pan with 5ml/2 tsp salt. Bring to the boil, skimming. When there is no more froth, add the parsley stalks and simmer for 15 minutes. Cool, then strain the stock and make up to 2 litres/3½ pints/8 cups with water.

2 Heat the oil in a pan. Stir in the flour. Stir over medium heat until golden. Add the pepper, onion, celery and garlic. Cook for 3 minutes until softened. Stir in the sausage. Reheat the stock.

3 Stir the brown crab meat into the roux, then ladle in the hot stock, stirring until it is smoothly incorporated. Boil, partially cover, then simmer gently for 30 minutes.

4 Meanwhile, cook the rice in plenty of lightly salted boiling water until the grains are tender.

5 Add the prawns, mussels, white crab meat and spring onions to the gumbo. Return to the boil and season with salt, cayenne and a dash or two of Tabasco. Simmer for a minute, then add the chopped parsley. Serve immediately, ladled over the rice.

Chicken Rice Soup with Ginseng and Red Dates

Traditionally eaten on the hottest day of summer, this Korean speciality is a smooth chicken broth with a revitalizing quality. It is usually served with a small dish of salt and ground pepper, for seasoning the chicken while eating. All the ingredients are available from Thai, Indonesian or sometimes Chinese supermarkets.

Serves 2

180g/7oz/1 cup short grain or pudding rice
800g/28oz whole small chicken or poussin
4 chestnuts, peeled
4 garlic cloves, peeled
2 red dates
2 fresh ginseng roots
4 gingko nuts
salt and ground black pepper
finely shredded spring onions (scallions), to garnish

1 Soak the rice in a bowl of cold water for 20 minutes. Meanwhile, remove the wing tips and neck from the chicken, clean it thoroughly and sprinkle with salt.

2 Drain the rice and combine with the chestnuts and garlic to make a stuffing. Pack the stuffing into the neck end of the body cavity and pull down the skin before trussing the chicken.

3 Place the stuffed chicken into a heavy pan and add enough cold water to cover. Bring to the boil.

4 Once the water is boiling add the red dates, ginseng roots and gingko nuts. Reduce the heat and simmer the soup for about 1 hour, or until it thickens.

5 To serve, lift the chicken or poussin from the pan, draining off the stock. Place on a platter or board and cut in half. Use a heavy knife and rolling pin to chop through the bones, or a pair of strong poultry shears.

6 Transfer to two bowls, dividing the stuffing between the bowls. Ladle over the soup and serve garnished with spring onions.

Seafood and Rice: Energy 559kcal/2336kJ; Protein 31.1g; Carbohydrate 57.6g, of which sugars 3.7g; Fat 23g, of which saturates 3.4g; Cholesterol 183mg; Calcium 145mg; Fibre 1.9g; Sodium 474mg.
Chicken Rice Soup: Energy 630kcal/2654kJ; Protein 56.3g; Carbohydrate 93.1g, of which sugars 12.3g; Fat 3.6g, of which saturates 0.8g; Cholesterol 140mg; Calcium 60mg; Fibre 2.2g; Sodium 128mg.

Chicken Rice Soup

Light and refreshing, this soup is the perfect choice for a hot day. In the great tradition of chicken soup recipes, it also acts as a wonderful pick-me-up when you are feeling low or a little tired.

Serves 4

2 lemon grass stalks, trimmed, cut into 3 pieces, and lightly bruised
15ml/1 tbsp fish sauce
90g/3½oz/½ cup short grain rice, rinsed
ground black pepper
sea salt
chopped coriander (cilantro) and 1 fresh green or red chilli, seeded and cut into thin strips, to garnish
1 lime, cut in wedges, to serve

For the stock

1 small chicken, about 900g/2lb
1 onion, quartered
2 garlic cloves, crushed
25g/1oz fresh root ginger, sliced
2 lemon grass stalks, cut in half lengthways and bruised
2 dried red chillies
30ml/2 tbsp fish sauce

1 For the stock, put the chicken into a deep pan. Add all the other stock ingredients and pour in 2 litres/3½ pints/8 cups water. Bring to the boil for a few minutes, then reduce the heat and simmer gently with the lid on for 2 hours.

2 Skim off any fat from the stock, sieve (strain) and reserve. Remove the skin from the chicken and shred the meat with your fingers, or chop roughly using a sharp knife. Set aside.

3 Pour the stock back into the deep pan and bring to the boil. Reduce the heat and stir in the lemon grass stalks and fish sauce. Stir in the rice and simmer, uncovered, for about 40 minutes. Add the shredded chicken and season with the black pepper and sea salt to taste.

4 Ladle the piping hot soup into warmed individual bowls; garnish with chopped coriander and the thin strips of chilli. Put the lime wedges into a separate bowl and serve for squeezing over the soup if desired.

Pumpkin, Rice and Chicken Soup

This is a comforting, full-flavoured soup.

Serves 4

450g/1lb wedge of pumpkin
15ml/1 tbsp sunflower oil
25g/1oz/2 tbsp butter
6 green cardamom pods
1 large skinless boneless chicken breast
2 leeks, chopped
900ml/1½ pints/3¾ cups chicken stock
115g/4oz/generous ½ cup basmati rice, soaked
350ml/12fl oz/1½ cups milk
salt and ground black pepper
generous strips of pared orange rind, to garnish

1 Skin the pumpkin and remove all seeds and pith, so that you have about 350g/12oz flesh. Cut the flesh into 2.5cm/1in cubes.

2 Heat the oil and butter in a pan and fry the cardamom pods for 2–3 minutes until slightly swollen. Add the chicken breast and cook for 1–2 minutes on each side. Add the leeks and pumpkin. Cook, stirring and turning the chicken once, for 3–4 minutes over a medium heat, then lower the heat, cover and sweat for 5 minutes more or until the pumpkin is soft, stirring occasionally.

3 Pour in 600ml/1 pint/2½ cups of the stock and bring to the boil, then lower the heat, cover and simmer gently for 15 minutes, until the pumpkin is soft and the chicken is cooked.

4 Pour the remaining stock into a pan. Drain the rice and add it to the stock. Bring to the boil, then reduce the heat, cover and simmer for about 10 minutes until the rice is tender. Add seasoning to taste.

5 Remove the chicken and cardamom pods from the soup. Discard the cardamoms and cut the chicken into strips.

6 Process the soup in a food processor or blender until smooth. Pour back into a clean pan and stir in the milk, chicken and rice (with any stock that has not been absorbed). Heat until simmering. Garnish with the strips of pared orange rind and freshly ground black pepper, and serve with Granary or wholemeal bread.

Chicken Rice Soup: Energy 147kcal/615kJ; Protein 12.8g; Carbohydrate 19.8g, of which sugars 1.4g; Fat 1.7g, of which saturates 0.4g; Cholesterol 53mg; Calcium 37mg; Fibre 0.8g; Sodium 317mg.
Pumpkin, Rice Soup: Energy 336kcal/1406kJ; Protein 25.4g; Carbohydrate 33.9g, of which sugars 7.8g; Fat 11g, of which saturates 5g; Cholesterol 71mg; Calcium 168mg; Fibre 2.9g; Sodium 122mg.

Tagine-style Lamb Soup with Butternut Squash

This soup is inspired by the simmered stews of Morocco.

Serves 6

30ml/2 tbsp olive oil
450g/1lb lamb fillet, cubed
1 large onion, chopped
2 garlic cloves, crushed
2 celery sticks, diced
15ml/1 tbsp harissa
10ml/2 tsp plain (all-purpose) flour
1.2 litres/2 pints/5 cups hot vegetable stock
400g/14oz can chopped tomatoes
75g/3oz/⅓ cup ready-to-eat dried apricots
900g/2lb butternut squash, seeded, peeled and cubed
salt and ground black pepper

For the minted couscous

300ml/½ pint/1¼ cups vegetable stock
175g/6oz/1 cup couscous
2 tomatoes, peeled and diced
30ml/2 tbsp chopped fresh mint

1 Heat the oil in a pan. Add the lamb and cook until browned all over. Use a draining spoon to remove the lamb; set aside.

2 Add the onion and garlic, and cook for 5 minutes, until softened. Add the celery, cover and cook gently for 5 minutes. Stir in the harissa and flour, and cook for 2 minutes. Gradually whisk in the hot vegetable stock.

3 Stir in the tomatoes and apricots and bring to the boil. Cover and simmer gently for 20 minutes. Season well.

4 Add the cubes of butternut squash and return the lamb to the soup. Cover and cook for about 25 minutes more, stirring occasionally, until both lamb and squash are tender.

5 Meanwhile, prepare the couscous. Bring the stock to the boil in a large pan. Stir in the couscous and cook for 1 minute, then remove from the heat, cover and leave to stand for 5 minutes. Mix in the tomatoes and mint with a fork.

6 Ladle the soup into bowls and pile a spoonful of couscous into the centre. Serve at once, offering extra harissa.

Lamb Soup with Rice and Coconut

This meaty soup thickened with long grain rice is based on Indian mulligatawny soup.

Serves 6

2 onions, chopped
6 garlic cloves, crushed
5cm/2in piece fresh root ginger, grated
90ml/6 tbsp olive oil
30ml/2 tbsp black poppy seeds
5ml/1 tsp cumin seeds
5ml/1 tsp coriander seeds
2.5ml/½ tsp ground turmeric
450g/1lb boneless lamb chump chops, trimmed and cut into bitesize pieces
1.5ml/¼ tsp cayenne pepper
1.2 litres/2 pints/5 cups lamb stock
50g/2oz/generous ⅓ cup long grain rice
30ml/2 tbsp lemon juice
60ml/4 tbsp coconut milk
salt and ground black pepper
fresh coriander (cilantro) sprigs and toasted flaked coconut, to garnish

1 Process the onions, garlic, ginger and 15ml/1 tbsp of the oil in a food processor or blender to form a paste. Set aside.

2 Heat a small, heavy-based frying pan. Add the poppy, cumin and coriander seeds and toast for a few seconds, until aromatic. Transfer the seeds to a mortar and grind them to a powder with a pestle. Stir in the turmeric. Set aside.

3 Heat the rest of the oil in a pan. Fry the lamb in batches over a high heat for about 4–5 minutes until browned all over. Remove the lamb and set aside.

4 Add the onion, garlic and ginger paste to the pan and cook for 1–2 minutes, stirring continuously. Stir in the ground spices and cook for 1 minute. Return the meat to the pan with any meat juices that have seeped out while it has been standing. Add the cayenne, stock and seasoning. Bring to the boil.

5 Reduce the heat, cover and simmer for 30 minutes until the lamb is tender. Stir in the rice. Cover and cook for 15 minutes. Add the lemon juice and coconut milk. Simmer for 2 minutes.

6 Ladle the soup into six warmed bowls and garnish with sprigs of coriander and lightly toasted flaked coconut.

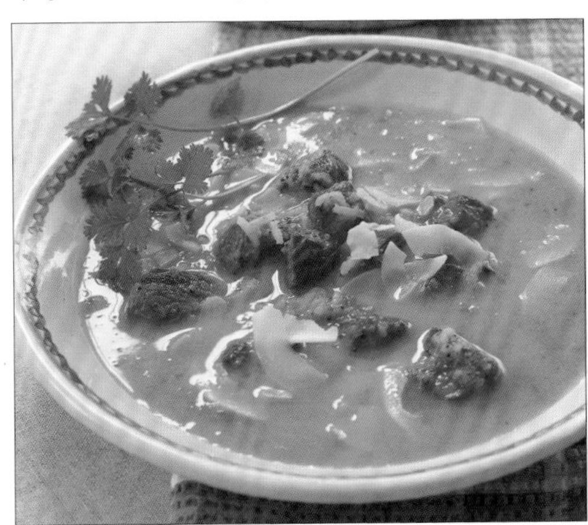

Tagine-style Lamb: Energy 300kcal/1256kJ; Protein 19.1g; Carbohydrate 27.8g, of which sugars 10.3g; Fat 13.1g, of which saturates 4.7g; Cholesterol 57mg; Calcium 95mg; Fibre 3.5g; Sodium 83mg.
Lamb with Rice: Energy 249kcal/1036kJ; Protein 15.8g; Carbohydrate 7.5g, of which sugars 0.8g; Fat 17.3g, of which saturates 4.5g; Cholesterol 56mg; Calcium 14mg; Fibre 0.2g; Sodium 64mg.

Lamb and Yogurt Soup with Rice and Mint

This is a classic Turkish soup. Based on well-flavoured stock and yogurt, it usually contains a little rice, bulgur, chickpeas or barley, depending on the local version. Occasionally it is coloured with saffron or sprinkled with paprika.

Serves 4

15ml/1 tbsp butter or sunflower oil
1 large onion, finely chopped
scant 15ml/1 tbsp plain (all-purpose) flour
1.2 litres/2 pints/5 cups lamb or chicken stock
75g/3oz/scant ½ cup long grain rice (wild or plain), well rinsed
15–30ml/1–2 tbsp dried mint
400ml/14fl oz/1⅔ cups thick and creamy natural (plain) yogurt, such as Greek (US strained plain) yogurt
salt and ground black pepper

1 Melt the butter or oil in a heavy pan, add the onion and cook until soft.

2 Take the pan off the heat and stir in the flour, then pour in the stock, stirring constantly. Return to the heat and bring the stock to the boil, stirring often.

3 Stir in the rice and most of the mint, reserving a little for the garnish. Lower the heat, cover the pan and simmer for about 20 minutes, until the rice is cooked. Season to taste with salt and pepper.

4 Beat the yogurt until smooth, then spoon almost all of it into the soup. Keep the heat low and stir vigorously to make sure the yogurt remains smooth and creamy and becomes well blended. Do not boil or it may curdle.

5 Ladle the soup into serving bowls, swirl in the remaining yogurt. Garnish with the remaining mint and serve immediately, while the soup is piping hot.

Chinese Rice Porridge with Salt Pork

Originating in China, this dish has now spread throughout much of Asia and is loved for its comforting textures. It is invariably served with a few strongly flavoured accompaniments.

Serves 2

900ml/1½ pints/3¾ cups vegetable stock
200g/7oz/1¾ cups cooked rice
225g/8oz minced (ground) pork
15ml/1 tbsp fish sauce
2 heads pickled garlic, finely chopped
1 celery stick, finely diced
salt and ground black pepper

To garnish

30ml/2 tbsp groundnut (peanut) oil
4 garlic cloves, thinly sliced
4 small red shallots, finely sliced

1 Make the garnishes by heating the groundnut oil in a frying pan and cooking the garlic and shallots over a low heat until brown. Drain well on kitchen paper and reserve for the soup.

2 Pour the stock into a large pan. Bring to the boil and add the rice. Season the minced pork. Add it by taking small teaspoons and tapping the spoon on the side of the pan so that the meat falls into the soup in small lumps.

3 Stir in the fish sauce and pickled garlic and simmer for about 10 minutes, until the pork is cooked. Stir in the celery.

4 Serve the rice porridge in individual warmed bowls. Sprinkle the prepared garlic and shallots on top and season with plenty of ground pepper.

Cook's Tip

Pickled garlic has a distinctive flavour and is available in many Asian food stores. Once opened, it will keep for about one month in the refrigerator.

Lamb and Yogurt: Energy 187kcal/781kJ; Protein 7.6g; Carbohydrate 30.3g, of which sugars 11.1g; Fat 4.4g, of which saturates 2.5g; Cholesterol 9mg; Calcium 215mg; Fibre 1g; Sodium 108mg.
Rice Porridge: Energy 152kcal/636kJ; Protein 15.2g; Carbohydrate 17g, of which sugars 1.8g; Fat 2.5g, of which saturates 0.3g; Cholesterol 34mg; Calcium 12mg; Fibre 0.3g; Sodium 45mg.

Rice Soup with Spicy Sausage

Oriental soups prepared with soft rice are known as congee. Gentle on the stomach, this dish is often eaten for breakfast or served to convalescents.

Serves 2–3

115g/4oz/generous ½ cup long grain rice
25g/1oz/3 tbsp glutinous rice
1.2 litres/2 pints/5 cups water
about 2.5ml/½ tsp salt
5ml/1 tsp sesame oil
thin slice of fresh root ginger, peeled and bruised
2 Chinese sausages
1 egg, lightly beaten (optional)
2.5ml/½ tsp light soy sauce

For the garnish

roasted peanuts, chopped
thin shreds of spring onion (scallion)

1 Wash both rices thoroughly. Drain and place in a large pan. Add the water, bring to the boil and immediately reduce to the lowest heat, using a heat diffuser if you have one.

2 Cook gently for 1¼–1½ hours, stirring from time to time. If the congee thickens too much, stir in a little boiling water. It should have the consistency of creamy pouring porridge.

3 About 15 minutes before serving, add salt to taste and the sesame oil, together with the piece of ginger.

4 Steam the Chinese sausages for about 10 minutes, then slice and stir into the congee. Cook for 5 minutes.

5 Just before serving, remove the ginger and stir in the lightly beaten egg, if using. Serve hot, garnished with the peanuts and spring onions and topped with a drizzle of soy sauce.

Variation

Use roast duck instead of Chinese sausages. In the East, congee is often served with boiled eggs simmered in tea.

Rice Soup with Pork and Roasted Garlic

Made with pork or chicken, this warming and sustaining rice soup combines the ancient traditions of the Filipino rice culture with the Spanish colonial culinary techniques of browning and sautéeing.

Serves 4–6

15–30ml/1–2 tbsp palm or groundnut (peanut) oil
1 large onion, finely chopped.
2 garlic cloves, finely chopped
25g/1oz fresh root ginger, finely chopped
350g/12oz lean boneless pork, cut into bitesize slices
5–6 black peppercorns
115g/4oz/1 cup plus 15ml/1 tbsp short grain rice
2 litres/3½ pints/8 cups pork or chicken stock
30ml/2 tbsp fish sauce
salt

To serve

2 garlic cloves, finely chopped
2 spring onions (scallions), white parts only, finely sliced
2–3 fresh green or red chillies, seeded and quartered lengthways

1 Heat the oil in a wok or deep, heavy pan that has a lid. Stir in the onion, garlic and ginger and fry until fragrant and beginning to colour. Add the pork and fry, stirring frequently, for 5–6 minutes, until lightly browned. Stir in the peppercorns.

2 Meanwhile, put the rice in a sieve (strainer), rinse under cold running water until the water runs clear, then drain. Toss the rice into the pan, making sure that it is coated in the mixture. Pour in the stock, add the fish sauce and bring to the boil. Reduce the heat and partially cover. Simmer for about 40 minutes, stirring ocassionally to make sure that the rice does not stick to the bottom of the pan. Season with salt to taste.

3 Just before serving, dry-fry the garlic in a small, heavy pan, until golden brown then stir it into the soup. Ladle the soup into individual warmed bowls and sprinkle the spring onions over the top. Serve the chillies separately, to chew on.

Rice with Sausage: Energy 301kcal/1254kJ; Protein 7.2g; Carbohydrate 40.4g, of which sugars 0.8g; Fat 12g, of which saturates 4.2g; Cholesterol 16mg; Calcium 23mg; Fibre 0.2g; Sodium 610mg.
Rice with Pork: Energy 195kcal/813kJ; Protein 14.8g; Carbohydrate 19.9g, of which sugars 3.4g; Fat 6.2g, of which saturates 1.3g; Cholesterol 37mg; Calcium 24mg; Fibre 0.8g; Sodium 399mg.

Mussel Soup with Pumpkin

Pumpkin is excellent in this French mussel soup.

Serves 4

1kg/2¼lb mussels, cleaned
300ml/½ pint/1¼ cups dry white wine
1 large lemon
1 bay leaf
15ml/1 tbsp olive oil
1 onion, chopped
1 garlic clove, crushed
675g/1½lb pumpkin or squash, seeded, peeled and roughly chopped
900ml/1½ pints/3¾ cups vegetable stock
30ml/2 tbsp chopped fresh dill
salt and ground black pepper
lemon wedges, to serve

1 Discard any open mussels that do not shut when tapped sharply, and put the rest into a large pan. Pour in the wine.

2 Pare large pieces of rind from the lemon and squeeze the juice, then add both to the mussels with the bay leaf. Cover and bring to the boil, then cook for 4–5 minutes, shaking the pan occasionally until all the mussels have opened. Drain the mussels in a colander over a large bowl. Reserve the liquid.

3 Discard the lemon rind and bay leaf, and any mussel shells that have not opened. Set aside a few mussels in their shells for the garnish. Remove the remaining mussels from their shells. Strain the reserved cooking liquid through a muslin- (cheesecloth) lined sieve.

4 Heat the oil in a large, clean pan. Add the onion and garlic and cook for 4–5 minutes, until softened. Add the pumpkin flesh and the strained mussel cooking liquid. Bring to the boil and simmer, uncovered, for 5–6 minutes. Pour in the vegetable stock and cook for a further 25–30 minutes, until the pumpkin has almost disintegrated.

5 Cool the soup slightly, then process it in a food processor or blender until smooth. Return the soup to the rinsed-out pan and season well. Stir in the chopped dill and the shelled mussels, then bring just to the boil. Ladle the soup into warmed bowls. Garnish with the reserved mussels in shells. Serve lemon wedges with the soup.

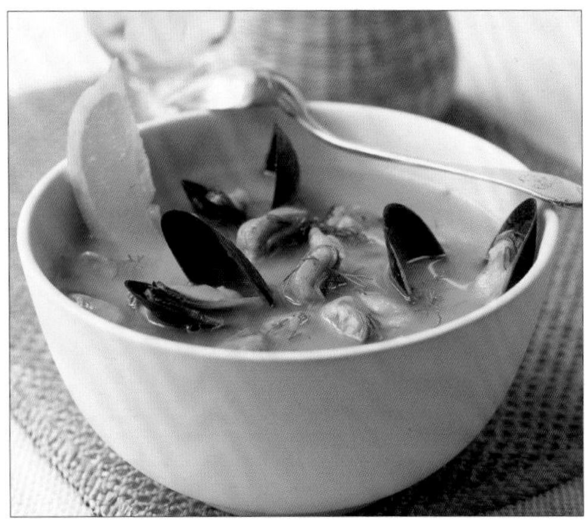

Spiced Mussel Soup

Chunky and colourful, this Turkish fish soup is like a chowder in its consistency. It is flavoured with harissa sauce which is more familiar in north African cookery.

Serves 6

1.5 kg/3–3½ lb fresh mussels
900ml/1½ pints vegetable stock
150ml/¼ pint/⅔ cup white wine
2 bay leaves
30ml/2 tbsp olive oil
1 onion, finely chopped
2 garlic cloves, crushed
2 celery sticks, finely sliced
bunch of spring onions (scallions), finely sliced
1 potato, diced
7.5ml/1½ tsp harissa sauce
3 tomatoes, peeled and diced
45ml/3 tbsp chopped fresh parsley
freshly ground black pepper
thick natural (plain) yogurt, to serve (optional)

1 Scrub the mussels, discarding any damaged ones or any open ones that do not close when tapped with a knife.

2 Bring the stock and wine to the boil in a large pan with the bay leaves. Add the mussels and cover with a lid. Cook for 4–5 minutes until the mussels have opened wide. Discard any mussels that remain closed. Drain the mussels, reserving the cooking liquid. Reserve a few mussels in their shells to use as a garnish and shell the rest.

3 Heat the oil in a pan and fry the onion, garlic, celery and spring onions for 5 minutes.

4 Add the reserved liquid from the shelled mussels, potato, harissa sauce and tomatoes. Bring to the boil, reduce the heat and cover. Simmer gently for 25 minutes or until the potatoes are breaking up.

5 Stir in the parsley and pepper and add the shelled mussels. Heat through for 1–2 minutes. Ladle into bowls and garnish with the unshelled mussels. Serve hot with a spoonful of yogurt, if liked.

Mussel with Pumpkin: Energy 126kcal/532kJ; Protein 13g; Carbohydrate 7.5g, of which sugars 4g; Fat 5g, of which saturates 0.8g; Cholesterol 40mg; Calcium 113mg; Fibre 2.5g; Sodium 245mg.
Spiced Mussel Soup: Energy 153kcal/644kJ; Protein 14.5g; Carbohydrate 7.8g, of which sugars 3.2g; Fat 5.6g, of which saturates 0.9g; Cholesterol 30mg; Calcium 178mg; Fibre 1.5g; Sodium 175mg.

Saffron-flavoured Mussel Soup

This creamy soup, with the jet black shells and plump mussels, tastes as delicious and colourful as it looks. The flavours are subtle yet distinctive – just right for shellfish soup.

Serves 4

1.5kg/3–3½lb fresh mussels
600ml/1 pint /2½ cups white wine
few fresh parsley stalks
50g/2oz/¼ cup butter
2 leeks, finely chopped
2 celery sticks, finely chopped
1 carrot, chopped
2 garlic cloves, chopped
large pinch of saffron threads
600ml/1 pint/2½ cups double (heavy) cream
3 tomatoes, peeled, seeded and chopped
salt and ground black pepper
30ml/2 tbsp chopped fresh chives, to garnish

1 Scrub the mussels and pull away the beards. Put into a large pan with the wine and parsley stalks. Cover, bring to the boil and cook for 4–5 minutes, shaking the pan occasionally, until the mussels have opened. Discard the stalks and any mussels that refuse to open.

2 Drain the mussels over a large bowl, reserving the cooking liquid. When cool enough to handle, remove about half of the cooked mussels from their shells. Set aside with the remaining mussels in their shells.

3 Melt the butter in a large pan and add the leeks, celery, carrot and garlic, and cook for 5 minutes until softened. Strain the reserved mussel cooking liquid through a fine sieve (strainer) or muslin (cheesecloth). Add to the pan and cook over a high heat for 8–10 minutes to reduce slightly. Strain into a clean pan, add the saffron strands and cook for 1 minute.

4 Add the cream and bring back to the boil. Season well. Add all the mussels and the tomatoes and heat gently to warm through. Ladle the soup into four bowls, then scatter with the chopped chives and serve immediately.

Seafood Wonton Soup

This is a variation on the popular Chinese wonton soup that is traditionally prepared using pork.

Serves 4

50g/2oz raw tiger prawns (jumbo shrimp)
50g/2oz queen scallops
75g/3oz skinless cod fillet, roughly chopped
15ml/1 tbsp finely chopped fresh chives
5ml/1 tsp dry sherry
1 small egg white, lightly beaten
2.5ml/½ tsp sesame oil
1.5ml/¼ tsp salt
large pinch of ground white pepper
20 wonton wrappers
2 cos lettuce leaves, shredded
900ml/1½ pints/3¾ cups fish stock
fresh coriander (cilantro) leaves and garlic chives, to garnish

1 Peel and devein the prawns. Rinse, dry on kitchen paper and cut into small pieces.

2 Rinse and dry the scallops. Chop them into small pieces the same size as the prawns.

3 Place the cod in a food processor or blender and process until a paste is formed. Scrape into a bowl and stir in the prawns, scallops, chives, sherry, egg white, sesame oil, salt and pepper. Mix well, cover and leave in a cool place to marinate for 20 minutes.

4 Make the wontons. Place 5ml/1 tsp of the seafood filling in the centre of a wonton wrapper, then bring the corners together to meet at the top. Twist them together to enclose the filling. Fill the remaining wonton wrappers in the same way. Tie with a fresh chive if desired.

5 Bring a large pan of water to the boil. Drop in the wontons. When the water returns to the boil, lower the heat and simmer gently for 5 minutes or until the wontons float to the surface. Drain the wontons and divide them among four heated soup bowls.

6 Add a portion of lettuce to each bowl. Bring the fish stock to the boil. Ladle it on top of the lettuce and garnish with coriander leaves and garlic chives. Serve immediately.

Saffron Mussel Soup: Energy 441kcal/1825kJ; Protein 9.6g; Carbohydrate 3.1g, of which sugars 3.1g; Fat 39.1g, of which saturates 23.9g; Cholesterol 116mg; Calcium 137mg; Fibre 0.6g; Sodium 156mg.
Seafood Wonton Soup: Energy 92kcal/388kJ; Protein 10.7g; Carbohydrate 10.8g, of which sugars 0.9g; Fat 0.7g, of which saturates 0.2g; Cholesterol 39mg; Calcium 44mg; Fibre 0.7g; Sodium 74mg.

Clam and Basil Soup

Subtly sweet and spicy, this soup is an ideal starter for serving as part of a celebration dinner.

Serves 4–6

30ml/2 tbsp olive oil
1 onion, finely chopped
leaves from 1 fresh or dried sprig of thyme, chopped or crumbled
2 garlic cloves, crushed
5–6 fresh basil leaves, plus extra to garnish
1.5–2.5ml/¼–½ tsp crushed red chillies, to taste
1 litre/1¾ pints/4 cups fish stock
350ml/12 fl oz/1½ cups passata (bottled strained tomatoes)
5ml/1 tsp sugar
90g/3½oz/scant 1 cup frozen peas
65g/2½oz/⅔ cup small pasta shapes, such as chifferini
225g/8oz frozen shelled clams
salt and ground black pepper

1 Heat the oil in a large pan, add the onion and cook gently for about 5 minutes until softened but not coloured. Add the thyme, then stir in the garlic, basil leaves and chillies.

2 Add the stock, passata and sugar to the pan, with salt and pepper to taste. Bring to the boil, then lower the heat and simmer gently for 15 minutes, stirring from time to time. Add the frozen peas and cook for a further 5 minutes.

3 Add the pasta and bring to the boil, stirring. Lower the heat and simmer for about 5 minutes or according to the packet instructions, stirring frequently, until the pasta is *al dente*.

4 Turn the heat down to low, add the frozen clams and heat through for 2–3 minutes. Taste and adjust the seasoning. Serve hot in warmed bowls, garnished with basil leaves.

Cook's Tip

Frozen shelled clams are available at good fishmongers and supermarkets. If you can't get them, use bottled or canned clams in natural juice (not vinegar). Italian delicatessens sell jars of clams in their shells. These both look and taste delicious and are not too expensive.

Clam, Wild Mushroom and Potato Chowder

The delicate, sweet shellfish taste of clams and the soft earthiness of wild mushrooms combine with potatoes to make this a great meal on its own – fit for any occasion.

Serves 4

48 clams, scrubbed
50g/2oz/4 tbsp unsalted (sweet) butter
1 large onion, chopped
1 celery stick, sliced
1 carrot, sliced
225g/8oz assorted wild mushrooms, such as chanterelles, saffron milk-caps, chicken of the woods or St George's mushrooms, sliced
225g/8oz floury potatoes, thickly sliced
1.2 litres/2 pints/5 cups light chicken or vegetable stock, boiling
1 thyme sprig
4 parsley stalks
salt and ground black pepper
fresh thyme, to garnish

1 Place the clams in a large pan, discarding any that are open. Put 1cm/½ in of water in the pan, cover, bring to the boil and steam over a medium heat for 6–8 minutes until the clams open (discard any clams that do not open).

2 Drain the clams over a bowl, remove the shells, reserving a few clams in their shells for garnish. Chop the shelled clams. Strain the cooking juices into the bowl, add the chopped clams and set aside.

3 Add the butter, onion, celery and carrot to the pan and cook gently for about 10 minutes, until the vegetables are softened but not coloured.

4 Add the mushrooms and cook for 3–4 minutes until their juices begin to seep out. Add the potatoes, the clams and their juices, the stock, thyme and parsley stalks.

5 Bring the soup to the boil then reduce the heat, cover and simmer for 25 minutes, stirring occasionally. Season, ladle into bowls and garnish with the reserved clams and fresh thyme.

Clam and Basil Soup: Energy 123kcal/518kJ; Protein 8.9g; Carbohydrate 13g, of which sugars 3g; Fat 4.3g, of which saturates 0.7g; Cholesterol 25mg; Calcium 42mg; Fibre 1.5g; Sodium 585mg.
Clam and Potato: Energy 203kcal/848kJ; Protein 10.8g; Carbohydrate 15.8g, of which sugars 5.2g; Fat 11.2g, of which saturates 6.8g; Cholesterol 60mg; Calcium 66mg; Fibre 2.4g; Sodium 696mg.

Clam and Corn Chowder

Canned or bottled clams in brine, once drained, can be used as an alternative to fresh ones in their shells. Discard any clam shells that remain closed during cooking as this means they were already dead.

Serves 4

300ml/½ pint/1¼ cups double (heavy) cream
75g/3oz/6 tbsp unsalted (sweet) butter
1 small onion, finely chopped
1 apple, cored and sliced
1 garlic clove, crushed
45ml/3 tbsp mild curry powder
350g/12oz/3 cups baby corn
225g/8oz new potatoes, cooked
24 baby onions, boiled
600ml/1 pint/2½ cups fish stock
40 small clams
salt and ground black pepper
8 lime wedges, to garnish (optional)

1 Pour the cream into a small pan and cook over a high heat until it is reduced by half.

2 In a larger pan, melt half the butter. Add the onion, apple, garlic and curry powder. Sauté until the onion is translucent. Add the reduced cream and stir well.

3 In another pan, melt the remaining butter and add the baby corn, potatoes and baby onions. Cook for 5 minutes. Increase the heat and add the cream mixture and stock. Bring to the boil.

4 Add the clams. Cover and cook until the clams have opened. Discard any that do not open. Season well to taste with salt and freshly ground black pepper and serve, garnished with lime wedges, if liked.

Cook's Tip
Scrubbed shells make interesting serving vessels. Scrub them and wash in sterilizing fluid before rinsing and drying.

Spinach and Clam Soup

The leafy flavour of the fresh spinach marries perfectly with the nutty taste of the doenjang soybean paste to make this delicious soup with clams.

Serves 3

9 clams
90g/3½oz spinach
2 spring onions (scallions)
40g/1½oz/scant ¼ cup minced (ground) beef
15ml/1 tbsp doenjang soybean paste
15ml/1 tbsp crushed garlic
salt

1 Scrub the clams in cold running water, and rinse the spinach. Cut the spring onions in half lengthways and then across into 5cm/2in strips.

2 Place the minced beef and soybean paste in a pan, and stir over medium heat until the beef is well cooked. Pour in 750ml/1¼ pints/3 cups water, cover, bring to the boil and add the clams and spinach.

3 Once the clams have opened, add the spring onions and garlic. Discard any clams that remain closed. Add salt to taste, and serve.

Cook's Tip
Doenjang soybean paste is a Korean fermented soybean paste. It is the same as miso but slightly milder. Miso, available from wholefood and healthfood stores as well as Asian supermarkets, can be used instead.

Variations
- *Use fish stock instead of water and omit the beef.*
- *Use shredded pak choi (bok choy) instead of the spinach.*
- *For a vegetarian soup, omit the beef and use vegetable stock. Add tofu instead of the clams.*

Clam and Corn: Energy 676kcal/2798kJ; Protein 18.2g; Carbohydrate 24.2g, of which sugars 11.3g; Fat 56.9g, of which saturates 35g; Cholesterol 193mg; Calcium 136mg; Fibre 3.8g; Sodium 2038mg.
Spinach and Clam: Energy 90kcal/377kJ; Protein 11.1g; Carbohydrate 4.7g, of which sugars 3.8g; Fat 3.1g, of which saturates 1.1g; Cholesterol 30mg; Calcium 119mg; Fibre 2.2g; Sodium 1471mg.

Chilli Clam Broth

This soup of succulent clams in a tasty stock could not be easier to prepare. Popular in coastal areas of Colombia, it makes the perfect lunch on a hot summer's day.

Serves 6

30ml/2 tbsp olive oil
1 onion, finely chopped
3 garlic cloves, crushed
2 fresh red chillies, seeded and finely chopped
250ml/8fl oz/1 cup dry white wine
400ml/14fl oz can plum tomatoes, drained
1 large potato, about 250g/9oz, peeled and diced
400ml/14fl oz/1⅔ cups fish stock
1.3kg/3lb fresh clams
15ml/1 tbsp chopped fresh coriander (cilantro)
15ml/1 tbsp chopped fresh flat leaf parsley
salt
lime wedges, to garnish

1 Heat the oil in a pan. Add the onion and sauté for 5 minutes over a low heat. Stir in the garlic and chillies and cook for a further 2 minutes. Pour in the wine and bring to the boil, then simmer for 2 minutes.

2 Add the tomatoes, diced potato and stock. Bring to the boil, cover and lower the heat so that the soup simmers.

3 Season with salt and cook for 15 minutes, until the potatoes are beginning to break up and the tomatoes have broken down and made a rich sauce.

4 Meanwhile, wash the clams thoroughly under cold running water. Gently tap any that are open, and discard them if they do not close.

5 Add the clams to the soup, cover the pan and cook for about 3–4 minutes, or until the clams have opened, then stir in the chopped herbs. Season with salt to taste.

6 Check over the clams and throw away any that have failed to open. Ladle the soup into warmed bowls. Offer the lime wedges separately, to be squeezed over the soup just before eating.

Mediterranean Seafood Soup

This seafood soup contains all the colours and flavours of the Mediterranean.

Serves 4

675g/1½lb raw prawns (shrimp), in the shell
1 onion, chopped
1 celery stick, chopped
1 bay leaf
45ml/3 tbsp olive oil
2 slices stale bread, crusts removed
1 small onion, finely chopped
1 large garlic clove, chopped
2 large tomatoes, seeded and chopped
½ large green (bell) pepper, finely chopped
500g/1¼lb cockles (small clams) or mussels, cleaned
juice of 1 lemon
45ml/3 tbsp chopped fresh parsley
5ml/1 tsp paprika
salt and ground black pepper

1 Pull the heads off the prawns and put them in a pan with the 900ml/1½ pints/3¾ cups water. Add the onion, celery and bay leaf and simmer for 20–25 minutes. Peel the prawns, replacing the shells in the pan and setting the prawns aside. Keep the stock and shells simmering while continuing with the next step.

2 Heat the oil in a pan and fry the bread slices quickly, then reserve them. Fry the onion until it is soft, then add the garlic. Add the tomatoes and green pepper. Fry briefly, stirring occasionally. Strain the stock into the pan and bring to the boil. Discard the vegetables and prawn shells.

3 Add half the cockles or mussels. When open, use a slotted spoon to transfer them to a plate. Reserve some in their shells, and shell the remainder, setting them all aside. Repeat the process to cook the remaining cockles or mussels.

4 Return the cockles or mussels, shelled and in shells, to the soup and add the peeled prawns. Add the bread, torn into little pieces, and the lemon juice and chopped parsley.

5 Season to taste with paprika, salt and pepper and stir gently to dissolve the bread. Serve at once in soup bowls, providing a plate for the empty shells.

Chilli Clam: Energy 290kcal/1217kJ; Protein 36.2g; Carbohydrate 14.1g, of which sugars 3.5g; Fat 7.2g, of which saturates 1.3g; Cholesterol 145mg; Calcium 184mg; Fibre 1.5g; Sodium 151mg.
Seafood Soup: Energy 305kcal/1283kJ; Protein 38.9g; Carbohydrate 13.8g, of which sugars 6.9g; Fat 10.9g, of which saturates 1.6g; Cholesterol 344mg; Calcium 262mg; Fibre 2.6g; Sodium 486mg.

Seafood Soup

This is a Portuguese version of seafood soup, which is prepared in a variety of different ways all along the coast of Portugal.

Serves 6

60ml/4 tbsp olive oil
2kg/4½lb prawn (shrimp) heads and fish bones
1kg/2¼lb mixed onions, carrots, leek and garlic, chopped
1 bay leaf
6 black peppercorns
105ml/7 tbsp dry white wine
1 green (bell) pepper, seeded and finely diced
1 red (bell) pepper, seeded and finely diced
1 onion, chopped
2 ripe tomatoes, peeled and diced
1 garlic clove, chopped
15ml/1 tbsp chopped fresh thyme
185g/6½oz live clams, scrubbed
125g/4¼oz prepared squid
300g/11oz white fish fillet, cut into chunks
12 prawns (shrimp), peeled
chopped fresh coriander (cilantro), to garnish

1 Heat 30ml/2 tbsp of the olive oil in a large pan. Add the prawn heads and cook over a low heat, stirring, for 5 minutes.

2 Add the mixed vegetables, bay leaf and peppercorns and cook for a further 5 minutes, mashing the prawn heads.

3 Pour in the wine and 2 litres/3½ pints/8¾ cups water. Bring to the boil, then lower the heat and simmer gently for 1 hour.

4 Add the fish bones and bring back to the boil. Lower the heat and simmer very gently for 20 minutes. Remove the pan from the heat and strain the stock into a bowl.

5 Heat the remaining olive oil in a large, clean pan. Add the red and green peppers, onion and tomatoes and cook over a low heat, stirring occasionally, for 5 minutes, until softened. Add the garlic and thyme, pour in the stock and bring just to the boil.

6 Add the clams and squid. Cook for 2–3 minutes, until the clams have opened. Add the fish and prawns and simmer for 5 minutes to cook the fish. Sprinkle with coriander and serve.

Bouillabaisse

Perhaps the most famous of all fish soups, this recipe originates from Marseilles in the south of France.

Serves 4–6

1.5 kg/3–3½ lb mixed fish and raw shellfish, such as red mullet, John Dory, monkfish, red snapper, whiting, large raw prawns (jumbo shrimp) and clams
225g/8oz well-flavoured tomatoes
pinch of saffron strands
90ml/6 tbsp olive oil
1 onion, sliced
1 leek, sliced
1 celery stick, sliced
2 garlic cloves, crushed
1 bouquet garni
1 strip orange rind
2.5ml/½ tsp fennel seeds
15ml/1 tbsp tomato purée (paste)
10ml/2 tsp Pernod
salt and ground black pepper
4–6 thick slices French bread and 45ml/3 tbsp chopped fresh parsley, to serve

1 Remove the heads, tails and fins from the fish and set the fish aside. Put the trimmings in a large pan with 1.2 litres/2 pints/ 5 cups water. Bring to the boil and simmer for 15 minutes. Strain and reserve the liquid.

2 Cut the fish into large chunks. Leave the shellfish in their shells. Scald the tomatoes, then drain and refresh in cold water. Peel them and chop roughly. Soak the saffron in 15–30ml/ 1–2 tbsp hot water.

3 Heat the oil in a large pan, add the onion, leek and celery and cook until softened. Add the garlic, bouquet garni, orange rind, fennel seeds and tomatoes, then stir in the saffron and its soaking liquid and the reserved fish stock. Season with salt and pepper, then bring to the boil and simmer for 30–40 minutes.

4 Add the shellfish and boil for about 6 minutes. Add the fish and cook for 6–8 minutes more, until it flakes easily.

5 Using a slotted spoon, transfer the fish to a warmed serving platter. Keep the liquid boiling, to allow the oil to emulsify with the broth. Add the tomato purée, Pernod, and seasoning.

6 Ladle into bowls, scatter with chopped parsley and serve.

Seafood Soup: Energy 267kcal/1112kJ; Protein 20.1g; Carbohydrate 25.2g, of which sugars 18.7g; Fat 9g, of which saturates 1.3g; Cholesterol 96mg; Calcium 96mg; Fibre 4.8g; Sodium 262mg.
Bouillabaisse: Energy 454kcal/1895kJ; Protein 53.8g; Carbohydrate 17g, of which sugars 6.4g; Fat 19.3g, of which saturates 3.1g; Cholesterol 135mg; Calcium 138mg; Fibre 2.5g; Sodium 345mg.

Corn Soup with Cockles

The basis of this Portuguese soup is coarse cornmeal, which is the meal that remains after fine cornmeal has been produced.

Serves 4

300g/11oz live cockles
1 litre/1¾ pints/4 cups water or light chicken stock
50ml/2fl oz/¼ cup olive oil
1 onion, finely chopped
150g/5oz/1¼ cups coarse cornmeal or semolina
30ml/2 tbsp chopped fresh parsley

1 Wash the cockles thoroughly and discard any with broken shells. Bring the water to the boil, add the cockles and cook until they open, for about 4–5 minutes.

2 Discard any cockles that remain closed. Strain the cooking liquid through a fine sieve (strainer) into a bowl and reserve. Set the cockles aside.

3 Heat the olive oil in a large pan, add the onion and cook over a low heat, stirring occasionally, for 5 minutes, until soft.

4 Add the reserved cooking liquid to the pan and sprinkle in the cornmeal, stirring constantly. Simmer for 5 minutes, and then add the cockles and parsley and heat through briefly. Pour into a warmed tureen and serve immediately.

Variation

Live cockles are not widely available from fish stores. You can substitute mussels or small clams in this recipe.

Cook's Tip

You can dig up live cockles on the shoreline of sandy beaches, but you must be sure that the sea is not polluted. Soak them in a bowl of salted water or clean seawater overnight.

Seafood Soup with Saffron Rouille

Vary the fish content of this soup according to the freshest available, but choose firm varieties that will not flake and fall apart easily.

Serves 4

450g/1lb fresh clams, scrubbed
120ml/4fl oz/½ cup white wine
15ml/1 tbsp olive oil
4 garlic cloves, crushed
5ml/1 tsp fennel seeds
pinch of dried chilli flakes
1 fennel bulb, halved and sliced
1 red (bell) pepper, seeded and sliced
8 plum tomatoes, halved
1 onion, cut into thin wedges
225g/8oz small waxy potatoes, sliced
1 bay leaf
1 sprig fresh thyme
600ml/1 pint/2½ cups fish stock
1 mini French stick
225g/8oz monkfish fillet, sliced
350g/12oz red mullet, scaled, filleted and cut into wide strips
45ml/3 tbsp Pernod
salt and ground black pepper
fennel fronds, to garnish

For the rouille

a few saffron strands
150ml/¼ pint/⅔ cup mayonnaise
dash of Tabasco

1 Discard open clams that do not shut when tapped. Place the rest in a large pan with the wine. Cover and cook over high heat for 4 minutes, until opened. Drain, strain the cooking liquid and set it aside. Discard unopened shells and reserve eight clams in their shells. Shell the remaining clams.

2 Heat the oil in a pan. Add the garlic, fennel seeds and chilli flakes and cook for 2 minutes, until softened. Add the fennel, pepper, tomatoes, onion and cooking liquid. Cover and cook gently for 10 minutes, stirring occasionally. Stir in the potatoes, bay leaf, thyme and stock. Cover and cook for 15–20 minutes.

3 For the rouille, pound the saffron to a powder in a mortar, then beat it into the mayonnaise with the Tabasco. Cut the French stick into eight slices and toast them on both sides.

4 Add the monkfish, red mullet and Pernod to the soup and cook for 3–4 minutes. Add all the clams and heat through for 30 seconds. Season well. Spoon the rouille on to the toasts. Serve the soup garnished with fennel, with the toasts.

Corn with Cockles: Energy 240kcal/999kJ; Protein 8.4g; Carbohydrate 28.8g, of which sugars 1g; Fat 9.8g, of which saturates 1.3g; Cholesterol 20mg; Calcium 52mg; Fibre 1.4g; Sodium 186mg.
Soup with Rouille: Energy 728kcal/3048kJ; Protein 50.2g; Carbohydrate 40g, of which sugars 10.9g; Fat 37.1g, of which saturates 5.4g; Cholesterol 111mg; Calcium 238mg; Fibre 4.7g; Sodium 1200mg.

Tomato Seafood Soup with Rouille

Hot, spicy rouille is served separately for swirling into this soup to flavour.

Serves 4

3 gurnard, red mullet or snapper, scaled, gutted, filleted with heads and bones
675g/1½lb white fish, such as cod, haddock or halibut
12 large prawns (shrimp)
225g/8oz live mussels, cleaned
1 onion, quartered
½ litre/1 pints/2½ cups vegetable stock
5ml/1 tsp saffron threads
75ml/5 tbsp olive oil
1 fennel bulb, roughly chopped
4 garlic cloves, crushed
3 strips pared orange rind
4 fresh thyme sprigs
900g/2lb tomatoes, peeled and chopped
30ml/2 tbsp sun-dried tomato purée (paste)
3 bay leaves

For the rouille

1 red (bell) pepper, seeded
1 fresh red chilli, seeded
2 garlic cloves, chopped
75ml/5 tbsp olive oil
15g/½oz/¼ cup fresh breadcrumbs

1 To make the rouille, purée all the ingredients until smooth. Transfer to a serving dish and chill.

2 Cut all the fish fillets into small chunks. Shell half the prawns and reserve the trimmings. Discard mussels that do not close when sharply tapped. To make the stock, put the fish and prawn trimmings in a pan with the onion and the water. Bring to the boil, then simmer gently for 30 minutes. Cool slightly and strain.

3 Soak the saffron in ½ litre/1 pint/2½ cups vegetable stock. Heat 30ml/2 tbsp of the oil in a large sauté pan. Add all the fish and fry over a high heat for 1 minute. Drain and set aside.

4 Heat the remaining oil and fry the fennel, garlic, orange rind and thyme until beginning to colour. Make up the strained stock to about 1.2 litres/2 pints/5 cups with the vegetable stock. Add to the pan with the saffron, tomatoes, tomato purée and bay leaves. Season, then simmer gently, covered, for 20 minutes.

5 Stir in the seafood. Cover and cook for 3–4 minutes. Discard any unopened mussels and serve. Offer the rouille separately.

Tamarind Seafood Vegetable Soup

From the Philippines, this is a soured soup-like stew, considered by many Filipinos to be their national dish.

Serves 4–6

15ml/1 tbsp tamarind pulp or 5ml/1 tsp concentrated tamarind pulp
150ml/¼ pint/⅔ cup warm water
2 tomatoes, roughly chopped
115g/4oz spinach or Chinese kangkong leaves
115g/4oz peeled, cooked large prawns (jumbo shrimp), thawed if frozen
1.2 litres/2 pints/5 cups fish stock
½ Chinese white radish, peeled and finely diced
115g/4oz/¾ cup French (green) beans, cut into 1cm/½in lengths
225g/8oz cod or haddock fillet, skinned and cut into strips
fish sauce, to taste
squeeze of lemon juice, to taste
salt and ground black pepper
plain boiled rice or noodles, to serve

1 Put the tamarind pulp in a large bowl, if using, and pour over the warm water. Set aside. Peel and chop the tomatoes, and discard the seeds. Strip the spinach or kangkong leaves from the stems and tear into small pieces. Set aside.

2 Using your hands, remove the heads and shells from the prawns, if necessary, leaving the tails intact.

3 Pour the prepared fish stock into a large pan and add the radish. Cook the radish for 5 minutes, then add the French beans. Continue to cook the stew gently for 3–5 minutes more.

4 Add the fish strips, tomatoes and spinach or kangkong leaves. Strain in the tamarind juice or add the concentrated tamarind, stir until dissolved, and cook for 2 minutes. Stir in the prawns and cook for 1–2 minutes to heat through.

5 Season the stew with salt and freshly ground black pepper, and add a little fish sauce and lemon juice to taste. Serve with either plain boiled rice or noodles.

Tomato Seafood: Energy 349kcal/1462kJ; Protein 45.5g; Carbohydrate 9.6g, of which sugars 6.5g; Fat 14.5g, of which saturates 1.7g; Cholesterol 100mg; Calcium 117mg; Fibre 2.6g; Sodium 318mg.
Tamarind Seafood: Energy 164kcal/686kJ; Protein 21.8g; Carbohydrate 4.9g, of which sugars 3.5g; Fat 6.5g, of which saturates 0.8g; Cholesterol 52mg; Calcium 33mg; Fibre 1.3g; Sodium 69mg.

Octopus and Watercress Soup

This refreshing seafood soup has a wonderfully restorative quality. Delicious octopus is cooked in a rich vegetable broth, with white radish and watercress adding an elusive flavour that is quintessentially Korean.

Serves 2–3

1 large octopus, cleaned and gutted
150g/5oz Chinese white radish, peeled
½ leek, sliced
20g/¾oz kelp or spinach leaves
3 garlic cloves, crushed
1 fresh red chilli, seeded and sliced
15ml/1 tbsp light soy sauce
75g/3oz watercress or rocket (arugula)
salt and ground black pepper

1 Rinse the octopus in salted water and cut into pieces about 2.5cm/1in long. Finely dice the white radish.

2 Pour 750ml/1¼ pints/3 cups water into a large pan and bring to the boil. Reduce the heat and add the radish, leek, kelp or spinach, and crushed garlic. Simmer over medium heat until the radish softens and becomes clear. Discard the kelp and leek and then add the sliced chilli.

3 Add the octopus, increase the heat and boil for 5 minutes. Season with soy sauce, salt and pepper, and then add the watercress or rocket. Remove from the heat, cover the pan and leave to stand for 1 minute while the leaves wilt into the liquid. Ladle into bowls and serve.

Variations

- *For a spicier version of this soup try adding a teaspoon of Korean chilli powder. This gives the dish a really tangy kick!*
- *The soup can be made with prepared squid or squid rings instead of octopus.*
- *Use peeled raw prawns (shrimp) instead of the octopus and add some chopped spring onions (scallions) with the watercress or rocket (arugula).*
- *Use chunks of white fish fillet instead of the octopus.*

Tomato Soup with Chilli Squid

Oriental-style seared squid mingles with the pungent tomato and garlic flavours in this superlative soup.

Serves 4

4 small squid, cleaned
60ml/4 tbsp olive oil
2 shallots, chopped
1 garlic clove, crushed
1.2kg/2½lb ripe tomatoes, roughly chopped
15ml/1 tbsp sun-dried tomato purée (paste)
450ml/¾ pint/2 scant cups vegetable stock
about 2.5ml/½ tsp sugar
2 fresh red chillies, seeded and chopped
30ml/2 tbsp chopped fresh tarragon
salt and ground black pepper
crusty bread, to serve

1 Cut the squid bodies into fine rings. Cut the tentacles into short pieces. Set the rings and pieces of tentacle aside.

2 Heat 30ml/2 tbsp of the oil in a pan. Add the shallots and garlic, and cook for 4–5 minutes, until just softened.

3 Stir in the tomatoes and tomato paste, and season. Cover and cook for 3 minutes. Add half the stock and simmer for 5 minutes, until the tomatoes are very soft.

4 Cool the soup, then purée it in a food processor or blender until smooth and rub it through a sieve (strainer) to remove all seeds. Return it to the rinsed-out pan. Stir in the remaining stock and sugar, and reheat gently.

5 Meanwhile, heat the remaining oil in a large frying pan. Add the squid rings and tentacles, and the chillies. Cook for 4–5 minutes, stirring continuously, then remove from the heat and stir in the chopped tarragon.

6 Taste the soup and adjust the seasoning if necessary. If the soup tastes slightly sharp, add a little extra sugar.

7 Ladle the soup into four warmed serving bowls and carefully spoon the chilli squid in the centre. Serve immediately with crusty bread.

Octopus Soup: Energy 106kcal/449kJ; Protein 19.9g; Carbohydrate 2.6g, of which sugars 2.3g; Fat 1.9g, of which saturates 0.5g; Cholesterol 48mg; Calcium 108mg; Fibre 1.7g; Sodium 386mg.
Tomato with Squid: Energy 186kcal/777kJ; Protein 8.1g; Carbohydrate 10.9g, of which sugars 10.2g; Fat 12.6g, of which saturates 2g; Cholesterol 84mg; Calcium 30mg; Fibre 3.2g; Sodium 69mg.

Coconut and Seafood Soup

The marriage of flavours works beautifully in this soup, which is easy to make.

Serves 4

600ml/1 pint/2½ cups fish stock
5 thin slices fresh root ginger
2 lemon grass stalks, chopped
3 kaffir lime leaves, shredded
bunch of garlic chives, about 25g/1oz
small bunch of fresh coriander (cilantro), about 15g/½oz
15ml/1 tbsp vegetable oil
4 shallots, chopped
400ml/14fl oz can coconut milk
30–45ml/2–3 tbsp fish sauce
45–60ml/3–4 tbsp green curry paste
450g/1lb raw large prawns (jumbo shrimp), peeled and deveined
450g/1lb prepared squid
a little fresh lime juice (optional)
salt and ground black pepper
60ml/4 tbsp crisp fried shallot slices, to serve

1 Pour the fish stock into a large pan and add the slices of ginger, the lemon grass and half the shredded lime leaves.

2 Reserve a few garlic chives for the garnish, then chop the remainder. Add half the chopped garlic chives to the pan. Strip the coriander leaves from the stalks and set the leaves aside. Add the stalks to the pan. Bring to the boil, reduce the heat to low and cover the pan, then simmer gently for 20 minutes. Strain the stock into a bowl.

3 Rinse and dry the pan. Add the oil and shallots. Cook for 5–10 minutes, until the shallots begin to brown.

4 Stir in the strained stock, coconut milk, the remaining kaffir lime leaves and 30ml/2 tbsp of the fish sauce. Heat gently until simmering and cook over a low heat for 5–10 minutes.

5 Stir in the curry paste and prawns, then cook for 3 minutes. Add the squid and cook for a further 2 minutes. Add the lime juice, if using, and season, adding more fish sauce to taste. Stir in the remaining chives and the reserved coriander leaves. Serve in bowls sprinkled with fried shallots and chives.

Haddock Fishball Soup with Prawns

Delicious small brown prawns or shrimp have lots of flavour but they are fiddly to peel, so allow time.

Serves 2

1 small haddock, filleted with head and bones reserved
50g/2oz/½ cup cooked peeled brown prawns (shrimp)
½ rusk, crumbled
1 egg, lightly beaten
40g/1½oz/3 tbsp butter
1 leek, cut into rings
15ml/1 tbsp cornflour (cornstarch)
5ml/1 tsp Dijon mustard
15ml/1 tbsp chopped celery leaves
salt and ground black pepper
50–100g/2–3½oz/½–scant 1 cup cooked peeled prawns (shrimp), to garnish

For the stock

½ leek
2 carrots
2 potatoes
8 celery leaves
1 bay leaf
salt

1 Discard the gills from the fish head. To make the stock, pour 750ml/1¼ pints/3 cups water into a pan. Add the fish head and bones, leek, carrots, potatoes, celery leaves, bay leaf and a pinch of salt. Boil, lower the heat and simmer for 30 minutes.

2 Skin and chop the haddock. Process in a food processor or blender, then mix with the shrimp, rusk and seasoning with enough of the egg to make a firm mixture. Form into balls and leave to rest.

3 Melt the butter in a non-stick frying pan. Add the fish balls and leeks. Cook gently, stirring occasionally, for 10 minutes, until evenly browned. Remove with a slotted spoon and set aside.

4 Add the remaining beaten egg to the pan, season with salt and cook until set. Remove and cut into strips.

5 Strain the stock. Dice and replace the carrots and potatoes Discard the remaining flavourings. Pour it back into the pan.

6 Mix the cornflour with 30ml/2 tbsp water to a paste and stir into the stock. Add the mustard, celery leaves, fish balls, leeks and egg strips. Garnish with the peeled prawns and serve.

Coconut and Seafood: Energy 205kcal/871kJ; Protein 37.7g; Carbohydrate 7.5g, of which sugars 5.8g; Fat 3g, of which saturates 0.8g; Cholesterol 473mg; Calcium 144mg; Fibre 0.4g; Sodium 449mg.
Haddock Soup: Energy 496kcal/2082kJ; Protein 43.8g; Carbohydrate 29.7g, of which sugars 9.2g; Fat 23.8g, of which saturates 11.5g; Cholesterol 289mg; Calcium 230mg; Fibre 1.1g; Sodium 373mg.

Curried Prawn Soup

The cuisine of the Indian island of Goa is well known for its excellent range of fish and shellfish-based recipes, such as this one for prawns.

Serves 4

15g/½oz/1 tbsp ghee or butter
2 garlic cloves, crushed
450g/1lb small raw prawns (shrimp), peeled and deveined
15ml/1 tbsp groundnut (peanut) oil
4 green cardamom pods
4 cloves
5cm/2in piece cinnamon stick
15ml/1 tbsp mustard seeds
1 large onion, finely chopped
½–1 fresh red chilli, seeded and sliced
4 tomatoes, peeled, seeded and chopped
350ml/12fl oz/1½ cups fish stock or water
350ml/12fl oz/1½ cups coconut milk
45ml/3 tbsp fragrant spice mix (see Cook's Tip)
10–20ml/2–4 tsp chilli powder
salt
turmeric-seasoned basmati rice, to serve

1 Melt the ghee or butter in a large pan, add the garlic and stir over a low heat for a few seconds. Add the prawns and stir-fry briskly to coat. Transfer to a plate and set aside.

2 In the same pan, heat the oil and fry the cardamom, cloves and cinnamon for 2 minutes. Add the mustard seeds and fry for 1 minute. Add the onion and chilli and fry for 7–8 minutes or until softened and lightly browned.

3 Add the remaining ingredients and bring to a slow simmer. Cook gently for 6–8 minutes and add the prawns. Simmer for 5–8 minutes until the prawns are cooked through. Serve the soup with turmeric-coloured basmati rice.

Cook's Tip
To make a fragrant spice mix, dry-fry 25ml/1½ tbsp coriander seeds, 15ml/1 tbsp mixed peppercorns, 5ml/1 tsp cumin seeds, 1.5ml/¼ tsp fenugreek seeds and 1.5ml/¼ tsp fennel seeds until aromatic, then grind finely in a spice mill.

Hot and Sour Prawn Soup

This is a classic seafood soup, combining sour, salty, spicy and hot flavours. Variations on the theme are enjoyed throughout Asia.

Serves 4–6

450g/1lb raw king prawns (jumbo shrimp), thawed if frozen
1 litre/1¾ pints/4 cups chicken stock or water
3 lemon grass stalks
10 kaffir lime leaves, torn in half
225g/8oz can straw mushrooms
45ml/3 tbsp fish sauce
60ml/4 tbsp lime juice
30ml/2 tbsp chopped spring onion (scallion)
15ml/1 tbsp fresh coriander (cilantro) leaves
4 fresh red chillies, seeded and thinly sliced
salt and ground black pepper

1 Shell the prawns, putting the shells in a colander. Devein the prawns and set them aside on a plate.

2 Rinse the shells under cold water, then put in a large pan with the stock or water. Bring to the boil.

3 Bruise the lemon grass stalks and add them to the stock with half the kaffir lime leaves. Simmer gently for 5–6 minutes, until the stock is fragrant.

4 Strain the stock, return it to the clean pan and reheat. Add the drained mushrooms and the prawns, then cook until the prawns turn pink.

5 Stir in the fish sauce, lime juice, chopped spring onion, fresh coriander, chillies and the remaining kaffir lime leaves. Taste and adjust the seasoning if necessary. The soup should be sour, salty, spicy and hot.

Cook's Tip
For the best flavour, be sure to buy uncooked prawns (shrimp) in the shell. These are usually available frozen, in large bags that are relatively economical, from Asian or Chinese supermarkets. Alternatively, shell cooked prawns and simmer the shells.

Prawn Soup: Energy 251kcal/1054kJ; Protein 23.8g; Carbohydrate 20g, of which sugars 13g; Fat 9.1g, of which saturates 2.8g; Cholesterol 227mg; Calcium 228mg; Fibre 5g; Sodium 397mg.
Hot and Sour Prawn: Energy 96kcal/404kJ; Protein 20.9g; Carbohydrate 0.8g, of which sugars 0.5g; Fat 1g, of which saturates 0.2g; Cholesterol 219mg; Calcium 94mg; Fibre 0.7g; Sodium 217mg.

Prawn and Pineapple Broth

This simple dish is often served as an appetite enhancer because of its hot and sour flavour. It is also popular as a tasty accompaniment to plain rice or noodles. A nice touch is to serve the broth in a hollowed-out pineapple, which has been halved lengthways. It looks great and contributes to the fruity flavour.

Serves 4

30ml/2 tbsp vegetable oil
15–30ml/1–2 tbsp tamarind paste
15ml/1 tbsp sugar
450g/1lb raw prawns (shrimp), peeled and deveined
4 thick fresh pineapple slices, cored and cut into bitesize chunks
salt and ground black pepper
fresh coriander (cilantro) and mint leaves, to garnish
steamed rice or plain noodles, to serve (optional)

For the spice paste

4 shallots, chopped
4 fresh red chillies, seeded and chopped
25g/1oz fresh root ginger, peeled and chopped
1 lemon grass stalk, chopped
5ml/1 tsp shrimp paste

1 Make the spice paste. Using a mortar and pestle or a food processor or blender, grind the shallots, chillies, ginger and lemon grass to a paste. Add the shrimp paste and mix well.

2 Heat the oil in a wok or heavy pan. Stir in the spice paste and fry until fragrant. Stir in the tamarind paste and the sugar, then pour in 1.2 litres/2 pints/5 cups water. Mix well and bring to the boil. Reduce the heat and simmer for 10 minutes. Season the broth with salt and pepper.

3 Add the prawns and pineapple to the broth and simmer for 4–5 minutes, or until the prawns are cooked. Using a slotted spoon, lift the prawns and pineapple out of the broth and divide them among four warmed bowls. Ladle over some of the broth and garnish with coriander and mint leaves. The rest can be served separately as a drink, or spooned over steamed rice or plain noodles, if you want to transform this into a slightly more substantial dish.

Spicy Shrimp Soup with Pumpkin and Coconut

The natural sweetness of the pumpkin is balanced by chillies, shrimp paste and dried shrimp in this colourful soup. The cooked shellfish adds further colour and a decent amount of bite, making this dish a real delight to the senses.

Serves 4–6

2 garlic cloves, crushed
4 shallots, finely chopped
2.5ml/½ tsp shrimp paste
1 lemon grass stalk, chopped
2 fresh green chillies, seeded
15ml/1 tbsp dried shrimp, soaked for 10 minutes in warm water
600ml/1 pint/2½ cups chicken stock
450g/1lb pumpkin, peeled, seeded and diced
600ml/1 pint/2½ cups coconut cream
30ml/2 tbsp fish sauce
5ml/1 tsp sugar
115g/4oz peeled cooked prawns (shrimp)
salt and ground black pepper

To garnish

2 fresh red chillies, seeded and thinly sliced
10–12 fresh basil leaves

1 Put the garlic, shallots, shrimp paste, lemon grass, green chillies and salt to taste in a mortar. Drain the dried shrimp, discarding the soaking liquid, and add them to the mortar, then use a pestle to grind the mixture into a paste. Alternatively, place all the ingredients in a food processor or blender and process until you have a paste.

2 Bring the chicken stock to the boil in a large pan. Add the ground paste and stir well to dissolve. Add the pumpkin chunks and simmer for 10–15 minutes, or until tender.

3 Stir in the coconut cream, then bring the soup back to simmering point. Do not let it boil. Add the fish sauce, sugar and ground black pepper to taste.

4 Add the prawns and cook for a further 2–3 minutes, until they are heated through. Serve in warm soup bowls, garnished with chillies and basil leaves.

Prawn and Pineapple: Energy 192kcal/808kJ; Protein 20.4g; Carbohydrate 14.2g, of which sugars 13.9g; Fat 6.4g, of which saturates 0.8g; Cholesterol 219mg; Calcium 111mg; Fibre 1.3g; Sodium 216mg.
Spicy Shrimp Soup: Energy 73kcal/310kJ; Protein 6.5g; Carbohydrate 10.4g, of which sugars 9.8g; Fat 0.9g, of which saturates 0.4g; Cholesterol 56mg; Calcium 102mg; Fibre 1.3g; Sodium 399mg.

Spicy Shrimp and Squash Soup

This highly flavoured soup comes from northern Thailand. It is quite hearty and something of a cross between a soup and a stew.

Serves 4

1 butternut squash, about 300g/11oz
1 litre/1¾ pints/4 cups vegetable stock
90g/3½oz/scant 1 cup French beans, cut into 2.5cm/1in pieces
45g/1¾oz dried banana flower (optional)
15ml/1 tbsp fish sauce
225g/8oz raw prawns (shrimp)
small bunch of fresh basil
cooked rice, to serve

For the chilli paste

115g/4oz shallots, sliced
10 drained bottled green peppercorns
1 small fresh green chilli, seeded and finely chopped
2.5ml/½ tsp shrimp paste

1 Peel the butternut squash and cut it in half. Scoop out the seeds with a teaspoon and discard them, then cut the flesh into neat cubes. Set aside.

2 Make the chilli paste by pounding the shallots, peppercorns, chilli and shrimp paste together using a mortar and pestle or puréeing them in a spice blender.

3 Heat the stock gently in a large pan, then stir in the chilli paste. Add the squash, beans and banana flower, if using. Bring to the boil and cook for 15 minutes.

4 Add the fish sauce, prawns and basil. Bring to simmering point, then simmer for 3 minutes. Serve in warmed bowls, accompanied by rice.

Variation
Use pumpkin instead of butternut squash, or try acorn squash instead if you like.

Crab and Vegetable Soup

Generally, jars of asparagus preserved in brine are used for this recipe, but fresh asparagus that has been steamed until tender is, of course, excellent.

Serves 4

15ml/1 tbsp vegetable oil
2 shallots, finely chopped
2 garlic cloves, finely chopped
15ml/1 tbsp rice flour or cornflour (cornstarch)
225g/8oz/1⅓ cups cooked crab meat, chopped
450g/1lb preserved asparagus, finely chopped, or 450g/1lb fresh asparagus, trimmed and steamed
salt and ground black pepper
basil and coriander (cilantro) leaves, to garnish
fish sauce, to serve

For the stock

1 meaty chicken carcass
25g/1oz dried shrimp, soaked in water for 30 minutes, rinsed and drained
2 onions, peeled and quartered
2 garlic cloves, crushed
15ml/1 tbsp fish sauce
6 black peppercorns
sea salt

1 To make the stock, put the chicken carcass into a large pan. Add all the other stock ingredients, except the salt, and pour in 2 litres/3½ pints/8 cups water. Bring to the boil, boil for a few minutes, skim off any foam, then reduce the heat and simmer with the lid on for 1½–2 hours. Remove the lid and simmer for a further 30 minutes to reduce the stock. Skim off any fat, season, then strain the stock and measure out 1.5 litres/2½ pints/6¼ cups.

2 Heat the oil in a deep pan or wok. Stir in the shallots and garlic, until they begin to colour. Remove from the heat, stir in the flour, and then pour in the stock. Put the pan back over the heat and bring to the boil, stirring constantly, until smooth.

3 Add the crab meat and asparagus, reduce the heat and leave to simmer for 15–20 minutes. Season to taste with salt and pepper, then ladle the soup into bowls, garnish with fresh basil and coriander leaves, and serve with a splash of fish sauce.

Shrimp and Squash: Energy 68kcal/287kJ; Protein 11.2g; Carbohydrate 4.7g, of which sugars 3.4g; Fat 0.7g, of which saturates 0.2g; Cholesterol 110mg; Calcium 82mg; Fibre 1.7g; Sodium 108mg.
Crab and Vegetable: Energy 158kcal/652kJ; Protein 9.8g; Carbohydrate 7.6g, of which sugars 4g; Fat 9.9g, of which saturates 5.6g; Cholesterol 38mg; Calcium 87mg; Fibre 3.2g; Sodium 147mg.

Chinese Crab and Corn Soup

There's no denying the delightful combination of shellfish and corn in this universal favourite, but dressing fresh crab does increase the preparation time somewhat. Using frozen white crab meat will work just as well.

Serves 4

600ml/1 pint/2½ cups fish or chicken stock
2.5cm/1in piece fresh root ginger, peeled and very finely sliced
400g/14oz can creamed corn
150g/5oz cooked white crab meat
15ml/1 tbsp arrowroot or cornflour (cornstarch)
15ml/1 tbsp rice wine or dry sherry
15–30ml/1–2 tbsp light soy sauce
1 egg white
salt and ground white pepper
shredded spring onions (scallions), to garnish

1 Put the stock and ginger in a large pan and bring to the boil. Reduce the heat a little while you stir in the creamed corn, then bring the mixture back to the boil.

2 Switch off the heat and add the crab meat to the pan. Put the arrowroot or cornflour in a cup and stir in the rice wine or sherry to make a smooth paste; stir this into the soup. Cook over a low heat for about 3 minutes until the soup has thickened and is slightly glutinous in consistency. Add light soy sauce, salt and white pepper to taste.

3 In a bowl, whisk the egg white to a stiff foam. Gradually fold it into the soup. Ladle the soup into heated bowls, garnish each portion with spring onions and serve.

Cook's Tip
This soup is sometimes made with whole kernel corn, but creamed corn gives a better texture. If you can't find it in a can, use thawed frozen creamed corn instead; the result will be just as good.

Crab, Prawn and Corn Gumbo

A well-flavoured chicken and shellfish stock gives this dish the authentic taste of a traditional Louisiana gumbo.

Serves 6

30ml/2 tbsp vegetable oil
1 onion, chopped
1 garlic clove, chopped
115g/4oz rindless streaky (fatty) bacon, chopped
40g/1½oz/⅓ cup plain (all-purpose) flour
1 celery stick, chopped
1 red (bell) pepper, seeded and chopped
1 fresh red chilli, seeded and chopped
450g/1lb tomatoes, chopped
2 large cobs of corn
4 soft-shell crabs, washed well
30ml/2 tbsp chopped fresh parsley
small bunch of spring onions (scallions), roughly chopped
salt and ground black pepper

For the stock

350g/12oz whole uncooked prawns (shrimp)
2 large chicken wings
1 carrot, thickly sliced
3 celery sticks, sliced
1 onion, sliced
handful of parsley stalks
2 bay leaves

1 To make the stock, peel the prawns and put the shells into a pan. Set the prawns aside. Add the remaining ingredients to the pan with 1.5 litres/2½ pints/6¾ cups water. Bring to the boil and skim. Cover and cook for 1 hour.

2 Heat the oil in a large pan, add the onion and garlic and cook for 3–4 minutes. Add the bacon and cook for 3 minutes. Stir in the flour and cook for 3–4 minutes. When the mixture is turning golden, strain in the stock, stirring. Add the celery, pepper, chilli and tomatoes. Boil and simmer for 5 minutes. Cut the corn cobs into 2.5cm/1in slices, and add to the stock.

3 Clean each crab: use scissors to cut off the eyes and mouth. Cut across the face and hook out the stomach, a jelly-like sac, with your fingers. Turn the crab over and pull off the tail flap. Lift the sides of the shell and pull out the gills or dead man's fingers. Cut into quarters and add to the soup with the prawns.

4 Simmer for 15 minutes until the crabs and corn are cooked. Season, then stir in the parsley and spring onions. Serve hot.

Chinese Crab Soup: Energy 201kcal/852kJ; Protein 11.3g; Carbohydrate 33.8g, of which sugars 9.9g; Fat 3.2g, of which saturates 0.5g; Cholesterol 27mg; Calcium 17mg; Fibre 1.4g; Sodium 695mg.
Crab, Prawn and Corn: Energy 166kcal/694kJ; Protein 10.2g; Carbohydrate 11.1g, of which sugars 5.5g; Fat 9.3g, of which saturates 2.2g; Cholesterol 37mg; Calcium 94mg; Fibre 2.2g; Sodium 1280mg.

Scottish Crab Soup

Ideally this should be made with the little velvety-shelled crabs mostly caught off the west coast of Scotland, but common or brown crabs can be used instead.

Serves 4

1kg/2¼lbs shore or velvet crabs
50g/2oz/¼ cup butter
50g/2oz leek, chopped
50g/2oz carrot, chopped
30ml/2 tbsp brandy
225g/8oz ripe tomatoes, chopped
15ml/1 tbsp tomato purée (paste)
120ml/4fl oz/½ cup dry white wine
1.5 litres/2½ pints/6¼ cups fish stock
sprig of fresh tarragon
60ml/4 tbsp double (heavy) cream
lemon juice

1 Bring a large pan of water to a rolling boil and plunge the live crabs into it. They will be killed very quickly. Once the crabs are dead – a couple of minutes at most – take them out of the water, place in a large bowl and smash them up. This can be done with either a wooden mallet or the end of a rolling pin.

2 Melt the butter in a heavy pan, add the leek and carrot and cook gently until soft but not coloured.

3 Add the crabs and when very hot pour in the brandy, stirring to allow the flavour to pervade the whole pan. Add the tomatoes, tomato purée, wine, stock and tarragon. Bring to the boil and simmer gently for 30 minutes.

4 Strain the soup through a metal sieve (strainer), forcing as much of the tomato mixture through as possible. (If you like you could remove the big claws and purée the remains in a food processor or blender.)

5 Return to the heat, simmer for a few minutes then season to taste. Add the cream and lemon juice, and serve.

Cook's Tip
If you don't have fish stock then water will do, or you could use some of the water used to boil the crabs initially.

Crab, Coconut and Coriander Soup

Quick and easy to cook, this soup has all the flavours associated with the Bahia region of Brazil: creamy coconut, palm oil, coriander and, of course, chilli.

Serves 4

30ml/2 tbsp olive oil
1 onion, finely chopped
1 celery stick, finely chopped
2 garlic cloves, crushed
1 fresh red chilli, seeded and chopped
1 large tomato, peeled and chopped
45ml/3 tbsp chopped fresh coriander (cilantro)
1 litre/1¾ pints/4 cups fresh crab or fish stock
500g/1¼lb crab meat
250ml/8fl oz/1 cup coconut milk
30ml/2 tbsp palm oil
juice of 1 lime
salt

For serving
hot chilli oil
lime wedges

1 Heat the olive oil in a pan over a low heat. Stir in the onion and celery, and sauté gently for 5 minutes, until softened and translucent. Stir in the garlic and chilli and cook for a further 2 minutes.

2 Add the tomato and half the coriander and increase the heat. Cook, stirring, for 3 minutes, then add the stock. Bring to the boil, then reduce the heat and simmer for 5 minutes.

3 Stir the crab, coconut milk and palm oil into the pan and simmer over a very low heat for a further 5 minutes. The consistency should be thick, but not stew-like, so add some water if needed.

4 Stir in the lime juice and remaining coriander, then season with salt to taste. Serve in heated bowls with the chilli oil and lime wedges on the side.

Variation
Try chunks of white fish fillet instead of crab for a change.

Scottish Crab: Energy 419kcal/1741kJ; Protein 35.1g; Carbohydrate 3.8g, of which sugars 3.6g; Fat 25.7g, of which saturates 15.1g; Cholesterol 196mg; Calcium 252mg; Fibre 1.1g; Sodium 1122mg.
Crab and Coconut: Energy 228kcal/951kJ; Protein 23.6g; Carbohydrate 5.4g, of which sugars 5g; Fat 12.6g, of which saturates 3.7g; Cholesterol 90mg; Calcium 199mg; Fibre 1.1g; Sodium 767mg.

Chunky Asparagus and Crab Soup

Asparagus is used to great effect in this chunky and comforting soup – whole stems are simmered in stock until just tender, and then combined with delicious crab and threads of cooked egg.

Serves 4–6

350g/12oz asparagus spears, trimmed and halved
900ml/1½ pints/3¾ cups chicken stock, preferably home-made
30–45ml/2–3 tbsp sunflower oil
6 shallots, chopped
115g/4oz crab meat, fresh or canned, chopped
15ml/1 tbsp cornflour (cornstarch), mixed to a paste with water
30ml/2 tbsp fish sauce
1 egg, lightly beaten
chopped chives, plus extra chives to garnish
salt and ground black pepper to taste

1 Cook the asparagus spears in the chicken stock for 5–6 minutes until tender. Drain, reserving the stock.

2 Heat the oil and stir-fry the shallots for 2 minutes. Add the asparagus spears, crab meat and chicken stock.

3 Bring the mixture to the boil and cook for 3 minutes, then remove the wok or pan from the heat and spoon some of the liquid into the cornflour mixture. Return this to the wok or pan and stir until the soup begins to thicken slightly.

4 Stir in the fish sauce, with salt and pepper to taste, then pour the beaten egg into the soup, stirring briskly so that the egg forms threads. Finally, stir the chopped chives into the soup and serve immediately, garnished with chives.

Cook's Tip
If fresh asparagus isn't available, use 350g/12oz can asparagus. Drain and halve the spears.

Lobster and Tomato Soup

This luxurious lobster soup is for special occasions. The Norwegian lobster is smaller than those caught in the US, but its flesh is just as delicious. The soup can also be made with prawns, if you are feeling less extravagant, and is equally good. It is important to keep the lobster shells as well as the flesh because they are used to provide additional flavour to the soup.

Serves 4

1 large cooked lobster or 500g/1¼lb/3 cups cooked prawns (shrimp)
25g/1oz/2 tbsp butter
30ml/2 tbsp finely chopped shallot
2 red (bell) peppers, seeded and chopped
2.5cm/1in fresh root ginger, finely chopped
1 garlic clove, finely chopped
60ml/4 tbsp brandy
30ml/2 tbsp tomato purée (paste)
15ml/1 tbsp sherry vinegar
15ml/1 tbsp sugar
4 ripe tomatoes, skinned, seeded and chopped, or 400g/14oz can tomatoes
juice of 1 lime
salt and ground black pepper
chopped fresh dill, to garnish

1 Remove the lobster or prawn meat from their shells, reserving the shells. Set the meat aside. Melt the butter in a pan, add the shallots, peppers, ginger and garlic and cook for 5 minutes. Add the shells and cook gently, stirring occasionally, for a further 10 minutes.

2 Add the brandy to the pan and set alight. Stir in the tomato purée. Add 1.25 litres/2¼ pints/5½ cups water, season lightly with salt and pepper, and bring slowly to the boil. Lower the heat, cover and simmer very gently for 40 minutes.

3 Strain the stock through a fine sieve (strainer), preferably lined with muslin (cheesecloth), into a clean pan. Add the vinegar, sugar, tomatoes and lime juice to taste, and check the seasonings, adding salt and pepper only if necessary.

4 Divide the lobster or prawn meat among four individual serving bowls. Bring the soup to the boil then pour over the shellfish. Serve garnished with chopped dill.

Asparagus and Crab: Energy 158kcla/652kJ; Protein 9.7g; Carbohydrate 7.6g, of which sugards 4g; Fat 9.9g, of which saturates 5.6g; Cholesterol 38mg; Calcium 87mg; Fibre 3.2g; Sodium 147mg.
Lobster and Tomato: Energy 275kcal/1155kJ; Protein 29.6g; Carbohydrate 14.1g, of which sugars 13.5g; Fat 7.8g, of which saturates 3.7g; Cholesterol 151mg; Calcium 99mg; Fibre 2.6g; Sodium 479mg.

Hearty Fish Chowder

Hand around freshly made brown bread with this soup.

Serves 4–6

50g/2oz/¼ cup butter
1 large onion, chopped
115g/4oz bacon, rind removed, diced
4 celery sticks, diced
2 large potatoes, diced
450g/1lb ripe, juicy tomatoes, chopped
450ml/¾ pint/2 cups fish stock
450g/1lb white fish fillets, such as cod, flounder or haddock, skinned and cut into chunks
225g/8oz shellfish, such as prawns (shrimp), scallops or mussels
about 300ml/½ pint/1¼ cups milk
25g/1oz/¼ cup cornflour (cornstarch)
salt and ground black pepper
lightly whipped cream and chopped parsley, to garnish

1 Melt the butter in a large pan, add the onion, bacon, celery and potatoes and coat with the butter. Cover and sweat over a very gentle heat for 5–10 minutes, without colouring.

2 Meanwhile purée the tomatoes in a food processor or blender, and strain them to remove the skin and pips. Add with the fish stock to the pan. Bring to the boil, cover and leave to simmer gently until the potatoes are tender, skimming the top occasionally as required.

3 Prepare fresh prawns by plunging briefly in a pan of boiling water. Remove from the pan as the water boils. Cool and peel.

4 If using mussels, scrub the shells and discard any that do not open when tapped. Put the mussels into a shallow, heavy pan, without adding any liquid. Cover tightly and cook over a high heat for a few minutes, shaking occasionally, until all the mussels have opened. Discard any that fail to open. Remove the cooked mussels from their shells. Leave raw shelled scallops whole.

5 Add the shellfish to the soup. Blend the milk and cornflour together in a jug (pitcher), stir into the soup and bring to the boil. Reduce the heat, cover and simmer for a few minutes until the fish is tender. Add extra milk or stock if necessary and seasoning. Serve garnished with cream and some parsley.

Hot and Sour Filipino Fish Soup

Chunky, filling and satisfying, the Filipino fish soups are meals in themselves. There are many variations on the theme, depending on the region, usually packed with shellfish, flavoured with sour tamarind combined with hot chilli, and served with coconut vinegar flavoured with garlic.

Serves 4–6

2 litres/3½ pints/8 cups fish stock
250ml/8fl oz/1 cup white wine
15–30ml/1–2 tbsp tamarind paste
30–45ml/2–3 tbsp fish sauce
30ml/2 tbsp palm sugar (jaggery)
2–3 fresh red or green chillies, seeded and finely sliced
50g/2oz fresh root ginger, grated
2 tomatoes, skinned, seeded and cut into wedges
350g/12oz fresh fish, such as trout, sea bass, swordfish or cod, cut into bitesize chunks
12–16 fresh prawns (shrimp), in their shells
bunch of fresh basil, roughly chopped
bunch of fresh flat leaf parsley, roughly chopped
salt and ground black pepper

For serving

60–90ml/4–6 tbsp coconut vinegar
1–2 garlic cloves, finely chopped
1–2 limes, cut into wedges
2 fresh red or green chillies, seeded and quartered lengthways

1 In a wok or large pan, bring the stock and wine to the boil. Stir in the tamarind paste, fish sauce, sugar, chillies and ginger. Reduce the heat and simmer for 15–20 minutes.

2 Add the tomatoes to the broth and season with salt and pepper. Add the fish and prawns and simmer for 5 minutes, until the fish is cooked.

3 Meanwhile, mix the coconut vinegar and garlic for serving. Stir half the basil and half the parsley into the broth and ladle into bowls. Garnish with the remaining basil and parsley and serve. Offer the coconut vinegar, lime wedges to squeeze into the soup, and the chillies to chew on for extra heat.

Fish Chowder: Energy 488kcal/2050kJ; Protein 46g; Carbohydrate 36.2g, of which sugars 11.3g; Fat 18.7g, of which saturates 9.6g; Cholesterol 127mg; Calcium 163mg; Fibre 3.5g; Sodium 771mg.
Hot and Sour Fish: Energy 137kcal/576kJ; Protein 17.7g; Carbohydrate 8.1g, of which sugars 8g; Fat 1g, of which saturates 0.1g; Cholesterol 92mg; Calcium 76mg; Fibre 1.3g; Sodium 644mg.

Anchovy and Beansprout Soup

This gentle Korean broth is simple and quick to make and easy on the palate, with just a hint of spiciness and a refreshing nutty flavour. It is reputed to be the perfect solution for calming your stomach after a heavy drinking session.

Serves 4

200g/7oz/generous 2 cups soya beansprouts, washed and ends trimmed
1 fresh red or green chilli, washed, seeded and cut into thin diagonal slices
15 dried anchovies
1 spring onion (scallion), finely sliced
3 garlic cloves, chopped
salt

1 Boil 750ml/1¼ pints/3 cups water in a pan and add the dried anchovies. Bring to the boil, then reduce the heat slightly and part-cover the pan. Boil for 15 minutes, then remove the anchovies and discard them.

2 Add the soya beansprouts to the stock and bring back to the boil. Reduce the heat slightly and cook for 5 minutes, ensuring the lid is kept tightly on. Add the spring onion, chilli and garlic, and boil for a further 3 minutes. Add salt to taste, and serve.

Variation
To make a spicier version simply add 5ml/1 tsp of chilli powder to each bowl – great for curing a cold!

Cook's Tip
• *Wear protective gloves when seeding the chillies.*
• *Soya beansprouts and dried anchovies are available at some Asian stores. If you are unable to find dried anchovies, then 5ml/1 tsp Thai fish sauce can be used instead.*

Chunky Fish Soup

With some fresh crusty home-made brown bread or garlic bread, this quick-and-easy soup can be served like a stew and will make a delicious first course or supper dish.

Serves 6

25g/1oz/2 tbsp butter
1 onion, finely chopped
1 garlic clove, crushed or finely chopped
1 small red (bell) pepper, seeded and chopped
salt and ground black pepper
2.5ml/½ tsp sugar
a dash of Tabasco sauce
25g/1oz/¼ cup plain (all-purpose) flour
about 600ml/1 pint/2½ cups fish stock
450g/1lb ripe tomatoes, skinned and chopped, or 400g/14oz can chopped tomatoes
115g/4oz/1½ cups mushrooms, chopped
about 300ml/½ pint/1¼ cups milk
225g/8oz white fish, such as haddock or whiting, filleted and skinned, and cut into bitesize cubes
115g/4oz smoked haddock or cod, skinned, and cut into bitesize cubes
12–18 mussels, cleaned (optional)
chopped fresh parsley or chives, to garnish

1 Melt the butter in a large heavy pan and cook the onion and garlic gently until soft but not brown. Add the red pepper, salt and pepper, sugar and Tabasco sauce. Sprinkle the flour over and cook for 2 minutes, stirring. Gradually stir in the stock and add the tomatoes, with their juices and the mushrooms.

2 Bring to the boil, stirring and then reduce the heat and simmer gently until the vegetables are soft. Add the milk and bring back to the boil.

3 Add the fish to the pan and simmer for 3 minutes, then add the mussels, if using, and cook for another 3–4 minutes, or until the fish is just tender but not breaking up. Discard any mussels that remain closed.

4 Adjust the consistency with a little extra fish stock or milk, if necessary. Check the seasoning and serve immediately, garnished with parsley or chives.

Anchovy and Beansprout: Energy 41kcal/173kJ; Protein 4.6g; Carbohydrate 2.7g, of which sugars 1.2g; Fat 1.4g, of which saturates 0.2g; Cholesterol 7mg; Calcium 46mg; Fibre 1g; Sodium 445mg.
Chunky Fish Soup: Energy 142kcal/597kJ; Protein 13.9g; Carbohydrate 10.7g, of which sugars 7.1g; Fat 5.2g, of which saturates 2.9g; Cholesterol 36mg; Calcium 84mg; Fibre 1.7g; Sodium 91mg.

Mixed Fish in Vegetable Broth

Liguria is famous for its fish soups. In this one, the fish is cooked in a vegetable-flavoured broth and then puréed. The soup can also be used as a dressing for pasta when cooked down to the consistency of a sauce.

Serves 6

900g/2lb mixed fish, such as cod, haddock, whiting and monkfish
90ml/6 tbsp olive oil, plus extra to serve
1 onion, finely chopped
1 celery stick, chopped
1 carrot, chopped
60ml/4 tbsp chopped fresh parsley
175ml/6fl oz/¾ cup dry white wine
3 tomatoes, peeled and chopped
2 garlic cloves, finely chopped
1.5 litres/2½ pints/6¼ cups boiling water
salt and ground black pepper
rounds of French bread, to serve

1 Scale and clean the fish, discarding all innards, but leaving the heads on. Cut into large pieces. Rinse well in cool water.

2 Heat the oil in a large pan and add the onion. Cook over low to medium heat until it begins to soften. Stir in the celery and carrot and cook for 5 minutes more. Add the parsley.

3 Pour in the wine, increase the heat and cook until it reduces by about half. Stir in the tomatoes and garlic. Cook for 3–4 minutes, stirring occasionally. Pour in the boiling water and bring back to the boil. Cook over medium heat for 15 minutes.

4 Stir in the fish, and simmer for 10–15 minutes, or until the fish are tender. Season with salt and pepper.

5 Remove the fish from the soup with a slotted spoon. Discard the head and any bones. Purée the soup in a food processor or blender, reheat and adjust seasoning. If the soup is too thick, add a little more water.

6 To serve, bring the soup to a simmer. Toast the rounds of bread and drizzle one side with olive oil. Place two or three in each soup bowl before pouring over the soup.

Spinach, Shrimp and Tofu Soup

This is an extremely delicate and mild-flavoured soup, which can be used to counterbalance the heat from a spicy Thai curry. The tofu cubes add bulk and texture.

Serves 4–6

30ml/2 tbsp dried shrimp
1 litre/1¾ pints/4 cups chicken stock
225g/8oz tofu, drained and cut into 2cm/¾in cubes
30ml/2 tbsp fish sauce
350g/12oz spinach
freshly ground black pepper
2 spring onions (scallions), finely sliced, to garnish

1 Rinse and drain the dried shrimp. Combine the shrimp with the chicken stock in a large pan and bring to the boil. Add the tofu and simmer for about 5 minutes. Season with fish sauce and black pepper to taste.

2 Wash the spinach leaves thoroughly and tear into bitesize pieces. Add to the soup. Cook for another 1–2 minutes.

3 Pour the soup into warmed bowls, sprinkle the chopped spring onions on top to garnish, and serve.

Variations

- *For a lighter flavour, omit the dried shrimps but be sure to use good chicken stock.*
- *Use broccoli instead of the spinach – dice the stems and cook with the tofu, then add the very tender florets instead of the spinach in step 2.*
- *Use chicken intead of the tofu. Dice 1–2 skinless, boneless chicken breast fillets quite small and add to the stock instead of the tofu.*
- *For a light but full-flavoured soup, add the grated rind of 1 lime, a chopped bunch of garlic chives and a handful of small basil leaves with the spring onions (scallions).*

Fish in Broth: Energy 268kcal/1120kJ; Protein 31.1g; Carbohydrate 3.6g, of which sugars 3.3g; Fat 12.4g, of which saturates 1.8g; Cholesterol 77mg; Calcium 29mg; Fibre 1g; Sodium 112mg.
Spinach, Shrimp and Tofu: Energy 55kcal/231kJ; Protein 7.6g; Carbohydrate 1.4g, of which sugars 1.1g; Fat 2.2g, of which saturates 0.3g; Cholesterol 25mg; Calcium 352mg; Fibre 1.3g; Sodium 300mg.

Prawn and Tomato Soup

Cayenne pepper brings its fiery flavour to this soup.

Serves 4

675g/1½ lb raw unpeeled prawns (shrimp)
45ml/3 tbsp olive or vegetable oil
175g/6oz/1½ cups onions, very finely chopped
75g/3oz/½ cup celery, chopped
75g/3oz/½ cup green (bell) pepper, finely chopped
25g/1oz/½ cup chopped fresh parsley
1 garlic clove, crushed
15ml/1 tbsp Worcestershire sauce
1.5ml/¼ tsp cayenne pepper
120ml/4fl oz/½ cup dry white wine
50g/2oz/1 cup chopped peeled plum tomatoes
5ml/1 tsp salt
1 bay leaf
5ml/1 tsp sugar
fresh parsley, to garnish
boiled rice, to serve

1 Peel and devein the prawns. Put the prawn heads and shells in a pan with 475ml/16fl oz/2 cups water. Bring to the boil and simmer for 15 minutes. Strain and reserve 350ml/12fl oz/1½ cups of the stock.

2 Heat the oil in a heavy pan. Add the onions and cook gently for 8–10 minutes until soft. Add the celery and green pepper and cook for 5 minutes. Stir in the parsley, garlic, Worcestershire sauce and cayenne. Cook for another 5 minutes.

3 Raise the heat to medium. Stir in the wine and simmer for 3–4 minutes. Add the tomatoes, reserved prawn stock, salt, bay leaf and sugar and bring to the boil. Stir well, then reduce the heat to low and simmer for about 30 minutes, until the tomatoes have fallen apart and the sauce has reduced slightly. Remove from the heat and cool slightly.

4 Discard the bay leaf. Pour the sauce into a food processor or blender and purée until quite smooth. Taste and adjust the seasoning as necessary.

5 Return the tomato sauce to the pan and bring to the boil. Add the prawns and simmer for 4–5 minutes until they turn pink. Ladle into bowls, garnish with parsley and serve with rice.

Chilli-spiced Fish and Okra Soup

Okra grows well in many parts of West Africa and the Sudan, and soups like this one were the inspiration for gumbo, which slaves introduced to the Caribbean islands and North America. Okra thickens the soup and gives it a unique texture and flavour.

Serves 4

2 green bananas
50g/2oz/¼ cup butter
1 onion, finely chopped
2 tomatoes, peeled and finely chopped
115g/4oz okra, trimmed
225g/8oz smoked haddock or cod fillet, cut into bitesize pieces
900ml/1½ pints/3¾ cups fish stock
1 fresh red or green chilli, seeded and chopped
salt and ground black pepper
chopped fresh parsley, to garnish

1 Slit the skins of the bananas and place in a large pan. Cover with water, bring to the boil and cook over a medium heat for 25 minutes. Drain.

2 Melt the butter in a large pan and sauté the onion for about 5 minutes. Stir in the tomatoes and okra and sauté for a further 10 minutes.

3 Add the fish, fish stock, chilli and seasoning. Bring to the boil, then reduce the heat and simmer for about 20 minutes, until the fish is cooked through and flakes easily.

4 Peel the cooked bananas and cut into slices. Stir into the soup, heat through for a few minutes and then ladle into soup bowls. Sprinkle with chopped parsley and serve.

Cook's Tip

The bananas used in this recipe are plantain, not under-ripe dessert bananas. If they are not available, try using tiny new potatoes or chunks of peeled yam – they are different but equally as delicious in the soup.

Prawn and Tomato: Energy 252kcal/1054kJ; Protein 30.9g; Carbohydrate 6.2g, of which sugars 5g; Fat 9.6g, of which saturates 1.4g; Cholesterol 329mg; Calcium 177mg; Fibre 1.6g; Sodium 875mg.
Chilli-spiced Fish: Energy 295kcal/1233kJ; Protein 20g; Carbohydrate 24.6g, of which sugars 21.2g; Fat 13.8g, of which saturates 7.5g; Cholesterol 47mg; Calcium 477mg; Fibre 12.7g; Sodium 532mg.

Spicy Prawn and Tofu Soup

In this fiery seafood dish, clams and prawns are served in a piquant soup with a medley of vegetable. The creamy tofu melts beautifully into the sauce, and adds a healthy touch of non-dairy richness.

Serves 4

1 block soft tofu
15ml/1 tbsp light soy sauce
6 raw unpeeled prawns (shrimp)
6 clams
25g/1oz enoki mushrooms
15ml/1 tbsp vegetable oil
50g/2oz beef, finely chopped
7.5ml/1½ tsp Korean chilli powder
5ml/1 tsp crushed garlic
500ml/17fl oz/generous 2 cups water or beef stock
⅓ leek, sliced
½ red chilli, sliced
½ green chilli, sliced
2.5ml/½ tsp dark soy sauce
1.5ml/¼ tsp Thai fish sauce
salt

1 Break the tofu into small pieces, place in a bowl and marinate with the light soy sauce and a pinch of salt for 1 hour.

2 Peel and devein the prawns, and rinse them well. Scrub the clams in cold running water. Discard the caps from the enoki mushrooms.

3 In a flameproof casserole dish or heavy pan, heat the vegetable oil over high heat. Add the chopped beef and stir-fry until the meat has browned. Then add the chilli powder, garlic and a splash of water. Quickly stir-fry, coating the meat with the spices. Add the water or stock and bring to the boil. Add the clams, prawns and tofu, and boil for a further 4 minutes.

4 Reduce the heat slightly and add the leek, chillies and mushrooms. Continue to cook until the leek has softened. Stir in the dark soy sauce and Thai fish sauce. Season with salt if desired and serve.

Variation
Add firm-bodied white fish instead of the prawns (shrimp) or clams, and brown off chicken pieces rather than beef before adding stock.

Hot and Spicy Fish Soup

This Korean soup delivers a delicious spicy kick. Halibut or sea bass work as well as cod. The white fish flakes have the bite of red chilli, and the watercress and spring onions add a refreshing zesty quality.

Serves 3–4

1 cod, filleted and skinned, head separate
225g/8oz Chinese white radish, peeled
½ onion, chopped
2 garlic cloves, crushed
22.5ml/4½ tsp Korean chilli powder
5ml/1 tsp gochujang chilli paste
2 spring onions (scallions), roughly sliced
1 block firm tofu, cubed
90g/3½oz watercress or rocket (arugula)
salt and ground black pepper

1 Slice the cod fillets into three or four large pieces and set the head aside. Cut the white radish into 2cm/¾in cubes.

2 Bring 750ml/1¼ pints/3 cups water to the boil in large pan, and add the fish head. Add the radish, onion, crushed garlic and a pinch of salt. Then add the chilli powder and gochujang chilli paste, and boil for 5 minutes more.

3 Remove the fish head and add the sliced fillet to the pan. Simmer until the fish is tender, about 4 minutes, and then add the spring onions, tofu, and watercress or rocket. Simmer the soup without stirring for 2 minutes more.

4 Season with salt and pepper, and serve the soup immediately.

Cook's Tip
Gochujang chilli paste is a very hot fermented chilli paste. Korean chilli powder is milder than the Indian type. Both ingredients are widely used in Korean cooking and available from specialist stores. For a mild fish soup, omit the chilli powder and gochujang chilli paste. The soup will still be wonderfully hearty and flavoursome.

Spicy Prawn and Tofu: Energy 170kcal/709kJ; Protein 21.4g; Carbohydrate 2.1g, of which sugars 1.5g; Fat 8.4g, of which saturates 1.5g; Cholesterol 140mg; Calcium 378mg; Fibre 0.8g; Sodium 734mg.
Hot and Spicy Fish: Energy 132kcal/554kJ; Protein 23.4g; Carbohydrate 2.8g, of which sugars 2.3g; Fat 3g, of which saturates 0.5g; Cholesterol 46mg; Calcium 300mg; Fibre 1.1g; Sodium 80mg.

Dogfish Soup

Dogfish, a member of the shark family, is found along the Alentejo coast of Portugal, where this soup is very popular. This fish is also known as huss, flake, tope and rock salmon. This recipe is sufficient for a meal-in-a-bowl soup for four or, alternatively, a first course for eight.

Serves 4–8

4 dogfish fillets, about 4cm/1½in thick, or about 150g/5oz each
75ml/5 tbsp olive oil
2 garlic cloves, chopped
1 bunch of fresh coriander (cilantro), chopped
1 bay leaf
15ml/1 tbsp plain (all-purpose) flour
50ml/2fl oz/¼ cup white wine vinegar
salt

For the marinade
1 bay leaf
50ml/2fl oz white wine vinegar
salt

1 First make the marinade by combining all the ingredients with 500ml/7fl oz/2 cups water in a jug (pitcher). Place the fish fillets in a dish and pour the marinade over them. Leave to marinate for at least 2 hours, then rinse in water.

2 Heat the olive oil in a large pan. Add the garlic and coriander and cook, stirring, for a few minutes. Add the fish and bay leaf, and pour in 1 litre/1¾ pints/4 cups water. Season with salt.

3 Bring to the boil, then lower the heat and simmer for 10 minutes. Reserve the fish and throw away the bay leaf.

4 Mix the flour to a smooth paste with the vinegar. Gradually stir this into the soup. Simmer for 10 minutes until the flour is combined, and add more water if necessary. Add the fish and serve immediately.

Variation
This soup can also be made with swordfish or shark fillets, which have a similar texture to dogfish.

Fish Soup with Dumplings

This delicious soup is a classic recipe from Jewish cookery. It takes very little time to prepare, so is ideal as a quick supper.

Serves 4–8

675g/1½lb assorted fresh fish, skinned, boned and diced
15–30ml/1–2 tbsp vegetable oil
15ml/1 tbsp paprika, plus extra to garnish
1.5 litres/2½ pints/6¼ cups fish stock or water
3 firm tomatoes, peeled and chopped
4 waxy potatoes, peeled and grated
5–10ml/1–2 tsp chopped fresh marjoram, plus extra to garnish

For the dumplings
75g/3oz/½ cup semolina or plain (all-purpose) flour
1 egg, beaten
generous pinch of salt
15ml/1 tbsp chopped fresh parsley

1 Fry the pieces of assorted fish in the vegetable oil for about 1–2 minutes, taking care not to break them up.

2 Sprinkle in the paprika, pour in the fish stock or water, bring to the boil and simmer for 10 minutes.

3 Stir the tomatoes, grated potato and marjoram into the pan. Cook for 10 minutes, stirring occasionally.

4 Meanwhile, make the dumplings. Mix all the ingredients together adding 45ml/3 tbsp water, then leave to stand, covered with clear film (plastic wrap), for 5–10 minutes.

5 Drop spoonfuls of the dumpling mixture into the soup and cook for 10 minutes. Serve hot, sprinkled with a little marjoram and paprika.

Cook's Tip
For the fish, use a variety of whatever fresh fish is available. Good options include perch, cod, snapper or carp.

Dogfish Soup: Energy 174kcal/724kJ; Protein 18.8g; Carbohydrate 2.2g, of which sugars 0.2g; Fat 10g, of which saturates 1.4g; Cholesterol 46mg; Calcium 29mg; Fibre 0.5g; Sodium 63mg.
Fish Soup with Dumplings: Energy 154kcal/649kJ; Protein 18g; Carbohydrate 14.5g, of which sugars 1.8g; Fat 3g, of which saturates 0.5g; Cholesterol 63mg; Calcium 29mg; Fibre 1g; Sodium 67mg.

Cod and Omelette Soup with Prawn Balls

Omelette works well in soup, and is often used to add protein to light Oriental dishes like this one. Here it is cut into long strips and tied into knots – the familiar "egg-knot" of traditional Far Eastern cuisine.

Serves 4

1 spring onion (scallion), thinly shredded
800ml/1⅓ pints/3½ cups well-flavoured stock or instant dashi (Japanese stock)
5ml/1 tsp soy sauce
dash of sake or dry white wine

For the prawn balls

200g/7oz/generous 1 cup raw large prawns (shrimp), shelled and deveined
65g/2½oz cod fillet, skinned
5ml/1 tsp egg white
5ml/1 tsp sake or dry white wine, plus a dash extra
22.5ml/4½ tsp cornflour (cornstarch)
2–3 drops soy sauce
pinch of salt

For the omelette

1 egg, beaten
dash of mirin
pinch of salt
oil, for cooking

1 To make the prawn balls, place the prawns, cod, egg white, sake or dry white wine, cornflour, soy sauce and a pinch of salt in a food processor and process to a thick, sticky paste. Shape the mixture into 4 balls, place in a steaming basket and steam over a pan of vigorously boiling water for about 10 minutes.

2 Soak the spring onion in iced water for about 5 minutes, until the shreds curl, then drain.

3 To make the omelette, mix the egg with the mirin and salt. Heat a little oil in a frying pan and pour in the egg mixture, coating the pan evenly. When the omelette has set, turn it over and cook for 30 seconds. Leave to cool.

4 Cut the omelette into strips and tie each in a knot. Heat the stock or dashi, then add the soy sauce, sake or wine and salt. Divide the prawn balls and egg-knots among four bowls and add the soup. Garnish with the spring onion.

Mullet and Fennel Soup

Olives and tomato toasts are delicious in this soup.

Serves 4

25ml/1½ tbsp olive oil
1 onion, chopped
3 garlic cloves, chopped
2 fennel bulbs, thinly sliced
4 tomatoes, chopped
1 bay leaf
sprig of fresh thyme
1.2 litres/2 pints/5 cups fish stock
675g/1½lb red mullet or snapper, scaled and filleted
salt and ground black pepper

For the toasts

8 slices baguette, toasted
1 garlic clove
30ml/2 tbsp tomato purée (paste)
12 black olives, stoned (pitted) and quartered
fresh fennel fronds, to garnish

For the aioli

2 egg yolks
1–2 garlic cloves, crushed
10ml/2 tsp lemon juice
300ml/½ pint/1¼ cups extra virgin olive oil

1 Heat the olive oil in a large, heavy pan. Add the onion and garlic and cook for 5 minutes, until soften. Add the fennel and cook for 2–3 minutes. Stir in the tomatoes, bay leaf, thyme and stock. Boil, reduce the heat, cover and simmer for 30 minutes.

2 Meanwhile, make the aioli in a large bowl. Whisk the egg yolks, garlic, lemon juice and seasoning together. Whisk in the oil, drops at a time. As the mixture begins to thicken, add the oil in a slow trickle. Transfer to a large bowl and set aside.

3 Cut each mullet fillet into two or three pieces, then add them to the soup and cook gently for 5 minutes. Use a slotted spoon to remove the mullet and set aside.

4 Strain the cooking liquid, pressing the vegetables well. Whisk a ladleful of soup into the aioli, then whisk in the remaining soup in one go. Return the soup to a clean pan and cook very gently, whisking continuously, until the mixture is very slightly thickened. Add the mullet to the soup.

5 Rub the toasted baguette with garlic, spread with tomato purée and top with olives. Serve the soup topped with the toasts and garnished with fennel.

Cod and Omelette: Energy 98kcal/412kJ; Protein 13.6g; Carbohydrate 7.1g, of which sugars 0.2g; Fat 1.9g, of which saturates 0.5g; Cholesterol 153mg; Calcium 51mg; Fibre 0.1g; Sodium 218mg.
Mullet and Fennel: Energy 492kcal/2079kJ; Protein 41.2g; Carbohydrate 53.6g, of which sugars 10g; Fat 14.1g, of which saturates 1.2g; Cholesterol 0mg; Calcium 256mg; Fibre 6.1g; Sodium 965mg.

Curried Salmon Soup

A hint of mild curry paste really enhances the flavour of this soup, without making it too spicy. Grated creamed coconut adds a luxury touch, while helping to amalgamate the flavours. Served with chunks of warm bread, this makes a substantial and rich appetizer.

Serves 4

50g/2oz/¼ cup butter
2 onions, roughly chopped
10ml/2 tsp mild curry paste
150ml/¼ pint/⅔ cup white wine
300ml/½ pint/1¼ cups double (heavy) cream
50g/2oz/½ cup creamed coconut, grated or 120ml/4fl oz/½ cup coconut cream
2 potatoes, about 350g/12oz, cubed
450g/1lb salmon fillet, skinned and cut into bitesize pieces
60ml/4 tbsp chopped fresh flat-leaf parsley
salt and ground black pepper

1 Melt the butter in a large pan, add the onions and cook for about 3–4 minutes until beginning to soften. Stir in the curry paste. Cook for 1 minute more.

2 Add 475ml/16fl oz/2 cups water, the wine, cream and creamed coconut or coconut cream, with seasoning. Bring to the boil, stirring until the coconut has dissolved.

3 Add the potatoes and simmer, covered, for about 15 minutes or until they are almost tender. Do not allow them to break down into the liquid.

4 Add the fish and cook gently so as not to break it up for about 2–3 minutes until just cooked. Add the parsley and adjust the seasoning. Serve immediately.

Cook's Tip

There is a wide choice of curry pastes available. Select a concentrated paste for this recipe, rather than a 'cook-in-sauce' type of paste. If you cannot find a suitable paste, cook a little curry powder in melted butter over low heat and use instead.

Leek, Fish and Tomato Soup

This chunky Mediterranean soup, boasting spice and a hint of citrus, could almost be called a stew.

Serves 4

2 large thick leeks
30ml/2 tbsp olive oil
5ml/1 tsp crushed coriander seeds
good pinch of red chilli flakes
300g/11oz small salad potatoes, peeled and thickly sliced
400g/14oz can chopped tomatoes
600ml/1 pint/2½ cups fish stock
150ml/¼ pint/⅔ cup white wine
1 fresh bay leaf
1 star anise
strip of pared orange rind
good pinch of saffron threads
450g/1lb white fish fillets, such as monkfish, sea bass or haddock
450g/1lb small squid, cleaned
250g/9oz peeled raw prawns (shrimp)
30–45ml/2–3 tbsp chopped flat leaf parsley
salt and ground black pepper

For serving

1 short French loaf, sliced and toasted
garlic mayonnaise

1 Slice the leeks, keeping the green separate from the white pieces. Set the white slices aside for later.

2 Heat the oil in a heavy pan over a low heat, then add the green leek slices, the crushed coriander seeds and the dried red chilli flakes. Cook, stirring occasionally, for 5 minutes.

3 Add the potatoes and tomatoes, and pour in the stock and wine. Add the bay leaf, star anise, orange rind and saffron. Bring to the boil, lower the heat and partially cover the pan. Simmer for 20 minutes until the potatoes are tender. Add seasoning.

4 Cut the white fish into chunks. Cut the squid sacs into rectangles and score a criss-cross pattern into them. Add the fish to the soup and cook gently for 4 minutes. Add the prawns and cook for 1 minute. Add the squid and the white part of the leek and cook, stirring occasionally, for a further 2 minutes.

5 Finally, stir in the chopped parsley and serve immediately, ladling the soup into warmed bowls. Offer the toasted French bread and the garlic mayonnaise with the soup.

Curried Salmon: Energy 837kcal/3466kJ; Protein 26.3g; Carbohydrate 16.6g, of which sugars 3.6g; Fat 71.8g, of which saturates 41.2g; Cholesterol 186mg; Calcium 74mg; Fibre 0.9g; Sodium 158mg.
Fish and Tomato: Energy 326kcal/1379kJ; Protein 49.7g; Carbohydrate 17.5g, of which sugars 4.4g; Fat 4.2g, of which saturates 0.9g; Cholesterol 421mg; Calcium 106mg; Fibre 2.9g; Sodium 333mg.

Smoked Haddock Chowder with Sweet Thai Basil

Based on a traditional Scottish recipe, this soup combines the sweetness of sweet potatoes and butternut squash with aromatic Thai basil.

Serves 6

400g/14oz sweet potatoes (pink-fleshed variety), diced
225g/8oz peeled butternut squash, cut into 1cm/½in slices
50g/2oz/¼ cup butter
1 onion, chopped
450g/1lb Finnan haddock fillets, skinned
300ml/½ pint/1¼ cups water
600ml/1 pint/2½ cups milk
small handful of Thai basil leaves
60ml/4 tbsp double (heavy) cream
salt and ground black pepper

1 Cook the sweet potatoes and butternut squash separately in boiling salted water for 15 minutes or until tender. Drain well.

2 Meanwhile, melt half the butter in a large, heavy-based pan. Add the onion and cook for 4–5 minutes, until softened but not browned. Add the haddock fillets and water.

3 Bring to the boil, reduce the heat and simmer for 10 minutes, until the fish is cooked. Use a draining spoon to lift the fish out of the pan and leave to cool. Set the liquid aside.

4 When cool enough to handle, carefully break the flesh into large flakes, discarding the skin and bones. Set the fish aside.

5 Press the sweet potatoes through a sieve and beat in the remaining butter with seasoning to taste. Strain the reserved fish cooking liquid and return it to the rinsed-out pan, then whisk in the sweet potato. Stir in the milk and bring to the boil. Simmer for about 2–3 minutes.

6 Stir in the butternut squash, fish, Thai basil leaves and cream. Season the soup to taste and heat through without boiling. Ladle the soup into six warmed soup bowls and serve immediately.

North African Monkfish Soup

The fish for this tagine is marinated in chermoula for authentic Moroccan flavour.

Serves 4

900g/2lb monkfish fillet, cut in chunks
45–60ml/3–4 tbsp olive oil
4–5 garlic cloves, thinly sliced
15–20 cherry tomatoes
2 green (bell) peppers, grilled (broiled) until black, skinned, seeded and cut into strips
15–20 small new potatoes
large handful of black olives
salt and ground black pepper

For the chermoula

2 garlic cloves
5ml/1 tsp coarse salt
10ml/2 tsp ground cumin
5ml/1 tsp paprika
juice of 1 lemon
small bunch of fresh coriander (cilantro), roughly chopped
15ml/1 tbsp olive oil

1 Using a mortar and pestle to make the chermoula: pound the garlic with the salt to a smooth paste. Add the cumin, paprika, lemon juice and coriander, and gradually mix in the olive oil to emulsify the mixture slightly. Reserve a little chermoula for cooking, then rub the rest over the chunks of monkfish. Cover and leave to marinate for about 1 hour.

2 Heat the olive oil in a heavy pan and stir in the garlic. When the garlic begins to colour, add the tomatoes and cook until just softened. Add the peppers and the remaining chermoula, and season with salt and pepper.

3 Add the potatoes and stir well. Pour in enough water to cover the vegetables by about 2.5–5cm/1–2in and bring to the boil. Reduce the heat, cover and simmer for 15 minutes. Stir and taste, adding more salt and pepper, if required.

4 Add the fish chunks, scraping in all their marinade, and the olives. Drizzle a little extra olive oil over and pour. Bring back to simmering point, then cover and cook gently for about 15 minutes, or until the fish is cooked through.

5 Ladle the ingredients into bowls and take the pan to the table. Ladle on more broth as the fish is easten. Offer lots of fresh, warm crusty bread to mop up the delicious broth.

Haddock Chowder: Energy 285kcal/1196kJ; Protein 19.1g; Carbohydrate 20.7g, of which sugars 9.9g; Fat 14.7g, of which saturates 8.9g; Cholesterol 64mg; Calcium 166mg; Fibre 2.1g; Sodium 173mg.
African Monkfish: Energy 401kcal/1693kJ; Protein 40.6g; Carbohydrate 31.7g, of which sugars 10.2g; Fat 13.4g, of which saturates 2.2g; Cholesterol 32mg; Calcium 70mg; Fibre 4.6g; Sodium 561mg.

Monkfish Broth

Lemon grass, chillies and galangal are among the flavourings used in this fragrant soup.

Serves 2–3

1 litre/1¾ pints/4 cups fish or light chicken stock
4 lemon grass stalks
3 limes
2 small fresh hot red chillies, seeded and thinly sliced
2cm/¾in piece fresh galangal, peeled and thinly sliced
6 coriander (cilantro) stalks, with leaves
2 kaffir lime leaves, coarsely chopped (optional)
350g/12oz monkfish fillet, skinned and cut into 2.5cm/1in pieces
15ml/1 tbsp rice vinegar
45ml/3 tbsp fish sauce
30ml/2 tbsp chopped coriander (cilantro) leaves, to garnish

1 Pour the stock into a pan and bring it to the boil.

2 Meanwhile, slice the bulb end of each lemon grass stalk diagonally into pieces about 3mm/⅛in thick. Peel off four wide strips of lime rind with a potato peeler, taking care to avoid the white pith underneath, which would make the soup bitter. Squeeze the limes and reserve the juice.

3 Add the sliced lemon grass, lime rind, chillies, galangal and coriander stalks to the stock, with the kaffir lime leaves, if using. Simmer for 1–2 minutes.

4 Add the monkfish, rice vinegar and fish sauce, with half the reserved lime juice. Simmer for about 3 minutes, until the fish is just cooked.

5 Lift out and discard the coriander stalks, taste the broth and add more lime juice if necessary; the soup should taste quite sour. Sprinkle with the coriander leaves and serve.

Variation

Prawns (shrimp), scallops, squid, sole or flounder can be substituted for the monkfish. If you use kaffir lime leaves, you will need the juice of only 2 limes.

Hot-and-Sour Fish Soup

This style of soup is found all over South-east Asia.

Serves 4

1 catfish, sea bass or red snapper, about 1kg/2¼lb, filleted
60ml/4 tbsp fish sauce
2 garlic cloves, finely chopped
25g/1oz dried squid, soaked in water for 30 minutes
15ml/1 tbsp vegetable oil
2 spring onions (scallions), sliced
2 shallots, sliced
4cm/1½in fresh root ginger, peeled and chopped
2–3 lemon grass stalks, cut into strips and crushed
30ml/2 tbsp tamarind paste
2–3 Thai chillies, seeded and sliced
15ml/1 tbsp sugar
225g/8oz fresh pineapple, peeled and diced
3 tomatoes, skinned, seeded and roughly chopped
50g/2oz canned sliced bamboo shoots, drained
small bunch of fresh coriander (cilantro), stalks removed, leaves finely chopped
salt and ground black pepper
115g/4oz/½cup beansprouts

For the garnish

bunch of dill, fronds roughly chopped
1 lime, cut into quarters, to serve

1 Cut the fish into bitesize pieces, mix with 30ml/2 tbsp of the fish sauce and garlic and leave to marinate. Save the head, tail and bones for the stock. Drain and rinse the dried squid.

2 Heat the oil in a pan. Add the spring onions, shallots, ginger, lemon grass and squid. Add the reserved fish trimmings and cook gently for 1–2 minutes. Pour in 1.2 litres/2 pints/5 cups water and oil. Reduce the heat and simmer for 30 minutes.

3 Strain the stock into another pan and bring to the boil. Stir in the tamarind paste, chillies, sugar and remaining fish sauce. Simmer for 2–3 minutes. Add the pineapple, tomatoes and bamboo shoots and simmer for 2–3 minutes. Stir in the fish and chopped fresh coriander, and cook until the fish turns opaque.

4 Season to taste and ladle the soup into hot bowls. Garnish with beansprouts and dill, and serve with the lime quarters to squeeze over.

Monkfish Broth: Energy 92kcal/394kJ; Protein 19.8g; Carbohydrate 1.8g, of which sugars 1.6g; Fat 0.8g, of which saturates 0.1g; Cholesterol 16mg; Calcium 50mg; Fibre 0.8g; Sodium 1096mg.
Hot-and-Sour Fish Soup: Energy 335kcal/1415kJ; Protein 44g; Carbohydrate 24g, of which sugars 19g; Fat 7g, of which saturates 1g; Cholesterol 108mg; Calcium 138mg; Fibre 2.3g; Sodium 1.2g.

Fish Soup with Egg and Chillies

In Burma this delicious one-course meal, known as Mohingha, is sold by hawkers, carrying a bamboo pole carried across their shoulders. At one end is a container with a charcoal fire and at the other end are the ingredients for the soup.

Serves 8

675g/1½lb huss, cod or mackerel, cleaned on the bone
3 lemon grass stalks
2.5cm/1in piece fresh root ginger
30ml/2 tbsp fish sauce
3 onions, roughly chopped
4 garlic cloves, roughly chopped
2–3 fresh red chillies, seeded and chopped
5ml/1 tsp ground turmeric
75ml/5 tbsp groundnut (peanut) oil, for frying
400g/14oz can coconut milk
25g/1oz/¼ cup rice flour
25g/1oz/¼ cup gram flour
540g/1lb 5oz can bamboo shoots, drained and sliced
salt and ground black pepper
wedges of hard-boiled egg, thinly sliced red onions, finely chopped spring onions (scallions), deep-fried prawns (shrimp) and fried chillies, to garnish
rice noodles, to serve

1 Place the fish in a large pan with water to cover. Bruise two lemon grass stalks and half the ginger and add to the pan. Bring to the boil, add the fish sauce and cook for 10 minutes. Lift out the fish and cool. Strain the stock into a bowl. Discard skin and bones from the fish and break the flesh into pieces, using a fork.

2 Trim and roughly chop the remaining lemon grass. Process to a paste in a food processor or blender with the remaining ginger, onions, garlic, chillies and turmeric. Heat the oil in a pan and fry the paste until aromatic. Remove from the heat and add the fish.

3 Make up the coconut milk and stock to 2.5 litres/4 pints/10 cups with water. Mix a little into the rice and gram flours to make a paste. Pour into a pan with the rest of the stock. Bring to the boil, stirring. Add the bamboo shoots, fish mixture and seasoning. Heat through. Guests pour the soup over the noodles and add egg, onions, spring onions, prawns and chillies as garnishes, as required.

Soup Niçoise with Seared Tuna

Ingredients for the famous salad from Nice in the South of France are transformed into a simple, yet elegant soup by adding a hot garlic-infused stock.

Serves 4

12 bottled anchovy fillets, drained
30ml/2 tbsp milk
115g/4oz French (green) beans, halved
4 plum tomatoes, peeled, halved and seeded
16 black olives, stoned (pitted)
1 litre/1¾ pints/4 cups good vegetable stock
3 garlic cloves, crushed
30ml/2 tbsp lemon juice
15ml/1 tbsp olive oil
4 tuna steaks, about 75g/3oz each
small bunch of spring onions (scallions), shredded lengthways
handful of fresh basil leaves, shredded
salt and ground black pepper
fresh crusty bread, to serve

1 Soak the anchovies in the milk for 10 minutes. Drain well and dry on kitchen paper. Cook the French beans in boiling salted water for 2–3 minutes. Drain, refresh under cold running water and drain. Cut the tomatoes into thin wedges. Wash the olives, then cut into quarters. Set all the prepared ingredients aside.

2 Bring the stock and garlic to the boil in a pan. Reduce the heat, simmer for 10 minutes, season and add the lemon juice.

3 Meanwhile, brush a griddle pan with the oil and heat until very hot. Season the tuna and cook for about 2 minutes each side. Do not overcook the tuna or it will become dry.

4 Gently toss the French beans, tomatoes, spring onions, anchovies, black olives and shredded basil leaves. Put the seared tuna into four bowls and pile the vegetables on top. Ladle the stock around the ingredients. Serve at once, with crusty bread.

Cook's Tip
Buy anchovy fillets that have been bottled in extra virgin olive oil if you can, as they have a far superior flavour to the smaller anchovy fillets.

Fish Soup with Egg: Energy 166kcal/699kJ; Protein 19.8g; Carbohydrate 18.3g, of which sugars 8.6g; Fat 1.9g, of which saturates 0.4g; Cholesterol 39mg; Calcium 66mg; Fibre 2.2g; Sodium 514mg.
Soup Niçoise with Tuna: Energy 217kcal/909kJ; Protein 27.4g; Carbohydrate 3g, of which sugars 2.7g; Fat 10.7g, of which saturates 2.2g; Cholesterol 34mg; Calcium 76mg; Fibre 2g; Sodium 829mg.

Whitefish Soup with Orange

The old name for this Spanish soup is "sopa cachorreña" – Seville orange soup – and it is good served post-Christmas, when bitter Seville oranges are in season. The fish used is normally small hake, but any white fish is suitable.

Serves 6

1kg/2¼lb small hake or whiting, whole but cleaned
4 bitter oranges or 4 sweet oranges and 2 lemons
30ml/2 tbsp olive oil
5 garlic cloves, unpeeled
1 large onion, finely chopped
1 tomato, peeled, seeded and chopped
4 small potatoes, cut into rounds
5ml/1 tsp paprika
salt and ground black pepper
15–30ml/1–2 tbsp finely chopped fresh parsley, to garnish

1 Fillet the fish and cut each fillet into three, reserving all the trimmings. Put the fillets on a plate, salt lightly, cover and chill while preparing the stock.

2 Put the trimmings in a pan, add 1.2 litres/2 pints/5 cups water and a spiral of orange rind. Bring to a simmer, skim, then cover and cook gently for 30 minutes.

3 Heat the oil in a large pan over a high heat. Smash the garlic cloves with the flat of a knife and fry until they are well-coloured. Discard them and turn down the heat. Fry the onion gently until it is softened, adding the tomato halfway through.

4 Strain in the hot fish stock (adding the orange spiral as well if you wish) and bring back to the boil. Add the potatoes to the pan and cook them for about 5 minutes.

5 Add the fish pieces to the soup, a few at a time, without letting it go off the boil. Cook for about 15 minutes.

6 Finally, stir in the squeezed orange juice and lemon juice, if using, and the paprika, with salt and pepper to taste. Ladle into bowls and serve garnished with a little parsley.

Smoked Mackerel and Tomato Soup

All the ingredients for this unusual soup are cooked in a single pan, so it is not only quick and easy to prepare, but requires little clearing up afterwards. Smoked mackerel gives the soup a robust flavour, but it is tempered by the citrus tones provided by the lemon grass and tamarind.

Serves 4

200g/7oz smoked mackerel fillets
4 tomatoes
1 litre/1¾ pints/4 cups vegetable stock
1 lemon grass stalk, chopped
5cm/2in piece fresh galangal or root ginger, finely diced or sliced
4 shallots, finely chopped
2 garlic cloves, finely chopped
2.5ml/½ tsp dried chilli flakes
15ml/1 tbsp fish sauce
5ml/1 tsp palm sugar (jaggery) or light muscovado (brown) sugar
45ml/3 tbsp thick tamarind juice, made by mixing tamarind paste with warm water
small bunch fresh chives or spring onions (scallions), to garnish

1 Prepare the smoked mackerel fillets. Remove and discard the skin, if necessary, then chop the flesh into large pieces. Carefully remove any stray bones with your fingers or by using a pair of sterilized tweezers.

2 Cut the tomatoes in half, squeeze out and discard most of the seeds, then finely dice the flesh with a sharp knife. Place in bowls and set aside.

3 Pour the stock into a large pan and add the lemon grass, galangal or ginger, shallots and garlic. Bring to the boil, reduce the heat and simmer for 15 minutes.

4 Add the fish, tomatoes, chilli flakes, fish sauce, sugar and tamarind juice. Bring back to simmering point, then continue to simmer for around 4–5 minutes, until the fish and tomatoes are heated through.

5 Ladle the soup into individual bowls, garnish with the chives or spring onions and serve.

Whitefish Soup: Energy 263kcal/1105kJ; Protein 27.1g; Carbohydrate 23.9g, of which sugars 12.2g; Fat 7.2g, of which saturates 1.1g; Cholesterol 30mg; Calcium 81mg; Fibre 3.2g; Sodium 155mg.
Smoked Mackerel: Energy 226kcal/940kJ; Protein 11.2g; Carbohydrate 10.2g, of which sugars 8.5g; Fat 15.9g, of which saturates 3.3g; Cholesterol 53mg; Calcium 39mg; Fibre 2.1g; Sodium 653mg.

Fish Soup with Chunky Vegetables

This Grecian fish soup makes a complete meal. The liquid soup is served first, followed by a platter of the fish and vegetables.

Serves 4

1.5 litres/2½ pints/6¼ cups water or fish stock
75–90ml/5–6 tbsp extra virgin olive oil
2kg/4½lb whole fish, such as Mediterranean scorpion fish or red gurnard, cleaned and scaled
8 small potatoes, peeled
8 small onions, peeled
2 carrots, peeled and cut into 5cm/2in lengths
1 or 2 celery sticks, with leaves
2 courgettes (zucchini), quartered lengthways
juice of 1 lemon
salt and ground black pepper
extra virgin olive oil, juice of 1 lemon and dried oregano, to serve

1 Mix the water or stock and olive oil in a pan. Bring to the boil, and boil rapidly for 4 minutes. Add the fish with seasoning. Bring slowly back to the boil. Skim the surface until it is clear.

2 Add the potatoes, onions, carrots, celery sticks and leaves, and courgettes with a little more hot water, if needed, to cover.

3 Put a lid on the pan and cook over a medium heat until the fish is cooked and the flesh flakes when tested with the tip of a sharp knife. Large fish will take up to 35 minutes; smaller ones a little less. Make sure that the fish does not disintegrate.

4 Carefully lift the fish out of the pan and place it on a warm platter. Scoop out the hot vegetables with a draining spoon and arrange them around the fish. Cover and keep hot.

5 Stir the lemon juice into the soup. Serve it first, then bring out the platter of fish and vegetables. Invite guests to help themselves to a piece of fish and a selection of vegetables.

6 Quickly whisk the extra virgin olive oil with the lemon juice and dried oregano. This makes an excellent dressing for the fish and vegetables.

Cod, Bean and Spinach Chowder

Granary croûtons complete this delicious soup.

Serves 6

1 litre/1¾ pints/4 cups milk
150ml/1/4 pint/⅔ cup double (heavy) cream
675g/1½lb cod fillet, skinned and boned
45ml/3 tbsp olive oil
1 onion, sliced
2 garlic cloves, finely chopped
450g/1lb potatoes, thickly sliced
450g/1lb fresh broad (fava) beans, podded
225g/8oz baby spinach leaves
pinch of grated nutmeg
30ml/2 tbsp snipped fresh chives
salt and ground black pepper
fresh chives, to garnish

For the Granary croûtons
60ml/4 tbsp olive oil
6 slices Granary (whole-wheat) bread, crusts removed and cut into large cubes

1 Pour the milk and cream into a large pan and bring to the boil. Add the cod and bring back to the boil. Reduce the heat and simmer for 2–3 minutes, then remove from the heat and leave to stand for about 6 minutes, until the fish is just cooked. Use a slotted spoon to remove the fish from the cooking liquid.

2 Using a fork, flake the cooked cod into chunky pieces, removing any bones or skin, then cover and set aside.

3 Heat the olive oil in a large pan and add the onion and garlic. Cook for about 5 minutes, until softened, stirring occasionally. Add the potatoes, stir in the milk mixture and bring to the boil. Reduce the heat and cover. Cook for 10 minutes. Add the broad beans; cook for 10 minutes, until tender.

4 Meanwhile, make the croûtons. Heat the oil in a frying pan and add the bread cubes. Cook over a medium heat, stirring often, until golden all over. Remove and drain on kitchen paper.

5 Add the cod to the soup and heat through gently. Just before serving, add the spinach and stir for 1–2 minutes, until wilted. Season the soup well and stir in the nutmeg and chives.

6 Ladle the soup into bowls and pile the croûtons on top. Garnish with fresh chives and serve at once.

Fish Soup: Energy 454kcal/1,895kJ; Protein 53.8g; Carbohydrate 17g, of which sugars 6.4g; Fat 19.3g, of which saturates 3.1g; Cholesterol 135mg; Calcium 138mg; Fibre 2.5g; Sodium 345mg.
Cod and Spinach: Energy 603kcal/2525kJ; Protein 37.9g; Carbohydrate 44.7g, of which sugars 12.2g; Fat 31.6g, of which saturates 12.5g; Cholesterol 96mg; Calcium 398mg; Fibre 7.5g; Sodium 375mg.

Rice and Bean Soup with Salt Cod

Based on the classic Caribbean dish of rice and peas, this soup is made with black-eyed beans, but kidney beans or, more traditionally, pigeon peas can be used.

Serves 6

15ml/1 tbsp sunflower oil
75g/3oz/6 tbsp butter
115g/4oz thick rindless bacon rashers (strips), cut into strips
1 onion, chopped
2 garlic cloves, chopped
1 fresh red chilli, seeded and chopped
225g/8oz/generous 1 cup long grain rice
2 fresh thyme sprigs
1 cinnamon stick
400g/14oz can black-eyed beans (peas), drained and rinsed
350g/12oz salt cod, soaked for 24 hours, changing the water several times
plain (all-purpose) flour, for dusting
400g/14oz can coconut milk
175g/6oz baby spinach leaves
30ml/2 tbsp chopped fresh parsley
salt and ground black pepper

1 Heat the oil and 25g/1oz/2 tbsp of the butter in a large pan. Add the bacon and cook for 3–4 minutes, until golden. Stir in the onion, garlic and chilli and cook for a further 4–5 minutes.

2 Stir in the rice and cook for 1–2 minutes, until the grains are translucent. Stir in the thyme, cinnamon and black-eyed beans and cook for 1–2 minutes. Pour in 900ml/1⅓ pints/3¾ cups water and boil. Cook over low heat for 25–30 minutes.

3 Meanwhile, wash the soaked salt cod under cold running water. Pat dry with kitchen paper and remove the skin. Cut into large bitesize pieces and toss in the flour until evenly coated. Shake off the excess flour.

4 Melt the remaining butter in a large, heavy-based frying pan. Add the cod, in batches if necessary, and cook for 4–5 minutes until tender and golden. Remove the cod and set aside.

5 Stir the coconut milk into the rice and beans. Remove the cinnamon stick and cook the soup for 2–3 minutes. Stir in the spinach and cook for 2–3 minutes. Add the cod and parsley, season and heat through. Ladle the soup into bowls and serve.

Salt Cod and Okra Soup with Creamed Yam

Inspired by the ingredients of the Caribbean, this chunky soup is served in deep bowls around a chive-flavoured sweet yam mash.

Serves 6

200g/7oz salt cod, soaked for 24 hours, changing the water several times
15ml/1 tbsp olive oil
1 garlic clove, chopped
1 onion, chopped
1 green chilli, seeded and chopped
6 plum tomatoes, peeled and chopped
250ml/8fl oz/1 cup white wine
2 bay leaves
225g/8oz okra, trimmed and cut into chunks
225g/8oz callaloo or spinach
30ml/2 tbsp chopped fresh parsley
salt and ground black pepper

For the creamed yam

675g/1½lb yam, peeled and cut into chunks
juice of 1 lemon
50g/2oz/¼ cup butter
30ml/2 tbsp double (heavy) cream
15ml/1 tbsp chopped fresh chives

1 Drain and skin the cod, then rinse it under cold running water. Cut into bitesize pieces, removing bones, and set aside. Heat the oil in a pan. Add the garlic, onion and chilli. Cook for 4–5 minutes until soft. Add the cod and cook for 3–4 minutes, until it begins to colour. Stir in the tomatoes, wine and bay leaves. Pour in 900ml/1⅓ pints/3¾ cups water, bring to the boil, reduce the heat and simmer for 10 minutes.

2 Add the okra and cook for 10 minutes. Stir in the callaloo or spinach and cook for 5 minutes, until the okra is tender.

3 Prepare the creamed yam. Place the yam in a pan with the lemon juice and add cold water to cover. Bring to the boil and cook for 15–20 minutes, until tender. Drain well, return to the pan and dry it out over the heat for a few seconds. Mash with the butter and cream, and season well. Stir in the chives.

4 Season the soup and stir in the parsley. To serve, divide the creamed yam between six bowls and ladle the soup around it.

Rice and Bean: Energy 323kcal/1358kJ; Protein 10.7g; Carbohydrate 37g, of which sugars 5.6g; Fat 12.9g, of which saturates 6.7g; Cholesterol 40mg; Calcium 159mg; Fibre 4.6g; Sodium 138mg.
Salt Cod and Okra: Energy 322kcal/1352kJ; Protein 10.7g; Carbohydrate 36.7g, of which sugars 5.3g; Fat 12.8g, of which saturates 6.6g; Cholesterol 40mg; Calcium 159mg; Fibre 4.6g; Sodium 137mg.

Chicken and Ginger Soup

This aromatic soup is rich with coconut milk and intensely flavoured with galangal, lemon grass and kaffir lime leaves.

Serves 4–6

4 lemon grass stalks, roots trimmed
2 x 400ml/14fl oz cans coconut milk
475ml/16fl oz/2 cups chicken stock
2.5cm/1in piece fresh root ginger, peeled and thinly sliced
10 black peppercorns, crushed
10 kaffir lime leaves, torn
300g/11oz skinless boneless chicken breast portions, cut into thin strips
115g/4oz/1 cup button (white) mushrooms
50g/2oz/½ cup baby corn cobs, quartered lengthways
60ml/4 tbsp lime juice
45ml/3 tbsp fish sauce

For the garnish

fresh red chillies, seeded and chopped
spring onions (scallions), chopped
fresh coriander (cilantro) leaves, chopped

1 Cut off the lower 5cm/2in from each lemon grass stalk and chop it finely. Bruise the remaining pieces of stalk.

2 Bring the coconut milk and chicken stock to the boil in a large pan. Add the bruised lemon grass, the ginger, peppercorns and half the lime leaves, lower the heat and simmer gently for 10 minutes. Strain into a clean pan.

3 Return the soup to the heat, then add the chopped lemon grass, chicken, mushrooms and corn. Simmer for 5–7 minutes or until the chicken is cooked.

4 Stir in the lime juice and fish sauce, then add the remaining lime leaves. Serve hot, garnished with chillies, spring onions and coriander.

Cook's Tip

Store root ginger in the freezer. It thaws rapidly or can be shaved or grated while frozen.

Chicken Soup with Crispy Shallots

This Thai-inspired soup is topped with crisp shallots.

Serves 6

40g/1½oz/3 tbsp butter
1 onion, finely chopped
2 garlic cloves, chopped
2.5cm/1in piece fresh root ginger, finely chopped
10ml/2 tsp green curry paste
2.5ml/½ tsp turmeric
400ml/14fl oz can coconut milk
475ml/16fl oz/2 cups chicken stock
2 lime leaves, shredded
1 lemon grass stalk, finely chopped
8 skinless, boneless chicken thighs
350g/12oz spinach, chopped
10ml/2 tsp fish sauce
30ml/2 tbsp lime juice
30ml/2 tbsp vegetable oil
salt and ground black pepper
2 shallots, thinly sliced
handful of Thai basil leaves, to garnish

1 Melt the butter in a large, heavy pan. Add the onion, garlic and ginger, then cook for 4–5 minutes, until softened. Stir in the curry paste and turmeric, and cook for a further 2–3 minutes, stirring continuously.

2 Pour in two-thirds of the coconut milk; cook for 5 minutes. Add the stock, lime leaves, lemon grass and chicken. Heat until simmering; cook for 15 minutes or until the chicken is tender.

3 Remove the chicken thighs with a draining spoon and set them aside to cool. Add the spinach to the pan and cook for 3–4 minutes. Stir in the remaining coconut milk and seasoning, then process the soup in a food processor or blender until almost smooth. Return the soup to the rinsed-out pan.

4 Cut the chicken thighs into bitesize pieces and stir these into the soup with the fish sauce and lime juice.

5 Reheat the soup gently until hot, but do not let it boil. Meanwhile, heat the oil in a frying pan and cook the shallots for 6–8 minutes, until crisp and golden, stirring occasionally. Drain on kitchen paper. Ladle the soup into bowls, then top with the basil leaves and fried shallots, and serve.

Chicken and Ginger: Energy 87kcal/371kJ; Protein 13.1g; Carbohydrate 6.8g, of which sugars 6.7g; Fat 1.1g, of which saturates 0.4g; Cholesterol 35mg; Calcium 42mg; Fibre 0.3g; Sodium 620mg.
Chicken with Shallots: Energy 198kcal/827kJ; Protein 16.5g; Carbohydrate 6.5g, of which sugars 5.5g; Fat 12g, of which saturates 4.6g; Cholesterol 84mg; Calcium 157mg; Fibre 2.3g; Sodium 266mg.

Hot and Spicy Chicken Soup with Charmoula Butter

Inspired by the ingredients of North Africa, this soup is spiced with chilli and served with pungent lemon butter.

Serves 6

50g/2oz/¼ cup butter
450g/1lb skinless boneless chicken breast, cut into strips
1 onion, chopped
2 garlic cloves, crushed
7.5ml/1½ tsp plain (all-purpose) flour
15ml/1 tbsp harissa
1 litre/1¾ pints/4 cups chicken stock
400g/14oz can chopped tomatoes
400g/14oz can chickpeas, drained and rinsed
salt and ground black pepper
lemon wedges, to serve

For the charmoula butter
50g/2oz/¼ cup butter
30ml/2 tbsp chopped fresh coriander (cilantro)
2 garlic cloves, crushed
5ml/1 tsp ground cumin
1 fresh red chilli, seeded and chopped
pinch of saffron threads
finely grated rind of ½ lemon
5ml/1 tsp paprika
25g/1oz/1 cup coarse dried white breadcrumbs

1 Melt the butter in a large pan. Add the chicken and cook for 5–6 minutes, until beginning to brown, then use a draining spoon to remove the strips and set aside. Add the onion and garlic and cook over a gentle heat for 4–5 minutes, until soft.

2 Stir in the flour and cook for 3–4 minutes, stirring, until beginning to brown. Stir in the harissa and cook for 1 minute. Gradually stir in the stock and bring to the boil, stirring.

3 Stir in the tomatoes. Replace the chicken and add the chickpeas. Cover and simmer for 20 minutes. Season well.

4 For the charmoula butter, beat the coriander, garlic, cumin, chilli, saffron strands, lemon rind and paprika into the butter. When well combined, stir in the breadcrumbs.

5 Ladle the soup into bowls. Spoon a little charmoula butter into each and serve with lemon wedges.

Chicken Soup with Corn and Butter Beans

Based on a vegetable dish from the southern states of America, this soup includes succulent fresh corn kernels with bacon and chicken. They are a delicious, and favourite, combination of complementary ingredients.

Serves 4

750ml/1¼ pints/3 cups chicken stock
4 boneless, skinless chicken breasts
50g/2oz/¼ cup butter
2 onions, chopped
115g/4oz piece rindless smoked streaky (fatty) bacon, chopped
25g/1oz/¼ cup plain (all-purpose) flour
4 cobs of corn, kernels removed
300ml/½ pint/1¼ cups milk
400g/14oz can butter (lima) beans, drained
45ml/3 tbsp chopped fresh parsley
salt and ground black pepper

1 Bring the chicken stock to the boil in a large pan. Add the chicken breasts and bring back to the boil. Reduce the heat and cook for 12–15 minutes, until cooked through and tender. Use a draining spoon to remove the chicken from the pan and leave to cool. Reserve the stock.

2 Melt the butter in a pan. Add the onions and cook for 4–5 minutes, until softened.

3 Add the bacon and cook for a 5–6 minutes, until beginning to brown. Sprinkle in the flour and cook for 1 minute, stirring continuously. Gradually stir in the hot stock and bring to the boil, stirring until thickened. Remove from the heat.

4 Stir in the corn and half the milk. Return the pan to the heat and cook, stirring occasionally, for 12–15 minutes until the corn is tender.

5 Cut the chicken into bitesize pieces and stir into the soup. Stir in the butter beans and the remaining milk. Bring to the boil and cook for 5 minutes, season well and stir in the parsley.

Hot and Spicy Chicken: Energy 493kcal/2050kJ; Protein 36g; Carbohydrate 8.5g, of which sugars 1g; Fat 35.1g, of which saturates 9.1g; Cholesterol 258mg; Calcium 46mg; Fibre 0.8g; Sodium 178mg.
Chicken with Corn: Energy 570kcal/2395kJ; Protein 52.6g; Carbohydrate 44.6g, of which sugars 16.6g; Fat 21.4g, of which saturates 10.3g; Cholesterol 155mg; Calcium 159mg; Fibre 7.3g; Sodium 1119mg.

Chicken Soup with Egg and Lemon

There are many variations of this classic soup – here, the egg-lemon contingent is added as a sauce, rather than used as the stock.

Serves 4–6

1 chicken, about 1.6kg/3½lb
2 onions, halved
2 carrots
3 celery sticks, cut into chunks
a few sprigs of flat leaf parsley
3 or 4 black peppercorns
50g/2oz/generous ⅓ cup short grain rice
salt
lemon wedges, to serve

For the egg and lemon sauce
5ml/1 tsp cornflour (cornstarch)
2 large (US extra large) eggs, at room temperature
juice of 1–2 lemons

1 Place the chicken in a pan. Add 1.75 litres/3 pints/7½ cups water. Bring to the boil and skim off scum. Add the vegetables, parsley and peppercorns, season with salt and bring to the boil. Lower the heat, cover and simmer for 1 hour (longer if using a boiling fowl or stewing chicken), until the chicken is very tender.

2 Lift out the chicken. Strain the stock and set it aside, but discard the vegetables. Pull away the chicken breasts, skin them and dice the flesh. Do the same with the legs. Pour the stock back into the pan and add the chicken meat.

3 Shortly before serving, heat the stock and diced chicken. When the stock boils, add the rice. Cover and cook for about 8 minutes, until soft. Set aside off the heat to cool slightly.

4 For the sauce, mix the cornflour to a paste with a little water. Beat the eggs in a separate bowl, add the lemon juice and the cornflour mixture and beat until smooth.

5 Gradually beat a ladleful of soup into the egg and beat for 1 minute. Add a second ladleful in the same way. Gradually, but vigorously, stir the sauce into the soup. Warm the soup over a gentle heat for 1–2 minutes. Do not simmer or it will curdle. Serve immediately in warmed bowls, with a plate of lemon wedges for those who wish to add extra juice.

Chicken, Leek and Barley Soup

This recipe is based on the traditional Scottish soup, cock-a-leekie.

Serves 6

115g/4oz/⅔ cup pearl barley
1 chicken, weighing about 2kg/4¼lb
900g/2lb leeks
1 bouquet garni
1 large carrot, thickly sliced
2.4 litres/4 pints/10 cups chicken or beef stock
400g/14oz ready-to-eat prunes
salt and ground black pepper
chopped fresh parsley, to garnish

1 Rinse the pearl barley in a sieve (strainer) under cold water, then cook it in a large pan of boiling water for 10 minutes. Drain, rinse well and drain thoroughly. Set aside in a cool place.

2 Cut the breast portions from the chicken and set aside, then place the remaining carcass in the pan. Cut half the leeks into 5cm/2in lengths and add them to the pan with the bouquet garni, carrot and stock.

3 Bring the stock to the boil, then reduce the heat and cover the pan. Simmer gently for 1 hour, skimming occasionally. Add the chicken breasts and cook for another 30 minutes until they are just cooked. Leave until cool enough to handle.

4 Strain, and skim the fat from, the stock. Reserve the chicken breasts and the meat from the carcass. Discard the skin, bones, cooked vegetables and herbs. Return the stock to the pan.

5 Add the barley. Bring to the boil, then lower the heat and cook very gently for 15–20 minutes, until the barley is just tender. Season the soup to taste and add the prunes. Thinly slice the remaining leeks and add them to the pan. Bring to the boil, cover and simmer gently for 10 minutes, or until the leeks are cooked.

6 Slice the chicken breast portions and then add them to the soup with the remaining chicken meat from the carcass, sliced or cut into neat pieces. Reheat the soup, if necessary, then ladle it into warm, deep soup plates and sprinkle with plenty of chopped parsley to garnish.

Chicken with Egg: Energy 599kcal/2,488kJ; Protein 53.5g; Carbohydrate 8.5g, of which sugars 3g; Fat 39.1g, of which saturates 10.9g; Cholesterol 359mg; Calcium 50mg; Fibre 1.2g; Sodium 236mg.
Chicken, Leek, Barley: Energy 326kcal/1383kJ; Protein 33.7g; Carbohydrate 44.4g, of which sugars 27.2g; Fat 2.7g, of which saturates 0.5g; Cholesterol 82mg; Calcium 73mg; Fibre 7.5g; Sodium 85mg.

Chicken, Leek and Celery Soup

This makes a substantial main course soup with fresh crusty bread.

Serves 4–6

1.4kg/3lb chicken
1 small head of celery, trimmed
1 onion, coarsely chopped
1 bouquet garni
3 large leeks
65g/2½oz/5 tbsp butter
2 potatoes, cut into chunks
150ml/¼ pint/⅔ cup dry white wine
30–45ml/2–3 tbsp single (light) cream (optional)
salt and ground black pepper
90g/3½oz pancetta, grilled until crisp, to garnish

1 Cut the breasts from the chicken and set aside. Chop the rest of the chicken carcass into 8–10 pieces and place in a pan. Chop 4–5 of the celery sticks and add them to the pan with the onion and bouquet garni. Pour in 2.4 litres/4 pints/10 cups water to cover the ingredients and bring to the boil. Reduce the heat and cover the pan, then simmer for 1½ hours.

2 Remove the chicken and cut off and reserve the meat. Strain the stock, then return it to the pan and boil rapidly until it has reduced to about 1.5 litres/2½ pints/6¼ cups.

3 Set about 150g/5oz leeks aside. Slice the remaining leeks and the remaining celery, reserving any celery leaves. Melt half the butter in a pan. Add the sliced leeks and celery, cover and cook over a low heat for 10 minutes, until soft but not brown. Add the potatoes, wine and 1.2 litres/2 pints/5 cups of the stock. Season, bring to the boil and reduce the heat. Part-cover and simmer for 15–20 minutes, or until the potatoes are cooked.

4 Dice the reserved uncooked chicken. Melt the remaining butter in a pan and fry the chicken for 5–7 minutes, until cooked. Slice the remaining leeks, add to the chicken and cook, stirring occasionally, for a further 3–4 minutes, until just cooked.

5 Purée the soup and diced chicken from the stock. Season and add more stock if the soup is thick. Stir in the cream and chicken and leek mixture. Reheat gently and serve topped with pancetta and the chopped reserved celery leaves.

Corn and Chicken Soup

A combination of chicken, creamed corn and whole kernels gives this classic Chinese soup its characteristic texture. It tastes delicious, is suitably warming on a cold day and, above all, is easy to make if you are in a hurry or have friends for lunch.

Serves 4–6

1 skinless boneless chicken breast, about 115g/4oz, cubed
10ml/2 tsp light soy sauce
15ml/1 tbsp Chinese rice wine
5ml/1 tsp cornflour (cornstarch)
5ml/1 tsp sesame oil
15ml/1 tbsp vegetable oil
5ml/1 tsp grated fresh root ginger
1 litre/1¾ pints/4 cups chicken stock
425g/15oz can creamed corn
225g/8oz can corn
2 eggs, beaten
salt and ground black pepper
2–3 spring onions (scallions), green parts only, sliced into tiny rounds, to garnish

1 Mince (grind) the chicken in a food processor or blender, taking care not to overprocess. Transfer the chicken to a bowl and stir in the soy sauce, rice wine, cornflour, 60ml/4 tbsp water, sesame oil and seasoning. Cover with clear film (plastic wrap) and leave for about 15 minutes so the chicken absorbs the flavours.

2 Heat a wok over medium heat. Add the vegetable oil and swirl it around. Add the ginger and stir-fry for a few seconds. Pour in the stock with the creamed corn and corn kernels. Bring to just below boiling point.

3 Spoon about 90ml/6 tbsp of the hot liquid into the chicken mixture until it forms a smooth paste and stir. Return to the wok. Slowly bring to the boil, stirring constantly, then simmer for 2–3 minutes or until the chicken is cooked.

4 Pour the beaten eggs into the soup in a slow steady stream, using a fork or chopsticks to stir the top of the soup in a figure-of-eight pattern. The egg will set in lacy shreds. Serve immediately with the spring onions on top.

Chicken, Leek, Celery: Energy 294kcal/1246kJ; Protein 40.5g; Carbohydrate 22.1g, of which sugars 5.9g; Fat 2.8g, of which saturates 0.7g; Cholesterol 105mg; Calcium 69mg; Fibre 4.8g; Sodium 124mg.
Corn and Chicken: Energy 196kcal/831kJ; Protein 10g; Carbohydrate 29.9g, of which sugars 10.7g; Fat 4.7g, of which saturates 1g; Cholesterol 77mg; Calcium 17mg; Fibre 1.6g; Sodium 447mg.

Chicken and Tomato Soup with Smoked Haddock

Christophene is a pale green gourd. In southern Africa is is called cho-cho, while elsewhere it is called choko, chayote or vegetable pear. The flesh has a delicate flavour.

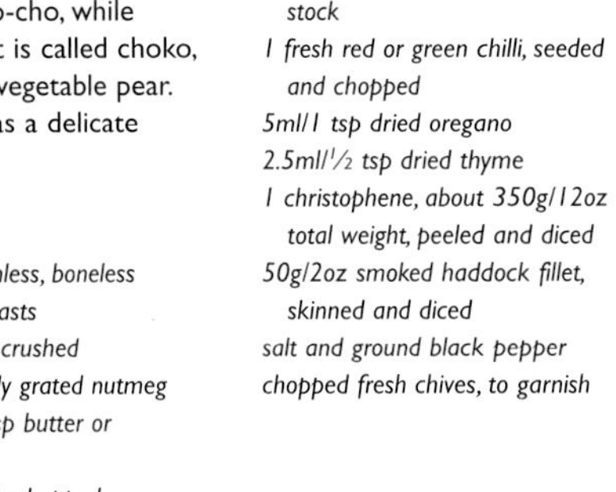

Serves 4

225g/8oz skinless, boneless chicken breasts
1 garlic clove, crushed
pinch of freshly grated nutmeg
25g/1oz/2 tbsp butter or margarine
½ onion, finely chopped
15ml/1 tbsp tomato purée (paste)
400g/14oz can tomatoes, puréed
1.2 litres/2 pints/5 cups chicken stock
1 fresh red or green chilli, seeded and chopped
5ml/1 tsp dried oregano
2.5ml/½ tsp dried thyme
1 christophene, about 350g/12oz total weight, peeled and diced
50g/2oz smoked haddock fillet, skinned and diced
salt and ground black pepper
chopped fresh chives, to garnish

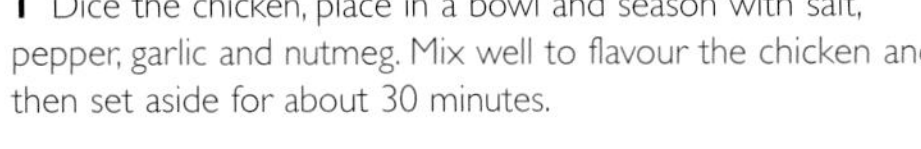

1 Dice the chicken, place in a bowl and season with salt, pepper, garlic and nutmeg. Mix well to flavour the chicken and then set aside for about 30 minutes.

2 Melt the butter or margarine in a large pan, add the chicken and sauté over a medium heat for 5–6 minutes. Stir in the onion and sauté gently for a further 5 minutes, until the onion is slightly softened.

3 Add the tomato purée, puréed tomatoes, stock, chilli, dried herbs and christophene. Bring to the boil, reduce the heat and cover the pan. Then simmer gently for 35 minutes, until the christophene is tender.

4 Add the smoked fish, and simmer for a further 5 minutes, until the fish is cooked through. Taste the soup and adjust the seasoning, then pour it into warmed soup bowls. Garnish with a sprinkling of chopped chives and serve.

Chicken Soup with Cheese and Chickpeas

This simple chicken soup originates from Tlalpan, in Mexico City. The soup is made more substantial by the addition of cheese and chickpeas.

Serves 6

1.5 litres/2½ pints/6¼ cups chicken stock
½ chipotle chilli, seeded
2 skinless, boneless chicken breasts
1 avocado
4 spring onions (scallions), finely sliced
400g/14oz can chicpeas, drained
salt and ground black pepper
75g/3oz Cheddar cheese, grated, to serve

1 Pour the stock into a large pan and add the dried chilli. Bring to the boil, add the chicken breasts, then lower the heat and cover the pan. Simmer the soup gently for about 15 minutes or until the chicken is cooked. Remove the chicken from the pan and let it cool a little.

2 Using two forks, shred the chicken into small pieces. Set it aside. Pour the stock and chilli into a food processor or blender and process until smooth. Return the stock to the pan.

3 Cut the avocado in half, remove the skin and stone, then slice the flesh into 2cm/¾in pieces. Add it to the stock, with the spring onions and chickpeas. Return the shredded chicken to the pan, with salt and pepper to taste, and heat gently.

4 Spoon the soup into heated bowls. Serve with a bowl of grated cheese at the table, for adding to the soup as required.

Cook's Tip

When buying the avocado for this soup choose one that is slightly under-ripe; not only does this makes it easier to handle when peeling and slicing, but it also means the pieces will retain their shape and texture in the soup. Unripe avocadoes feel hard to the touch; ripened fruits give to gentle pressure.

Chicken and Tomato: Energy 133kcal/558kJ; Protein 16.7g; Carbohydrate 3.2g, of which sugars 2.4g; Fat 6g, of which saturates 3.5g; Cholesterol 57mg; Calcium 36mg; Fibre 1.1g; Sodium 167mg.
Chicken with Cheese: Energy 163kcal/686kJ; Protein 17.3g; Carbohydrate 11.3g, of which sugars 0.5g; Fat 5.7g, of which saturates 1g; Cholesterol 35mg; Calcium 36mg; Fibre 3.4g; Sodium 178mg.

Chicken Soup with Coconut, Ginger and Lime

A fragrant blend of lemon grass, ginger and lime, with a hint of chilli.

Serves 4

5ml/1 tsp oil
1–2 fresh red chillies, seeded and chopped
2 garlic cloves, crushed
1 large leek, thinly sliced
600ml/1 pint/2½ cups chicken stock
400ml/14fl oz/1⅔ cups coconut milk
450g/1lb boneless skinless chicken, cut into pieces
30ml/2 tbsp Thai fish sauce
1 lemon grass stalk, split
1–2 kaffir lime leaves (optional)
2.5cm/1in piece fresh root ginger, peeled and finely chopped
5ml/1 tsp sugar
75g/3oz/¾ cup frozen peas, thawed
45ml/3 tbsp coriander (cilantro), chopped

1 Heat the oil in a large pan and cook the chillies and garlic for about 2 minutes. Add the leek and cook, stirring frequently, for a further 2 minutes.

2 Stir in the stock and coconut milk and bring to the boil.

3 Add the chicken, with the fish sauce, lemon grass, lime leaves (if using), ginger and sugar. Reduce the heat so that the soup just simmers and cover the pan.

4 Simmer for 15 minutes, or until the chicken is tender, stirring occasionally. Add the thawed peas and cook for a further 3 minutes. Remove the lemon grass and stir in the coriander just before serving.

Cook's Tip
Fish sauce is widely used in Thai, Indonesian and Malaysian cooking. It is strong and distinctive but can be omitted from this recipe and light soy sauce used instead. Light soy sauce is extremely salty, so add it in small amounts, tasting as you add.

Chicken and Asparagus Broth

This is a very delicate and delicious soup. When fresh asparagus is not in season, frozen asparagus is an acceptable substitute. Soy sauce boosts the flavour.

Serves 4

140g/5oz skinless boneless chicken breast
5ml/1 tsp cornflour (cornstarch)
pinch of salt
5ml/1 tsp egg white
115g/4oz asparagus
700ml/1¼ pints/3 cups chicken stock
10ml/2 tsp dark soy sauce
salt and ground black pepper
fresh coriander (cilantro) leaves, to garnish

1 Cut the chicken meat into small, thin slices each about the size of a postage stamp. Mix the cornflour with just a little water to make a smooth paste. Mix with a pinch of salt, then add the egg white and stir to make a smooth thin paste.

2 Cut off and discard the tough stems of the asparagus (or use for stock, see Cook's Tip, below) and diagonally cut the tender ends of the spears into short, even lengths.

3 In a wok or pan, bring the stock to a rolling boil, add the asparagus and soy sauce, and bring back to the boil, cooking for 2 minutes.

4 Add the chicken, stir to separate and bring back to the boil once more. Adjust the seasonings. Serve hot, garnished with fresh coriander leaves.

Cook's Tip
Instead of discarding the slightly tough stems use them to flavour the stock. Slice them and simmer in the stock for 30 minutes, then strain the stock, pressing all the liquid out of the asparagus. For a cloudy or creamy soup, cook the asparagus trimmings in the stock, then leave to cool for a while before puréeing in a food processor or blender. Press through a sieve (strainer) to remove all the fibrous bits of asparagus. The stock will have a delicious, pronounced asparagus flavour.

Chicken with Coconut: Energy 127kcal/543kJ; Protein 19.5g; Carbohydrate 9.6g, of which sugars 9.4g; Fat 1.6g, of which saturates 0.6g; Cholesterol 53mg; Calcium 61mg; Fibre 0.5g; Sodium 395mg.
Chicken and Asparagus: Energy 49kcal/208kJ; Protein 9.4g; Carbohydrate 1.7g, of which sugars 0.6g; Fat 0.6g, of which saturates 0.1g; Cholesterol 25mg; Calcium 10mg; Fibre 0.5g; Sodium 24mg.

Chicken Soup with Roasted Ham and Prawns

This delicious, simple dish combines chicken, ham and prawns in a no-frills, high-protein Chinese soup.

Serves 4

115g/4oz skinless boneless chicken breast
115g/4oz honey-roast ham
115g/4oz peeled cooked prawns (shrimp)
700ml/1¼ pints/3 cups chicken stock
salt
chopped spring onions (scallions), to garnish

1 Thinly slice the chicken breast and ham into small pieces. If the prawns are large, cut them in half lengthways.

2 In a wok or pan, bring the stock to a rolling boil and add the chicken, ham and prawns. Bring back to the boil, add salt to taste and simmer for 1 minute.

3 Ladle into individual soup bowls. Serve hot, garnished with chopped spring onions.

Variation
For a mixed meat and vegetable soup, add some shredded Chinese cabbage with the chicken and ham. For a crunchy contrasting texture, try stirring in a few drained and sliced canned water chestnuts. Serve the soup with shredded Chinese pickled ginger and pickled garlic for sprinkling over after serving.

Cook's Tip
This simple everyday soup is just fine made with economical peeled cooked shellfish even though raw prawns (shrimp) would be superior. The ideal stock would be home-made using chicken and pork (such as a carcass and bones from belly pork or meaty spare ribs) but, to be practical, simply use good bought stock or a superior bouillon powder or cube.

Spiced Chicken and Vegetable Broth

This is perhaps the most popular of Indonesian soups.

Serves 4–6

30ml/2 tbsp palm, groundnut (peanut) or corn oil
25g/1oz fresh root ginger, finely chopped
25g/1oz fresh turmeric root, finely chopped, or 5ml/1 tsp ground turmeric
1 lemon grass stalk, finely chopped
4–5 kaffir lime leaves, crushed with fingers
4 candlenuts, coarsely ground
2 garlic cloves, crushed
5ml/1 tsp coriander seeds
5ml/1 tsp terasi (Indonesian shrimp paste)
2 litres/3½ pints/8 cups chicken stock
corn or vegetable oil, for deep-frying
2 waxy potatoes, finely sliced
350g/12oz skinless boneless chicken breast, thinly sliced widthways
150g/5oz leafy green cabbage, finely sliced
150g/5oz/generous ½ cup beansprouts
3 hard-boiled eggs, thinly sliced
salt and ground black pepper

For serving

1 bunch fresh coriander (cilantro) leaves, roughly chopped
2–3 spring onions (scallions), finely sliced
2–3 fresh hot red or green chillies, seeded and finely sliced
2 limes, cut into wedges
Indonesian sweet soy sauce

1 Heat the oil in a pan, stir in the ginger, turmeric, lemon grass, lime leaves, candlenuts, garlic, coriander seeds and terasi and fry until darker and fragrant. Pour in the stock, bring to the boil, then reduce the heat and simmer for about 20 minutes.

2 Heat the oil for deep-frying in a wok. Fry the potatoes until crisp and golden. Drain on kitchen paper and put aside.

3 Strain the stock, pour back into the pan and season. Return to the boil, then reduce the heat and add the chicken. Simmer for 2–3 minutes until cooked but still tender.

4 Divide the cabbage and beansprouts among serving bowls and ladel in the broth, dividing the chicken equally between the bowls. Top with the eggs and potatoes. Serve at once, with the coriander, spring onions, chillies, lime wedges and soy sauce.

Chicken with Ham: Energy 83kcal/350kJ; Protein 17.4g; Carbohydrate 0.3g, of which sugars 0.3g; Fat 1.5g, of which saturates 0.5g; Cholesterol 93mg; Calcium 27mg; Fibre 0g; Sodium 562mg.
Spiced Chicken Broth: Energy 296kcal/1238kJ; Protein 21.1g; Carbohydrate 14.8g, of which sugars 3g; Fat 17.5g, of which saturates 2.8g; Cholesterol 136mg; Calcium 63mg; Fibre 2.7g; Sodium 96mg.

Mulligatawny Soup

Mulligatawny (which literally means "pepper water") was introduced into Scotland in the late 18th century by members of the colonial services returning home from India.

Serves 4

50g/2oz/4 tbsp butter or 60ml/4 tbsp oil
2 large chicken joints (about 350g/12oz each)
1 onion, chopped
1 carrot, chopped
1 small turnip, chopped
about 15ml/1 tbsp curry powder, to taste
4 cloves
6 black peppercorns, lightly crushed
50g/2oz/¼ cup lentils
900ml/1½ pints/3¾ cups chicken stock
40g/1½oz/¼ cup sultanas (golden raisins)
salt and ground black pepper

1 Melt the butter or heat the oil in a large pan, then brown the chicken over a brisk heat. Transfer the chicken to a plate and set aside.

2 Add the onion, carrot and turnip to the pan and cook, stirring occasionally, until lightly coloured. Stir in the curry powder, cloves and crushed peppercorns and cook for 1–2 minutes, then add the lentils.

3 Pour the stock into the pan, bring to the boil, then add the sultanas, the chicken and any juices from the plate. Cover and simmer gently for about 1¼ hours.

4 Remove the chicken from the pan and discard the skin and bones. Chop the flesh, return to the soup and reheat. Check the seasoning before serving the soup piping hot.

Cook's Tip

Choose red split lentils for the best colour, although either green or brown lentils could also be used. The soup is also delicious made with split peas but these should be soaked overnight in cold water, then drained and added instead of the lentils.

Smoked Turkey and Lentil Soup

Lentils seem to enhance the flavour of smoked turkey, and combined with four tasty vegetables they make a fine meal-in-a-pot.

Serves 4

25g/1oz/2 tbsp butter
1 large carrot, chopped
1 onion, chopped
1 leek, white part only, chopped
1 celery stick, chopped
115g/4oz mushrooms, chopped
50ml/2fl oz/¼ cup dry white wine
1.2 litres/2 pints/5 cups chicken stock
10ml/2 tsp dried thyme
1 bay leaf
115g/4oz/½ cup green lentils
75g/3oz smoked turkey meat, diced
salt and ground black pepper

1 Melt the butter in a large pan. Add the carrot, onion, leek, celery and mushrooms. Cook for 3–5 minutes until golden.

2 Stir in the wine and chicken stock. Bring to the boil and skim off any foam that rises to the surface. Add the thyme and bay leaf. Lower the heat, cover and simmer gently for 30 minutes.

3 Add the lentils and continue cooking, covered, for a further 30–40 minutes until they are just tender. Stir the soup occasionally.

4 Add the turkey and season to taste with salt and pepper. Cook until just heated through. Ladle into bowls and serve.

Variation

Try smoked chicken instead of the turkey in this soup. Follow the recipe, using dry (hard) cider, if preferred, instead of wine and adding a good dash of medium sherry. This enriches the soup and balances the tart cider. Use smoked chicken breast instead of turkey and add the grated rind of 1 lemon to bring a little zesty flavour. Finally, stir in a little single (light) or soured cream before serving, if liked.

Mulligatawny: Energy 347kcal/1447kJ; Protein 28.7g; Carbohydrate 16g, of which sugars 9.6g; Fat 19.1g, of which saturates 8.9g; Cholesterol 142mg; Calcium 54mg; Fibre 2.1g; Sodium 160mg.
Turkey and Lentil: Energy 201kcal/844kJ; Protein 15g; Carbohydrate 20.4g, of which sugars 4.1g; Fat 6.3g, of which saturates 3.5g; Cholesterol 27mg; Calcium 39mg; Fibre 3.4g; Sodium 73mg.

Curried Chicken Soup

With a culinary culture born from Indian, Malay, Chinese and European traditions, the Eurasians have some distinct dishes of their own. This is one such example – a delicious spicy chicken soup. Traditionally, chicken feet are added with the chicken!

Serves 4–6

1 chicken, about 1kg/2¼lb
2 cinnamon sticks
5ml/1 tsp black peppercorns
5ml/1 tsp fennel seeds
5ml/1 tsp cumin seeds
15 ml/1 tbsp ghee or vegetable oil with a little butter
15–30ml/1–2 tbsp brown mustard seeds
a handful of fresh curry leaves
salt and ground black pepper
2 limes, quartered, to serve

For the curry paste

40g/1½oz fresh root ginger, peeled and chopped
4 garlic cloves, chopped
4 shallots, chopped
2 lemon grass stalks, trimmed and chopped
4 dried red chillies, soaked to soften, drained, seeded and the pulp scraped out
15–30ml/1–2 tbsp Indian curry powder

1 To make the curry paste, grind the ginger with the garlic, shallots and lemon grass, using a mortar and pestle or food processor or blender. Add the chilli pulp and curry powder and set aside.

2 Put the chicken and the chicken feet, if using, in a deep pan with the cinnamon sticks, peppercorns, fennel and cumin seeds. Add enough water to just cover, and bring it to the boil. Reduce the heat and cook gently for about 1 hour, until the chicken is cooked. Remove the chicken from the broth, skin it and shred the meat. Strain the broth.

3 In a pan or wok, heat the ghee or oil. Stir in the mustard seeds and, once they begin to pop and give off a nutty aroma, add the curry paste. Fry the paste until fragrant, then pour in the strained broth. Bring the broth to the boil and season to taste with salt and pepper. Add the curry leaves and shredded chicken, and ladle the soup into bowls. Serve with wedges of lime to squeeze into the soup.

Chicken and Ginger Broth with Papaya

In the Philippines, this is a traditional peasant dish that is still cooked every day in rural areas. Generally the chicken and broth are served with steamed rice, but the broth is also sipped during the meal to cleanse and stimulate the palate.

Serves 4–6

15–30ml/1–2 tbsp palm or groundnut (peanut) oil
2 garlic cloves, finely chopped
1 large onion, sliced
40g/1½oz fresh root ginger, finely grated
2 whole dried chillies
1 chicken, left whole or jointed, trimmed of fat
30ml/2 tbsp patis (fish sauce)
600ml/1 pint/2½ cups chicken stock
1 small green papaya, cut into fine slices or strips
1 bunch fresh young chilli or basil leaves
salt and ground black pepper
cooked rice, to serve

1 Heat the oil in a wok or a large pan that has a lid. Stir in the garlic, onion and ginger and fry until they begin to colour. Stir in the chillies, add the chicken and fry until the skin is lightly browned all over. Pour in the patis, stock and 1.2 litres/2 pints/ 5 cups water, adding more water if necessary so that the chicken is completely covered. Bring to the boil, reduce the heat, cover and simmer gently for about 1½ hours, until the chicken is very tender.

2 Season the stock with salt and pepper and add the papaya. Continue to simmer for a further 10–15 minutes, then stir in the chilli or basil leaves. Serve the chicken and broth in warmed bowls, with bowls of steamed rice.

Variation

Young chilli leaves, plucked off the chilli plant, are added at the end to spike the soup with their unique flavour. There is no similar substitute for these leaves, but, if you don't have any, you can use fresh basil instead.

Curried Chicken: Energy 264kcal/1093kJ; Protein 20.7g; Carbohydrate 1.6g, of which sugars 1g; Fat 19.4g, of which saturates 6.3g; Cholesterol 112mg; Calcium 19mg; Fibre 0.5g; Sodium 104mg.
Chicken and Ginger: Energy 290kcal/1219kJ; Protein 46.4g; Carbohydrate 9.8g, of which sugars 8.7g; Fat 7.5g, of which saturates 1.5g; Cholesterol 169mg; Calcium 40mg; Fibre 2.2g; Sodium 150mg.

Chicken Drumsticks in Lemon Grass Broth

This quick and easy recipe from Vietnam contains the unusual combination of ginger and lemon grass with mandarin orange and chillies. The dish is served topped with peanuts, which are first roasted, then skinned.

Serves 4–6

3 chicken legs (thighs and drumsticks)
15ml/1 tbsp vegetable oil
2cm/¾in piece fresh root ginger, finely chopped
1 garlic clove, crushed
1 small fresh red chilli, seeded and finely chopped
5cm/2in piece lemon grass, shredded
150ml/¼ pint/⅔ cup chicken stock
15ml/1 tbsp fish sauce
10ml/2 tsp sugar
2.5ml/½ tsp salt
juice of ½ lemon
50g/2oz raw peanuts
2 spring onions (scallions), shredded
zest of 1 mandarin or satsuma, shredded
plain boiled rice or rice noodles, to serve

1 With the heel of a knife, chop through the narrow end of each of the chicken drumsticks. Remove the jointed parts of the chicken, then remove the skin. Rinse and pat dry with kitchen paper.

2 Heat the oil in a wok or large pan. Add the chicken, ginger, garlic, chilli and lemon grass and cook for 3–4 minutes. Add the chicken stock, fish sauce, sugar, salt and lemon juice. Cover the pan and simmer for 30–35 minutes.

3 To prepare the peanuts, the red skin must be removed. To do this grill (broil) or roast the peanuts under a medium heat until evenly brown, for 2–3 minutes. Turn the nuts out on to a clean cloth and rub briskly to loosen the skins.

4 Transfer the chicken from the pan to a warmed serving dish, and sprinkle with the roasted peanuts, shredded spring onions and the zest of the mandarin or satsuma. Serve hot with plain boiled rice or rice noodles.

Clay-pot Chicken Soup

This deliciously spiced dish is a refined version of the ancient cooking method, whereby the food was placed in a clay pot and buried in the dying embers of an open fire.

Serves 4–6

1.3–1.6kg/3–3½lb chicken
45ml/3 tbsp grated fresh coconut
30ml/2 tbsp vegetable oil
1 small onion, finely chopped
2 garlic cloves, crushed
5cm/2in piece lemon grass
2.5cm/1in piece fresh galangal or fresh root ginger, thinly sliced
2 green chillies, seeded and chopped
12mm/½in cube shrimp paste
400g/14oz can coconut milk
600ml/1 pint/2½ cups chicken stock
2 kaffir lime leaves (optional)
15ml/1 tbsp sugar
15ml/1 tbsp rice vinegar
2 ripe tomatoes, peeled, seeded and diced
30ml/2 tbsp chopped fresh coriander leaves (cilantro), to garnish

1 To joint the chicken, remove the legs and wings with a sharp knife. Skin the pieces, divide the drumsticks from the thighs and, using kitchen scissors, remove the lower part of the chicken, leaving only the breast piece. Remove as many of the bones as you can, to make the dish easier to eat. Cut the breast piece into four or six and set aside.

2 Dry-fry the coconut in a large wok until evenly browned. Add the vegetable oil, onion, garlic, lemon grass, galangal or ginger, chillies and shrimp paste. Fry for 2–4 minutes. Preheat the oven to 180°C/350°F/Gas 4. Add the chicken joints to the wok and brown evenly with the spices for 2–3 minutes.

3 Strain the coconut milk, and add the thin part with the chicken stock, lime leaves, if using, sugar and vinegar. Transfer to a glazed clay pot or oven-proof dish, cover and bake in the centre of the oven for 50 minutes, or until the chicken is tender. Stir in the thick part of the coconut milk and return to the oven for 5–10 minutes.

4 Add the tomatoes to the finished dish, sprinkle with the chopped coriander and serve.

Drumsticks in Lemon Grass: Energy 128kcal/535kJ; Protein 13g; Carbohydrate 3.2g, of which sugars 2.6g; Fat 7.1g, of which saturates 1.3g; Cholesterol 53mg; Calcium 14mg; Fibre 0.6g; Sodium 224mg.
Clay-pot Chicken: Energy 296kcal/1238kJ; Protein 21.1g; Carbohydrate 14.8g, of which sugars 3g; Fat 17.5g, of which saturates 2.8g; Cholesterol 136mg; Calcium 63mg; Fibre 2.7g; Sodium 96mg.

Chicken Broth with Dumplings

This is the classic comfort-and-cure Jewish recipe.

Serves 6–8
1–1.5kg/2¼–3¼lb chicken, cut into portions
2–3 onions, halved
3–5 carrots, thickly sliced
3–5 celery sticks, thickly sliced
1 small parsnip, cut in half
30–45ml/2–3 tbsp roughly chopped fresh parsley
30–45ml/2–3 tbsp chopped fresh dill
1–2 pinches ground turmeric
2 garlic cloves, finely chopped
salt and ground black pepper

For the dumplings
175g/6oz/¾ cup medium matzo meal
2 eggs, lightly beaten
45ml/3 tbsp vegetable oil
1 garlic clove, finely chopped
30ml/2 tbsp chopped fresh parsley, plus extra to garnish
½ onion, finely grated
salt and ground black pepper

1 Put the chicken, onions, carrots, celery, parsnip, parsley, half the dill and the turmeric in a pan. Add plenty of salt and pepper and 3–4 litres/5–7 pints/12–16 cups water.

2 Boil; immediately lower the heat and simmer, skimming scum that rises. This first scum will spoil the soup; once it is removed, cover and simmer for 2–3 hours. Remove the chicken, discard skin and bones, dice the meat and add to the soup.

3 For the dumplings combine the matzo meal with the eggs, oil, garlic, if using, parsley, onion and salt and pepper. Add about 90ml/6 tbsp water, mixing the ingredients to a thick, soft paste. Cover and chill for 30 minutes to firm up the mixture.

4 Bring a pan of water to the boil, then regulate the heat so that is simmers when adding dumplings. Have a bowl of cold water and wet your hands. Dip a spoon in cold water, take a spoonful of matzo batter and roll it into a ball by hand, then add to the pan. Quickly shape and add all the mixture. Cover and simmer the dumplings gently for 15–20 minutes. Drain and transfer to a plate for about 20 minutes to firm up.

5 Reheat the soup. Add the garlic and remaining dill. Serve the soup ladled over the dumplings and garnish with parsley.

Chicken, Pork and Sweet Potato Soup with Aubergine Sauce

This can be served as two courses or all together.

Serve 6–8
225g/8oz/generous 1 cup chickpeas, soaked overnight
1.3kg/3lb chicken, cut into eight
350g/12oz belly of pork, rind removed or pork fillet, cubed
2 chorizo, thickly sliced
2 onions, chopped
60ml/4 tbsp vegetable oil
2 garlic cloves, crushed
3 large tomatoes, peeled, seeded and chopped
15ml/1 tbsp tomato purée (paste)
1–2 sweet potatoes, cut into 1cm/½ in cubes
2 plantains, sliced (optional)
salt and ground black pepper
chives or chopped spring onions (scallions), to garnish
½ head Chinese leaves (Chinese cabbage), shredded, to serve

For the aubergine sauce
1 large aubergine (eggplant), skin pricked in places
3 garlic cloves, crushed
60–90ml/4–6 tbsp wine vinegar or cider vinegar

1 Put the drained chickpeas in a pan with water to cover; boil rapidly for 10 minutes. Reduce the heat and simmer for 30 minutes until the chickpeas are half tender. Drain.

2 Put the chickpeas, chicken, pork, chorizo and half of the onions in a pan with 2.5 litres/4 pints/10 cups water. Boil, lower the heat, cover and simmer for 1 hour until the meat is tender.

3 Preheat the oven to 200°C/400°F/Gas 6 for the aubergine sauce. Bake the aubergine for 30 minutes. Cool, peel and mash with the garlic, seasoning and vinegar to sharpen the sauce.

4 Heat the oil in a pan and fry the remaining onion and garlic for 5 minutes. Add the tomatoes and tomato purée and cook for 2 minutes. Add to the soup, with the sweet potato and plantains, if using. Simmer for 20 minutes until the sweet potato is cooked. Add the Chinese leaves for the last minute or two.

5 Serve the soup and vegetables separately, garnished with chives or spring onions. Serve with the aubergine sauce.

Chicken with Dumplings: Energy 266kcal/1115kJ; Protein 25.7g; Carbohydrate 24g, of which sugars 6.6g; Fat 7.5g, of which saturates 1.2g; Cholesterol 109mg; Calcium 48mg; Fibre 2.7g; Sodium 86mg.
Chicken, Pork, Potato: Energy 290kcal/1219kJ; Protein 46.4g; Carbohydrate 9.8g, of which sugars 8.7g; Fat 7.5g, of which saturates 1.5g; Cholesterol 169mg; Calcium 40mg; Fibre 2.2g; Sodium 150mg.

Potted Chicken Soup

This slow-cooked Eastern European dish can be eaten as a hotpot or soup. It is traditionally cooked in a flameproof dish over the hob, so that the chicken is allowed to cook steadily in its own juices until delightfully tender. It is then served in a broth laced with herbs and port.

Serves 6–8

8 chicken portions
6–8 firm ripe tomatoes, chopped
2 garlic cloves, crushed
3 onions, chopped
60ml/4 tbsp vegetable oil or melted lard
250ml/8fl oz/1 cup good quality chicken stock
2 bay leaves
10ml/2 tsp paprika
10 white peppercorns, bruised
handful of parsley, stalks reserved and leaves finely chopped
salt

1 Place the chicken, tomatoes and garlic in the flameproof pot. Cover and cook gently for 10–15 minutes.

2 Add the remaining ingredients, except the parsley, and stir well to combine.

3 Cover tightly and cook over a very low heat, stirring occasionally, for about 1¾–2 hours, or until the chicken is tender. Five minutes before the end of cooking, stir in the finely chopped parsley leaves. Serve with crusty bread or plain boiled white rice.

Variation

The vegetables in this dish can be varied to taste – try cannellini beans, sliced button (white) mushrooms or sliced courgettes (zucchini).

Cook's Tip

To add a bit of heat and spice to the soup, finely seed a red or green chilli and add in step 2.

Chicken Soup with Red Peppers and Herbs

This superb dish, with its colourful medley of sweet and crunchy vegetables, is one of the best potted chicken soups around. The secret of its success is when to add the vegetables so that they are cooked to perfection. For the best results, it is important to use fresh herbs rather than dried, although a mixture of fresh and dried herbs would not compromise the flavour too much.

Serves 6

60ml/4 tbsp vegetable oil or melted lard
1 mild onion, thinly sliced
2 garlic cloves, crushed
2 red peppers, seeded and sliced
about 1.5kg/3½lb chicken, jointed into six pieces
90ml/6 tbsp tomato purée (paste)
3 potatoes, diced
5ml/1 tsp chopped fresh rosemary
5ml/1 tsp chopped fresh marjoram
5ml/1 tsp chopped fresh thyme
3 carrots, cut into chunks
½ small celeriac, cut into chunks
120ml/4fl oz/½ cup dry white wine
2 courgettes (zucchini), sliced
salt and freshly ground black pepper
chopped fresh rosemary and marjoram, to garnish

1 Heat the oil in a large flameproof casserole. Add the onion and garlic and cook for 1–2 minutes until softened. Add the peppers and cook for a further 2 minutes.

2 Place the chicken to the casserole and brown over the hob for about 15 minutes.

3 After about 15 minutes add the tomato purée, potatoes, herbs, carrots, celeriac and white wine, and season to taste with salt and pepper. Cook over a gentle heat, covered, for a further 40–50 minutes.

4 Add the courgettes 5 minutes before the end of cooking. Adjust the seasoning to taste. Garnish with the herbs and serve with rye bread if liked, or with herb bread or warm crusty rolls.

Potted Chicken: Energy 225kcal/946kJ; Protein 29.3g; Carbohydrate 11g, of which sugars 8.5g; Fat 7.5g, of which saturates 1.1g; Cholesterol 79mg; Calcium 50mg; Fibre 2.7g; Sodium 119mg.
Chicken/Red Peppers: Energy 430kcal/1807kJ; Protein 49.6g; Carbohydrate 28.5g, of which sugars 12.9g; Fat 12.3g, of which saturates 2.3g; Cholesterol 175mg; Calcium 61mg; Fibre 4.4g; Sodium 202mg.

Duck Consommé

This soup is a good example of the influence the Vietnamese community in France has had on modern French cooking.

Serves 4

1 duck carcass (raw or cooked), plus 2 legs or any giblets, trimmed of fat
1 large onion, unpeeled, root off
2 carrots, cut into chunks
1 parsnip, cut into chunks
1 leek, cut into chunks
2–4 garlic cloves, crushed
2.5cm/1in piece fresh root ginger, peeled and sliced
15ml/1 tbsp black peppercorns
4–6 sprigs of fresh thyme
small bunch of coriander (cilantro), leaves and stems separated

For the garnish

1 small carrot
1 small leek, halved lengthways
4–6 shiitake mushrooms, sliced
soy sauce
2 spring onions, sliced
watercress or finely shredded Chinese leaves
ground black pepper

1 Put the duck carcass and legs or giblets, onion, carrots, parsnip, leek and garlic in a large, heavy pan or flameproof casserole. Add the ginger, peppercorns, thyme and coriander stems, cover with cold water and bring to the boil, skimming off any foam that rises to the surface.

2 Reduce the heat and simmer gently for 1½–2 hours, then strain through a muslin-lined (cheesecloth) sieve (strainer) into a bowl, discarding the bones and vegetables. Cool the stock and chill for several hours or overnight. Skim off congealed fat and blot with kitchen paper.

3 For the garnish, cut the carrot and leek into 5cm/2in pieces and slice into thin strips. Place in a pan with the mushrooms.

4 Pour in the stock and add a few dashes of soy sauce and some pepper. Bring to the boil, skimming any foam that rises to the surface. Taste and adjust the seasoning. Stir in the spring onions and watercress or Chinese leaves. Ladle the consommé into warmed bowls and sprinkle with the coriander leaves before serving.

Duck Broth with Spiced Dumplings

Handle the dumplings gently for a light texture to match their delicious flavour.

Serves 4

1 duckling, about 1.75kg/4–4½lb, with liver
1 large onion, halved
2 carrots, thickly sliced
½ garlic bulb
1 bouquet garni
3 cloves
bunch of chives, in short lengths

For the spiced dumplings

2 thick slices white bread
60ml/4 tbsp milk
2 rashers (strips) rindless streaky (fatty) bacon
1 shallot, finely chopped
1 garlic clove, crushed
1 egg yolk, beaten
grated rind of 1 orange
2.5ml/½ tsp paprika
50g/2oz/½ cup plain (all-purpose) flour
salt and ground black pepper

1 Set the duck liver aside. Cut off the breasts and set them aside. Put the carcass into a pan and pour in enough water to cover. Bring to the boil and skim the scum off the surface.

2 Add the onion, carrots, garlic, bouquet garni and cloves. Reduce the heat, cover, then simmer for 2 hours, skimming off scum occasionally.

3 Lift the carcass from the broth. Remove all meat from the carcass and shred it finely, then set it aside. Strain the broth and skim off any fat. Return the broth to the pan and then simmer, uncovered, until reduced to 1.2 litres/2 pints/5 cups.

4 For the dumplings, soak the bread in the milk for 5 minutes. Remove the skin and fat from the duck breasts. Mince the meat with the duck liver and bacon. Squeeze the milk from the bread, then mix the bread into the meat with the shallot, garlic, egg yolk, orange rind, paprika, flour and seasoning.

5 Shape the mixture into balls, a little smaller than walnuts to make 20 small dumplings. Bring a pan of lightly salted water to the boil. Poach the dumplings for 4–5 minutes, until just tender.

6 Boil the broth. Add the dumplings. Divide the shredded duck among bowls and ladle in the broth. Sprinkle with chives.

Duck Consommé: Energy 12kcal/51kJ; Protein 1.4g; Carbohydrate 1.9g, of which sugars 1.6g; Fat 0.6g, of which saturates 0.2g; Cholesterol 0mg; Calcium 13mg; Fibre 1g; Sodium 550mg.
Duck with Dumplings: Energy 289kcal/1214kJ; Protein 29.9g; Carbohydrate 19g, of which sugars 2.8g; Fat 13g, of which saturates 3.1g; Cholesterol 196mg; Calcium 63mg; Fibre 1.3g; Sodium 373mg.

Fruity Duck Soup

This rich soup originates in the Chiu Chow region of southern China. This recipe can be made with chicken stock and leftover duck meat from a roasted duck, or by roasting a duck, slicing off the breast portion and thigh meat for the soup.

Serves 4–6

I lean duck, about 1.5kg/3lb 5oz
2 preserved limes (see Cook's Tip)
25g/1oz fresh root ginger, thinly sliced
salt and ground black pepper

For the garnish

vegetable oil, for frying
25g/1oz fresh root ginger, thinly sliced into strips
2 garlic cloves, thinly sliced into strips
2 spring onions (scallions), finely sliced

1 Place the duck in a large pan with enough water to cover. Season with salt and pepper and bring the water to the boil. Reduce the heat, cover the pot, and simmer for 1½ hours.

2 Add the preserved limes and ginger. Continue to simmer for another hour, skimming off the fat from time to time, until the liquid has reduced a little and the duck is so tender that it almost falls off the bone.

3 Meanwhile heat some vegetable oil in a wok. Stir in the ginger and garlic strips and fry until gold and crispy. Drain them well on kitchen paper and set aside for garnishing.

4 Remove the duck from the broth and shred the meat into individual bowls. Check the broth for seasoning, then ladle it over the duck in the bowls. Sprinkle the spring onions with the fried ginger and garlic over the top and serve.

Cook's Tip

Preserved limes have a distinct bitter flavour. Look for them in Asian markets.

Duck, Nut and Date Soup

This rich soup is delicious. Packed with nuts and sweetened with jujubes (dried Chinese red dates). Served on its own, or with rice and pickles, it is a meal in itself.

Serves 4

30–45ml/2–3 tbsp vegetable oil
4 duck legs, split into thighs and drumsticks
water from 1 coconut
60ml/4 tbsp fish sauce
4 lemon grass stalks, bruised
12 chestnuts, peeled
90g/3½oz unsalted cashew nuts, roasted
90g/3½oz unsalted almonds, roasted
90g/3½oz unsalted peanuts, roasted
12 jujubes (see Variation)
sea salt and ground black pepper
1 bunch fresh basil leaves, to garnish

1 Heat the oil in a wok or heavy pan. Brown the duck legs in the oil and drain on kitchen paper.

2 Bring 2 litres/3½ pints/7¾ cups water to the boil. Reduce the heat and add the coconut water, fish sauce, lemon grass and duck legs. Cover the pan and simmer over a gentle heat for 2–3 hours. Skim off any fat.

3 Add the nuts and jujubes and cook for 40 minutes, until the chestnuts are soft and the duck is very tender. Skim off any fat, season to taste and sprinkle with basil leaves to serve.

Variation

Chinese red dates are sold in Chinese supermarkets but it is also worth looking in healthfood or wholefood shops for small dried red dates that can be used instead. Otherwise use ordinary dried dates.

Cook's Tip

To extract the water from a coconut, pierce the eyes on top and turn the coconut upside down over a bowl.

Fruity Duck Soup: Energy 124kcal/520kJ; Protein 19.8g; Carbohydrate 0.3g, of which sugars 0.3g; Fat 6.5g, of which saturates 1.3g; Cholesterol 110mg; Calcium 19mg; Fibre 0g; Sodium 110mg.
Duck, Nut and Date: Energy 604kcal/2512kJ; Protein 43.8g; Carbohydrate 8.9g, of which sugars 3.6g; Fat 44g, of which saturates 9.2g; Cholesterol 165mg; Calcium 49mg; Fibre 3.1g; Sodium 231mg.

Tomato and Beef Soup

Another wholesome and much-loved classic, the tomatoes and spring onions give this light beef broth a superb flavour. It is quick and easy to make, and ideal as an appetizer or light lunch.

Serves 4

75g/3oz rump (round) steak
900ml/1½ pints/3¾ cups beef stock
30ml/2 tbsp tomato purée (paste)
6 tomatoes, halved, seeded and chopped
10ml/2 tsp caster (superfine) sugar
15ml/1 tbsp cornflour (cornstarch)
1 egg white
2.5ml/½ tsp sesame oil
salt and ground black pepper
2 spring onions (scallions), finely shredded

1 Cut the beef into thin strips and place in a pan. Pour over boiling water to cover. Cook for 2 minutes, then drain thoroughly and set aside.

2 Bring the stock to the boil in a clean pan. Stir in the tomato purée, then the tomatoes and sugar.

3 Add the beef strips, allow the stock to boil again, then lower the heat and simmer for 2 minutes.

4 Mix the cornflour to a paste with 15ml/1 tbsp water. Add the mixture to the soup, stirring constantly. Bring to the boil, stirring, and cook for a few minutes, until the soup thickens slightly. Lightly beat the egg white in a cup.

5 Pour the egg white into the soup, stirring. When the egg white changes colour, season, stir and pour the soup into heated soup bowls. Drizzle with sesame oil, sprinkle with spring onions and serve.

Variation
It's tempting to use canned, rather than fresh, tomatoes to cut down on preparation time, but the flavour will not be the same.

Beef and Ginger Soup

This and similar fragrant soups are often eaten for breakfast in Asian countries.

Serves 4–6

1 onion
1.5kg/3–3½lb beef shin or leg (shank) with bones
2.5cm/1in fresh root ginger
1 star anise
1 bay leaf
2 whole cloves
2.5ml/½ tsp fennel seeds
1 piece of cinnamon stick
fish sauce, to taste
juice of 1 lime
150g/5oz fillet (tenderloin) steak
450g/1lb fresh flat rice noodles
salt and ground black pepper

For the accompaniments
1 small red onion, sliced into rings
115g/4oz/½ cup beansprouts
2 fresh red chillies, seeded and sliced
2 spring onions (scallions), sliced
coriander (cilantro) leaves
lime wedges

1 Cut the onion in half. Grill (broil) under a high heat, cut side up, until the exposed sides are caramelized. Set aside.

2 Cut the meat into large chunks and then place with the bones in a large pan. Add the caramelized onion with the ginger, star anise, bay leaf, cloves, fennel seeds and cinnamon.

3 Add 3 litres/5 pints/12 cups water, bring to the boil, then reduce the heat. Cover and simmer gently for 2–3 hours, skimming off the fat and scum occasionally.

4 Remove the meat from the stock and cut into small pieces, discarding the bones. Strain the stock and return to the pan together with the meat. Bring back to the boil and season with the fish sauce and lime juice.

5 Slice the fillet steak very thinly and then chill until required. Place the accompaniments in separate bowls.

6 Cook the noodles in boiling water until just tender. Drain and divide among soup bowls. Top with steak, pour the hot stock over and serve, offering the accompaniments separately so that each person may garnish their soup as they like.

Tomato and Beef Soup: Energy 79kcal/337kJ; Protein 6.2g; Carbohydrate 11.1g, of which sugars 7.6g; Fat 1.5g, of which saturates 0.5g; Cholesterol 11mg; Calcium 16mg; Fibre 1.5g; Sodium 58mg.
Beef and Ginger: Energy 532kcal/2222kJ; Protein 36.7g; Carbohydrate 63.6g, of which sugars 1.6g; Fat 13.4g, of which saturates 5.4g; Cholesterol 82mg; Calcium 26mg; Fibre 0.6g; Sodium 102mg.

Braised Beef and Peanut Soup

This meaty soup is a variation on a stew taken to the Philippines by early Spanish settlers.

Serves 4–6

30ml/2 tbsp vegetable oil
15ml/1 tbsp annatto seeds, or 5ml/1 tsp paprika and a pinch of ground turmeric
2 onions, chopped
2 garlic cloves, crushed
275g/10oz celeriac or swede (rutabaga), roughly chopped
900g/2lb stewing beef, cubed
1.2 litres/2 pints/5 cups beef stock
350g/12oz new potatoes, peeled and cut into large dice
15ml/1 tbsp fish sauce
30ml/2 tbsp tamarind sauce
10ml/2 tsp sugar
1 bay leaf
1 sprig thyme
90ml/6 tbsp long grain rice
50g/2oz/⅓ cup peanuts or 30ml/2 tbsp peanut butter
15ml/1 tbsp white wine vinegar
salt and ground black pepper

1 Heat the vegetable oil in a large pan. Add the annatto seeds, if using, and stir until the oil is dark red. Remove the seeds with a slotted spoon and discard. (Add paprika and turmeric later.)

2 Cook the onions, garlic and celeriac or swede in the oil until soft but not brown. Add the beef and cook briefly over high heat. Stir in the paprika and turmeric, if using, with the beef.

3 Add the stock, potatoes, fish sauce and tamarind sauce, sugar, bay leaf and thyme. Bring to a simmer, cover and cook gently for about 2 hours.

4 Cover the rice with cold water and leave to stand for 30 minutes. Roast the peanuts under a hot grill (broiler), if using, then rub the skins off in a clean cloth. Drain the rice and grind with the peanuts or peanut butter, using a mortar and pestle, or food processor or blender.

5 When the beef is tender, add some of the cooking liquid to the ground rice and nuts. Blend smoothly and stir into the soup. Bring to the boil, stirring, reduce the heat and simmer gently for 5–20 minutes, until thickened. To finish, stir in the wine vinegar and season well.

Aubergine-Beef Soup with Lime

A delicious soupy stew from Indonesia. If you like, serve the soup with a bowl of rice and a chilli sambal, bearing in mind that the quantity of rice should be great, as the role of the soup is to moisten and flavour it.

Serves 4

30ml/2 tbsp palm, groundnut (peanut) or corn oil
150g/5oz lean beef, cut into thin strips
500ml/17fl oz/generous 2 cups coconut milk
10ml/2 tsp sugar
1 large aubergine (eggplant), cut into wedges
3–4 kaffir lime leaves
juice of 1 lime
salt

For the spice paste

4 shallots, chopped
4 fresh red Thai chillies, seeded and chopped
25g/1oz fresh root ginger, chopped
15g/½oz fresh turmeric root, chopped or 2.5ml/½ tsp ground turmeric
2 garlic cloves, chopped
5ml/1 tsp coriander seeds
2.5ml/½ tsp cumin seeds
2–3 candlenuts

To serve

cooked rice
1 lime, quartered
chilli sambal

1 To make the spice paste, using a mortar and pestle, grind all the ingredients together to form a textured paste, or whiz them together in a food processor or blender.

2 Heat the oil in a pan, stir in the spice paste and fry until fragrant. Add the beef, stirring to coat it well in the spice paste, then add the coconut milk and sugar. Bring to the boil, then reduce the heat and simmer gently for 10 minutes.

3 Add the aubergine wedges and kaffir lime leaves to the pan and cook gently for a further 5–10 minutes, until tender but not mushy. Stir in the lime juice and season with salt to taste.

4 Ladle the soup into individual warmed bowls and serve with bowls of cooked rice to spoon the soup over, wedges of lime to squeeze on the top and a chilli sambal.

Beef and Peanut: Energy 482kcal/2012kJ; Protein 39.6g; Carbohydrate 32.3g, of which sugars 9.6g; Fat 22g, of which saturates 6.9g; Cholesterol 87mg; Calcium 62mg; Fibre 2.9g; Sodium 646mg.
Aubergine-Beef Soup: Energy 224kcal/938kJ; Protein 12.1g; Carbohydrate 14.6g, of which sugars 12.6g; Fat 13.6g, of which saturates 3.2g; Cholesterol 22mg; Calcium 79mg; Fibre 3g; Sodium 181mg.

Chillied Beef Soup

This is a hearty dish based on a traditional chilli recipe. It is ideal served with fresh, crusty bread as a warming start to any meal.

Serves 4

15ml/1 tbsp oil
1 onion, chopped
175g/6oz/¾ cup minced (ground) beef
2 garlic cloves, chopped
1 fresh red chilli, seeded and sliced
25g/1oz/¼ cup plain (all-purpose) flour
400g/14oz can chopped tomatoes
600ml/1 pint/2½ cups beef stock
225g/8oz/2 cups canned kidney beans, drained
30ml/2 tbsp chopped fresh parsley
salt and ground black pepper
crusty bread, to serve

1 Heat the oil in a large pan. Fry the onion and minced beef for 5 minutes until brown and sealed.

2 Add the garlic, chilli and flour. Cook for 1 minute, stirring continuously. Add the tomatoes and pour in the stock, still stirring, and bring to the boil while stirring.

3 Stir in the kidney beans, reduce the heat so that the soup just simmers and add salt and pepper to taste. Cover and cook for 20 minutes.

4 Add the chopped parsley, reserving a little to garnish the finished dish. Pour the soup into warm bowls, sprinkle with the reserved parsley and serve with crusty bread.

Cook's Tip

For a hot flavour, leave the seeds in the chilli. Soured cream or yogurt and avocado are delicious finishing touches for the soup and have a cooling effect. Swirl a little cream or yogurt into each portion, top with diced avocado and sprinkle with a little chopped fresh green chilli and/or chopped spring onion (scallions) and grated lemon or lime rind.

Clear Chinese Mushroom Soup with Meatballs

In this soup the meatballs are combined with lightly cooked vegetables in a tasty stock. The reserved liquid from the soaked mushrooms contributes really well to the flavour of the latter.

Serves 8

4–6 dried Chinese mushrooms, soaked in warm water for 30 minutes
30ml/2 tbsp groundnut (peanut) oil
1 large onion, finely chopped
2 garlic cloves, finely crushed
1cm/½in piece fresh root ginger, bruised
2 litres/3½ pints/9 cups beef or chicken stock, including soaking liquid from the mushrooms
30ml/2 tbsp soy sauce
115g/4oz curly kale, spinach or Chinese leaves (Chinese cabbage), shredded

For the meatballs

175g/6oz/¾ cup finely minced (ground) beef
1 small onion, finely chopped
1–2 garlic cloves, crushed
15ml/1 tbsp cornflour (cornstarch)
half an egg white, lightly beaten
salt and freshly ground black pepper

1 Prepare the meatballs. Mix the beef with the onion, garlic, cornflour and seasoning using a food processor or blender, and then bind with the egg white to make a firm mixture. With wet hands, roll into tiny, bitesize balls and set aside.

2 Drain the mushrooms. Reserve the soaking liquid. Trim off and discard the stalks. Slice the caps finely and set aside.

3 Heat a wok or large pan and add the oil. Fry the onion, garlic and ginger to bring out the flavour, but do not burn.

4 When the onion is soft, pour in the stock. Bring to the boil, then stir in the soy sauce and mushroom slices and simmer for 10 minutes. Add the meatballs and cook for a further 10 minutes.

5 Just before serving, remove the ginger. Stir in the shredded curly kale, spinach or Chinese leaves. Heat through for 1 minute so as not to overcook the leaves. Serve immediately.

Chillied Beef Soup: Energy 226kcal/946kJ; Protein 14.2g; Carbohydrate 19.4g, of which sugars 6.2g; Fat 10.7g, of which saturates 3.5g; Cholesterol 26mg; Calcium 78mg; Fibre 5.3g; Sodium 267mg.
Chinese Mushroom Soup: Energy 103kcal/426kJ; Protein 5.8g; Carbohydrate 5.8g, of which sugars 3g; Fat 6.6g, of which saturates 1.9g; Cholesterol 13mg; Calcium 39mg; Fibre 0.9g; Sodium 493mg.

Oxtail and Butter Bean Soup

This soup is based on a traditional Caribbean stew – old-fashioned, economical and full of goodness. It requires patience because of the long cooking time.

Serves 4

1.6kg/3½lb oxtail, chopped into pieces
1 onion, finely chopped
3 bay leaves
4 fresh thyme sprigs
3 cloves
175g/6oz/scant 1 cup dried butter (lima) beans, soaked overnight
2 garlic cloves, crushed
15ml/1 tbsp tomato purée (paste)
400g/14oz can chopped tomatoes
5ml/1 tsp ground allspice
1 fresh hot chilli
salt and ground black pepper

1 Put the pieces of oxtail in a large pan, add the onion, bay leaves, thyme and cloves and cover with water. Bring to the boil.

2 Reduce the heat, cover the pan and simmer gently for at least 2½ hours or until the meat is very tender. If the meat looks like it might dry out, add a little extra water, being careful not to add too much at one time.

3 Meanwhile, drain the butter beans and tip them into a large pan. Pour in water to cover. Bring to the boil, lower the heat, part cover the pan and simmer for about 1–1¼ hours or until just tender. Drain and set aside.

4 When the oxtail is cooked, add the garlic, tomato purée, tomatoes, allspice, and chilli with seasoning to taste.

5 Add the beans, bring back to the boil and simmer the soup for 20 minutes, until the beans are tender and infused with flavour. Ladle into bowls and serve.

Variation
Haricot (navy) beans can be used in the same way as butter (lima) beans in the recipe.

Beef and Cassava Soup

This simple, tasty soup is almost a stew. Such soups, made in one pot, are everyday fare in Latin America. The addition of wine is not traditional, but it enhances the flavour.

Serves 4

450g/1lb stewing beef, cubed
1.2 litres/2 pints/5 cups beef stock
300ml/½ pint/1¼ cups white wine
15ml/1 tbsp soft brown sugar
1 onion, finely chopped
1 bay leaf
1 bouquet garni
1 fresh thyme sprig
15ml/1 tbsp tomato purée (paste)
1 large carrot, sliced
275g/10oz cassava or yam, peeled and cubed
50g/2oz fresh spinach, chopped
a little hot pepper sauce, to taste
salt and ground black pepper

1 Mix the beef, stock, white wine, sugar, chopped onion, bay leaf, bouquet garni, thyme and tomato purée in a large pan.

2 Bring to the boil, then reduce the heat, cover and simmer very gently for about 1¼ hours. The meat will be cooked but still quite chewy – often preferred this way. For very tender meat, allow about 2½–3 hours.

3 Add the sliced carrot, cubed cassava or yam, spinach and a few drops of hot pepper sauce. Season with salt and ground black pepper to taste and simmer the soup for a further 15 minutes, until the meat and vegetables are both tender.

4 Remove the bouquet garni and any remnants of the thyme and ladle the soup into bowls to serve.

Variation
Make this with pork and potato instead of beef and cassava. Use boneless pork – sparerib chops, knuckle or leg – cut into chunks and chicken stock instead of beef stock. Then add big chunks of peeled old, or main crop, potatoes instead of yam. Include a couple of sage sprigs in the bouquet garni.

Oxtail/Butter Bean: Energy 510kcal/2147kJ; Protein 57.1g; Carbohydrate 24.1g, of which sugars 5.6g; Fat 21.4g, of which saturates 0.2g; Cholesterol 130mg; Calcium 76mg; Fibre 8.2g; Sodium 314mg.
Beef and Cassava: Energy 336kcal/1410kJ; Protein 24.7g; Carbohydrate 27.2g, of which sugars 7.8g; Fat 9.7g, of which saturates 3.9g; Cholesterol 58mg; Calcium 55mg; Fibre 1.9g; Sodium 100mg.

Classic Oxtail Soup

This is the familiar oxtail recipe – from the days when it was natural to use up every part of an animal.

Serves 4–6

1 oxtail, cut into joints, total weight about 1.3kg/3lb
25g/1oz/2 tbsp butter
2 medium onions, chopped
2 medium carrots, chopped
2 celery sticks, sliced
1 bacon rasher (strip), chopped
2 litres/3½ pints/8 cups beef stock
1 bouquet garni
2 bay leaves
30ml/2 tbsp flour
squeeze of fresh lemon juice
60ml/4 tbsp port, sherry or Madeira
salt and ground black pepper

1 Wash and dry the pieces of oxtail, trimming off excess fat. Melt the butter in a large pan, and, when foaming, add the oxtail and brown quickly on all sides. Remove and set aside.

2 To the same pan, add the vegetables and bacon. Cook over a medium heat for 5–10 minutes until golden brown.

3 Return the oxtail to the pan and add the stock, bouquet garni, bay leaves and seasoning. Bring to the boil and skim off any foam. Cover and simmer gently for about 3 hours or until the meat is so tender that it is falling away from the bone.

4 Strain the mixture, discarding the vegetables, bouquet garni and bay leaves, and leave to stand.

5 When the oxtail has cooled sufficiently to handle, pick all the meat off the bones and cut it into small pieces. Skim off any fat that has risen to the surface of the stock, then tip the stock into a large pan. Add the pieces of meat and heat through.

6 Whisk the flour with a little cold water to make a smooth paste. Stir in a little of the hot stock then stir the mixture into the pan. Bring to the boil and stir until thickened slightly. Reduce the heat and simmer gently for about 5 minutes.

7 Add the lemon juice and stir in the port, sherry or Madiera. Season to taste, and serve.

Oxtail and Leek Soup

This is a Spanish-style oxtail dish – more substantial than broth but with lots of liquid. Add plenty of potatoes to turn it into a real meal.

Serves 6

30ml/2 tbsp plain (all-purpose) flour
60ml/4 tbsp olive oil
1.6kg/3½ lb oxtail, chopped up
2 onions, chopped
6 carrots, cut into short lengths
2 large garlic cloves, crushed
1 bay leaf
2 thyme sprigs
2 leeks, sliced thinly
1 clove
pinch of freshly grated nutmeg
350ml/12fl oz/1½ cups red wine
30ml/2 tbsp vinegar
750ml/1¼ pints/3 cups stock
30ml/2 tbsp fino sherry
60ml/4 tbsp chopped fresh parsley
salt, paprika and black pepper
boiled potatoes (optional)

1 Season the flour with salt, paprika and pepper, and dust the oxtail pieces all over. Heat the oil in a large pan. Add the oxtail in batches and brown the pieces all over, removing them as they are ready.

2 Add the onions, carrots, garlic, bay leaf, thyme sprigs and leeks. Cook, stirring, for about 5 minutes, to reduce the leeks in volume. Stir in the clove, grated nutmeg and more black pepper.

3 Replace the oxtail, nesting the pieces among the vegetables. Pour in the wine, vinegar and enough stock to cover. Bring to simmering point, then cover and simmer very gently, stirring occasionally, for 3 hours, or longer, until the meat is falling off the bones.

4 Lift out the oxtail and cut the meat off the bones. Skim the fat off the stock. Discard the bay leaf and thyme. Spoon the garlic and some of the soft vegetables into a food processor or blender and purée with the sherry.

5 Return the meat and purée to the pan. Add the boiled potatoes, if using, and heat through. Stir in the parsley, check the seasonings and ladle into bowls or deep plates to serve.

Classic Oxtail Soup: Energy 459kcal/1914kJ; Protein 45.4g; Carbohydrate 6.5g, of which sugars 2.6g; Fat 26.8g, of which saturates 11.8g; Cholesterol 176mg; Calcium 36mg; Fibre 0.7g; Sodium 403mg.
Oxtail and Leek: Energy 416kcal/1737kJ; Protein 33.4g; Carbohydrate 12.2g, of which sugars 6.1g; Fat 21.5g, of which saturates 1.1g; Cholesterol 159mg; Calcium 63mg; Fibre 2.6g; Sodium 201mg.

Beef Steak and Vegetable Soup

This old-English soup was particularly popular during the reign of Queen Victoria, when it is said to have featured regularly on state banquet menus. It is smooth, meaty, full of flavour and pleasantly substantial.

Serves 4

225g/8oz lean stewing steak
30ml/2 tbsp plain (all-purpose) flour
25g/1oz/2 tbsp butter
1 onion, finely chopped
1 carrot, finely chopped
1 small parsnip, finely chopped
1 litre/1¾ pints/4 cups beef stock
1 bouquet garni
salt, black pepper and chilli powder
cooked rice, to serve
fresh herbs, to garnish

1 Cut the stewing steak into 2.5cm/1in cubes and coat with the flour.

2 Melt the butter in a large saucepan. Add the steak a few pieces at a time and brown them on all sides. Lift the meat out and set aside.

3 Add the onion, carrot and parsnip to the fat remaining in the pan and cook over a medium heat for about 5 minutes, stirring occasionally until softened and golden brown.

4 Return the steak to the pan and pour in the stock. Stir in the bouquet garni and seasoning. Bring just to the boil; reduce the heat so that the stock just simmers. Cover and simmer the soup very gently for about 3 hours, or until the steak is very tender and can be broken up with a fork.

5 Purée the soup in a blender until smooth, adding a little extra hot stock or water to thin it if necessary. (A food processor can be used but the soup will not be as fine.)

6 Reheat the soup and season it to taste. Ladle into bowls, and add a spoonful of cooked rice to each one. Garnish with herbs.

Spicy Tripe Soup with Citrus

This popular Indonesian soup is packed with spices, lemon grass and lime. Locally, tripe is served chewy in this spicy soup, with its sambal on the side. Supermarkets and butchers usually sell tripe boiled, so step 1 may not be needed.

Serves 4

250ml/8fl oz/1 cup rice wine vinegar
900g/2lb beef tripe, cleaned
2 litres/3½ pints/8 cups beef stock or water
2–3 garlic cloves, crushed whole
2 lemon grass stalks
25g/1oz fresh root ginger, finely grated
3–4 kaffir lime leaves
225g/8oz white radish or turnip, finely sliced
15ml/1 tbsp palm, groundnut (peanut) or vegetable oil
4 shallots, finely sliced
salt and ground black pepper

For the sambal

2 garlic cloves, crushed
2–3 hot red chillies, seeded and finely chopped
15ml/1 tbsp palm, groundnut (peanut) or vegetable oil
15ml/1 tbsp chilli and shrimp paste
25ml/1½ tbsp tomato purée (paste)

1 Simmer the tripe in a large pan of salted water with the vinegar added. Allow 1 hour for a chewy result or 4–5 hours for tender tripe, topping up the water as necessary. Drain and cut into squares.

2 For the sambal, fry the garlic and chillies in the oil. Stir in the chilli, shrimp and tomato pastes until thoroughly mixed. Tip the paste into a small dish and put aside.

3 Bring the stock or water to the boil. Reduce the heat and add the tripe, garlic, lemon grass, ginger, lime leaves and radish or turnip. Cook gently for 20 minutes.

4 Heat the oil in a small frying pan. Add the shallots and fry for about 5 minutes until golden brown. Drain on kitchen paper.

5 Serve the soup topped with shallots, with the spicy sambal, which can be added in a dollop and stirred in as required.

Spicy Tripe Soup: Energy 160kcal/668kJ; Protein 19.2g; Carbohydrate 5.5g, of which sugars 4.8g; Fat 7g, of which saturates 1.1g; Cholesterol 163mg; Calcium 198mg; Fibre 1.9g; Sodium 299mg.
Beef Steak Soup: Energy 182kcal/757kJ; Protein 13.8g; Carbohydrate 8g, of which sugars 3.4g; Fat 10.7g, of which saturates 5.5g; Cholesterol 46mg; Calcium 25mg; Fibre 1.7g; Sodium 81mg.

Hot and Spicy Beef Soup

Known as *yukgejang*, this is one of the most traditional Korean soups, often served with rice. The smoky taste of fern fronds gives it its unique flavour. The addition of the red chilli powder provides a fierce kick and fiery colour for the beef and leek.

Serves 2–3

75g/3oz dried fern fronds (see Cook's Tip)
75g/3oz enoki mushrooms, trimmed
250g/9oz braising steak
10ml/2 tsp sesame oil
30ml/2 tbsp chilli powder
1 garlic clove, finely chopped
15ml/1 tbsp vegetable oil
75g/3oz/½ cup beansprouts, trimmed
1 leek, sliced
1 spring onion (scallion), sliced
salt

1 Boil the dried fern fronds for about 3 minutes. Drain and rinse with cold water. Cut the fronds into thirds, and discard the tougher stem pieces, along with the enoki mushroom caps.

2 Place the beef in a medium pan and cover with water. Bring to the boil, cover and cook over high heat for 30 minutes. Then remove the beef and strain the stock into a jug (pitcher).

3 Cut the beef into thin strips and place in a bowl. Add the sesame oil, chilli powder and chopped garlic, and coat the meat.

4 Heat the oil in a large pan. Add the meat, fern fronds, beansprouts, leek and spring onion. Stir-fry for 2 minutes, then pour in the stock. Bring to boil, reduce the heat and cover. Simmer for 30 minutes or so until the meat is tender.

5 Add the enoki mushrooms and simmer for a further 2 minutes. Add salt to taste and serve.

Cook's Tip
If ferns are not available the best alternative is an equivalent amount of shiitake mushrooms.

Beef, Bread and Garlic Broth

This rich, dark garlic soup, known as *Sopa Castilliana* in its native central Spain, divides people into two groups – you either love or hate it. However, there are two fantastic sops to its rich, slightly sour flavour. Poaching a whole egg in each bowl – traditionally ovenproof – just before serving is one, while the broth-soaked fried bread adds texture and bulk.

Serves 4

30ml/2 tbsp olive oil
4 large garlic cloves, peeled
4 slices stale country bread
20ml/4 tbsp paprika
1 litre/1¾ pints/4 cups beef stock
1.5ml/¼ tsp ground cumin
4 eggs
salt and ground black pepper
chopped fresh parsley, to garnish

1 Preheat the oven to 230°C/450°F/Gas 8. Heat the olive oil in a large pan. Add the whole peeled garlic cloves and cook until they are golden, then remove and set aside. Fry the slices of bread in the oil until golden, then set these aside.

2 Add 15ml/1 tbsp of the paprika to the pan, and fry for a few seconds. Stir in the beef stock, cumin and remaining paprika, then add the reserved garlic, crushing the cloves with the back of a wooden spoon. Season to taste. Bring to the boil, reduce the heat slightly and cook for 5 minutes.

3 Break up the slices of fried bread into bitesize pieces and stir them into the soup.

4 Ladle the soup into four ovenproof bowls. Carefully break an egg into each bowl and place in the oven for about 3 minutes, until the eggs are set. Sprinkle the soup with chopped fresh parsley and serve immediately.

Cook's Tip
Instead of baking the eggs in the soup, poach them in a small amount of simmering water with a little vinegar added. Ladle the soup into bowls and add the drained eggs.

Hot and Spicy Beef: Energy 225kcal/935kJ; Protein 21.5g; Carbohydrate 3g, of which sugars 2g; Fat 14.1g, of which saturates 4g; Cholesterol 48mg; Calcium 28mg; Fibre 2.3g; Sodium 59mg.
Beef, Bread and Garlic: Energy 202kcal/845kJ; Protein 9.7g; Carbohydrate 15.3g, of which sugars 0.7g; Fat 12.5g, of which saturates 2.5g; Cholesterol 190mg; Calcium 69mg; Fibre 0.4g; Sodium 579mg.

Beef Dumpling Soup

Succulent dumplings taste fantastic in this simple broth. It is a great example of how to make the most of bought ingredients for a stylish snack or light meal.

Serves 4

750ml/1¼ pints/3 cups beef stock
16 frozen dumplings
1 spring onion (scallion), sliced
¼ green chilli, sliced
1 garlic clove, crushed
15ml/1 tbsp light soy sauce
salt and ground black pepper

1 Place the beef stock in a pan and bring to the boil. Add the frozen dumplings, cover, and boil for 6 minutes.

2 Add the spring onion, chilli, garlic and soy sauce, and boil for a further 2 minutes.

3 Season with salt and black pepper, and serve piping hot.

Variation

Use chicken stock and prawn (shrimp) or pork-filled dumplings. Add a little finely shredded very crisp lettuce and grated lemon rind to each bowl when serving.

Cook's Tips

- *The quality of stock and dumplings is important for the success of this soup, so start with good home-made stock or superior bought stock. Be guided by price when buying dumplings and check the lable for filling ingredients: cheap dumplings usually have inferior filling.*
- *If you want to use fresh dumplings, cook them for 5 minutes.*
- *Soy sauce with a drop of vinegar makes a good dipping sauce for the dumplings.*
- *When cooking dumplings don't stir the soup as this can often cause the dumplings to tear open.*

Beef and Radish Soup

The smoky flavour of the beef cooked in sesame oil is perfectly complemented by the sweet tanginess of Chinese white radish in this mild and refreshing soup, with a slightly sweet edge. A popular Korean soup.

Serves 4

200g/7oz Chinese white radish, peeled (see Cook's Tip)
50g/2oz tender frying (round) steak
15ml/1 tbsp sesame oil
½ leek, sliced
15ml/1 tbsp light soy sauce
salt and ground black pepper

1 Slice the white radish, and cut the pieces into 2cm/¾in squares. Roughly chop the beef into bitesize cubes.

2 Heat the sesame oil in a large pan, and stir-fry the beef until brown and just cooked. Add the white radish, and briefly stir-fry.

3 Add 750ml/1¼ pints/3 cups water to the pan. Bring to the boil, reduce the heat immediately, cover and simmer the soup for 7 minutes.

4 Stir in the leek and soy sauce. Simmer the soup for a further 2 minutes. Season to taste and serve.

Cook's Tips

- *The long white radish, or daikon, is used extensively in Korean cooking. It is readily available in general supermarkets but the prize examples are usually found in Asian stores, where they are extremely crisp and fresh.*
- *Buy good-quality steak for this soup: braising steak is too tough, so look for fine-grained, lean meat. Cut the meat across the grain into slices, and then into small squares. To avoid toughening the meat, it is important to reduce the cooking temperature as soon as the stock boils (beforehand if you have a heat-retentive pan) so that the meat simmers gently. Harsh boiling toughens meat.*
- *Remember that light soy sauce is salty and take care when adding seasoning to avoid making the soup too salty.*

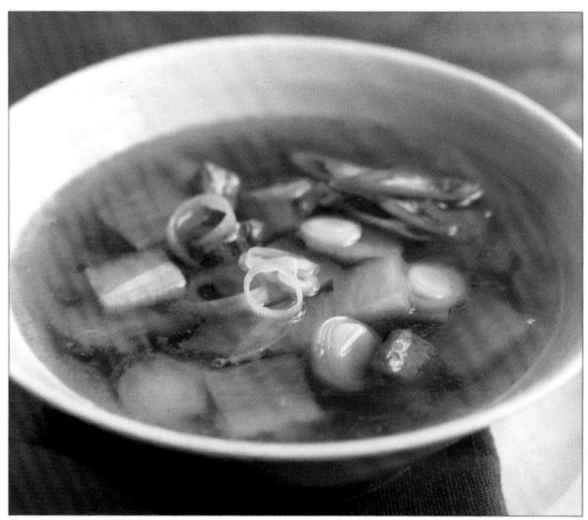

Beef Dumpling Soup: Energy 106kcal/445kJ; Protein 2g; Carbohydrate 12.6g, of which sugars 0.6g; Fat 6.1g, of which saturates 3.4g; Cholesterol 5mg; Calcium 30mg; Fibre 0.5g; Sodium 842mg.
Beef and Radish Soup: Energy 60kcal/247kJ; Protein 3.7g; Carbohydrate 2g, of which sugars 1.8g; Fat 4.1g, of which saturates 1g; Cholesterol 7mg; Calcium 17mg; Fibre 1g; Sodium 281mg.

Diced Beef and Seaweed Soup

This rich Korean broth is flavoured with tender beef and packed with silky green ribbons of seaweed. Seaweed soup is said to detoxify the body and help the circulation. If cooled, the soup can then be chilled and served as a summery side dish.

Serves 4
25g/1oz dried seaweed
40g/1½oz lean, tender frying (round) steak, diced
37.5ml/7½ tsp sesame oil
3 garlic cloves, finely chopped
45ml/3 tbsp light soy sauce
salt and ground black pepper
spring onion (scallion) finely shredded, to garnish

1 Soak the dried seaweed in plenty of cold water to cover for about 20 minutes, or until softened. Drain and cut into 2.5cm/1in lengths.

2 Place the steak in a dish. Add 15ml/1 tbsp of the sesame oil and ground black pepper, then mix well to coat the meat thoroughly and set aside for 10 minutes.

3 Place the beef and seaweed in a large pan. Add the remaining sesame oil and stir-fry the meat until the pieces are browned.

4 Pour in 750ml/1¼ pints/3 cups water. Bring the water to the boil and reduce the heat slightly, so that it just boils.

5 Add the garlic and soy sauce, stir well and bring back to a steady boil. Reduce the heat, if necessary, cover the pan and boil the soup until it has turned slightly milky in colour.

6 Taste and season before serving, garnished with fine shreds of spring onion.

Cook's Tip
Dried seaweed can be found at Asian food stores and health food stores. There are many different varieties, but this is best prepared with Korean miyuk or Japanese wakame. The soy sauce really brings out the flavour.

Beef Chilli Soup with Nachos

Steaming bowls of beef chilli soup, packed with beans, are delicious topped with crushed tortillas and cheese. The soup can be finished by putting the bowls under the grill (broiler) to brown the cheese.

Serves 4
45ml/3 tbsp olive oil
350g/12oz rump (round) steak, diced
2 onions, chopped
2 garlic cloves, crushed
2 green chillies, seeded and chopped
30ml/2 tbsp mild chilli powder
5ml/1 tsp ground cumin
2 bay leaves
30ml/2 tbsp tomato purée (paste)
900ml/1½ pints/3¾ cups beef stock
2 x 400g/14oz cans mixed beans, drained and rinsed
45ml/3 tbsp chopped fresh coriander (cilantro)
salt and ground black pepper

For the topping
bag of plain tortilla chips, lightly crushed
225g/8oz Monterey Jack or Cheddar cheese, grated

1 Heat the oil in a large pan over a high heat and brown the meat all over until golden. Use a draining spoon to remove the meat from the pan. Reduce the heat and add the onions, garlic and chillies, then cook for 4–5 minutes, until softened.

2 Stir in the chilli powder and cumin, and cook for a further 2 minutes. Return the meat to the pan, then stir in the bay leaves, tomato purée and beef stock. Bring to the boil.

3 Reduce the heat, cover and simmer for about 45 minutes or until the meat is tender.

4 Put a quarter of the beans into a bowl and mash with a potato masher. Stir these into the soup to thicken it slightly. Add the remaining beans and simmer for 5 minutes. Taste the soup and adjust the seasoning.

5 When ready to serve the soup, stir in the chopped coriander. Ladle the soup into bowls and sprinkle the tortilla chips over the surface. Pile the grated cheese over the tortilla chips and serve immediately.

Diced Beef and Seaweed: Energy 77kcal/318kJ; Protein 2.5g; Carbohydrate 0.7g, of which sugars 0.6g; Fat 7.2g, of which saturates 1.3g; Cholesterol 6mg; Calcium 3mg; Fibre 0.1g; Sodium 274mg.
Chilli with Nachos: Energy 631kcal/2629kJ; Protein 38.7g; Carbohydrate 25.6g, of which sugars 2.5g; Fat 41g, of which saturates 17.7g; Cholesterol 103mg; Calcium 500mg; Fibre 4.5g; Sodium 788mg.

Beef Broth with Water Spinach

Water spinach is a popular vegetable throughout Vietnam. When cooked, the stems remain crunchy while the leaves soften, lending a delightful contrast of texture to the dish. Served as an appetizer, this is a light soup with tender bites of beef and lemon juice.

Serves 4–6

30ml/2 tbsp fish sauce
5ml/1 tsp sugar
175g/6oz beef fillet, finely sliced across the grain into 2.5cm/1in strips
1.2 litres/2 pints/5 cups beef or chicken stock
175g/6oz water spinach, trimmed, rinsed, leaves and stalks separated
juice of 1 lemon
ground black pepper
1 fresh red or green chilli, seeded and finely sliced, to garnish

1 In a bowl, stir the fish sauce with the sugar until the sugar has dissolved. Add the beef strips and mix thoroughly, then leave to marinate for 30 minutes.

2 Pour the stock into a pan and bring it to the boil. Reduce the heat, so that the stock is simmering and add the water spinach. Stir in the lemon juice and season with pepper.

3 Divide the meat strips among soup bowls. Ladle the broth, straight from the stove so it is very hot, over the beef. Garnish with chillies and serve.

Cook's Tip
It is important to marinate the beef strips so that they take on the flavourings. If you have time to prepare them in advance, they can be left to marinate overnight.

Variation
You can sprinkle coriander (cilantro) and mint or fried garlic and ginger over the top if you prefer.

Beef and Barley Soup

This traditional Irish farmhouse soup makes a wonderfully restorative dish on a cold day. The flavours develop particularly well if it is made in advance and reheated to serve.

Serves 6–8

450–675g/1–1½lb stewing beef, such as leg, on the bone
2 large onions
50g/2oz/¼ cup pearl barley
50g/2oz/¼ cup green split peas
3 large carrots, chopped
2 white turnips, chopped
3 celery stalks, chopped
1 large or 2 medium leeks, thinly sliced
salt and ground black pepper
chopped fresh parsley, to serve

1 Bone the meat, put the bones and half an onion, roughly sliced, into a large pan. Cover with cold water and bring to the boil. Skim, reduce the heat and cover the pan. Simmer for 1½ hours or longer, until required. Do not salt the stock.

2 Trim any fat or gristle from the meat and cut it into small pieces. Chop the remaining onions finely.

3 Strain the stock, discard the bones, and add water to make up to 2 litres/3½ pints/9 cups. Return the stock to the rinssed pan. Add the meat, onions, barley and split peas. Do not add salt yet. Bring to the boil, and skim if necessary. Reduce the heat, cover and simmer for about 30 minutes.

4 Add the rest of the vegetables and simmer for 1 hour, or until the meat is tender. Add seasoning to taste and simmer the soup for a further 5 minutes. Serve in large warmed bowls, generously sprinkled with parsley.

Cook's Tip
Buying stewing beef on the bone is not easy. Ask the butcher for bones separate from the meat, if necessary. Alternatively, use minced (ground) beef to make a full-flavoured stock or buy ready made stock. Adding salt before the split peas are tender will prevent them from softening properly.

Beef Broth with Spinach: Energy 61kcal/254kJ; Protein 7.4g; Carbohydrate 1.2g, of which sugars 1.1g; Fat 3g, of which saturates 1.1g; Cholesterol 17mg; Calcium 51mg; Fibre 0.6g; Sodium 60mg.
Beef and Barley Soup: Energy 194kcal/816kJ; Protein 20.3g; Carbohydrate 21.6g, of which sugars 12g; Fat 3.5g, of which saturates 1.2g; Cholesterol 50mg; Calcium 84mg; Fibre 5g; Sodium 88mg.

Sliced Beef Soup

This dish is great for sharing with friends, as the cooking is done at the table.

Serves 4

600g/1⅓ lb rump (round) steak
2 thin leeks, cut into thin strips
4 spring onions (scallions), quartered
8 shiitake mushrooms caps
175g/6oz/2 cups oyster mushrooms, base part removed, torn into small pieces
½ head Chinese leaves (Chinese cabbage), cut into squares
300g/11oz spinach leaves, halved
275g/10oz firm tofu, halved and cut crossways in slices
10 x 6cm/4 x 2½in dashi-konbu or wakame, wiped with a damp cloth

For the lime sauce

1 lime
20ml/4 tsp mirin
60ml/4 tbsp rice vinegar
120ml/4fl oz/½ cup Japanese soy sauce (shoyu)
4 x 6cm/1½ x 2½in dashi-konbu or wakame

For the pink daikon

1 piece Chinese white radish (daikon), 6cm/2½in in length, peeled
1 dried chilli, seeded and sliced

1 To make the lime sauce, squeeze the lime and make up the juice to 120ml/4fl oz/½ cup with water. Pour into a bowl and add the mirin, rice vinegar, shoyu and dashi-konbu. Cover and leave to stand overnight.

2 Make the pink daikon. Pierce the mooli in several places and insert the chilli strips. Leave for 20 minutes, then grate, squeeze out the liquid and divide among four small bowls.

3 Slice the meat thinly. Arrange the meat, vegetables and tofu on platters. Fill a casserole three-quarters full of water and add the dashi-konbu. Boil, then transfer to a table burner. Strain the citrus sauce and add 45ml/3 tbsp to each bowl of daikon.

4 Remove the konbu from the stock. Add some tofu and vegetables to the pot. Each guest cooks a slice of beef in the stock, then dips it in sauce. Tofu and vegetables are removed and dipped in the same way, and more are added to the pot.

Braised Beef and Cabbage Soup

This is a main course in a bowl. Cook the beef as rare or as well done as you like.

Serves 6

900g/2lb red cabbage, finely shredded
2 onions, finely sliced
1 large cooking apple, peeled, cored and chopped
45ml/3 tbsp soft brown sugar
2 garlic cloves, crushed
1.5ml/¼ tsp grated nutmeg
2.5ml/½ tsp caraway seeds
45ml/3 tbsp red wine vinegar
1 litre/1¾ pints/4 cups beef stock
675kg/1½lb beef sirloin
30ml/2 tbsp olive oil
salt and ground black pepper
watercress, to garnish

For the horseradish cream

15–30ml/1–2 tbsp grated fresh horseradish
10ml/2 tsp wine vinegar
2.5ml/½ tsp Dijon mustard
150ml/¼ pint/⅔ cup double (heavy) cream

1 Preheat the oven to 150°C/300°F/Gas 2. Butter a casserole. Mix the cabbage, onions, apple, sugar, garlic, nutmeg, caraway seeds, red wine vinegar and 45ml/3 tbsp of the stock in the casserole. Season well, cover, tightly and bake for 2½ hours. Stir every 30 minutes to ensure that the cabbage is not too dry. If necessary, add a few more tablespoons of the stock. Set aside.

2 Increase the oven temperature to 230°C/450°F/Gas 8. Trim excess fat from the meat, leaving a thin layer. Heat the oil in a frying pan and brown the beef thoroughly all over. Transfer to a roasting pan and roast for 15–20 minutes for a medium-rare result or 25–30 minutes for well-done beef.

3 To make the horseradish cream, mix the grated horseradish, wine vinegar, mustard and seasoning with 45ml/3 tbsp of the cream. Lightly whip the remaining cream and fold in the horseradish mixture. Chill until required.

4 Place the cabbage in a pan, pour in the remaining stock and bring to the boil. Set the roast beef aside to rest for 5 minutes before carving into slices. Ladle the cabbage soup into bowls, top with beef slices and add a little horseradish cream. Garnish with watercress and serve.

Sliced Beef Soup: Energy 290kcal/1216kJ; Protein 42.2g; Carbohydrate 8.3g, of which sugars 7.4g; Fat 9.9g, of which saturates 3.1g; Cholesterol 89mg; Calcium 425mg; Fibre 3.9g; Sodium 1000mg.
Beef and Cabbage: Energy 395kcal/1645kJ; Protein 29.4g; Carbohydrate 19.4g, of which sugars 18.5g; Fat 22.5g, of which saturates 11.1g; Cholesterol 92mg; Calcium 104mg; Fibre 3.8g; Sodium 97mg.

Mixed Meat Soup

This Norwegian equivalent of French pot-au-feu, consists of broth followed by the meat and potatoes.

Serves 8–10

500g/1¼lb boneless beef, such as brisket
500g/1¼lb boneless pork, such as leg or lean belly
500g/1¼lb boneless mutton or lamb, such as shoulder
20ml/4 tsp salt
5ml/1 tsp peppercorns
2.5cm/1in piece fresh root ginger
1 bay leaf
250g/9oz sausagemeat (bulk sausage), rolled into balls
15ml/1 tbsp chopped onion
4 carrots, cut into strips
1 turnip or swede (rutabaga), diced
½ small white cabbage, cut into small pieces
boiled potatoes, to serve

For the dumplings
200ml/7fl oz/scant 1 cup single (light) cream
25ml/1½ tbsp sugar
130g/4½oz plain (all-purpose) flour
2 eggs
pinch of grated nutmeg
pinch of salt

1 Put the three pieces of meat in a large pan. Add 3 litres/5 pints/12½ cups water, salt, peppercorns, ginger and bay leaf and bring to simmering point. Simmer gently for 1–1½ hours.

2 Remove and cool the meat. Slice, arrange on a dish, add a little cooking liquid to prevent the slices from drying out and cover.

3 Skim the stock, add the onion, carrots, turnip or swede and cabbage. Boil, lower the heat and simmer for 10 minutes until the vegetables are just tender.

4 For the dumplings, put the cream and sugar in a pan and bring to the boil. Beat in the flour. Remove from the heat and beat in the eggs, one at a time. Season with nutmeg and salt. Wet your hands and roll the mixture into 16–20 small balls.

5 Add the balls of sausagemeat to the stock and simmer for 5 minutes. Add the dumplings and simmer for 5 minutes. Serve the soup followed by the meat accompanied by potatoes.

Gammon and Potato Broth

In this hearty soup, the potatoes cook in the gammon stock, absorbing its flavour and saltiness. Take care not to add too much salt and spoil the soup.

Serves 4

450g/1lb gammon (smoked or cured ham), in one piece
2 bay leaves
2 onions, sliced
10ml/2 tsp paprika
675g/1½lb baking potatoes, cut into large chunks
225g/8oz spring greens (collards)
425g/15oz can haricot (navy) or cannellini beans, drained
salt and ground black pepper

1 Soak the gammon overnight in cold water. Drain and put in a large pan with the bay leaves and onions. Pour in 1.5 litres/2½ pints/6¼ cups cold water. Bring to the boil, reduce the heat and simmer very gently for about 1½ hours until the meat is tender.

2 Remove the meat from the cooking liquid and leave to cool slightly. Discard the skin and any excess fat and cut the meat into small chunks. Return to the pan with the paprika and potatoes. Bring back to the boil, then reduce the heat, cover and simmer for 20 minutes until the potatoes are tender.

3 Trim the greens. Roll up the leaves and cut into thin shreds. Add to the pan with the beans and simmer, uncovered, for about 10 minutes. Remove the bay leaves. Season with salt and pepper to taste and serve hot.

Cook's Tip
Peel the potatoes if you prefer, but the flavour is best with the skin left on.

Variation
Bacon knuckle can be used instead of the gammon (smoked or cured ham) – they are economical and the bones will give the stock a delicious flavour. Freeze any stock you don't use.

Mixed Meat: Energy 453kcal/1892kJ; Protein 38.4g; Carbohydrate 22.9g, of which sugars 10.2g; Fat 23.7g, of which saturates 10.5g; Cholesterol 158mg; Calcium 111mg; Fibre 2.9g; Sodium 351mg.
Gammon and Potato: Energy 405kcal/1703kJ; Protein 31.7g; Carbohydrate 48.8g, of which sugars 8.2g; Fat 10.5g, of which saturates 3.2g; Cholesterol 26mg; Calcium 216mg; Fibre 10g; Sodium 1411mg.

Bean and Smoked Gammon Soup

This classic Spanish soup features haricot beans with young turnips. Do all the preparation a full day in advance, to allow time for the flavours to develop. The soup is then simply reheated the following day.

Serves 6

150g/5oz/⅔ cup haricot (navy) beans, soaked overnight in water
1kg/2¼lb smoked gammon (smoked or cured ham) hock
3 potatoes, quartered
3 small turnips, sliced in rounds
150g/5oz purple sprouting broccoli
salt and ground black pepper

1 Put the drained beans and gammon into a flameproof casserole and cover with 2 litres/3½ pints/8 cups water. Slowly bring to the boil, skim off any scum, then turn down the heat and cook gently, covered, for about 1¼ hours.

2 Drain, reserving the broth. Return the broth to the casserole and add the potatoes, turnips and drained beans.

3 Meanwhile, strip all the gammon off the bone and return the bone to the broth. Discard the rind, fat and gristle. Dice half the meat. Reserve the remaining meat for another recipe.

4 Add the diced meat to the casserole. Discard the hard stalks from the broccoli and add the leaves and florets to the broth. Simmer for 10 minutes. Season with pepper, then remove the bone and leave the soup to stand for at least half a day.

5 To serve, reheat the soup, add a little more seasoning if necessary, and ladle into soup bowls.

Cook's Tip
The leftover meat can be used in many ways, for example, chopped into bitesize pieces and added to rice or vegetable dishes, or Spanish omelettes (tortillas).

Kale, Chorizo and Potato Soup

This hearty winter soup has a spicy kick from the chorizo sausage. The soup becomes more potent if chilled overnight. It is worth buying the best possible chorizo sausage to achieve superior flavour.

Serves 6–8

225g/8oz kale, stems removed
225g/8oz chorizo sausage
675g/1½lb potatoes, cut into chunks
1.75 litres/3 pints/7½ cups vegetable stock
5ml/1 tsp ground black pepper
pinch of cayenne pepper (optional)
12 slices French bread, toasted on both sides
salt and ground black pepper

1 Place the kale in a food processor or blender and process for a few seconds to chop it finely. Alternatively, shred it finely by hand.

2 Prick the sausages and place in a pan with enough water to cover. Bring just to boiling point, then reduce the heat immediately before the water boils too rapidly and simmer for 15 minutes. Drain and cut into thin slices.

3 Boil the potatoes for about 15 minutes or until the slices are just tender. Drain, and place in a bowl, then mash adding a little of the cooking liquid to form a thick paste.

4 Bring the vegetable stock to the boil and add the kale. Bring back to the boil. Reduce the heat and add the chorizo, then simmer for 5 minutes. Gradually add the potato paste, stirring it into the soup, then simmer for 20 minutes. Season with black pepper and cayenne.

5 Divide the freshly made toast among serving bowls. Pour the soup over and serve immediately, sprinkled with pepper.

Cook's Tip
Select maincrop, floury potatoes for this soup rather than new potatoes or waxy salad potatoes.

Bean and Gammon: Energy 242kcal/1020kJ; Protein 22.6g; Carbohydrate 23.4g, of which sugars 3g; Fat 7.1g, of which saturates 2.3g; Cholesterol 19mg; Calcium 61mg; Fibre 5.8g; Sodium 751mg.
Kale, Chorizo, Potato: Energy 411kcal/1740kJ; Protein 13.2g; Carbohydrate 69.3g, of which sugars 6.2g; Fat 11g, of which saturates 4.1g; Cholesterol 15mg; Calcium 140mg; Fibre 4g; Sodium 812mg.

Golden Chorizo and Chickpea Soup

Small uncooked chorizo sausages are available from Spanish delicatessens, but ready-to-eat chorizo can be cut into chunks and used.

Serves 4

115g/4oz/⅔ cup dried chickpeas, soaked overnight
pinch of saffron strands
45ml/3 tbsp olive oil
450g/1lb uncooked mini chorizo sausages
5ml/1 tsp dried chilli flakes
6 garlic cloves, finely chopped
450g/1lb tomatoes, roughly chopped
350g/12oz new potatoes, quartered
2 bay leaves
450ml/¾ pint/scant 2 cups water
60ml/4 tbsp chopped fresh parsley
salt and ground black pepper
30ml/2 tbsp extra virgin olive oil, to garnish
crusty bread, to serve

1 Place the chickpeas in a large pan. Cover with plenty of fresh water and bring to the boil, skimming off any scum. Cover and simmer for 2–3 hours, until tender. Add more boiling water, if necessary, to keep the chickpeas well covered. Drain, reserving the liquid. Soak the saffron strands in a little warm water.

2 Heat the oil in a large, deep frying pan. Add the chorizo and fry for 5 minutes, until a lot of oil has seeped out of the sausages and they are pale golden brown. Drain and set aside.

3 Add the chilli flakes and garlic to the fat in the pan and cook for a few seconds. Stir in the saffron with its soaking water, tomatoes, chickpeas, potatoes, chorizo and bay leaves. Pour in 450ml/¾ pint/scant 2 cups of the chickpea cooking liquor and 450ml/¾ pint/scant 2 cups water. Season to taste.

4 Bring to the boil, reduce the heat and simmer for 45–50 minutes, stirring gently occasionally, until the potatoes are tender and the soup has thickened slightly.

5 Add the chopped parsley to the soup and adjust the seasoning. Ladle the soup into four large, warmed soup plates and drizzle a little extra virgin olive oil over each portion. Serve with crusty bread.

Tamarind Pork and Vegetable Soup

Sour soups, usually flavoured with tamarind or lime, are very popular in South-east Asia. They can be made with any combination of meat or fish and vegetables. Tamarind pods or kamias, a sour fruit similar in shape to star fruit, are the common souring agents in Filipino recipes.

Serves 4–6

2 litres/3½ pints/8 cups pork or chicken stock, or a mixture of stock and water
15–30ml/1–2 tbsp tamarind paste (see Cook's Tip)
30ml/2 tbsp patis (fish sauce)
25g/1oz fresh root ginger, finely grated
1 yam or sweet potato, cut into bitesize chunks
8–10 snake beans (yardlong beans)
225g/8oz kangkong (water spinach) or ordinary spinach, well rinsed
350g/12oz pork tenderloin, sliced widthways
2–3 spring onions (scallions), white parts only, finely sliced
salt and ground black pepper

1 Bring the stock to the boil In a wok or deep pan. Stir in the tamarind paste, patis and ginger, reduce the heat and simmer for about 20 minutes. Season with salt and lots of pepper.

2 Add the yam and snake beans to the pan and bring back to the boil, then immediately reduce the heat and cook gently for 3–4 minutes, until the yam is tender.

3 Stir in the spinach and the sliced pork and simmer gently for 2–3 minutes, until the pork is just cooked and turns opaque.

4 Ladle the soup into individual warmed bowls and sprinkle the sliced spring onions over the top.

Cook's Tip
Fresh tamarind pods, packaged tamarind pulp and pots of tamarind paste are all available in Middle-Eastern, Indian, African and South-east Asian food shops.

Chorizo and Chickpea: Energy 642kcal/2674kJ; Protein 21.7g; Carbohydrate 42.3g, of which sugars 8.1g; Fat 44g, of which saturates 12.5g; Cholesterol 68mg; Calcium 174mg; Fibre 6.1g; Sodium 997mg.
Pork and Vegetable: Energy 126kcal/532kJ; Protein 14g; Carbohydrate 12.3g, of which sugars 4.1g; Fat 2.7g, of which saturates 0.9g; Cholesterol 37mg; Calcium 31mg; Fibre 2g; Sodium 417mg.

Bacon, Mushroom and Herb Potage

Do not worry if this soup is not completely smooth – it is especially nice when it has a slightly nutty, textured consistency.

Serves 4

50g/2oz smoked streaky (fatty) bacon
1 onion, chopped
15ml/1 tbsp sunflower oil
350g/12oz open field (portabello) mushrooms or a mixture of wild and brown mushrooms
600ml/1 pint/2½ cups good meat stock
30ml/2 tbsp sweet sherry
30ml/2 tbsp chopped fresh mixed herbs, such as sage, rosemary, thyme and marjoram, or 10ml/2 tsp dried herbs
salt and ground black pepper
a few sprigs of sage or marjoram, to garnish
60ml/4 tbsp thick Greek (US strained plain) yogurt or crème fraîche, to serve

1 Roughly chop the bacon and place it in a large pan. Cook gently until all the fat comes out of the bacon.

2 Add the onion and cook, stirring, until it has softened, adding the oil if necessary. Wipe the mushrooms clean, roughly chop them and add to the pan. Cover and sweat until they have completely softened, reduced and yielded their liquid.

3 Add the stock, sherry, herbs and seasoning. Bring to the boil, reduce the heat and cover the pan. Simmer for 10–12 minutes. Process the soup in a food processor or blender until smooth or, if preferred, slightly coarsely textured.

4 Taste and adjust the seasoning and heat through. Ladle the soup into bowls and top each portion with a little yogurt or crème fraîche. Garnish with sprigs of fresh sage or marjoram and serve immediately.

Cook's Tip

Any mushrooms can be used – for maximum flavour from the ordinary, closed cap type, use more than suggested and cook them uncovered to evaporate and concentrate their juices.

Pork and Vegetable Soup

Gobo is a Japanese root vegetable with a mild, sweet taste. Konnyaku is a gelatinous thickening agent, suitable for vegetarians. The latter can be replaced by another agent such as agar agar, or by 5ml/1 tsp arrowroot mixed with water.

Serves 4

50g/2oz gobo (burdock – optional)
5ml/1 tsp rice vinegar
½ black konnyaku (about 115g/4oz)
10ml/2 tsp vegetable oil
200g/7oz pork belly, cut into thin 3–4cm/1¼–½in long strips
115g/4oz Chinese white radish (mooli), peeled and thinly sliced
1 carrot, thinly sliced
1 potato, thinly sliced
4 shiitake mushrooms, stems removed and thinly sliced
800ml/scant 1½ pints/3½ cups kombu and bonito stock or instant dashi
15ml/1 tbsp sake or dry white wine
45ml/3 tbsp red or white miso
2 spring onions (scallions), thinly sliced, to garnish

1 Scrub the skin off the gobo, if using, and use a peeler to slice it into fine shavings. Soak for 5 minutes in plenty of water with the vinegar added to remove any bitter taste, then drain.

2 Put the piece of konnyaku in a small pan and add enough water just to cover it. Bring to the boil over a moderate heat, then drain and allow to cool. This removes any bitter taste. Break the konnyaku into 2cm/¾in lumps. Do not use a knife as a smooth cut surface will not absorb any flavour.

3 Heat the oil in a pan and stir-fry the pork. Add the gobo, white radish, carrot, potato, mushrooms and konnyaku, then stir-fry for 1 minute. Pour in the stock and sake or wine. Bring the soup to the boil, then skim it and simmer for 10 minutes, until the vegetables have softened.

4 Ladle a little of the soup into a small bowl and stir the miso into it until dissolved. Pour back into the pan and bring back to the boil. Remove from the heat immediately or flavour will be lost if the soup continues to boil. Pour the soup into bowls. Sprinkle with the spring onions and serve immediately.

Bacon, Mushroom and Herb: Energy 111kcal/460kJ; Protein 4.7g; Carbohydrate 2g, of which sugars 1.4g; Fat 8.7g, of which saturates 2.4g; Cholesterol 8mg; Calcium 33mg; Fibre 1.2g; Sodium 174mg.
Pork and Vegetable: Energy 310kcal/1299kJ; Protein 42.3g; Carbohydrate 6.8g, of which sugars 6g; Fat 12.8g, of which saturates 3.4g; Cholesterol 110mg; Calcium 73mg; Fibre 2g; Sodium 1235mg.

Gammon and Herb Gumbo

The variety of green ingredients is important, so buy substitutes if you cannot find individual types of them.

Serves 6–8
350g/12oz smoked gammon (cured ham)
30ml/2 tbsp lard or cooking oil
1 large Spanish (Bermuda) onion, roughly chopped
2–3 garlic cloves, crushed
5ml/1 tsp dried oregano
5ml/1 tsp dried thyme
2 bay leaves
2 cloves
2 celery sticks, finely sliced
1 green (bell) pepper, seeded and chopped
½ green cabbage, finely shredded
2 litres/3½ pints/9 cups light stock or water
200g/7oz spring greens (collards) or kale, finely shredded
200g/7oz Chinese mustard cabbage, finely shredded
200g/7oz spinach, shredded
bunch of watercress, shredded
6 spring onions (scallions), finely shredded
25g/1oz fresh parsley, chopped
2.5ml/½ tsp ground allspice
¼ nutmeg, grated
pinch of cayenne pepper
salt and ground black pepper
warm French or garlic bread, to serve

1 Dice the gammon quite small, keeping any fat and rind in one separate piece. Put the fat with the lard or oil in a deep pan and cook until it sizzles. Stir in the diced ham, onion, garlic, oregano and thyme and cook over a medium heat for 5 minutes, stirring occasionally.

2 Add the bay leaves, cloves, celery and green pepper and stir over a medium heat for 2–3 minutes. Add the cabbage and stock or water. Boil, reduce the heat and simmer for 5 minutes.

3 Add the spring greens or kale and mustard cabbage. Boil for a further 2 minutes, then add the spinach, watercress and spring onions. Return to the boil, then lower the heat and simmer for 1 minute. Add the parsley, allspice and nutmeg, salt, black pepper and cayenne to taste.

4 Remove the piece of ham fat and, if you can find them, the cloves. Ladle into individual soup bowls and serve immediately, with warm French bread or garlic bread.

Sweet-Sour Pork Soup with Coconut

This coconut-flavoured, sharp soup is a variation on adobo hotpots cooked in Philippines.

Serves 4–6
675g/1½lb lean boneless pork, diced
1 garlic clove, crushed
5ml/1 tsp paprika
5ml/1 tsp crushed black peppercorns
15ml/1 tbsp sugar
175ml/6fl oz/¾ cup palm vinegar or cider vinegar
2 small bay leaves
750ml/1¼ pints/3 cups chicken stock
50g/2oz creamed coconut (coconut cream) (see Cook's Tip)
150ml/¼ pint/⅔ cup vegetable oil, for frying
1 under-ripe papaya, peeled, seeded and chopped
salt

For the garnish
½ cucumber, peeled and cut into batons
2 firm tomatoes, skinned, seeded and chopped
small bunch of chives, chopped

1 Place the pork in a bowl. Add the garlic, paprika, black pepper, sugar, vinegar and bay leaves. Mix well to coat the meat thoroughly, cover and leave in a cool place for 2 hours.

2 Pour the meat and marinade into a pan or wok. Stir in the chicken stock and coconut. Bring to the boil, reduce the heat and simmer gently for 30–35 minutes.

3 Remove the pork using a slotted spoon. Heat the oil in a pan and fry the pork until golden. Drain the pork well and return it to the soup.

4 Add the papaya, season with salt and simmer the soup for 15–20 minutes. To serve, ladle the soup into bowls and garnish with the cucumber batons, chopped tomatoes and chives.

Cook's Tip
If creamed coconut (coconut cream) is not available, use 50ml/2fl oz/10 tsp coconut milk

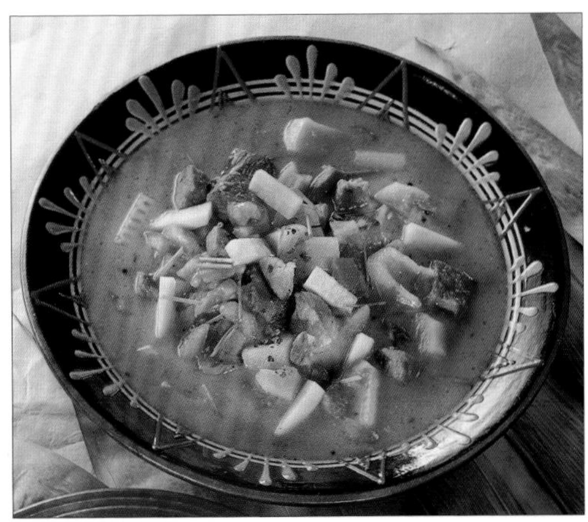

Gammon Gumbo: Energy 138kcal/573kJ; Protein 10.8g; Carbohydrate 8.8g, of which sugars 7.8g; Fat 6.8g, of which saturates 1.5g; Cholesterol 10mg; Calcium 129mg; Fibre 3.6g; Sodium 440mg.
Sweet-Sour Pork: Energy 229kcal/963kJ; Protein 32.8g; Carbohydrate 11.1g, of which sugars 10.9g; Fat 6.2g, of which saturates 2.1g; Cholesterol 95mg; Calcium 37mg; Fibre 2.3g; Sodium 111mg.

Pork Wonton Soup

The freshly cooked crisp wontons are supposed to sizzle and "sing" in the hot soup as they are taken to the table.

Serves 6

2 cloud ear (wood ear) mushrooms, soaked for 30 minutes in warm water to cover
1.2 litres/2 pints/5 cups home-made chicken stock
2.5cm/1in piece fresh root ginger, peeled and grated
4 spring onions (scallions), chopped
2 rich-green inner spring greens (collards) leaves, finely shredded
50g/2oz drained canned bamboo shoots, sliced
25ml/1½ tbsp dark soy sauce
2.5ml/½ tsp sesame oil
salt and ground black pepper

For the wontons

2.5ml/½ tsp sesame oil
½ small onion, finely chopped
10 drained canned water chestnuts, finely chopped
115g/4oz minced (ground) lean pork
24 wonton wrappers
1 egg white
5ml/1 tsp sunflower oil

1 For the wontons. Heat the sesame oil in a small pan. Add the onion, water chestnuts and pork and cook, stirring often, until the meat is just cooked. Season to taste and leave to cool.

2 Dampen the edges of a wonton wrapper. Place 5ml/1 tsp filling in the centre. Gather up the wrapper, pinching it to seal in the filling. Repeat with the remaining wrappers and filling.

3 Make the soup. Drain the cloud ears, trim stems, then slice them. Bring the stock to the boil. Add the ginger and spring onions and simmer for 3 minutes. Add the cloud ears, spring greens, bamboo shoots and soy sauce. Simmer for 10 minutes, then stir in the sesame oil. Season, cover and keep hot.

4 Preheat the oven to 240°C/475°F/Gas 9. Lightly whisk the egg white with the sunflower oil and water. Brush the wontons generously with this and place on a non-stick baking sheet. Bake for about 5 minutes, until browned and crisp. Ladle the soup into six warmed soup bowls and share the wontons among them. Serve immediately.

Prawn Tail and Pak Choi Broth with Pork Wontons

A well-flavoured chicken stock or broth is a must for this classic Chinese snack, which is popular on fast-food stalls in towns and cities throughout the regions of Southern China.

Serves 4

200g/7oz minced (ground) pork
200g/7oz peeled cooked prawns (shrimp), thawed if frozen
10ml/2 tsp rice wine or dry sherry
10ml/2 tsp light soy sauce
5ml/1 tsp sesame oil
24 thin wonton wrappers
1.2 litres/2 pints/5 cups chicken stock
12 raw tiger prawns (jumbo shrimp), shelled, with tails
350g/12oz pak choi (bok choy), coarsely shredded
salt and ground black pepper

For the garnish

4 spring onions (scallions), sliced
1cm/½in piece fresh root ginger, finely shredded

1 Put the pork, prawns, rice wine or sherry, soy sauce and sesame oil in a large bowl. Add plenty of seasoning and mix the ingredients thoroughly.

2 Put about 10ml/2 tsp of the pork mixture in the centre of each wonton wrapper. Bring up the sides of the wrapper and pinch them together to seal the filling in a small bundle.

3 Bring a large pan of water to the boil. Add the wontons and simmer for 3 minutes, then drain well and set aside.

4 Pour the stock into a large pan and bring to the boil. Season to taste. Add the tiger prawns and cook for 2–3 minutes, until they are just tender.

5 Add the wontons and pak choi, then simmer the soup for a further 1–2 minutes until the green vegetables are wilted and the wontons are reheated.

6 Ladle the soup into bowls and garnish with spring onions and ginger. Serve immediately.

Pork Wonton: Energy 132kcal/554kJ; Protein 8.4g; Carbohy. 17g, of which sugars 3.4g; Fat 3.9g, of which saturates 0.7g, of which polyunsaturates 1.9g; Cholesterol 12mg; Calcium 140mg; Fibre 2.7g; Sodium 332mg.
Prawn Tail and Pak Choi: Energy 273kcal/1148kJ; Protein 32.1g; Carbohydrate 21g, of which sugars 1.9g; Fat 7.2g, of which saturates 2.2g; Cholesterol 228mg; Calcium 267mg; Fibre 2.6g; Sodium 524mg.

Sausage and Pesto Soup

This is a satisfying one-pot meal with overtones of summer, thanks to the pesto and fresh basil.

Serves 4

15ml/1 tbsp olive oil, plus extra or frying
1 red onion, chopped
450g/1lb smoked pork sausages
225g/8oz/1 cup red lentils
400g/14oz can chopped tomatoes
1 litre/1¾ pints/4 cups water
oil, for deep-frying
salt and ground black pepper
60ml/4 tbsp pesto and fresh basil sprigs, to garnish

1 Heat the oil in large pan and cook the onion until soft. Coarsely chop all the sausage except for two, and add them to the pan. Cook for about 5 minutes, stirring, or until the sausage is cooked through.

2 Stir in the lentils, tomatoes and water, and bring to the boil. Reduce the heat, cover and simmer for about 20 minutes. Allow to cool slightly.

3 Purée the sausage mixture in a food processor or blender until smooth. Return to the rinsed-out pan.

4 Cook the remaining sausages in a little oil in a small frying pan for 10 minutes, turning often, until lightly browned and firm. Transfer to a chopping board or plate and leave to cool slightly, then slice thinly.

5 Heat the oil for deep-frying to 190°C/375°F or until a cube of day-old bread browns in about 60 seconds. Deep-fry the sausage slices and basil briefly until the sausages are brown and the basil leaves are crisp.

6 Lift the sausage slices out using a slotted spoon and drain on kitchen paper.

7 Reheat the soup, add seasoning to taste, then ladle into warmed bowls. Sprinkle with the deep-fried sausage slices and basil and swirl a little pesto through each portion. Serve with warm crusty bread.

Pork and Tofu Soup with Kimchi

Cabbage kimchi is a classic oriental condiment of marinated Chinese leaves, and it is available to buy in many Asian stores. It combines beautifully with the pork and meaty shiitake mushrooms in this spicy Korean soup. Be sure to use firm, rather than soft, tofu as it is less likely to break up during cooking.

Serves 4

4 dried shiitake mushrooms, soaked in warm water for about 30 minutes
150g/5oz firm tofu
200g/7oz boneless pork chop
300g/11oz cabbage kimchi
45ml/3 tbsp vegetable oil
1 garlic clove, crushed
15ml/1 tbsp chilli powder
750ml/1¼ pints/3 cups vegetable stock or water
2 spring onions (scallions), finely sliced
salt

1 When the soaked shiitake mushrooms have reconstituted and become soft, drain and slice them, discarding the stems. Dice the tofu into cubes approximately 2cm/¾in square. Dice the pork into bitesize cubes, and slice the kimchi into similar size pieces.

2 Pour the vegetable oil into a pan or wok and place over medium heat. Add the pork and garlic, and sauté until crisp. Once the pork has turned dark brown add the kimchi and chilli powder, and stir-fry for 60 seconds more.

3 Add the stock or water and bring to the boil. Add the tofu, mushrooms and spring onions, cover and simmer for 10–15 minutes. Season with salt and serve bubbling from the pan.

Variation
Create a lighter dish by substituting canned tuna for the pork. Use fish stock to emphasize the flavour.

Sausage and Pesto: Energy 656kcal/2741kJ; Protein 30.9g; Carbohydrate 46.7g, of which sugars 8.2g; Fat 39.7g, of which saturates 13.1g; Cholesterol 75mg; Calcium 250mg; Fibre 4.8g; Sodium 1109mg.
Pork and Tofu Soup: Energy 185kcal/770kJ; Protein 15.1g; Carbohydrate 4.2g, of which sugars 4g; Fat 12.1g, of which saturates 1.9g; Cholesterol 32mg; Calcium 234mg; Fibre 1.8g; Sodium 534mg.

Pork Soup with Cloud Ears

One of China's most popular hot and sour soups, this is famed for its clever balance of flavours, notably the vinegar and pepper.

Serves 6

4–6 Chinese dried mushrooms
2–3 small pieces of cloud ear (wood ear) mushrooms
115g/4oz pork fillet (tenderloin), cut into fine strips
45ml/3 tbsp cornflour (cornstarch)
150ml/¼ pint/⅔ cup water
15–30ml/1–2 tbsp sunflower oil
1 small onion, finely chopped
1.5 litres/2½ pints/6 cups good quality beef or chicken stock
150g/5oz fresh firm tofu, diced
60ml/4 tbsp rice vinegar
15ml/1 tbsp light soy sauce
1 egg, beaten
5ml/1 tsp sesame oil
salt and ground black pepper
2–3 spring onions (scallions), shredded, to garnish

1 Place the dried mushrooms in a bowl, with the pieces of cloud ear. Add sufficient warm water to cover and leave to soak for about 30 minutes.

2 Drain the mushrooms, reserving the soaking water. Cut off and discard the mushroom stems and slice the caps finely. Trim away any tough stem from the wood ears, then chop them.

3 Lightly dust the strips of pork with some of the cornflour. Mix the remaining cornflour to a smooth, thin paste with 150ml/¼ pint/⅔ cup water.

4 Heat the oil in a wok and fry the onion until soft. Increase the heat and fry the pork until it changes colour. Add the stock, mushrooms, soaking water and cloud ears. Bring to the boil, then simmer for 15 minutes. Stir in the cornflour paste and bring to the boil, stirring, to thicken. Add the tofu, vinegar, soy sauce, and salt and pepper.

5 Bring the soup to just below boiling point, then drizzle in the beaten egg so that it forms threads. Stir in the sesame oil and serve at once, garnished with spring onion shreds.

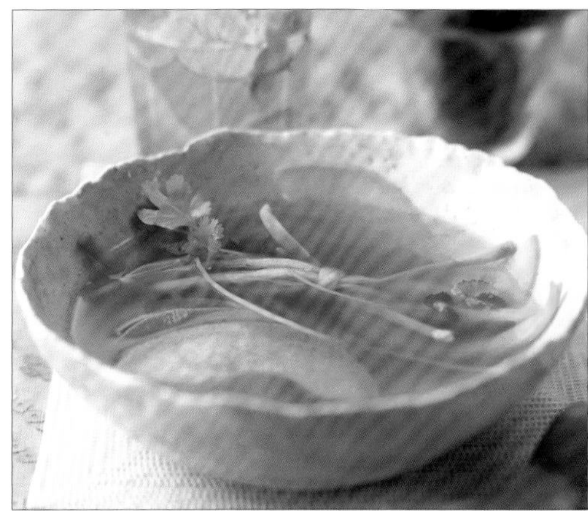

Pork Broth with Winter Melon

Winter melon is excellent for absorbing the rich flavours of this recipe.

Serves 4

350g/12oz winter melon
salt and ground black pepper
1 small bunch each coriander (cilantro) and mint, stalks removed, leaves chopped, to garnish

For the stock

25g/1oz dried shrimp, soaked in water for 15 minutes
500g/1¼lb pork ribs
1 onion, peeled and quartered
175g/6oz carrots, peeled and cut into chunks
15ml/1 tbsp fish sauce
15ml/1 tbsp soy sauce
4 black peppercorns

1 To make the stock, drain and rinse the dried shrimp. Put the pork ribs in a large pan and cover with 2 litres/3½ pints/8 cups water. Bring the water to the boil, skim off any fat, and add the dried shrimp and the remaining stock ingredients. Cover and simmer for 1½ hours, then skim again.

2 Continue simmering the stock, uncovered, for 30 minutes. Strain the stock and check the seasoning. You should have about 1.5 litres/2½ pints/6 cups.

3 Halve the winter melon lengthways and remove the seeds and inner membrane. Finely slice the flesh into half-moons. Squeeze the soaked tiger lilies dry and tie them in a knot.

4 Bring the stock to the boil in a pan or wok. Reduce the heat and add the winter melon and tiger lilies. Simmer for 15–20 minutes, or until the melon is tender.

5 Season the soup to taste with salt and pepper, and serve in heated bowls, sprinkled with the herbs.

Cook's Tip

If you can find them, golden tiger lilies make an excellent addition. Soak for 20 minutes, then tie in a knot and add with the melon.

Pork with Cloud Ears: Energy 109kcal/458kJ; Protein 7.8g; Carbohydrate 8.3g, of which sugars 1g; Fat 5.3g, of which saturates 1g; Cholesterol 44mg; Calcium 141mg; Fibre 0.4g; Sodium 210mg.
Pork Broth with Melon: Energy 25kcal/103kJ; Protein 1.6g; Carbohydrate 2.6g, of which sugars 1.9g; Fat 0.9g, of which saturates 0.1g; Cholesterol 0mg; Calcium 55mg; Fibre 1.5g; Sodium 616mg.

Sweet and Sour Pork Soup

This very quick, sharp and tangy soup is perfect for an impromptu supper. It can also be made with shredded chicken breast.

Serves 6–8

900g/2lb pork fillet (tenderloin), trimmed
1 unripe papaya, halved, seeded, peeled and shredded
3 shallots, chopped
5ml/1 tsp crushed black peppercorns
5 garlic cloves, chopped
15ml/1 tbsp shrimp paste
30ml/2 tbsp vegetable oil
1.5 litres/2½ pints/6 cups chicken stock
2.5cm/1in piece fresh root ginger, grated
120ml/4fl oz/½ cup tamarind water
15ml/1 tbsp honey
juice of 1 lime
4 spring onions (scallions), sliced
salt and ground black pepper
2 small fresh red chillies, seeded and sliced, to garnish

1 Cut the pork into very fine strips, 5cm/2in in length. Mix with the papaya and set aside.

2 Process the shallots, peppercorns, garlic and shrimp paste together in a food processor or blender to form a paste.

3 Heat the oil in a heavy pan and fry the shallot paste for 1–2 minutes. Add the stock and bring to the boil, stirring. Stir in the pork and papaya, ginger and tamarind water.

4 Bring the soup to the boil, then reduce the heat and cover the pan. Simmer the soup for 7–8 minutes, or until the pork strips are tender.

5 Stir in the honey, lime juice, most of the chillies and spring onions. Season to taste. Ladle the soup into bowls and serve at once, garnished with the remaining chillies and onions.

Cook's Tip
Unripe papayas are often served in salads in Asia and are also cooked as a vegetable.

Peppered Pork Broth

This aromatic, peppery broth is a favourite at late-night hawker stalls.

Serves 4–6

500g/1¼lb meaty pork ribs, trimmed and cut into 5cm/2in lengths
225g/8oz pork loin
8 garlic cloves, unpeeled and bruised
2 cinnamon sticks
5 star anise
120ml/4fl oz/½ cup light soy sauce
50ml/2fl oz/¼ cup dark soy sauce
15ml/1 tbsp sugar
salt and ground black pepper
steamed rice, to serve

For the dipping sauce
120ml/4fl oz/½ cup light soy sauce
2 fresh red chillies, seeded and finely chopped

For the spice bag
6 cloves
15ml/1 tbsp dried orange peel
5ml/1 tsp black peppercorns
5ml/1 tsp coriander seeds
5ml/1 tsp fennel seeds

1 To make the dipping sauce, stir the soy sauce and chillies together in a small bowl and set aside. To make the spice bag, lay a piece of muslin (cheesecloth) flat and place all the spices in the centre. Gather up the edges and tie together.

2 Put the pork ribs and loin into a deep pan. Add the garlic, cinnamon sticks, star anise and spice bag. Pour in 2.5 litres/4½ pints/10 cups water and bring to the boil.

3 Skim off any fat from the surface, then stir in the soy sauces and sugar. Reduce the heat and simmer, partially covered, for about 2 hours, until the pork is almost falling off the bones. Season to taste with salt and lots of black pepper.

4 Remove the loin from the broth and cut it into bitesize pieces. Divide the meat and ribs among four to six bowls and ladle steaming broth over the top.

5 Serve the soup immediately, with the soy and chilli sauce, as a dip for the pieces of pork. Ladle over more broth as required.

Sweet and Sour Pork: Energy 229kcal/963kJ; Protein 32.8g; Carbohydrate 11.1g, of which sugars 10.9g; Fat 6.2g, of which saturates 2.1g; Cholesterol 95mg; Calcium 37mg; Fibre 2.3g; Sodium 111mg.
Peppered Pork Broth: Energy 49kcal/206kJ; Protein 8.1g; Carbohydrate 0.8g, of which sugars 0.8g; Fat 1.5g, of which saturates 0.5g; Cholesterol 24mg; Calcium 3mg; Fibre 0g; Sodium 145mg.

Pork and Lotus Root Broth

In this clear broth, which is served as an appetizer, the thin, round slices of fresh lotus root look like delicate flowers floating in water.

Serves 4–6

450g/1lb fresh lotus root, peeled and thinly sliced
ground black pepper

For the garnish
1 fresh red chilli, seeded and finely sliced, and 1 small bunch basil leaves, to garnish

For the stock
450g/1lb pork ribs
1 onion, quartered
2 carrots, cut into chunks
25g/1oz dried squid or dried shrimp, soaked in water for 30 minutes, rinsed and drained
15ml/1 tbsp fish sauce
15ml/1 tbsp soy sauce
6 black peppercorns
sea salt

1 First prepare the stock. Put the ribs into a pan and cover with 1.5 litres/2½ pints/6¼ cups water. Bring to the boil, skim, and add the other ingredients. Reduce the heat, cover, and simmer for 2 hours.

2 Take off the lid and simmer the soup for a further 30 minutes to reduce the stock and intensify its flavour. Strain the stock and shred the meat off the pork ribs.

3 Pour the stock back into the pan and bring it to the boil. Reduce the heat and add the lotus root. Part cover the pan and simmer the soup gently for 30–40 minutes, until the lotus root is tender.

4 Stir in the shredded meat and season the broth with salt and pepper. Ladle the soup into bowls and garnish with the chilli and basil leaves.

Cook's Tip
The lotus, an edible water lily, has been grown in China for centuries and is prized for its delicate flavour.

Stuffed Cabbage Leaves in Broth

This Thai-style soup is spicy and deliciously different.

Serves 4

10 Chinese cabbage leaves
4 spring onions (scallions), green tops left whole, white part finely chopped
5–6 dried cloud ear (wood ear) mushrooms, soaked in hot water for 15 minutes
115g/4oz minced (ground) lean pork
115g/4oz prawns (shrimp), shelled, deveined and chopped
1 fresh Thai chilli, seeded and chopped
30ml/2 tbsp shrimp paste
45ml/3 tbsp soy sauce
1.5 litres/2½ pints/6¼ cups chicken stock
4 garlic cloves, crushed
4cm/1½ in fresh root ginger, peeled and very finely sliced
chopped fresh coriander (cilantro), to garnish

1 Blanch the cabbage leaves in boiling water for about 2 minutes, or until tender. Remove with a slotted spoon and refresh under cold water. Add the green tops of the spring onions to the boiling water and blanch for a minute, or until tender, then drain and refresh under cold water. Carefully tear each piece into five thin strips and set aside.

2 Squeeze dry the cloud ear mushrooms, then trim and finely chop. Mix with the pork, prawns, spring onion whites, chilli, shrimp paste and 15ml/1 tbsp soy sauce. Lay a cabbage leaf flat on a surface and place a teaspoon of the filling about 1cm/½in from the bottom edge.

3 Fold the bottom edge over the filling, and then fold over the sides of the leaf. Roll up all the way to the top of the leaf to form a tight bundle. Wrap a piece of blanched spring onion green around the bundle and tie it so that it holds together. Repeat with the remaining leaves and filling.

4 Bring the stock, remaining soy sauce, garlic and ginger to the boil in pan. Reduce the heat and add the cabbage bundles. Bubble very gently over a low heat for about 20 minutes to ensure that the filling is thoroughly cooked. Serve immediately, ladled into bowls, with a sprinkling of fresh coriander leaves.

Pork and Lotus Root: Energy 181kcal/756kJ; Protein 23.8g; Carbohydrate 4g, of which sugars 3.1g; Fat 7.8g, of which saturates 2.7g; Cholesterol 74mg; Calcium 65mg; Fibre 1.4g; Sodium 269mg.
Stuffed Cabbage Leaves: Energy 80kcal/334kJ; Protein 12.7g; Carbohydrate 3.9g, of which sugars 3.7g; Fat 1.5g, of which saturates 0.5g; Cholesterol 74mg; Calcium 68mg; Fibre 1.4g; Sodium 891mg.

Celeriac and Bacon Soup

Versatile, yet often overlooked, celeriac is a winter vegetable that makes excellent soup.

Serves 4

50g/2oz butter
2 onions, chopped
675g/1½lb celeriac, roughly diced
450g/1lb potatoes, roughly diced
1.2 litres/2 pints/5 cups vegetable stock
150ml/¼ pint/⅔ cup single (light) cream
salt and ground black pepper
sprigs of fresh thyme, to garnish

For the topping

1 small savoy cabbage
50g/2oz/¼ cup butter
175g/6oz rindless streaky (fatty) bacon, roughly chopped
15ml/1 tbsp roughly chopped fresh thyme
15ml/1 tbsp roughly chopped fresh rosemary

1 Melt the butter in a pan. Add the onions and cook for 4–5 minutes, until softened. Add the celeriac. Put a lid on the pan and cook gently for 10 minutes.

2 Stir in the potatoes and stock. Bring to the boil, reduce the heat and simmer for 20 minutes or until the vegetables are very tender. Leave to cool slightly. Using a slotted spoon, remove about half the celeriac and potatoes from the soup and set them aside.

3 Purée the soup in a food processor or blender. Return it to the rinsed-out pan with the reserved celeriac and potatoes.

4 Prepare the topping. Discard the tough outer leaves from the cabbage. Roughly tear the remaining leaves, discarding any hard stalks, and blanch them in boiling salted water for 2–3 minutes. Refresh under cold running water and drain.

5 Melt the butter in a large frying pan and cook the bacon for 3–4 minutes. Add the cabbage, thyme and rosemary, and stir-fry for 5–6 minutes, until tender. Season well.

6 Add the cream to the soup and season it well, then reheat gently. Ladle the soup into bowls and pile the cabbage mixture in the middle. Garnish with sprigs of fresh thyme.

Bacon and Green Pea Soup with Spinach

This lovely green soup was supposedly invented by the wife of a 17th-century British member of parliament and it has stood the test of time.

Serves 6

450g/1lb/generous 3 cups podded fresh or frozen peas
1 leek, finely sliced
2 garlic cloves, crushed
2 rindless back bacon rashers (slices), finely diced
1.2 litres/2 pints/5 cups ham or chicken stock
30ml/2 tbsp olive oil
50g/2oz fresh spinach, shredded
40g/1½oz/⅓ cup white cabbage, finely shredded
½ small lettuce, finely shredded
1 celery stick, finely chopped
a large handful of parsley, finely chopped
½ carton mustard and cress
20ml/4 tsp chopped fresh mint
a pinch of ground mace
salt and ground black pepper

1 Put the peas, leek, garlic and bacon in a large pan. Add the stock, bring to the boil, then lower the heat and cover the pan. Simmer for 20 minutes.

2 About 5 minutes before the pea soup is ready, heat the oil in a frying pan. Add the spinach, cabbage, lettuce, celery and herbs to the frying pan. Cover and sweat the mixture over a low heat until the vegetables are soft.

3 Transfer the pea soup to a food processor or blender and process until smooth. Return the soup to the rinsed-out pan.

4 Add the sweated vegetables and herbs to the soup. Stir them in and reheat the soup. Season to taste with mace, salt and pepper, and serve piping hot.

Cook's Tip

For the best flavour use tender young fresh peas or petit pois (baby peas) if using frozen peas. The economy frozen peas are fine, but they tend to be less sweet and coarser in texture.

Celeriac and Bacon: Energy 462kcal/1919kJ; Protein 12.3g; Carbohydrate 24.3g, of which sugars 7.3g; Fat 35.8g, of which saturates 20.4g; Cholesterol 97mg; Calcium 144mg; Fibre 4.3g; Sodium 954mg.
Bacon and Green Pea: Energy 127kcal/527kJ; Protein 7.7g; Carbohydrate 10.3g, of which sugars 3.3g; Fat 6.4g, of which saturates 1.3g; Cholesterol 4mg; Calcium 62mg; Fibre 5.1g; Sodium 145mg.

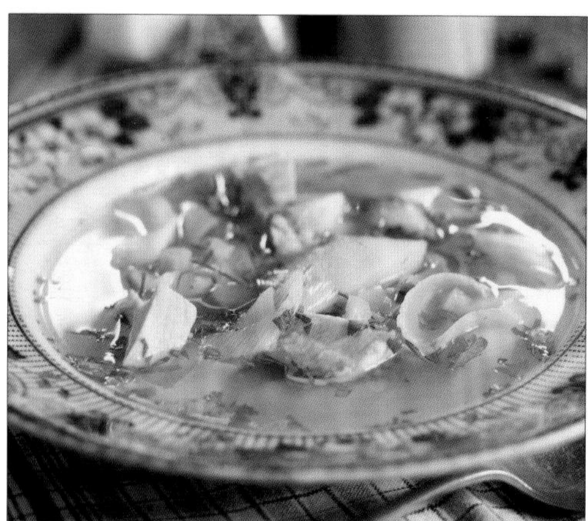

Leek and Bacon Soup

Traditionally, this often made two courses or even two meals – the bacon and vegetables for one and the broth for the other.

Serves 4–6

1 piece unsmoked bacon, weighing about 1kg/2¼lb
500g/1lb 2oz/4½ cups leeks
1 large carrot, finely chopped
1 large potato, sliced
15ml/1 tbsp fine or medium oatmeal
handful of fresh parsley
salt and ground black pepper

1 Trim the bacon of excess fat, put it in a large pan and pour over enough cold water to cover. Bring to the boil, then discard the water. Add 1.5 litres/2¾ pints cold water, bring to the boil, then cover and simmer gently for 30 minutes.

2 Thickly slice the white and pale green parts of the leeks, reserving the dark green leaves. Add the sliced leek to the pan with the carrot, potato and oatmeal. Bring the soup back to the boil. Cover the pan and simmer gently for a further 30–40 minutes, until the vegetables and bacon are tender.

3 Slice the reserved dark green leeks very thinly and finely chop the parsley.

4 Lift the bacon out of the pan and either slice it and serve separately or cut it into bitesize chunks and stir these back into the soup.

5 Adjust the seasoning to taste, adding pepper, but it may not be necessary to add salt. Bring the soup to the boil. Add the sliced dark green leeks and parsley, and simmer very gently for about 5 minutes before serving.

Cook's Tip
This is a traditional Welsh soup, known as cawl. A chunk of beef or lamb may be used instead of bacon, and other root vegetables may be added. Shredded cabbage is also popular.

Bacon Broth

A hearty meal in a soup bowl. The bacon hock contributes flavour and some meat to this dish, but it may be salty so remember to taste before seasoning, and add salt only if required.

Serves 6–8

1 bacon hock, about 900g/2lb
75g/3oz/⅓ cup pearl barley
75g/3oz/⅓ cup lentils
2 leeks, sliced, or onions, diced
4 carrots, diced
200g/7oz swede (rutabaga), diced
3 potatoes, diced
small bunch of herbs (thyme, parsley, bay leaf)
1 small cabbage, trimmed and quartered or sliced
salt and ground black pepper
chopped fresh parsley, to garnish
brown bread, to serve

1 Soak the bacon in cold water overnight. Drain the bacon and put it into a large pan with enough fresh cold water to cover. Bring to the boil, skim off any scum that rises to the surface, and then add the barley and lentils. Bring back to the boil and simmer for about 15 minutes.

2 Add the vegetables to the pan with some black pepper and the herbs. Bring the broth back to the boil, then reduce the heat and cover the pan, leaving a small space for steam to escape. Simmer gently for 1½ hours, or until the meat is tender.

3 Lift the bacon hock from the pan with a slotted spoon. Remove the skin, then take the meat off the bones and cut it into bitesize pieces. Return the meat to the pan and add the cabbage. Discard the herbs and simmer the soup for a little longer, until the cabbage is cooked to your liking.

4 Adjust the seasoning and ladle the soup into large serving bowls. Garnish with shopped parsley and serve with warmed brown bread.

Cook's Tip
Traditionally, the cabbage is simply trimmed and quartered, although it may be sliced if you prefer.

Leek and Bacon: Energy 337kcal/1422kJ; Protein 51.4g; Carbohydrate 11.3g, of which sugars 3.3g; Fat 10g, of which saturates 3.6g; Cholesterol 33mg; Calcium 44mg; Fibre 2.7g; Sodium 1860mg.
Bacon Broth: Energy 306kcal/1284kJ; Protein 17.7g; Carbohydrate 33.5g, of which sugars 8.3g; Fat 12.1g, of which saturates 4.3g; Cholesterol 35mg; Calcium 74mg; Fibre 4.6g; Sodium 1050g.

Kidney and Bacon Soup

Although there is a modern twist in the seasonings, the two main ingredients of this meaty soup are still very traditionally Irish. For a lighter flavour, lamb's kidney can be used with chicken stock instead of beef stock.

Serves 4–6

225g/8oz ox kidney
15ml/1 tbsp vegetable oil
4 streaky (fatty) bacon rashers (strips), chopped
1 large onion, chopped
2 garlic cloves, finely chopped
15ml/1 tbsp plain (all-purpose) flour
1.5 litres/2½ pints/6¼ cups beef stock or water
good dash of Worcestershire sauce
good dash of soy sauce
15ml/1 tbsp chopped fresh thyme, or 5ml/1 tsp dried thyme
4–6 slices French bread
75g/3oz/¾ cup grated cheese
salt and ground black pepper

1 Wash the kidney in cold, salted water. Drain, dry well on kitchen paper and remove the core and any blood vessels and membrane. Then chop the pieces of kidney.

2 Heat the vegetable oil in a large pan over a medium heat. Add the bacon and sauté for a few minutes. Add the prepared kidney and continue cooking, stirring, until evenly browned. Stir in the onion and garlic, and continue to cook, stirring often, until the onion is just soft.

3 Stir in the flour and cook for 2 minutes. Gradually pour in the water, stirring constantly. Add the Worcestershire and soy sauces, thyme and seasoning to taste. Reduce the heat and simmer gently for 30–35 minutes.

4 Preheat the grill (broiler) on the hottest setting. Toast the bread on one side, then turn the slices. Sprinkle with the cheese, covering the slices completely and and grill until the cheese is bubbling and golden.

5 Pour the soup into bowls and top each portion with the cheese on toast. Serve immediately.

Sausage and Tomato Soup

The bread makes this both a nourishing and a substantial soup. The recipe originates from Alentejo, in southern Portugal, where people created fantastic soups with basic ingredients such as water and a combination of simple wild herbs and vegetables, such as coriander or asparagus, as well as garlic and olive oil.

Serves 4

50ml/2fl oz/¼ cup olive oil
1 onion, chopped
1 small sausage, preferably from black pork, cut into small pieces
1 garlic clove, chopped
4 ripe tomatoes, peeled, seeded and diced
1 fresh oregano sprig
1 litre/1¾ pints/4 cups chicken stock or water
4 small slices of dry bread, cut into cubes
1 tbsp chopped fresh coriander (cilantro)
salt

1 Heat the oil in a large pan. Add the onion and sausage and cook over a low heat, stirring occasionally, for 5 minutes, until the onion has softened. Add the garlic, tomatoes and oregano and cook for a further 5 minutes.

2 Pour in the stock, season to taste with salt, and cook, stirring frequently, until completely heated through.

3 Add the bread and coriander and cook, stirring, until the bread is fully incorporated. Serve immediately.

Cook's Tip

To peel a tomato, cut a cross in the top, immerse in boiling water for 1 minute. Drain and peel off the skins.

Variation

This soup can also be prepared without the sausage. You can also add a poached egg to each bowl just before serving.

Kidney and Bacon: Energy 445kcal/1866kJ; Protein 26.8g; Carbohydrate 40.7g, of which sugars 5.4g; Fat 20.2g, of which saturates 8.1g; Cholesterol 192mg; Calcium 241mg; Fibre 2.4g; Sodium 1180g.
Sausage and Tomato: Energy 326kcal/1360kJ; Protein 9.7g; Carbohydrate 24.2g, of which sugars 6.4g; Fat 21.8g, of which saturates 5.9g; Cholesterol 30mg; Calcium 120mg; Fibre 2.8g; Sodium 600mg.

Sausage Soup with Borlotti Beans and Breadcrumbs

A big-filler soup, this recipe is based loosely on cassoulet. French sausages and Italian beans contribute flavour and substance, and the soup is topped with golden breadcrumbs.

Serves 6

250g/9oz/generous 1½ cups borlotti beans, soaked overnight and drained
115g/4oz pancetta, finely chopped
6 Toulouse sausages, thickly sliced
1 large onion, finely chopped
2 garlic cloves, chopped
2 carrots, finely diced
2 leeks, finely chopped
6 tomatoes, peeled, seeded and chopped
30ml/2 tbsp tomato purée (paste)
1.27 litres/2¼ pints/5⅔ cups vegetable stock
175g/6oz spring greens (collards), roughly shredded
25g/1oz/2 tbsp butter
115g/4oz/2 cups fresh white breadcrumbs
50g/2oz/⅔ cup Parmesan cheese, grated
salt and ground black pepper

1 Place the beans in a pan. Cover with plenty of cold water and bring to the boil, then boil for 10 minutes. Drain well.

2 Heat a large pan. Dry fry the pancetta until it is browned and yields its fat. Add the sausages and cook for 4–5 minutes, stirring occasionally, until beginning to brown. Add the onion and garlic and cook for 3–4 minutes until softened.

3 Stir in the beans, carrots, leeks, tomatoes, tomato purée and stock. Bring to the boil, reduce the heat and cover, then simmer for about 1¼ hours or until the beans are tender.

4 Stir in the spring greens and cook for 12–15 minutes more. Season well. Melt the butter in a frying pan and fry the breadcrumbs for 4–5 minutes, stirring, until golden, then stir in the Parmesan.

5 Ladle the soup into six bowls. Sprinkle the fried breadcrumb mixture over, then serve.

Pancetta, Tomato and Onion Soup

This warming winter soup comes from Umbria, central Italy, where it is sometimes thickened with beaten eggs and lots of grated Parmesan cheese. It is then served on top of hot toasted croûtes – rather like savoury scrambled eggs.

Serves 4

115g/4oz pancetta, roughly chopped
30ml/2 tbsp olive oil
15g/½oz/1 tbsp butter
675g/1½lb onions, thinly sliced
10ml/2 tsp sugar
about 1.2 litres/2 pints/5 cups chicken stock
350g/12oz ripe plum tomatoes, peeled and roughly chopped
a few basil leaves, shredded
salt and ground black pepper
freshly grated Parmesan cheese, to serve

1 Put the pancetta in a large pan and heat gently, stirring constantly, until the fat runs. Increase the heat to medium, add the oil, butter, onions and sugar and stir well to mix.

2 Half cover the pan and cook the onions gently for about 20 minutes, until golden. Stir frequently and lower the heat if necessary, to prevent the onions from sticking.

3 Stir in the stock, tomatoes and salt and pepper and bring to the boil, stirring. Lower the heat, half cover the pan and simmer, stirring occasionally, for about 30 minutes. Regularly check the consistency of the soup and add a little more stock or water if it is too thick.

4 Just before serving, stir in most of the basil and adjust the seasoning. Serve hot, garnished with the remaining shredded basil. Hand around the freshly grated Parmesan separately.

Cook's Tip

Look for Vidalia onions to make this soup. They are available at large supermarkets, and have a very sweet flavour and attractive yellowish flesh.

Sausage Soup: Energy 574kcal/2405kJ; Protein 29g; Carbohydrate 47.7g, of which sugars 10.2g; Fat 31g, of which saturates 12.5g; Cholesterol 75mg; Calcium 284mg; Fibre 10.7g; Sodium 1179mg.
Pancetta, Tomato, Onion: Energy 232kcal/963kJ; Protein 7.2g; Carbohydrate 16.1g, of which sugars 12.2g; Fat 16g, of which saturates 5.2g; Cholesterol 27mg; Calcium 51mg; Fibre 3.2g; Sodium 398mg.

Squash, Bacon and Cheese Soup

This is a lightly spiced squash soup, enriched with melting cheese.

Serves 4

900g/2lb butternut squash
225g/8oz smoked rindless bacon
15ml/1 tbsp oil
225g/8oz onions, roughly chopped
2 garlic cloves, crushed
10ml/2 tsp ground cumin
15ml/1 tbsp ground coriander
275g/10oz potatoes, diced
900ml/1½ pints/3¾ cups vegetable stock
10ml/2 tsp cornflour (cornstarch)
30ml/2 tbsp crème fraîche
Tabasco sauce, to taste
salt and ground black pepper

For serving

175g/6oz/1½ cups Gruyère cheese, grated
crusty bread

1 Halve the squash, discard the seeds and peel the flesh, then cut it into small chunks. Roughly chop the bacon.

2 Heat the oil in a large pan and cook the onions and garlic for 3 minutes, or until beginning to soften. Add the bacon and cook for about 3 minutes. Stir in the spices and cook on a low heat for a further minute.

3 Add the squash, potatoes and stock. Bring to the boil, reduce the heat and cover. Simmer for 15 minutes, or until the squash and potatoes are tender.

4 Blend the cornflour with 30ml/2 tbsp water and add to the soup with the crème fraîche. Bring to the boil, stirring, and simmer, uncovered, for 3 minutes. Adjust the seasoning and add Tabasco sauce to taste.

5 Ladle the soup into warm bowls and sprinkle the cheese on top. Serve immediately with crusty bread to scoop up the melted cheese.

Cook's Tip

Pumpkin can be used instead of butternut squash and is equally delicious.

Spare Rib, Sausage, and Pea Soup

This traditional Danish recipe is a great example of combining classic ingredients to make a delicious and successful soup for all the family.

Serves 4

800g/1¾lb/3½ cups green split peas
500g/1¼lb uncured gammon (smoked ham)
250g/9oz pork spare ribs
1 split pig's trotter (foot)
250g/9oz lean bacon in a single piece
1 small celeriac
bunch of celery leaves
500g/1¼lb leeks, thickly sliced
1 carrot, sliced
1 smoked (Guelders) sausage, about 250g/9oz
salt
rye bread spread with mustard, to serve

1 Rinse the peas under cold running water and place in a large pan. Add 2.5 litres/4¼ pints/10⅔ cups water, bring to the boil and skim off any scum that rises to the surface.

2 Add the gammon, spare ribs, pig's trotter and bacon. Simmer over low heat for about 3 hours, until the meat is tender. Remove the bacon from the pan and leave to cool.

3 Peel and dice the celeriac. Chop half the celery leaves and reserve the remainder for garnish. Add the celeriac, chopped celery leaves, leeks and carrot to the soup and simmer for 30 minutes, until tender.

4 Put the smoked sausage in a pan, add enough water to cover and poach the sausage over low heat for 20 minutes.

5 Using a slotted spoon, remove the meat from the soup. Cut the meat from the bones and dice it. Return the meat to the soup and add the sausage.

6 Ladle the soup into bowls and garnish with the reserved celery leaves.

7 As a tasty accompaniment, slice the bacon and serve on thin slices of rye bread spread with mustard.

Squash and Bacon: Energy 438kcal/1823kJ; Protein 24g; Carbohydrate 23g, of which sugars 8.1g; Fat 27.4g, of which saturates 15.3g; Cholesterol 81mg; Calcium 414mg; Fibre 3.7g; Sodium 1195mg.
Spare Rib and Sausage: Energy 914kcal/3843kJ; Protein 68.5g; Carbohydrate 87g, of which sugars 8.4g; Fat 34.8g, of which saturates 12.5g; Cholesterol 75mg; Calcium 222mg; Fibre 18.1g; Sodium 2216mg.

Lamb and Turnip Soup

Traditionally being the everyday food of the poor, soup often reflects old regional ingredients and seasonal produce of a country. Even in a small country, such as the Netherlands, tastes differ from region to region. This soup originates in Limburg where it is made with Geuldal lamb that live on the moors and turnips that are enjoyed in spring.

Serves 4

300g/11oz boneless shin (shank) of lamb, diced
1 rosemary sprig
4 bay leaves
500g/1½lb young turnips, diced
100g/3¾oz carrots, diced
100g/3¾oz potatoes, diced
salt and ground black pepper

To garnish

8 thin rashers (slices) smoked streaky (fatty) bacon
chopped fresh chervil

1 Put the lamb, rosemary and bay leaves in a large pan, Pour in 1.5 litres/2½ pints/6¼ cups water and add salt and pepper to taste. Bring to the boil, lower the heat and cover the pan. Simmer the soup for 3 hours, until the lamb is completely tender and succulent.

2 Discard the rosemary and bay leaves from the stock. Add the turnips, carrots and potatoes to the pan, re-cover and simmer for a further 15 minutes, until the vegetables are tender. Do not overcook the vegetables or they will become mushy.

3 Dry-fry the bacon in a heavy frying pan until crisp, turning once. Remove the bacon from the pan, drain on kitchen paper and crumble it into pieces.

4 Ladle the soup into bowls, garnish with the chervil and bacon and serve immediately.

Cook's Tip

This is also a good recipe for best end of neck of lamb. If using a fatty cut, cook the lamb a day in advance, cool and chill it in the stock, then skim off the fat before continuing.

Chunky Lamb and Vegetable Soup

This is based on a traditional Jewish dish of baked meats and beans. A parcel of rice is often added to the broth part way through cooking, to produce pressed, chewy rice.

Serves 8

250g/9oz/1 cup chickpeas, soaked overnight
45ml/3 tbsp olive oil
1 onion, chopped
10 garlic cloves, chopped
1 parsnip, sliced
3 carrots, sliced
5–10ml/1–2 tsp ground cumin
2.5ml/½ tsp ground turmeric
15ml/1 tbsp chopped fresh root ginger
2 litres/3½ pints/8 cups beef stock
1 potato, cut into chunks
½ marrow (large zucchini), sliced
400g/14oz fresh or canned tomatoes, diced
45–60ml/3–4 tbsp brown or green lentils
2 bay leaves
250g/9oz salted meat such as salt beef
250g/9oz piece of lamb
½ large bunch fresh coriander (cilantro), chopped
200g/7oz/1 cup long grain rice

For serving

chopped fresh chillies
1 lemon, cut into wedges

1 Preheat the oven to 120°C/250°F/Gas ½. Drain the chickpeas. Heat the oil in a deep flameproof casserole, add the onion, garlic, parsnip, carrots, cumin, turmeric and ginger and cook for 2–3 minutes. Add the chickpeas, stock, potato, marrow, tomatoes, lentils, bay leaves, salted meat, lamb and coriander. Cover and cook in the oven for 1 hour.

2 Tie the rice in a double thickness of muslin (cheesecloth), allowing enough room for it to expand while it is cooking. Place the rice parcel in the casserole, anchoring the edge of the muslin parcel under the lid so it is held above the soup and allowed to steam. Return the casserole to the oven and continue cooking for a further 2 hours.

3 Carefully remove the lid and the rice. Skim any fat off the top of the soup. Ladle the soup into bowls. Open the rice and add a scoop to each bowl with one or two pieces of meat. Sprinkle with chopped fresh chillies and serve with lemon.

Lamb and Turnip: Energy 345kcal/1437kJ; Protein 25.3g; Carbohydrate 11.9g, of which sugars 7.8g; Fat 22.2g, of which saturates 8.6g; Cholesterol 94mg; Calcium 77mg; Fibre 3.9g; Sodium 801mg.
Chunky Lamb: Energy 463Kcal/1941kJ; Protein 28.5g; Carbohydrate 60.5g, of which sugars 17g; Fat 12.7g, of which saturates 3.5g; Cholesterol 47mg; Calcium 130mg; Fibre 9.4g; Sodium 409mg.

Lamb Dumpling and Beetroot Soup

This is a substantial, meaty version of borscht.

Serves 6–8

15ml/1 tbsp vegetable oil
1 onion, finely chopped
6 garlic cloves
1 carrot, diced
1 courgette (zucchini), diced
½ celery stick, diced (optional)
5ml/1 tsp curry powder
4 cooked beetroot (beets), diced
1 litre/1¾ pints/4 cups stock
400g/14oz can tomatoes
45–60ml/3–4 tbsp chopped fresh coriander (cilantro) leaves
2 bay leaves
15ml/1 tbsp sugar
a little vinegar
salt and ground black pepper

For the lamb dumplings
115g/4oz/1 cup plain (all-purpose) flour
5ml/1 tsp ground turmeric
2 pinches saffron threads infused in 15ml/1 tbsp hot water
15ml/1 tbsp vegetable oil
1 large onion, finely chopped
250g/9oz minced (ground) lamb
5ml/1 tsp vinegar
½ bunch fresh mint, chopped

For the spice paste
4 garlic cloves, chopped
15–25ml/1–1½ tbsp chopped fresh root ginger
½–4 fresh mild chillies
bunch of fresh coriander (cilantro)
30ml/2 tbsp white wine vinegar
a little extra virgin olive oil

1 For the dumplings, make a dough from the flour, salt and turmeric, adding just enough water. Knead, cover and stand for 30 minutes. Fry the onion in the oil, then mix with the remaining ingredients to make the meat filling. Roll 10–15 thin circles of dough and fill with meat, sealing the edges.

2 For the soup, heat the oil in a pan. Fry the onion, garlic, carrot, courgette, celery and curry powder until the vegetables are softened, Add three of the beetroot, the stock, tomatoes, coriander, bay leaves and sugar. Boil, reduce the heat and simmer for 20 minutes. Add the remaining beetroot.

3 Poach the dumplings in boiling water for about 4 minutes: using a slotted spoon, remove them as they are cooked. Purée all the ingredients together for the spice paste.

4 Ladle the soup into bowls. Add a dash of vinegar, dumplings and a small spoonful of the paste to each. Serve immediately.

Lamb Broth

Sustaining and warming, lamb broth, or Scotch broth as it is traditionally known, is custom-made for the chilly Scottish weather, and makes a delicious winter soup anywhere. In days gone by it used to be the custom to make a large pot of it is to last a few days, as the flavour improves all the time.

Serves 6–8

1kg/2¼lb lean neck (US shoulder or breast) of lamb, cut into large, even-sized chunks
1 large onion, chopped
50g/2oz/¼ cup pearl barley
bouquet garni
1 large carrot, chopped
1 turnip, chopped
3 leeks, chopped
1 small white cabbage, finely shredded
salt and ground black pepper
chopped fresh parsley, to garnish
fresh bread, to serve

1 Put the lamb and 1.75 litres/3 pints/7½ cups water in a large pan over a medium heat and gently bring to the boil. Skim off the scum with a spoon. Add the onion, pearl barley and bouquet garni, and stir in thoroughly.

2 Bring the soup back to the boil, then reduce the heat, partly cover the pan and simmer gently for a further 1 hour. Make sure that it does not boil too furiously or become too dry.

3 Add the carrot, turnip, leeks and cabbage to the pan and season with salt and ground black pepper. Bring the soup back to the boil and then reduce the heat. Partly cover the pan again and simmer the soup for about 35 minutes, until the vegetables are tender.

4 Remove the surplus fat from the top of the soup by skimming it off a spoon and then blotting it with a sheet of kitchen paper.

5 Serve the soup piping hot, garnished with chopped parsley, with big chunks of fresh bread.

Lamb Dumpling Soup: Energy 175kcal/732kJ; Protein 9.2g; Carbohydrate 18.6g, of which sugars 6.6g; Fat 7.6g, of which saturates 2.4g; Cholesterol 24mg; Calcium 69mg; Fibre 2.8g; Sodium 50mg.
Lamb Broth: Energy 387kcal/1619kJ; Protein 36.2g; Carbohydrate 17.7g, of which sugars 9.1g; Fat 19.5g, of which saturates 8.8g; Cholesterol 127mg; Calcium 86mg; Fibre 4.3g; Sodium 157mg.

Roast Lamb in Pearl Barley Broth

Succulent roasted lamb shanks studded with garlic and rosemary make a fabulous meal when served in a hearty vegetable, barley and tomato broth.

Serves 4

4 small lamb shanks
4 garlic cloves, cut into slivers
handful of small fresh rosemary sprigs
30ml/2 tbsp olive oil
2 carrots, diced
2 celery sticks, diced
1 large onion, chopped
1 bay leaf
few sprigs of fresh thyme
1.2 litres/2 pints/5 cups lamb stock
50g/2oz pearl barley
450g/1lb tomatoes, peeled and chopped
grated rind of 1 large lemon
30ml/2 tbsp chopped fresh parsley
salt and ground black pepper

1 Preheat the oven to 150°C/300°F/Gas 2. Make small cuts all over the lamb and insert slivers of garlic and sprigs of rosemary into them.

2 Heat the oil in a flameproof casserole and brown the shanks two at a time. Remove and set aside. Add the carrots, celery and onion in batches and cook until lightly browned. Put all the vegetables in the casserole with the bay leaf and thyme. Pour in stock to cover, place the lamb on top and roast for 2 hours.

3 Meanwhile, pour the remaining stock into a large saucepan. Add the pearl barley, then bring to the boil. Reduce the heat, cover and simmer for 1 hour, or until the barley is tender.

4 Remove the lamb shanks from the casserole using a slotted spoon. Skim the fat from the surface of the roasted vegetables, then add them to the broth. Stir in the tomatoes, lemon rind and parsley.

5 Bring the soup back to the boil. Reduce the heat and simmer for 5 minutes. Add the lamb shanks and heat through, then season. Put a lamb shank into each of four large bowls, then ladle the barley broth over the meat and serve at once.

Lamb and White Cabbage Soup

This is a good modern adaptation of the traditional recipe for Irish mutton broth, Brachán caoireola, and is delicious served with wholemeal bread.

Serves 6

675g/1½lb neck of lamb on the bone
1 large onion
2 bay leaves
3 carrots, chopped
½ white turnip, diced
½ small white cabbage, shredded
2 large leeks, thinly sliced
15ml/1 tbsp tomato purée (paste)
30ml/2 tbsp chopped fresh parsley
salt and ground black pepper

1 Trim any excess fat from the meat. Chop the onion coarsely and put in a large pan. Add the lamb and bay leaves. Then pour in 1.5 litres/2½ pints/6¼ cups water and bring to the boil.

2 Skim the surface of the stock as it comes to the boil. Then reduce the heat and cover the pan. Simmer the soup for about 1½–2 hours or longer, if necessary, until the lamb is thoroughly tender and almost falling off the bone.

3 Remove the lamb, draining it well, and transfer it to a platter. Then cut all the meat off the bones. Discard the bones and dice the meat.

4 Return the meat to the broth. Add the vegetables, tomato purée and parsley. Stir in seasoning to taste. Bring the soup back to the boil, reduce the heat and cover the pan.

5 Simmer the soup for another 30 minutes, or until the vegetables are tender. Ladle the soup into big bowls and serve piping hot.

Variation

Try making the same broth using other meat on the bone – beef or bacon, for example. It is also ideal for one or two large turkey drumsticks that are delicious when well boiled in soup.

Lamb with Barley: Energy 287kcal/1199kJ; Protein 22.5g; Carbohydrate 19.5g, of which sugars 7.6g; Fat 13.7g, of which saturates 0.9g; Cholesterol 0mg; Calcium 35mg; Fibre 2.3g; Sodium 24mg.
Lamb and Cabbage Soup: Energy 162kcal/675kJ; Protein 13.1g; Carbohydrate 8.5g, of which sugars 7g; Fat 8.6g, of which saturates 3.8g; Cholesterol 44mg; Calcium 42mg; Fibre 3g; Sodium 55mg.

Lamb Meatball and Vegetable Soup

A variety of vegetables makes a tasty base for meatballs in this substantial soup, which will make a hearty meal served with crusty bread.

Serves 4

1 litre/1¾ pints/4 cups lamb stock
1 onion, finely chopped
2 carrots, finely sliced
½ celeriac, finely diced
75g/3oz/¾ cup frozen peas
50g/2oz green beans, cut into 2.5cm/1in pieces
3 tomatoes, seeded and chopped
1 red (bell) pepper, seeded and diced
1 potato, coarsely diced
2 lemons, sliced
salt and ground black pepper
crusty bread, to serve

For the meatballs

225g/8oz/1 cup very lean minced (ground) lamb
40g/1½oz/¼ cup short grain rice
30ml/2 tbsp chopped fresh parsley
plain (all-puspose) flour, for coating

1 Pour the stock into a large pan and place over medium heat. Stir in the onion, carrot, celeriac and peas.

2 Add the beans, tomatoes, red pepper and potato with the slices of lemon. Stir in a little salt and freshly ground black pepper and bring the mixture to the boil. Reduce the heat, cover the pan and simmer for 15–20 minutes.

3 Meanwhile, prepare the meatballs. Mix the meat, rice and parsley together in a bowl and season well. The best way of mixing meat for meatballs is by hand, squeezing and kneading the mixture so that the meat mixes with the rice.

4 Take out a rounded teaspoon of the meat mixture and roll it into a small ball, roughly the size of a walnut. Toss it in the flour. Repeat with the remaining mixture.

5 Add the meatballs to the soup and simmer gently for 25–30 minutes, stirring occasionally, to prevent the meatballs from sticking. The rice should be plumped up and cooked in the meat. Adjust the seasoning and serve in warm bowls, accompanied by crusty bread.

Country-style Lamb Soup

Traditionally, Irish soda bread would be served with this hearty one-pot meal based on classic Irish stew.

Serves 4

15ml/1 tbsp vegetable oil
675g/1½lb boneless lamb chump chops, trimmed and cut into small cubes
2 small onions, quartered
2 leeks, thickly sliced
1 litre/1¾ pints/4 cups lamb stock or water
2 large potatoes, cut into chunks
2 carrots, thickly sliced
sprig of fresh thyme, plus extra to garnish
15g/½oz/1 tbsp butter
30ml/2 tbsp chopped fresh parsley
salt and ground black pepper
Irish soda bread, to serve

1 Heat the oil in a pan. Add the lamb and brown in batches. Use a slotted spoon to remove the lamb from the pan.

2 Add the onions and cook for 4–5 minutes, until browned. Return the meat to the pan and add the leeks. Pour in the stock or water, then bring to the boil. Reduce the heat, cover and simmer gently for about 1 hour.

3 Add the potatoes, carrots and thyme, and continue cooking for a further 40 minutes, until the lamb is tender. Remove from the heat and leave to stand for 5 minutes to allow the fat to settle on the surface of the soup.

4 Skim off the fat. Pour off the stock from the soup into a clean pan and whisk in the butter. Stir in the parsley and season well, then pour the liquid back over the soup ingredients.

5 Ladle the soup into warmed bowls and garnish with sprigs of fresh thyme. Serve with chunks of brown or Irish soda bread.

Variation

The vegetables in this rustic soup can be varied according to the season. Swede (rutabaga), turnip, celeriac and even cabbage could be added in place of some of the listed vegetables.

Lamb Meatball Soup: Energy 226kcal/948kJ; Protein 15.7g; Carbohydrate 25.1g, of which sugars 11.4g; Fat 7.7g, of which saturates 3.2g; Cholesterol 43mg; Calcium 75mg; Fibre 5.2g; Sodium 102mg.
Country-style Lamb: Energy 500kcal/2092kJ; Protein 38.2g; Carbohydrate 30.2g, of which sugars 12.2g; Fat 26g, of which saturates 11.3g; Cholesterol 136mg; Calcium 104mg; Fibre 6.1g; Sodium 197mg.

Meatball Soup with Spinach

This soup (or similar) is standard fare throughout the Middle East.

Serves 6

2 large onions
45ml/3 tbsp oil
15ml/1 tbsp turmeric
90g/3½oz/½ cup yellow split peas
225g/8oz minced (ground) lamb
450g/1lb spinach, chopped
50g/2oz/½ cup rice flour
juice of 2 lemons
1–2 garlic cloves, very finely chopped
30ml/2 tbsp chopped fresh mint
4 eggs, beaten
salt and ground black pepper

1 Chop one of the onions, heat a little of the oil in a pan and fry the onion until golden. Add the turmeric, split peas and 1.2 litres/2 pints/5 cups water, bring to the boil, then reduce the heat and cover the pan. Simmer for 20 minutes.

2 Grate the remaining onion into a bowl, add the minced lamb and seasoning and mix. With your hands, form into small balls, about the size of walnuts. Add to the pan and simmer for 10 minutes. Add the spinach, cover and simmer for 20 minutes.

3 Mix the rice flour with about 250ml/8fl oz/1 cup cold water to a smooth paste. Slowly add to the pan, stirring. Stir in the lemon juice and seasoning and cook gently heat for 20 minutes.

4 Meanwhile, heat the remaining oil in a small pan and fry the garlic briefly until golden. Stir in the chopped mint and remove the pan from the heat.

5 Remove the soup from the heat and stir in the beaten eggs. Ladle the soup into warmed soup bowls. Sprinkle the garlic and mint garnish over the soup and serve.

Cook's Tip
If preferred, use less lemon juice to begin with and then add more to taste once the soup is cooked. Use minced (ground) beef or pork in place of minced lamb.

Lamb and Cucumber Soup

This is a very simple soup to prepare, but it tastes delicious nevertheless.

Serves 4

225g/8oz lamb steak
15ml/1 tbsp light soy sauce
10ml/2 tsp Chinese rice wine or dry sherry
2.5ml/½ tsp sesame oil
7.5cm/3in piece cucumber
750ml/1¼ pints/3 cups chicken or vegetable stock
15ml/1 tbsp rice vinegar
salt and ground white pepper

1 Trim off any excess fat from the lamb. Thinly slice the lamb into small pieces and place in a bowl. Add the soy sauce, wine or sherry and sesame oil. Mix well. then cover and set aside to marinate for 25–30 minutes. Discard the marinade.

2 Halve the cucumber lengthways (do not peel), then cut it into thin slices diagonally.

3 In a wok or saucepan, bring the stock to a rolling boil, add the lamb and stir to separate.

4 Bring the soup back to the boil, then add the cucumber slices, vinegar and seasoning. Bring back to the boil, remove from the heat and serve at once.

Variations
- *Use fine cut, lean boneless pork instead of lamb. Add a little chopped fresh root ginger to spice up the soup.*
- *For a sweet-sour soup, stir in honey to taste – it is delicious with the lamb or with pork.*
- *For a punchy flavour, thinly slice a milld to medium fresh green chilli and add it to the soup with a good handful of chopped fresh mint. Sprinkle in a little sugar for a sweet-sour, piquant minted soup.*
- *For additional crunch, cut some celery and spring onions (scallions) into fine shreds and soak them in iced water until they curl. Drain, dry and use as a garnish.*

Meatball Soup: Energy 293kcal/1222kJ; Protein 18.3g; Carbohydrate 21.6g, of which sugars 5.2g; Fat 15.2g, of which saturates 4.3g; Cholesterol 156mg; Calcium 179mg; Fibre 3.4g; Sodium 185mg.
Lamb and Cucumber: Energy 105kcal/438kJ; Protein 11.2g; Carbohydrate 0.4g, of which sugars 0.3g; Fat 6.6g, of which saturates 3g; Cholesterol 43mg; Calcium 6mg; Fibre 0g; Sodium 316mg.

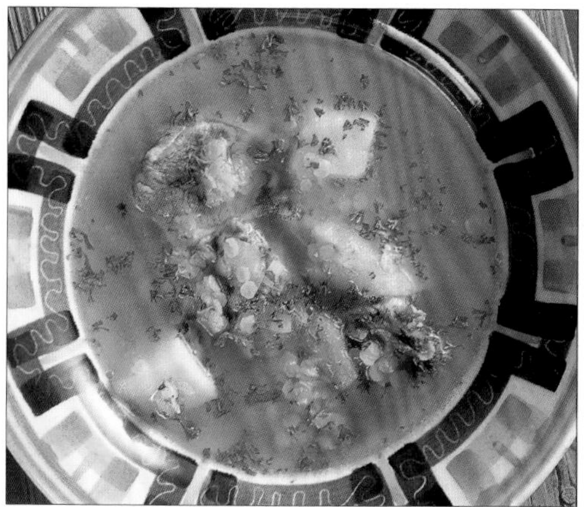

Lamb and Red Lentil Soup

Lentils are popular on Caribbean islands, such as Trinidad and Tobago, where they were introduced by South-east Asian labourers recruited to work the sugar cane plantations.

Serves 4

1.5–1.75 litres/2½–3 pints/ 6¼–7½ cups water or stock
900g/2lb neck of lamb, cut into chops
½ onion, chopped
1 garlic clove, crushed
1 bay leaf
1 clove
2 fresh thyme sprigs
225g/8oz potatoes
175g/6oz/¾ cup red lentils
600ml/1 pint/2½ cups water
salt and ground black pepper
chopped fresh parsley

1 Pour 1.5 litres/2½ pints/6¼ cups of the water or stock into a large pan and add the lamb, chopped onion, crushed garlic, bay leaf, clove and thyme sprigs. Bring to the boil, then lower the heat and simmer gently for about 1 hour, until the lamb is completely tender.

2 Peel the potatoes and cut them into 2.5cm/1in cubes. Add them to the soup and bring back to the boil. Reduce the heat and cook for a further 5 minutes.

3 Add the red lentils to the pan, stirring them gently into the stock, then season the soup with a little salt and plenty of ground black pepper. Pour in an additional 300ml/½ pint/ 1¼ cups of warm water or stock, if necessary, to completely cover the meat and vegetables.

4 Bring the soup back to the boil, then lower the heat, cover the pan and simmer for 25 minutes or until the lentils are cooked, stirring occasionally. Check the liquid level during cooking and add a little more water or stock if the soup becomes too thick.

5 Just before serving, taste the soup for seasoning and more salt and pepper if necessary. Stir in the chopped parsley and serve immediately, while the parsley still tastes fresh and uncooked to complement the lentils.

Lamb, Bean and Pumpkin Soup

Aside from the green bananas, which are very much an African touch, this soup could have come from any of the lands of the Middle East. Pumpkin, carrot and turmeric give it a rich colour and the spices provide a warmth designed to banish winter chills.

Serves 4

115g/4oz black-eyed beans (peas), soaked for 1–2 hours, or overnight
675g/1½lb neck of lamb, cut into medium-size chunks
5ml/1 tsp chopped fresh thyme, or 2.5ml/½ tsp dried
2 bay leaves
1.2 litres/2 pints/5 cups stock or water
1 onion, sliced
225g/8oz pumpkin, diced
2 black cardamom pods
7.5ml/1½ tsp ground turmeric
15ml/1 tbsp chopped fresh coriander (cilantro)
2.5ml/½ tsp caraway seeds
1 green chilli, seeded and chopped
2 green bananas
1 carrot
salt and ground black pepper

1 Drain the beans, place in a pan and cover with cold water. Bring to the boil and boil rapidly for 10 minutes, then reduce the heat and simmer, covered, for 40–50 minutes until tender, adding more water if necessary. Set aside to cool.

2 Meanwhile, put the lamb in a large pan, add the thyme, bay leaves and stock or water and bring to the boil. Cover and simmer over a medium heat for 1 hour, until tender.

3 Add the onion, pumpkin, cardamoms, turmeric, coriander, caraway seeds, chilli and seasoning and stir. Bring back to a simmer and then cook, uncovered, for 15 minutes, until the pumpkin is tender, stirring occasionally.

4 When the beans are cool, spoon into a food processor or blender with their liquid and process to a smooth purée.

5 Cut the bananas into medium slices and the carrot into thin slices. Stir into the soup with the bean purée. Cook for 10–12 minutes, until the vegetables are tender. Adjust the seasoning and serve.

Lamb and Lentil: Energy 587kcal/2465kJ; Protein 55.7g; Carbohydrate 34.9g, of which sugars 2.6g; Fat 26g, of which saturates 11.9g; Cholesterol 171mg; Calcium 48mg; Fibre 2.9g; Sodium 216mg.
Lamb, Bean, Pumpkin: Energy 442kcal/1855kJ; Protein 40.8g; Carbohydrate 27.2g, of which sugars 13.1g; Fat 19.7g, of which saturates 9g; Cholesterol 128mg; Calcium 74mg; Fibre 6.4g; Sodium 155mg.

Lamb and Paprika Soup

This is Turkish wedding soup. Steeped in tradition, it varies little throughout the country, the only difference being the cinnamon.

Serves 4–6

500g/1¼lb lamb on the bone – neck, leg or shoulder
2 carrots, roughly chopped
2 potatoes, roughly chopped
1 cinnamon stick
45ml/3 tbsp thick and creamy (natural) plain yogurt
45ml/3 tbsp plain (all-purpose) flour
1 egg yolk
juice of ½ lemon
30ml/2 tbsp butter
5ml/1 tsp kırmızı biber, or paprika
salt and ground black pepper

1 Place the lamb in a deep pan with the carrots, potatoes and cinnamon. Pour in 2 litres/3½ pints/8 cups water and bring to the boil, then skim off any scum and lower the heat. Cover and simmer for 1½ hours, until the meat almost falls off the bone.

2 Lift the lamb out of the pan. Remove the meat from the bone and dice it.

3 Strain the stock and discard the carrots and potatoes. Pour the stock back into the pan, season and bring to the boil.

4 Beat the yogurt with the flour. Add the egg yolk and lemon juice and beat well again, then pour in about 250ml/8fl oz/1 cup of the hot stock, beating all the time so that the hot liquid doesn't cook the yolk.

5 Lower the heat under the pan and pour the yogurt mixture into the stock, beating constantly. Add the meat to the pan and warm gently, ensuring the meat heats through but the mixture does not boil.

6 Melt the butter in a small pan and stir in the kırmızı biber or paprika. Ladle the soup into bowls and drizzle the pepper butter over the top.

Sour Lamb Soup

This traditional sour soup uses lamb, though pork and poultry are popular alternatives.

Serves 4–5

30ml/2 tbsp oil
450g/1lb lean lamb, trimmed and cubed
1 onion, diced
30ml/2 tbsp plain (all-purpose) flour
15ml/1 tbsp paprika
1 litre/1¾ pints/4 cups hot lamb stock
3 sprigs of fresh parsley
4 spring onions (scallions)
4 sprigs of fresh dill
25g/1oz/scant ¼ cup long grain rice
2 eggs, beaten
30–45ml/2–3 tbsp or more vinegar or lemon juice
salt and ground black pepper

For the garnish

25g/1oz/2 tbsp butter, melted
5ml/1 tsp paprika
a little fresh parsley or lovage and dill

1 In a large pan heat the oil and fry the meat until brown. Add the onion and cook until it has softened. Sprinkle in the flour and paprika. Stir well, add the stock and cook for 10 minutes.

2 Tie the parsley, spring onions and dill together with string and add to the large pan with the rice and seasoning. Bring to the boil, then simmer for about 30–40 minutes, or until the lamb is tender.

3 Remove the pan from the heat and stir in the eggs. Add the vinegar or lemon juice. Discard the tied herbs and season the soup to taste.

4 For the garnish, melt the butter in a pan and add the paprika. Ladle the soup into warmed serving bowls. Garnish with the herbs and a little red paprika butter.

Cook's Tip

Trimmed leg of lamb is ideal for this soup and the bone from the meat can be used to make the stock.

Lamb and Paprika: Energy 226kcal/943kJ; Protein 15g; Carbohydrate 14.4g, of which sugars 3.6g; Fat 12.4g, of which saturates 6.2g; Cholesterol 88mg; Calcium 54mg; Fibre 1.4g; Sodium 87mg.
Sour Lamb Soup: Energy 281kcal/1173kJ; Protein 21.6g; Carbohydrate 11.3g, of which sugars 2g; Fat 16.9g, of which saturates 5.8g; Cholesterol 145mg; Calcium 39mg; Fibre 0.7g; Sodium 107mg.

Spiced Kofta Soup with Lemon

This North African dish can be found in the tiniest rural villages, in street stalls in the towns and cities, and in the finest restaurants of Fez. Bread for mopping up the juices is essential.

Serves 4

450g/1lb finely minced (ground) lamb
3 large onions, grated
small bunch of fresh flat leaf parsley, chopped
5–10ml/1–2 tsp ground cinnamon
5ml/1 tsp ground cumin
pinch of cayenne pepper
40g/1½oz/3 tbsp butter
25g/1oz fresh root ginger, peeled and finely chopped
1 fresh hot chilli, seeded and finely chopped
pinch of saffron threads
small bunch of fresh coriander (cilantro), finely chopped
juice of 1 lemon
1.2 litres/2 pints/5 cups lamb or chicken stock or water
1 lemon, quartered
salt and ground black pepper

1 For the kofta, pound the lamb in a bowl by hand. Knead in half the onions, parsley, cinnamon, cumin and cayenne pepper. Season with salt and pepper, and continue pounding the mixture by hand for a few minutes. Break off pieces of the mixture and shape them into walnut-size balls.

2 In a large pan, melt the butter and add the remaining onions with the ginger, chilli and saffron. Cook until the onions just begin to colour, stirring frequently, then stir in the chopped coriander and lemon juice.

3 Pour in the stock or water, season with salt and bring to the boil. Drop in the kofta, reduce the heat and cover the pan. Poach the kofta gently, turning them occasionally, for about 20 minutes or until they are cooked.

4 Remove the lid, tuck the lemon quarters around the kofta, raise the heat a little and cook, uncovered, for a further 10 minutes to impart the lemon flavour and sharpness.

5 Garnish with parsley and serve the kofta hot, straight from the pan with lots of fresh crusty bread to mop up the juices.

Curried Mutton Soup

In Malaysia and Singapore, this a popular dish at the hawker stalls as well as in the coffee shops. It is a soup that comes into its own late at night, when it is valued for its restorative qualities. It also makes a great supper dish, served with chunks of crusty bread or any of the Indian flatbreads.

Serves 4 to 6

25g/1oz fresh root ginger, peeled and chopped
4–6 garlic cloves, chopped
1 fresh red chilli, seeded and chopped
15ml/1 tbsp ghee or vegetable oil
5ml/1 tsp coriander seeds
5ml/1 tsp cumin seeds
5ml/1 tsp ground fenugreek
5ml/1 tsp sugar
450g/1lb meaty mutton ribs, cut into bitesize pieces
2 litres/3½ pints/7¾ cups lamb stock or water
10ml/2 tsp tomato purée (paste)
1 cinnamon stick
4–6 green cardamom pods, bruised
2 tomatoes, peeled and quartered
salt and ground black pepper
fresh coriander (cilantro) leaves, roughly chopped, to garnish

1 Using a mortar and pestle, food processor or a blender, grind the ginger, garlic and chilli to a smooth paste. Scrape the paste down into the pot several times to ensure the ingredients are properly ground.

2 Heat the ghee or oil in a heavy pan and stir in the coriander and cumin seeds. Add the ginger, garlic and chilli paste along with the fenugreek and sugar. Stir until fragrant and beginning to colour. Add the chopped mutton ribs and turn them to sear the meat on both sides.

3 Pour in the stock or water and stir in the tomato purée, cinnamon stick and cardamom pods. Bring to the boil, then reduce the heat, cover the pan and simmer the soup gently for 1½ hours, until the meat is very tender.

4 Season to taste with salt and pepper. Stir in the tomatoes, and garnish with coriander. Serve hot with chunks of fresh crusty bread or Indian flatbread.

Spiced Kofta: Energy 362kcal/1503kJ; Protein 24.5g; Carbohydrate 12.9g, of which sugars 9.3g; Fat 24g, of which saturates 12.2g; Cholesterol 108mg; Calcium 134mg; Fibre 4g; Sodium 155mg.
Curried Mutton: Energy 166kcal/693kJ; Protein 15.2g; Carbohydrate 2.8g, of which sugars 2.5g; Fat 10.6g, of which saturates 5.2g; Cholesterol 62mg; Calcium 12mg; Fibre 0.5g; Sodium 87mg.

Index

NOTES

Notes

Notes

Notes

NOTES

Notes